First published in Great Britain 2018



FIRST EDITION

Cover image: 2 Loud Creative

Illustrations: Heath Gascoigne

ISBN 978-0-9957779-0-3 Paperback
ISBN 978-0-9957779-1-0 E-book
ISBN 978-0-9957779-2-7 Audio book
ISBN 978-0-9957779-3-4 Hardcover

# Dedication

To my late great Aunt and Uncle Dawn and Asen Georgiv, thank you for planting the seed.
To my parents, Debbie and Joe Gascoigne, thank you for nurturing the seed.
This one's for you.

# Foreword

I first met Heath on the first day commencing my MBA studies in 2007, some 10 years ago. We have kept in close contact ever since and throughout this time I have known Heath to be not only a keen student, but a highly dedicated and focused professional. Back then while completing my completing our MBA I founded my own business "Acclimation" and found myself frequently calling on Heath for his insights and critique of my strategy and implementation. Acclimation has since gone on from 3 co-founders, to 40-plus staff with offices across Australia and Singapore.

Heath would have to be one of the most critical thinkers of this generation. He is a pragmatic, logical, analytical and methodical thinker and has an uncanny ability to quickly assess and understand big picture issues affecting an Organisation strategically, as well as the implications of implementing an Organisation's strategy down to the operational level, where the implementation and execution actually takes place.

One of the most admirable traits I like about Heath, is his ability to cut through noise and get straight to the point. He's not afraid to speak his mind, or challenge the status quo and ask the *'Why?'* questions and skillfully so, both in a professional and personal sense.

Heath also displays the charisma and natural ability to read a room and understand people's different personalities and motivations to tactfully discuss the most critical issues (including taboo subjects). This approach is highly relevant as we have become very 'PC' in this day and age where 'group think' has almost become common place with individuals wanting to avoid discussing the 'elephant in the room', which is arguably, the cause of many failed Programmes and even organisations.

In ***The Business Transformation Playbook®***, Heath has been able to merge his academic business studies with his vast experience and impressive list of industry certificates and qualifications on some of the biggest and smallest Programmes (i.e. mine)in different industries across and the world, and developed a unique approach and framework to ensure the Organisation's strategy is implemented as intended, and the outcomes are realized as expected.

This is one of those rare books, that gives you information you can put directly into practice. Additionally, this book offers the personal insights of a practitioner who is 'walking the talk', unlike other alternatives, which might sound sound good on paper, but aren't actually useful in practice.

Heath takes a relatively simple approach to solving a rather complex problem. It is good to see that Heath has now taken the time to share with the world what I have been privy too for so many years.

Rod Taubman

Rod Taubman
Founder & CEO
Acclimation

# Preface

Hi, my name is Heath Gascoigne, and this book came about out of frustration and a belief that there had to be a better way of way of delivering projects which delivered real value to an organisation. As a Business Architect, my job is to help companies design and implement their complex Target Operating Models (TOM's) as part of their business and digital transformation. My clients are mainly government agencies and big banks undertaking enterprise wide transformation Programmes with budgets between £5M-£500M.

I'm the guy the client calls to come in and clean up the consultants' mess, set up and implement the framework and processes to realign the Programme to deliver the business and system changes into the organisation.

When I get called in, in a lot of cases it is after a the Programme has started (in some cases up to 2 years after a Programme has commenced, which is not ideal, which I will get into later in the book, even worse – there is usually a team of management consultants there, that they should know better) I'm normally greeted with explicit instructions "to reign in the Programme", and "realign it to the Business Strategy". Some of these Programmes I have been asked to rescue have been reincarnations of large scale failed transformation Programmes[1,2,3] that are being tackled for a second time.

The first thing I do when I arrive on the Client site is start off with three (3) simple questions:

1. **What is the problem?**
2. **What are you doing (to solve that problem)? and**
3. **Have you been through this before?**

The answers to these simple questions provide me with a good indication of the state of the Programme and how far off track it is from the intended outcomes the Programme was originally tasked to deliver.

When I ask those involved "what is the problem?" and to describe the problem, they almost immediately start by telling me about the solution. I have to remind them that what they are describing to me is not in fact the problem, but the solution. They go on to tell me about how *"What we are building is going to solve all the business' problems".* I say *"Great! So what are those problems?"*. The answer to that question is often, *"it's not that simple"*, or *"it's not that easy to describe"* (so they tell me). **This is my first red flag.**

The next question , "What are you doing to solve that problem?" is almost always met with a description or presentation of what they are building and delivering, which again I ask them to clarify "and for what problem was that solving?". Again, that answer is not that clear. **This is my second red flag.**

The third question, "Have you (and/or the Organisation) been through this before?", is almost always answered with a resounding "yes". To which I reply "Great, let's look at the lessons learned" (so

---

[1] UK Campaign 4 Change: After two IT disasters, immigration officials launch £208m agile project (Jul 2014) https://ukcampaign4change.com/2014/07/22/after-two-it-disasters-immigration-officials-launch-208m-agile-project/

[2] National Audit Office (NOA): Reforming the UK border and immigration system (Jul 2014) https://www.nao.org.uk/report/reforming-uk-border-immigration-system-2/

[3] The Register: MPs question value of canning Raytheon from e-borders 'Some 80 per cent of £1.1bn project has been written off' (Dec 2015) http://www.theregister.co.uk/2015/12/17/mps_question_value_of_canning_raytheon_from_eborders/

we can learn what worked last time, do the things that worked, and avoid the things that didn't), It's often at this point when I am greeted with the response "umm, well there aren't any".

**And that, my friends is when my trifecta of red flags highlights to me why I've been brought in on the job.**

Apart from these answers being a cause of massive concern to me, the truly frustrating part of it all is that while the Programmes themselves vary (in terms of scale, complexity, drivers and motivations), the stakeholders seem to always insist that their situation is unique, and that no one else is going through or has gone through these situations before.

In reality, **all of these Programmes face and share one of the most overlooked and under rated issues, in that the stakeholder is simply too close to the problem. This is because:**

- They are **focusing on the wrong thing**. They are focusing on 'delivery' and less on 'discovery', and by not defining or describing the problem properly or clearly (or by the right people), you can end up solving the wrong problem – which isn't the one that they were originally meant to solve (I will provide plenty of examples later in this book);
- They are unable tosee that what they are **going through is a clearly defined process** – that has a beginning, middle and an end. The problem with the process is not just that they have virtually started in the middle (i.e. building a solution) and skimmed over the beginning (i.e. understanding clearly what they problem is they are solving), they have almost always not finished the Programme at the actual *'end'.* The Programme doesn't *actually* end when the solution is implemented, actually ends at *'Programme close'* - after the solution is delivered, and most importantly after the 'lessons learned' are captured and agreed. By the time the solution is implemented however everyone involved in the Programme (mainly the Business stakeholders – whose original problem it was to solve) are no longer interested or no longer have the patience to capture the lessons learned due to reasons ranging from their needs not being met to feeling their time has not been valued (from skimming over the 'beginning' of the process not understanding the real problems). Lessons learned are often only partially recorded or not to a sufficient level that is re-usable the next time around, so that when the next time comes, its literally starting from scratch; and
- They are **looking at it with the wrong lens.** They are looking at business problems often through a 'technical' lens. This is like holding a hammer and thinking every problem is a nail. Not every business problem needs to be solved with technology, and in most cases, it's a combination of business-changes, and technology but not technology alone (but don't tell Technical stakeholders that!).

So, what's the cause of these problems? How did they come about in the first place? Well, they came about because ***"there wasn't a structured framework"*** that put the Business first (rather than the solution or technology) *first.* One which defined the problem in Business' words, that the Business could understand and encompassed all phases of the process, capturing all the work and activities along the way in an agile fashion that recorded the changes and lessons learnt and built them into future iterations of the process. What they needed was a framework that clearly traced everything, from the needs and concerns raised at the CXO, Portfolio and Programme level, all the way through to the actual physical changes implemented in the Organisation as well as record if they were delivered as originally specified. Most importantly the framework should allow the Business stakeholders to see that their concerns have been addressed, and the effort they have contributed to the Programme has been worthwhile.

So, what is the answer? The answer (and answers to many other questions) is this framework - **HOBA® - House of Business Architecture®**, which is covered within this book – **'The Business Transformation Playbook® – *How to Implement Your Organisation's Target Operating Model (TOM) and Achieve a Zero Percent Fail Rate Using the 6-Step Agile Framework'.*** **HOBA®** is the framework I developed in answer to remedy my frustration (and that of my peers) and have been using over the years as an independent consultant. It addresses the problems mentioned above and has been designed with the Business, by the Business, for the Business – and most importantly, to be owned by the Business. **HOBA®** puts the control back into Business's hands, in a language the Business understands to drive and deliver the changes that allows an Organisation to execute on its Business Strategy and transformation and realise it's planned Business Benefits.

I hope you enjoy it.

Heath Gascoigne
Founder and CEO
HOBA Tech Ltd

# Acknowledgement

This book would not have been possible without the endless support from my parents, Debbie and Joe Gascoigne, my sisters Natalie and Renee and my brother in-laws Jeff Wichmann, and Hans Wesche, and my nieces Tayla, Maddi and Ashley. Thank you.

This list is endless, so apologies to anyone I omitted. I would also like to make a mention to the following people:

My MBA classmates (and lecturers) - Rod Taubman, Kwabena Aforo-Addo, Geoff Anderson, Dale Lawrence, Jonathan Lathlei, Lisa Walton, Leharna Black, David Watson, David Williams (and Dr Geoff 'Head of Strategy' Waring). Thank you for pushing me, and keeping me honest.

My former Programme and Project Managers, Business Architects, Technical Architects, Data Architects and Business Analyst colleagues – Val Smith, Helen Smith, Catherine Lewis McNulty, Charles Symonds, Julius Abensur, Tim Hook, Ben(jamin) Kopic, Liane Jackson, Alistair Cooke, Nick Dawes, Benjamin Slasberg, Chris Jarvis, Andy Frost, David Webb, Jeremy Vickers, Wayne Horkan, Beju Shah, Damien Bere and Jeb Cordery. Thank you for the comradeship, the challenges and bringing out the best in me.

My Sydney family, friends and former colleagues - Euta Roberts, William Toilolo, Danny Saluni, Matthew Fautua, Rob Williams, Arthur Basha, Gunnar Krueger, Hemathri Balakrishnan, Lisa Barker, Sam Tomaras and Tobin Fonseca. Thank you for the best early lessons any young 21-year-old man arriving in Australia could ask for.

My Melbourne friends and former colleagues - Cliff Moss, Ross Johnston, Mario Kukec, Luke & Roberta Chisholm, Dipen Patel, Adrian Thomas, Justin Baldaccino, Sally Milne, Euan Walker, Amy Thompson, Emma Sharrock, Wael Khudraj, Johnny & Paula Rogers, Phil & Alana Read, Cole Boulter, Adrian Hanley, Ben Kushinsky, Alex Louey, Taylor Tran, Hayden Rumble and Luke Bruce. Thank you for your friendship and the inspiration, and making that 4-day long weekend trip to Melbourne the most enjoyable 7-years of my life.

My New Zealand whanau (family) – Alastair Manihera, Richard Lancaster, Levani Lumon, Mike Honore, Wetex Kang, Adrian Tawhiti, Kylie Smith, Amanda Workman, Kellie Peyroux , Kristin McIntosh, Geoff Woodcock and Steve Parker.. Although most of you are now half way across the other side of the world, your support is always there, thank you.

My London family - Liam Buckley-Markey, Colin Schabort, Michael Goodacre, Noe Inigo, Erika Bernstedt, Ivan Panfilov. Carl McCrow, Moses Rashid, Wes Rashid, Andy Gray, Alex Zomignani, Cath Till, Christian & Helen Kypreos, Damian Miranda, Hayden & Lorena Smart, Lucian & Julia Pataki, Mark & George Barnes, Boyd & Katya Smart, David & Gillian van Klick, Narelle Ryan, Grazi Bittencourt and, Marisa Sefton. You make being half way across the world feel like home, thank you.

Thanks are also due to Agile evangelist and Agile Scrum Master Extraordinaire Joseph Cruickshank, for the ongoing expert Agile critique.

A special mention to Meredith Rogers. Thank you for introducing me to the Minto Principle (perhaps 'drumming into me' would be more appropriate?). I hope I was able to do your excellent tutelage justice.

And last but no means least, a very special mention to Aidan (& Vicki) Clark, for your constant inspiration and motivation, and Vicki, because as I have always said 'behind every good man is a good woman, and behind every good woman, is a good man'. Thank you.

# Contents

# PART 1
# PLAN

Part 1 sets the scene, and provides the background to Business Strategy and Business Architecture development and implementation. It explains the rationale for the book, where Business Architecture sits in terms of overall Enterprise Architecture, the challenges Business Architecture faces; the value it brings (and how to overcome them), and what **HOBA®** and the **Design Process** are about and how to use them.

- **Chapter 1: Introduction**, explains the purpose of this book, who should read it, how the book is organised, an assessment of current state of the problems, causes and answers to why there is such a high failure rate in transformation Programmes and how Business Architecture has the answers, scope, assumptions, case study and disclaimers.

- **Chapter 2: The Business Architecture Challenge**, discusses (and addresses) the 'elephant in the room'- the biggest challenges facing Business Architecture, and Business Architects today and how **HOBA®** and the **Design Process** overcomes them; as well as describing what Business Architecture is (and for completeness what it isn't) to clear up any confusion.

- **Chapter 3: HOBA® (House of Business Architecture®)**, discusses **HOBA®**, the complete Business Architecture framework to design and implement Organisation's, Business Strategy and Target Operating Model (TOM), **HOBA®**s four (4) complementary frameworks, and components, and **HOBA®**s alignment with other approaches.

- **Chapter 4: Design Process,** introduces the Target State Architecture Design Process ('**Design Process**'), its purpose and the objectives of each of the six (6) design steps. The detail (the actual 'activities' needed to complete each step) is discussed in the following section, Part 2 – Act.

# Why This Book?

**The Business Transformation Playbook® – *How to Implement Your Organisation's Target Operating Model (TOM) and Achieve a Zero Percent Fail Rate Using the 6-Step Agile Framework.* This book and framework guides you through implementing your Business Strategy and Target Operating Model (TOM) as part of your Organisation's business transformation - from start (concept), right the way through to the end (implementation).**

For those that know about Business Architecture, or any of the other architecture disciplines (Data, Information, Application, Technology, Security etc.) you might think this is a bold statement. Well, without causing any controversy, it is...and for good reason (as you will discover in this book).

Business Architecture, and 'Business Architecture concepts' are relatively simple, but their execution and implementation in practice are often not. Well, that's what a lot of management consultancies would like to tell you. That's how they make their money after all, usually charging exorbitant consultancy fees to solve supposedly "complex" problems. This my friends is also where the problem usually starts. And like any good problem solving scenario, the place to start addressing the problem is at the root cause.

Those of you currently in (or considering in embarking on) a business/technology change or transformation programme (or know someone who is), will know what this is all about. You've probably already brought a team of top notch consultants in to assess the current state of the organisation (aka 'the problem') and been given a 'recommendation' – consisting of fancy images hung on the programme wall along with a roadmap on how to implement the Target Operating Model ('the solution'). It will come as no surprise then that they've probably also told you 'we have a template for that' (known in the industry as a 'cookie cutter', not that they would actually tell you that). What they probably conveniently forget to mention is that it hasn't actually been tested in the market. Yes, they did have a team of top business professionals (school graduates) work on it tirelessly (as part of their internship) to provide a solid solution (which doesn't really make a lot of sense but is very colourful with 300+ pages of double sided A4 PowerPoint slides which you must admit looks very convincing!).

While colourful PowerPoint presentations are lovely, they can also be somewhat annoying. I say annoying because the 'recommended solution' or 'final recommendation' presented in them, is often very close to (if not word for word verbatim) what your internal team presented in terms of approach, recommendation and implementation path just 6-months earlier! If that's not annoying enough, the 300-page pack was so impressive and convincing that your Senior Executive board was so taken in by it (that's code for 'completely confused and bewildered') that they approved it. I have seen first-hand, time and again a bewildering situation in board meetings where CxO's had no clue about the execution strategy but signed off on it anyway rather than 'risk' looking silly or be perceived as 'incompetent' for having no real idea what the pack was saying.

But the real problem was 'what' the board signed off on. They didn't just sign off on the *'design'* of the TOM, they also signed off on the '*implementation*' of the TOM as well. But this make's perfect sense, right? Why get another third party to implement their design – the consultants who had their design approved, would also be the best to implement it, right? Well true, but here comes the worrying part. Some 12 months later (after the consultant team has doubled in size and is now occupying two floors of the building), the Organisation still finds itself in a position where there is still no operational 'final solution' to show for it, despite the huge printed artefacts on the wall that get incrementally and ceremonially updated with great bravado, as if they were the milestones of the project themselves!?

Added to this however are a whole bunch of new issues and concerns, which are 'promptly' now recorded on the Programme's ever growing Issues log. There's also a plethora of lovely new colourful artefacts on the wall, and a 'war room' now exists with a User Journey Map stuck to it (which took some 30-plus people more than 3 months to create when the project first started, none of whom are now around to explain what it is, or what it means!?
And it doesn't stop there. Each of these 'newly found' issues now require even more money, more resources, and more meetings with the CxO's to ask for (you guessed it) even more time and money – none of which was originally in scope or budgeted for but is now expected to be fixed along with the original problems the consultants were originally contracted to solve!

Are you starting to see the problem? But what's the answer? How do you and your Organisationstop being caught up in this ever revolving scenario (cue image of Bill Murry in the film 'Ground Hog Day')? Well my friends, that's the reason why I wrote this book.

**The first and primary purpose of this book** is to provide you with a complete, end-to-end framework and process to develop both the design and physical implementation of the TOM. And this end-to-end framework is called **HOBA®** or **House of Business Architecture®**, and the supporting process is the Target State Architecture Design Process **(AKA the 'Design Process')**.

Both **HOBA®** and the **Design Process** are intended to provide you with the right amount and level of information needed to develop and implement your **Business Strategy** and **Target Operating Model (TOM)** with a minimal amount of time, cost and effort. This includes ensuring you have ticked all your boxes, and is designed to give you a full view of the business to identify and capture the needs, concerns and issues the TOM is there to address, while minimalising your risks and providing the right level (and number) of impacted and inflected stakeholders involved to review and approve decisions in a timely manner.

By learning, and applying **HOBA®** and the **Design Process**, the aim of this book is to provide you with the ability to break down 'consultant speak' and get back to the root cause while understanding what your Organisation's fundamental objective is and how to achieve it. For the Business Architect and Business Architecture, that fundamental objective is developing the design of the **Target Operating Model (TOM)** that supports the Vision and aligns the Business to the Business Strategy. It's also managing the alignment of the implementation of the physical Business Architecture as well as the other architectures (e.g. technical, data etc.) that the design describes.

As you will see, if you aren't familiar with this already, the design of the Business Architecture and the Technology Architecture don't always develop at the same pace or rate for similar (but also other) reasons. For example, the programme is a technology driven change or transformation programme; the Sponsor is a CTO or CIO, or the funding is provided by the IT budget, so more focus, attention and even priority is (mistakenly, as I will argue later) given to technology.

The skill of the Business Architect is to ensure, that as the two architectures develop, they remain aligned throughout their development, and ultimately together support the Organisations Business Strategy.

**The second purpose of this book** is to provide a practical guide. As we will discuss, Business Architecture is relatively new to being recognised as a methodology and because of this it is (among other matters we'll delve into within these pages) suffering from an identity crisis. Business Architecture is often being confused with other methodologies, such as Enterprise Architecture or Business Analysis. Business Architecture as a concept is often thought of as "it's a good idea, we think we need to do it, but we don't know exactly what it looks like or how to do it?"

Business Architecture as a methodology is getting more visibility of late, as a number of programmes, companies, and professionals are noticing and experiencing that it is quickly becoming one of the common denominators in programmes that are successful in transforming the business and delivering on its vision, strategy and planned benefits. These programmes did it through a structured transparent approach that identifies and manages the identification of the Vision, Strategy and Business Benefits from conception, right through to implementation. That methodology my friends is Business Architecture.

From my experience (which I will share with you throughout this book), there's a lot of material out there. However, it's almost entirely based on theory and lacking in practical applications, especially around actual real-world examples of '*how to do Business Architecture*'. At least none that were showing *'what a day in the life'* of a Business Architect looks like – what they really do on a day to day basis, why they do it, what value do those activities have and what do those deliverables that make up the Business Architecture actually look like.

I will discuss, in a conceptual, logical and practical sense what that process is and what it looks like. That process is the Target State Architecture Design Process ('**Design Process**'), and the end result – the model of the Target State Architecture, which is both a model and a framework of the Target State Architecture, called **HOBA®** - the '**House of Business Architecture®'.**

After the frustrations I've felt and witnessed in the clients and companies that I've assisted, it's now time to share with you what I've done, how I did it, what the end result looked like and what the process was that I followed to get there.

Please use **HOBA®** to cut through the noise, (re) align your organisation to its Business Strategy, implement your business transformation and start realising your organisations Business Benefits and reaching its full potential!

# Who Should Read This Book

**The intended audience for this book is anyone who is involved in and/or interested in Business Architecture or Business Transformation. That includes current Business Architects (BA's), junior or senior BA's; stakeholders on a business or digital transformation programme where the Organisation is implementing a new Target Operating Model (TOM), fellow architects of other related disciplines (data, technology etc.), as well as Business Analysts of all levels interested in Business Architecture and/or looking to make the jump to becoming a Business Architect.**

This book is also equally intended for Start-ups, Founders, Entrepreneurs and those involved or interested in Start-ups. A Start-up has the advantage over a mature Organisation in that, as a new Organisation, they don't have overburdened and embedded processes, high levels of bureaucracy or an established culture which can hinder change by taking a long (or longer) time to make a decision and act on it.

With a Start-up, there is less bureaucracy, less obstacles in the way to prevent change. If the Start-up or Entrepreneur needs or wants to pivot or change the direction of the company, strategy or product range (due to changing market conditions, real or perceived barriers, potential competitor rivalry etc.), then no problem, the decision is made, and the change is usually almost immediately implemented. The only problem with this scenario is, while the ability to change quickly is often an advantage, if a change to the company's direction is made quickly, the rest of the company doesn't always get informed of the decision at the same speed the Entrepreneur would like to think they have, thereby not giving the rest of the company sufficient time to assess the impact of a change and how it might affect their existing work activities.

> **In fact, I have seen this with several Start-ups I've been involved in. A founder (or co-founder) often "sees an opportunity" and changes the direction of the company, but despite the business' relatively small size, fails to communicate those changes to the rest of the company.**

Once the 'rest' of the company learns of the 'changed direction', they soon realise that their time and efforts have been spent working on executing a now 'out of date' strategy (when they could have been working on developing and executing the 'new strategy'). The usual outcome is an inevitable and avoidable resentment and mistrust developing within the business, simmering just under the surface and negatively impacting the business.

Within this book we will also explore together the main challenges that Business Architecture faces today in both recognition and usage (and how to overcome them). This includes having a clear sight of the entire business so that changes (or potential changes in one part of the business; i.e. strategy) can be seen where it impacts other parts of the business (i.e. operations, and implementation) to prevent scenarios such as the one I've mentioned above. This is achieved through a transparent process (the '**Design Process**') and structured framework - **HOBA®**, the **House of Business Architecture®.**

The approach and process to design and

implementation is based on an Agile project management approach of iterative (continuous) design and implementation to clearly show all the affected stakeholders impacted by the implementation of the Business Strategy and Business Architecture and how the Business Architecture supports the organisations Vision, as well as how Business Architecture aligns all parts of the business to execute the organisations Business Strategy effectively and efficiently.

> **I will also briefly discuss the *Transformation Test*, which is a set of questions designed to score you on each of the six areas (and overall score) of the HOBA® framework and Design Process described in this book.**

This free online test is based on the same philosophy behind designing the **Target Operating Model (TOM)** and starting with the Current Operating Model - *"you can only improve on what you measure"*. Your individual (and overall) score becomes the agreed baseline to build from. You will get a customised *Transformation Scorecard®* report with tips and access to tools and training to improve your score and speed up your progress and the success implementing your Organisations transformation.

This book is not intended to explain the origins of Agile or Agile Scrum project management in depth. Neither will it provide details about how to set up a Business Architect department in your Organisation or the details of effective stakeholder management. There isimply aren't enough pages within this book to truly do justice to these subjects, and there is already a lot of useful information regarding these and related topics available out there. I have as a result provided links in the additional reading section for your benefit should you wish to investigate these areas further. All referenced sources are provided in the footnotes.

> **What you *will* learn by reading this book however is the practical application of applying a transparent design process and structured Business Strategy and Business Architecture framework (HOBA®) to maximise the full and true value of Business Architecture.**

Your Transformation Scorecard® will provide you a report on your strengths and weaknesses and tips and tools on how to improve your score and improving the success of your Organisations transformation. My goal is to help you to be a successful and competent Business Architect and *hopefully*, overcome some of the common problems facing Business Architecture, and the Business Architecture community today. The models, diagrams and tables found within these pages (including Case Study examples) are intended to provide you with not only context and visual aids of what's discussed, but to be reproduced and used as you see fit.

There is a distinct lack of understanding of the value of Business Architecture is today, what it is and how to develop it. We will discuss these (and other points) in more detail in *Chapter 2 The Business Architecture Challenge*.

# How This Book Is Organised

**This book is divided into the following three (3) parts* - 'Plan, Act, Do', based off the following Plan-Act-Do-Review Action-Learning-Cycle:**

- **Plan** – Identify the areas of study (i.e. **HOBA®** framework and the **Design Process**);
- **Act** – Knowledge acquisition (i.e. learn the 'Activities' (Act) needed to carry out the work);
- **Do** – Knowledge application (i.e. implement what you just learnt), and
- **Review** – Review and reflect (i.e. assess progress and process and feedback lessons learned into the next cycle of work).

(*) Note:

- Review' doesn't have its own separate part in this book, as 'review' (and reflection) is included in and carried out throughout **HOBA®** and the **Design Process. HOBA®** and the **Design Process** are closely aligned to the Agile Scrum ('Scrum') project management methodology. Scrum is based on the three (3) pillars of Transparency, Inspection and Adaption, which provides the 'review and reflection'. **HOBA®** uses the Scrum methodology for managing the development and delivery of Business Architecture deliverables. Scrum also provides the control to manage the incremental development and delivery of usable Business Architecture deliverables to the Business at regular intervals.
- We will discuss Scrum, and **HOBA®**'s alignment to other approaches in the *Alignment with Other Approaches* section later in this book.

## Part 1 – Plan

**Part 1 sets the scene, and provides the background to Business Strategy and Business Architecture development and implementation. It explains the rationale for the book, where Business Architecture sits in terms of overall Enterprise Architecture, the challenges Business Architecture faces (and how to overcome them); the value Business Architecture brings, what HOBA® and the Design Process are about and how to use them.**

- **Chapter 1: Introduction**, explains the purpose of this book, who should read it, how the book is organised, an assessment of the current state of the problems, causes and answers to why there is such a high failure rate in transformation programmes and how Business Architecture has the answers, scope, assumptions, case study and disclaimers.
- **Chapter 2**: **The Business Architecture Challenge,** discusses (and addresses) the "elephant in the room" - the biggest challenges facing Business Architecture, and Business Architects today and how **HOBA®** and the **Design Process** overcome them; as well as what Business Architecture is (and isn't - just' to clear up any confusion).

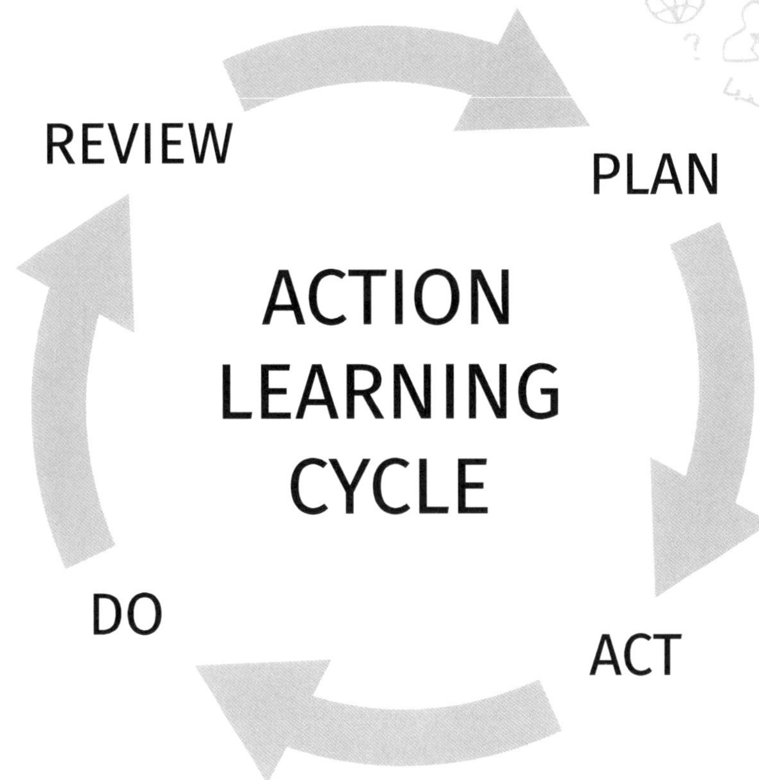


**Figure 1.1** – Plan-Act-Do-Review Action Learning Cycle.

- **Chapter 3**: **HOBA®** (**House of Business Architecture®**), discusses **HOBA®**, the complete Business Architecture framework to design and implement Organisations Business Strategy and Target Operating Model (TOM), **HOBA®**'s four (4) complementary frameworks, and components, and **HOBA®**'s alignment with other approaches.
- **Chapter 4: Design Process**, introduces the Target State Architecture Design Process ('**Design Process**'), its purpose and objectives of each of the six (6) design steps. The detail (the actual 'activities' needed to complete each step) is discussed in the following section, Part 2 – Act).

# Part 2 – Act

**Here I outline 'the activities' to be carried out in designing and implementing the Target Operating Model (TOM). These 'activities' are the actual steps needed to design and implement the TOM.**

- **Chapter 5:** Step 1 - **Focus,** explains the first step of the **Design Process**, which is about setting the focus and direction of the Organisation, and the Business Architecture. It defines the roles, expectations and scope of the Programme as well as the Business Architecture. Focus is provided through defining the **HOBA®** Business Motivation Model Reference Model.
- **Chapter 6:** Step 2 - **Control**, explains the second step of the **Design Process**, which is about setting and agreeing the governance structures and processes, the key stakeholder's roles, and design principles. Control is provided through defining the **HOBA®** Governance Reference Model.
- **Chapter 7:** Step 3 - **Analyse**, explains the third step of the **Design Process,** which is about assessing the state of the Current Operating Model (i.e. the Organisation intends to realise from both the business' strategy and transformation Programme. 'Evaluate' is provided through defining the **HOBA®** Benefits Model Reference Model.
- **Chapter 8:** Step 4 - **Evaluate**, explains the fourth step of the **Design Process**, which is *'evaluation'* of the both the Business Benefits the organisation intends to realise from both the business' strategy and transformation programme. 'Evaluate' is provided through defining the **HOBA®** Benefits Model Reference Model.
- **Chapter 9:** Step 5 – **Design**, explains the fifth step of the **Design Process**, which is the 'design' of the future state operating model – the **Target Operating Model (TOM).** The development of the TOM is based on the elements of the Business Capabilities (people, process and technology) that were identified from the previous Step (4- Evaluate).. 'Design' is provided through the **HOBA®** Target Operating Model (TOM) Reference Model.

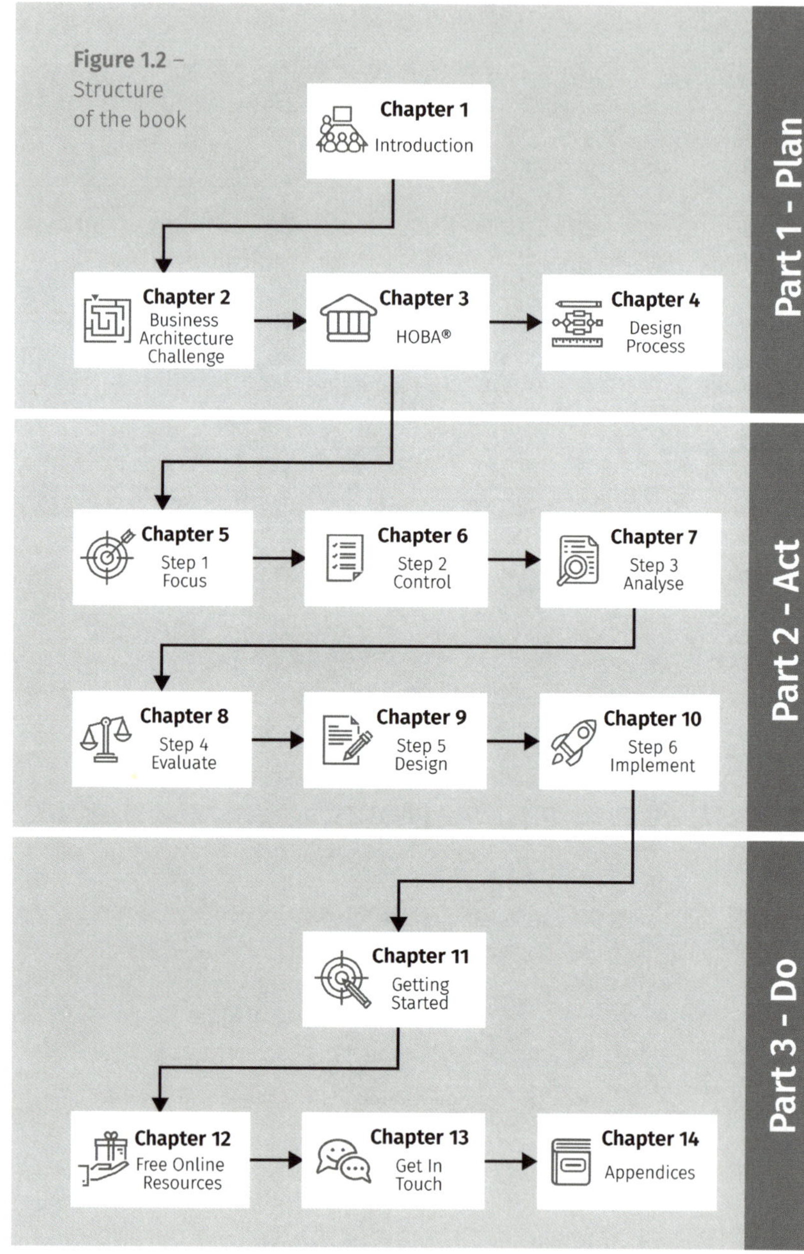


**Figure 1.2** – Structure of the book

- **Chapter 10:** Step 6 – **Implement**, explains the sixth step of the **Design Process,** which is the delivery of both the 'design' of the Target Operating Model (TOM) and managing the alignment of the implementation of the 'physical' Business Architecture with the 'design' of the TOM. 'Implementation' is provided through the **HOBA®** Road Map Model Reference Model.

# Part 3 – Do

**Part 3 describes the practical approaches to getting started and using HOBA® in your Programme or work place immediately (i.e. today), starting with a recap of the key points of HOBA® framework and the Design Process, Getting Started options, Online Resources, Get in Touch (with the Author - me!) and finally, the Appendices.**

- **Chapter 11 – Getting Started**, recaps the key points of **HOBA®** and the Design Process, Getting Started options (where and how to start using **HOBA®** now), Next Book, **HOBA®** Cheat Sheet (reference) of the different elements of **HOBA®,** and the aspect's (Why, Who, What, Where, How, and When) they address to get you off to a flying start!
- **Chapter 12 – Free Online Resources**, take the free online Transformation Test and get your Transformation Scorecard®, assess your strengths and weaknesses to successfully implement your Organisations Target Operating Model (TOM) as part of the business transformation and get your personalised report and tips to improve your score, visiting www.hoba.tech and download the latest free resources – templates, checklists, toolkits and case studies.
- **Chapter 13 –** Get in Touch, comments, credits, training, consulting and talk details, contact details on how to connect with the Author (me)!
- **Chapter 14 –** Appendices – contains the important facts that you may want to look up now (as you read), and/or refer to later. Includes the Glossary, Tables list, Figures list, Reference Models, Building Blocks and Blueprints, Additional Reading List and Index.

# How To Read This Book

**In terms of what to read and where to start, that will depend on a lot of things, including your interest, experience and objectives.**

I would suggest starting at **Part 1 – Plan** (and related chapters 1, 2, 3 and 4). This will give you an understanding of the background issues facing Business Architecture and todays Business Architects. This will provide some context, and a mutual baseline of understanding of where this book is coming from, after which you can start flipping through to specific sections that may be of the greatest interest or focus on your objectives. From there, although each chapter builds on the previous chapter (or rather – each Building Block, and design step builds on the predecessor Building Block and design step), it is possible to focus on areas of greater interest to you, by skipping straight to and between the chapters.

To help you get the most out of this book, **Part 2 – Act**, is structured in the following intentional order intentionally structured as follows:

- Introduction - provides an overview of the section;
- Reference Model (e.g. Business Motivation Model) – brief description,
- Reference Model aspect:
  - Process
  - Perspective
  - Context
  - Content
- High Level Process (SIPOC) - high level SIPOC (Supplier-Input-Process-Output-Customer) diagram showing:
  - Who is the **(S)**upplier involved in this step,
  - What **(I)**nputs are required,
  - the **(P)**rocess (Building Blocks) that is carried out,
  - **(O)**utputs (Blueprints) that are generated, and

- Who are the **(C)**ustomers who receives it.

An example of the SIPOC diagram is shown in *Figure 1.3* below.

Each Output listed in the SIPOC is a specifically number referenced Blueprint. The numbering referencing sequence easily helps identify where you are in the **Design Process**, and the related Reference Model, Building Blocks and Blueprints.

The number referencing starts at 1.0 (for Step 1), and increases incrementally 0.1 for each lower level **HOBA®** requirement – from Reference Model (e.g. 1.0); Building Block (e.g. 1.1) to Blueprints (e.g. 1.1.1). An example of the **numbering sequence** is shown below:

- **Design Process Step** e.g. **Step 1** - Focus
- **Reference Model** e.g. **1.0** - Business Motivation Model
- **Building Block** e.g**. 1.1** - Business Architecture Approach
- **Blueprint** e.g. **1.1.1** – Statement of Work (SOW)

The objective of the intentional structuring of **HOBA®** referencing is as follows:

- It makes it easy to identify which step in the **Design Process** is related to which element of the **HOBA®** model (Reference Model, Building Block or Blueprint. For example, Step 1 Focus, covers and address the '1.0 - Business Motivation Model'.
- Predefined reference numbers for all the steps, Reference Models, Blueprints and Building Blocks make it a closed 'system' of all the activities and deliverables to streamline the process, activities and reduce the amount of work needed to develop and implement the design of the TOM.
- There is a finite number of possible Blueprints that are worth using, that add the most value, and don't cause (unnecessary) work (or rework) or provide little to no value.
- This *'streamlining'* effect will help, doing the minimum amount of work possible in the least amount of time, but most importantly

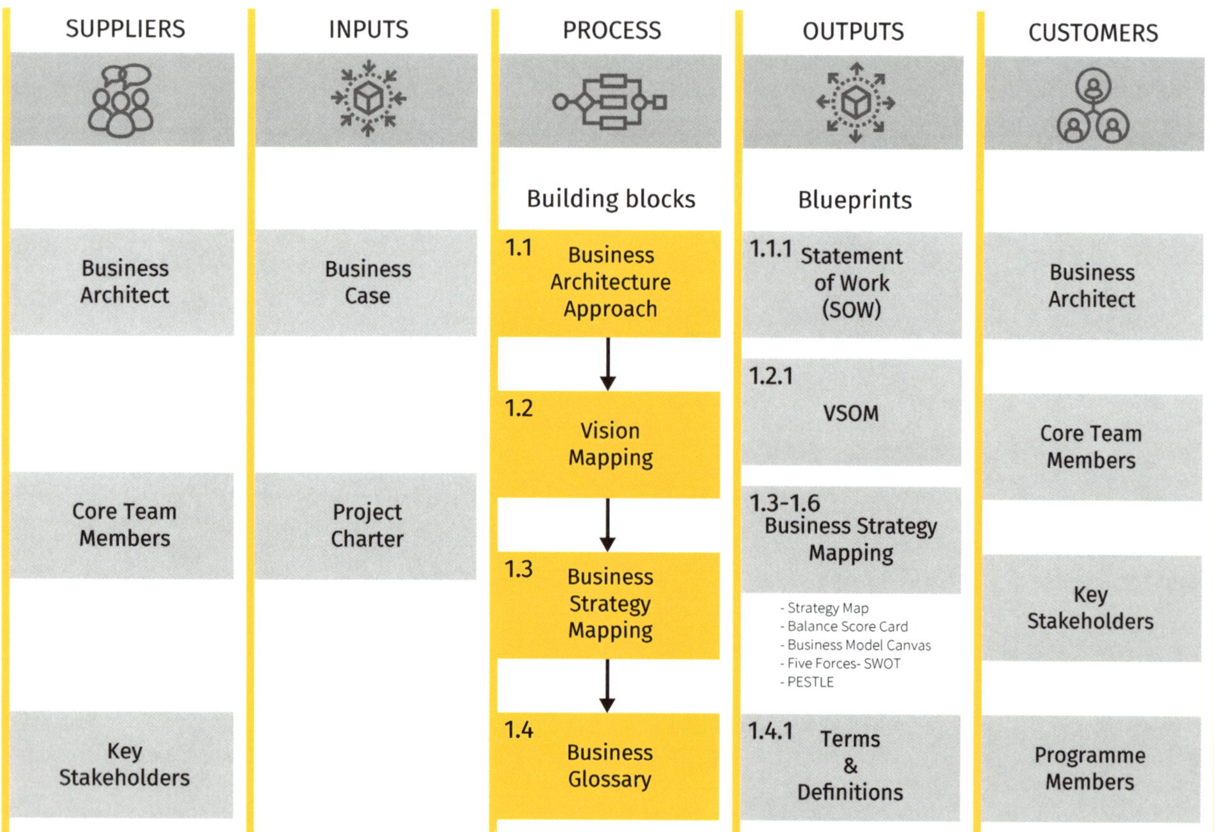


**Figure 1.3** - Example SIPOC diagram

help avoid the numerous distracting conversations that certain Blueprints or views of the Business Architecture "should and need to be considered" they say. The guess work has been removed (and time saved), as **HOBA®** provides the superset of Reference Models, Building Blocks and Blueprints to be considered and completed.

Following on from the Introduction section is the related Blueprint that was listed as an (O) utput in the SIPOC diagram. Each Blueprint section is sign-posted with the following headings:

- **Introduction** – covers objective, purpose, benefits;
- **Inputs** – lists the Blueprints needed to begin and complete this section;
- **Outputs** – covers the expected outputs (i.e. Blueprints) produced;
- **Steps** – the steps required to complete the Building Block (and respective Blueprints), in order to produce the stated Outputs (above);
- **Risks and Mitigations** – things to watch out for that could derail your efforts;
- **Building Block Wrap-up** – brief wrap up of the Building Block just covered,
- **Reference Model Recap** – quick recap of the Reference Model so far,
- **Next Steps** – The next step in the Design Process.

## Current Situation

Like every Programme, it's always important to begin with getting everyone on the same page and creating common understanding of the current situation with strategy planning, implementation and where Business Architecture fits in.

Now, despite existing frameworks and leading experts (and even management consultancies) specialising in strategy planning and implementation, there are unfortunately high failure rates (as high as 70%[4]) in the transformation Programmes that implement these strategic transformations (namely I.T or 'digital transformation' Programmes).

These high failure rates in implementing a new or change of Business Strategy or new **Target Operating Model (TOM)** aren't isolated to just existing businesses but new business start-ups as well. Alarmingly, 75% of crowdfunding business start-ups also fail. A recent study by Anglia Ruskin University[5] looked at why such a high proportion of crowdfunding projects the study primarily looked at success factors (such as reputation, reciprocity, timing social networks, ambition and impatience), it also looked at modelling and predictability of the success of these crowd funding campaigns using the 'Kickstarter' website. The reasons why they failed could be found in the opposite argument to why they succeeded, of which I would argue aren't inherently isolated to crowdfunding projects, but shared with IT transformation Programmes as well.

Crowdfunding projects fail for a number of reasons, one of which was covered by the study 'ambition', which questioned if these businesses were too ambitious, competed in a red ocean and ended up getting eaten alive? The first question any founder (and indeed Business Architect) needs to ask should be 'Is there a hole in the market, and if there is, is there a market in that hole?' What usually happens, is the founder has a bias (normally a confirmation bias) where they form a hypothesis or belief and use the research they conduct to confirm that belief, and reject everything that doesn't. If the founder is very convincing, through group-think with the rest of the business, they are able to quickly (and effectively) get everyone singing from the same hymn sheet, singing the same (inadvertently incorrect) song, leading to the wrong outcomes, or worse – no outcomes at all (project fail). When you read The Problem section below, you would wonder if Start-ups suffer from the same issues too.

---

[4] McKinsey, Quarterly Transformation Executive Survey (2008)

[5] Anglia Ruskin University: Why 3 out of 4 crowdfunding projects fail (Sep 2016) http://www.anglia.ac.uk/news/why-3-out-of-4-crowdfunding-projects-fail

## The Problem

According to the Chaos Report, there are two (2) types of problem Programmes:

- **Challenged Programmes** (completed but over budget, time and fewer features and functions than originally specified), and
- **Impaired Programmes** (cancelled at some point during the development phase).

Factors contributing to challenged projects, ranked lack of user input, incomplete requirements or specifications and changing statement of requirements at the top of the list:

Project Challenged Factors (top 4)[6]

**Table 1.1**

| Project Challenged Factors | % of Responses |
|---|---|
| Lack of User Input | 13% |
| Incomplete Requirements & Specifications | 12% |
| Changing Requirements & Specifications | 12% |
| Lack of Executive Support | 8% |

Factors that were present in impaired projects, ranked incomplete requirements, lack of user involvement and lack of resources and unrealistic expectations as the top 4.

Project Impaired Factors (top 4)[7]

**Table 1.2**

| Project Impaired Factors | % of Responses |
|---|---|
| Incomplete Requirements | 13% |
| Lack of User Involvement | 12% |
| Lack of Resources | 11% |
| Unrealistic Expectations | 10% |

[6, 7, 8] The Standish Group (2014), Chaos Report

## The Solution

So, what does that tell us? Its tells us if you want to increase the 'chance' of success for your transformation Programme, the common following success factors are almost certainly mandatory:

- **get users involved,**
- **get support from the top, and**
- **be clear about the why (objective), how (strategy) and when (implementation).**

The Chaos report surveyed those success criteria, and ranked the factors contributing to project success (completed on time and on budget, with all features and functions as initially specified) as follows:

Project Success Factors (top 4)[8]

**Table 1.3**

| Project Success Factors | % of Responses |
|---|---|
| User Involvement | 16% |
| Executive Management Support | 14% |
| Clear Statement of Requirements | 13% |
| Proper Planning | 10% |

So, in terms of developing and implementing your Business Strategy and **Target Operating Model (TOM)**, to increase the chance of your success, you must ensure you have in place and do the following:

- **Involve the Users** (and stakeholders, including executive management) in the development of the design and implementation of the Business Strategy and TOM from the start (to finish),
- **Establish the Governance Model** (Reference Model) that ensures the right level and coverage of executive support and decision making is in place,
- **Provide a robust requirements framework and process** where requirements are captured, validated and released (published) when agreed in an approved and suitable state for others to continue working from, and
- **Provide a clear plan of the activities, deliverables** to be produced, and roles and responsibilities outlining who is (R)esponsible, (A)ccountable, (C)onsulted, and (I)nformed (RACI) to complete each activity.

I will discuss in the following chapters how **HOBA®** and the **Design Process** addresses each of the success criteria (and more).

# Scope

## In Scope

The goal in writing this book was to provide you with a structured approach, framework and model – **HOBA®**, the **House of Business Architecture®** for designing and implementing your Business Strategy and Target Operating Model (TOM), and the process for doing that, the **Design Process.**

The purpose of **HOBA®** and the **Design Process** is to align the Business to the Business Strategy, which also means ensuring the developing Business Architecture and Technology (IT) Architecture are aligned, as they will (and do) develop often in parallel (but not always, in an ideal world they should develop in sync) over the life cycle of the Programme.

The scope of this book is based around the business scenario where Business Architecture (and Business Architects) are required or requested on a project or Programme that is either in-flight (i.e. has passed the conception) or in the planning phase having already defined the Organisations Business Strategy. This scenario is chosen because it is the area right now in need of the greatest attention with the big questions being asked of (and by) Executive and Senior Management who are looking for answers from Business Architecture.

What this scenario means in terms of scope is that the activities needed and covered in this book focus on on taking the agreed Business Strategy and developing the *design* of the Business Architecture that aligns the business to that Business Strategy. It will also include the implementation steps and Blueprints necessary to implement that design – the *physical* Business Architecture.

## Out of Scope

The following areas are deemed out of scope for this book:

- How to facilitate walkthrough's, workshops and stakeholder management.
- Other architecture domains - data, application, technology, data, information etc.
- Business Strategy Mapping - e.g. market penetration, expansion, diversification etc. (see assumptions section).
- Setting up a Business Architecture department or unit in your Organisation*.
- Using Business Architecture as a Strategic Tool*.

I think that there is a lot of useful information regarding these (above) topics that can be found online, in other books, manuals, and even certifications that cover them. To cover them here would require an entire new book(s) to do them justice. The latter two bullets (*) however, will possibly come in later editions of this book or subjects of future books.

# Assumptions

The following assumptions have been made in writing this book - about you, Your Project or Programme and Organisation:

**You:**

- You may have some level of knowledge of Projects, Project Management and Programme Management, and are therefore familiar with related terms and acronyms, which means not a lot of time is spent on elaborating (assumed) *'known'* terms. For any unknown terms, refer to the glossary, reference or additional reading section(s).

**Your Project or Programme:**

- Your project is a Business Transformation Programme, with Information Technology (IT) /system/service and/or software as the Enabler. In other words, it is not 'construction' or 'building' architecture based or related, which 'business' architecture is often wrongly confused with. The frameworks, principles, and design process(es) outlined in this book however, are industry agnostic and can be applied across a range of sectors and industries (including construction and building architecture).
- Your project scale and size would be classified as *'medium to large'.* Examples of these projects would include the decommissioning or on-boarding of new and legacy IT and software systems and applications, business process, process re-engineering as well as regulatory and policy driven business and system changes. Although the recommendations supplied and promoted here are applicable

and transferable across sectors and industries, developing a full-blown architecture for a *'small'* project (e.g. adding new features to an existing website) would be over doing it, and you probably don't or didn't need a Business Architect to do that job for you (a Business aAnalyst might do).

- The project management methodology promoted here is *Agile*. Scrum Agile to be specific. Scrum is an iterative and incremental agile software development methodology. Scrum method is preferred over the gated waterfall method, as Scrum produces high velocity and quality output over the traditional gated waterfall process.
- Your project or Programme governance is established, with the proper design authorities or boards in place, proper distribution of stakeholders across the Organisation, with the right level of management oversight and authority (Responsible (R), Accountable (A), Consulted (C) and Informed (I)) to contribute to the design and delivery of the Business Architecture. This also includes the right level of management oversight and approval for the Business Architecture. We all know in reality that this never turns out to be the case, which I address in **HOBA®** Governance Reference Model, Step 2 – Control of the Design Process.

**Your Organisation:**

- Your Organisation is established and has an operating model, existing products, services and customers (i.e. is not a new business or Start-up or planning a Start-up). This is important for two (2) reasons:

1. As the Target State Architecture (model), **HOBA®** makes the assumption that there is an existing current ('as-is') Operating Model, to serve as the baseline model and;
2. Your business's strategy and Business Strategy development has already been developed, completed and is in place. With a new business, concept or Start-up, there is effectively no current operating model (as it doesn't exist), only a future or Target Operating Model. While the principles and frameworks contained within this book are applicable to both types of Organisations (existing and new/start-ups), this book will focus on already, operating Organisations.

- Business Strategy, Mapping, Building Block and Blueprint(s) will be covered 'lightly', to show what you should expect to see and do to develop and validate the Business Strategy for a new business start-up. Business Strategy Mapping maybe looked at in future versions or later releases of this book.

# Case Study

To make reading this book as real and practical as possible (not the conceptual approach that Business Architecture is often accused of), an example case study has been used throughout the book.

The case study scenario used is a topical subject in a lot of pubs and workplaces around London. As a fairly large segment of people arrived in the country via the process, (which I was personally involved in), so hopefully many of you out there can relate or appreciate the scale, complexity, or the large number of individuals that use or are subjected to this process.

Without giving too much away, that case study is 'roughly' based on a government digitisation Programme - which included digitalising (a 'digital transformation') a predominantly manual (paper-based) Visa Application process, with an online (digital) application process and supporting IT systems.

For simplicity (although in reality a relatively complicated process), we are only going to be concerned with and focus on the Student Visa 'postal' application route, process and project within the Programme. To give you a sense of the size and scale of this Programme and how this project had to ensure it was aligned with the other projects (not just within the same Programme, but with others too), and to keep the case study scope manageable, the following changes have been excluded from the case study scenario:

- The different Visa types (e.g. Highly Skilled, Entrepreneur, Sponsored, Seasonal Worker etc.);
- The different application routes - Priority Postal, and Premium Service - which requires making and booking an appointment for a face-to-face interview, made via a separate (booking application) system was also being replaced as part of the overall transformation Programme, by another Programme;
- Replacing a legacy case working system, which was handled by another project within

the Programme, with its different sets of stakeholders and Business Benefits; and

- Creating (and maintaining) a person centric database, which was being delivered by another project within the Programme, again with its different set of stakeholders and Business Benefits.

Once the new online application system and process was ready, it would be extended and rolled out to 'out of country' visa applications, and other Visa types and application routes (i.e. premium service centres which require booking an appointment at the time of application), which is out of scope for the case study.

There are so many stakeholders involved in developing and delivering the Business Architecture, both internal stakeholders (departments, business functions and business units), and external (Applicants, outsourced suppliers and vendor suppliers) that their needs and concerns need to be catered for. This not only makes it interesting for a case study, but is also typical of most large Programmes with their various and different perspectives, objectives and goals. These large number of stakeholders also present additional challenges in managing the changes and dependencies both within the Programme and across the Organisation that need to be managed.

As we will step through **HOBA®** - with its Reference Models, Building Blocks, Blueprints, and the Design Process (with its clearly articulated SIPOC process - outlining what is needed, who is providing the inputs, the process steps, outputs and customer, to develop the Business Architecture that will deliver the Business Strategy), we will use the case study as the working example.

With **HOBA®** and the **Design Process,** you will see how you and your Programme can manage the end to end design and implementation of the Target Operating Model, align the Business to the Business Strategy, and set up to realise the intended Business Benefits, ideally to a greater level of success and confidence than ever before.

All or any private or confidential information regarding the 'actual' Programme is not shown, discussed or mentioned. The case study is used for example and illustration purposes only.

# Disclaimer

This book was only made possible due to the number of companies and consultancies I have been fortunate enough to have worked in (and alongside). Examples within these pages have therefore been 'amended' as deemed necessary to ensure those Organisation's privacy and anonymity.

It goes without saying that I could not have written this book, particularly as a practical guide, without basing it on real world practical experience. I have drawn on years of my experience across a range of industries, clients, countries, education and qualifications to provide you with as much ammunition to face your challenges head on. Having said this, I am compelled to say that all examples, references, comments and/or remarks are the expressions and opinions of the authors alone, unless otherwise specified or referenced via an (external) source(s). Sources are provided in the foot-notes.

Some of the projects and programmes I've had the privilege to work on (and with) have required high security clearance due to the sensitivity of the information that the project encompassed. As a result, and in respect of this sensitivity (and where practical), examples within this book will and have been referred to as 'on a company I assisted' or similar, to protect the identification of all parties concerned.

# Chapter 2 The Business Architecture Challenge



## Introduction

As you might have guessed from *Chapter 1 Business Architecture* is facing a few challenges right now. It shouldn't be surprising, Business Architecture and Business Architects are currently competing with some well-established practices and disciplines, cultures and project acceptance issues, and possibly some (misdirected?) frustrations.

To the uninitiated, this lack of recognition and acceptance could be quite daunting for anyone considering a career in Business Architecture, or promoting themselves as a Business Architect. However, to the unintimidated this should be considered as an 'opportunity' (I personally like to see it this way!). The opportunity is to show the real value and benefits of Business Architecture. A recent report by Gartner[9] said:

> **"Organisations that support Business Architecture have a significantly higher ability to execute on their Business Strategy, because they have a clear understanding of the strategy and its impact on business and IT, and guidance to drive delivery."**

But before we (you, and I) discuss the real value and benefits of Business Architecture, let's first understand what the real problems are (not just the symptoms) that Business Architecture is facing. What we are seeing, or have seen, are the symptoms of the problems. What we should be asking, and we will address here, is the underlying root cause(s).

In a recent Business Architecture conference I attended in Berlin, it was remarked that the issues facing Business Architecture and Business Architects today aren't isolated events but are common issues faced across the industry. These issues (and common misconceptions) are so prevalent that they have even been given a name. They are collectively called 'The Business Architecture Challenge', which are summed up into the following five (5) questions:

1. What is Business Architecture?
2. What is the value of Business Architecture?
3. What does this value look like?
4. When can I see the value of Business Architecture?
5. What is the role of the Business Architect (and when do we engage them)?

Each one of these questions (and challenges) are discussed in the following section.

[9] Gartner (2014), 'Business Architecture Is Not Optional for Business Outcome Driven EA'

# Challenge #1: What is Business Architecture?

In answering a question like this, it's helpful to define what something both is as well as what it isn't. With this in mind I propose splitting this question into two parts:

1. What is Business Architecture? and
2. What isn't Business Architecture?

Each of these questions are discussed in more detail below.

## What is Business Architecture?

There are two ways to answer this question – in 'text-book' terms, and in 'practical' terms (one is almost always more helpful than the other):

1. In 'text book' terms (according to TOGAF® – The Open Group Architecture Framework), Business Architecture is defined as:

**"A description of the structure and interaction between the business strategy, organisation, functions, business processes and information needs."**

As a reminder (or introduction to those not familiar with TOGAF®), The Open Group Architecture Framework (TOGAF®) is a framework owned by The Open Group, for developing Enterprise Architecture (EA). The Open Group and TOGAF® view and place Business Architecture as a single phase within the TOGAF®'s process of developing the Enterprise Architecture, the Architecture Development Method (ADM) and as an element within a traditional IT based Enterprise Architecture, as shown in *Figure 2.1*:

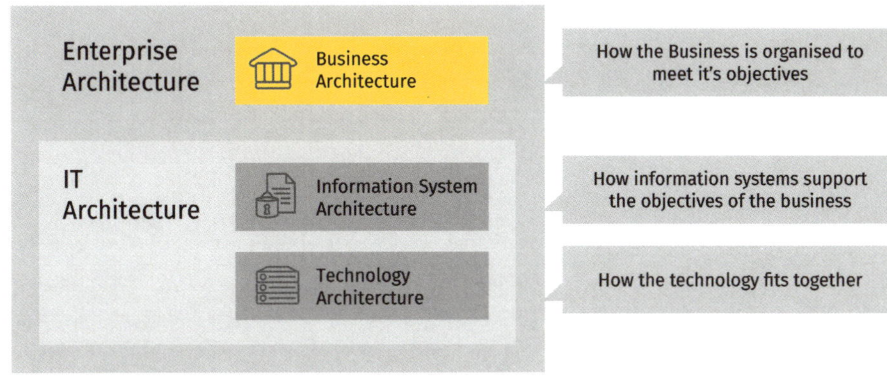


**Figure 2.1** - Business Architecture and IT Architecture make up Enterprise Architecture[10]

While TOGAF® doesn't see Business Architecture as its discipline, methodology or framework in its own right, TOGAF® (to its credit) does introduce Business Architecture to a predominately IT driven industry (Enterprise Architecture), and the concept of – process, iterative development, and re-use of architecture assets (i.e. Blueprints), all of which are core parts **HOBA®** and discussed in detail in later sections of this book.

2. In 'practical' terms, the definition of Business Architecture is:

**"The 'why, who, what, where, how and when' of a business - how it is set up and organised to deliver the Organisations Business Strategy"**

Specifically, Business Architecture answers the following questions concerning an Organisation and its processes:

- **WHY** do they do it?
- **WHO** does it?

[10] Martin, C. (2013) 'An introduction into the design of business using Business Architecture' http://www.slideshare.net/craigrmartin/togdiscobiz?related=1

- **WHAT** do they do?
- **WHERE** do they do it?
- **HOW** do they do it? and
- **WHEN** do they do it?

To put Business Architecture in context of the process of strategic planning and strategy execution, Business Architecture is the bridge that makes 'strategy' happen in the real life, as illustrated by *Figure 2.2* below:

**Figure 2.2** - Business Architecture is the bridge between Strategy Planning & Strategy Execution

Business Architecture's goal is to support the Organisations vision through aligning the business to support the Organisations Business Strategy. It is only through setting up and structuring the Business in such a way, that allows it to execute the Business Strategy effectively and efficiently.

Business Architecture's unique position between strategic planning and strategic execution, allows it to identify opportunities for investment (i.e. business capabilities), what explicitly those capabilities look like, and the outcomes that will be achieved[12].

In a recent 'Aligning Enterprise Architecture and Business Architecture' presentation by Export Development Canada (EDC)[13] , EDC showed how Business Architecture is accountable for taking the Business Strategy, to identify projects (and initiatives), and through the identification of Business Benefits, using Technology Architecture, Project Management and Programme Management Office (PMO), identify the projects and initiatives that the develop the Business Capabilities to produce the Outcomes (i.e. implemented Target Operating Model), that when used by the Business, realise the intended Business Benefits, as shown in *Figure 2.3* on the next page.

What is worth noting from *Figure 2.3*, the Business Architect is firmly seated in what would be the 'planning' phases and not 'delivery' (i.e. Project Management) of the Outcomes the business is seeking. Business Architectures role in Outcomes is to identify (and prioritise) the projects and initiatives that produce those Outcomes, that when used by the Business, realise the intended Business Benefits. 'How' Business Architecture identifies those investment opportunities (i.e. business capabilities) to develop the Target Operating Model (TOM) is covered in *Chapter 8 Step 4 – Evaluate* using the Benefits Model Reference Model.

## What isn't Business Architecture?

Business Architecture has been (and still is) suffering from an identity crisis – admittedly partly its own fault and partly based on its naming association, tools and the techniques used. We will now quickly look at the differences and similarities (and thus confusion) with the following:

- Business Architecture is *not* Enterprise Architecture
- Business Architecture is *not* Technology Architecture
- Business Architecture is *not* Business Analysis
- Business Architecture is *not* Business Change

I will clear up this confusion and discuss each of these in the following sections.

### Business Architecture is *not* Enterprise Architecture

This is one of the biggest misconceptions, that 'Business Architecture is Enterprise Architecture'. As discussed in the *What is Business Architecture?* section above, Business Architecture is an element of Enterprise Architecture, it is not "Enterprise Architecture" per se. Enterprise Architecture is made up of Business Architecture and Technology Architecture. To call Business Architecture – 'Enterprise Architecture' is incorrect.

There are Business Architects who call themselves or are called 'Enterprise-Business Architects', which raises the question: are you responsible for

---

[12] Export Development Canada (EDC) - Business Architecture Innovation Summit, OMG/Business Architecture Guild, Reston, VA, 'Aligning Enterprise Architecture and Business Architecture' (March 2014)
[13] Business Architecture Innovation Summit, OMG/Business Architecture Guild, Reston, VA, (Mar 2014)
[14] Export Development Canada (EDC) - Business Architecture Innovation Summit, OMG/Business Architecture Guild, Reston, VA, 'Aligning Enterprise Architecture and Business Architecture' (March 2014)

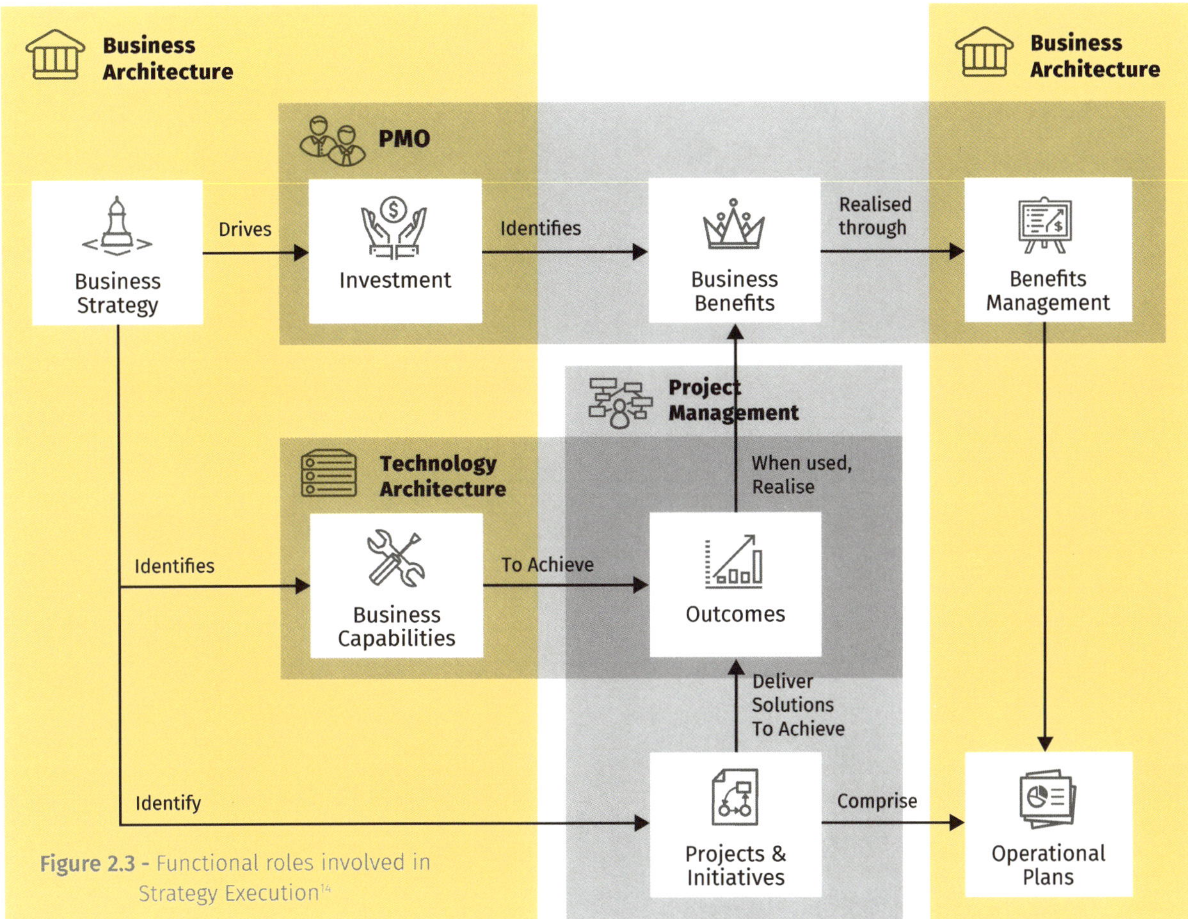


**Figure 2.3** - Functional roles involved in Strategy Execution[14]

both Enterprise Architecture (i.e. Business and Technical) and therefore really an 'Enterprise Architect'? or are you a Business Architect who's scope of work and responsibility is across the whole Organisation (i.e. Enterprise), and therefore, are a Business Architect, whose scope of work and responsibility is across the Organisation?'

An 'Enterprise-Business Architect' who is responsible for the Technology elements of the Enterprise Architecture (i.e. Technology Architecture), would not be considered an Enterprise-Business Architect nor a Business Architect, instead they would be a 'Technology Architect' who would be responsible for the Technology Architecture across the enterprise (Organisation).

To be more effective, we need to be clear on our terminology, and how it should be used. Enterprise Architecture looks at both Business and Technology Architecture. We should also help and educate others, especially Recruitment Consultants who often confuse the two when attempting to fill a position.

## Business Architecture is *not* Technology Architecture

This is the biggest misconception – confusing Business Architecture with Technical Architecture.

As stated in the *What is Business Architecture?* section above, Technology Architecture and Business Architecture are actually two pieces of the same puzzle, that together form Enterprise Architecture (EA). A simplified illustration of this is shown in *Figure 2.4*.

To clear up any confusion, Technology Architecture encompasses the technical elements (only) of an Organisation. These aspects and elements are otherwise referred to as technical Enablers (or just 'Enablers') – in that they 'enable' the business to be able to execute its Business Strategy, and include technology elements such as networks, servers, storage mediums, communications, platforms etc.

The issue with Business Architecture being confused or mistaken as Technology Architecture, is often that Technology Architecture is looking at the Business through a 'technology' lens, and business concepts, issues or concerns, not through a 'business' lens.

And I'm not the first person to say it either. In a recent report, Gartner described it best, stating:

> **"Without Business Architecture, "EA" efforts are just IT architecture and will fail to demonstrate and deliver significant business value outcomes"**[15]

[15] Gartner (2014), 'Business Architecture Is Not Optional for Business Outcome Driven EA'

**Figure 2.4** - Business & Technology Architecture – two pieces of the Enterprise Architecture puzzle

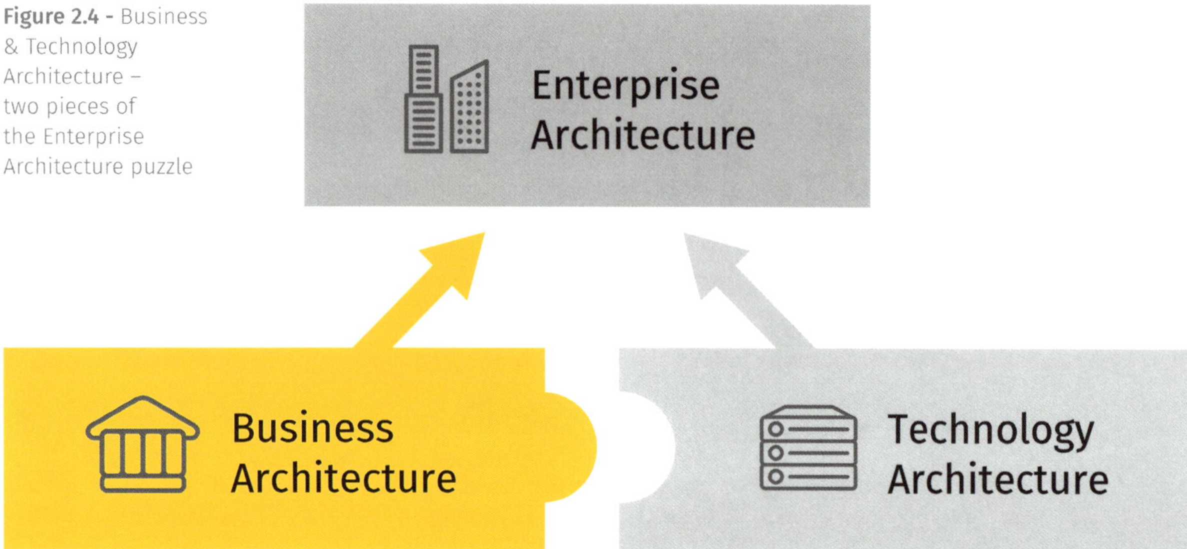


Although by definition, Business Architecture is an equal contributing part of Enterprise Architecture, according to BPTrends (2010), the reality is Business Architecture is now playing a less significant role in comparison to Technology Architecture, as illustrated in *Figure 2.5 below*:

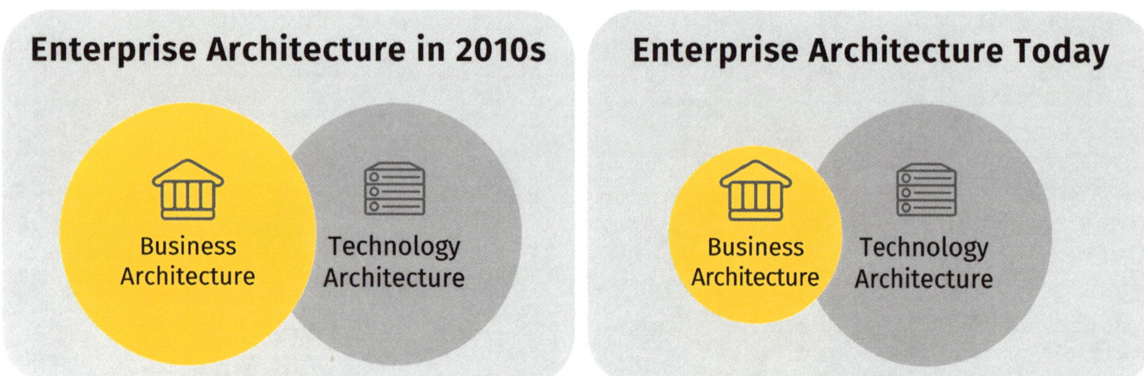


**Figure 2.5** - Business Architecture 'relative' Representation in EA in 2017[16]

According to BPTrends (2010), the reason for this current 'miss-representation' or imbalance between Business and Technology Architecture is a

**"Historical emphasis on the technology side of Enterprise Architecture, the development of the Zachman Framework in 1987, and later with TOGAF® and others as setting the foundations of any architectures that we designed to support an IT Strategy."**

What also usually happens with Enterprise Architecture is that Enterprise Architects themselves usually come from a technology background – as either an Application, Solution, Information or Data Architect, IT Project lead or developer[17]. So, when they perform 'Business Architecture' activities, they do so using a 'technical' lens, seeing and believing all business concerns, problems and issues can be addressed and solved by a technology solution (and in a lot of cases, a technology solution alone), which in practice is not always the case, and doesn't always work (hence the high failure rate in transformation programmes!)

### Business Architecture is *not* Business Analysis

The second biggest misconception about Business Architecture is that 'Business Architecture' is 'Business Analysis', which also includes the misconception that a 'Business Architect' is a 'Business Analyst' both in terms of the role they perform on the programme, and the activities they do. )

Although both are related (even sharing similar tools and techniques), both elements are necessary in developing the design (and implementing) the **Target Operating Model (TOM)**, however they differ in the following ways:

- They have a different focus,
- They operate at a different Organisation level,

[16] BPTrends (2010) 'Business Architecture: The Missing Link between Business Strategy and Enterprise Architecture'
[17] Scott, J., (2012) 'Will the Real Business Architect Please Stand Up'

- They are engaged at different times (or phases) within the Programme,
- They share similar tools, but use them differently, and
- The scale of change they deal in is different.

A more detailed description about each of these points is outlined below.

### They have a different focus

Business Architecture's focus is on the planning, strategy, and long term time horizons (it also takes place earlier on in the Programme life cycle), helping set and define the direction of the Organisation and Programme. They help the Business determine the Business Strategy, and answer the big questions like 'is there a hole in that market, and a market in that hole?'.

Business Analysis (and Business Analysts) focus on the other more tactical, short term time horizons. In terms of the Programme life cycle, Business Analysts are usually involved later in the business and project life cycle than Business Architects, once the *'market in the hole'* has been determined. Business Analysis/Analysts help the Business develop and implement the solution, now the Business Architecture has given the 'green light' (i.e. *'there is a hole in the market and this is how we can compete'.)*

### They operate at a different Organisation level

Business Architects operate at the Organisation (or Strategic) level, whereas Business Analysis (generally) work at the lower operational, implementation levels (see *Figure 2.6*).

Business Architecture's (and Business Architects) main focus is looking at the *'What is possible?'*, and 'Why?' for the Organisation at a strategic or enterprise wide level, whereas Business Analysis and the Business Analyst works at the project level and translates (with the Business) their requirements to define *'how?'* those requirements will be implemented.

In a well organised Programme, there is clear delineation between Business Architecture and Business Analysis as well as clear touch and handover points between the two. The overlaps (as shown in *Figure 2.6*) below occur when the Business Architect hands over and works with the Business Analyst (and the Business) to translate those high level strategic requirements into lower level detailed level implementation requirements.

In a 'not so well' organised programme, where that delineation and handover points are not clear, role confusion, and even (dare I say) 'tensions' often occur.

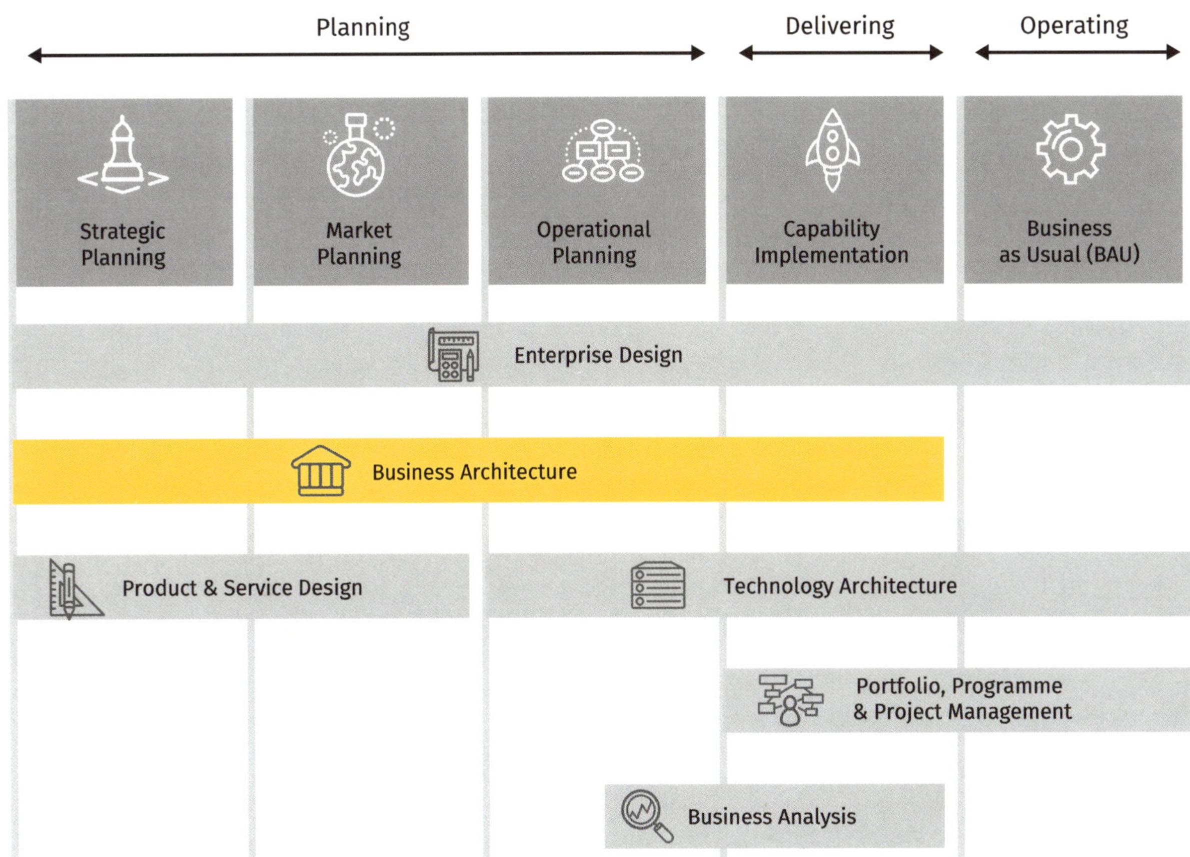


**Figure 2.6 -** Disciplines involved with Enterprise Design[18]

[18] Adapted from Martin, C., (2014) 'Driving your BA Career - From Business Analyst to Business Architect'

**To avoid these situations and confusion between the Business Architecture/ Architect and Business Analysis/Analyst, it is essential that the specific roles and responsibilities are established early in the Programme lifecycle. Roles and responsibilities are discussed in more detail as part of governance, in Step 2 – Control with the Governance Model and Stakeholder's Role and Responsibilities (RACI).**

### *They are engaged at different times (or phases) within the Programme*

The third area of difference between the Business Architect and the Business Analyst is timing. The Business Architect should be brought into and onto the Organisation (or Programme) early in the Business or Programme lifecycle to *lead* the design. By contrast, the Business Analyst is generally (or usually) brought into the Organisation (or Programme) later in the business or Programme cycle, as part of the *implementation* of the design.
The Business Architect intentionally comes in early in the Programme (compared to the Business Analyst) to lead the development of the design and implementation of the TOM. What this means in practice is that the Business Architect does the majority of their work *'upfront'*, in the planning stages as shown in *Figure 2.6*.

The Business Analyst on the other hand, joins the Programme 'later' in the Programme lifecycle. This is usually during or after the Business Architect has agreed with the Business (or at least drafted a working version of the Vision and Business Strategy) that analysis of the Current Operating Model, and planning the design of the Target Operating Model (TOM) can begin.

When the Business Analyst joins the Programme (in the second half of the Planning phase), they will carry out the detailed analysis of the current state of the Organisation. They will also translate those high-level business/strategic requirements into lower level, detailed implementation requirements, working with the Business Architect ensuring that the implementation requirements are aligned to the architecture requirements and the design of the TOM.

### *They have similar tools, but use them differently*

The fourth area of difference between the Business Architect and the Business Analyst is in their different use of similar tools. The Business Architect and Business Analyst share some common tools and techniques, but use these tools differently. Just like a weight-lifter and a body builder use weights in their respective disciplines, the outcome of using these same tools is very different (one is focused on strength, the other on aesthetics). These differences are mainly due to the differences in focus, as in how they use the tools, and who they use them on.

One example is impact and gap analyses. The Business Architect will carry out a gap analysis on existing business capabilities, to assess their ability to meet future strategic objectives whereas the Business Analyst will use gap analysis to assess the differences, and changes required between an existing (current) process, and the proposed (future) process, to fulfil an objective (in fact this list can be virtually endless).

Just because a Business Architect uses the same tool (or technique) as a Business Analyst, doesn't make the Business Architect a Business Analyst, and vice-versa. They may be the same tools, but in more cases than not, they will be used very differently, often from a different perspective, with a different focus, which ultimately leads to a different result.

### *The 'scale' of change they deal in is different*

The fifth area of differentiation between the Business Architect and Business Analyst, is *scale.* Business Architecture and Business Architects deal with 'big scale'. This is not to say 'more important or more significant', this is saying they focus on 'larger size' tasks.

To use renovating a house as an analogy, if you are a home owner renovating the bathroom, you have two options - you can do it yourself or bring in an expert. As it's only a single room (i.e. not physically that big - relatively speaking to the size of rest of other rooms in the house), it doesn't impact too many other rooms by changes made inside it (i.e. low interactions and dependencies on other rooms, particularly the *'structure'* of the house). As a result, you assess its a relatively small job. You work out it is a relatively small job, you could manage it yourself, but you still need specialists to complete specific parts of it - a Plumber (for the plumbing), an Electrician (for the wiring), and lastly a Carpenter (for the woodwork).

If on the other hand, you're renovating the whole house, from front to back and top to bottom, then all the rooms would be impacted, not just the bathroom (of the small job example above). As a result, you would likely think you only had one option (unless you're a master builder) and that would be to bring in an expert. You would need someone that can see across the whole house, and understand the impacts and dependencies of changes in one part of the house, and the knock-on effects to other parts of the house. You're also thinking of removing a few walls to open up the living space but this adds a new level of complexity and risk, and these risks need to be managed. You need someone to come up with the design and manage the implementation of that design, factoring in the dependencies and impacts of changes in one part of the house with timing of changes in the other. That specialist is the Architect, and in the case of an Organisation or Business, that specialist is the Business Architect.

### Business Architecture is *not* Business Change

The Business Architect is not a Business Change person (represented by the Portfolio, Programme and Project Management row in *Figure 2.6* above), who compiles the detailed people change impact analyses, plans and leads the implementation of the final solution with the Project Manager.

The point where Business Architecture and Business Change cross over, is in the Delivery phase, where the Business Architect works with Business Change to oversee that the physical implementation aligns with the design (as shown *in Figure 2.6 above*).

The role of the Business Architect here is to highlight the 'Business Changes' (the changes the Organisations business capabilities i.e. people, process and technology) to the 'Business Change' Manager, who are candidates for change as part of the design of the TOM. The actual detail of the business change activities (i.e. what that change means to the business on a day-to-day operational level, and how the business will transition from existing processes, old systems, roles and responsibilities to new processes, new systems, roles and responsibilities) is not the role of the Business Architect.

What does happen in practise however, is the Business Architect is drawn into Business Change conversations (as they should be), to confirm and assure the Business Change activities will lead to the implementation of the design of the TOM. But this is where the confusion sets in. The Business Architect is inadvertently tasked with coming up with the above mentioned business change plan and activities due to their familiarity with the subject matter, having also come up with the design.

Business Change however, is a specialist skillset, with its own frameworks, tools and techniques, as is Business Architecture. I would highly recommend if you find yourself in this situation, to push back (subtly of course) and redirect the questioning to Business Change.

**To avoid these situations and confusion between the Business Architecture/Architect and Business Change, it is essential that roles and responsibilities are established early in the Programme lifecycle. Roles and responsibilities are discussed later as part of governance, in *Chapter 6: Step 2 – Control* with the Governance Model and Stakeholder's Role and Responsibilities (RACI)**

## Challenge #2: What is The Value of Business Architecture?

The value of Business Architecture is simply – *Transparency*. Business Architecture's value is to:

- **Provide the transparency of 'why, where and how?'** the Organisation needs to invest in its Business Capabilities (i.e. people, process, technology) in order to realise the Organisations planned Business Benefits and execute its Business Strategy as efficiently and effectively as possible. Just as importantly it also -
- **Translates the Business Strategy into actionable plans** to implement the physical Business Architecture.

Business Architecture as a practice or methodology would only solve half the problem if it was tasked to only come up with the *'design'* of the Target Operating Model (TOM). To solve the other half of the problem and finish the job, Business Architecture's value is to also come up with the actionable plans – and oversee the *implementation* of the *physical* Business Architecture, to ensure it aligns to the *design* of the TOM.

In providing this design of the TOM, Business Architecture must identify and prioritise the Business Benefits the Organisation intends to realise. It is the Business Benefits that drive the investment decisions. The Business Architecture must also take into account the dependencies and impacts those investment decisions have on the different parts of the Organisation to minimise delivery risk and change to and in the Business, including the accumulation of any change debt (technical or business – where change is) in implementing the *physical* TOM.

'How' Business Architecture (and **HOBA®** and the **Design Process**) provide the value is addressed in the next section below.

## Challenge #3 : What does this value look like?

The challenge here is asking 'how' does Business Architecture do that (provide its value)?'

How Business Architecture, **HOBA®** and the **Design Process** provides its value of developing the design of the TOM, driven by investment in the necessary Business Capabilities (i.e. People, Process and Technology), that lead to the realisation of the identified and prioritised Business Benefits, as well providing actionable plans to implement the physical TOM, is via the following:

1. **Benefits Model** – to identify and prioritise the Business Benefits the Organisation intends to realise and drive the investment options; and
2. **Impact Mapping** – to assess the scale of change to the Organisation by the proposed investment (solution) options, and align and co-ordinate all changes across the Programme and Organisation.

We will briefly discuss each of these points below:

### 1. Benefits Model

The Benefits Model Reference Model defines the Business Benefits the Organisation is intending to achieve from the Programme and the Business Architecture. The Benefits Model identifies and prioritises the changes to the Business Capabilities (i.e. People, Process and Technology) of the Current Operating Model that are needed, in order for the Organisation to realise the planned Business Benefits.

The Benefits Model is made up of the specific Building Blocks and Blueprints that identify and prioritise not just the Business Benefits the Organisation intends to realise, but identify and prioritise the Enablers (i.e. technology aspects of Business Capabilities) and Business Changes (i.e. the people and process aspects of Business Capabilities) needed to realise the intended Business Benefits in the order the Business requires them.

**For more information on the Benefits Model, refer to *Chapter 8 Step 4 – Evaluate***

### 2. Impact Mapping

Impact Mapping is a Building Block within the **Target Operating Model (TOM)** Reference Model. Impact Mapping is about assessing the scale of change associated with delivering the changes to the Business Capabilities (People, Process and Technology) that directly support the realisation of the identified benefits, and align the business to the Business Strategy.

The objective of the **Impact Mapping** Building Block (and Blueprints) is to:

- **Establish a common understanding of the scale and impact** on the enterprise Current. Operating Model, in terms of its capabilities (people, process and technology);
- **Align your project, and Programme with other Programme efforts** to enable coordinated activities across the Programme and Portfolio;
- **Quickly identify and address critical activities, highlight dependences and gaps** in changes and work to enable mitigation actions ahead of delivery and communicating with internal and external stakeholders, and
- **Develop a set of solution and implementation options** (and recommended an option) as the set of changes needed to realise the Business Benefits and align the business to the Business Strategy.

**For more information on the Benefits Model, refer to *Chapter 8 Step 4 – Evaluate***

# Challenge #4: When can I see the value of Business Architecture?

This challenge is asking about 'timing' – when can the Organisation, and the Programme, see the value that Business Architecture brings?

Before addressing this challenge, lets briefly discuss the context. This challenge comes about as Business Architecture has (historically) been accused of being a *'dark art'*. Business Architecture and Business Architects would disappear from sight, hide themselves in a room, work on their designs (seemingly in isolation), and appear many days (or weeks) later with their *'new view of the future'* to share with the world.

The problem of (allegedly) working *'out of sight'*, is the process Business Architecture and the Business Architect(s) followed aren't, nor are the Blueprints they produced (i.e. deliverables) visible. The outcome is one where stakeholders are unable to set any expectations about the timing and amount of effort required, thereby undermining the ability to build confidence in the overall process.

To address this challenge, **HOBA®** and the **Design Process** make the *'value'* of Business Architecture both available and visible to the Organisation, and Programme at the following two (2) crucial times:

1. Upfront (i.e. quickly, in a short amount of time), and
2. Iteratively (i.e. frequently, through continuous delivery).

We will discuss each of these areas in the sections below.

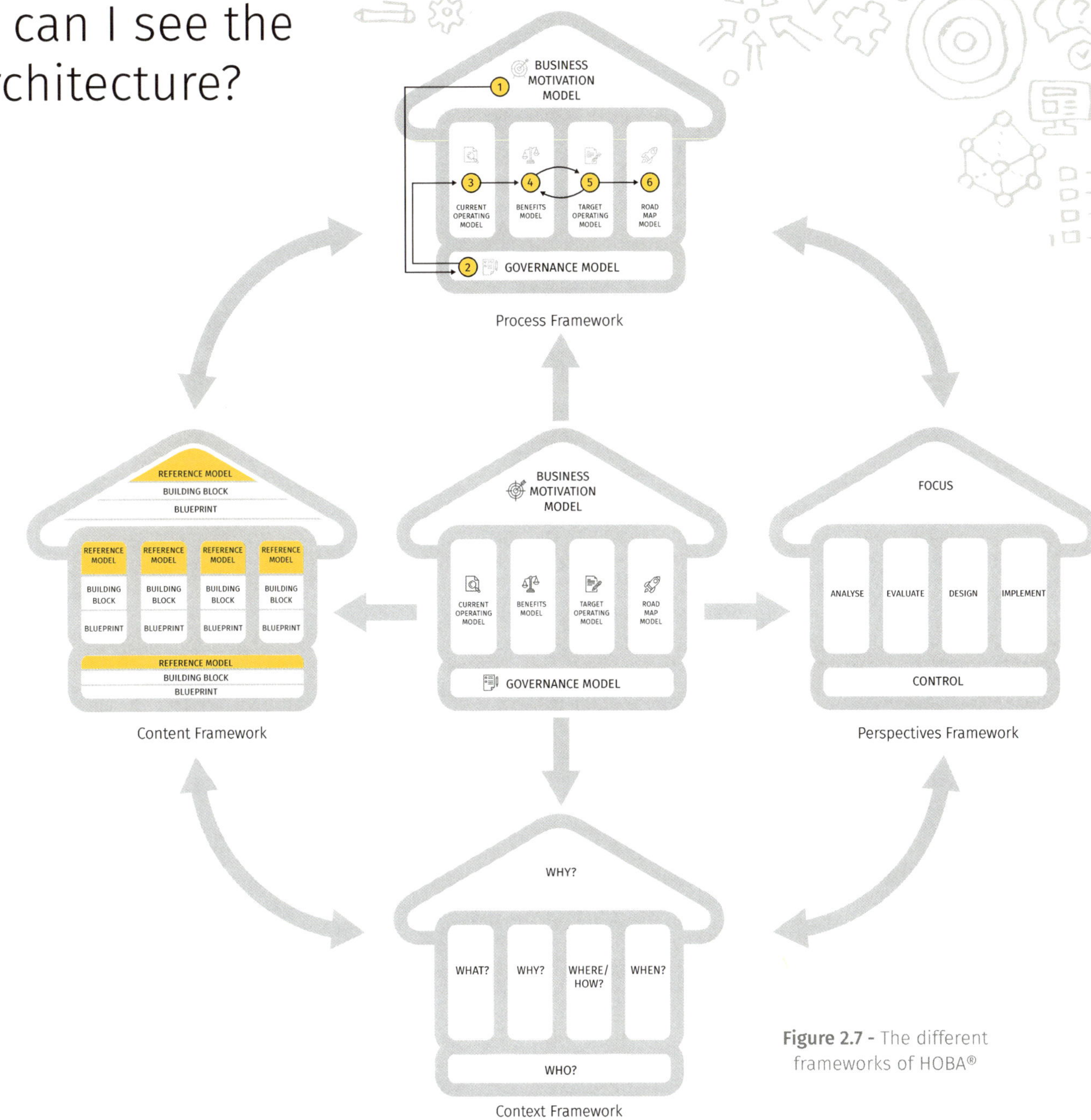


**Figure 2.7 -** The different frameworks of HOBA®

## 1. Upfront

**HOBA®** and the **Design Process are** able to show the value of Business Architecture *'upfront'* to the Organisation and the Programme.

In terms of **HOBA®**, it provides the answers to the 'Why, Who, What, Where, How and When?' questions asked of the Organisation and Business Architecture.

In terms of a framework, **HOBA®** is actually four (4) frameworks in one (1), as shown in *Figure 2.7.*

**HOBA®**'s four (4) complementary frameworks are as follows:

- **Process Framework** - provides the framework for the specific order and number of steps needed to develop the design and implement the Target Operating Model (TOM);
- **Perspectives Framework** - provides the framework for the different views (i.e. focus, control, analyse, evaluate, design, implement) of the Organisation to address the unique concerns of the Organisation and Business Architecture stakeholders;
- **Context Framework** - provides the framework that addresses the different aspects or 'Why, What, Who, How, Where and When?' questions that are asked of both the Organisation and the Business Architecture.
- **Content Framework** - provides the framework of the Reference Models, Building Blocks and Blueprints that describes a specific view or perspective of the Organisation. Blueprints take the form of diagrams, catalogues or matrices.

When looking at the **HOBA®** Business Motivation Reference Model for example, the Business Architect, and Programme will know:

- Which step in the 'Process' they are they are dealing in (Step 1);
- Which *'Perspective'* they are working on (Focus);
- Which *'Aspect'* of the Organisation they are addressing (i.e. 'Why' is the Organisation doing this?); and
- Which *'Content'* (i.e. Reference Model, Building Blocks and Blueprints) will be used to articulate and visualise these views.

**For more information on HOBA® framework, refer to *Chapter 3 House of Business Architecture® (HOBA®).***

In terms of the **Design Process**, the **Design Process** actually fulfils the 'Process Framework' role mentioned above. The **Design Process** provides the framework of the specific order and number of steps needed to develop the design and implement the **Target Operating Model (TOM).**

The **Design Process** is shown in *Figure 2.8.*

The upfront value the *Design Process* has to the Organisation and Programme is all parties and stakeholders can quickly see visually what steps are required (i.e. what they are, and their purpose) to develop the design and implement the TOM. They can quickly 'upfront' set their expectations in terms of the process,

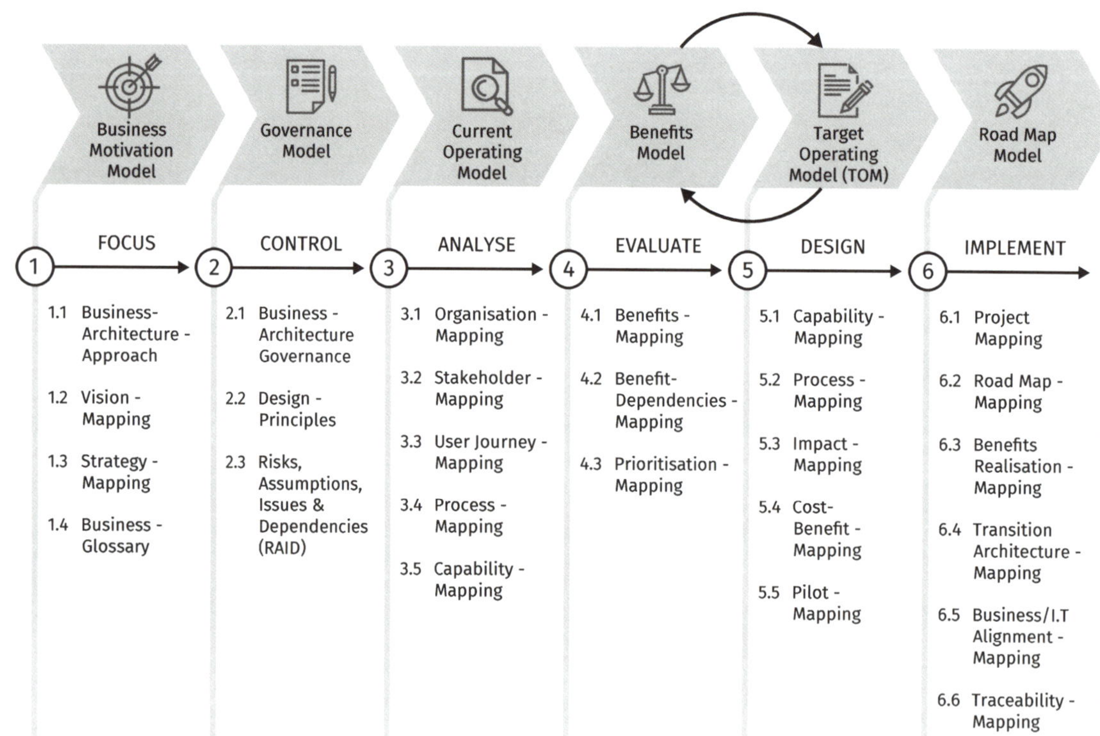


**Figure 2.8** - The different frameworks of HOBA®

timing and amount of work (and potential effort) are required to complete the design and implementation activities. is iteratively, as the design of the **Target Operating Model (TOM)** develops *'iteratively'* overtime.

**For more information on the Design Process, refer to *Chapter 4 - Design Process***

## 2. Iteratively

The second part of how **HOBA®** and the **Design Process** shows its value is iteratively, as the design of the **Target Operating Model (TOM)** develops *'iteratively'* overtime.

**HOBA®** and the **Design Process** is based around the Agile Scrum Project Management method of iterative continuous development.

The aim of Scrum, is to produce high velocity, iterative releases of usable output at the end of set period of work (called sprint). For those that aren't familiar with Scrum, Scrum is popular in software development, where is it 'helps Organisations deliver working software more frequently'[19] .

The benefit of using Scrum with **HOBA®** and the **Design Process** in developing the design and implementation of the Target Operating Model (TOM), is that usable, incremental versions of the Business Architecture are released to the Organisation and Programme on a regular basis.

How this iterative approach helps the Organisation and the Programme is that as the development of the Business Architecture develops incrementally, it keeps aligned with the Technology Architecture and software development as the Technology Architecture and software also develop in parallel over time.

# Challenge #5 : What is the role of the Business Architect (and when do we engage them)?

The role of the Business Architect is really two things. Firstly, they are responsible for developing and delivering the design of the **Target Operating Model (TOM)** that aligns the Business to the Business Strategy, driven by investment and changes in the Organisations Business Capabilities (People, Process and Technology). This alignment also includes ensuring the Business Architecture is *aligned* with the other architectures across the Organisation and Programme as part of the design.

An illustration of this alignment with the other architectures is shown in *Figure 2.9* below.

The **second role of the Business Architect, is to ensure (and assure) that the *implementation* of the physical Business Architecture is aligned to the *design* of the Business Architecture.** This is a crucial point, the role of the Business Architect is *not only* to develop and deliver the *design* (which would effectively be 'lugging the design over the fence' for someone else to

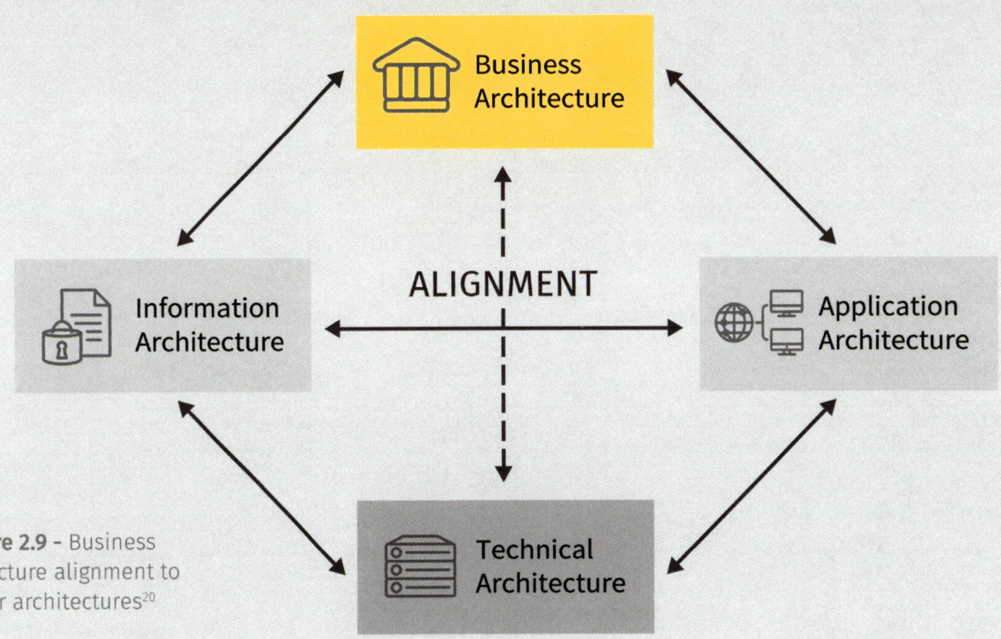


**Figure 2.9** - Business Architecture alignment to other architectures[20]

[20] Sousa, P et al. (2005) 'Enterprise Architecture Alignment Heuristics'
[19] Adapted from Schwaber, Ken (February 1, 2004). Agile Project Management with Scrum.

implement, and *'hope'* the expected outcomes are achieved). The Business Architects job is not finished when the *design* is delivered, the Business Architects job is finished when the physical architecture that the design describes is *implemented*. The Business Architects role here is to oversee the implementation of the physical Business Architecture (the physical Target Operating Model), that the implemented changes (Business Changes and Enablers, discussed later in this book) produce the outcomes as expected, handing over to the Business the responsibility to monitor and manage the realisation of the planned Business Benefits, as part of Business As Usual (BAU). The details of how the Business Architect does this and what it looks like, is all discussed later in this book.

In terms of when the Business Architect should be engaged, as mentioned in the *What isn't Business Architecture?* section. *They are engaged at different times (or phase) within the Programme* section, Business Architecture and Business Architects should be engaged early in the Project or Programme (i.e. in the conception and planning phases). This is to agree the direction of the Organisation with developing and/or validating the Vision and Business Strategy, and high level/strategic business requirements before the detailed analysis (on both the Current Operating Model and Target Operating Model (TOM)). Detailed level/implementation requirements are defined, when and where the Business Analyst comes in.

What is happening in the market and industry right now (albeit this is slowing changing, hopefully aided by with what is recommended in this book, using **HOBA®** and the **Design Process**) is that Business Architecture and the Business Architects are brought late into a Programme, at the end of the planning phase, or worse – in the delivery phase, which causes all sorts of problems down the track.

In order to combat this, **HOBA®** promotes the 'Proactive' and 'Interactive' aspects of the Business Architecture Engagement Model, as shown in *Figure 2.10*. **HOBA®** and Business Architecture work best proactively shaping the direction of the Programme, leading (and driving) the change from a Business perspective, as opposed to a 'Reactive' or 'Inactive' action, where Business Architecture is brought in late into the Programme, as an 'after thought', often to justify (not validate) the proposed technology solution or a compliance box ticking exercise in order for a Programme to pass the Programme stage exit criteria.

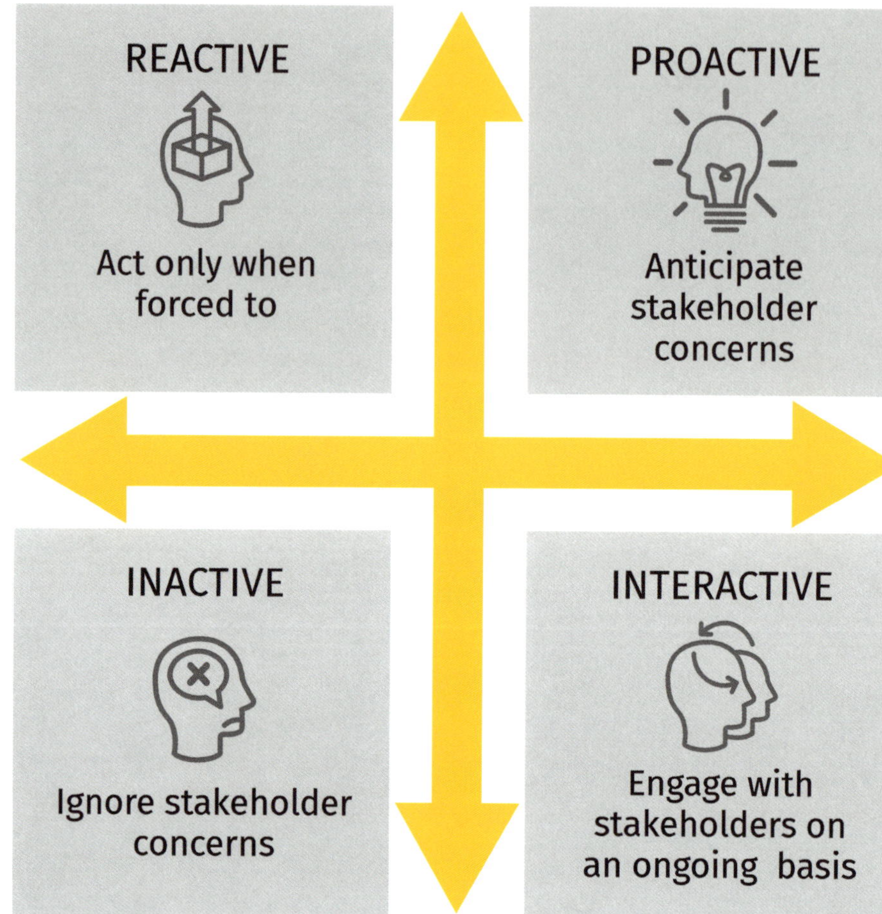


**Figure 2.10** - Business Architecture Engagement Model[21]

## Building Block Wrap-up

In this section, we discussed the Business Architecture Challenges.

Despite Organisations that use Business Architecture, and reports that Organisations that use Business Architecture as a methodology, practice and discipline 'have a significantly higher ability to execute on their Business Strategy', Business Architecture none the less has significantly suffered from a lack of recognition and acceptance.

[21] Adapted from Subramaniam, A (2009) 'Stakeholder Mapping: Game plan to influence stakeholder groups'

Business Architecture is often confused and mistaken for similar related, often interdependent disciplines and practices (but that is changing, and hopefully aided with what is recommended in this book, using **HOBA®** and the **Design Process**). Explicitly, Business Architecture isn't Enterprise Architecture, Technology Architecture, Business Analysis, nor Business Change.

Business Architecture *addresses* the different aspects or questions, the 'why, who, what, where, how and when?' asked of the Business – how it is set up and organised to deliver the Organisation's Business Strategy.

Business Architecture *is* the bridge between Strategic Planning and Strategy Execution - it is the bridge that makes strategy happen in real life.

Business Architecture's unique position between strategic planning and strategic execution, make it able to *identify* opportunities for investment (i.e. business capabilities), explicitly what those capabilities look like, what the Benefits will be and the actionable plans to get there.

Its *goal* is to support the Organisation's Vision through aligning the Business to support the Organisation's Business Strategy.

Business Architectures *value* is Transparency, in that it:

- Provides the transparency of why, where and how the Organisation needs to invest in its capabilities (people, process, technology) that realise the Organisations intended Business Benefits and execute its Business Strategy as efficiently and effectively as possible. Just as importantly it also –
- Translates the Business Strategy in actionable plans to implement the physical Business Architecture.

Business Architectures *value* takes the form of:

- **Benefits Model** – that is used to identify and prioritise the Business Benefits the Organisation intends to realise, and the necessary business capabilities (people, process and technology) the Business needs to invest in; and
- **Impact Mapping** – that is to assess the scale of change to the Organisation by the proposed investment (solution) options, and align and co-ordinate all changes across the Programme and Organisation.

The *value* of Business Architecture can be seen at two (2) crucial times:

- Upfront (i.e. quickly, in a short amount of time), and
- Iteratively (i.e. frequently, through continuous delivery).

The Business Architects *role* has two parts:

- Develop the design and alignment of the implementation of the physical Target Operating Model (TOM) that aligns the business to the Business Strategy, and
- Ensure the design of the TOM is aligned with the other architectures across the Organisation and Programme.

The best time to engage the Business Architect and Business Architecture is early in the Programme (and business) lifecycle, in the conception and planning phases, to agree the direction of the Organisation, Programme, Vision and Business Strategy, to then design the Target Operating Model (TOM), and oversee the implementation of the physical TOM that it aligns with the design.

### Next Steps

Now we have discussed (and hopefully addressed) the biggest challenges facing Business Architecture and Business Architects today, we shall next discuss **HOBA®**, the **House of Business Architecture®**, what it is as well as its key features and benefits.

# Chapter 3
# House of Business Architecture® (HOBA®)

## Purpose

**HOBA®**, the **House of Business Architecture®** is the Target State Architecture framework developed to support the design and implementation of the Organisations Business Strategy and Target Operating Model (TOM).

**HOBA®**'s greatest strength of supporting the design and implementation of the Organisations strategy and Target Operating Model (TOM) is being able to capture and present business facing and business driven information in a coherent and comprehensive way, that:

- **Simplifies the complexity of the issues and questions asked of the Organisation** when it comes to aligning the business to the Business Strategy and creating and implementing the Target Operating Model (TOM). **HOBA®** is made up of six (6) Reference Models, which address the big 'Why, Who, What, Where, How and When? questions asked of the Organisation and Business Architecture;
- **Provides the full picture of all the work** that is needed and required to both develop the *design* of the Target Operating Model (TOM), and implement the *physical* TOM as well.
- **Provides managers throughout an Organisation at their various levels with the right level of information** needed to make the decisions and changes to the Organisation that enable the Organisation to execute its Business Strategy effectively and efficiently (i.e. Executive level, the big strategic questions and answers with the Reference Models and Building Blocks, down to the Operations level, the implementation questions and answers with Blueprints), and
- **Puts the control back into the Business' hands,** as it is a tool and framework designed, owned and driven *by* the Business.

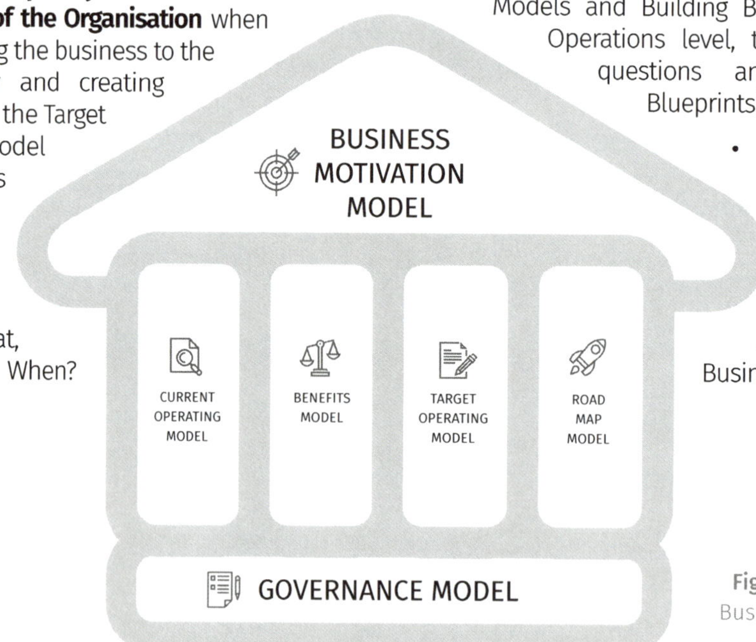


**Figure 3.1** - House of Business Architecture® (HOBA®)

# HOBA® Components

**HOBA®, House of Business Architecture®** - intentionally takes its shape and name from the physical shape of a house, made up of three (3) core components.

Each core component represents a different aspect and Reference Model making up the complete view of both the design of the Organisations Business Architecture, but the activities to implement the Organisations Target Operating Model (TOM) as well.

The relationship between **HOBA®'s** core components, Reference Models and aspects are shown in the *Table 3.1*.

**HOBA®** Reference Models describe an aspect or specific view of the Organisation and Business Architecture. Reference Models provide a high level conceptual view of the Organisation and Business Architecture, and are made up of Building Blocks and Blueprints, which provide an increasingly focused and detailed level view of that aspect.

**HOBA® is made up of the following six (6) Reference Models:**

- **1.0 Business Motivation Model (BMM)** – used to define the desired outcomes the Organisation is hoping to achieve, as well the Organisations outcomes for the Business Architecture.
- **2.0 Governance Model (GOV)** – used to define the governance structure and processes that manage the Programme decisions.

**Figure 3.2 -** HOBA® Core Components

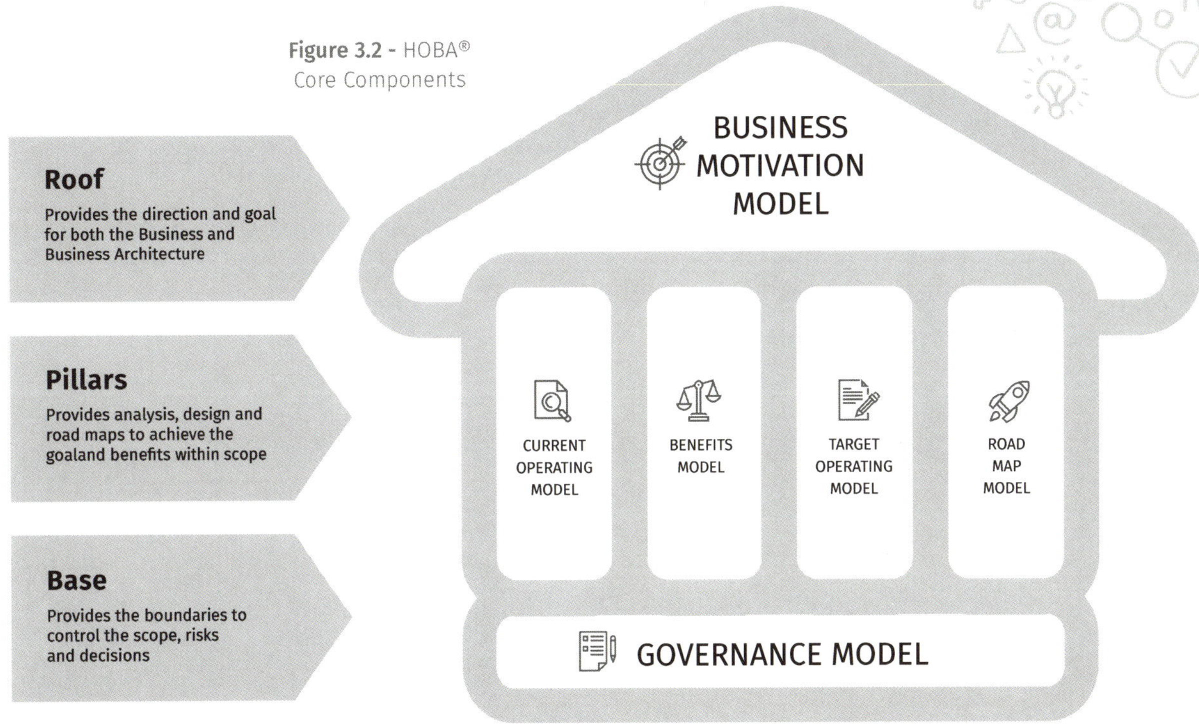


HOBA® Core Components, Reference Models and Aspects

**Table 3.1**

| HOBA® Core Component | HOBA® Reference Model(s) | Aspect of the Business |
|---|---|---|
| Roof | Business Motivation Model | WHY do they do it? (vision) |
| Pillars | · Current (As-Is) Operating Model<br>· Benefits Model<br>· Target (To-Be) Operating Model<br>· Road Map Model | · WHAT do they do?<br>· WHY do they do it? (Benefits)<br>· WHERE/HOW do they do it?<br>· WHEN do they do it? |
| Base | Governance Model | · WHO does the work (Stakeholders)? also<br>· WHAT is their role (RACI)? and<br>· WHAT is the process(es) to manage the work (Requirements), control scope (Principles) and manage risks (RAIDS)? |

- **3.0 Current Operating Model (COM)** – used to define the current (As-Is) business operating model for the Organisation.
- **4.0 Benefits Model (BEN)** – used for identifying and prioritising the Business Benefits the Organisation intends to realise from the business and Business Architecture, that will drive investment decisions.
- **5.0 Target Operating Model (TOM)** – used to define the target (To-Be) operating model for the Organisation.
- **6.0 Road Map Model (RMM)** – used to define the road map, and activities to implement the design and physical TOM.

Each Reference Model (and related Building Blocks and Blueprints) are discussed further in the *HOBA® Reference Models section.*

# HOBA® - the 'Target State Architecture'

**HOBA®**, the **House of Business Architecture®** is the complete model and framework of the Target State Architecture. That is, the complete framework and process to both develop the design of the Organisation's Target Operating Model (TOM), as well as the development of the plans, Blueprints and roadmaps to manage the alignment of the implementation of the physical Business Architecture with the design of the TOM.

**The scope of HOBA® doesn't just stop at developing the 'design' of the TOM, it stops *when* the physical TOM has been implemented.**

The current misconception in (and of) Business Architecture today is when the Business Architect/Architecture is tasked with developing the 'design' of the TOM, they are only responsible for developing the design and explicitly not responsible or accountable for developing the plans, Blueprints and roadmaps to manage the alignment of the implementation the physical TOM - to ensure the implementation of the physical TOM maintains alignment to the design of the TOM.

Implementation is where the biggest risk lies with any Programme. The best person(s) to oversee the physical implementation of the design (of the TOM) would naturally be the person or people who developed the design of the TOM – the Business Architect.

The current misconception of the Business Architect only being responsible for the design of the TOM (and not the overseeing of the implementation of the physical TOM) means that when the Business Architect is tasked to 'develop the design of Target Operating Model (TOM)', it also often means developing the design of the TOM without the consideration of one or multiple of the following:

- **An assessment of the Current Operating Model** (to identify and validate the issues, concerns and needs of the Organisation to be incorporated into the design of the TOM).
- **Agreeing or confirming the Organisations or Business Architecture's** vision (which all requirements and the design of the TOM will align and trace back to).
- **Agreeing the governance structure or processes** (which will manage all decisions on and across the Programme).
- **Identifying, validating or prioritising the Business Benefits** that are intended to be realised by the Organisation (which all changes to the business and Business Architecture are to support).

As a Business Architect, developing the design of the TOM that excludes an assessment of the Organisations Current Operating Model would be opening oneself up to scrutiny, or at worse, jumping into *'solution mode'. In other words,* proposing changes to the Organisation where there hasn't been a clear or robust challenge of what is actually currently going on (i.e. designing based on treating the symptoms of the problems, not the cause of the problems) within and across the Organisation today.

**HOBA®** overcomes the shortcomings of how Business Architecture is currently perceived and used (i.e. only assuming responsibility for the 'design of the TOM', and not overseeing the implementation of the physical TOM), by the explicit and intentional *inclusion* of the areas that have been previously ignored. These areas are represented by the Governance Model, Current Operating Model, Benefits Model and Road Map Reference Models, as mentioned in the *HOBA® Components* section.

While each of the Reference Models that make up **HOBA®** are discussed in more detail in later chapters, the main elements of each of **HOBA®**'s Reference Models as discussed in the *HOBA® Reference Models* section below.

# HOBA® Reference Models

As previously mentioned in the ***HOBA®*** *Components section*, **HOBA®** is made up of six (6) Reference Models:

- 1.0 Business Motivation Model
- 2.0 Governance Model
- 3.0 Current Operating Model
- 4.0 Benefits Model
- 5.0 Target Operating Model
- 6.0 Road Map Model

We will discuss each of these Reference Models in the following sections below.

## 1.0 Business Motivation Model

The Business Motivation Reference Model defines the vision and objectives for the Organisation and the Business Architecture. It establishes a clear and single focal point for both the Organisation, the Business Architecture, and what they each intend to achieve.

The Business Motivation Model answers the *'WHY do they do it?'* aspect and question asked of the business, and Business Architecture, and is the starting point of any Business Architecture and Business Architect engagement with the Project or Programme (and some cases with the Organisation). This is because it sets both the direction and Vision for the Organisation, as well as the Business Architecture in helping the Organisation achieve that Vision.
The Business Motivation Model is made up of the Building Blocks and example Blueprints as shown in Figure 3.3.

**Business Motivation Model**

| Design Step | Building Block | Blueprint (example) |
|---|---|---|
| 1.1 | Business Architecture Approach | Statement of Work (SOW) |
| 1.2 | Vision Mapping | Vision, Strategy, Objectives & Measures (VSOM) |
| 1.3 | Business Strategy Mapping | Business Canvas Model |
| 1.4 | Business Glossary | Terms & Definitions |

**Figure 3.3** - Business Motivation Model, Building Blocks and example Blueprints

## 2.0 Governance Model

The Governance Reference Model defines the Business Architecture governance framework, processes, and roles and responsibilities to make decisions regarding the design and implementation of the Business Architecture, and ultimately the Target Operating Model (TOM).

The Governance Model answers primarily the 'WHO?' question and aspect of the Business and Business Architecture, 'Who are the stakeholders involved?' (but also, secondary 'WHAT?' is their role, and processes these stakeholders use to manage the work, control the scope and manage the risks?').

The Governance Model is made up of the following Building Blocks and example Blueprints ,shown in Figure 3.4.

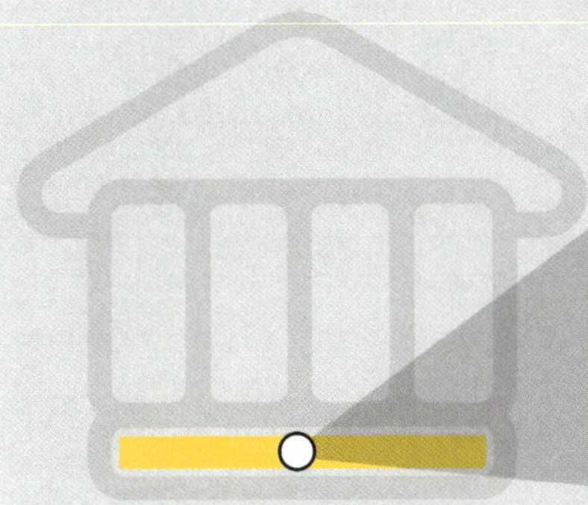

**Governance Model**

| Design Step | Building Block | Blueprint (example) |
|---|---|---|
| 2.1 | Architecture Governance | Business Architecture Governance Framework |
| 2.2 | Design Principles | Design Principles Register |
| 2.3 | Risks, Assumptions, Issues & Dependencies (RAID) | RAID Log |

**Figure 3.4** - Governance Model, Building Blocks and example Blueprints

## 3.0 Current Operating Model

The Current Operating Model defines the current (As-Is) operating model and provides a baseline to design and build from. The Current Operating Model answers the 'What?' is the current state of the Organisation, aspect or question that is asked of the Business or Business Architecture.

The Current Operating Model is the first (of four) pillars of **HOBA®**, and is intentionally positioned as the first pillar, as this is first and critical piece of analysis that needs to happen in order to fully and accurately understand the current state of the Organisation, which will form the baseline that improvements or changes will be made.

Explicitly calling out the Current Operating Model and putting it at the forefront of any design work, ensures it is actually done and not over looked, or dismissed as unnecessary, which I have regrettably seen with many clients I have assisted. A common error I have seen is Project and Programme members who are a little too ambitious and keen *'to get on with it'* (as they would say) and *'build and deliver'* something. Keenness is great, provided any design work built on a solid foundation of a clear and robust understanding of the current state of the Organisation, *not* a loosely understood or rapidly changing one (or worse - one that was never formally documented and agreed).

The Current Operating Model is made up of the following Building Blocks and example Blueprints:

**Current Operating Model**

| Design Step | Building Block | Blueprint (example) |
|---|---|---|
| 3.1 | Organisation Mapping | Organisation Chart |
| 3.2 | Stakeholder Mapping | Stakeholder Map |
| 3.3 | User Journey Mapping | User Journey Map |
| 3.4 | Process Mapping | Process Model Map |
| 3.5 | Capability Mapping | Capability Model Map |

**Figure 3.5 -** Current Operating Model, Building Blocks and example Blueprints



## 4.0 Benefits Model

The Benefits Reference Model defines the Business Benefits the business is intending to realise from the changes the implementation of the Target Operating Model (TOM) will bring about. The Benefits Model identifies and prioritises the changes (people, process and technology) needed to the Current Operating Model in order for the Organisation to realise the identified and planned benefits.

The Benefits Model is made up of the following Building Blocks and example Blueprints:

**Benefits Model**

| Design Step | Building Block | Blueprint (example) |
|---|---|---|
| 4.1 | Benefits Mapping | Benefits Map |
| 4.2 | Benefits-Dependencies Mapping | Benefits-Dependencies Map |
| 4.3 | Prioritised Changes | Prioritised Changes Map |

**Figure 3.6 -** Benefits Model, Building Blocks and example Blueprints

## 5.0 Target Operating Model

The Target Operating Model (TOM) Reference Model defines the future state (To-Be) operating model for the Organisation. The TOM design is driven by the identified benefits and prioritised changes (i.e. people, process and technology - elements of the Organisations business capabilities) that were identified in the Benefits Model.

The TOM answers the *'HOW?'* and *'WHERE do they do it?'* aspect or questions asked of the business and Business Architecture – how, and where are the changes to the Current Operating Model needed to realise the intended

Business Benefits (and Business Objectives, and ultimately, the Business Strategy).

The TOM is made up of the following Building Blocks and example Blueprints:

**Target Operating Model**

| Design Step | Building Block | Blueprint (example) |
|---|---|---|
| 5.1 | Capability Mapping | Capability Model Map (To-Be) |
| 5.2 | Process Mapping | Process Model Map (To-Be) |
| 5.3 | Impact Mapping | Impact Map |
| 5.4 | Cost-Benefit Mapping | Cost-Benefit Analysis |
| 5.5 | Pilot Mapping | Pilot Brief |

**Figure 3.7 -** Target Operating Model, Building Blocks and example Blueprints

### 6.0 Road Map Model

The Road Map Reference Model defines the implementation path and activities required to implement the Target Operating Model. This also includes overseeing the design and implementation of the physical TOM to ensure it aligns to the design of the TOM.

The Road Map model answers the *'WHEN do they do it?'* aspect and question asked of the Business and Business Architecture, as well as the *'When will the changes be implemented?'*, and *'When will the Business Benefits be realised?'*.
The Road Map Model is made up of the following Building Blocks and example Blueprints.

Now we have discussed **HOBA®** and each of its components, 'what they are' and 'what they mean', next we will discuss 'how to use **HOBA®**'.

**Road Map Model**

| Design Step | Building Block | Blueprint (example) |
|---|---|---|
| 6.1 | Project Mapping | Project Benefits Map |
| 6.2 | Road Map Mapping | Business Architecture Road Map |
| 6.3 | Benefits Realisation Mapping | Benefits Realisation Map |
| 6.4 | Transition Architecture Mapping | Transition Architecture Alignment Map |
| 6.5 | Business/I.T Alignment Mapping | Business/I.T Alignment Map |
| 6.6 | Traceability Mapping | Stakeholder Concerns Traceability Matrix |

**Figure 3.8 -** Road Map Model, Building Blocks and example Blueprints

# How To Use HOBA®?

### HOBA® Frameworks

**HOBA®** is made up of four (4) complementary frameworks, with each one playing a separate but key role:

- **Process framework** – as a process framework, **HOBA®** provides the 'design process' for both developing the design of the Target Operating Model (TOM), as well as managing the alignment of the implementation of the physical Business Architecture with the design of the TOM;
- **Perspectives framework** – as a perspectives framework, **HOBA®** provides the different perspectives (views) of the Organisation to address the unique concerns of the Business ('Organisation') and Business and Technical Architecture stakeholders;
- **Context framework** – as a context framework, **HOBA®** addresses the different aspects or *'Why, Who, What, Where, How and When?'* questions that are asked of both the Organisation and the Business Architecture; and
- **Content framework** – as a content framework, **HOBA®** provides the Reference Models, Building Blocks and Blueprints needed to capture the necessary information about the Organisation in order to develop the design and manage the alignment of the implementation of the Target Operating Model (TOM).

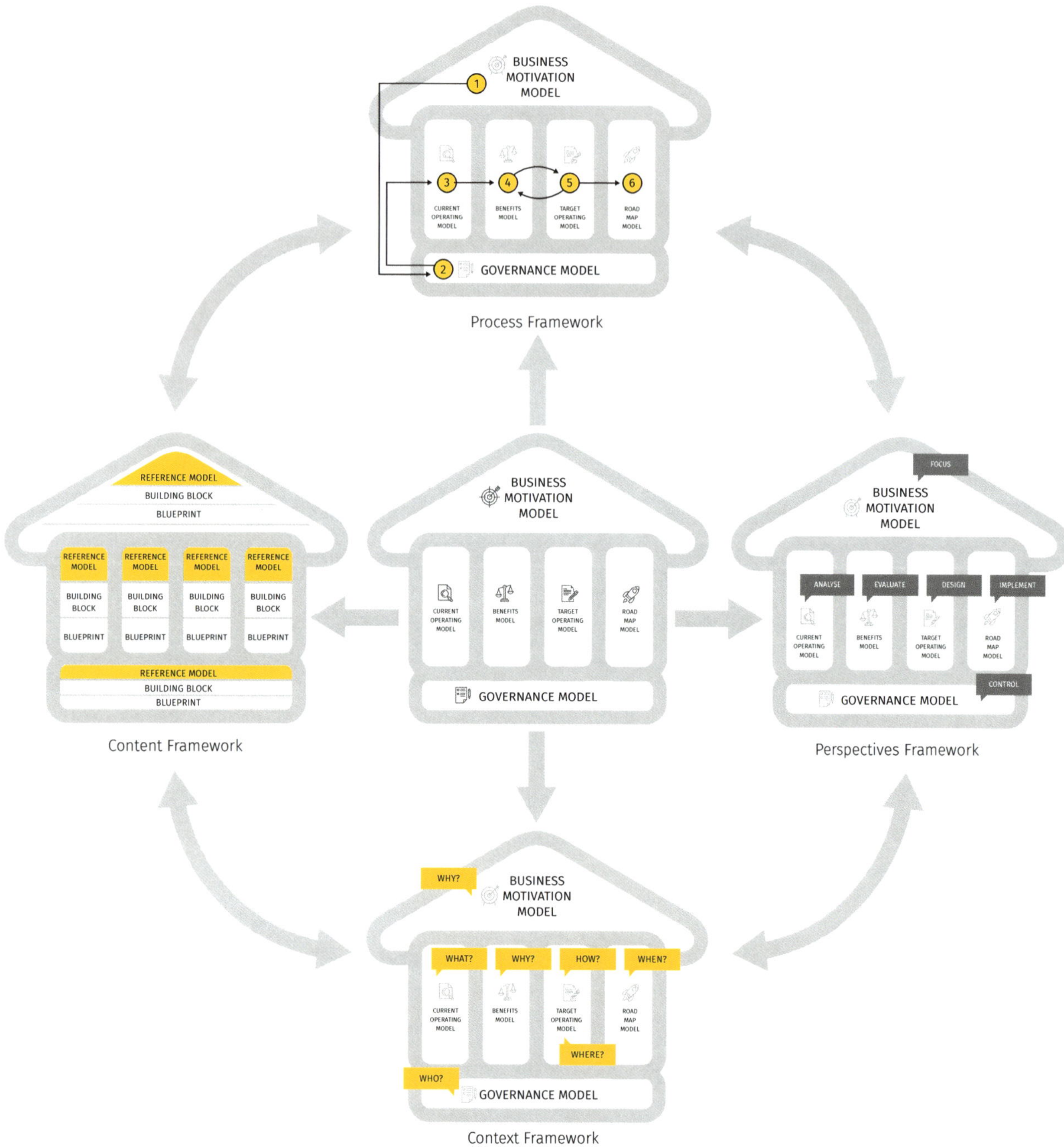


**Figure 3.9** - The different HOBA® frameworks

An expanded view of each of these four (4) complementary frameworks is shown in *Figure 3.9*.

Each of these frameworks (and roles) are discussed in the sections below.

## Process Framework

As a process framework, **HOBA®** provides the actual process and steps that are required and needed to both develop the design of the Target Operating Model (TOM), as well as managing the alignment of implementation of the physical Business Architecture with the design of the TOM.

Each **HOBA®** Reference Model is actually a specific and intentional step in the **Design Process** – the process of developing the 'design' of the TOM, and implementation of the 'physical' TOM.

The order of the design steps and the relationship to the Reference Models is shown in *Figure 3.10* below.

As discussed earlier in **HOBA®** Components section, each Reference Model addresses a different and specific aspect of the Organisation and Business Architecture. The relationship between the **Design Process** step, Reference Model and Aspect of the Business is shown in the Table 3.2 (on the next page).

You will notice that from *Figure 3.10*, the approach to develop the design and implement the Target Operating Model (TOM) follows a top-down (and left to right) approach – starting with the Business Motivation Model at the top (roof), then Governance Model at the bottom (base), followed by Current Operating Model, Benefits Model, Target Operating Model and then the Road

Map Model from left to right. This order and direction of the steps (namely top down) and their respective Reference Model each step covers is deliberate.

Each step of the **Design Process** looks at the Organisation and the Business Architecture from a very different perspective, as a Perspective Framework. As a Perspective Framework **HOBA®** helps build up a complete view of both the design of the whole Organisation and Target Operating Model (TOM), as well as development of the plans, maps and roadmap to manage the alignment of the implementation of the physical Business Architecture with the design of the TOM. **HOBA®** as a *Perspectives Framework* is discussed in the following section.

## Perspectives Framework

As a Perspectives Framework, **HOBA®** provides the different perspectives (i.e. views) of the Organisation to address the unique concerns of the Business Organisation ('Organisation') and Business and Technical Architecture stakeholders.

The immediate question that comes to mind when looking at **HOBA®** and each step is *'What is the point, or role of each Reference Model in developing the design and implementation of the TOM?'*

Well, each aspect or Reference Model fulfills a specific role in developing the design and implementation of the TOM, as shown by the diagram below.

The specific role of each **HOBA®** Reference Model is shown in the following table.

What this means in practice, is that when you are going through (or about to go through) one of the Reference Models - the Governance Model Reference Model for example, you know that this activity is focused around the 'control(ling)' governance structure, processes and roles the different stakeholders will have in making decisions affecting both the scope of the Programme, and ultimately the design of the TOM.

All of the Reference Models are important and must be completed to some degree (more detail on this later in the book). There is also a specific order and sequence each Reference Model is to be addressed. That order was discussed as part of the Process Framework section above.

## Context Framework

There are two (2) aspects of Context for HOBA®:

1. **HOBA®** as a Context Framework
2. Context of **HOBA®** Model

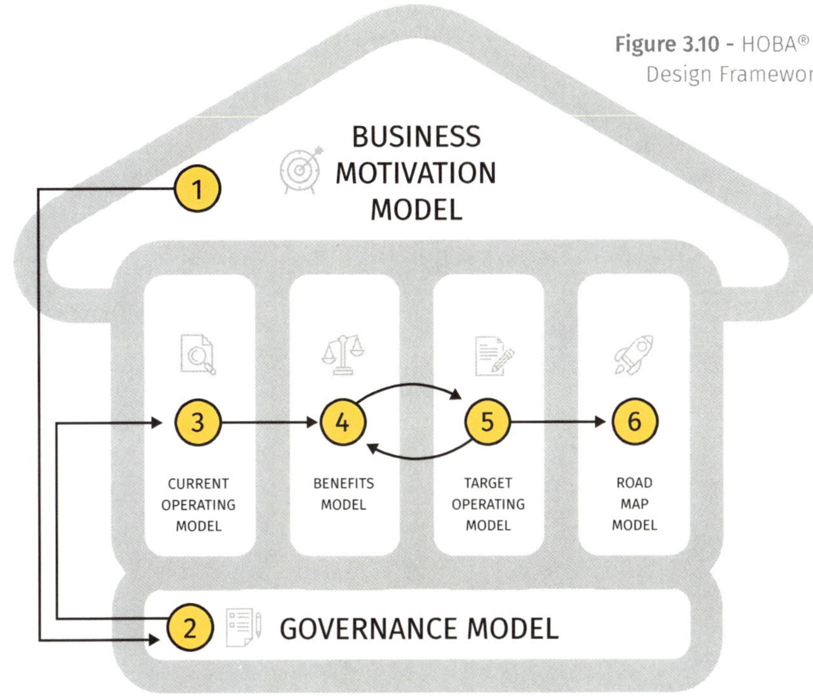


**Figure 3.10** - HOBA® as a Design Framework

**Table 3.2** Design Process Steps, HOBA® Reference Models and Aspects

| Design Step | HOBA® Reference Model | Aspect of the Business |
|---|---|---|
| 1 | Business Motivation Model | WHY do they do it? (vision) |
| 2 | Governance Model | WHO does it?<br>WHAT is their role? (i.e. RACI)<br>HOW do we control scope? (Design Principles)<br>HOW do we manage work? (Requirements framework)<br>HOW do we manage risks? (RAIDs) |
| 3 | Current Operating Model | WHAT do they do? |
| 4 | Benefits Model | WHY do they do it? (benefits) |
| 5 | Target Operating Model | WHERE/HOW do they do it? |
| 6 | Road Map Model | WHEN do they do it? |

Figure 3.11 - HOBA® - As A Perspectives Framework

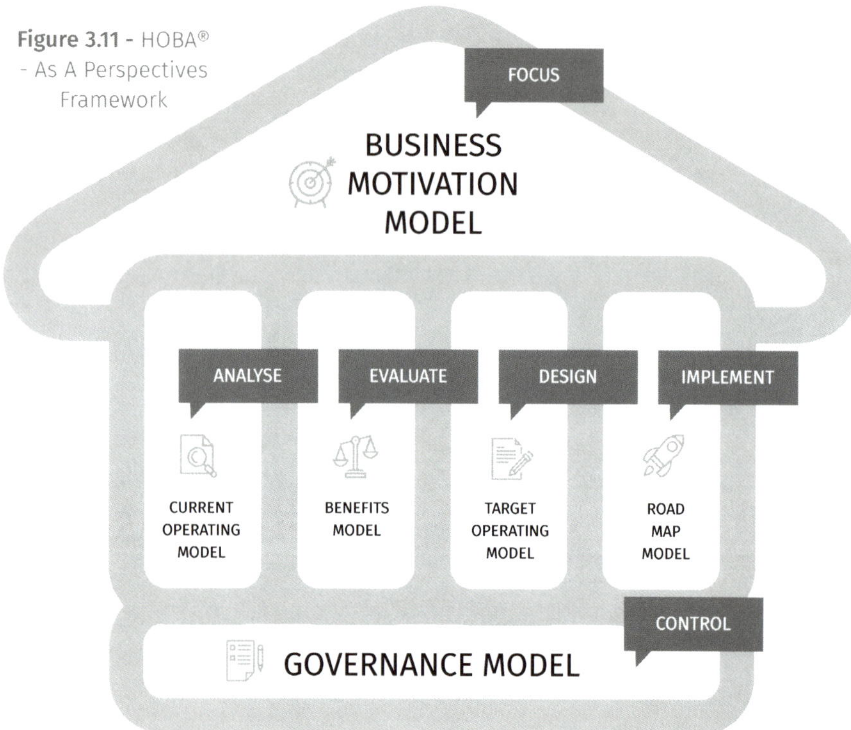


## 1. HOBA as a Context Framework

As a Context Framework, **HOBA®** provides the context to understand (and address) the different aspects and questions asked of the Organisation and the Business Architecture in the development of design of the TOM and managing the alignment of the implementation of the physical Business Architecture with the design of the TOM.

As a Context Framework, **HOBA®** is able to surface these different questions facing the Organisation and the design and implementation of the TOM, so a suitable solution (or range of solution options) can be presented, agreed and implemented as part of the TOM that explicitly addresses those questions asked of the Organisation.
The different aspects or questions asked of the Organisation and Business Architecture, and their relationship to **HOBA®** Reference Models are shown in *Figure 3.12*.

Table 3.3 below summarises the different aspects and questions addressed by each of the HOBA® Reference Models.

What this means in practise, is that when you are going through (or about to go through) the different Reference Models you are addressing a different aspect of the Organisation and Business Architecture. For the Benefits Model Reference Model for example, you and your stakeholders will know and learn two (2) things - *first* – what are the Business Benefits the Organisation intends to realise from the TOM, and *second* – what are the new or changes to existing business capabilities needed in order for the Business to realise the intended

Table 3.3 Roles of HOBA® Reference Models

| # | Reference Model | Role | Description |
|---|---|---|---|
| 1 | Business Motivation Model | Focus | Provides the focus for the Business, and the Business Architecture effort. |
| 2 | Governance Model | Control | Provides the boundaries in which decisions must be taken, and by whom, and how scope, work and risks are managed. |
| 3 | Current Operating Model | Analyse | Provides the context of the 'problem area' to be analysed (the 'As-Is' operating model) |
| 4 | Benefits Model | Evaluate | Provides the criteria and method to identify and evaluate the benefits the Business intends to realise and the Business Changes and Enablers (i.e. people, process and technology elements of business capabilities) needed for the Business to realise its planned Benefits and Business Strategy. |
| 5 | Target Operating Model (TOM) | Design | Provides the design of the 'To-Be' operating model, taking into account the prioritised Business Changes and Enablers identified the 'Evaluate' step. This step also has a feedback loop into the Evaluate step to (re)validate and (re) confirm the solution 'design' can still achieve the planned benefits the business is intending to achieve. |
| 6 | Road Map Model | Implement | Provides the road map and necessary Blueprints required to implement the chosen Business Changes and Enablers, and tools to manage and monitor its implementation and traceability back to the stakeholder's concerns and Business Benefits. |

Business Benefits and ultimately the Business Strategy. Having this as an outcome you want to achieve you should keep any discussions and work focused on the Benefits Model. going into any discussion relating to the Benefits Model should keep the discussions and work focused.

### Context of HOBA® Model

The context of **HOBA®** as a model of what is needed to design and implement the Organisations TOM, the context of **HOBA®** Model puts the different Reference Models in context to show they help in the development of the design and the implementation of the physical TOM.

The context of each Reference Model and their role and the nature of the relationship and interaction between each other, is shown in *Figure 3.13* below.

This 'Context of HOBA® Model' (*Figure 3.13 below)* is a useful tool for yourself, and more importantly helping your stakeholders understand and appreciate the necessity to complete each and every Reference Model for the respective role they play in developing the *design* of the Target Operating Model (TOM) and the implementation of the *physical* TOM.

Due to their *'cause and effect'* relationship with each other, each Reference Model is important to adequately develop the design of the TOM that explicitly addresses the stakeholder's concerns (defined in the problem statement), and implement the physical Business Architecture to enable the Organisation to effectively and efficiently executive its Business Strategy, realise its planned Business Benefits and fulfil its Vision.

### Content Framework

As a Content Framework, **HOBA®** provides the complete list of the content (i.e. deliverables) that are both required and necessary to develop the design, and manage the alignment of the implementation of the physical Business Architecture with the design of the TOM, which you are required to produce, as the Business Architect.

**Figure 3.12 -** HOBA® - As A Context Framework

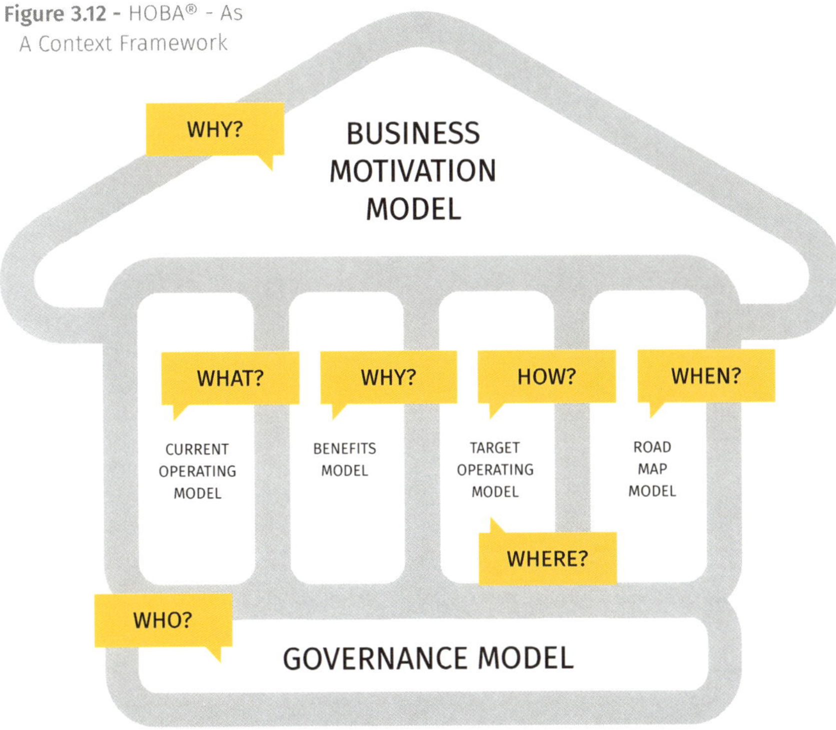


**HOBA® Reference Models, Aspects and Questions**

**Table 3.4**

| HOBA® Reference Model | Aspect | Question |
|---|---|---|
| Business Motivation | WHY | Why are we doing this?<br>What are the objectives we are seeking to achieve? |
| Governance Model | WHO | Who are the people, the stakeholders involved?<br>What is their role? (i.e. Responsible, Accountable, Consulted, Informed)<br>How do we control scope?<br>How do we manage work?<br>How do we manage risks? |
| Current Operating Model | WHAT | What is the current issues, and concerns with the existing operating model? |
| Benefits Modell | WHY | Why are we doing this?<br>What are the benefits we/the Organisation intend to realise? and What are the new or changes to existing business capabilities needed that drive the realisation of the intended Business Benefits? |
| Target Operating Model | HOW<br>WHERE | How will the operating model change in the future?<br>Where are the changes made to the current operating model? |
| Road Map Model | WHEN | When will the changes be implemented? |

**HOBA®** deliverables consist of Reference Models, Building Blocks and Blueprints. Reference Models address the aspects or 'Why, Who, What, Where, How and When' questions (i.e. 'big picture' questions) asked of the Organisation and Business Architecture discussed earlier.

Reference Models are broken down into Building Blocks, which are further broken down or made up of Blueprints. Building Blocks are a collection of Blueprints that describe a specific view or perspective of the Business Architecture, and break down and address a specific aspect of the Reference Model they belong too (i.e. the 'middle picture'). Blueprints address an even more focused view of the Building Block they belong too (i.e. the 'small picture').

The relationship between Reference Models, Building Blocks and Blueprints is shown in Figure 3.14 (on the next page).

Building Blocks and Blueprints are where a good percentage of your time is spent - gathering information, speaking with stakeholders both within and across the Organisation, validating their requirements, negotiating trade-offs etc., and capturing them in the appropriate deliverable.

While each of the Blueprints that make up each of **HOBA®**'s Building Blocks are discussed in more detail in later chapters, Figure 3.15 (on the next page) shows each Reference Model with their respective Building Blocks.

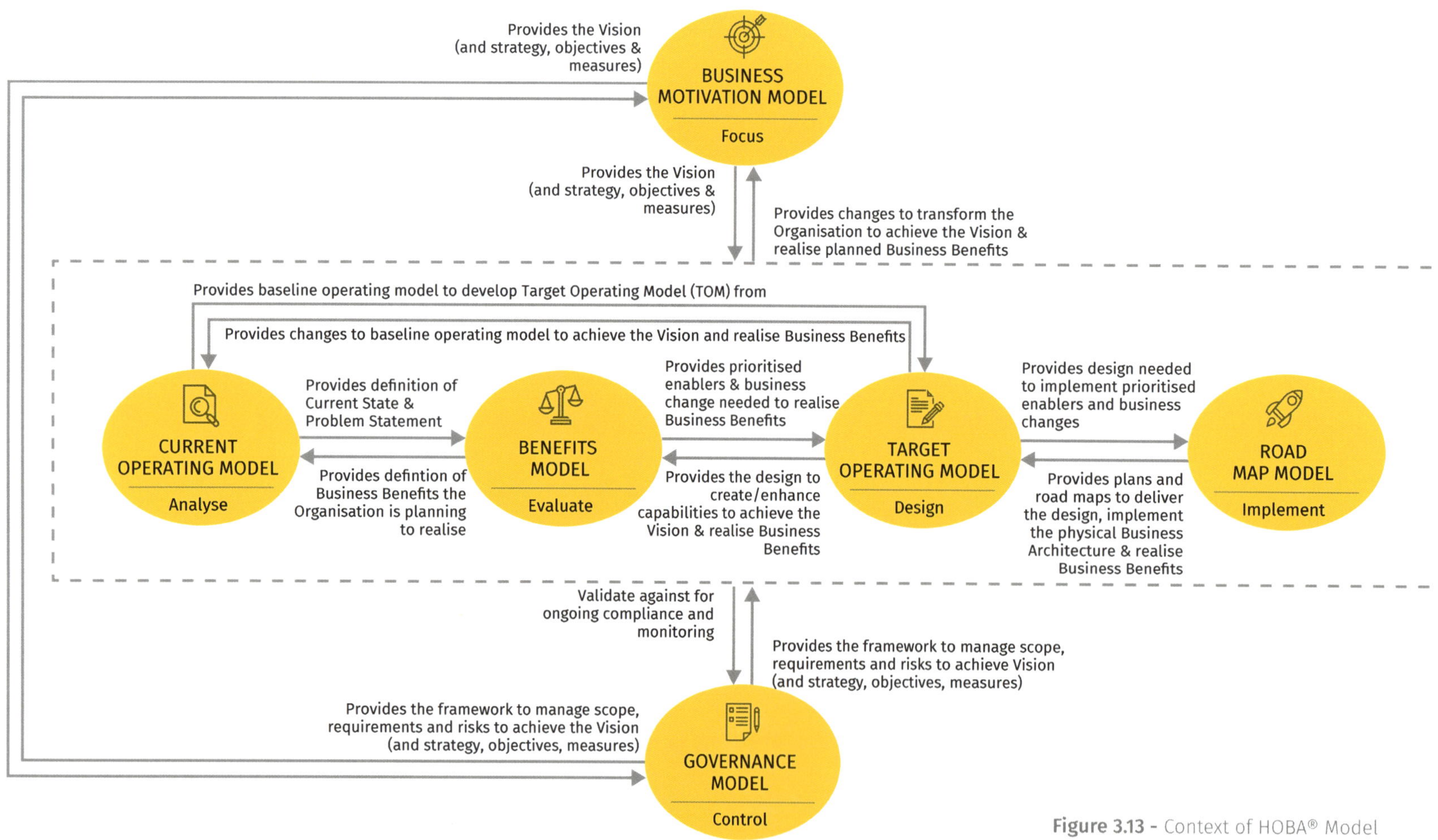


**Figure 3.13** - Context of HOBA® Model

The Blueprints that make up each of the afore mentioned Building Blocks are discussed in detail in later chapters, however Figure 3.16 (on the following page) will give you an idea of what form the Blueprints take, and how the different Blueprints address a different specific aspect or one of the *'Why, Who, What, Where, How and When?'* questions asked of the business and the Business Architecture.

**Note – The 'Where' aspect/question asked of the Business and Business Architecture is covered and addressed in the 'To-Be' versions of the 'What' (capability model) and 'How' (Process Model), shown in the above diagram.**

**HOBA®** represents the best practises in Project and Programme Management, Process Management, and Architecture Frameworks (not to mention the culmination of years of experience), but most importantly developed with input and feedback from the key Business Stakeholders, from the CxO level with their strategic concerns, right through to the Operational level with their implementation concerns. There is no guesswork about which Building Blocks or Blueprints (or Reference Models for that matter) are needed to represent a certain view of the Business or Business Architecture, including how to implement the Target Operating Model (TOM), to ensure not only are the different stakeholder concerns are addressed, but the TOM is implemented as expected, and the Business Benefits are realised as planned.

Because the *'guess work'* is removed, as Business Architect you can focus on getting the ***design*** of the TOM together to best meet the needs of the Organisation and then focus on managing the alignment of the *implementation* of the TOM with the design.

**For a full list of all Building Blocks and their respective Blueprints and artefacts, refer to *Appendix D – Reference Models, Building Blocks and Blueprints.***

[22] Adapted from Walker, M. (2014) 'Business Architecture the key to Enterprise Transformation: Business Architecture Content Framework' [sic]

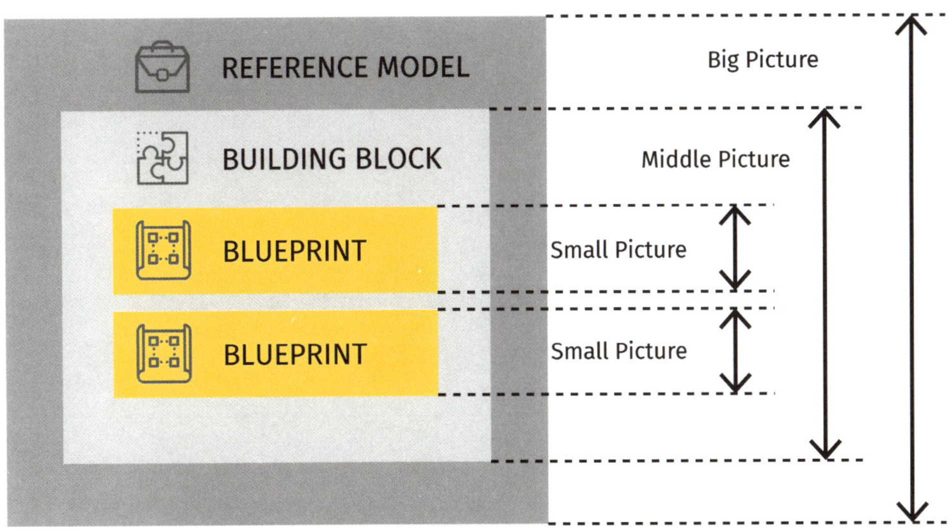


Figure 3.14 - Relationship between Reference Models, Building Blocks and Blueprints

Figure 3.15 - HOBA* as a Content Framework

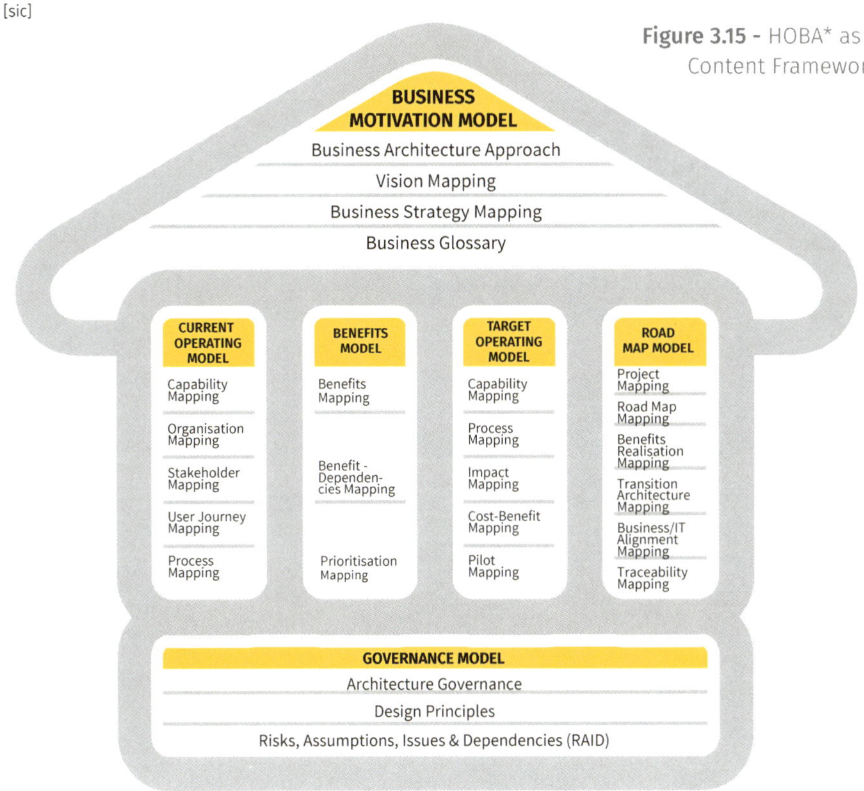

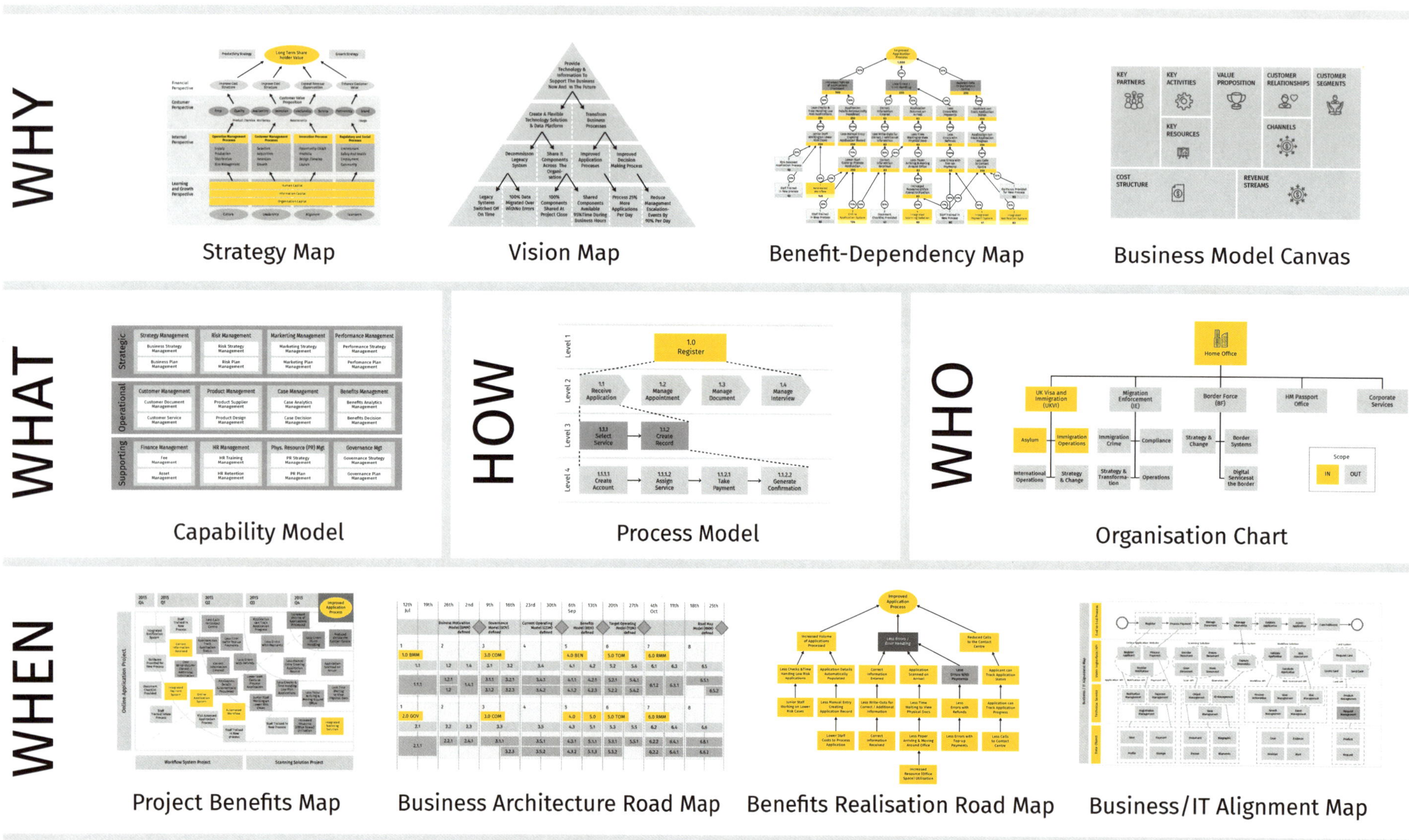


**Figure 3.16** - HOBA® Blueprints Address Context Framework Questions[22]

# Alignment with Other Approaches

**HOBA®** and the **Design Process** have been developed over a decade of strategy and implementation work with clients and alongside various consultancies and subject matter experts within the private and public sector, combined with certifications in PRINCE2, Scrum, Lean Six Sigma, and Masters of Business Administration (MBA), as well as other architecture frameworks (albeit more IT focused).

**HOBA®** is intentionally designed with other approaches in mind. Explicitly, **HOBA®** is aligned with the following approaches:

1. The Open Group Architecture Framework (TOGAF®),
2. Zachman,
3. Project Management,
4. Agile Scrum,
5. Scaled Agile Framework (SAFe®),
6. APQC Process Classification Framework (PCF®), and
7. Business Realisation Management (BRM),

We will discuss each of these approaches in the section below.

## The Open Group Architecture Framework (TOGAF®)

**HOBA®** is aligned with TOGAF®, for the most part, in that they both share a similar approach to Business Architecture and the process to develop it (i.e. it's a good idea, and Organisations must have it).

As a reminder (or quick introduction to TOGAF® for those that are unfamiliar with it), TOGAF® is designed and owned by the Open Management Group (OMG). According to their website, they are:

**"An international, open membership, not-for-profit technology standards consortium, founded in 1989."**

Note the key word – *"technology"*. As mentioned in the Introduction, first and foremost, the idea behind HOBA® is getting back to *'first principles'*, only doing the things that add direct value to designing and implementing the Business Architecture while always questioning what we're doing, and why are we are doing it.

**We all know that 'if the only tool you have is a hammer, don't be too surprised when you starting seeing every problem is a nail?!'**

It also helps to check what tools we have in our hands when we are asking those questions. (i.e. not every business problem is going to be, or needs to be solved by technology, contrary to what a lot of technical folk will tell you!).

The similarities between **HOBA®** and TOGAF® are as follows:

- They both share a defined process for developing their respective architectures (TOGAF®'s design process is the Architecture Development Method (ADM).
- The order of activities to be completed in developing the design and implementation activities are similar, the key ones being; starting with the Vision, assessment of the current state, future state, solution options, and end with actual implementation).
- Both support iterative development of their respective architectures.
- Both share the concept of deliverables – namely Building Blocks and Blueprints, where all the work is captured.

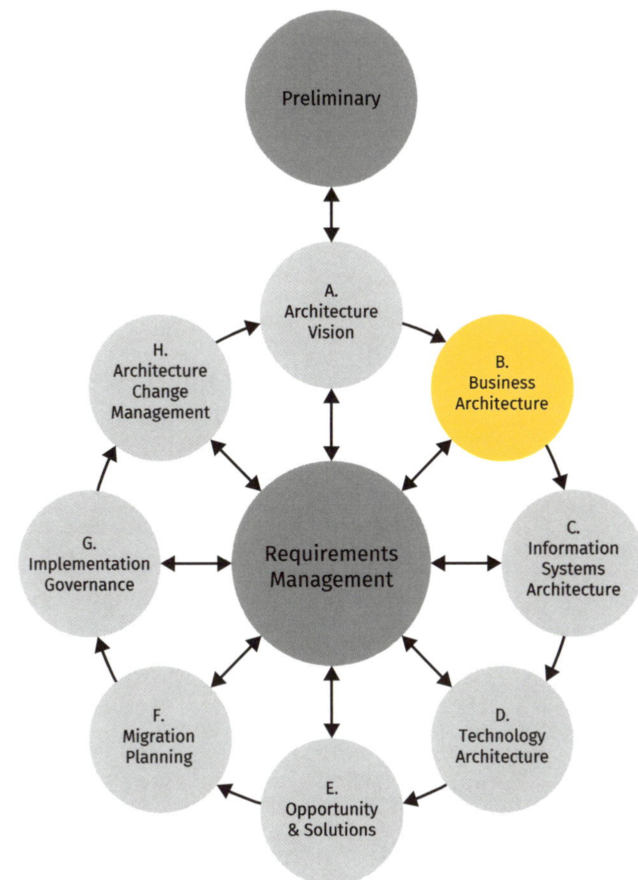


**Figure 3.17 -** TOGAF® ADM highlighting where Business Architecture comes in

All credit should be given to OMG and TOGAF® however, for:

- Collectively heightening the awareness of Business Architecture in the Enterprise Architecture field, and
- Rightfully placing Business Architecture as the first architecture (domain) in the Enterprise to be developed and defined, before any other architecture domains (i.e. the correct way - the horse leading the cart, as opposed to that cart leading the horse).

Although TOGAF® and the ADM cover Business Architecture in their framework and processes, they do not go into great detail of what Business Architecture actually looks like or its value and how to effectively use it. This is where **HOBA®** and the Design Process comes in, to address these areas (among others).

## Zachman Framework

Before we start with Zachman, we should (as when starting any Business Architecture engagement), agree on terms. **HOBA®** is aligned with Zachman, for the parts that relate to Business Architecture, however, Zachman in itself is not an actual framework.

Although Zachman is referred to as an Enterprise Architecture *'framework'*, it is not a framework per se. Zachman is actually a *taxonomy* (or structure) of how to classify or organise different elements or deliverables of an Enterprise Architecture.

To be clear, according to the Oxford dictionary, a 'framework' is defined as:

> **"An essential supporting structure of a building, vehicle, or object; A basic structure underlying a system, concept, or text; the theoretical framework of political sociology"[23]**

Whereas, a taxonomy is defined as:

> **"The classification of something, especially organisms; A scheme of classification"[24]**

While Zachman is therefore not a framework but actually a taxonomy for classifying and organising architectural Blueprints and artefacts to address the needs and perspectives of a particular stakeholder, **HOBA®** is aligned to the areas of the taxonomy that relate to Business Architecture.

As a reminder (or quick introduction to Zachman for those that are unfamiliar), Zachman 'framework' is divided into 2 parts: **columns** (which represent perspectives, views or viewpoints), and **rows** (representing the 'total view' of the architecture, through that perspective), as shown in *Figure 3.18* below.

The rows and columns that are important and applicable to Business Architecture span the width of the columns (from *'why, how, what, who, where and when'*) and the first three (3) rows - contextual, conceptual and logical.

The first three (3) rows (i.e. contextual, conceptual and logical) also have their specific business facing, and Business Architecture perspectives and audience, which is true for **HOBA®**:

- **Row 1** – Executive / Contextual Perspective
- **Row 2** – Business Management / Conceptual Perspective
- **Row 3** – Architect / Logical Perspective

[23] Oxford dictionary (2017) http://www.oxforddictionaries.com/definition/english/framework
[24] Oxford dictionary (2017) http://www.oxforddictionaries.com/definition/english/taxonomy
[25] Adapted from O'Rourke, C. et al (2003) 'Enterprise Architecture: Using the Zachman Framework'

**Figure 3.18** - Zachman Framework[25]

| | Why | How | What | Who | Where | When |
|---|---|---|---|---|---|---|
| Contextual | Goal List | Process List | Material List | Organisational Unit & Role List | Geographical Locations List | Event List |
| Conceptual | Goal Relationship | Process Model | Entity Relationship | Organisational Unit & Role Relationship Model | Locations Model | Event Model |
| Logical | Rules Diagram | Process Diagram | Data Model Diagram | Role Relationship Diagram | Locations Diagram | Event Diagram |
| Physical | Rules Specification | Process Function Specification | Data Entity Specification | Role Specification | Location Specification | Event Specification |
| Detailed | Rules Detail | Process Details | Data Details | Role Details | Location Details | Event Details |

The last two (2) rows also, have their specific perspective and audiences (i.e. physical and detailed). As Business Architects we naturally share an interest, and are concerned with these areas also as they make up the complete view of the 'enterprise architecture'. The difference between Zachman and **HOBA®** however is in the scope of work for that level is instead covered by our co-workers whom we work closely with (the Business Analyst, and Technical Architect), as shown in *Figure 3.19*.

In terms of alignment and coverage, **HOBA®** addresses each of the first three (3) rows through the different perspectives, which are covered and addressed through **HOBA®**'s the three (3) core elements as follows:

- **Row 1 - HOBA® Reference Models** (e.g. Business Motivation Model, Governance Model, Current Operating Model, Benefits Model etc.) – address the contextual/strategic (Row 1) aspects and *'Why, Who, When, Where, Why and How?'* questions asked of the Business and Business Architecture;
- **Row 2 - HOBA® Building Blocks** - (i.e. Vision Mapping, Strategy Mapping, Benefits Mapping etc.) address the conceptual (Row 2) aspects of the Business and Business Architecture; and
- **Row 3 - HOBA® Blueprints -** (i.e. Vision, Strategy, Objectives, Measures (VSOM), Terms & Definitions, Organisation Mapping, Stakeholder Mapping etc.) address the logical/operational (Row 3) aspects of the Business and Business Architecture.

## Project Management

In terms of Project Management, *HOBA®* is aligned with the Scaled Agile Framework (SAFe®), Agile and the 'traditional' Project Management approach known as 'waterfall' (the latter discussed below).

Mentioning 'waterfall' could actually be a *taboo* subject and at risk of criticism from 'Agilests' for its inclusion, however working on some big Programmes, and in particularly with government agencies, in my experience I have discovered not everyone is on board 'the Agile train'. As a result, waterfall is also discussed here for those more familiar with waterfall (rather than agile) principles.

As a quick recap, the traditional 'waterfall' approach for managing projects (depending on your school of thought) essentially follows 4 life cycle stages – discovery, design, build and delivery (some approaches also call it the 4D's – Discovery, Design, Develop and Deploy).

**HOBA®** and the steps in the **Design Process** align to the different stages of the traditional project management approach, as shown in *Figure 3.20:*

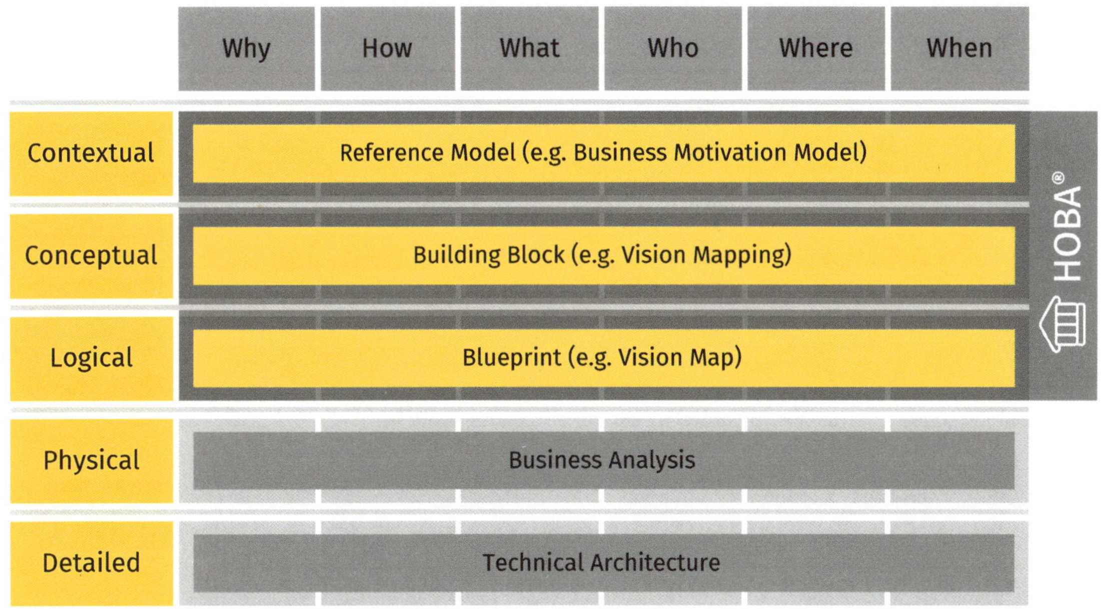


**Figure 3.19 -** HOBA® alignment with Zachman Framework

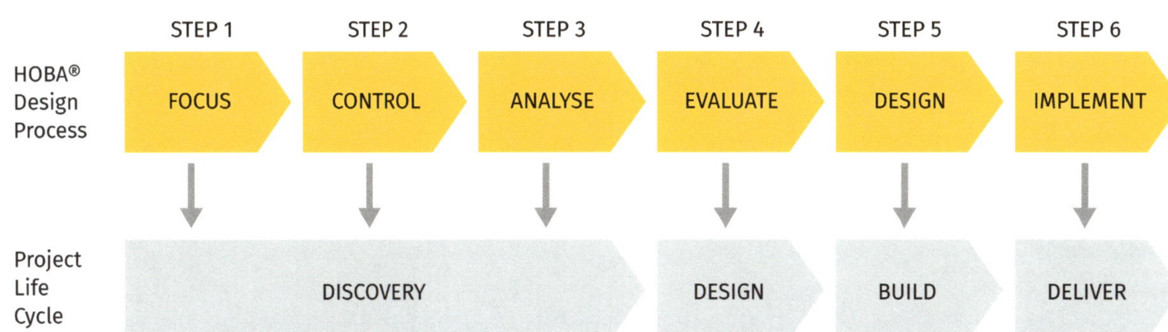


**Figure 3.20 -** HOBA® Design Process Alignment to Project Life-Cycle Phases

How HOBA® and the Design Process align with the respective traditional Project management phases is as shown in Table 3.5.

**(*) Note – What the Table 3.5 doesn't show, is that the change of 'role' the Business Architect performs moving from Step 5 to Step 6. From Step 5 to Step 6 is where the Business Architects role changes from a 'Design-Lead' to a 'Design-Steward' role, which is one that moved from 'designing' to 'stewarding' the alignment of the implementation of the physical Target Operating Model (TOM) aligns with the agreed design of the TOM.**

What this alignment also means is that if you, as the Business Architect, are ever in the unfortunate position of getting brought into (or dropped into, depending on how late into the process it is) a project that is part way through its lifecycle, **HOBA®** and the **Design Process** are both sufficiently flexible to allow the Business Architect to adopt where to start the **Design Process**, depending on where in its life cycle the project or Programme is.

A caveat with this 'mid-project' approach is of course, a big assumption that the activities, and Blueprints, and all the decisions that needed to have happened in order to get those Blueprints drafted and signed off have already happened.

Project Life-Cycle Phase alignment to HOBA® Design (Process) Steps

Table 3.5

| Project Life Cycle Phase | Aspect | Question |
|---|---|---|
| Discovery | Step 1 - Focus | Step-1 Focus is about 'discovering' what is important for the Business, and Business Architecture, the Vision.<br>Step-1 Focus sets the direction and agrees the intended outcomes both the Programme and Business Architecture are aiming for, which corresponds neatly to the 'discovery' phase of the traditional project life cycle. |
| | Step 2 - Control | Step-2 Control, is about discovering and agreeing the scope of the Programme and Business Architecture, and the approval and governance processes |
| | Step 3 – Analyse | Step-3 Analyse is about discovering and agreeing the issues and opportunities facing the business today. |
| Design | Step 4 – Evaluate | Step-4 Evaluate is about identifying the 'design' of the Target Operating Model (TOM) based on the benefits that are evaluated as part Benefits Reference Model covered in Step 4. |
| Build* | Step 5 – Build | Step-5 Design aligns neatly with 'build' phase, as this is where both approaches build (or develop) the changes identified from the previous Step 4 Evaluate. |
| Delivery* | Step 6 - Implement | Step-6 Implement aligns neatly with 'delivery' phase, as this where both approaches implement the physical changes to the business. |

As I have discussed previously in *The Business Architecture Challenge* section Business Architecture is (or should be) involved in early in the project (in terms of the project and Programme lifecycle), ideally in the planning phases, well before any Design or Build work takes place.

Business Architecture should begin in a projects infancy, early enough in the projects life cycle (ideally 'Discovery' phase), to help shape the scope and direction of the project or Programme. This should be before any (solution) design occurs, and definitely before any build (and delivery for that matter) occurs. It may seem like common sense, but I cannot over emphasised how important this is to the success or failure of a project.

Bringing in a Business Architect after kick off (i.e. past the Discovery phase, and into the Design or later) is *not* an ideal situation because, given the level and scope of the view the Business Architect has (i.e. strategic and Organisation wide), they will likely unearth previously unseen dependencies and issues that need to be addressed. To address these at a later point in time becomes a costly and expensive exercise. It is always more expensive to solve unforeseen or unplanned problems later in a project lifecycle, because resources (i.e. time and money) have already been expended leaving little time and budget to resolve those unplanned or unexpected issues.

I recall one particular instance where I assisted one company with their business digitalisation transformation Programme that amongst the number of changes, was decommissioning its online application website. The Programme was tasked with removing and migrating what they thought was 'all application forms on the current website', to a newly built 'service'. Unfortunately, the Programme experienced scope creep after it was revealed the projects objectives and measures had been ill defined and not agreed to. A very small wording change, 'all application forms *online*' was miss-read as 'all application forms' (i.e. the scope was 'thought' to be application forms just the website being decommissioned, not all application forms '*online*') created a very big project scope change. This was due to the fact that there were literally hundreds of additional application forms on other company websites that would also need to be included within the new service, which included providing the means for them to be maintained and updated as and when needed. This resulted in extensive increases in the cost and time need to complete the project. Had the Business Architect been brought into the Programme early, and the objectives and measures been quantified via the Business Motivation Model (at least the Statement of Work (SOW) Blueprint, or the Vision, Strategy, Objectives and Measures (VSOM) Blueprint) the number of application forms that were to be migrated, and at least the quantified source of application forms agreed (i.e. exact name of website or website, as opposed to '*online*'), this situation could have been avoided.

## Agile Scrum

Agile Scrum is a Project Management methodology which encourages a highly structured, iterative and incremental development approach where solutions evolve through collaboration between self-organising, cross-functional teams, with the emphasis on collaboration.

Although the term 'Agile' was not coined until the 1990s, versions of the methodology existed as far back as the early 1900s. Agile is most frequently used in software delivery environments but it can be used to manage any type of project.

In Agile delivery, the product evolves over the lifecycle of the project. From a customer perspective, each delivery cycle (two to four-week time-boxed periods called sprints), adds value and produces a potentially shippable product enhancement which is measurable and can in theory be deployed to a production environment. Agile Scrum (which is closely aligned to **HOBA®** (and the **Design Process**) has become popular because of its collaborative and structured approach to Project Management.

**HOBA®** follows the same collaborative, structured and iterative approach to developing the design and implementation of the physical TOM and Business Architecture. The approach, much like Scrum, aims to produce a continuous delivery of up-to-date, working and useable design views (Reference Models, Building Blocks and Blueprints) of the Business Architecture.

Much like Agile Scrum, **HOBA®** also subscribes to the same 3-pillars principle:

- **Transparency** - development and implementation of the Business Architecture is transparent and therefore visible and available to any interested parties;
- **Inspection** - the Reference Models, Building Blocks and Blueprints that make up the Business Architecture are inspected frequently so unexpected variances in the process (and output) can be detected; and
- **Adaptation** - the 'inspector' (you, the Business Architect in this case) can adjust the process and output as required to ensure alignment with the strategic objectives.

Scrums 3 pillars of Transparency, Inspection and Adaptation, are shown in Figure 3.21 below:

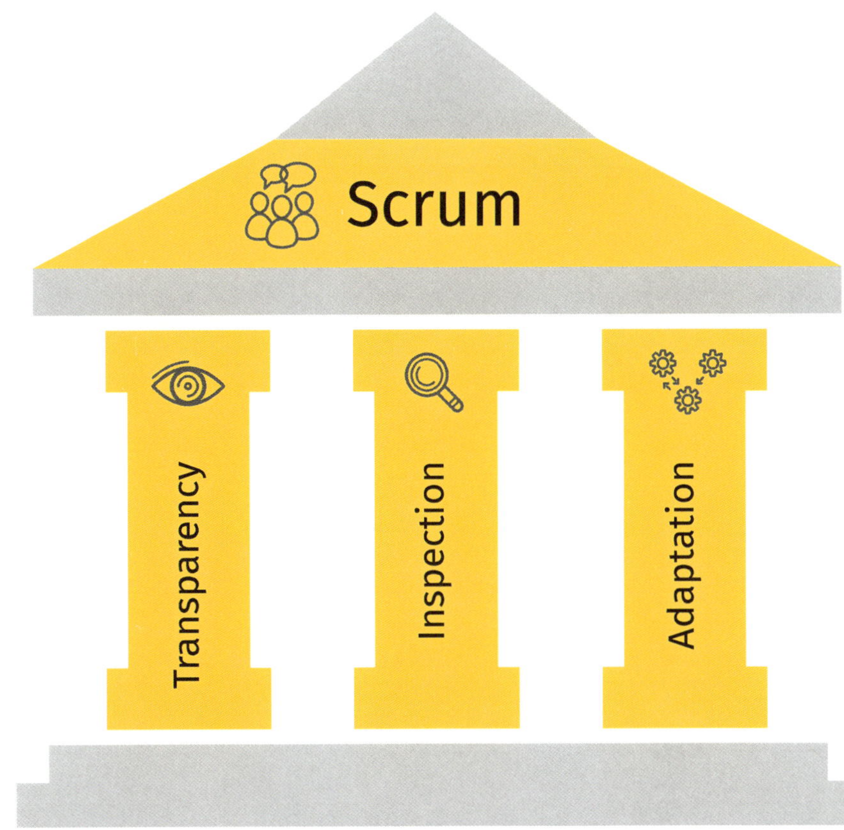


**Figure 3.21** - 3-Pillars of Scrum

What this means in practice is that when short periods of work (called sprints, usually 1, 2 or sometimes 4 weeks in duration) are planned and carried out, frequent inspections take place, and adjustments are carried out to ensure, that:

- All work is still moving in the right direction;
- Any new external (and internal) changes or impacts to the business or Programme can be factored in and included into current and upcoming planned work, and
- Lessons learned from the current and previous phase of work can be fed back into the process and future work.

The illustration below (*Figure 3.22*) shows a graphical representation of the three (3) principles (Transparency, Inspection, Adaption) in action, in the Scrum process (Transparency, Inspection, Adaptation):

Ceremonies within the Agile Scrum framework for example, the 'daily scrum', additionally serve to maintain delivery momentum by encouraging collaboration and conversation between the team members. The 'daily scrum', facilitated by the Scrum Master, is a time-boxed meeting, usually held in the morning and ideally lasting up to a maximum of 15-minutes. Team members take turns to update each other on:

- **What they achieved** the day before,
- **What their plans are** for the day and;
- If they have faced **any impediments**.

Other ceremonies include Sprint Planning where the team, for example Sprint Review and Sprint Retrospectives, facilitate the 'inspect and adapt' process which allow any lessons learnt to be fed into subsequent sprints.

**We will discuss Scrum Ceremonies and governance in more detail later in *'Chapter 6 Step 2 – Control'* and in the *'Governance Model'* Reference Model.**

**Figure 3.22 -**
The Scrum Process[26]

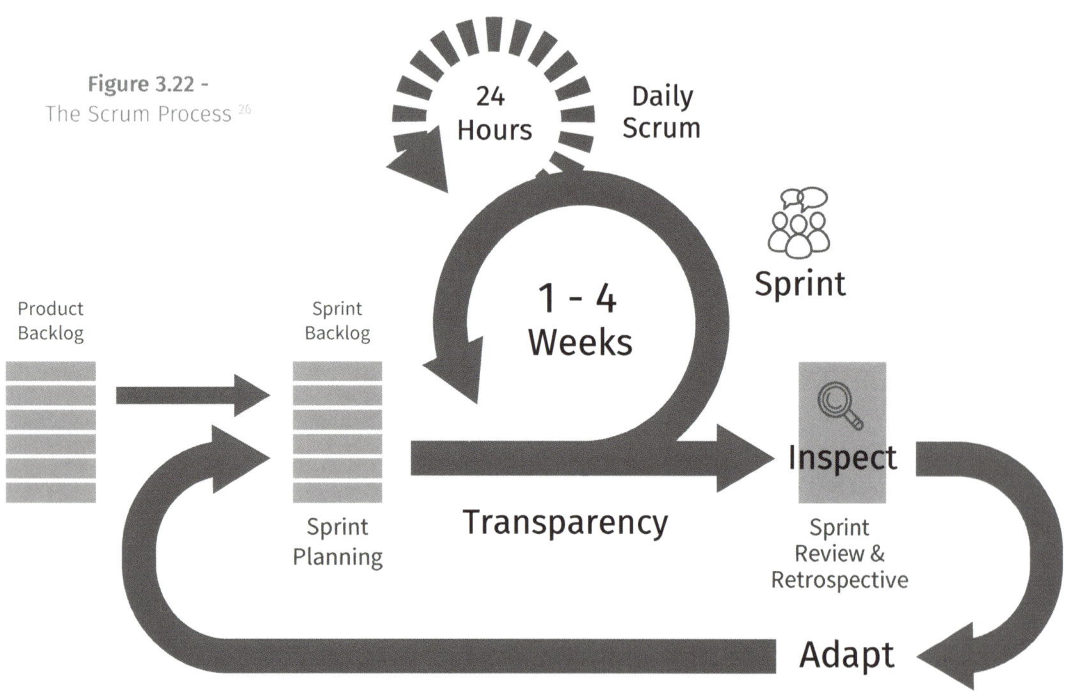


## Scaled Agile Framework (SAFe®)

**HOBA®** is aligned with the Scaled Agile Framework (SAFe®). SAFe® is an Agile iterative and incremental framework for managing mainly software, systems and product development.

SAFe® is based around Scrum (discussed in the previous section *Agile Scrum* above) and LEAN processes of continuous incremental delivery of a workable or working product or service.

The premise behind SAFe® is first and foremost – scale. Enterprise-scale to be more precise. That is, suitable for large Programmes of change, that span across the 'entire' Organisation. Second, it's about ensuring the right information and decisions are taken at the right level of the Organisation to ensure three (3) factors:

- From a **risk** management perspective - the right level of management and management oversight (i.e. review, monitor and supervision) is given to needs, issues and concerns that, rightly so, concern them.
- From a work and **operational** perspective – as the decisions and work disseminates down through the Programme, from the top with the Executive and Senior Management (who have the scope and responsibility across the Organisation), to Middle Management (who have the scope and responsibility for their specific departments and business units), to Operations staff (who are on the 'shop floor'), the people closest to the work, are the ones doing the work.
- From an **alignment** perspective – all work that is going on across the Organisation, from the Executive level to Operations, is all pulling in the same direction, focused on achieving the same set of agreed outcomes.

[26] Adapted from Verheyen, G., (2013) 'Scrum – A Pocket Guide'

How HOBA® uses the SAFe® approach to ensure the above three (3) factors (risk, operations and alignment) are addressed, and the right information and decisions are taken at the right level in the Organisation, different HOBA® components (i.e. Reference Models, Building Blocks and Blueprints) with their different perspective, focus and audience are taken to the respective Portfolio, Programme, and Team levels across the Organisation, as shown in *Figure 3.23* below:

---

[27] Adapted from Cockburn, A., et al. (2011) Agile Software Requirements The Agile Enterprise Big Picture'

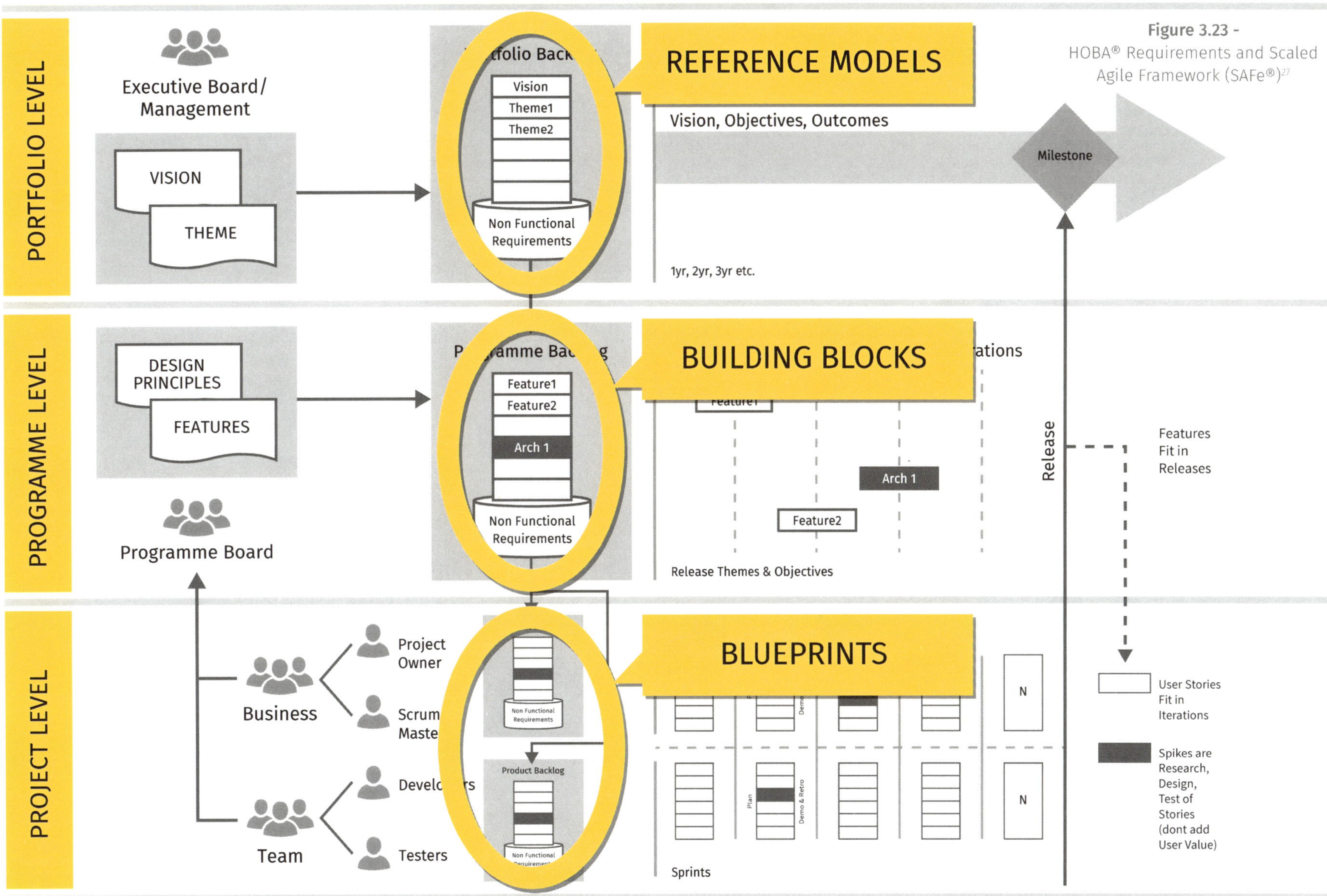


Figure 3.23 - HOBA® Requirements and Scaled Agile Framework (SAFe®)[27]

What this means in practice, in terms of developing and delivering the Business Architecture, is that the different levels of the Organisation (i.e. Portfolio, Programme and Team/Project) are responsible for approving and developing the specific level of requirements applicable at that level of the Organisation. For example:

- **The Portfolio level** (consisting of the Portfolio board) should agree and sign off the scope of the Business Architecture through the agreement of the Vision, and Reference Models (Theme level architecture requirements).
- **The Programme level** (consisting of the Programme board) should inherit this list of Building Blocks (Feature level architecture requirements), and is responsible for their review and approval.
- **The Team level** (consisting of internal project governance boards) should do the work in their respective projects and agree and manage the Blueprints (Epic and Story level requirements), within the respective projects.

By incorporating the SAFe® approach into HOBA®, and in developing and implementing the Organisations Target Operating Model (TOM), HOBA® ensures that all work under the Vision (approved by the Portfolio), and carried out in the Programme are completely aligned. So, no more scope creep (among other things)!

**Note – The commonality in the way HOBA® is aligned to SAFe® is that they are both enterprise wide facing frameworks that require certain decisions be taken to (and by) the relevant level of authority and responsibly in the Organisation (i.e. the high level strategic components such as Reference Models – Vision and Theme level requirements) are taken at the Portfolio Level, and lower detailed implementation components (e.g. Building Blocks and Blueprints – Epic and User Story level requirements) are taken at respective Programme and Project level. Where HOBA® differs from SAFe® is in the naming convention and requirement hierarchy. In HOBA®, Theme level requirements are equivalent to an Epic in SAFe®, taken to, and taken by the Portfolio Level for definition and approval.**

The iterative and incremental approach of developing and releasing up to date, usable versions of the Blueprints making up the Business Architecture, also ensures that the process and progress of how the Business Architecture is developing is transparent.

This transparent approach ensures that all stakeholders are informed and kept up to date as the Business Architecture develops. Most importantly, input and feedback loops are built into the process so that feedback can be obtained and incorporated back into the design in short iterations. As a result, not only does the Business Architecture keep up to date, but it maintains alignment with the other architectures across the Programme and Organisation so they too can develop incrementally over time.

**Governance, the Governance Model and the Requirements Management Framework, including how to manage changes and approval of the different level requirements is discussed later in *'Chapter 6 Step 2 – Control'.***

## Business Process Classification Framework (PCF)

**HOBA®** and the **Design Process** is also aligned with the leading industry standard in process classification, the American Productivity & Quality Centre (APQC) Business Process Classification Framework (PCF), shown in Figure 3.24 (on the next page).

The PCF provides the common language to communicate and define business processes comprehensively and without redundancies[28]. That is, PCF provides a framework to standardise the processes across the Organisation in such a way that they are categorised and decomposed at the same and consistent levels so that there is no duplication nor forgotten (overlooked) processes.

The benefits to **HOBA®** and the **Design Process** of standardising how the Organisations processes are categorised and decomposed are to:

- **Identify the processes that are 'in scope',** but also as importantly the processes that are 'out of scope' for the Programme.
- **Identify and define the processes that are the responsibility of the Business Architect** (and therefore Business Architecture), and
- **Identify the handover points** between when Business Architecture finishes, and Business Analysis begins.

As discussed previously *(Challenge #1: What is Business Architecture? - Business Architecture is not Business Analysis)*, Business Architects focus on the different Organisation level, phases and time when they are initially engaged onto and work on the Programme, compared with the Business Analyst. The PCF helps define and draw the line between when and where the Business Architect operates (on the high level Organisational wide processes - level 1 to 3), and engages with and hands over work to the Business Analyst (who operates on the lower level processes - level 4 to 5). This can be seen in Figure 3.25.

[28] American Productivity & Quality Centre (APQC) (2015), Process Classification Framework (PCF) ver 7.0.2

## LEVEL 1 - CATEGORY

**1.0 Develop Vision and Strategy**

Represent the highest level of process in the enterprise, such as Manage Customer Service, Supply Chain, Financial Organisation, and Human resouces.

## LEVEL 2 - PROCESS GROUP

**1.1 Define the Business Concept and Long Term Vision**

Indicates the next level of processes and represent a group of processes. Perfom after Sales Repairs, Procurement, Accounts Payable, Recruit/Spource And Develop Sales Strategy are example of process group.

## LEVEL 3 - PROCESS

**1.1 .5 Conduct Organisation Restructuring Opportunities**

A series of interrelated activities that convert inputs into results (outputs): processes consume resources and require standards for repeatable perfromance; and processes respond to control systems that quality, rate and cost of performance.

## LEVEL 4 - ACTIVITY

**1.1 .5.3 Analyse Deal Options**

Indicates key events performed when exciting a process. Examples of activities include Receive Customer Request, Resolve CustomerComplaints, and Negotiate Purchasing Contracts.

## LEVEL 5 - TASK

**1.1 .5.3.1 Evaluate Acquisition Options**

Tasks represent the next level of hierachical ecomposition after activities. Tasks are generallly much more fine grained and may vary widely across indus industries. Example include: Create Businesss Case and Obtain Funding and Design Recognition and Reward Approaches.

**Figure 3.24 -** APQC Process Classification Framework (PCF)

What this means in practice is that the Business Architect identifies the Organisations' high-level (i.e. Level 1, 2, and 3) processes across the Organisation. As the Business Architect, your role is to validate and confirm with the Business and Key Stakeholders, including the Business Analyst, that they are captured completely and correctly at that high level (i.e. Level 1, 2 and 3), and identify any gaps between the strategic needs of the business, and their ability to meet those needs in terms of the Organisations current processes.

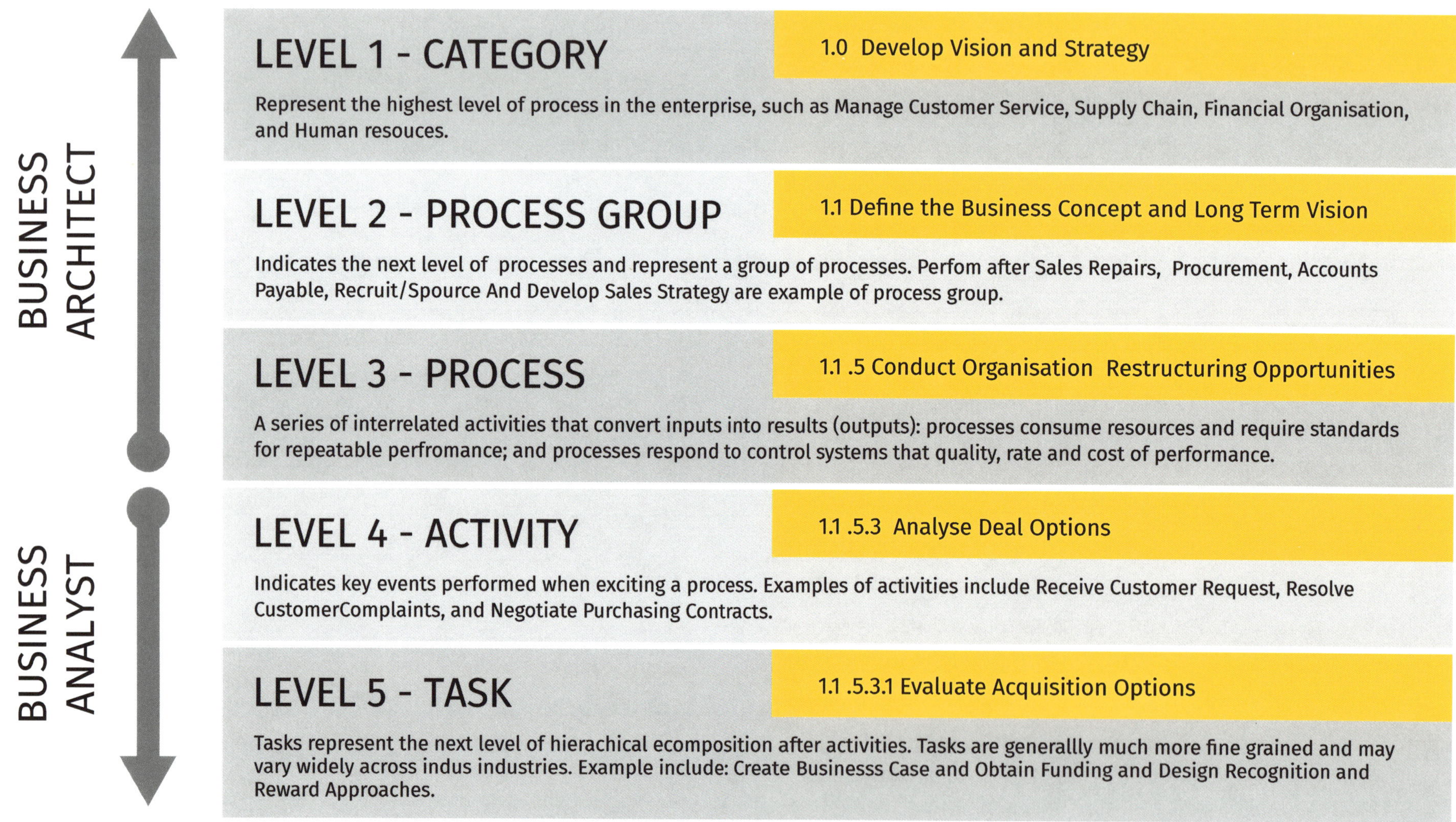


**Figure 3.25 -** The Different Process Focus for the Business Architect and Business Analyst

The next step is to then work with the Business Analyst, handing over the high-level processes to carry out the deeper decomposition and levelling standardisation and analysis activities.

What is important to know here is that the Business Architect is intentionally not caught in the detail or *'the weeds'* (as it is often referred to in Programme Management) of the process mapping, delivery and implementation activities. This allows a Business Architect to then remain focused on the more strategic and planning level work and activities.

As the Business Architect, your concern and strength is in developing the high level strategic functional and structural views (equivalent to PCF levels 1 to 3) across the Organisation, capturing the capabilities and modelling the inter and intra business relationships and dependencies, so that you can uncover any capability and process gaps, and to identify solutions and roadmaps to address these gaps.

The Business Analyst, with their primary concern and strong(er) understanding of the information and (sometimes) software application interdependencies within those (high level strategic functional and structural) views, will use their specialist modelling and analysis skills, elicit and develop the system (functional and non-functional) requirements that will address those gaps[29] (equivalent to PCF levels 4 & 5). Examples of what the different process levels and mapping by the Business Architect and the Business Analyst look like, are discussed later in the *3.4 Process Mapping (As-Is) section.*

## Benefits Realisation Management (BRM)

HOBA® is tightly aligned with the Benefits Realisation Management (BRM) framework. In fact, HOBA® is so tightly aligned that the BRM framework (and specifically, the Benefits Reference Model) can be found right in the middle of it (literally, at Step-4 of the Design Process).

The importance Business Benefits (often referred to as 'Benefits') has (and should have) in Business Architecture is so significant that Benefits (via the Benefits Reference Model) are at the centre of HOBA® and the Design Process, as shown in the *Figure 3.26.*

In his book 'Benefits Realisation Management (2010)' Bradley stated:

**"The purpose of change should always be the realisation of benefits. It is therefore worth investing time and energy in:**

- **Identifying a comprehensive set of benefits;**
- **Classifying and validating them;**
- **Creating high-quality, robust Benefits Maps;**
- **Determining high priority paths;**
- **Securing ownership;**
- **Assessing impact on stakeholders (including dis-benefits)"**

Although according to Bradley, *'Benefits are a fundamental outcome goal for any change Programme'*, Benefits (and the Benefits Model) are unfortunately the missing link in Business Architecture today. Benefits are what *should* be used to drive the decision for the creation of or changes to existing Business Capabilities (people, process, technology) to align the Business to the Business Strategy to aid in forming the Target Operating Model (TOM).

[29] Adapted from Mailk, N., (The Difference Between Business Architect and Business Analyst) https://blogs.msdn.microsoft.com April 2012

**Figure 3.26** - HOBA® – Benefits Model (Step 4)

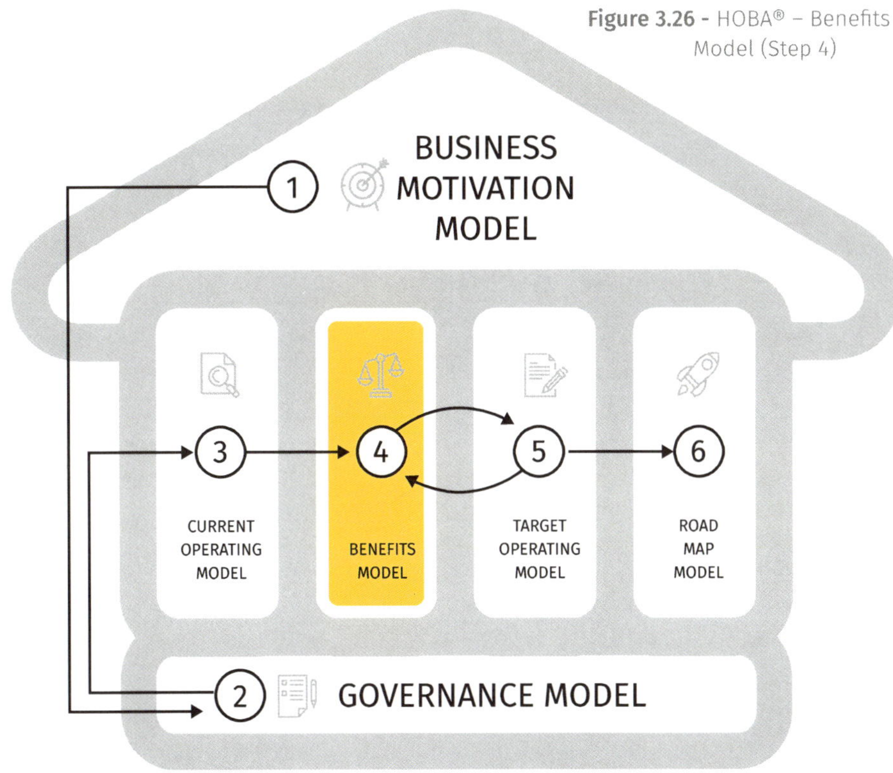

It is in these Business Capabilities (often referred to as 'capabilities') that investments are made, and costs are incurred to either develop new capabilities, or to pay for enhancements to existing ones. It is also only when the forecast '*benefits*', that are to be realised from their use, outweigh the costs of creating or enhancing them should any decision be made to proceed building those new capabilities (or make changes to existing ones).

What happens in practice, is the structured Benefits identification, validation and prioritisation is often not brought into or onto the Programme until *after* the investment in the Business Capabilities has been committed. This is similar to what happens currently with the current reactive (retrospective) engagement model with Business Architecture and Business Architects on a Programme is currently subjected to (as was discussed earlier in the *Challenge #5: What is the role of the Business Architect (and when do we engage them)?* section).

On several Programmes I have been involved in, by the time Business Architecture, Business Benefits or the Benefits Manager were brought onto a Programme, neither the Business Architect nor the Benefits Manager had been involved in the identification, analysis and planning of benefits management or benefits realisation. Their role at that point was to use the Benefits to *validate* the investment in the already selected capabilities, as opposed to using the Benefits to *guide* the investment options needed to directly drive the realisation of the planned Benefits.

While it is not the purpose of this book to provide a detailed overview of Benefits Management is fundamental in (and to) **HOBA®**, as well as the **Design Process.** As a result, it is still important to discuss the process, and the role Benefits Realisation Management plays in Business Architecture in developing the design and implementation of the Target Operating Model (TOM). It is also important to discuss some common terms, what the Programmes actually deliver (outcomes, not benefits) as well as identifying who is responsible for what.

According to *Managing Successful Programmes* (MSP), (2011)[30] , the definition of Benefits Realisation is:

> **"Identification, definition, tracking, realization and optimization of benefits within and beyond a Programme [sic]"**

MSP's definition provides the context in terms of project and Programme scope, which in my experience isn't very well understood currently. The primary misunderstanding is that the Benefits management process (or lifecycle) actually spans across the Programme, from the pre-delivery, into post-delivery phases. What that means in practise is that the benefits management process starts (ideally) at Programme inception, but actually finishes *after* it is finished. The key point is that the 'end' dates of the Programme and the benefits realisation process are not the same.

This difference in end dates between the Programme and the Benefits Management process highlights two (2) important points, which generates a lot of current misunderstanding:

- Programmes end *before* the Benefits Management Process, and
- A Business Architect's 'Benefits Management' responsibility ends when the Programme ends (i.e. not when the Benefits are realised).

In terms of Programmes and their scope, Programmes have historically been (incorrectly) held accountable for the 'realisation' of the Benefits from the changes the Programme was implementing into the Organisation. Programmes are actually responsible for implementing the creation of (or changes to) existing capabilities, as shown in *Figure 3.27* (on the next page).

As with many of the companiesI have assisted over the years, I have seen this common confusion between who is responsible for Programme outputs (i.e. capabilities) and who is responsible for '*realising benefits*'. The general misconception is Programmes are responsible for the delivery of benefits – when in fact, they are actually responsible for the creation of (or changes to) existing capabilities. It is not until these capabilities are embedded and in use within the Business, can the Business realise the planned Benefits.

What actually happens in practice is, the Programme produces outcomes (e.g. a new Case Working system), this 'outcome' then provides a new (or changed) capability (e.g. Application Management, which automatically risks assesses applications between high and low risk and auto-approves low risk applications, diverting high risk applications to a Case Worker for manual, in depth assessment and processing), which is integrated and embedded into the Business. The Business' use of that capability then produces an outcome (e.g. faster identification of 'low risk' applications; better Applicant experience), which

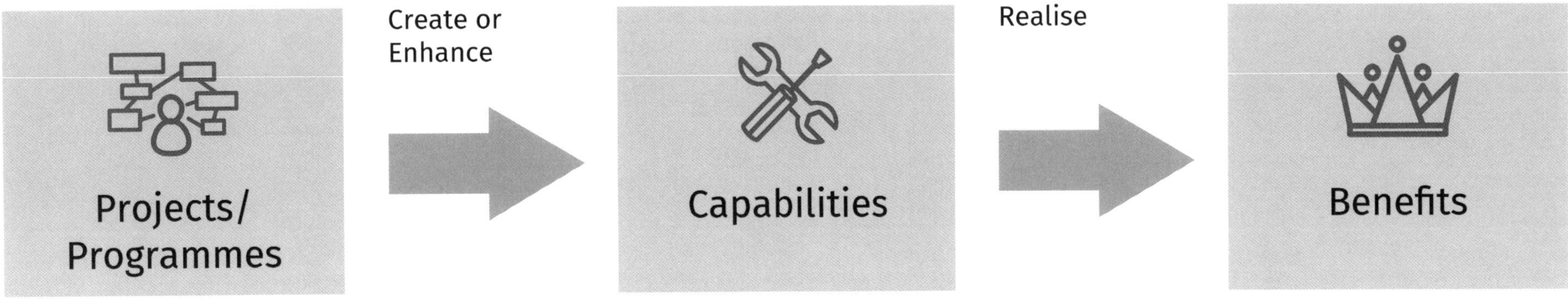


**Figure 3.27 -** Perceived Relationship Between Capabilities and Benefits [31]

through the ongoing use of that new capability can the Business Benefits be 'realised' (e.g. increased volume of applications processed). This actual capability/benefits *cause-and-effect* relationship is shown in *Figure 3.28* below.

In terms of HOBA® and who is responsible for what, it's the Business Architecture and the Business Architect who are responsible for the identification and prioritisation of the Benefits. It is those Benefits that directly contribute to the Organisation achieving its Strategic Objectives, which are the same Strategic Objectives that are identified in the Vision, Strategy, Objectives and Measures (VSOM) Blueprint as part of the Business Motivation Model. It is also important to point out that it's the Benefits Reference Model that capabilities are identified and that drive the realisation of the intended Benefits and Strategic Objectives, as shown in *Figure 3.29*.

The Benefits Management Process – the process of managing the identification of benefits right the way through to their realisation according to Managing Successful Programmes (MSP) (2011)[32], consists of five (5) phases, as shown in *Figure 3.30*.

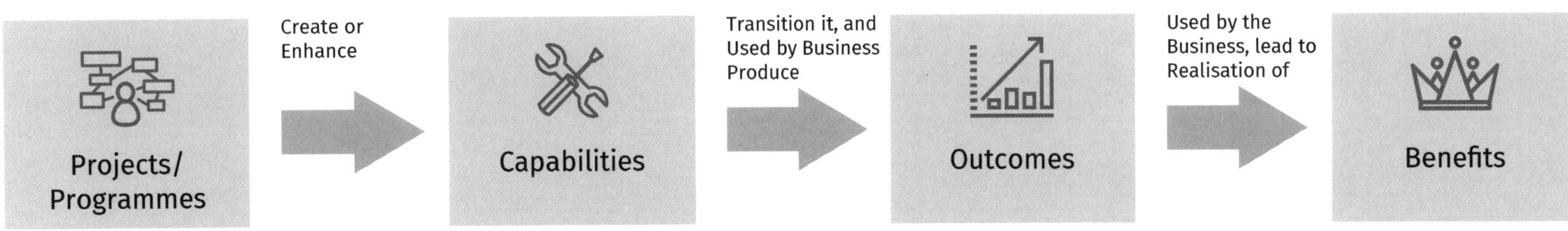


**Figure 3.28 -** Actual Relationship Between Capabilities and Benefits

[31] Letavec, C., (2014) Strategy Benefits Realisation: Optimizing Value through Programs, Portfolios and Organizational Change Management [sic]
[32] Managing Successful Programmes (MSP) (2011), Cabinet Office

Figure 3.29 - Strategic Objective relationship to Benefits

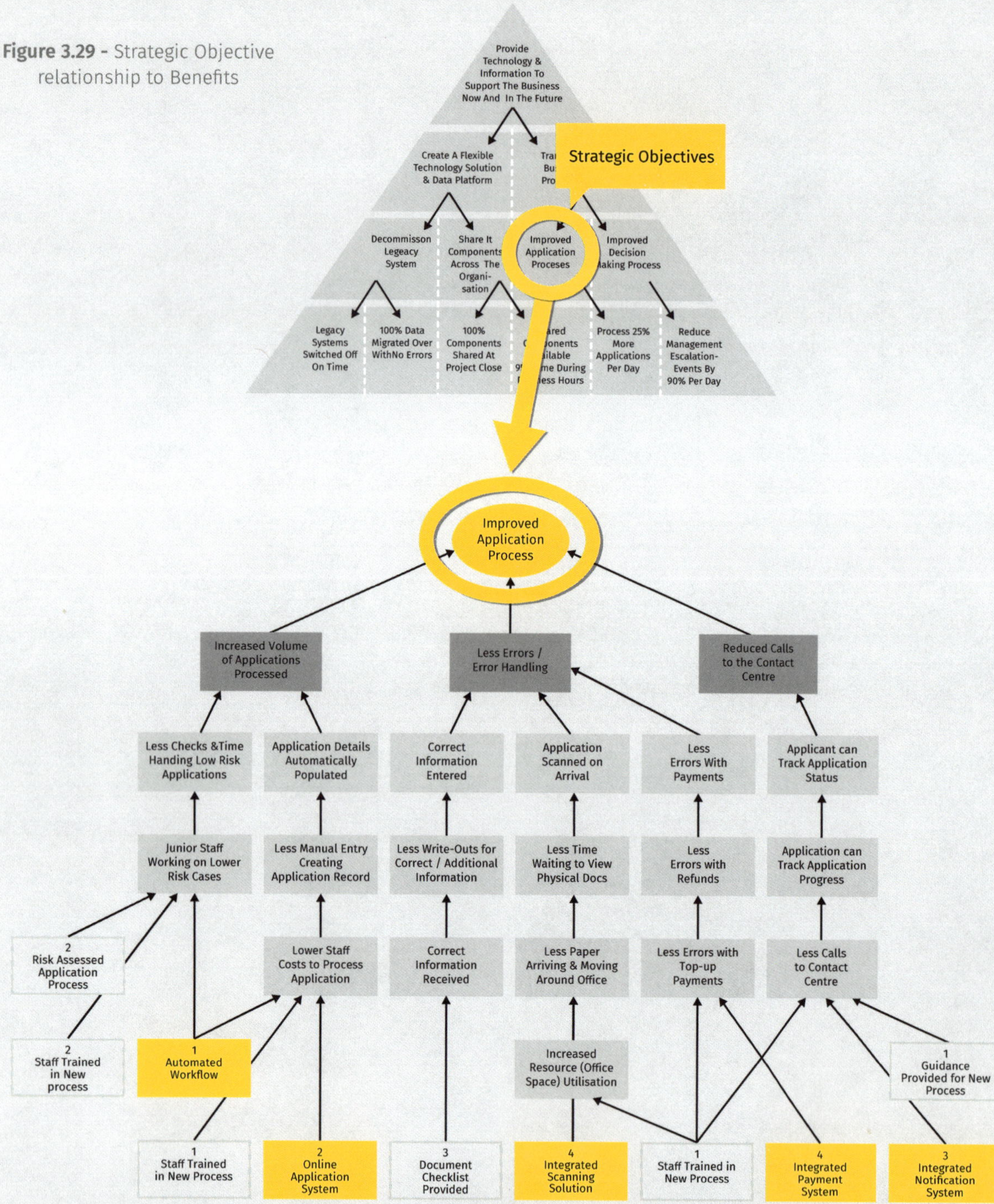


According to MSP, the Business Delivery phase is where the Benefit is initially *'delivered'.* This is however *not* entirely correct. It is not the 'benefit' per se that is delivered, but new (or changes) to existing capabilities. At this point, the Benefit itself has not delivered business value (until it is used), it's only the capability that has been delivered.

What actually happens in practice, is at 'benefits delivery', the capability is delivered (remember, no business value as yet), and then over time, as the capability is used, the true value of the Benefit is 'realised' and increases, shown in *Figure 3.31* below.

So, to be clear on roles and responsibilities:

- The **Business Architect** (supported by the members of the Programme), is responsible for the design, delivery and for overseeing the alignment of the implementation of the capabilities (that become part of the TOM), that when used by the Business, realise the planned Benefits.
- The **Benefits Manager, or Business Change Manager** (if you are lucky enough to have one on your Programme) is responsible for managing the Benefits Realisation Management (BRM) process.
- The **Benefits Owner** is accountable that the Benefits themselves are actually realised from the use of the implemented (new or enhanced) capabilities. The Benefits Owner is usually the Senior Responsible Owner (SRO) or Sponsor for the Programme.

The primary roles and responsibilities in the BRM process are shown in the table below.

**For more information on Benefits and the Benefits Reference Model, refer to 'Chapter 8 Step 4 – Evaluate'.**

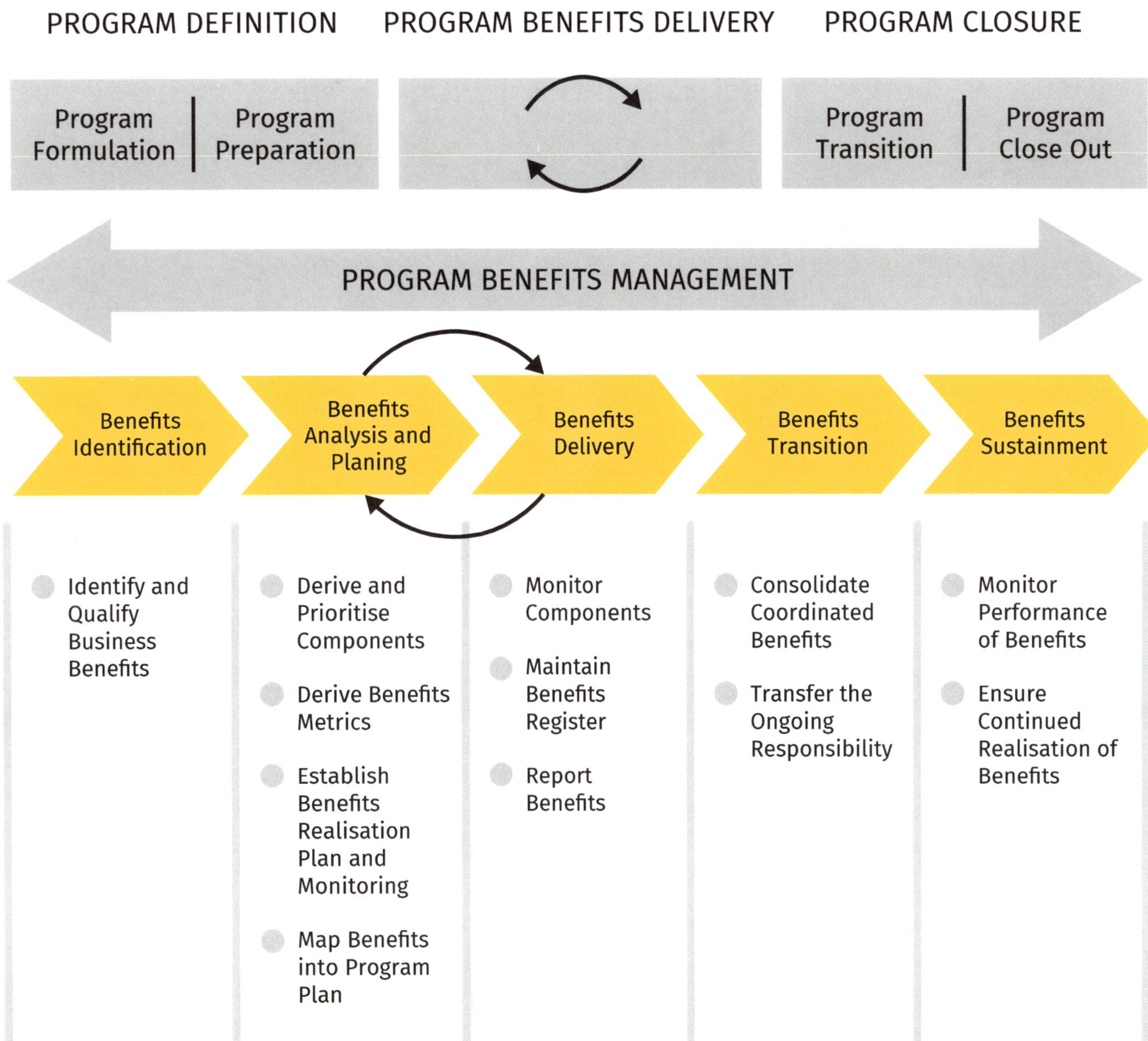


**Figure 3.30** - PMI Benefits Management Process[33]

[33] Benefits and Benefits Management (2008) PMI. The Standard for Program Management – Second Edition).

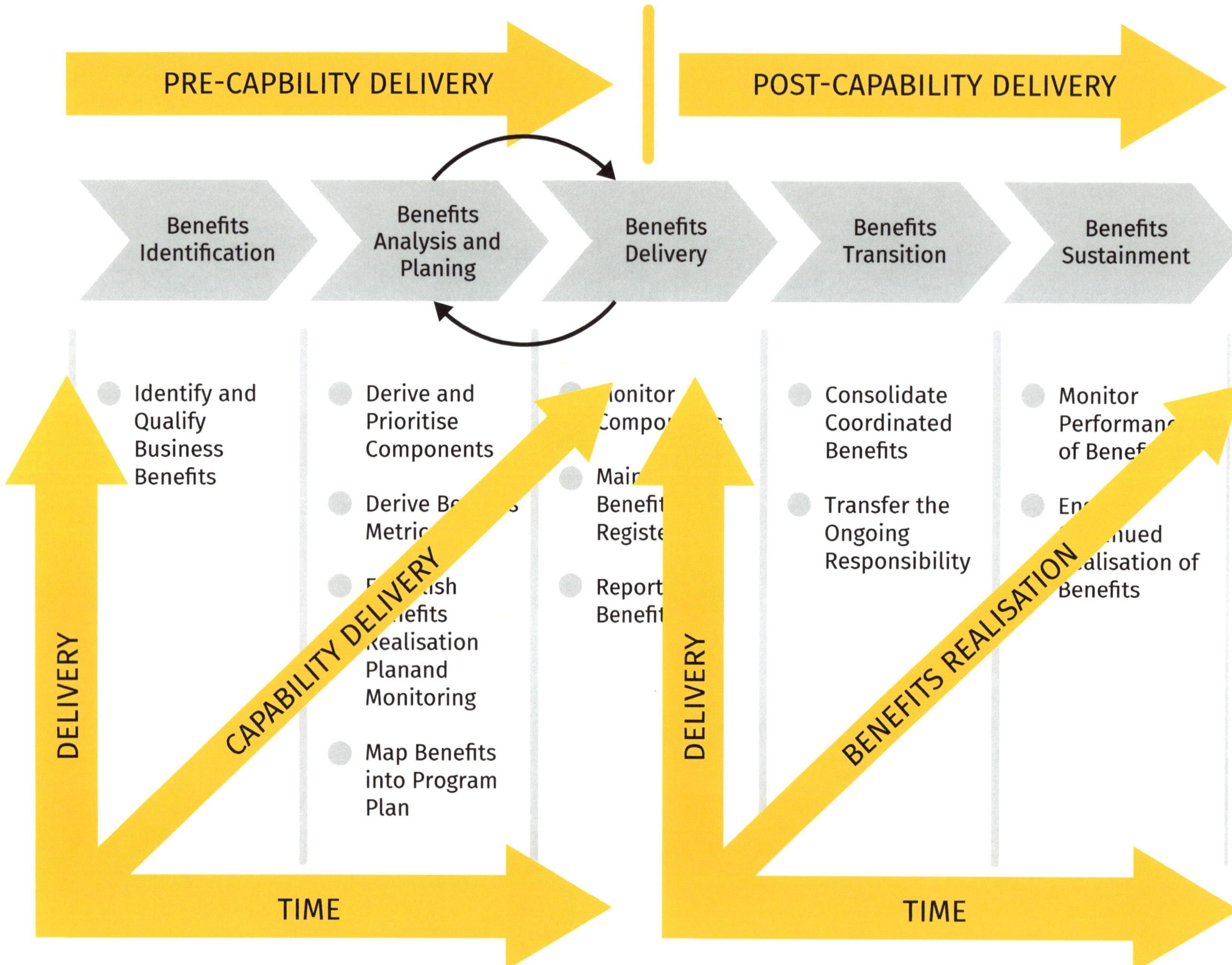


Figure 3.31 - PMI Benefits Management – Capability Delivery

BRM Roles and Responsibilities

Table 3.6

| Role | Responsibility |
|---|---|
| Senior Responsible Officer (SRO)/ Sponsor | The Benefit Owner. Overall accountability the project or Programme delivers identified benefits. However, may delegate the identification, definition and validation of benefit realisation to other senior / Programme staff. |
| Programme Manager | Provides leadership in the benefits realisation strategy and plan. |
| Business Architect | Design of, and managing the alignment of the implementation of capabilities (that when integrated and embedded into the business, are able to realise the planned benefits) that form part of the Target Operating Model (TOM). |
| Benefits Modell | Responsible the new (or enhanced) capabilities are integrated and embedded into the Organisation (in order for the business to realise their benefit). |
| Target Operating Model | Leads the benefits management process from identification, to sustainment. |
| Road Map Model | Support the effective delivery of the project or Programme, and the Benefits Management process. |

## Building Block Wrap-up

In this section, we discussed HOBA® as a 'framework of frameworks', and its alignment with other approaches. In terms of a framework:

- **HOBA®** is the complete framework to both develop the design of the Organisations TOM and also implement the physical Business Architecture.
- **HOBA®** is designed around three (3) core components (roof, pillars, base), made up of six (6) Reference Models (Business Motivation, Governance, Current Operating, Benefits, Target Operating and Road Map Models), each of which address different aspects, the *'Why, Who, What, Where, How and When?'* questions, asked of the Business and Business Architecture.
- Each Reference Model is made up of Building Blocks and Blueprints, which collectively describe a specific view or perspective of the Organisation and its Business Architecture.
- As a framework, **HOBA®** should be viewed as a 'framework of frameworks' – consisting of four (4) complementary frameworks:
  - **Process framework - HOBA®** provides a **'design process'** for both developing the design of the Target Operating Model (TOM), but also managing the alignment of the implementation of the physical Business Architecture with the design of the TOM;
  - **Perspectives framework - HOBA®** provides different views (perspectives) of the Organisation to address the unique concerns of the business and architecture (business and technical) stakeholders;
  - **Context framework - HOBA®** provides a context framework for the business and Business Architecture, and provides a context of the questions asked of both the Organisation and the Business Architecture – the Why, What, Who, How, Where and When;
  - **Content framework - HOBA®** provides the Reference Models, Building Blocks and Blueprints needed to both capture the necessary information about the Organisation in order to develop the design and implement the Target Operating Model (TOM).

In terms of alignment with other approaches:

- As outlined in the previous pages, **HOBA®** and the **Design Process** are aligned with the leading industry approaches and frameworks including TOGAF®, Zachman, Waterfall Project Management, Scaled Agile (SAFe®), Agile Scrum and APQC's Process Classification Framework (PCF).
- **HOBA®** and the **Design Process** address the gaps and missing pieces (specifically around Business Architecture, and delivering the design and physical Business Architecture in an Agile environment and process), in a comprehensive, complete, practical and usable framework that you can actually use today (based on actual work and not just theory and academia).

### Next Steps

Now that you have leant the value of **HOBA®** and its alignment with other approaches, the next area we will cover is the **Design Process**, which is the process that uses **HOBA®** to develop and deliver the design of the Organisations TOM, and oversee the implementation the physical architecture is aligned to the TOM design.

# Chapter 4 The Design Process

## Introduction

The Target State Architecture Design Process (**'Design Process'**) is the process to both develop the design of the Target Operating Model (TOM), as well as manage the alignment of the implementation of the physical Business Architecture with the design of the TOM.

The **Design Process** is a six (6) step process, and aligns neatly (and intentionally) to each of the Reference Models that make up the House of Business Architecture® (**HOBA®**): the Target State Architecture, as shown in *Figure 4.1* below.

Each 'sub-step' within each step of the **Design Process** aligns neatly to (and is made up) of the Building Blocks that make up that particular Reference Model. Building Blocks are in turn made up of Blueprints. The Reference Models (steps) and Building Blocks (sub-steps) are shown in *Figure 4.2* (on the next page).

The aim of intentionally ordering and sequencing the Steps (Reference Model) and sub-steps (Building Blocks) is, that by completing each step in sequence, you, as the Business Architect,

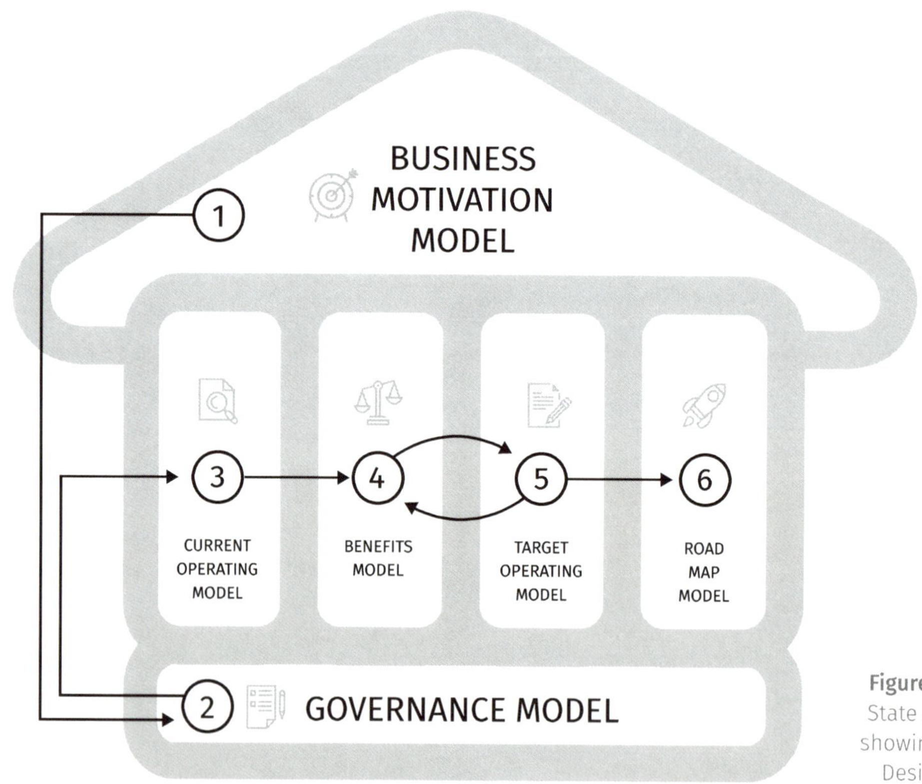


**Figure 4.1** - Target State Architecture showing the 6-Step Design Process

will have created not only a complete view of the Target State Architecture (the design of the TOM, and the actionable plans to implement it) – but also:

- **Provide the rationale for the changes required to the Current Operating Model**, that directly drives the realisation of the identified and validated Business Benefits.
- **Identified the changes to existing, or the creation of new business capabilities** (people, process and technology) needed to create the Target Operating Model (TOM).
- **Completed the gap, and cost-benefit analysis assessments that enable the selection of the best solution and implementation options** available to achieve the Business Benefits, Business Strategy.
- **Provide the Road Map and related Blueprints to manage the alignment of implementation of the physical Business Architecture with the design of the TOM**, and most importantly, alignment with the technical architecture.

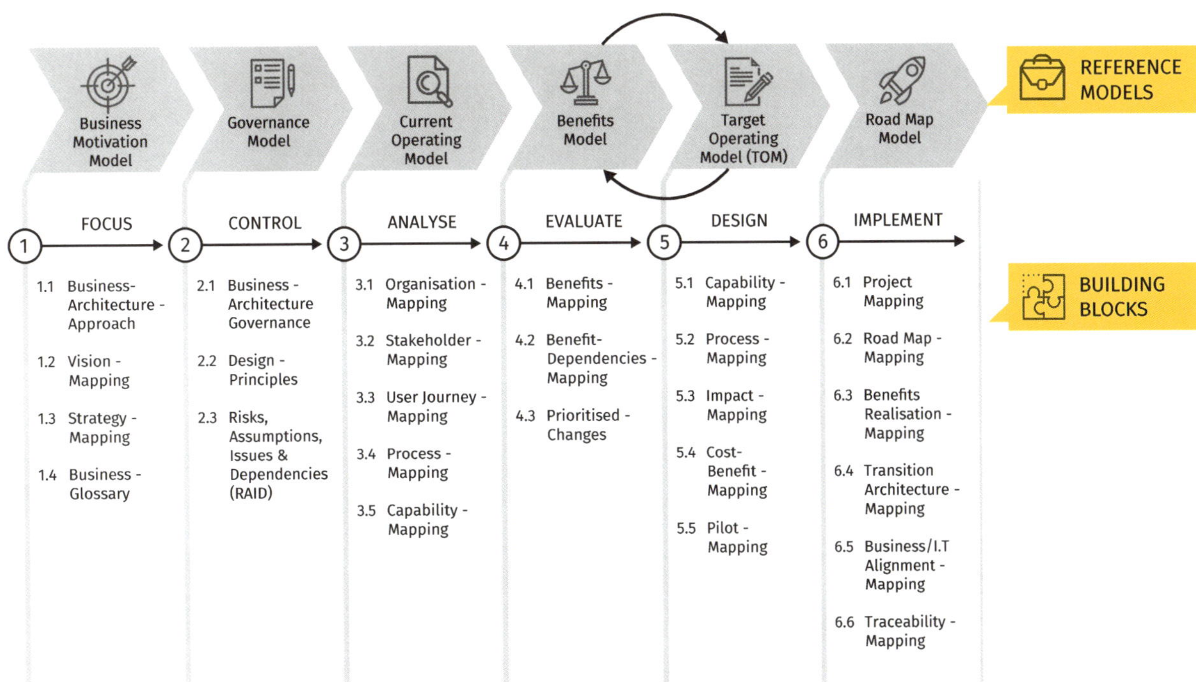


**Figure 4.2 -** Design Process steps (Reference Model) and sub-steps (Building Blocks)

# Objectives

As mentioned in the Introduction and in section *3.2 How To Use **HOBA®**?*, each step of the Design Process represents a Reference Model which addresses the different aspect or questions, the *'Why, Who, What, Where, How and When?'* that are asked of both the Organisation and the Business Architecture.

By addressing each of these aspects and questions asked of the Business, and of the Business Architecture, you will have a complete picture of the work involved in designing the TOM and managing the alignment of the implementation of the physical Business Architecture with the design of the TOM. Specifically, you will have addressed the different aspects and questions asked of the Business and the Business Architecture, the:

- **WHY** is the Organisation doing this? (i.e. what is the Vision, Strategy, Objectives, Measures?);
- **WHO** does it? (i.e. who are the stakeholders, what is their role, and how is work, decisions and risks managed?);
- **WHAT** do they do? (i.e. what is the current state of the Organisation – namely the business capabilities - people, process and technology?);
- **WHY** are they doing this? (i.e. what are the benefits the Business expects or intends to realise?);
- **WHERE/HOW** do they do it? (i.e. where are the changes needed, and how are the business capabilities changed?), and
- **WHEN** do they do it? (i.e. when will these changes be implemented?)

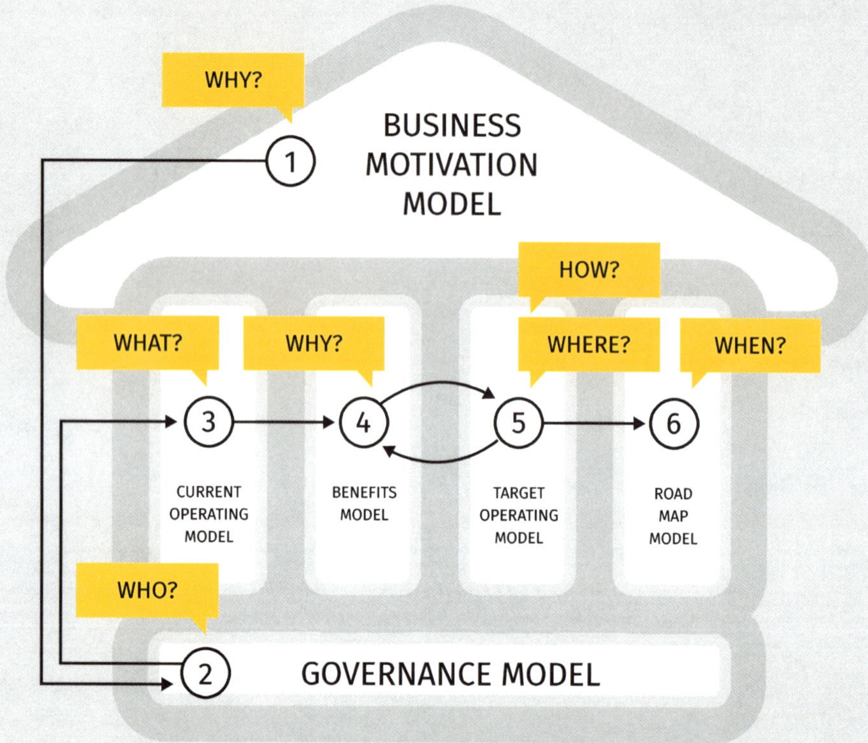


**Figure 4.3** - Target State Architecture Design Process & Aspects

How the view or description of the Target State Architecture (i.e. HOBA®) is developed and how the **Design Process** is executed in practice is in an Agile Scrum ('Scrum') Project Management approach. That is the Design Process is executed in short phases of work (called sprints), with the objective to publish to the Programme validated and agreed designs of the Business Architecture that contain the latest and agreed thinking, that further work can build on.

This Scrum approach aims to produce continuous delivery of up to date, working and usable views of the design (namely Reference Models, Building Blocks and Blueprints) of the Business Architecture, that results in faster and better quality output in comparison to the traditional gated waterfall process. *Agile Scrum* is discussed further in the *Alignment with Other Approaches* section. How Scrum is executed in practise with **HOBA®** and the **Design Process** is discussed later in the Business Architecture Governance section as part of *Chapter 6 Step 2 – Control.*



# HOBA® Principles

As mentioned above, **HOBA®** and the Design Process are based on based on Agile Scrum iterative continuous development. Similar to Agile, **HOBA®** has the following principles based on the three (3) themes of - *Regular Delivery of Architecture views* (i.e. Reference Models, Building Blocks, Blueprints), *Team Communication* and *Design Excellence.*

**HOBA®** Principles are based off Agile principles for software development and adapted applied to Business Architecture as follows.

Target State Architecture Model – Design Process Steps & Roles

Table 4.1

| | HOBA® Principles |
|---|---|
| | **Regular Delivery of Business Architecture Views** |
| 1 | Early and continuous delivery of valuable Architecture views |
| 2 | Provides leadership in the benefits realisation strategy and plan. |
| 3 | Delivering Architecture usable views is primary measure of progress |
| 4 | Maintain a sustainable pace of development |
| | **Team Communication** |
| 5 | Business people and Architects (Business & IT) must work together daily |
| 6 | Face-to-face conversation is most effective to convey information between teams |
| 7 | Best Architectures emerge from self-organizing teams |
| 8 | Build teams around motivated individuals and provide support and trust |
| 9 | Reflect regularly, tune and adjust process and behaviour to become more effective |
| | **Design Excellence** |
| 10 | Continuous focus on technical excellence |
| 11 | Simplicity is the art to minimising wasteful work |
| 12 | Welcome changing requirements for customer's advantage |

Figure 4.4 - Target State Architecture Design Process & Aspects

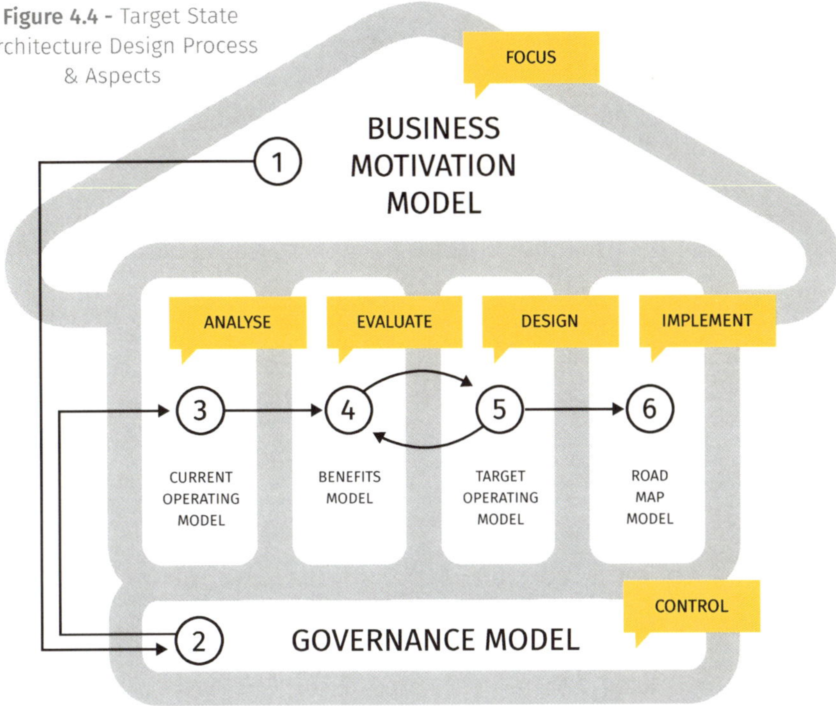


# Roles

Each step (and Reference Model) of the **Design Process**, as mentioned earlier has its specific role, as shown in the *Figure* 4.4 and Table 4.2.

The specific role of each step of the Design Process is shown in the Table 4.2 below.

## Benefits

As mentioned above, **HOBA®** and the Because **HOBA®** is a model of the Target State Architecture and provides transparency to the Organisation and the Programme, the major benefit of the Design Process is transparency. As stated earlier in *Chapter 1 Introduction* and *Chapter 2 The Business Architecture Challenge*, Business Architecture as a practice and discipline is facing some fundamental challenges for recognition and for the value that it brings - for several reasons, the most prominent of which is lack of transparency.

Design Process Step Role Descriptions

Table 4.2

| # | Role | Description |
|---|---|---|
| 1 | Focus | Provides the focus for the Business, and the Business Architecture effort. |
| 2 | Control | Provides the boundaries in which decisions must be taken, and by whom, and how scope, work and risks are managed. |
| 3 | Analyse | Provides the context of the 'problem area' to be analysed (the 'As-Is' operating model) |
| 4 | Evaluate | Provides the criteria and method for evaluate the options available to the business to reach its goals |
| 5 | Design | Provides the context for the design of the 'To-Be' operating model, taking into account the prioritised Business Changes and Enablers from the 'Evaluate' step. This step has a 'visible' feedback loop back to Step 4 – Evaluate, to (re)validate and (re)confirm the solution 'design' can still achieve the planned benefits the business is intending to realise. |
| 6 | Implement | Provides the Blueprints required to implement the chosen solution option, and tools to manage and monitor its implementation and traceability back to the benefits and the Vision. |

What the **Design Process** does, by clearly laying out the process, and steps (i.e. Reference Models) and sub-steps (i.e. Building Blocks and Blueprints) is that it addresses different aspects of the Organisation and its Business Architecture, and identifies what is needed to develop the design and implement the Target Operating Model (TOM) by providing transparency.

The **Design Process** provides transparency to the Organisation and Programme stakeholders identifying what the process you as the Business Architect will follow in developing the design of the TOM, and managing the alignment of the implementation of the physical Business Architecture with the design. It also outlines what that process actually looks like, what role each step plays, and what to expect in terms of activities and output.

The main benefits of the Design Process providing the transparency is that is builds confidence and thereby 'buy in' from all concerned.

Providing clear, understandable visibility early on of what the process of developing the design of the Target Operating Model (TOM) has the following benefits which address two (2) of the challenges faced by Business Architecture/ Architects today, in that it builds confidence in Business Architecture (and the Business Architect) by the Organisation and Programme stakeholders:

- That the process to be followed and the outputs produced (the Target State Architecture) will address the concerns and needs of the Organisation.
- That the practise and discipline is robust, structured and is aligned to industry leading approaches to project and Programme management (and also has been and is used in some of the biggest financial institutions and government agencies in the world).

One of the first tasks you will (and should) do following the **Design Process**, and as the Business Architect joining any Programme is provide a view of the Design Process, to the Organisation and Programme stakeholders (after first of course agreeing the terms of engagement, the vision for the Organisation and the Business Architecture, discussed later in *Chapter 5 Step 1 – Focus with the 1.1 Business Architecture Approach).*

Providing an early view (and walking your key stakeholders through the Design Process) will also aim to appease the dreaded *'burning platform'* syndrome. The *'burning platform'* is a typical (unwanted, and undesired) situation that is known to happen on Programmes (regardless of size) that results in the Programme getting lured away from the planned activities i.e. developing the design and implementing the TOM, and diverted to *'putting out fires'* on other activities or Programmes that are *'deemed'* more *'urgent and important'.*

In reality however, these 'fires' will usually prove to be just distractions. Soon after the *'urgency'* of the burning platform has been abated, the attention will return back to the previously thought *'lower priority and urgency'* Business Architecture design and implementation activities. The only difference now is that senior executives will be calling out for the latest version of the Business Architecture", claiming *"it should have been done already"*, while ignoring the fact that they themselves had requested *"all hands-on deck"* to put out the fires.
By getting the Design Process out in front of the Organisation and Programme stakeholders you will be able to clearly show how each step, and sub-step, builds on each other, producing workable and useful iterations of the Business Architecture. As a result of this, you can show how critical it is to keep the *'Agile Scrum Process'* working (and not stop for *'fire fighting'* minor issues).

The *Agile Scrum* process was discussed earlier in the *Alignment with Other Approaches* section.

We will discuss each Design Step in their respective sections below.

Part 2 describes 'the activities' to be carried out in designing and implementing the Target Operating Model (TOM). These 'activities' are the actual steps needed to design and implement the TOM.

- **Chapter 5: Step 1- Focus**, explains the first step of the Design Process, which is about setting the focus and direction of the Organisation, and the Business Architecture. It defines the roles, expectations and scope the Programme as well as the Business Architecture. Focus is provided through defining the HOBA® Business Motivation Model Reference Model.
- **Chapter 6: Step 2- Control**, explains the second step of the Design Process, which is about setting and agreeing the governance structures and processes, the key stakeholder's roles, and design principles. Control is provided through defining the HOBA® Governance Model Reference Model.
- **Chapter 7: Step 3- Analyse**, explains the third step of the Design Process, which is about assessing the state of the Current Operating Model (i.e. the current state of the business *'as-is'* today). This *'bottom up'* approach assesses the current state of the Organisation – starting at the foundation of the Organisation, the Organisation Mapping and ending with the Capability Mapping.
- **Chapter 8: Step 4 - Evaluate**, explains the fourth step of the Design Process, which is 'evaluation' of the both the Business Benefits the Organisation intends to realise from both the business' strategy and transformation Programme. *'Evaluate'* is provided through defining the HOBA® Benefits Model Reference Model.
- **Chapter 9: Step 5 – Design,** explains the fifth step of the Design Process, which is the 'design' of the future state operating model – the Target Operating Model (TOM). The development of the TOM is based off the elements of the Business Capabilities (people, process and technology) that were identified from the previous Step -4 Evaluate. *'Design'* is provided through the HOBA® Target Operating Model (TOM) Reference Model.
- **Chapter 10: Step 6 – Implement,** explains the sixth step of the Design Process, which is the delivery of both the 'design' of the Target Operating Model (TOM) and managing the alignment of the *'implementation'* of the 'physical' Business Architecture with the design of the TOM. Implementation is provided through the HOBA® Road Map Model Reference Model.

ACT

PART 2

# Chapter 5

# Step 1 – Focus

## Introduction

Step 1 – Focus, is naturally all about focus. Focusing on the direction and vision for the Organisation as well as the scope of work for the Programme and Business Architecture. Focus is provided via the Business Motivation Model.

*Figure 5.1* below shows where Step-1 Focus fits in the overall Design Process:

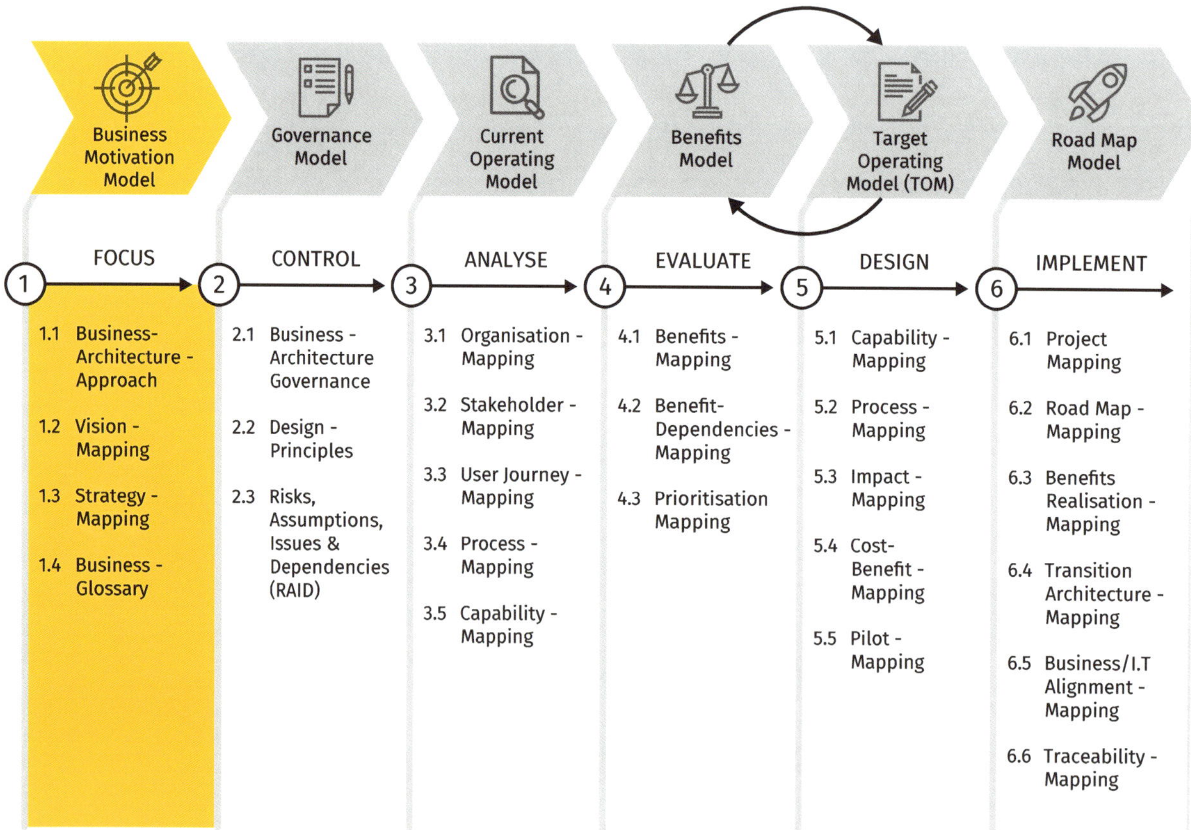


**Figure 5.1 -** Design Process - Step 1 Focus

# Business Motivation Model

Step 1 – Focus defines the **Business Motivation Model**. The Business Motivation Model is where the Vision for the Organisation, the Programme and the Business Architecture work is developed and agreed.

As mentioned earlier in House of Business Architecture® (HOBA®) section, each HOBA® Reference Model addresses a specific aspect in the design and implementation of the Target Operating Model (TOM). These different aspects are represented in the following different views:

- **Process**
- **Perspective**
- **Context**
- **Content**

We will briefly discuss each of these in the section below.

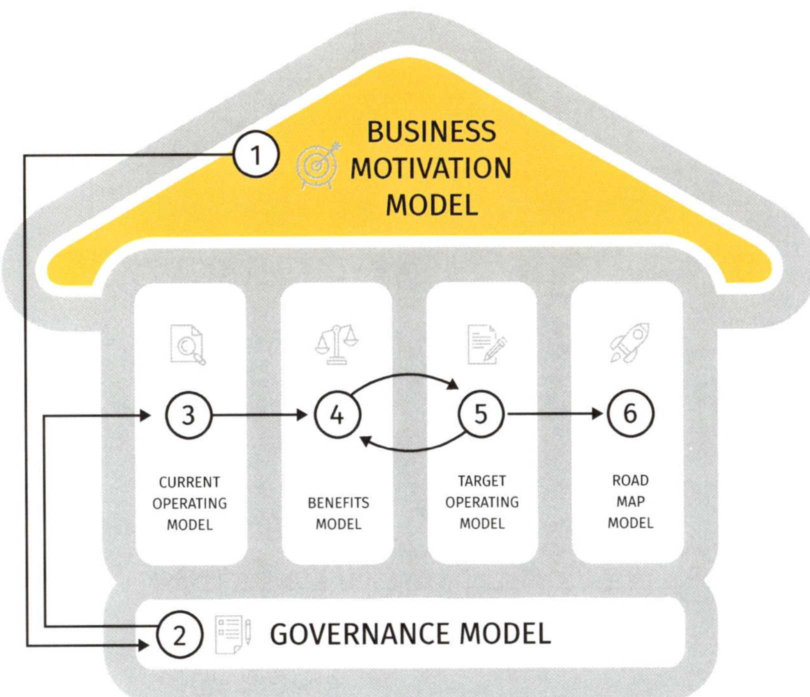


**Figure 5.2** - Business Motivation Model - Step 1

## Process

In terms of process, the Business Motivation Model is the first step in the Design Process.
Step 1 addresses the activities necessary to identify and validate the 'focus' (i.e. Vision, strategy and objectives) for the Business, as well as for the focus for the Business Architecture and Business Architect.

## Perspective

In terms of perspective, the Business Motivation Model provides the 'focus' perspective or point of view, where all activities help provide the 'focus' or direction for both the Business and Business Architecture.

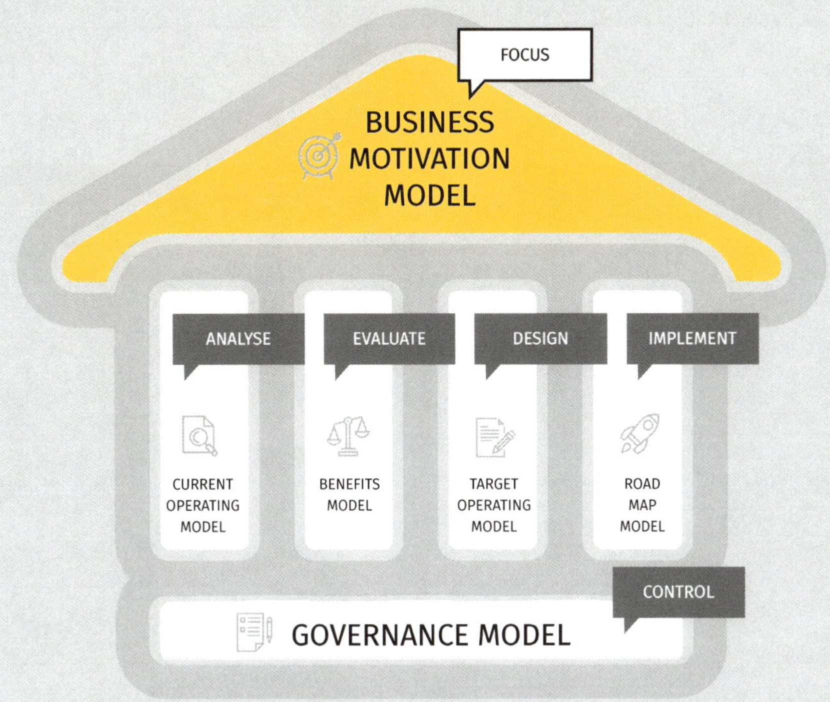


**Figure 5.3** - Business Motivation Model - Focus Perspective

## Context

In terms of context, the Business Motivation Model addresses the aspect or 'why' question (of the *'why, who, what, where, how and when'* questions) asked of the both the Business and the Business Architecture:

- 'Why is the Business doing this?' (i.e. what do they want or expect to achieve?)
- 'Why is the Business Architecture, and Business Architect involved?' (i.e. what does the Business want or need them to do and achieve?)

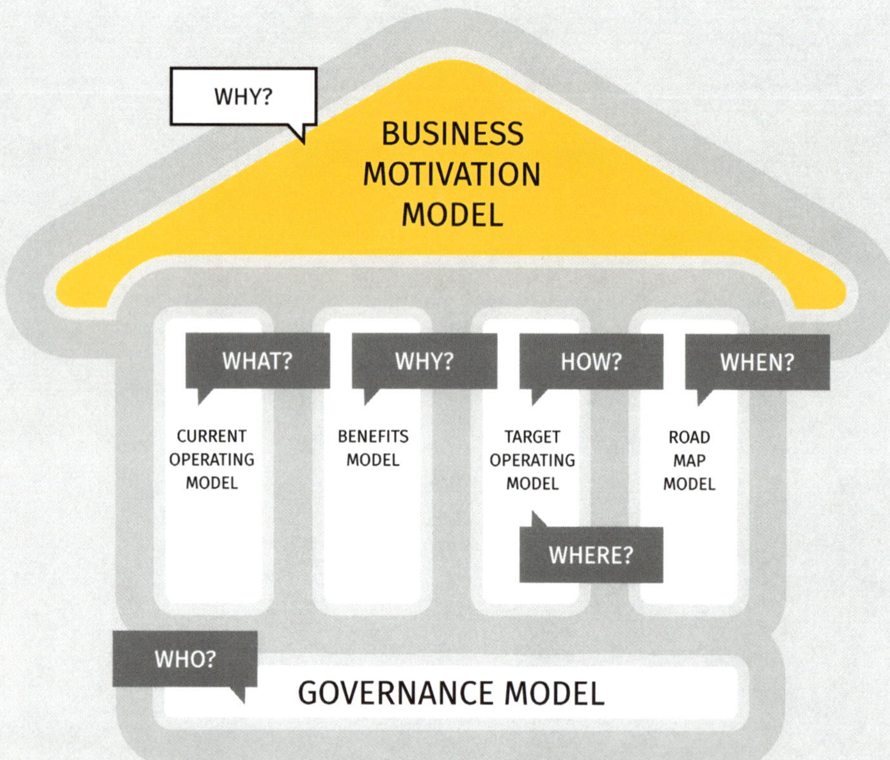


**Figure 5.4-** Business Motivation Model - 'Why?' Aspect

## Content

In terms of content, the Building Blocks and Blueprints developed here are the Business Architecture content used to identify, validate and agree the Vision, Business Strategy and Objectives of the Business, as well as defining the vision, objectives and role of Business Architecture in assisting the Business in achieving that Vision.

The list of Building Blocks and respective Blueprints that make up the Business Motivation Model are shown in *Table 5.5.*

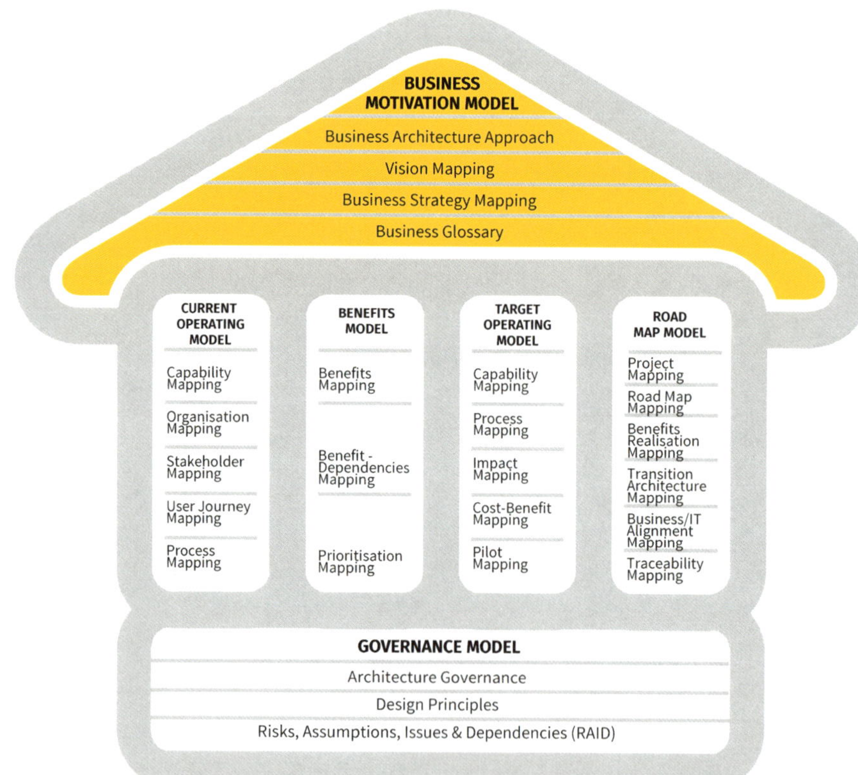


**Figure 5.5 -** Business Motivation Model Building Block Content

Business Motivation Model Building Blocks and Blueprints

**Table 5.1**

| Design Step | Building Block | Purpose | Blueprint |
|---|---|---|---|
| 1.1 | Business Architecture Approach ('Approach') | The physical 'contract' between the Business Architect and the Programme, outlining the Business Architects role, responsibilities, expectations and deliverables. | 1.1.1 Statement of Work (SOW) |
| 1.2 | Vision Mapping | Defines the Vision for the Programme and decomposes it into how the vision is going to be achieved (strategy) and how to measure progress and success (objectives, and measures). | • 1.2.1 Vision, Strategy, Objectives and Measures (VSOM) Map<br>• 1.2.2 VSOM Table |
| 1.3 | Business Strategy Mapping* | Business strategy Blueprints that collectively help the business define the Organisations Business Strategy, through an assessment of its chosen market(s), competitors and its ability to compete. | • 1.3.1 Business Strategy Map*<br>• 1.3.2 Balanced Score Card*<br>• 1.3.3 Business Model Canvas*<br>• 1.3.4 Porters Five Forces*<br>• 1.3.5 SWOT Analysis*<br>• 1.3.6 PESTLE* |
| 1.4 | Business Glossary | Contains all the key terms and definitions used on the Project or Programme. | 1.4.1 Terms & Definitions |

**(*) Note - As discussed earlier in the 'Scope' and 'Assumptions' sections, the Strategy Mapping Building Block (and the associated Blueprints) are out of scope for this book. They are have shown above for completeness only and will be discussed briefly in section '1.3 Business Strategy Mapping' below.**

## High Level Process (SIPOC)

Shown below is the high level 'Supplier-Input-Process-Output-Customer' (SIPOC) process used to complete step - Step-1 Focus, as well as the Business Motivation Model (*Figure 5.6*).

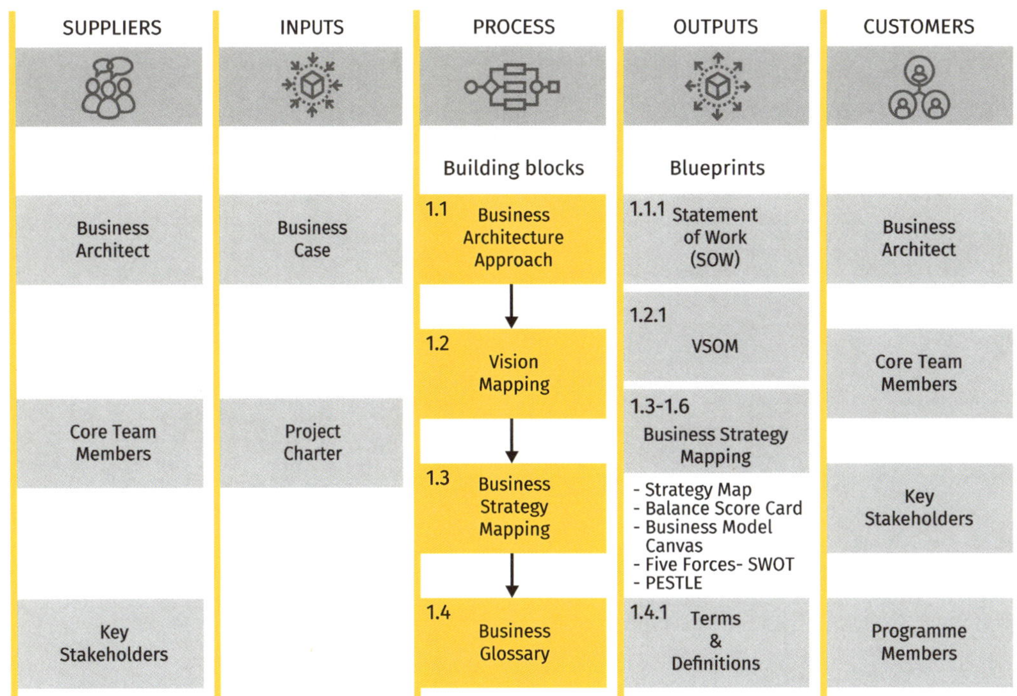


**Figure 5.6** - Business Motivation Model SIPOC

# 1.1 Business Architecture Approach

## Introduction

Defining and agreeing the Business Architecture Approach ('Approach') is the first activity the Business Architect should do on the Business Architecture engagement. The Approach comes first for several key reasons in the Business Architecture and transformation journey, as it is:

- The first step (Step-1 Focus) in the Design Process,
- The first step in the engagement with the Business Organisation ('Organisation'), and
- The first stage of developing the Business Motivation Reference Model.

Defining and agreeing the Approach is where you, as Business Architect define and agree your role, both in and on the Programme. According to TOGAF, the Approach is a 'contract' between the Business Architect and the Organisation. Once agreed, the Approach will become the documented and agreed way of working between yourself, as Business Architect, the activities you will carry out, and the outputs you are (and should be) expected to produce and deliver.

Being the Business Architect, the purpose of the Approach is to define the scope of your work, and the scope of the work for the Programme. Because the Approach sets the direction of your work, and the Programme, it must be (or should be) the first activity in your engagement with the Programme (if it's not you should have a very good reason why it isn't!). The Approach will clearly define the roles, responsibilities, expectations as well as agree a way of working and measure success.

The Blueprint that documents the Approach is the Statement of Work (SOW). The SOW will become a living document (i.e. updated as and when needed) and referred to often as it contains the criteria the successful delivery of the design and the implementation of the physical Business Architecture will be measured from.

## Inputs

The inputs used to complete this Building Block are shown in the Table 5.2 (on the next page).

## Outputs

The Blueprints (outputs) produced for this Building Block are shown in the table below.

# Steps

The Business Architecture Approach is made up of the following Blueprints.

**Business Architecture Approach Building Block Inputs**

**Table 5.2**

| Ref | Blueprint or Document | Use |
|---|---|---|
| N/A | Programme Request and Background | Provides the high-level context and business drivers that have created the need for the Programme and the request for Business Architecture services. |
| N/A | Problem Description | The problem description statement is a complete and concise statement that fully describes the problem domain, the current issues, stakeholders involved and any financials, dates or deadlines the issues be rectified by. It is the basis of what the project is trying to solve, and following the SMART format. |
| N/A | Programme Description and Scope | Describes what the Programme will accomplish. |

**Business Architecture Approach (Output) Blueprints**

**Table 5.3**

<table>
<tr><th>Ref</th><th>Blueprint</th><th>Purpose</th><th>Blueprint</th></tr>
<tr><td>1.1.1</td><td>Statement of Work (SOW)</td><td>Defines the scope and approach that will be used to develop and deliver the design of the Target State Business Architecture.</td><td>
<table>
<tr><th>Area</th><th>Description</th></tr>
<tr><td>Business Objectives</td><td>“Increase the application process output by 25% from 100,000 per year to meet current demand of 125,000 applications per year in the next 12 months”.</td></tr>
<tr><td>Business Architecture Objectives</td><td>Design and deliver the Business Architecture and Target Operating Model (TOM) that aligns the business to the Business Strategy and business vision, and oversee the implementation of the physical TOM is aligned to the design of the TOM.</td></tr>
<tr><td>Strategic Alignment</td><td>This piece of work supports the Organisations’ digital strategy to provide simpler, cleaner, faster and more cost-effective ways of meeting the needs of its users.</td></tr>
</table>
Example Objectives & Scope Section</td></tr>
</table>

### 1.1.1 Statement of Work (SOW)

The SOW Blueprint is made of the following sections:

1. Background
2. Objectives and Scope
3. Stakeholders, Concerns and Views
4. List of Issues and Scenarios to be Addressed
5. Roles and Responsibilities, and Deliverables
6. Business Architecture Plan
7. Work Plan
8. Communication Plan
9. Duration and Effort
10. Project Plan and Schedule
11. Risks and Mitigations
12. Acceptance Criteria and Procedures
13. Approvals

We will discuss the above sections in the sections below.

**1. Background**

The background section provides the high-level context of the history and drivers that have resulted in the formation of the Programme, and the request for Business Architecture services. The Background Information section is made up of the following three (3) areas, each with a specific purpose as shown in Table 5.4 below.

In a formal bid/acceptance process when requesting Business Architecture services and formal bids are solicited from suppliers or a formal tender for Business Architecture services is issued, the SOW should explicitly address the concerns and issues that are raised in the request. These concerns and issues are addressed as part of the objectives and scope areas of the SOW, discussed in the List of Scenarios and Issues section below.

**2. Objectives, Scope and Alignment**

This section lists both the Business and Business Architecture objectives, as well as the strategic alignment (how this work aligns to the overall Organisation strategy).

Below is an example of Objectives and Scope using the Case Study example.

Statement of Work – Background Information

Table 5.4

| # | Area | Purpose |
|---|---|---|
| 1 | Programme Request and Background | Provides the high-level context and business drivers that have created the need for the Programme and the request for Business Architecture services. |
| 2 | Problem Statement | The problem description statement is a complete and concise statement that fully describes the problem domain, the end-to-end business process(es) impacted or affected, the current issues, stakeholders involved and any financials, dates or deadlines the issues be rectified by. It is the basis of what the project is trying to solve, and following the SMART format. |
| 3 | Programme Description and Scope | Describes what the Programme will accomplish. |

Statement of Work – Objectives and Scope

Table 5.5

| # | Area | Purpose |
|---|---|---|
| 1 | Business Objectives | The business objectives are the objectives that are obtained from the business Organisation (as opposed to the objectives of the Programme/ Business Architecture).<br>The format should be SMART (as close to or as best as possible).<br>The source of the business objectives will be informed from the following sources:<br>1. Request for Architecture Work<br>2. Project Charter<br>3. Business Case<br>4. Sponsor |
| 2 | Business Architecture Objectives | This is effectively the Business Architecture Vision. This is the problem the Business Architecture is solving, and what that looks like from the Business Architects perspective (e.g. design or model of the Target State Architecture). |
| 3 | Strategic Alignment | Description how this piece of work will address and align to the overall Organisation strategy and strategic objectives. |

Example Statement of Work – Objectives and Scope

Table 5.6

| Area | Description |
|---|---|
| Business Objectives | "Increase the application process output by 25% from 100,000 per year to meet current demand of 125,000 applications per year in the next 12 months". |
| Business Architecture Objectives | Design and deliver the Business Architecture and Target Operating Model (TOM) that aligns the business to the Business Strategy and business vision, and oversee the implementation of the physical TOM is aligned to the design of the TOM. |
| Strategic Alignment | This piece of work supports the Organisations' digital strategy to provide simpler, cleaner, faster and more cost-effective ways of meeting the needs of its users. |

## 3. Stakeholder, Concerns and Views

This section captures the Stakeholder Concerns, and which view (i.e. Blueprint) those concerns will be addressed in. Be warned, as **HOBA®** and the **Design Process** follow an iterative design and continuous delivery approach, capturing the concerns here is *not* a one-off exercise. You should expect to review and update the Stakeholder Concerns (as well as previously agreed or published Blueprints) as the Programme progresses as the Business (and Business Stakeholders) become more clear about the problems they are facing. This also factors in how the ever changing business conditions and environment the Business operates in will challenge the business, revisiting and adjusting the baseline to some (hopefully not all) decisions and assumptions made previously. So, make sure to keep in mind, capturing the Stakeholder Concerns here, as part of the Statement of Work (SOW) is a *'first pass'*.

The identification and validation (and even elaboration, where needed) of Stakeholders and their Concerns, will be revisited in more depth – both through the review and approval cycle for this Blueprint and also when covered in the Current Operating Model (within the Stakeholder Mapping Blueprint) so make sure not to overdo it by spending unnecessary amounts of time and energy here as you will most likely revisit again later in the **Design Process.**

We will also discuss Stakeholder Analysis later as they are covered as part of the Governance Model *('Chapter 6 Step 2 – Control')*, and the Current Operating Model *('Chapter 7 Step 3 – Analyse')*.

An example of a Stakeholder, Concerns and Views Table is shown in Table 5.7 below.

**Ideally all Stakeholders identified and captured on the Stakeholder, Concerns and Views Table (example above), will either be physically or virtually allocated/assigned to (or on) the Programme. This is so you, as the Business Architect can elicit firsthand their concerns, issues and needs. Where this is not possible (due to geographic location, political or economic factors etc.), a nominated representative stakeholder (in most cases it is the Product Owner) needs to be delegated to represent the wishes and needs of those stakeholders (and recorded within the 'Stakeholder, Concerns and Views' table).**

Example Stakeholder, Concerns and Views Table

Table 5.7

| Stakeholder | Concern | View / Blueprint |
|---|---|---|
| Sponsor | Demonstrable benefits IT Budget | • 4.1.1 Benefits Profile<br>• 5.11.1 Cost-Benefit Assessment<br>• 6.2.1 Business Architecture Road Map<br>• 6.2.2 Programme Road Map |
| Business Unit Manager | New process will remove or reduce the amount of paper received and moving around the business.<br>New process will maintain or improve processing speed (and be able to handle peak volumes with ease)<br>Simplified process, Applicant able to submit application, and book appointment (if required) and pay online.<br>Applicants experience is improved<br>Applicant is not able to view application status, or progress majority of calls to contact centre are for application status and progress. | • 3.3.1 User Journey Map<br>• 5.1.2 Process Model Map (To-Be)<br>• 6.4.2 Transition Architecture<br>• 6.5.1 Business/IT Alignment Map |
| Caseworker | Work needs to be allocated fairly and proportionately<br>Currently need to check several systems to verify identity, takes time, and results unreliable.<br>Letters that could be automated are currently manually produced. | • 5.1.2 Process Model Map (To-Be) |
| Data Entry Operator | Too many typos from applicants require manual correction.<br>Letters that could be automated are currently manually produced. | • 5.1.2 Process Model Map (To-Be) |
| Mail Room Operator | Manual payment process could be automated<br>Physical documents sent between buildings could be digital and sent electronically | • 5.1.2 Process Model Map (To-Be) |
| Higher Education Institution (HEI) | No interruption of service during implementation (i.e. Students should still be able to submit applications during new solution being implemented). | • 5.1.2 Process Model Map (To-Be)<br>• 6.4.2 Transition Architecture<br>• 6.5.1 Business/IT Alignment Map |
| Payment Provider | Payment integration is secure and continuously connected (within service hours) | • 5.1.2 Process Model Map (To-Be) |
| Post Office | No interruption of service during implementation (i.e. students should still be able to enrol biometrics e.g. system integration operates throughout and post implementation) | • 5.1.2 Process Model Map (To-Be) |

The list of stakeholders here should include all the key – primary and secondary stakeholders of the Programme (directly, and indirectly impacted), if they are known at this point. As this activity is at the kick-off/early beginnings of the Programme, you should expect this list to be updated as the Programme progresses as the business learns more about the problem it is intending to solve and who needs to be involved in the Programme, and the business environment it operates in changes.

An example of what and who primary and secondary stakeholders are is shown in *Figure 5.7.*

These key stakeholders include (but are not limited to) the Service Manager, Product Owner, Domain Subject Matter Expert (SME), as well as other business representatives such as Human Resources, and I.T. If the complete key stakeholder list is not known at this point (or haven't been formally agreed, which is often the case on a newly started Programme or initiative), don't panic as these will be elaborated on further and validated as part of *Chapter 6 Step 2 – Control*, when completing the *Governance Model.*

## 4. List of Scenarios and Issues

This section helps provide the business context and problem description. Scenarios are the situations (high level business process) where the problem (and opportunity) the Organisation is experiencing, that the Business Architecture is attempting to address and resolve.

These scenarios will provide the input into creating the User Journey Blueprint, that will describe the interactions (and pain points) between the Organisation and the Customer.

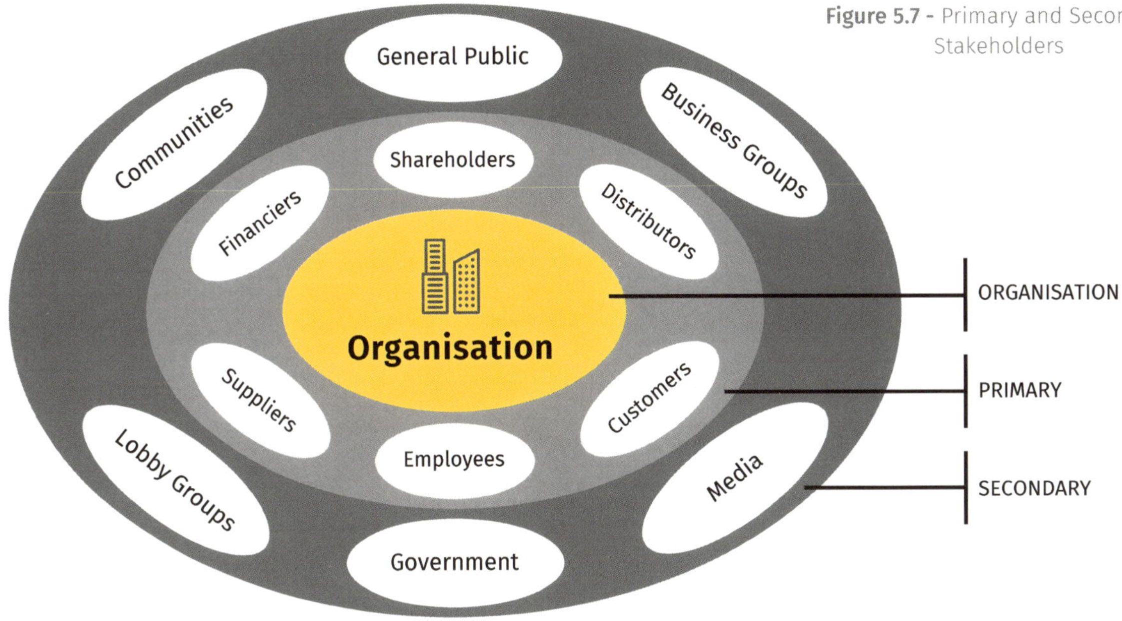


**Figure 5.7** - Primary and Secondary Stakeholders

Scenarios and Issues

**Table 5.8**

| Ref | Scenario | Ref | Issue |
|---|---|---|---|
| S01 | Description of outline of the high level business process(es) where the issues are present, or relevant that are in scope and impacted by the Programme. | I01 | Description of drivers for change, or opportunities the Organisation is not able to take advantage of due to a lack of or gap in capability |

Example Scenarios and Issues

**Table 5.9**

| Ref | Scenario | Ref | Issue |
|---|---|---|---|
| S01 | Online (Student) Visa application process | I01 | Large volume of Student Visa applications using current system and staff cannot cope with the volume and headcount (SLA are not being met). |
| | | I02 | There is no physical office space to accommodate additional staff to manually process more applications. |
| | | I03 | Changes to process or systems must be outside of peak periods (Sept to end of Oct) to provide minimal disruption to the business. |
| | | I04 | Changes to the overall process and systems should not introduce paper back into the building or process due to storage and capacity constraints. |

**When more than one issue appears, or occurs in a single scenario, or appears in more than one scenario this indicates a 'common' issue. This also highlights a particular issues' importance (and priority) in having it resolved. Resolving a major scenario often solves more than one problem but if left unchecked can create bigger problems down the road).**

## 5. Roles and Responsibilities

Roles and responsibilities represent the governance roles and responsibilities of the stakeholders involved on the Programme. These are the Roles and Responsibilities, captured in the (R)esponsible, (A)ccountable, (C)onsulted, (I) nformed (RACI) Matrix for the Core Team members, as follows.

(*) Note – These team members are usually (in most cases) shared across more than one project, both within the same Programme or involved in (i.e. sit on boards, design authorities or work streams) in other projects both within and outside of the existing Programme. This is both helpful and necessary in keeping abreast of dependencies and developments on both sides (internal and external sides of the Programme), as well as maintaining traceability and alignment between projects and Programmes.

**The RACI Matrix records the roles and responsibilities of the Core Team members. These are the Programme members that you will work with on a daily basis. It does not include members of the Programme that are a part of the Organisation, or business unit itself (with the exception of possibly the Product Owner). These key stakeholders are identified and assessed in section '*3.2 Stakeholder Mapping (As-Is)*' Building Block as part of defining the Current Operating Model.**

RACI Matrix

Table 5.10

| Position | R | A | C | I | Description |
|---|---|---|---|---|---|
| Programme Manager | R | | | | Responsible for the successful running and delivery of the Programme within agreed time, quality and budget. |
| Project Manager | | A | | | Responsible for the successful running and delivery of the project(s) within the Programme within agreed time, quality and budget. |
| Product Owner | | A | | | Represents the business to and on the Programme. Holds the vision for the product, owns the product backlog, orders (prioritizes) the items on the backlog, creates acceptance criteria for the backlog items. Accountable for the solution meeting the needs of the business. |
| Scrum Master | | A | | | Facilitates the self-organizing (core) team. While the team focus on delivering a product, the Scrum Master facilitates a performing, self-organising team. Accountable to facilitate the team, remove impediments or roadblocks that keep team from doing their work. |
| Business Architect* | | A | | | Accountable the Business Architecture aligns the business to the Business Strategy, and all requirements and activities on the Programme direct relate or trace to and from the product, Programme and Organisations Vision. |
| Business Analyst | | A | | | Accountable the Product Owners needs are articulated into requirements in the form of User Stories. |
| Benefits Manager | | A | | | Accountable the Programme needs are articulated and managed and tracked over the lifecycle/duration of the Programme (and handed over to the business to maintain once the product is handed over to the business) |
| Business Change | | A | | | Accountable for the business change activities, communication and training are provided and the changes are embedded into the Organisation. |
| Solution Architect* | | A | | | Accountable the underlying technology platform design meets the requirements of the technical architecture. |
| Technical Architect* | | A | | | Accountable for the definition and delivery of the technical architecture. |
| Security Architect* | | A | | | Accountable for technology platform and architecture has the appropriate security controls in place that to balance risk, delivery and cost. |
| Test Manager | | A | | | Accountable for the co-ordination of cross Programme teams in areas including system integration, testing accessibility, compatibility testing and performance testing. |

## 6. Business Architecture Plan

The Business Architecture Plan is the high-level plan (and steps) for you as the Business Architect to take and develop the design of the Target Operating Model (TOM) and manage the alignment of the physical TOM's implementation.

The Target State Architecture **Design Process** ('Design Process') provides the outline of the high-level steps that you will follow, and based on **HOBA®** and its Reference Models, Building Blocks and Blueprints.

This plan will act as a checklist to provide input into reporting (and managing) the process and progress of the development of the Business Architecture over the lifecycle of the Programme.

**This plan serves as a checklist and record of what was agreed between you, the Business Architect and the Programme, and can be called upon later to clarify or review, should there need to be any changes. This plan will also come in handy should you get pulled on to other 'unrelated' pieces of work, that have somehow 'slipped' into your scope, or have been mistaken for Business Architects' roles and responsibilities.**

## 7. Work Plan

The Work Plan section provides the following:

- A summary of the views (Reference Models and Building Blocks) necessary to fulfil the requirements of the Request for Architecture Work, and
- The list of deliverables you are expected to produce.

Together they provide a summary of each of

Business Architecture Plan

Table 5.11

| No. | Step | Purpose | Blueprint |
|---|---|---|---|
| 1 | Focus | | Define the Business Motivation Model, which includes:<br>· Business Architecture Approach<br>· Vision Mapping<br>· Strategy Mapping<br>· Business Glossary |
| 2 | Control | | Define the Governance Model, which includes:<br>· Architecture Governance<br>· Design Principles<br>· Risk, Assumptions, Issues and Dependencies (RAID) |
| 3 | Analyse | | Define the Current Operating Model, which includes:<br>· Organisation Mapping<br>· Stakeholder Mapping<br>· User Journey Mapping<br>· Process Mapping<br>· Capability Mapping |
| 4 | Evaluate | | Define the Benefits Model, which includes:<br>· Benefits Mapping<br>· Benefits-Dependencies Mapping<br>· Prioritised Changes |
| 5 | Design | | Define the Target Operating Model, which includes:<br>· Capability Mapping<br>· Process Mapping<br>· Impact Mapping<br>· Cost-Benefit Mapping<br>· Pilot Mapping |
| 6 | Implement | | Define the Road Map, which includes:<br>· Project Mapping<br>· Road Map Mapping<br>· Benefits Realisation Mapping<br>· Transition Architecture Mapping<br>· Business/IT Architecture Alignment Mapping<br>· Traceability Mapping |

the Building Blocks and Blueprints that make up the complete Target State Architecture, that is, both the design, and the implementation activities required to implement the physical Business Architecture.

Table 5.12 lists the complete list of Building Blocks that make up Target State Architecture.

**The differences between the Work Plan and the High-level plan is the Work Plan assumes all activities are in scope, and provides some insight into the activities that are carried out, which has most relevance for the Project Manager and Product Owner, whereas the High-Level Plan focuses on scope, and be of more interest to the Programme Director and Governance Boards and Design Authorities.**

## 8. Communications Plan

The purpose of this section is to outline the project communication activities throughout the Programme lifecycle from discovery to implementation. This plan, like the overall SOW is about setting the Organisations expectations for (and of) the Business Architecture and Business Architect, as well as increasingly the Organisations readiness to the forthcoming change.

The objectives of the communication plan are to provide a high-level overview of the events, objectives, formats and frequency of what will be communicated to the affected and impacted Organisation and the Programme. It also provides indicative times around communication and stakeholder engagement activities with the Organisation, the Programme and the Business Architecture.

Business Architecture Work Plan

Table 5.12

| Work Item | Reference Model | Building Block | Activities |
|---|---|---|---|
| 1 | Business Motivation Model | • Statement of Work (SOW)<br>• Vision Mapping<br>• Business Strategy<br>• Business Glossary | (Re)Confirm the Vision, Strategy, Objectives for the Organisation and Business Architecture, and capture the terms and definitions. |
| 2 | Governance Model | • RACI<br>• Tracking and Reporting<br>• Design Principles<br>• RAID | (Re)Confirm the architecture governance framework, processes, roles and responsibilities so the right decisions (and changes) are made at the right level by the right people. |
| 3 | Current Operating Model | • Organisation Mapping<br>• Stakeholder Mapping<br>• User Journey Mapping<br>• Process Mapping<br>• Capability Mapping | (Re)Confirm the current (As-Is) operating model, to establish and agree the baseline to design and build the TOM from. |
| 4 | Benefits Model | • Benefits Mapping<br>• Benefits-Dependencies Mapping<br>• Prioritisation Mapping | Define and prioritise the benefits, and changes (people, process and technology) to the Current Operating Model needed to realise the planned benefits. |
| 5 | Target Operating Model | • Capability Mapping<br>• Process Mapping<br>• Impact Mapping<br>• Cost-Benefit Mapping<br>• Pilot Mapping | Define the future (To-Be) state – Target Operating Model (TOM), and validating the prioritised changes from the Benefits Model are fit for purpose. |
| 6 | Road Map Model | • Project Mapping<br>• Road Map Mapping<br>• Benefits Realisation Mapping<br>• Transition Architectures<br>• Business/IT Arch. Alignment<br>• Traceability Mapping | Define the implementation path and activities required to implement the physical Target Operating Model (TOM), and oversee the alignment of the implementation the physical TOM with the design. |

Communication Plan

**Table 5.13**

| Event/ Comms' Activity | Objective | Who | Format | When/frequency |
|---|---|---|---|---|
| Project Launch | Provide general information to the Programme | All Staff | Face-to-face | Kick-off / [Date] |
| Product Owners, Super Users | Start engagement to move towards alignment | All Super Users, and their Managers | Face to face / presentation locations | Within Month of Kick-off |
| External Parties | Advise external parties of coming change | External Parties | Mail Out Face to Face | 1-2 Months following kick-off |
| End of Reference Model phase | Communicate success. Keep project "top of mind" | All staff | Newsletter / email | As milestones reached |
| Training Announcement* | Announce training activities, dates/locations | All impacted End Users Others for information | Email and newsletter | 8 weeks prior to go live |
| User Acceptance Testing Announcement* | Awareness raising | Testers Key Users SMEs Managers | Email Presentation Face to Face | 4 weeks prior to go live |
| System Integration Testing Announcement* | Awareness raising | All staff External parties | Email Face to Face Letter | 4 weeks prior to go live |
| Cutover Pack* | Practical Information | Impacted staff | Email link Printouts | 2 weeks before go-live |
| Countdown to Go Live* | Everyone to prepare Highlight timeline | All staff | Email | 1 week before go-live |
| Go Live reminder* | Final preparations | All staff External Parties | Email | 3 days before go-live |
| Go Live Announcement* | Announcement | All staff External Parties | Email | Go Live Day |
| Go Live celebration morning tea* | Celebrate success | All staff | Face to face | Go Live Day |

The following Table contains an example of the communication plan using the case study example:

### 9. Effort and Duration

The purpose of this section is to provide an indication of the estimated *effort* (the number of work units to complete the activity, often referred to as man hours, days or weeks) and estimated *duration* (total time to complete the activities based on resources available, and does not include holidays or non-working days, often referred to as work days or weeks). Effort is often determined first in order to determine duration.

**These are the activities and announcements that are important to Business Architecture, to ensure the Programme and external parties are informed and expectations are set. This plan should also dove-tail with the wider Programme communications plan. Activities marked (*) are shown for completeness (as the success of the Programme will depend on the changes successfully implemented into the Business, which as Business Architects, we have a vested interest in) and should be completed by the Programme Management Office (PMO) or Change Manager.**

Note – Duration and Effort are different to *Elapsed Time*. Elapsed Time is the total calendar time needed to complete the activities, which can include weekends and public holidays.

In some instances, you may not have a choice in defining duration times, as its already decided and dictated to you due to Programmes objectives and timelines. However, in instances where you do have a choice, you have two (2) options:

1. **A high-level guestimate** (based on past experience), or
2. **A detailed estimate**, based on Work Breakdown Structure (WBS) or similar.

Although option two (2) is preferred, option one (1) is, in most instances, a more sensible option to begin with to respond to the request for architecture work commencement. A fuller, more accurate estimate usually becomes clearer and known as the work progresses, particularly in Step-6 (Implement with the Projects, and Road Map Blueprints) which has a clear(er) view of schedules and dates.

For now, record the duration and effort estimates in the following table, and validate them in the Step-6 Road Map later.

**(*) Note – The below estimates assumes the effort of 640 hours work to develop and deliver the design is already known, and with one Business Architect committed to 40 hours per week, the duration would be 80 work days (Effort = 640 hours, Duration = 80 work days, Elapsed time = 16 weeks). This example is shown in *Figure 10.9 – Sample Business Architecture Road Map* as part of *6.2 Road Map Mapping.***

If there were two (2) Business Architects (of the same skill level) and each committed to 40 hours per week, in theory the duration could be halved to 40 work days (Effort = 640 hours, Duration = 40 work days, Elapsed time = 8 weeks), assuming other stakeholders the Business Architects need access to are also available (and they would not trip over each other).

However, if there were two (2) Business Architects committed to 20 hours per week, the duration would be 80 work days (Effort = 640 hours, Duration = 80 work days, Elapsed time = 16 weeks).

### 10. Project Plan and Schedule

The Project Plan and schedule provides the high-level plan and indicative timelines of the activities needed to design and deliver the Target State Architecture. These activities will be the deliverables from above, but with the addition of indicative dates as follows:

Note – a more accurate estimate of the time would involve estimating the time taken to complete each Blueprint within each of the models, however, for this example, are based on estimating at the Reference Model level. An illustration of this example is shown in *'Figure 10.9 – Sample Business Architecture Road Map'* as part of *6.2 Road Map Mapping.*

Example Effort and Duration*

Table 5.14

| Duration (to complete Programme) | Time |
|---|---|
| Effort | 640 hours |
| Duration | 80 work days |
| Elapsed Time | 16 weeks |

Example Project Plan and Schedule

Table 5.15

| Work Item | Building Block | Days (Duration) | Start | End | Notes |
|---|---|---|---|---|---|
| 1 | Business Motivation Model | 20 | 06/07/15 | 31/08/15 | (1) + (2) run in parallel |
| 2 | Governance Model | 20 | 06/07/15 | 31/08/15 | (1) + (2) run in parallel |
| 3 | Current Operating Model | 20 | 03/08/15 | 28/08/15 | |
| 4 | Benefits Model | 10 | 31/08/15 | 11/09/15 | (4) + (5) overlap |
| 5 | Target Operating Model | 10 | 07/09/15 | 25/09/15 | (4) + (5) overlap |
| 6 | Road Map Model | 20 | 28/09/15 | 20/10/15 | |

### 11. Risks and Mitigations

The Risks and Mitigations (and Assumptions, Issues and Dependencies) identified and recorded here will form part of the RAID Blueprint discussed in the *Governance Model* as part of *Chapter 6 Step 2 – Control*.

### A. Risks

Table 5.16 identifies the currently known risks and mitigations that will be verified and validated as part of the *Governance Model*.

SOW Risks Register

Table 5.16

| ID | Risk | Likelihood | Severity | Impact | Mitigation | Owner |
|---|---|---|---|---|---|---|
| R001 | Lack of Sponsor support for Programme | Low | High | High | Understand business & info needs & frequency & meet needs. | Business Architect |
| R002 | Business disengages commitment to Programme | Medium | High | High | Understand business & info needs & frequency & meet needs. | Business Architect |

SOW Assumptions Register

Table 5.17

| ID | Assumption | Impact | Criticality | Owner |
|---|---|---|---|---|
| A001 | The Vision, Strategic Objectives, and Measures are defined and agreed. | Should the Strategic measures the Programme is impacting not be as expected, this will result in a request and potential scope change. | Low | Business Architect |
| A002 | The scope is well defined and understood by the Programme. | High | Medium | Business Architect |

SOW Issues Register

Table 5.18

| ID | Issue | Impact | Owner |
|---|---|---|---|
| I001 | Projects across the Programme already indicate the decommission target dates are challenging. | Projects are placing stronger emphasis when planning to align to decommission agenda. | Technology Architect |
| I002 | The scope is well defined and understood by the Programme. | New ways of working (HOBA®) implemented, business providing earlier feedback through project lifecycle. Initial feedback is positive. | Project Manager |

SOW Dependencies Register

Table 5.19

| ID | Dependency | In/Outbound* | Priority | Owner |
|---|---|---|---|---|
| D001 | HQ to provide updated procurement process to on-board new suppliers | Inbound | High | Programme Manager |
| D002 | OAS Project is dependent on the Workflow Project to deliver the Workflow system before the OAS can be fully operational | Outbound | High | OAS Project Manager |

### B. Assumptions

Table 5.17 identifies the currently known assumptions and impacts that will be verified and validated as part of the *Governance Model.*

### C. Issues

Table 5.18 identifies the currently known issues and impacts that will be verified and validated as part of the *Governance Model.*

### D. Dependencies

Table 5.19 identifies the currently known dependencies and owner that will be verified and validated as part of the *Governance Model.*

**Note – an inbound dependency is where your project is dependent on receiving something from another project before you are able to start or begin a task. An outbound dependency is where another project/team cannot start an activity until you finish.**

## 12. Acceptance Criteria and Procedures

### A. Metrics and KPIs

In this section, state the metrics that will be used to determine the success of the architecture work.

Note - includes related and in-scope Blueprints.

## B. Acceptance Procedure

The acceptance procedure is the process used to sign-off/accept the Business Architecture work as complete and delivered. This is covered in more detail in *Chapter 6 Step 2 – Control*, as part of the Governance Reference Model, which covers the governance structure and review and approval process.

The review and approval ensures the right level of management review and approve the appropriate and relevant level of Business Architecture requirements for their level of management. It also ensures the right level of architecture requirements are taken to the most suitable level of management for review and approval.

The Requirements Pyramid in *Figure 5.8*, shows the relationship between the **HOBA®** components (Reference Model, Building Blocks, and Blueprints) and the different level and types of Business Architecture requirements.

These different level and type of Business Architecture requirements (Vision, Theme, Feature and User Story/Story) are signed off by different levels of management

Metrics and KPIs

Table 5.20

| ID | Metric | Measurement technique | Target Value (KPI) | Rationale/ Notes |
|---|---|---|---|---|
| M001 | Business Motivation Model* Complete | Reporting | · Statement of Work (SOW)<br>· Vision Mapping<br>· Business Strategy<br>· Business Glossary | Direction of the Programme and Business Architecture is confirmed. |
| M002 | Governance Model* Complete | Reporting | · RACI<br>· Tracking and Reporting<br>· Design Principles<br>· RAID | Architecture governance framework, processes, roles and responsibilities established and operational |
| M003 | Current Operating Model* Complete | Reporting | · Organisation Mapping<br>· Stakeholder Mapping<br>· User Journey Mapping<br>· Process Mapping<br>· Capability Mapping | Established and agreed the Current (As-Is) Operating odel as baseline to design and build the TOM from. |
| M004 | Benefits Model* Complete | Reporting | · Benefits Mapping<br>· Benefits-Dependencies Mapping<br>· Prioritisation Mapping | The Benefits, and changes (people, process and technology) to the Current Operating Model needed to realise the planned benefits have been defined & prioritised. |
| M005 | Target Operating Model* Complete | Reporting | · Capability Mapping<br>· Impact Mapping<br>· Cross-Mapping<br>· Process Mapping<br>· Cost-Benefit Mapping<br>· Pilot Mapping | The design of Target Operating Model (TOM), using the prioritised changes from the Benefits Model is confirmed. |
| M006 | Road Map* Model Complete | Reporting | · Project Mapping<br>· Road Map Mapping<br>· Benefits Realisation Mapping<br>· Transition Architectures<br>· Business/IT Arch. Alignment<br>· Traceability Mapping | The implementation path and activities required to implement the physical TOM, and oversee the implementation the physical TOM aligns to the design is confirmed |
| M007 | Physical Target perating Model implemented | Reporting | The physical TOM is implemented as per the design (of the TOM) | The Business Architect is best placed as the designer to oversee the implementation of the physical Business Architecture. |

across the Organisation, in line with the SAFe® Agile framework which was discussed in the *Alignment with Other Approaches* section.

The following diagram shows how each of the different level of requirement(s), require a different level of management oversight, review and approval, as follows:

- Vision and Themes level requirements (Reference Models), are agreed at the Portfolio level;
- Features level requirements (Building Blocks), are agreed at the Programme level;
- Epics and User Stories requirements (Blueprints) are agreed and managed at the Project level, within the projects.

Table 5.21 shows the different level of the Organisation that develops and owns the different types of Architecture requirements.

Requirements, requirements management, review and approval process and governance roles are discussed further as part of the Governance Model in *Chapter 6 Step 2 – Control*.

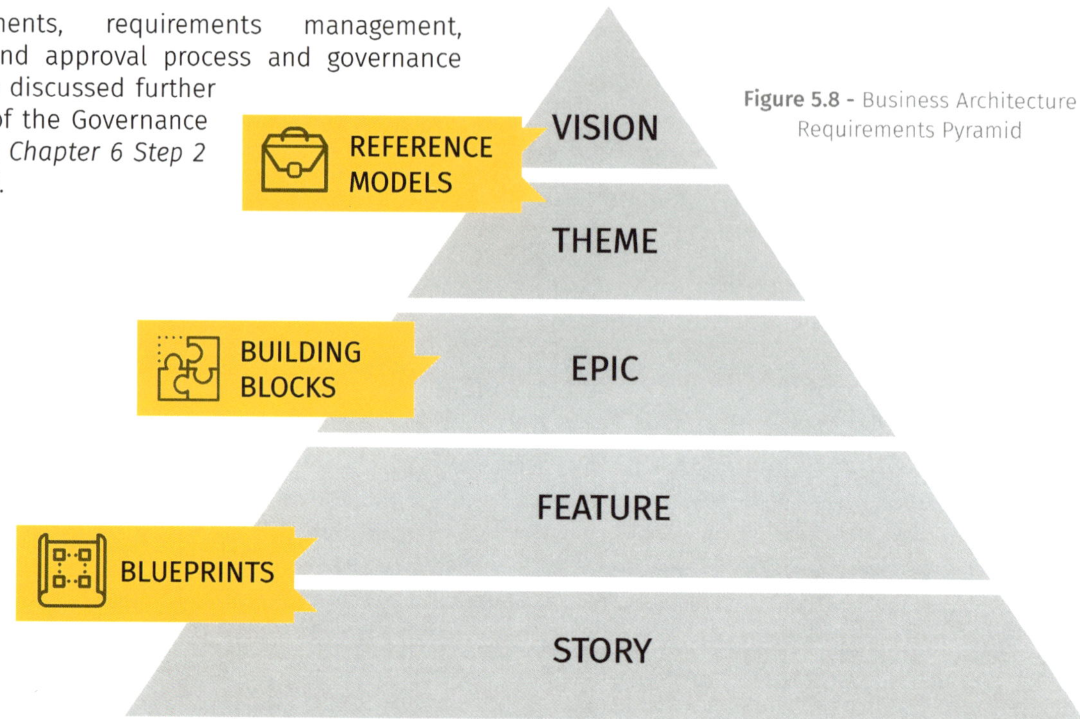


**Figure 5.8** - Business Architecture Requirements Pyramid

Approach to Managing Requirements Table

Table 5.21

| Architecture Requirement | Organisation Level | Description | Captured In | Approval of Changes |
|---|---|---|---|---|
| Vision (Business Architecture Approach) | Portfolio Level | The Vision for the Business Architecture, expected deliverables and ways of working between the Business Architect and Programme. | Statement of Work (SOW) | Changes to the Vision, priorities or delivery needs sign off from the Portfolio Board |
| Theme (Reference Models) | Programme Level | HOBA® Reference Models that, addresses specific aspects of the business and Business Architecture (e.g. Benefits Model). | Portfolio Backlog | As above |
| Feature (Building Blocks) | Programme Level | Group of components of HOBA® Reference Models that address a specific business concern (e.g. Benefit Mapping) | Programme Backlog | The addition or removal of Building Blocks from scope requires Programme Board approval |
| Epic (Blueprints) | Project Level | Discrete area of the Building Block that details a specific business concern (e.g. Benefit Map | Project Backlog | Changes to Blueprints and stories are managed within Scrum Team agreed with the Product Owner |
| User Story (Blueprint Story) | Project Level | Smallest chunk of a Blueprint that can be delivered within a sprint or release. | Sprint Backlog | As above |

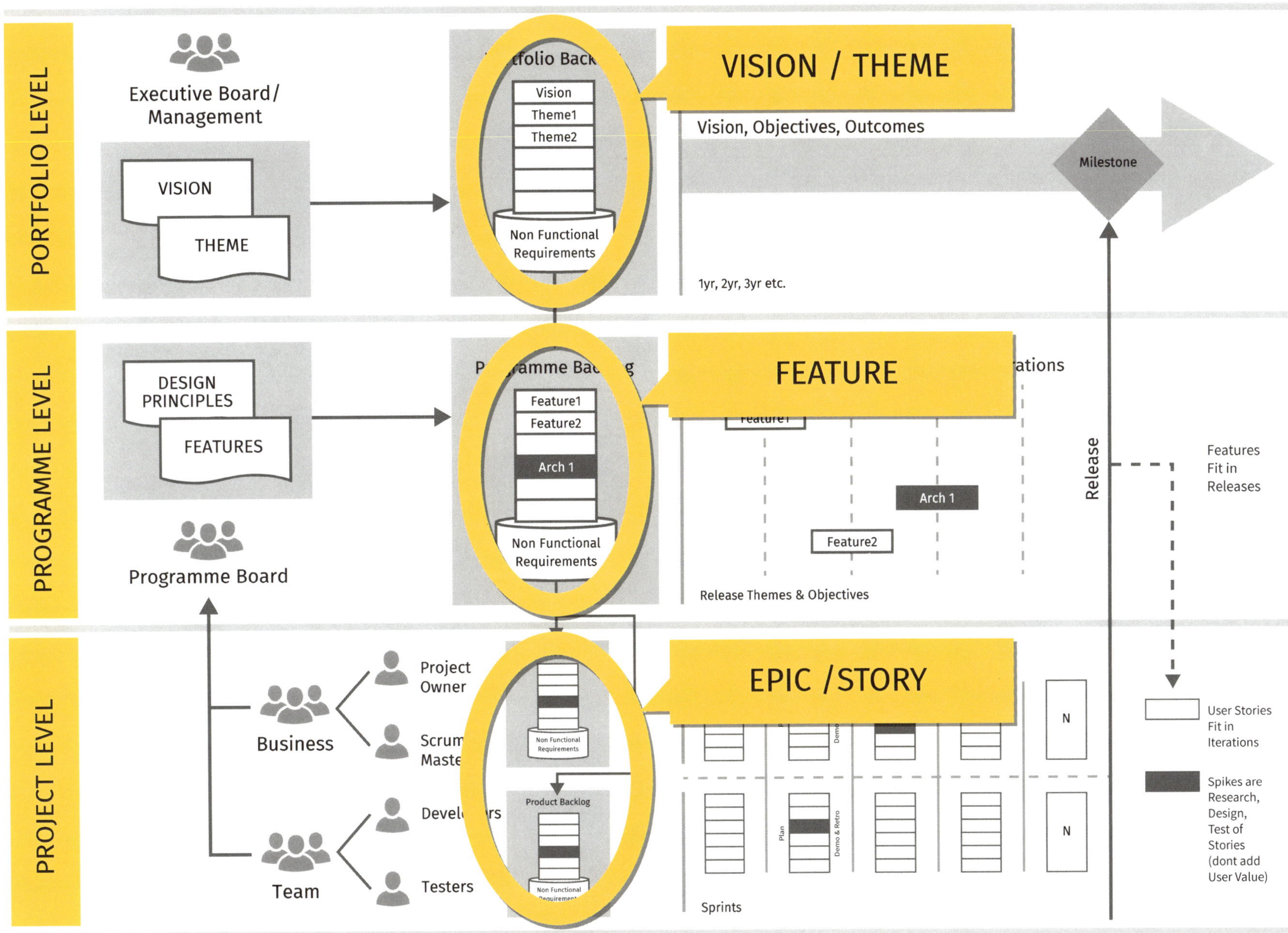


**Figure 5.9** - SAFe® Agile Framework Approval Process[14]

[14] Adapted from Cockburn, A., et al. (2011) Agile Software Requirements 'The Agile Enterprise Big Picture'

## 13. Approvals

This section covers the person or persons responsible for signing off the Statement of Work. This is different to the person or persons who are responsible for signing off each of the Business Architecture Deliverables (although this can be the same person/persons).

### Risks and Mitigations

The biggest risk with the 'Approach' is either it isn't done, or it isn't done in its entirety. The reason why the Approach and SOW is not written, agreed or even signed off, is often due to some form of hesitation, reluctance, or even dismissiveness that this activity (agreeing the Approach, and SOW) is even required. Often this is due to time constraints or a lack of understanding of its value.

Whatever the case, like with any engagement, it is in your best interests to get the terms of your engagement, how you will work, what are your expected deliverables, and by when are they needed – agreed, and agreed upfront.

This SOW was intentionally fairly comprehensive, and for good reason. Recall from *Chapter 2 The Business Architecture Challenge*, the five (5) challenges that Business Architects and Business Architecture is facing right now. Organisations know they need it, but don't know what it looks like, its value or how to use it. They're keen for you to just 'crack on' without the appropriate due diligence.

If you face some resistance getting this signed off, remember, its most likely an education process. Resist the temptation to *'crack on'* and set yourself up for success now, by defining what success looks like, and how to measure it by completing the SOW. Refer to *Chapter 2 The Business Architecture Challenge* for tips or recap how to address the Business Architecture challenges.

### Building Block Wrap-up

In this section, we discussed the Business Architecture Approach ('Approach') Building Block.

This Building Block captures and defines both the direction for the Programme, but most importantly the Business Architecture as well.

This Building Block is made up of the Statement of Work (SOW) Blueprint. The SOW will form the documented and agreed 'contract' between the Business Architect and the Programme, and sets out the scope of work and roles and responsibilities of the Business Architect on the Programme, set expectations as well as agree a way of working and measure success.

The SOW can be overlooked or dismissed on the Programme as unimportant, but it should not be overlooked. Often the reluctance with getting the SOW drafted and/or agreed to, is a lack of understanding of its value, almost like the misunderstanding of the value of Business Architecture. Should you encounter any resistance or reluctance, refer to *Chapter 2 The Business Architecture Challenge* for tips or recap how to address the Business Architecture challenges.

### Next Steps

Once you have agreed the *1.1.1 Statement of Work (SOW)* Blueprint, the next step in the Design Process is to complete the Vision Mapping Building Block to define the Vision for the Programme, which decomposes the Vision into how it is going to be achieved (strategy) and how to measure progress and success (objectives and measures).

The Vision Mapping Building Block is discussed in the next section below.

SOW Approvals Table

Table 5.22

| Name | Position | Approval | Date |
|---|---|---|---|
| Signatory1 | Programme Director | J Goodall | 29/06/2015 |
| Signatory2 | Sponsor | E Rutherford | 29/06/2015 |

# 1.2 Vision Mapping

## Introduction

Vision Mapping is the Building Block that defines and agrees the Programme Vision, and is the second activity you will do (and should do) with any Business Architecture engagement.

The purpose of this Building Block is to get a clear and agreed description of the Vision – the outcome the Organisation is aiming to achieve from the Programme, that the Programme and Business Architecture will and must support. For the Vision to be meaningful, it needs to be decomposed in such a way it is meaningful and measurable for all parties concerned – from the Executive level, down to the operational and Programme level.

Defining the Vision is one of the first, and possibly the most important task within the **Design Process,** as this becomes (and is) the single focus point for the entire Organisation and Programme.

The Vision Mapping consists of the 'Vision, Strategy, Objectives and Measures' (VSOM) Blueprint, and VSOM Table. The VSOM Map provides the view of the Vision decomposed into the Strategy(ies), Objectives and then Measures, and the VSOM Table records the necessary details behind the map, namely the information sources for each element of the VSOM Map.

Creating the VSOM Map is a practical planning process that helps define the Vision and laying out what needs to happen to achieve the Vision, and what the criteria are to measure success.

**Some of the more experienced amongst us might be thinking 'but we know what our Vision is', 'it's plastered on all the walls in the staff cafe', or 'it's on the footer of all my emails'. Yes true. The question is *'What does success look like for that Vision, and how do you measure it?'* What happens is although the Vision statements are 'out there', it is often too complex, too lofty, and not coherent. Like a game of 'whispers' played in primary school, the further away the whisper got from the source, the more the whisper changed. In primary school that was ok, and pretty funny, but in Business and Programme Management, it is not acceptable. The further the Vision gets from the source, the more 'diluted' it can become, and that can lead to miss-spending, failed Programmes and worse - not achieving the Vision. Hence its importance to not only define the Vision, and define it early in the Design Process, but define it in meaningful and measurable terms.**

Each of the elements of the VSOM, is broken down and discussed below:

- **Vision** – is the single focus or focal point of the Organisation or Programme. It is usually described in terms of what the 'end state' looks like. It is the aspirational statement of where the Organisation would like to be in the future. It addresses the 'Why is the business in business?' question) (or equally, why was the Programme requested?);
- **Strategy** – the options available to achieve the Vision. It is the 'means' or 'method' by which the Organisation will seek to achieve the Vision e.g. 'Create a flexible technology solution & data platform and transform business processes';
- **Objective** – are the outcomes to be achieved by the Strategy. This is the 'how' are the *outcomes* the Business is seeking going to be achieved. Robust objectives closely follow the S.T.A.R goal format – Specific, Time bound, Achievable and Realistic e.g. 'decommission [in scope] legacy systems (by end Q1 2017); share IT components across the Organisation (by end Q1 2017)'; and
- **Measures** – are Strategy and Objective outcome indicators, used to measure success or progress towards the Vision. Usually represented by Key Performance Indicators (KPI's) or Metrics. Measures are quantitative, as opposed to qualitative, and are used to accurately determine when the KPI/metric has been reached, or is at risk of not being reached e.g. 'legacy systems switched off on time, 100% data migrated over with no errors, 100% components shared at project close'.

For any Organisation or Programme to be successful, all 4 VSOM elements must be aligned, whether viewed from the top-down, or bottom-up. The relationship between the elements of the VSOM is shown in the diagram below.

Taking a top-down view, you will notice the deliberate and intentional cascading relationship between the upper elements of the VSOM with the lower elements. The Vision is decomposed into the Strategy, Strategy into Objectives, and Objectives into Measures. An example of a VSOM is shown in *Figure 5.11*.

**Figure 5.10-** Vision, Strategy, Objective and Measures (VSOM)

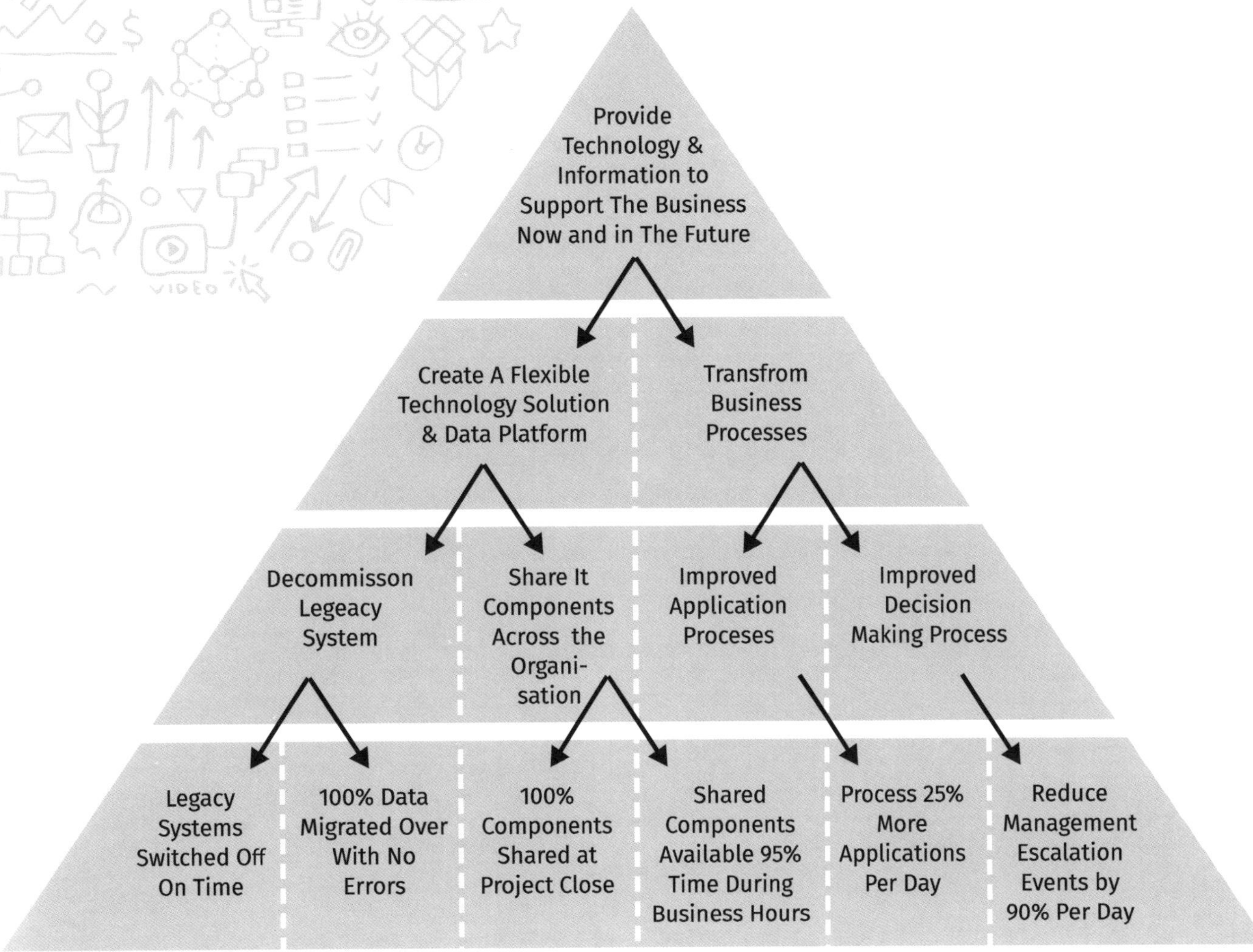


**Figure 5.11** -Sample VSOM

Measures should be **S.M.A.R.T** (Specific, Measurable, Achievable, Realistic and Time Bound). They need to be as this is what the Programme (and Organisation) will measure progress towards, and measure success off of. To be effective, Measures need to be quantitative, not qualitative. 'Improved Customer Satisfaction' for example, is weak and hard to measure. To make Customer Satisfaction a meaningful Measure, it needs a metric to measure against. A better measure for Improved Customer Service would be 'improved customer satisfaction star rating by 50% by end of 2015'. If there is no metric, or star rating, or way of measuring customer satisfaction, create one. If this is not possible, find another Measure.

## Inputs

The inputs used to complete this Building Block are shown in the Table 5.23.

## Outputs

The Blueprints produced for this Building Block are shown in the Table 5.24.

**Vision Mapping Building Block Inputs**

**Table 5.23**

| Ref | Blueprint | Use |
|---|---|---|
| N/A | Business Case-Business Objectives | Provide potential Objectives for the Vision,Strategy, Objectives and Measures (VSOM) Blueprints |
| N/A | Business Case-KPIs / Measures | Provide potential Measures for the VSOM Blueprints. |

**Vision Mapping (Output) Blueprints**

**Table 5.24**

| Ref | Blueprint | Description | Example |
|---|---|---|---|
| 1.2.1 | Vision, Strategy, Objectives and Measures (VSOM) Map | The VSOM Map provides the visual representation of the Vision (why) for the Organisation, decomposed into the Strategy (means), Objectives (how) and Measures that will be used to measure progress and success from. | 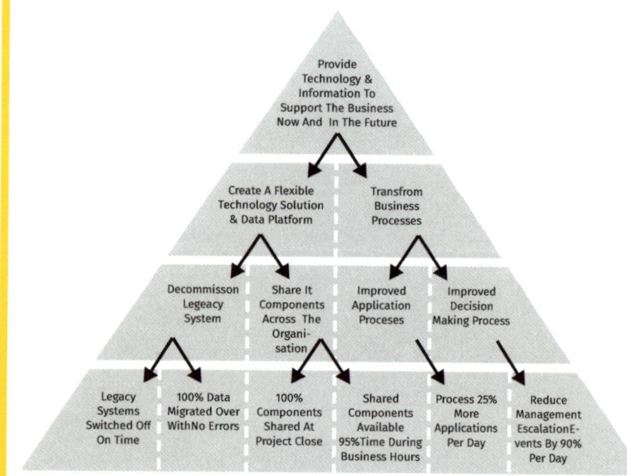 |
| 1.2.2 | VSOM Table | The VSOM Table provides the description and necessary sources of the details provided from the VSOM Map. | (see VSOM Table below) |



| Vision | Provide Technology & Information to support the business now and in the future<br>**Source: Programme Board Meeting Date 20160901** | |
|---|---|---|
| Strategies | Create flexible technology solution & data platform<br>**Source: Business Case v1.4** | Transform Business Processes<br>**Source: Business Case v1.4** |
| Objectives | Decommission legacy systems<br>**Source: Programme Charter v2.0** | Share IT components across the Organisation<br>**Source: Programme Charter v2.0** |
| | Improved decision making process<br>**Source: Business Case v1.4** | Improved Application Process<br>**Source: Business Case v1.4** |
| Measures | Legacy systems switched off on time<br>**Source: Business Case v1.4** | 100% data migrated over with no errors<br>**Source: Business Case v1.4** |
| | 100% components shared at Programme close<br>**Source: Business Case v1.4** | Shared components available 95% of time during business hours<br>**Source: Business Case v1.4** |
| | Reduce management escalation events by 90% per day<br>**Source: Business Case v1.4** | Process 25% more Applications per day<br>**Source: Business Case v1.4** |

## Steps

The steps to complete these Blueprints are as follows.

### 1.2.1 Vision, Strategy, Objectives and Measures (VSOM)

1. Obtain copies of the Blueprint Inputs, and existing business and Programme artefacts as shown in Table 5.23.
2. Plot the Vision, Strategies, Objectives and Measures on the VSOM Map. An example of a VSOM Map is shown in *Figure 5.12*.

### 1.2.2 VSOM Table

Record the description and source of each of the Vision, Strategies, Objectives and Measures from the VSOM Map for completeness and traceability. An example of a VSOM Table is shown below.

Validate and verify each Blueprint by iteratively socialising, validating and refining each Blueprint - including any Risk, Assumptions, Issues and Dependencies (RAID) addressed or raised as part of completing this step, and Package and publish the Blueprints and details – in line with your agreed sprint/release cycle, established in the *Governance Model* in *Chapter 6 Step 2 – Control*.

#### Risks and Mitigations

The risks with developing and agreeing the VSOM is really to do with how you engage the Business to get their buy-in. Walking into a room with a straw man (i.e. initial draft outline) of the VSOM would be the best, possibly quickest and the most pragmatic approach, as starting with a blank sheet of paper which is fraught with problems, as it almost always seems to open up unnecessary 'cans of worms' (or old wounds), and makes it difficult to focus the room or conversations on the task and definitions at hand.

Assuming your Programme budget has already been signed (and/or approved), sources for your strawman would include the Business Case, which would have been prepared and submitted. Check the different cases within it – the financial and economic cases. You should be able to find KPIs

**Figure 5.12** - Sample VSOM Map

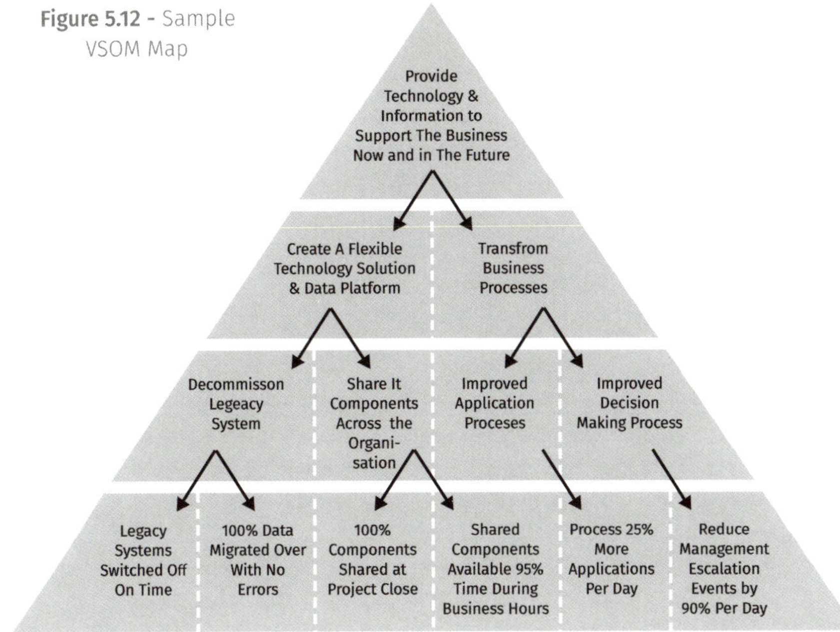


**VSOM (Supporting) Table**

Table 5.25

| | | |
|---|---|---|
| **Vision** | **Provide Technology & Information to support the business now and in the future**<br>Source: Programme Board Meeting Date 20160901 | |
| Strategies | Create flexible technology solution & data platform<br>Source: Business Case v1.4 | Transform Business Processes<br>Source: Business Case v1.4 |
| Objectives | Decommission legacy systems<br>Source: Programme Charter v2.0 | Share IT components across the Organisation<br>Source: Programme Charter v2.0 |
| | Improved decision making process<br>Source: Business Case v1.4 | Improved Application Process<br>Source: Business Case v1.4 |
| Measures | Legacy systems switched off on time<br>Source: Business Case v1.4 | 100% data migrated over with no errors<br>Source: Business Case v1.4 |
| | 100% components shared at Programme close<br>Source: Business Case v1.4 | Shared components available 95% of time during business hours<br>Source: Business Case v1.4 |
| | Reduce management escalation events by 90% per day<br>Source: Business Case v1.4 | Process 25% more Applications per day<br>Source: Business Case v1.4 |

(potential Measures), a statement about alignment to the Organisations strategic goals (potential Vision), and what risks it is hoping to mitigate and benefits to be gained (potential Objectives). The Project or Programme Charter should at least provide the reasons for undertaking the project (potential Vision), Objectives and constraints of the project including target project benefits (potential Objectives). These should all serve as a good conversation starter to get in front of the stakeholders to kick off discussions.

One company, I assisted failed to get the Measures agreed for one project within one of their Programmes. As a result, they churned through thousands of dollars building, and rebuilding components of a system, mainly because there was never an agreed definition of what success looked like (i.e. measures). The Business would take the *liberty* to change their mind and claim 'that's not what we said', or 'that's not what we meant'. The Business was (allegedly) pressed to provide the definition of what success meant to them, but for some unknown reason, it was never forthcoming. The common argument or response to 'how is the definition of the Measure's coming?' was 'it's coming', yet it was interesting how, the only thing that seemed to be eventuating was an open cheque book to continue paying someone for what seemed like a never-ending rollercoaster of building and rebuilding. Lesson learned: Make sure to make the Measures SMART, and if you want to save money and time, do it ASAP!

### Building Block Wrap-up

In this section, we discussed the Vision Mapping Building Block.

This Building Block captures and defines the Vision for the Programme, and provides a single focus point for the Programme that all other requirements within (and across) the Programme must support and align to.
This Building Block is made up of the following two (2) Blueprints:

- **VSOM Map** - provides the visual representation and decomposition of the Vision, and its relationship to the Strategy ('means' to achieve the Vision), Objectives ('how' the Strategy(ies) will be achieved); and Measures (Strategy and Objective outcome indictors, used to measure success or progress towards the Vision), and
- **VSOM Table** - provides the much needed and necessary sources of the details provided in the VSOM Map.

According to the Standish Report[35] a "clear statement of requirements" (i.e. the VSOM) is in the top three (3) factors contributing to the success of the project, which reiterates it's importance in increasing your chances of success for a Programme. So, make sure to get the VSOM agreed, and agreed early!

### Next Steps

Once you have agreed the Vision Mapping Building Block, the next step in the Design Process is to complete the Business Glossary Building Block to define the Terms and Definitions that are used on the Programme and Business Architecture.

Assuming however, the Organisation has not defined their Business Strategy (as mentioned earlier in the Assumptions section), the next logical (and actual) step in the **Design Process** is to complete the Business Strategy Mapping Building Block to define the Business Strategy.

[35] The Standish Group (2014), Chaos Report

# 1.3 Business Strategy Mapping

## Introduction

The Business Strategy Mapping Building Block is an area of analysis and assessment that shows the path (or general plan) the Organisation will take to achieve its Vision, and validates the two big questions for the Organisation: 'Is there a hole in the market?', and 'is there a market in the hole?', which is effectively saying – 'Is there a gap in the market (i.e. market opportunity)?, and given the Organisations' current – core (or otherwise potential) capabilities, can we compete?'.

There are various models and frameworks that help answer those questions. However, the Blueprints that are included in **HOBA®** are as follows:

- Business Strategy Map,
- Balanced Score Card,
- Business Model Canvas,
- Porters Five Forces,
- SWOT Analysis,
- PESTLE Analysis.

As mentioned in the *Scope* and *Assumptions* sections at the start of this book, Business Strategy Mapping as a Blueprint and activity which is out of scope for this book however for completeness, is discussed here briefly below.

In practice, by the time the Business Architect has been brought on board to the Organisation or Programme, the Organisation has (in most cases) already defined the Business Strategy. That

Business Strategy would be a key part of the terms of the Business Architects engagement - to develop the design and implementation of the Target Operating Model (TOM) that explicitly aligns the Business to the Business Strategy' (the Business Strategy that has already been determined). Examples of common strategies that already existed before the Business Architect started include 'decommissioning, (of a legacy system)', 'out sourcing (to a low labour cost market)', or 'developing a new product or service'.

Remember, the objective of **HOBA®** and this book is to get you up and running, establishing and maintaining the continuous delivery of iterations of the Building Blocks and Blueprints that the rest of the Programme (particularly the Technology Architecture) can continue developing.

The intention with **HOBA®**, and Business Architecture in general, is not to create Blueprints and artefacts just for 'Blueprint-and-artefacts-sake'. These pieces of work just end up becoming pretty and colourful shelf-ware. As each draft or updated Blueprint will need to go through a whole review and approval cycle, it will inevitably consume time and resources (mainly but not limited to) your Key Stakeholders day to day jobs to review and approve them. Everything you take to your Stakeholders, and everything **HOBA®** proposes needs to add clear value to the objective of the project or Programme, and not be just a box ticking exercise.

## Inputs

The inputs used to complete this Building Block are shown in the following table.

**Business Strategy Building Block Inputs**

Table 5.26

| Ref | Blueprint or Document | Use |
|---|---|---|
| N/A | Business Case | Provide background information and potential Strategy options. |
| N/A | Programme Request and Background | Provides the high-level context and background information and potential Strategy options. |

## Outputs

The Blueprints (outputs) produced for this Building Block are shown in the following table.

**Business Strategy (Output) Blueprints**

Table 5.27

| Ref | Blueprint | Description | Example |
|---|---|---|---|
| 1.3.1 | Business Strategy Map[36] | A strategy map is a diagram that is used to document the primary strategic goals being pursued by an organization or management team. | 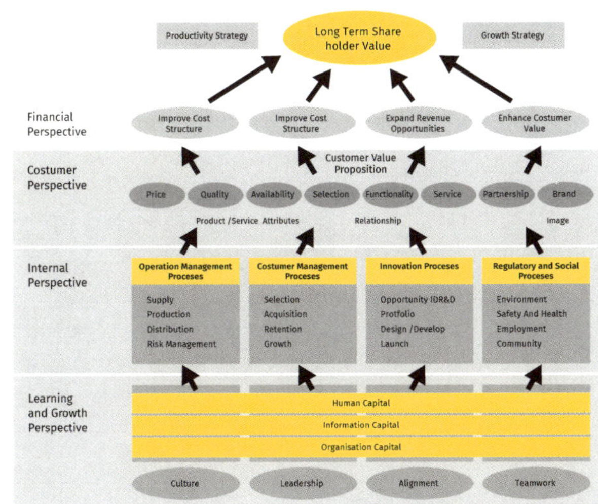 |



[36] Kaplan, R., and Norton, D., (2004) Strategy Maps – Converting Intangible Assets into Tangible Outcomes

Table 5.27

Business Strategy (Output) Blueprints

<table>
<tr><th>Ref</th><th>Blueprint</th><th>Description</th><th>Example</th></tr>
<tr><td>1.3.2</td><td>Balanced Score card[37]</td><td>A strategy performance management tool used by managers to keep track of the execution of activities by the staff within their control and to monitor the consequences arising from these actions.</td><td>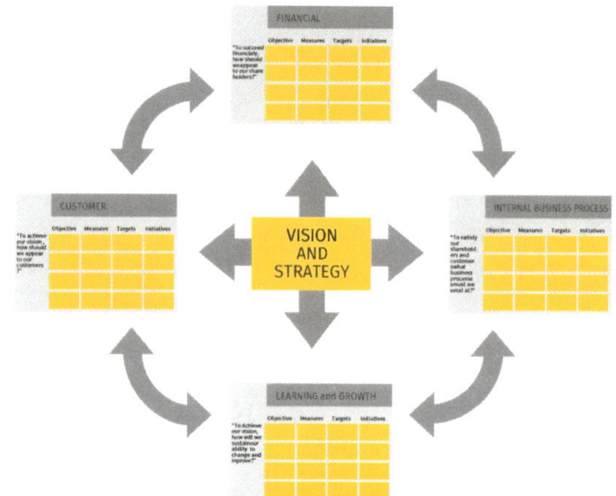
</td></tr>
<tr><td>1.3.3</td><td>Business Model Canvas[38]</td><td>A strategic management and lean start-up template for developing new or documenting existing business models. It is a visual chart with elements describing a firm's value proposition, infrastructure, customers, and finances.</td><td>
</td></tr>
<tr><td>1.3.4</td><td>Porters 5-forces[39]</td><td>A framework used to analyse the level of competition within the Organisation's industry and Business Strategy development</td><td>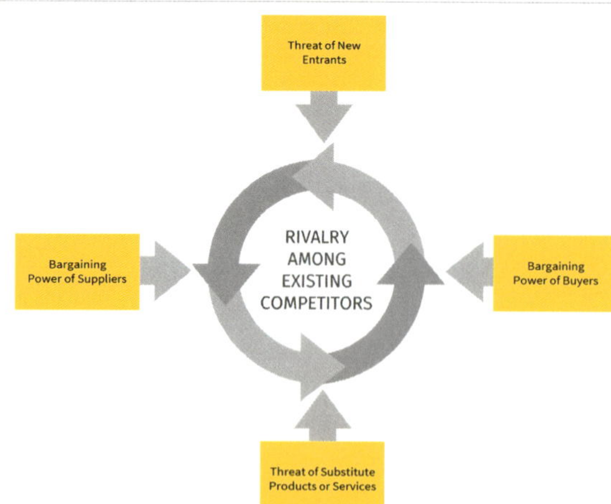
</td></tr>
</table>

## Steps

The steps for completing the Business Strategy Mapping Building Block consist of completing each of the afore-mentioned Blueprints, involving the necessary key stakeholders and having them agreed.

In practice, it may not require all Blueprints to be developed in order to get a clear view of the Organisations Business Strategy, and may stop after the first Blueprint, the Business Strategy Map. Subsequent Blueprints look at the Business Strategy from different areas and perspectives, aimed to provide a more robust argument and rationale behind why the Organisation would select its chosen Business Strategy (mainly that is had the capability to execute it, and means to defend it).

### Risks and Mitigations

There are many risks associated with Business Strategy Mapping, such as if the timing's right; is the business ready for (or want) it, or what the assumptions are in developing each Blueprint.

There is a great deal to cover here, (in terms of risks) but we will leave it for a later discussion in my next book, where I will take

[37] Kaplan, R., and Norton, D., (1996) The Balanced Scorecard – Translating Strategy into Action
[38] Osterwalder, A. & Pigneur Y., (2010) Business Model Generation
[39] Porter, M.E. (1979) How Competitive Forces Shape Strategy

the position (and assumption) that the Business Architect either joins the Organisation as a new starter, is a part of the Organisation already or the company they are joining is a Start-up. In any of these situations, the prime assumption is the Business Architect commences before a Programme is formed or agreed.

The Business Architects role in these situations is to look at the Organisations internal strengths (namely Business Capabilities) and both internal and external opportunities, and help them develop the Business Strategy, and then (as per the topics covered within this book) align the Business Architecture with the Business Strategy.

## Building Block Wrap-up

In this section, we briefly discussed the Business Strategy Mapping Building Block.

This Building Block captures and defines the Organisations Business Strategy – the 'HOW' is the business is going to achieve its Vision question.
This Building Block is made up of several Blueprints, each looking at Business Strategy from a slightly different area and perspective, that incrementally and collectively provide a more robust argument and rationale behind why the Organisation would select its chosen Business Strategy.



Table 5.27

| Ref | Blueprint | Description | Example |
|---|---|---|---|
| 1.3.5 | SWOT Analysis [40] | A framework for analysing Organisation's strengths, weaknesses, opportunities and threats. | 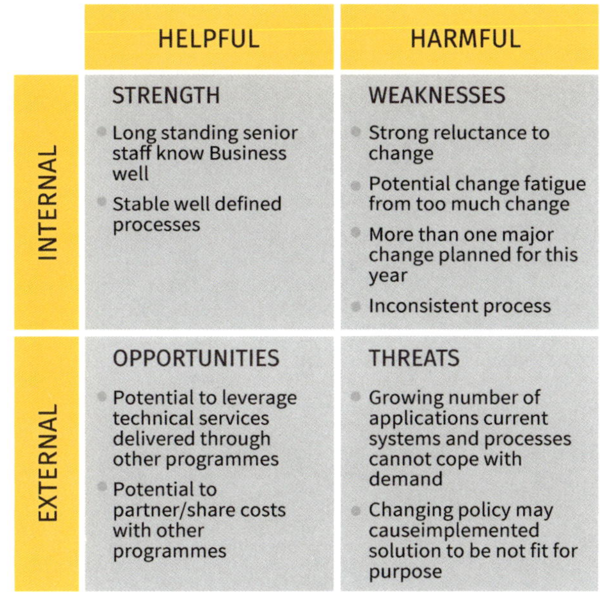 |
| 1.3.6 | PESTLE Analysis [41] | A framework to assess an Organisation's environmental influences using to guide and inform strategic decision-making. | 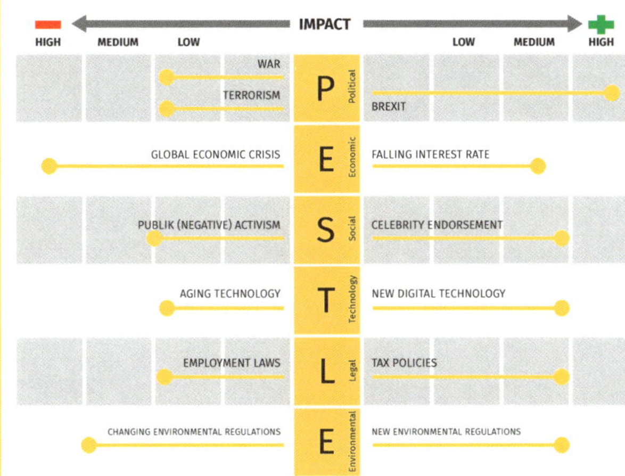 |

[40] Humphrey, A., (2005) SWOT Analysis for Management Consulting
[41] Aguilar, F., (1967) Scanning the Business Environment

This Building Block was only covered briefly for completeness, as deemed out of scope for this book and Programme that requires Business Architecture services (having already defined the Business Strategy).

Business Strategy Mapping will (most likely) be covered in a later book (or updated edition of this one), where the Business Architect joins the Organisation, is a pre-existing part of the Organisation, or the company they are joining joins is a Start-up where they are tasked to develop the Business Strategy.

**Next Steps**

Assuming the Business Strategy Blueprints were agreed in this step, the next step in the **Design Process** is to complete the Business Glossary Building Block and agree the common language (i.e. terms and definitions) that are to be used on the Programme and Business Architecture.

The Business Glossary Building Block is discussed in the section following.

# 1.4 Business Glossary

## Introduction

The Business Glossary Building Block is the activity that defines and agrees the business and technical terms and language for the Programme.

The Business Glossary (also referred to as 'the Glossary', or 'Programme Glossary' for the Programme) contains the Terms and Definitions Blueprint ('Terms and Definitions' or 'Ts and Ds').

The T's and D's contains all the Business facing, or Business-used terms and definitions. These Business terms are all the common (and not-so-common) terms used in (and by) both the Business and the Programme.

The purpose of the Business Glossary is two (2) fold:

- To provide the single source of the common terms used in and on the Programme, which will become known as 'the common language' between the business and the Programme, and
- To establish the correct definition and 'way' they are meant to be used to reduce or remove any ambiguity, misunderstanding and/or miscommunication between the Programme and the Business.

The T's and D's (where appropriate) should provide the following additional information to provide the context of where each term is used, and where the term originated from:

- **Example** – should be an actual example that everyone can relate to.
- **Source** – always quote the source where applicable and able, particularly a creditable or well-known and supported source.

**The 'example' should not be a controversial example where there is not a general consensus or agreement on the example given. If you find the Programme cannot agree on the example, this is a sign that the definition of the term is probably not clear or defined correctly. If there is heated or highly contested debate (which I have been privy too in the past), it is also a sign that the term is really one you need to agree the definition about in advance, as there will likely be issues around that term later on.**

Half the struggle with implementing any change or Transformation Programme is a lack of stakeholder involvement and engagement. As the Business Architect, you are representing the Business on the Programme, as the 'voice of the Business'. How you create and maintain your status, role as well as respect as their representative, is by using their language, and words, and speaking to them in a language they not only understand, but use themselves.

## Inputs

The inputs used to complete this Building Block are shown in Table 5.28 (on the next page).

## Outputs

The Blueprint (output) produced for this Building Block is shown in the Table 5.9.

Business Glossary Building Block Inputs

Table 5.28

| Ref | Blueprint/Documentation | Use |
|---|---|---|
| N/A | Exiting Programme Documentation | Business Case, Project and Programme Brief including terms and definitions on the Programme intranet or Programme wiki. |
| N/A | Existing Business Documentation | Existing policies and procedures, manuals and reference guides. |

Business Glossary (Output) Blueprint

Table 5.29

| Ref | Blueprint | Description | Example | | |
|---|---|---|---|---|---|
| | | | Acronym | Term | Description |
| 1.4.1 | Terms and Definitions | Common terms and definitions of terms, and acronyms used across the Business and Programme. | BDA | Business Design Authority | Authority that oversees and approves proposed Business solutions |
| | | | | Kanban | One of the techniques used in Agile project management to record and breakdown work packages to make progress and blockers visible to everyone within the Scrum team.<br><br>Source: Enterprise Architecture Glossary v1.2 |

Terms and Definitions Table Template

Table 5.30

| Acronym | Term | Description |
|---|---|---|
| BDA | Business Design Authority | Authority that oversees and approves proposed Business solutions |
| | Kanban | One of the techniques used in Agile project management to record and breakdown work packages to make progress and blockers visible to everyone within the Scrum team.<br><br>Source: Enterprise Architecture Glossary v1.2 |

## Steps

Putting together the Terms and Definitions is a fairly straight forward process, as follows.

**1. Develop the Terms and Definitions Table** using the *inputs* from the Inputs section above, and working with the necessary key stakeholders and owners of those documents where necessary to clarify any terms and input the terms, definition, example (if applicable) and source into Terms and Definitions Table template, as shown in the example in Table 5.30.

**2. Iteratively socialise, validate and refine the Blueprint** - including any Risks, Assumptions, Issues and Dependencies (RAID) raised or addressed as part of completing this Blueprint, and

**3. Package and publish the Blueprint(s)** – in line with your agreed sprint/release cycle, established back in *Step 2 – Control* with the *Governance Model*

### Risk and Mitigations

There are a two (2) commons errors when putting together the T's and D's that you should be aware of:

- Adding every and all terms in (and across) the Business, and

- Creating terms from the Programme, and imposing them on the Business.

Try and avoid adding every and all terms in (and across) the Business, try and avoid this. Stay focused on the common terms that are used in the Business and the Programme (hence the nickname *'common language'*).

In one of the companies I assisted, there were over 700 T's and D's in their Glossary (yes, over 700!). This was the accumulation of all the business and technical glossaries across the Organisation, including from areas that were outside of the scope of the Programme!? While all these terms are in some way important to the Organisation, they are not as important to everyone on the Programme, or in the Organisation affected by the changes the Programme was implementing.

What happens with all these terms (as in the above example), is they become a 'mash up' of all terms ever conceived in the Business, but weren't necessarily up to date (or validated), and because of this, the final product – the Term's and Definition's, weren't given the creditability or visibility they deserved.

In cases like this, the Term's and Definition's ends up becoming a dumping ground for all terms. To overcome this situation, restrict the source (input) documents (and terms) to those explicitly originating from the Business area undergoing the change and the scope of the Programme. This will also help you, and speed up the review and approval process when there is a smaller number of terms (and not 700+!) to review.

Also try to avoid creating terms from the Programme and imposing them on the Business. This is the situation where the Programme 'develops' a new term, to fit with the solution the Programme is building, but has done so without explicit consultation or input from the Business.

In one company I assisted, the Programme developed a term called *'Service Delivery'*, as their preferred term for a 'Case' when referring to the situation where 'an application received from an Applicant'. The new term 'Service Delivery' however wasn't a term familiar to the Business, as they already had a term for it, which worked well for them already.

When the Programme people started using this term (service delivery) and were talking to the Business using it, despite the Programme people trying to explain it and the context it was used in, people within the Business were confused. The Business in turn felt as though *'change was being forced upon them'*, as opposed to their role of *'helping drive the change'*, which unfortunately led to disengagement, a situation which is common on a lot of Programmes when changes are forced on people, being made to feel like they're no longer driving the change.

You will recall we discussed the stats that showed over *'70% of Transformation Programmes fail to deliver'* on time, scope and/or quality', with one of the top three (3) leading causes being *"lack of stakeholder engagement"*. This is because when the Business doesn't feel like their needs, wishes or desires are being met, their involvement almost becomes a 'head-nodding' activity, to comply to Programmes *'demands'* without providing any meaningful results. This eventually leads to the Programme delivering a solution that was (just) *'OK'ed'* by the Business that doesn't really fulfil the Business' needs, because the Business didn't want to argue with the Programme, they were willing to *'accept'* what the Programme 'demanded' so as not to cause any disagreements or confrontations.

Where ever possible, use terms that are familiar to and used by the Business, or *'invented'* by the Business, as opposed to imposing them on the Business. When there is a need to create, or change the definition of a common term, first determine if there is an actual need to create a new term (or change one), and raise it with the Business first (rather than imposing it on them).

### Building Block Wrap-up

In this section, we discussed the Business Glossary Building Block.

The Business Glossary Building Block, which agrees the terms and definitions and importantly, sets the *'common language'* to be used on the Programmes. It is used to avoid any confusion in terms, and consists of the Terms and Definitions Blueprint.

The **Terms & Definitions Blueprint** provided the documented and agreed clarification of terms and definitions within (and across) the Organisation and the Programme, forming the 'common language' to be used on the Programme.

Getting the Terms and Definitions agreed with both the Business and Programme stakeholders, and getting sign off early goes, along way to keeping stakeholders engaged. If everyone is speaking the same language, and you can avoid disagreements later when people claim 'that's not what I meant' (which when the Terms and Definitions is not defined, is almost certain to happen).

**Reference Model Recap**

Once the Business Glossary Blueprint is completed, this completes the Building Blocks (along with other Business Architecture Approach, Vision Mapping and Business Strategy Mapping Building Blocks) that make up the Business Motivation Reference Model. The Business Strategy Mapping Building Block was only briefly discussed (as out of scope for the Case Study example, and is more suited for Organisations and Programmes that don't already have their Business Strategy agreed).

By completing the Business Motivation model, this now means you have:

Clearly defined where the Programme (and Organisation) is going (i.e. the vision), how it will get there (i.e. strategy),

Defined what success looks like and how to measure process (i.e. objectives and measures), and

Reduced any ambiguity now by ensuring everyone is speaking the common language, having agreed the Terms and Definitions.

For a full recap of HOBA® and the Design Process, refer to the Recap section in *Chapter 11 Next Steps*.

**Next Steps**

The next step in the Design Process is Step 2 'Control', which addresses the Governance Reference Model. The Governance Model ensures the necessary controls are in place to make decisions, the right people are identified and in place to make them, and the right meetings, structure and format are in place to hold them.

# Chapter 6
# Step 2 – Control

## Introduction

Step 2 – Control, is naturally about control. Control of the processes, decision making, scope and risks for the Programme and Business Architecture. Control is provided via the Governance Reference Model.

*Figure 6.1* below shows where Step-2 Control fits into the overall Design Process.

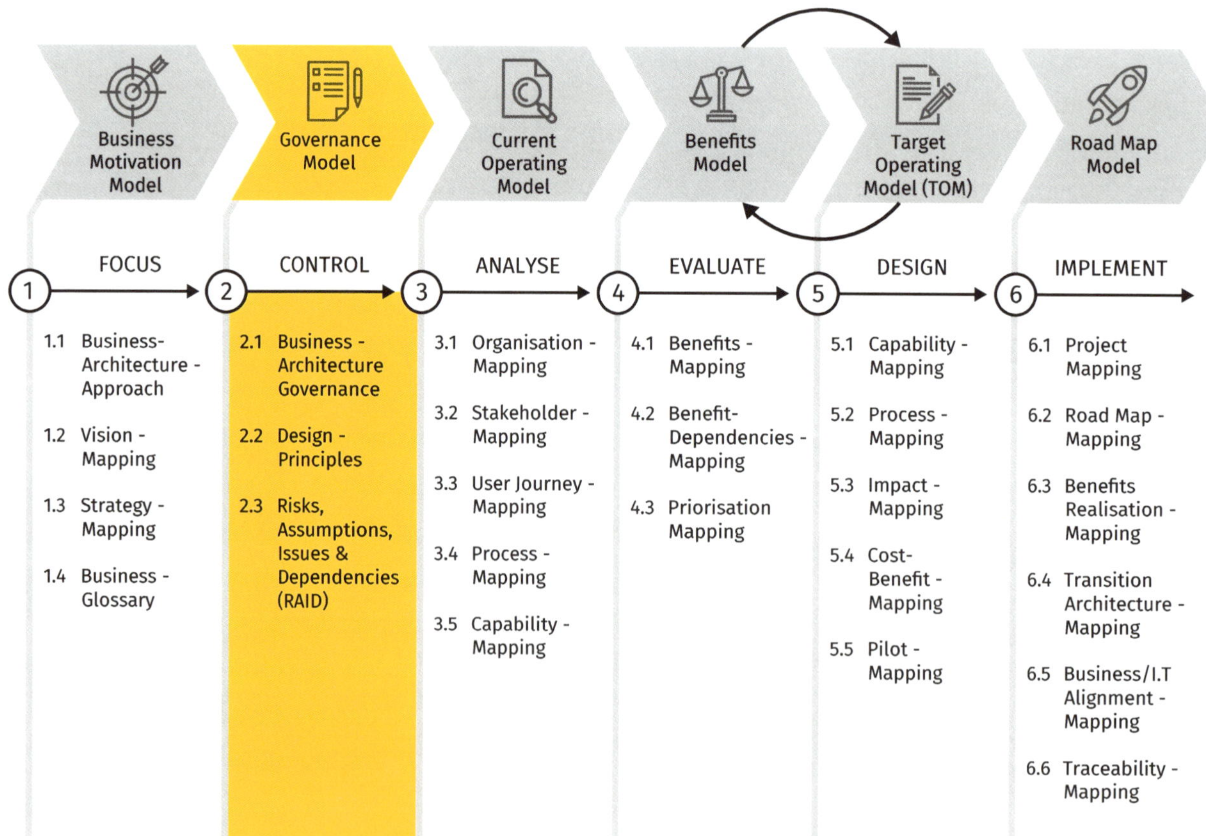


**Figure 6.1** - Design Process - Step 2 Control

# Governance Model

Step-2 Control defines the Governance Model. The Governance Model is where the process of managing the design, decisions, scope and risks of the Programme and Business Architecture are developed and agreed.

As mentioned earlier in *How To Use HOBA®?* section, each **HOBA®** Reference Model addresses a different aspect in the design and implementation of the Target Operating Model (TOM). These different aspects are represented in the following views:

- **Process**
- **Perspective**
- **Context**
- **Content**

We will briefly discuss each of these in the section below.

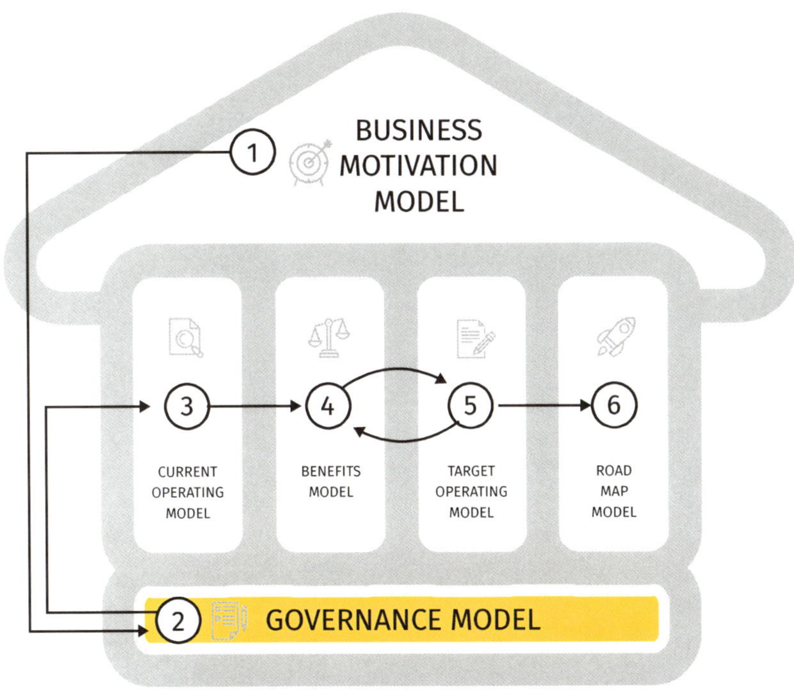


**Figure 6.2** - Governance Model - Step 2

## Process

In terms of process, the Governance Model is the second (2nd) step in the Design Process.

Step-2 addresses the areas and activities that are important and necessary to identifying, validating and implementing the process and frameworks to manage the design, decisions, scope and risks in developing and implementing the Target Operating Model (TOM).

## Perspective

In terms of perspective, the Governance Model provides the 'Control' perspective or point of view, where all areas and activities carried out in

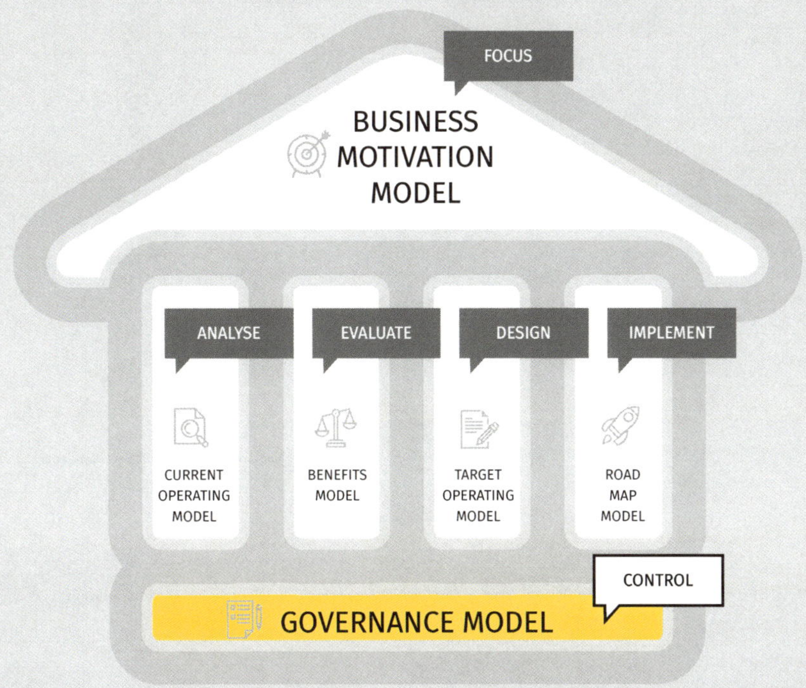


**Figure 6.3** - Governance Model - Control Perspective

defining the Governance Model help provide the 'Control' of the design, decisions, scope and risks for both the Business and Business Architecture. direction for both the Business and Business Architecture.

## Context

In terms of context, the Governance Model addresses the *'Who?' (and 'What?')* aspect of the *'Why, Who, What, Where, How and When?'* questions asked of the both the Business and the Business Architecture:

- 'Who is impacted and affected by the changes the Programme and Business Architecture is touching?' (i.e. what is their role and responsibilities?)
- 'Who is involved in the decisions and decision making on the Programme, and regarding the Business Architecture? (i.e. what is their role and level of impact and influence?).
- 'What are the process(es) for managing decisions, scope and risks on the Programme, affecting the Business Architecture?

## Content

In terms of content, the Building Blocks and Blueprints developed here are the Business Architecture content used to defining the framework and process needed to control the design, decisions, scope and risks in developing and implementing the Target Operating Model (TOM).

The list of Building Blocks and respective Blueprints that make up each section of the Governance Model are shown in Table 6.1 (on the next page).

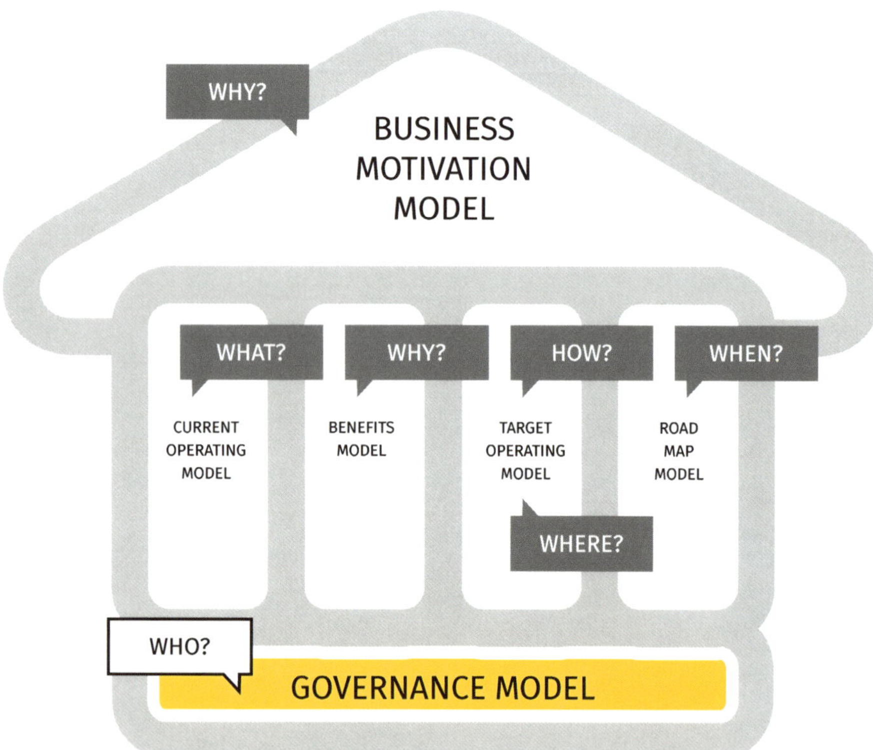


**Figure 6.4** – Governance Model - 'Who?' Context

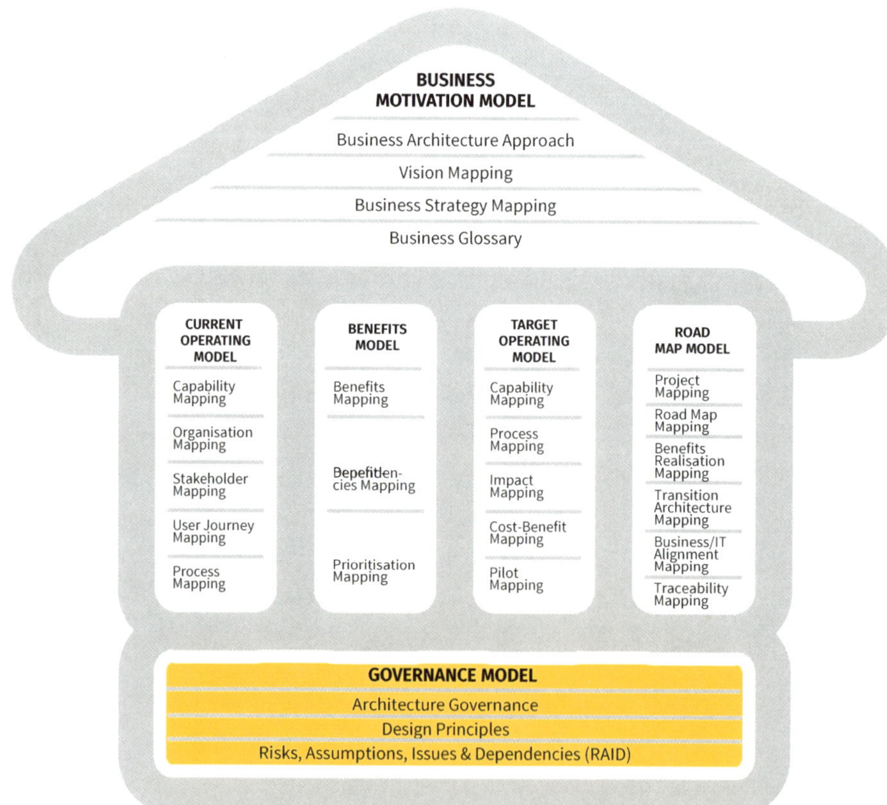


**Figure 6.5 -** Governance Model Building Block Content

Governance Model Building Blocks and Blueprints

**Table 6.1**

| Design Step | Building Block | Purpose | Blueprint |
|---|---|---|---|
| 2.1 | Business Architecture Approach ('Approach') | Provides the framework for managing the decisions and architecture requirements across the Programme. | • 2.1.1 Business Architecture Governance Framework |
| 2.2 | Vision Mapping | Provides the set of principles as the general rules and guidelines used to govern 'what is in' and 'what is out' of scope for the Programme and Business Architecture. | • 2.2.1 Design Principles Register |
| 2.3 | Risks, Assumptions, Issues & Dependencies (RAID) | Provides both the process and register to capture and manage Risks, Assumptions, Issues and Dependencies affecting the Programme and Business Architecture. | • 2.3.1 RAID Log |

# High Level Process (SIPOC)

The high-level Supplier-Input-Process-Output-Customer (SIPOC) process to completing this step: Step-2 Control and the Governance Model are shown in *Figure 6.6.*

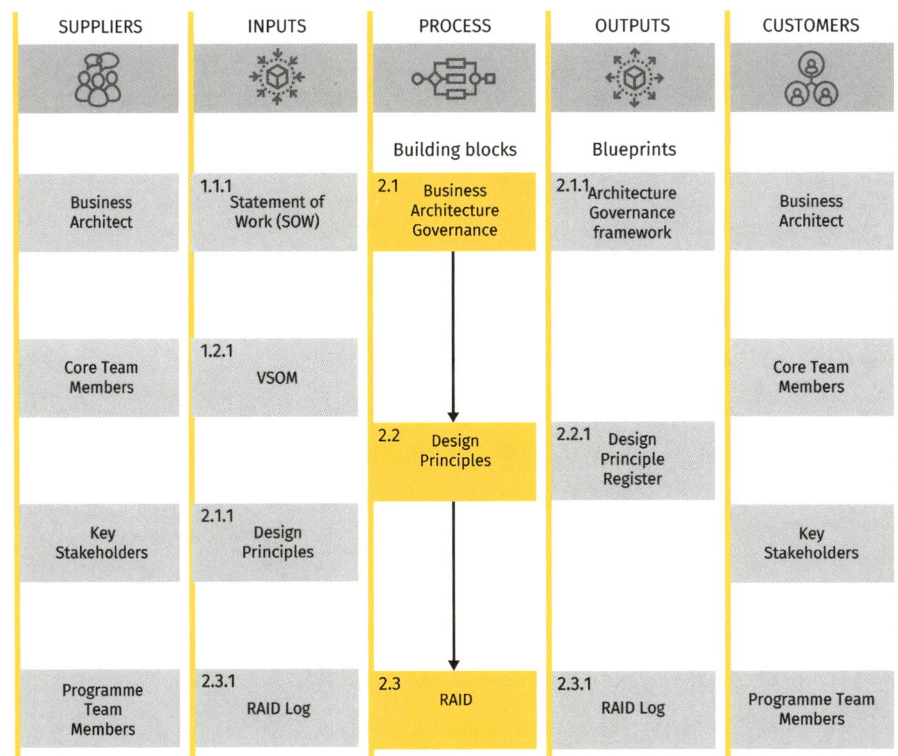


**Figure 6.6 -** Governance Model SIPOCFigure .Figure .Table .Table .

# 2.1 Business Architecture Governance

## Introduction

Business Architecture Governance is the Building Block that establishes the Business Architecture Governance Framework ('Governance Framework'), structure and boards, team members that sit on those boards, and the review and approval process for taking decisions to those boards.

The Governance Framework also includes assessing the key stakeholders to understand the influence they have on the Programme (to implement strategies to manage them and their expectations), their role and responsibilities in terms of contributing to the Business Architecture deliverables, the necessary meetings and ceremonies, and how to track and monitor progress.

The Blueprint that captures the Governance Framework is the 'Architecture Governance Framework', that consists of all the governance activities from the (Business Architecture) Requirements Management Framework to the necessary meetings and ceremonies and tracking and reporting to manage the development and delivery of the Business Architecture deliverables and requirements within (and across) the Programme.

The objective of the Governance Framework is to ensure (and assure) the Business Architecture and Blueprints get reviewed (and are approved) by the appropriate Stakeholders who are at the appropriate management level. They should also have the appropriate seniority and knowledge from their respective areas of responsibility within both the Organisation, as well as Stakeholders, who have the appropriate level of authority within the Organisational structure of the Programme.

Most importantly, the Governance Framework is about incorporating the needs of all the key stakeholders and known dependences both in and outside the Programme, setting up and establishing the framework to identify and manage the Risks, Assumptions, Issues and Dependencies (RAID) affecting the development of the design and implementation of the physical Business Architecture.

## Inputs

The inputs used to complete this Building Block are shown in the Table 6.2.

## Outputs

The Blueprint (output) produced for this Building Block is shown in the Table 6.3.

**Business Architecture Governance Building Block Inputs**

**Table 6.2**

| Ref | Blueprint/Documentation | Use |
|---|---|---|
| 1.1.1 | Statement of Work (SOW) | Provides the initial Stakeholder List, Concerns and Views. |
| 1.2.1 | Vision (VSOM) | Provides the Vision, and articulated business goals (strategy, objectives and measures) that all requirements including the 'improvement opportunities' should align to and support. |
| 2.2.1 | Design Principles | Provides the boundaries and scope of changes to the capabilities, that are needed to address the stakeholder's concerns, realise the identified benefits, and support the Vision. |

**Business Architecture Governance (Output) Blueprint**

**Table 6.3**

| Ref | Blueprint | Description | Example |
|---|---|---|---|
| 2.1.1 | Architecture Governance Framework | The Governance Framework provides the framework and process to manage, track and monitor the Business Architecture requirements on the Programme. | 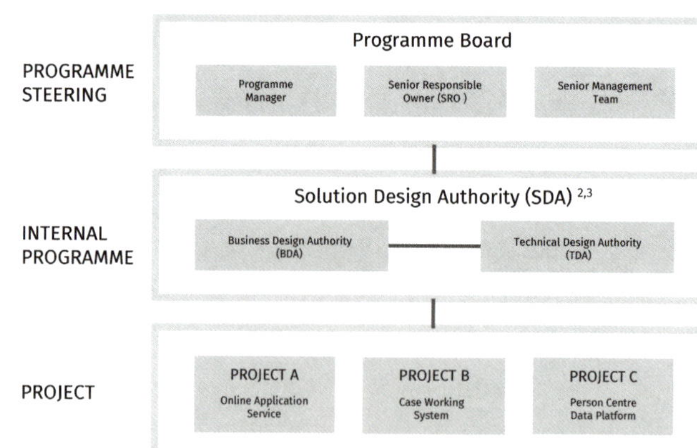 |

## Steps

The Blueprint to complete the Architecture Governance Building Block are discussed in the section following.

## 2.1.1 Architecture Governance Framework

The Blueprint to complete the Architecture Governance Building Block are discussed in the section following.

The Architecture Governance Framework is made up of the following areas:

1. Requirements Management Framework
2. Governance Structure
3. Governance Authorities
4. Review and Approval Process
5. Stakeholder (Influence/Impact) Matrix
6. Business Architecture Requirements RACI
7. Meetings and Ceremonies
8. Tracking and Reporting

Each of the above areas are discussed in more detail in the section below.

### 1. Requirements Management Framework

The first area in defining the Governance Framework is to determine and agree the Requirements Management Framework. That is, the approach and process for managing the Business Architecture Requirements.

There are five (5) areas to consider when defining the requirements management framework:

1.1 Requirements Pyramid
1.2 Requirements Deliverables
1.3 Requirements Development Process
1.4 Requirements Format (Story Card)
1.5 Requirements Versioning, and
1.6 Requirements Storage.

### 1.1. Requirements Pyramid

There is a hierarchy relationship of priority and size to Business Architecture requirements, represented by the HOBA® (Business Architecture) Requirements Pyramid shown in *Figure 6.7* below.

In terms of priority, the top of the pyramid represents the highest priority (i.e. first to be completed) and asks the big 'strategic level' questions requested of the Organisation and Business Architecture (the *'Why are you doing this?'*), while the bottom of the pyramid represents the relative lower level priorities (i.e. to be investigated, analysed and validated once the 'higher level' requirements have first been determined), and asks the 'implementation level' questions, the *'How are we going to implement the User requirements?'*.

In terms of size, the top of the pyramid represents with the 'largest' or most important requirement, the Vision is decomposed into Themes, Themes into Features, Features into Epics, and Epics into User Stories. User Stories being the lowest (smallest, detailed) level requirements (also referred to as 'Stories').

There is a direct relationship between these requirements and the **HOBA®** 'content' framework (i.e. Reference Model, Building Block and Blueprints), which the Business Architecture is tasked to produce as the set of deliverables that make up the Business Architecture. This is discussed in the *'Requirements Deliverables'* section below.

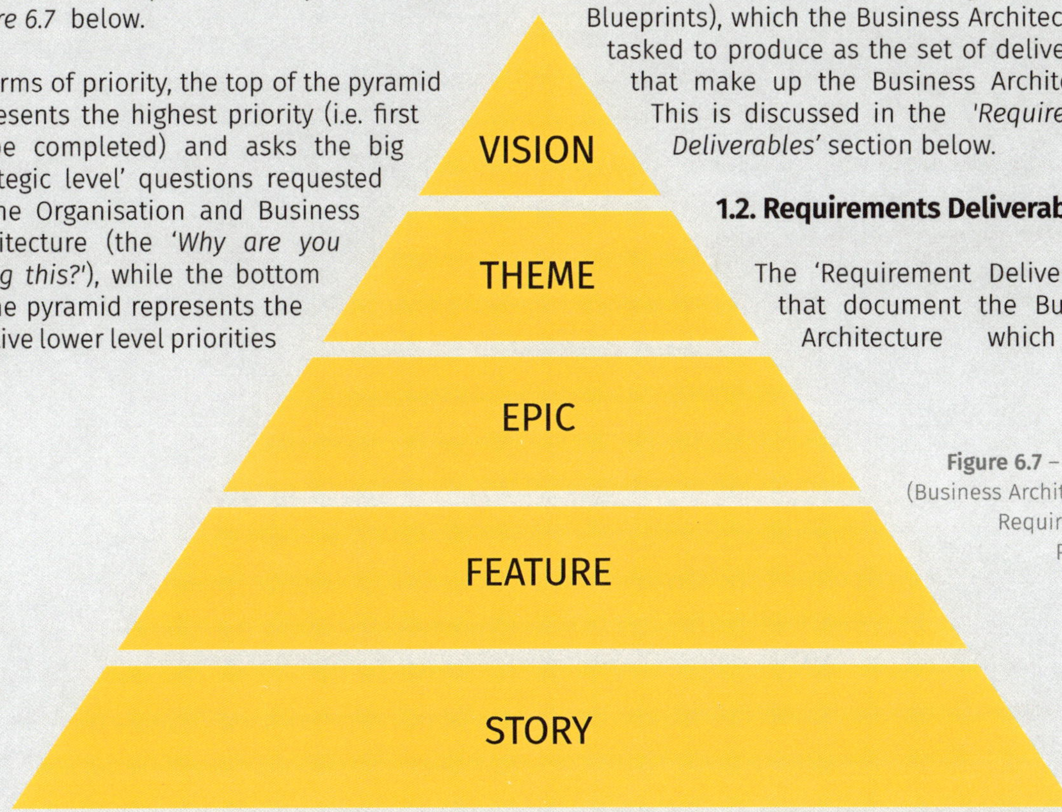


**Figure 6.7** – HOBA® (Business Architecture) Requirements Pyramid

### 1.2. Requirements Deliverables

The 'Requirement Deliverables' that document the Business Architecture which the

Business Architect is responsible to deliver, are the three (3) elements of the HOBA® Content Framework:

- **Reference Models** (e.g. Business Motivation Model, Governance Model, Current Operating Model etc.);
- **Building Blocks** (e.g. Vision Mapping, Benefits Mapping etc.) and
- **Blueprints** (e.g. SOW, the Vision etc.).

Each of these three (3) deliverables (e.g. Reference Model, Building Block, Blueprints) maps to the different level of Business Architecture Requirements as shown in *Figure 6.8* below.

The Requirement definitions are described below:

- **Vision** – The Vision for the Programme and Business Architecture, covered in the Statement of Work (SOW) Blueprint, covers the expected deliverables and ways of working between the Business Architect and Programme;
- **Theme – HOBA®** Reference Models make up the Target State Architecture that address a specific aspect of the Business and Business Architecture (e.g. Business Motivation Model, Governance Model, Benefits Reference Model etc.);
- **Feature – HOBA®** Building Block that addresses a specific business concern (e.g. Business Benefits, via the Benefit Mapping Building Block);
  - **Epic** – A discrete area of the Building Block that details a specific business perspective (e.g. Benefit Map Blueprint), and
    - **Story (or User Story)** – This is actually a *'Blueprint story'*, or the smallest chunk of a work (of a Blueprint) that can be delivered within a sprint or release. (e.g. draft version of the Benefits Map).

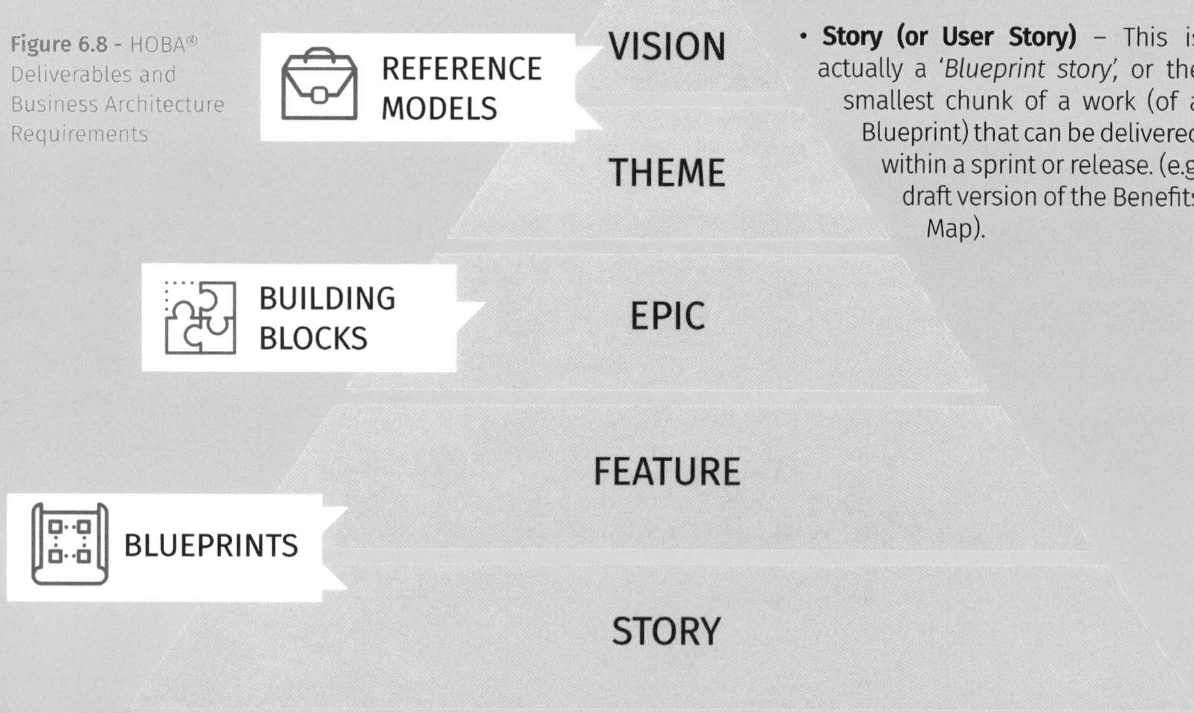


**Figure 6.8** - HOBA® Deliverables and Business Architecture Requirements

To provide the context of how the Business Architecture Requirements ('requirements') actually maps to the Requirements Pyramid, the following diagram shows how high level requirements (themes) map to (and decompose down into) features; features into epics; and epics into stories, as shown in *Figure 6.9* below.

Substituting the Business Motivation Model (BMM) Reference Model as the Theme level requirement, *Figure 6.10* (on the next page) shows how the BBM is made up of (and decomposes into) it's composite Building Blocks, Blueprints and User Stories.

This example shows the 'Theme' level requirement; the BMM broken down into its composite parts and to its 'Feature' level requirements (Business Architecture Approach; Vision Mapping, and Business Glossary), which in turn are each decomposed and broken down into their respective 'Epic' level ('Epics') requirements (SOW, VSOM and Terms & Definitions Blueprints). These Epics are then decomposed further into 'Story' level requirements – which are the smallest chunk of work that is expected to be delivered at the end of a sprint. These 'Stories' translate into a deliverable version of the Blueprint i.e. Draft SOW, Updated or Approved.

For those that aren't familiar with Agile, Scrum or the concept of continuous delivery, the main benefit of breaking the requirements down into the smallest chunks of work is:

- It's easier to estimate the size of work, expected effort and duration, which helps set expectations within the core team, Programme and key stakeholders, specifically:
  - What exactly you are working on,
  - When they can expect a finished product(s), and
  - What the product(s) looks like.

Figure 6.9 - Business Architecture Requirements Hierarchy

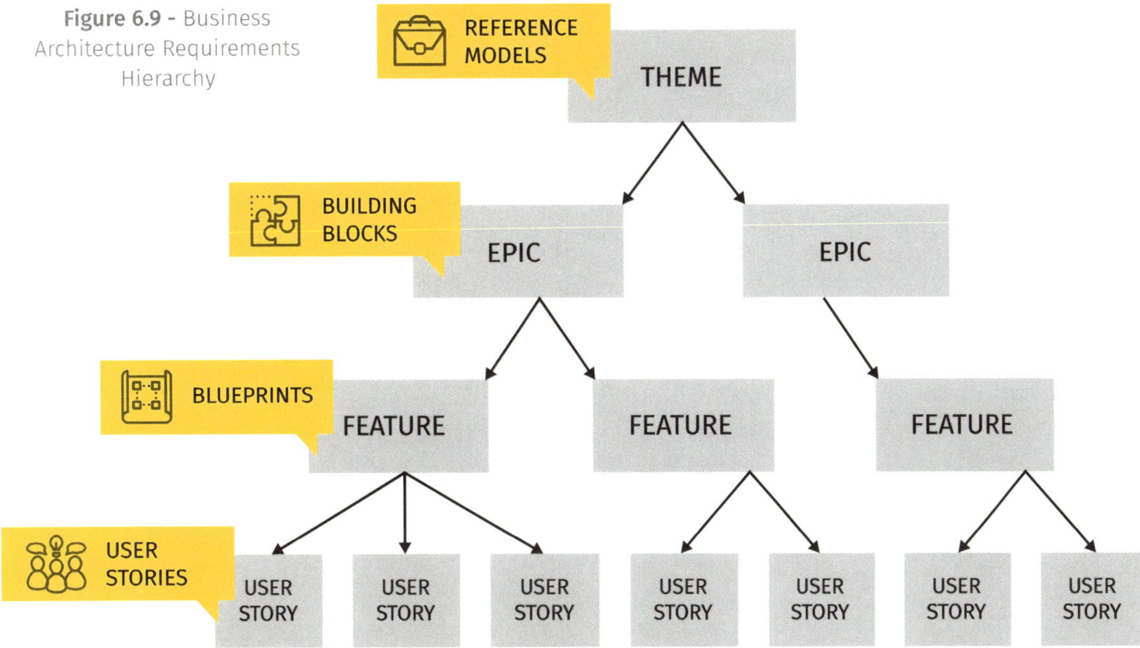


Figure 6.10 - Business Motivation Model Architecture Requirements

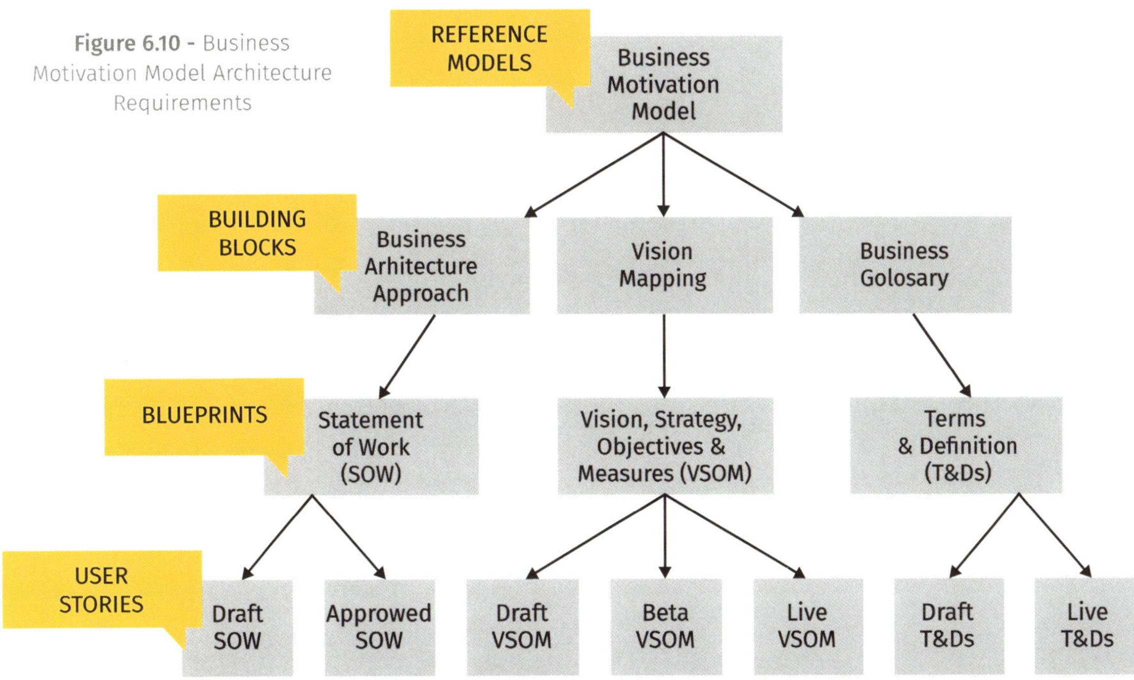


Once we have agreed the requirements-deliverables mapping, the next area we need to agree on is the process of developing the requirements. I discuss the requirement development process in the section below.

## 1.3. Requirements Development Process

The 'Requirements Development Process' is the approach and process of how requirements are developed, and owned.

**HOBA®** requirements development and management follows similar principles followed by the Scaled Agile Framework (SAFe®). SAFe® is an enterprise level lean and agile adaptive framework where the highest-level requirements (i.e. Vision and Themes) are defined at the highest level in the Organisation (i.e. the Portfolio), which then cascade down to the Programme as 'Investment Themes'. Programmes inherit these Investment Themes and derive Feature level requirements, which are then passed down to the Projects who in turn create Epics and Story level requirements to implement those high-level Investment Themes and the Vision.

The SAFe® approach is intended for large 'scale' Programmes or Portfolios of work (hence the name 'scaled').. How SAFe® works is the highest level of requirements (i.e. Vision and Themes) are defined at the highest level of the Organisation, which are cascaded down to the Programmes and Projects within the Portfolio, which these Programmes and Projects decompose into Epics and Stories. The outcome is there is complete visibility and traceability from the high-level requirements at the Portfolio level right through to the Project and Project level (as well as back up to the Portfolio). The requirements created at their respective level, are captured and managed in their respective backlogs at that level, as well as reported at that level.

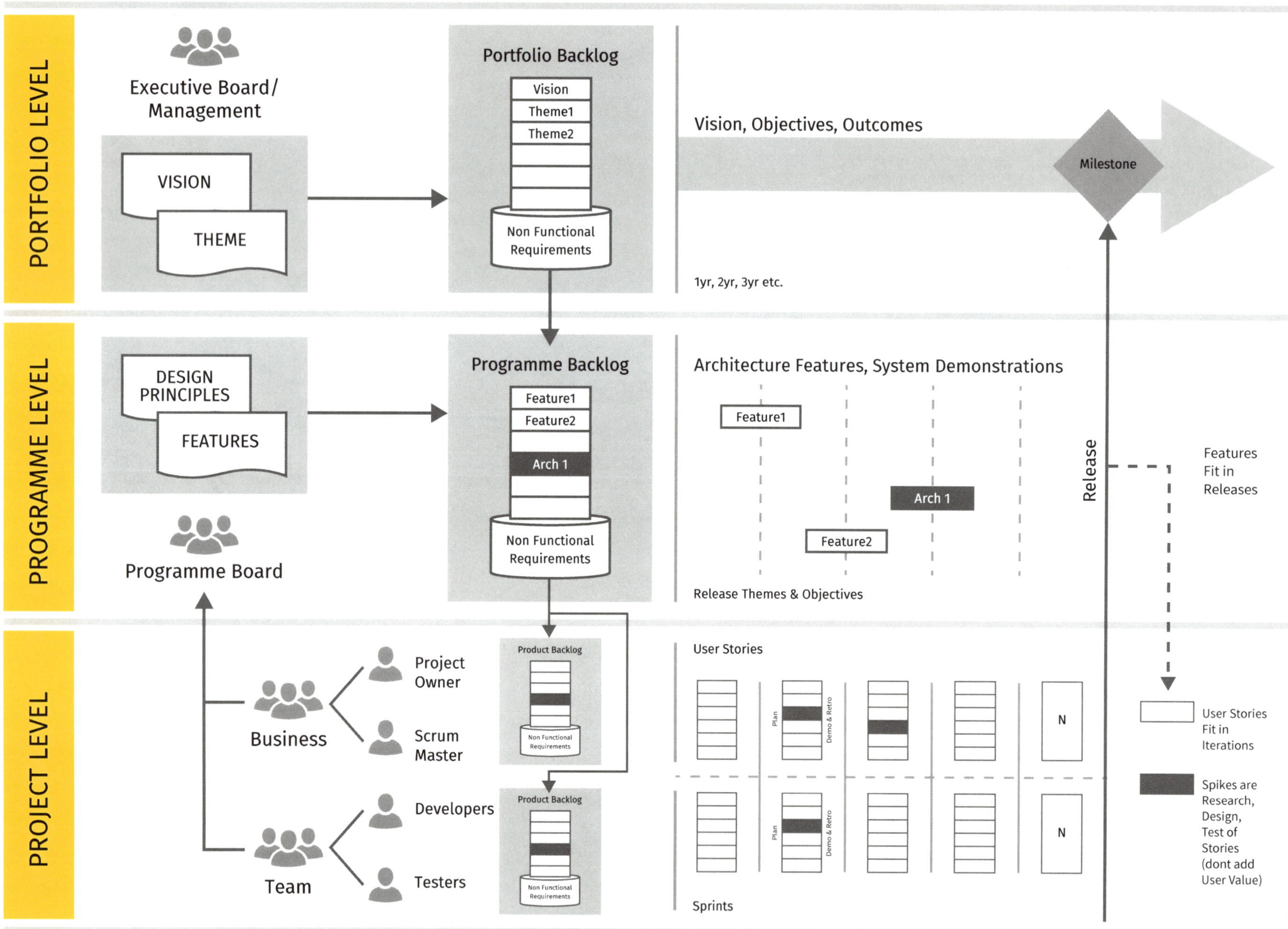


**Figure 6.11** - Simplified Scaled Agile Framework (SAFe®)[42]

[42] Adapted from Cockburn, A., et al. (2011) Agile Software Requirements 'The Agile Enterprise Big Picture'

**HOBA®** uses SAFe® in the requirement development process in the following way:

- **Programme Steering Level** - define and agree the Vision and Themes, which are cascaded down to the Internal Programme level.
- **Internal Programme level** - decomposes the Themes into Features, which are then cascaded to the Project and Scrum Teams.
- **Project & Scrum Teams** - decompose the Features in Epics and User Stories. Feedback loops are built into the process to raise changes at the appropriate level.

The above example is shown in Figure 6.12.

In the example above, HOBA® adopted SAFe® from a 'Portfolio' of work situation, to a 'Programme' of work. This is where the Programme is tasked with developing the Vision and Themes, as opposed to the Portfolio. At the Portfolio level, that is the highest-level requirements (i.e. Vision and Themes) are created at the top of the Organisation, which are developed and owned at that level, and are cascaded down and decomposed to the lower level requirements at their respective Programme and Project levels. Thus, full visibility and traceability is in place, in both directions (from top-down, and bottom-up). The roles and responsibilities of those involved in the requirements development process are discussed later in this section.

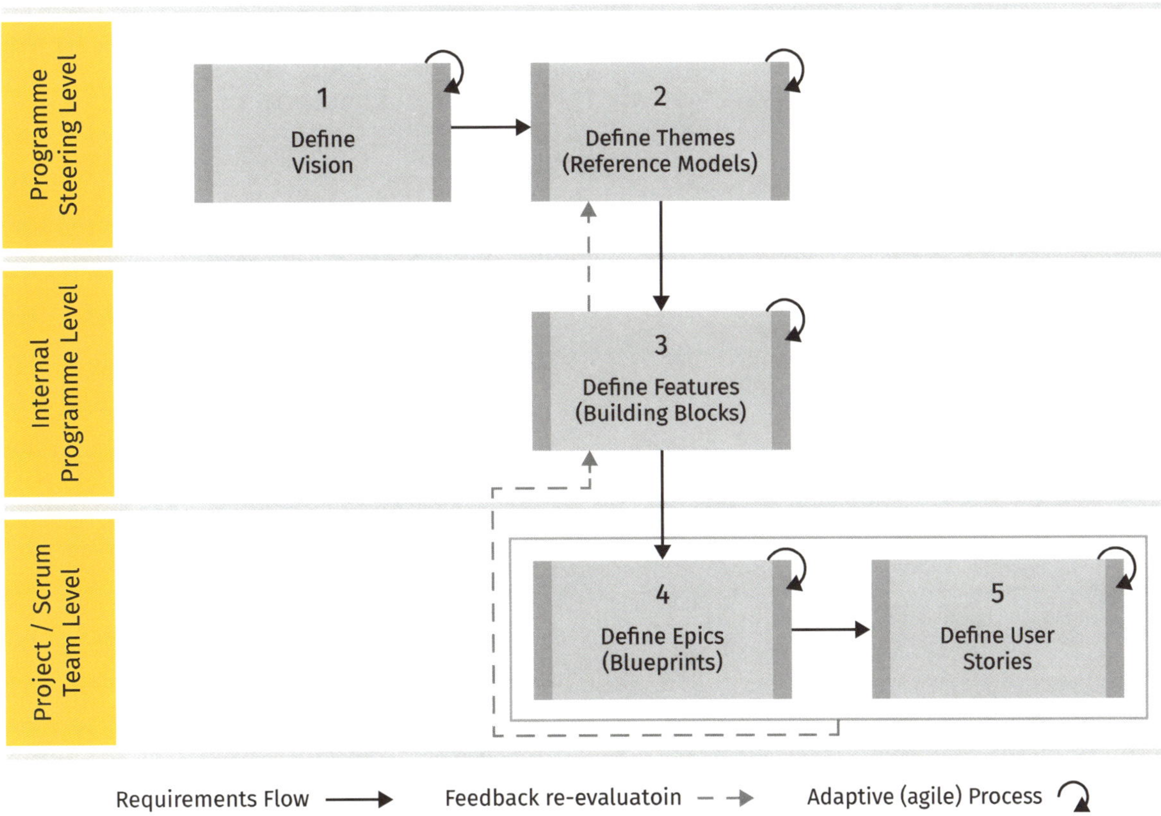


**Figure 6.12** - HOBA® Requirement Development Process

The next steps in requirements management is to understand what the requirements themselves look like (i.e. format), which is discussed in the '*Requirements Format* (Story Card)' section below.

## 1.4. Requirements Format (Story Card)

Business Architecture Requirements ('Requirements') are captured on User Story Cards. The following User Story Card ('Story Card') shows the Blueprint Story 'Draft Organisation Map' requirement.

User Story cards provide the description of the requirement that is made up of one (or two, but not more) sentences and everyday language of the End User that captures what the User does (or needs to do) in order to do their job or fulfil their role.

User Story cards are written in the format that captures the *'who', 'what'* and *'why'* of a requirement in a simple concise way, intentionally limited in detail. The intentional *'limited detail'* is enforced or constrained by both the structure of how the requirements are written, and how (and where) they are captured i.e. on a small notecard called a 'story card'.

Writing the Business Architecture requirements (or any other of the Programme requirements for that matter) on a Story card, in the prescribed format, provides a clear and concise *'agile'* approach to capture the details of the requirements compared to the document heavy *'waterfall'* approach.

Because Requirements and User stories are so concise and can be written and agreed relatively quickly with the Scrum Team and Product Owner, it is relatively faster (than Waterfall) to get the same requirement formally documented and agreed to with the same people.

The main benefits of using Story Cards and its concise format and quick decision making, are they help the Programme in the following two (2) ways:

**1. Velocity** **2. Cadence.**

In terms of *Velocity*, by getting requirements documented and the work started to deliver what is needed to complete the work under the requirement quicker (than waterfall), the Business Architect and the team can spend more time on *'doing the work'* that needs to be completed and relatively less time on the *'planning (and admin) work'* that needs to be completed, which increases the velocity (pace) that work gets picked up, started and completed.

In terms of *Cadence*, by having a framework that allows the team to get started on 'doing' and completing the work (as opposed to spending a lot of the time planning and describing what work needs to be done, which is typical with Waterfall requirements documentation), the Business Architect and the team will be able to deliver requirements more frequently, at a regular frequency or 'rhythm', which is known as '*cadence*' in Agile circles.

When putting together Business Architecture requirements and writing Story Cards, the following steps should be followed:

1. Use **HOBA®** as the starting point of the complete set of Building Blocks and Blueprints that need User Story requirements elaborated on and captured on a Story Card,
2. Work with the Scrum Team and Product Owner, and identify and agree the User Stories to be written,
3. Complete the following areas, format and details of the Story Card:

- **Story**, written in the following format:
  - I am [Role],
  - I want to be able to [perform role or function],
  - So that I can [fulfil role, complete this or next task]
- **Acceptance criteria** - the scenario situation which defines the conditions that this requirement is considered 'done', written in the format:
  - Scenario [situation where requirement is needed]
  - Given, When, Then, And [to provide context of how and why it is needed]
- **Owner** [who is responsible for delivery, and managing changes to the User Story]
- **Size** [relative size of the story, measured in points, agreed with the Scrum Team]
- **Priority** [ranked by business value, approved by the Product Owner]

4. **For the Sizing** – agree the relative 'story

| User Story: Draft Organisation Map | Owner: HG |
|---|---|
| Story | **I am a** Product Owner<br>**I want to** be able to see the draft version of the Organisation Map<br>**So I can** confirm the scope of impacted business units and divisions for our programme |
| Acceptance Criteria | **Scenario:** The programme has just kicked off and the scope of the impacted organisation needs to be verified and validated<br>**Given:** There is some uncertainty of the actual scope of the programme<br>**When:** deciding on who is impacted by the changes of this programme<br>**Then:** I will be able to use this blueprint to start conversations with our key stakeholders to confirm the identified in scope (and out of scope) areas are correct<br>**And:** I will use this view to inform the in-scope impacted stakeholders within the in-scope business units and division. |
| Priority 1 | Points 8 |

**Figure 6.13 -** Sample User Story Card[43]

[43] Adapted from Cohen, M., (2004) User Stories Applied – For Agile Software Development

point' size against, and relative to, other stories that could be (or are expected to be) completed in a single sprint. For example:

- If you agree it takes 1-week (5 business days) to complete a draft Organisation Map – and other stories of relatively the same size have been scored 10 points by the Scrum Team, then your Story will also be 10 points too. This would factor in obtaining and reviewing an existing Programme and business documentation/artefacts, drafting a first version for discussion, making contact, arranging and holding meetings with the necessary stakeholders (to provide input and feedback), and allowing enough time to make updates and be ready to present back to the Product Owner by the end of sprint as a *'draft'*.

5. **For the Priority** – working again with the Scrum Team and Product Owner, agree the priorities based on the business value that is described by the Acceptance Criteria. The Acceptance Criteria not only describes the definition of 'done' (the conditions needed to be achieved in order to say the requirement or story is complete and has been delivered), but also describes *'why'* it is needed and *'what'* purpose it serves.

6. **Kanban Boards** – Kanban Story Boards[44] , are a means of providing visibility and tracking User Stories and are arranged in terms of *'Not Doing'*, *'Doing'* and *'Done'*. Once the story is written and agreed, the Story Card is placed on the Kanban Board for *physical* visibility, and recorded on the Product Backlog for *online* visibility, tracking and monitoring. An example of a Kanban Story Board is shown in *Figure 6.14*.

7. **Product Backlogs** - are the repository of all the Requirements across the Programme. All Requirements entered and recorded on the Backlog from that point on are referred to as an 'item' in the product backlog, otherwise known as a *'Product Backlog Item' or 'PBI'*.

8. **Moving cards** – User Story cards are pulled through the process across the Kanban board, moving left to right from the *'To Do'*, *'Doing'* and finally *'Done'* columns when appropriate. The following rules for pulling cards should be followed:

- Cards should only move from *'To Do' to 'Doing'* when the team has collectively agreed (that is the Scrum Master, Product Owner and Scrum Team) that they have capacity to accept the card into *'Doing'*.
- Cards should only be moved from *'Doing' to 'Done'* under the instruction or guidance of the Scrum Master (who effectively owns the board), as and when the Acceptance Criteria is met, and work is agreed by the Product Owner as *'Done'*.

9. **Reporting** – at project meetings and ceremonies, Team members report status, progress and bottlenecks and speak directly to each 'in progress' card:

- **Daily Scrums** – Requirement status, progress and bottleneck updates are reported on a daily basis at the morning *'Daily Scrums'*, which are also called Stand-ups, as they are literally done *'standing up'*, where all participants must 'stand up' (i.e. no sitting allowed). It is aimed at keeping the meetings intentionally short, which is discussed in the *'Meetings and Ceremonies'* section below).
- **Sprint Planning,** Sprint Review and Sprint Retrospectives meetings are other meetings that the team plan the work ahead, show and tell work completed for that sprint, and discover and agree the lessons learned; what worked well (keep doing), what didn't work well (stop doing), and what needs to be done (start doing) are all discussed..

In addition to providing updates and sharing of information, all project meetings and ceremonies are intended to provide the *'visibility'* and *'transparency'* of the *process* but also the 'progress' of the developing Business Architecture. This visibility and transparency is also provided

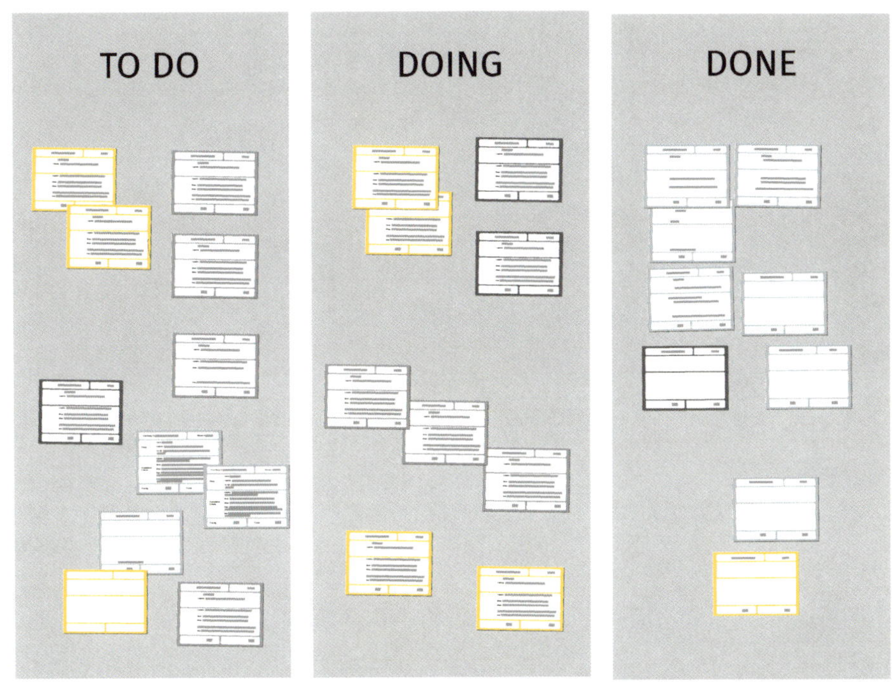


**Figure 6.14 -** Example Kanban board

[43] Adapted from Cohen, M., (2004) User Stories Applied – For Agile Software Development

through the continually delivering iterations of the Business Architecture as it develops incrementally over time, and most importantly ensures the two-way alignment from (and between) the Business Architecture, Technology Architecture, Programme and Organisation.

As creating, moving and completing User Stories (and requirements) are done in and as part of the Scrum Team, it is important that the 'User' who is the subject of the Story Cards is involved in the process. For Business Architecture, that User is the Product Owner who represents the Business or Business Representatives. However, it can and will also include members of the wider Programme, including Technology Architects. Irrespective of the User, it is important that all User Stories always add value, and trace back to the Vision. That is, you only want to be creating requirements and deliverables that add-value, and not be drawn into the need, desire or habit to be creating requirements for *'requirements sake'*. The intentional User Story format (e.g. I am [Role], I want to be able to [perform role or function], So that I can [fulfil role, complete this or next task]) helps ensure Stories are focused, add-value, and can be easily traced back to the Vision.

The added benefit of the way Stories and Story Cards are structured, created and managed, reported and moved through the Kanban board at regular meetings and intervals, is it addresses two (2) of the Business Architecture Challenge questions asked of the Business Architecture, and Business Architect:

- 'What does the Value (of Business Architecture) look like?',
- 'When can I see it (the value)?'

The 'What does the value look like?' question is addressed and described by the Story and Acceptance Criteria sections of the Story Card:

- Story - Who needs it and Why? and
- Acceptance Criteria - When they get it, what are they going to do with it? as shown previously in the example Story Card in *Figure 6.13*.

The 'When will I see it?' question is addressed partly by the Story Card itself, and through the life of the Story Card as it and the Blueprint Story Card it relates to is created and managed as the work is completed and the Story Card is moved across the Kanban board from *'to do'*, through *'doing'* and finally to *'done'*.

In terms of sizing, Business Architecture stories are decomposed down to manageable chunks of work that can be delivered within the respective sprint cycle, effectively becoming a *'User Story size'*. The objective with sizing is to break down large or big stories into manageable chucks of information and remove the variability and complexity. Smaller stories are easier and more accurate to estimate and have a higher level of confidence they will (and can) be completed to the accepted level of quality and completeness within a sprint.

There are two main methods to sizing used to measure the effort required to complete a story – *'t-shirt size'* (small, medium, large) or *'Story points'*. T-shirt sizing is an effective method to quickly make size estimates for work of the *'relatively'* the same size. Story points ('points') based sizing is more detailed where points based on a Fibonacci sequence (where every number after the first two is the sum of the two preceding ones) of 1, 2, 3, 5, 8, 13, and 21. By providing more metrics therefore become arguably more accurate, and is the method which **HOBA®** uses, as this is are more suitable for our purposes, especially reporting, tracking and monitoring the rate work is completed.

The objective with sizing is to establish a relative size of one story when compared to another. For example, the User Story *'define and approve Organisation mapping'* is the outcome and Blueprint the Business Architect would be expected to deliver by the end of a sprint, however it would be too large to complete in a 2-week sprint, for example. A story of this size, could be deemed 21-points, requiring more than a sprint cycle (e.g. 2 weeks) to not just draft, but also finalise it, considering the size of the Organisation, it's multiple locations (that are in scope for the Programme), and arranging and holding the necessary meetings with the different Stakeholders. It's not impossible, but it would be a tough ask to complete this task any sooner.

To set ourselves up for success, a better approach is to break the story (the 'define and approve Organisation mapping') into manageable chunks of work (stories) that could be delivered within a single sprint. Smaller chucks could then be completed within a single (and separate) sprint that shows the status (explained in '1.5.1 Status' below), as revealed in the example below:

- Draft Organisation Map [ALPHA v0.1];
- Draft Organisation Map [BETA v0.2], and
- Approve Organisation Map [LIVE v1.0].

These different versions of the Blueprint would become separate User Stories, written on separate Story Cards, form part of the Product Backlog, placed on the Kanban board under the applicable 'status' (*'To do', 'Doing' or 'Done'*) column, and 'pulled' through the process in, as, and when ready.

### 1.5. Requirements Versioning

There are four (4) areas to consider when defining how the requirements are versioned and communicated which are:

1.5.1 Status
1.5.2 Versioning
1.5.3 Storage
1.5.4 Managing Changes

We will discuss each of these areas in the sections below.

### 1.5.1 Status

To signal to the Business and Programme that the issued requirements and deliverables are in different and various status and levels of completeness as the Business Architecture develops overtime, the requirements and Blueprints need to follow an agreed 'status', which follows that same naming (and similar definitions) of the phases of the Programme. These phases are shown below:

- **Discovery** – phase of the project; where the user needs are researched, and identified.
- **Alpha** – phase of the project; where a core service or solution is built to meet the main user needs
- **Beta** – phase of the project; where the solution is in use and in the process of being improved, through testing within the Programme or in the public domain.
- **Live** – phase of a project; where the service is public and works well, and continually improved to meet user needs.

The Requirement status (i.e. discovery, alpha, beta and live), should match and be based on Programme phase (i.e. discovery, alpha, beta and live). This is to clearly signal the status and level of completeness of the Requirement, and where the final solution is. This status label is displayed both on the requirement and deliverable itself (i.e. in the file), as well as on the file name itself.

Table 6.4 shows an example of the file name format that appears on both the requirement and deliverable, as well as the file name itself.

Table 6.5 shows an example of the file name for the requirement and deliverable (e.g. Organisation Map Blueprint).

The status labels *'discovery, alpha, beta, live'* is used in preference to the commonly used *'draft'* status label. The reason for this, is that the *'draft'* status is often taken as (or represents) an *'unfinished state'*. The problem is everything remains *'unfinished'* until it is signed off or approved. 'Draft'

File Naming Convention Format

Table 6.4

| File Naming Convention Format |
|---|
| <Requirement / Deliverable name><Status><YYYY-MM-DD><Version> |

Example File Naming Convention Format

Table 6.5

| Sample File Naming Convention Format |
|---|
| Organisation Map BETA 2015-12-25 v0.2 |

doesn't offer or provide any insight into how much work has gone into the requirement at that point in time, or how much work is left remaining.

Using and aligning the Programme phases (e.g. discover, alpha, beta, live) as status labels provide a better signal of the amount of work that have gone into the requirement at that time, the likelihood of it changing, and the degree to which it may change in the near future.

The general *'rule of thumb'* for phase status labels is as follows:

- **Discovery** – signal initial thinking, high level objectives and elements only.
- **Alpha** – signals thinking has progressed, with thoughts recorded on paper, ready for wider discussion;
- **Beta** – signals *'we've firmed up our thinking and come to a consensus, its ready to be vigourously assessed and constructively criticized'*; and
- **Live** – signals *'we're good to go'*, this is our best version to date, containing less flaws, errors, or inaccuracies as possible and for all intents and purposes, meets the needs of the majority of the key stakeholders at that point in time.

### 1.5.2 Requirements Versioning

*Versioning* is about version control. Control and management of multiple versions of the same document. Version control enables us to tell one version of a document from another, and is critical when requirements and deliverables have been created and undergo a lot of revision (as they will on most Programmes, particularly with a Programme that has external stakeholders or stakeholders that aren't physically located in the same location).

Version is often an overlooked (and unaddressed) issue, where often different versions of the same document are often called the same thing, or where two authors work on two different versions of what they think are the same document, but inadvertently end up creating more work and then losing time having to collate changes into a single usable document.

Requirement and deliverable versions are controlled by an incrementally increasing '0.1' decimal place (1dp) version numbering notation. That is:

- 0.1, 0.2, 0.3 etc. - Any 'draft' version, in any status (i.e. discovery, alpha etc.)
- 1.0, 2.0, 3.0 etc. – First and subsequent Approved versions (using 1 significant figure)
- 1.1, 1.2; 2.1, 2.2; 3.1 ,3.2 etc. - Subsequent reversions after a version has been Approved

Using the example from Table 6.5 shown previously, for the now 'approved' version in the Programme Live stage, the file name of the Organisation Map Blueprint will appear as follows.

Sample File Naming Convention Format

Table 6.6

| Sample File Naming Convention Format |
|---|
| Organisation Map LIVE 2016-04-01 v1.0 |

**Setting up the versioning (and governance framework for that matter) is all about the 5Ps being 'Prior Preparation Presents Poor Performance'. The effort you spend here setting up the requirements management process (and governance framework), will save you time, money (mainly in labour costs), and unnecessary frustration later.**

### 1.5.3 Requirements Storage

Requirements and deliverables are stored in *Product Backlogs* ('Backlogs'). Backlogs are the repository and home for all the requirements, which take the form of a system, spreadsheet, file cabinet or Kanban wall. Requirements, once stored in the backlogs, become *Product Backlog Items* (PBI), and are referred to at that point as PBI's, or a PBI.

There are also different Backlogs for the different types of requirements (i.e. Theme, Feature, Epic, User Story), to reflect the type of requirements they hold, and the level of the Organisation that is managing them.

The following table summarises where the different Business Architecture requirements (Vision, Themes, Features, Epics and User Stories) are stored and managed.

Business Architecture Requirement Backlog List

Table 6.7

| The following Business Architecture Requirement... | Equates to Architecture Deliverable | Is a PBI is the following Backlog |
|---|---|---|
| Vision* | The Vision (Vision, Strategy, Objectives and Measures (VSOM) Blueprint) | Programme Backlog |
| Theme* | Reference Model (Business Motivation Model, overnance Model etc.) | Programme Backlog |
| Feature | Building Block (Benefits Mapping, Capability Mapping etc.) | Programme Backlog |
| Epic | Blueprint (Benefits Map, Capability Map etc.) | Project Backlog |
| User Story | Blueprint task (Draft Benefits Map, Approved Benefits Map etc.) | Sprint Backlog |

(*) Note - On a typical Programme, which is part of a Portfolio (of work), the Vision and Themes form part of a larger Portfolio of work. The process for managing requirements from the Portfolio level down (was discussed previously and shown in Figure 6.12) is as follows:

- The Portfolio will (or should) have defined and delegated requirements from the Portfolio to the Programme(s) – Vision and Theme level requirements;
- The Portfolio level requirements (the Vision and Themes) are defined at (and by) the Portfolio Board as shown and discussed earlier in Figure 6.12, and then
- The Portfolio Level 'Vision' and 'Themes' level requirements, are cascaded down and are inherited by the Programme(s) within the Portfolio.

### 1.5.4 Managing Changes

The last area in defining how requirements are versioned and communicated, is the process of managing changes to the requirements. As the different types of requirements are stored and reported at different levels (i.e. Portfolio, Programme etc.), changes to those requirements (i.e. additions, deletions etc.) need to be taken to their respective levels for approval.

Table 6.8 summarises where the different level and type of requirements are taken to approve changes.

**Approval to Managing Business Architecture Requirement Tables**

**Table 6.8**

| Business Architecture Requirement | Organisation Level | Description | Captured In | Approval of Changes |
|---|---|---|---|---|
| Vision (for the Organisation) | Portfolio Level | The Vision for the Organisation, or the Vision the Organisation has for the Programme. | Vision, Strategies, Objectives and Measures (VSOM) Map, in Portfolio Backlog. | Changes to the requirement, priority or delivery needs sign off from the Portfolio Board. |
| Vision (for the Business Architecture) | Portfolio Level | The Vision for the Business Architecture, expected deliverables and ways of working between the Business Architect and Programme. | Statement of Work (SOW), in Portfolio Backlog. | As above |
| Theme (Reference Models) | Portfolio Level | HOBA® Reference Models making up the Target State Architecture, addressing & delivering specific aspects of business and Business Architecture (e.g. Benefits Model). | Portfolio Backlog | As above |
| Feature (Building Blocks) | Programme Level | Group of components of HOBA® Reference Models that address a specific business concern (e.g. Benefit Mapping). | Programme Backlog | The addition or removal of Building Blocks from scope requires Programme Board approval. |
| Epic (Blueprints) | Project Level | Discrete area of the Building Block that details a specific business concern (e.g. Benefit Map). | Project Backlog | Changes to Blueprints and stories can be managed within Scrum Team agreed with the Product Owner. |
| User Story (Blueprint Story) | Project Level | Smallest chunk of a Blueprint that can be delivered within a sprint or release. | Sprint Backlog | As above |

**In practice, all these requirements – now stored on (and in) the respective backlogs, will actually be stored within one central backlog, and labelled accordingly (i.e. Portfolio, Programme, Project, Sprint Backlog) and reported at their respective levels.**

For the full list of Business Architecture requirements, refer to *Appendix D – Reference Models, Building Blocks and Blueprints.*

## 2. Governance Structure

The Governance Structure should (and does) reflect the Agile nature of the requirement development process, simple. The governance structure to manage decisions on both the Programme, and the Business Architecture, is based on an equally simple 3-tier model, as shown in *Figure 6.15* below.

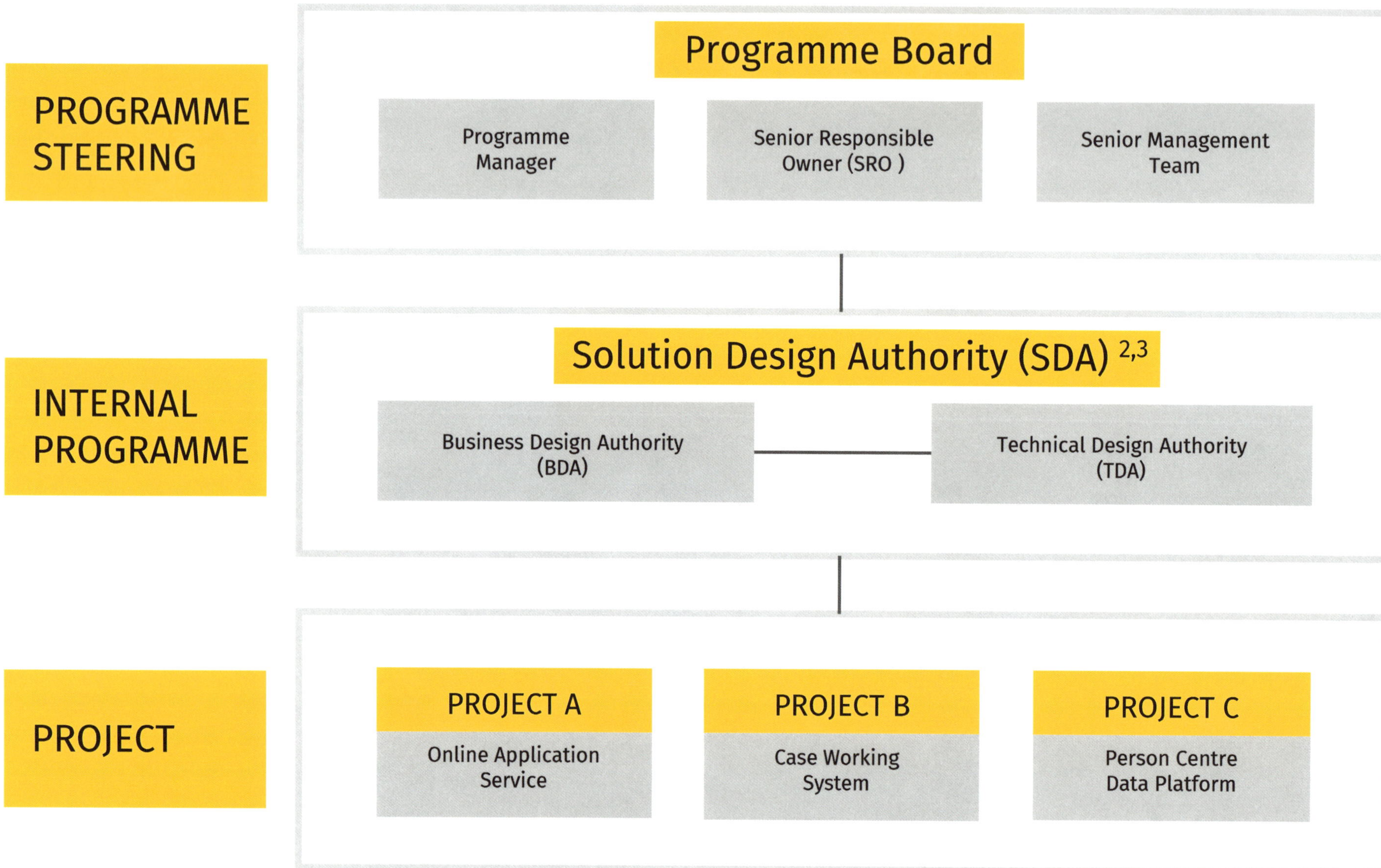


**Figure 6.15** - Example 3-Tier Programme Governance Structure

Notes:

1. The 'Portfolio' is represented at this level (Programme Steering) via the SRO, Programme Manager and Senior Management Team. These members would also be sitting on Portfolio level boards to feed in/out Portfolio level design requirements.
2. Represented on this level (internal Programme) are the Business Design and Technical Design Authorities and representatives that this group (the joint Solution Design Authority) consults with to share and feed in/out Programme level design requirements.
3. Where the role of the Business Architect is a more central strategic/Organisation facing role (as opposed to Programme facing role), there would be a separate and different governance structure for a 'central strategy' or 'strategic management office' at the Portfolio level.

The 3-tiers are divided between the following:

- **'Programme steering' decisions** are held and made at the top with the Programme Board,
- **'Design' decisions**, which are made in (and across) the Programme with the Solution Design Board (SDA), made up of the Business Design Authority (BDA), and Technical Design Authority (TDA), and
- **'Implementation and delivery' decisions,** which are made in (and on) the projects at the Project Level.

The Business Architect is part of the Business Design Authority (BDA), which makes (and takes) decisions at the Programme level, and considers the architectural requirements for the projects within the Programme while taking into account the needs of the consumers of the solutions the Programme delivers.

Business and Technical Architecture are intentionally separated into their own 'authorities' but come together to form a single Solution Design Authority (SDA). In this structure, Business design decisions are taken to, and discussed in the BDA, before being taken to the Technical Design Authority (TDA). The role of the SDA therefore is to ratify and align each other's designs. Decisions from this level are taken to the Programme Board for approval, ensuring alignment across the Portfolio (as well as within the Programme).

Table 6.9 shows the members of the Governance boards, authorities and teams from the Governance Structure.

**Governance Boards & Bodies**

**Table 6.9**

| Level | Board/ Authority/ Team | Core Members |
|---|---|---|
| Programme Steering | Programme Board | • Organisation Senior ManagementOfficers<br>• Senior Responsible Officer (Sponsor)<br>• Programme Director |
| Internal Programme | Solution Design Authority (SDA) | • Business Design Authority (BDA) Members<br>• Technical Design Authority (TDA) Members |
| | Business Design Authority (BDA) | • Product Owner(s)<br>• Business Architecture<br>• Business Change |
| | Technical Design Authority (TDA) | • Technical Architecture<br>• Data Architecture<br>• Application Architecture<br>• Security Architecture |
| Project Level | Project/Scrum Team(s) | • Project Manager<br>• Scrum Master<br>• Product Owner<br>• Developer(s)<br>• Test Manager<br>• Tester(s)<br>• Business Analyst(s) |

## 3. Governance Authorities

Table 6.10 (on the next page) shows the roles and responsibilities of the above Governance Board and Bodies ('Governance Authorities'), and members in the requirements management process.

## 4. Review and Approval Process

The review and approval of the Business Architecture requirements follows a similar Agile approach, as discussed in *Scaled Agile Framework* (SAFe®) section earlier. The review and approval of the different level of architecture requirements are reviewed, approved and reported at different levels of the Programme, depending on the type of Business Architecture requirement.

Table 6.10

| Level | Board/ Authority/ Team | Responsibilities |
|---|---|---|
| Programme Steering | Programme Board | • Defines Vision<br>• Approves Theme Requirements (Reference Models)<br>• Responsible for successful delivery of the Programme |
| Internal Programme | Solution Design Authority (SDA) | • Approves Feature Requirements (Building Blocks)<br>• Approves Architecture (Business &Technical)<br>• Approves the Release features and release dates |
| | Business Design Authority (BDA) | • Approves Business Architecture design |
| | Business Architect | • Define Business Architecture Deliverables<br>• Assure alignment with other Architectures and Programmes |
| | Business Change Lead | • Stakeholder Management & Communication<br>• Change Analysis & Change Management<br>• Training<br>• Business Readiness & Deployment |
| | Technical Design Authority (TDA) | • Approves Technical Architecture Design |
| | Technical Architect | • Defines Technical Architecture Design |
| | Data Architect | • Defines Data Architecture Design |
| | Application Architect | • Defines Application Architecture Design |
| | Security Architect | • Defines Security Architecture Design |
| Project Level | Scrum Team | • Deliver prioritised and committed User Stories |
| | Product Owner | • Owns the Product Backlog<br>• Approves the sign-off of User Stories<br>• Approves User Story Acceptance Criteria<br>• Prioritises User Stories (and Sprint Backlog)<br>• Contributes in Sprint Planning meeting(s)<br>• Approves delivery of User Stories<br>• Contributes to Release Planning |

Table 6.10

| Level | Board/ Authority/ Team | Responsibilities |
|---|---|---|
| Project Level | Scrum Master | • Co-ordinates and facilitates for the Scrum Team (Product Owner, Developers and Testers)<br>• Removes obstacles<br>• Ensures Scrum process |
| | Developer | • Create and implement code<br>• Fix bugs |
| | Test Manager | • Co-ordinate test approach and testing activities including regression testing, across the Programme. |
| | Test Manager | • Create Test Cases & test activities<br>• Create Test Scenarios<br>• Executive testing activities |
| | Business Analyst | • Consulted for User Story definition |

The SIPOC Table 6.10 (on the next page) summarises the activities that happen in (and through) each step of the Business Architecture requirements development process – identifying Who is responsible for the activity *(Supplier)*, What is required to complete the step *(Input)*; What is the outcome *(Output)*, and Who is the recipient *(Customer)*.

Note – For completeness, the following are included in the process summary on the following page:

1. **Non-Functional Requirements** - although Non-Functional Requirements (NFRs) are not 'Business Architecture' outcomes or deliverables. NFRs (e.g. Service Level Requirements, Performance & Capacity Requirements, Scalability, Operability Requirements etc.) are developed at the Feature level, and as the Business Architecture needs to support the NFRs (and vice versa), the Business Architect will still need to have visibility of them.
2. **Release Manager** - they are the customer of the 'non-Business Architecture' requirements (i.e. technical, and technical architecture requirements), and are responsible for the co-ordination of releasing those requirements into a production/live environment. The Business Architects role at this step is to oversee the implementation of those requirements that they maintain aligned to the design of the Business Architecture.

In practise, the Vision statement provided from the Programme Board is only high-level (e.g. 'Our vision is to be the market leader by 2020') and nothing more. It's therefore the role of the Programme Board to craft a complete 'Vision statement', which includes the breakdown into its decomposed parts: the Business Strategy, Objectives and (success) Measures. As the Business Architect, our role here is to lead this activity, as the 'Vision statement' is part of 'the Vision, Strategy, Objectives and Measures (VSOM)' Blueprint, which needs to be decomposed into its composite parts – Business Strategy, Objectives and Measures that all requirements in (and on) the Programme will map, trace and align to.

Business Architecture Requirements Development Process (SIPOC) Summary

Table 6.11

| # | Step | (S)upplier | (I)nput | (P)rocess | (O)utput | (C)ustomer |
|---|---|---|---|---|---|---|
| 1 | Define Vision | Programme Board (Programme Steering Level) | Organisation Goals | Review & Agree Vision | Vision Statement containing:<br>· Vision<br>· Strategy<br>· Objectives<br>· Measures/ Measures Indicators | Solution Design Board (Business Design Authority (BDA) & Technical Design Authority (TDA)) |
| 2 | Define Themes | Programme Board (Programme Steering Level) | Vision Statement | Define Themes | Themes (Approved) | |
| 3 | Define Features | Solution Design (BDA & TDA) (Internal Programme Level) | Themes (Approved) | Define & approve:<br>· Features<br>· NFRs[1] | · Features (Approved)<br>· NFRs (Approved | Scrum Team (Project Level) |
| 4 | Define Epics | Scrum Team (Project Level) | · Features (Approved)<br>· NFRs (Approved) | Define & approve:<br>· Epics | · Epics (Approved)<br>· NFRs (Approved | Scrum Team (Project Level) |
| 5 | Define User Stories | | · Epics (Approved)<br>· NFRs (Approved) | Define, develop & test User Stories | User Stories (Done) | Release Manager[2] |

**5. Stakeholder (Influence/Impact) Matrix**

In order for your requirements and Business Architecture to get successfully supported, approved and delivered, they need to be supported by the various stakeholders, and to do that, those stakeholders need to be assured that their interests and concerns are addressed.

The Stakeholder (Influence/Impact) Matrix provides a mechanism to identify and categorise the Stakeholders by their ability to promote, block or defend the changes brought about by the Business Architecture requirements.

The different quadrants and typical stakeholders of the matrix are as follows:

- **Key Players** (High Interest/High Power) – These are the 'promoters' of the Programme, and Business Architecture. Their requirements must be met, and managed closely. These include Programme management, Business Architecture Project Manager, PMO etc.
- **Keep Satisfied** (Low Interest/High power) – these are the 'latents'. They have a lot of power to influence the success of the Programme, but have a lower level of interest in the Programme. These would include Legal, Finance etc., including the Sponsor.

- **Keep Informed** (High Interest/Low Power) – These are the 'defenders', who either change happens to, or they are supporting the change. These include operations staff, Implementation staff (i.e. training manager) etc.
- **Monitor** (Low Interest/Low Power) – These are the 'bystander' stakeholders that change will 'happen' too. They have low power, but can kick up a stink. No one likes change 'happening to them', they (like everyone) want, and need to be 'part of the change', so monitor them and keep them informed. These stakeholders also include outsourced staff (i.e. Testers) etc.

Figures below show how the Stakeholder Matrix looks for our case study example, under their different quadrants, and management strategy (i.e. keep satisfied, manage closely etc.).

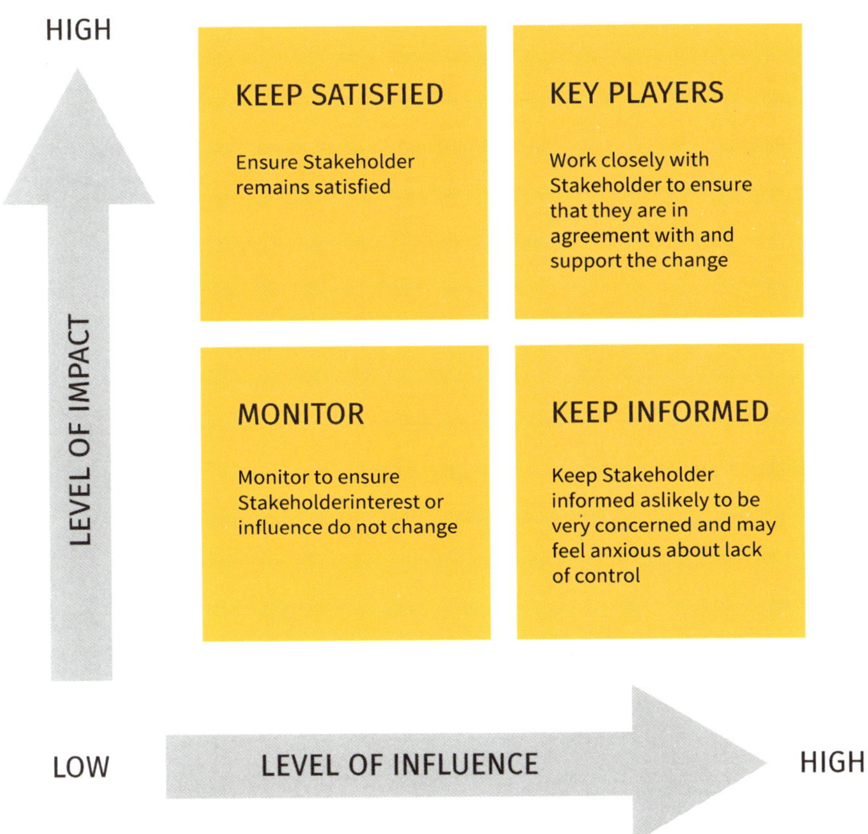


**Figure 6.16** – Stakeholder (Influence/Impact) Matrix[46]

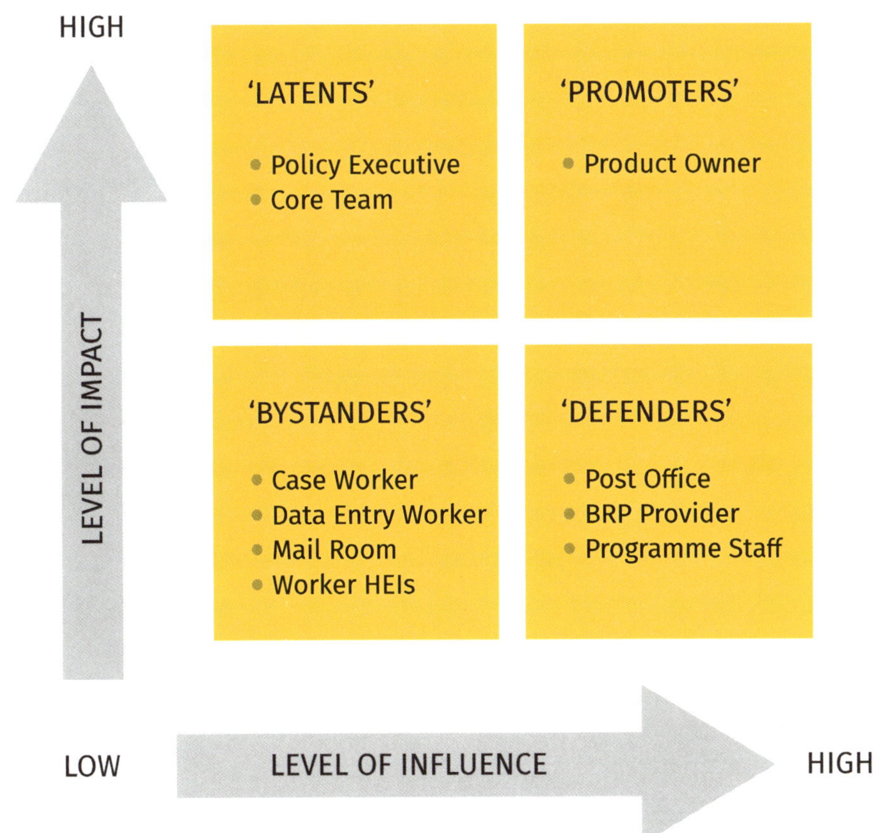


**Figure 6.17** – Sample Stakeholder Matrix[47]

---

[46] Mitchell, B. et al., Toward a Theory of Stakeholder Identification and Salience: Defining the Principle of Who and What Really Counts - The Academy of Management Review Vol. 22, No. 4 (Oct. 1997)

[47] Adapted from Mitchell, B. et al., Toward a Theory of Stakeholder Identification and Salience: Defining the Principle of Who and What Really Counts - The Academy of Management Review Vol. 22, No. 4 (Oct. 1997)

The objective of the Stakeholder Matrix is to identify the strategies necessary to manage these key stakeholders so that their needs are met, while balancing the needs of all the other interested and impacted stakeholders on the Programme.

The following Stakeholder Influence/Impact Table contains the communication needs to address their issues and concerns, using the case study example.

There are numerous strategies for managing and keeping stakeholders satisfied (over and above what is recommended in the table above), even for moving them from one quadrant to another. While that level of stakeholder management is important and necessary for the successful delivery of your remit, and the Programme, that level of stakeholder management, as mentioned in the *'Assumptions'* section is outside the scope of this book.

What is important with this activity of identifying and assessing the needs and concerns of your stakeholders however, is that these needs and concerns are actually addressed and are actively managed from the beginning to the end of the Programme.

**Sample Stakeholder Influence/Impact Table**

**Table 6.12**

| Stakeholder Name / Group | Impact | Influence | Classification | Issues/Concerns | Communication Plan/ Tactics |
|---|---|---|---|---|---|
| Product Owner | High | High | Manage Closely | Business Needs | Daily status report email<br>Weekly Progress Report |
| Post Office | Low | High | Keep Informed | Disruption to service/ loss of business | Weekly Progress Report |
| BRP Provider | Low | High | Keep Informed | Disruption to service/ loss of business | Weekly Progress Report |
| Policy | High | Low | Keep Satisfied | Legislation/non- compliance | Weekly face to face meeting |
| Core Team | High | Low | Keep Satisfied | Alignment/ Requirements | Daily status report email<br>Weekly Progress Report |
| Case Worker | Low | Low | Monitor | Automation/ time saving potential | Weekly Progress Report |
| Data Entry Operator | Low | Low | Monitor | Automation/ time saving potential | Weekly Progress Report |
| Mail Room | Low | Low | Monitor | Automation/ time saving potential | Weekly Progress Report |
| Higher Education Institute (HEI) | Low | Low | Monitor | Disruption to service/ loss of business | Weekly Progress Report |

## 6. Business Architecture Requirements RACI

The Business Architecture Requirements Responsible, Accountable, Consulted and Informed (RACI), captures the roles and responsibilities of the key stakeholders in defining and agreeing the different types and levels of Business Architecture requirements.

An example RACI – showing who is (and needs) to be involved in the development and sign off of the different Business Architecture requirements is shown in Table 6.13.

Note:

1. As mentioned earlier, if the Portfolio Board has defined the Vision for your Programme, your Programme will inherit that already *'agreed'* Vision. If this is not the case and there is no *'agreed'* Vision, the Business Architect will need to ensure the Vision is agreed at the earliest possible opportunity, as all requirements within the Programme will (and do) trace from (and back to) the Vision.
2. The Solution Design includes both the BDA and TDA which comprises a cross section of business representatives from the business who are assigned to the Programme. This includes Product Owners, Domain Subject Matter Experts (Domain SMEs), as well as Business Design representatives from the Programme (the Core Team) – Business Architects, Business Analysts, Technical Architects etc.
3. The Agile purists amongst us may argue that when in the Scrum Team/ Project Team level, the 'team' is collectively held responsible for the delivery of Epics and User Stories. Although you are welcome to assign this to the Scrum team, it is more effective in getting the Epics and Stories implemented when there is only one person responsible, as opposed to a group of people as there is no opportunity to pass on accountability to the *'next person'.*

## 7. Meetings and Ceremonies

All the work to develop the requirements are done over a 1, 2 or sometimes 4-week fixed periods of time called *'sprints', 'iterations'* or *'cycles'*. In software development terms, the objective of the sprint is to deliver workable, usable software. In Business Architecture terms, the objective is to issue the latest, up to date workable and usable iterations of the Business Architecture requirements and deliverables to allow further work to continue.

Over the course of the sprint, scope and deviations from the plan must be managed, including tracking the progress and status of the Business Architecture requirements and deliverables, managing changes as necessary.

Business Architecture Requirements RACI

Table 6.13

| # | Business Architecture Requirement | (R)esponsible | (A)ccountable | (C)onsulted | (I)nformed |
|---|---|---|---|---|---|
| 1 | Vision (e.g. Vision) | Portfolio Board[1] | Programme Board | Organisation (outside the Programme) | All / Programme & Portfolio |
| 2 | Theme (e.g. Reference Models) | Business Architect | Programme Board | Solution Design (including both BDA & TDA)[2] | |
| 3 | Feature (e.g. Building Blocks) | Business Architect | Product Owner | Solution Design (including both BDA & TDA)[2] | |
| 4 | Epic (e.g. Blueprints) | Business Architect[3] | Product Owner | Scrum Team | |
| 5 | Story (e.g. Blueprint tasks) | Business Architect[3] | Product Owner | Scrum Team | |

Example Meeting and Ceremonies List

Table 6.14

| Meeting | Description | Participants | Frequency | Duration |
|---|---|---|---|---|
| Sprint Planning | A core team exercise to estimate the amount of development and testing effort required to deliver a completed a backlog item. | Scrum Team | Fortnightly | 2 hours |
| Scrum Meeting | A daily 15 minute 'stand-up' meeting by the core members to present an update on progress and or impediments which require resolution. Each team member answers the following questions:<br>1. What did you achieve yesterday?<br>2. What are your plans today?<br>3. Do you have any impediments? | Scrum Team (plus any visitors. Visitors are welcome, but do not participate). | Daily | 15 mins |
| Sprint Review (Show & Tell) | At the end of the sprint, the Sprint Team present work that was completed and not completed during the Sprint. This can take the form of a live presentation of live/beta software, or presenting the status of a Business Architect deliverable. | Product Owner, Scrum Team, Management, Visitors and other Programme members. | Fortnightly[1] | 1 hour |
| Sprint Retrospective | Core team members discuss the past Sprint to identify areas for possible process improvements. Two main questions are asked:<br>1. What went well during the sprint?<br>2.What could be improved in the next sprint? | Scrum Team | Fortnightly[1] | 1 hour |
| Scrum of Scrums Meeting[1] | A meeting of Scrum Masters to discuss dependencies and blockers and issue resolutions on behalf of the teams they represent. | Scrum Master (or nominated Scrum Team representative) | Daily (following Scrum Meeting)[1] | 15 mins |
| Solution Design Meeting (similar to Work-Stream Alignment Meeting)[1] | A meeting is to ensure that all Product Owners are aligned and agree the order of delivery of Business and Technical Architecture and the business and technical requirements. | Scrum Master, Product Owner(s), Business Architecture, Technical Architecture and Business Change. | Fortnightly (following Scrum of Scrum Meeting)[1] | 15 mins |

This tracking progress and status is done through a series of specific meetings, held within (and at the end of) the sprint, which in Agile terms is called *'ceremonies'.*

Table 6.14 lists examples of the core meetings & ceremonies, participants, frequencies and duration (assuming a 2-week sprint).

Note:

1. These two (2) additional meetings (Scrum of Scrums, and Solution Design/Work Stream Alignment) are recommended for large Business Architecture Programmes with one or more Work Streams within its project or projects, to ensure (and assure) the parallel work in each of the work streams within the project or Programme is aligned.

A typical weekly ceremony schedule (based on a 1-week sprint cycle) is shown in *Figure 6.18* (on the next page).

**Note – The above Sprint Planning duration will vary depending on the size of Programme and sprint length. As a general rule, for a one-week sprint: allow a 1-hour sprint planning session, for a two-week sprint: a 2-hour sprint planning session may be required (both need to be time boxed to avoid running over time).**

**Daily Schedule for a One-Week Sprint**

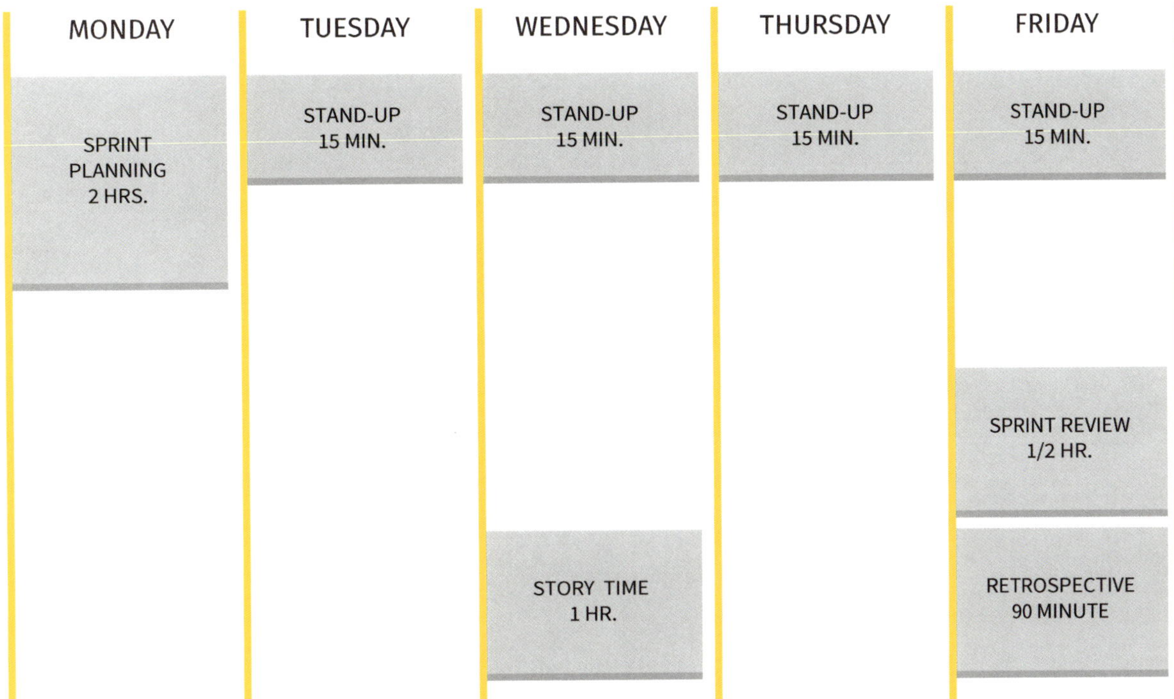


**Figure 6.18** – Typical Ceremony Timetable[48]

## 8. Tracking and Reporting

So now you've learnt about the Requirements Management Framework (e.g. what the process is, who does what, why they are doing it, what decisions are to be taken to what boards, and the meetings and ceremonies to progress the work and keep everything aligned and on track. The next step is tracking and reporting (e.g. tracking the status and reporting the progress of the Business Architecture requirements and deliverables).

Depending on your audience and their communication and information needs, the four (4) main tracking and reporting options available are as follows:

**8.1 3-Point**
**8.2 Kanban**
**8.3 Burn Down Chart**
**8.4 Dashboard**

We will discuss each of these reporting options in the next section.

### 8.1 3-Point

The *'3-Point'* is a status update tool which everyone can (and should) understand. It is the most straightforward option, providing the following simple highlights:

- **What you have been currently working on** (i.e. yesterday)?
- **What you are about to work on** (i.e. today)?
- **What could prevent you** (from doing your planned work today)?

The 3-Point bullet point update is the typical structure and information provided at the daily Scrum meetings. Scrum (or 'Stand-up') meetings, as discussed in the *Meetings and Ceremonies* section above, are both literally 'standing-up'. There is a method in the madness with the rationale to keeping meetings intentionally short and to the point. They should be, scheduled for 15 minutes maximum: just enough time to get everyone in the team to give their 3-point update and keep the team informed of progress. It's important to note here that the big issues and discussions are not brought up in these meeting in order to not disrupt the team 'flow', instead being taken offline (particularly addressing road blocks).

One of the keys to **HOBA®** and the **Design Process** being able to develop the design that aligns the Business to the Business Strategy and other architectures, is through making sure everyone involved in the process is aligned. The 3-Point approach is one of the means of making sure this happens, by keeping the key stakeholders up to date is through frequent communication – in both what is shared with the team, and as feedback that is received from them, so changes and updates can be incorporated quickly into ongoing work.

---

[48] Adapted from Sims, C., and Johnson, H.L., (2012) Scrum: A Breathtakingly Brief and Agile Introduction

## 8.2 Kanban

Kanban is a visual and physical representation of all the work (i.e. requirements) on a physical board (i.e. the Kanban board), written on Story (or User Story) Cards and placed into one of the three (3) columns, with placement depending on what status the work is in. These are either, About to/haven't Started (*To Do*), In Progress (*Doing*), or Complete (*Done*). Once the items are written on the Story cards they are stored and on display in the appropriate column.

The Kanban board usually sits on the Programme (or project) wall in clear sight and visibility of everyone on the project and Programme. The benefit and intention of Kanban boards (whether physically on the wall, or electronically in a system) is to show and report to the team (including interested stakeholders) the full scope of work that is planned, in progress, or completed, represented under the 3-headings.

A further benefit of this method is visitors to the Programme office (or floor) can quickly (and simply) gauge what is going on by visually seeing the volume of work being managed and the stage it is at without having to look into the detail (and reading the cards on the board). If they do want to know more however, the option then exists for them to take a closer look and read the detail on the cards to get a deeper understanding. It's a simple way to support engagement and understanding with minimal effort.

An example of the Kanban board is shown in *Figure 6.19*.

The issue with Kanban's is in the definition of '*Done*'. The definition '*Done*' has to be universally agreed from both within the Project (Scrum Team), and across the Programme, to ensure the entire Programme has the same definition and understanding of what 'Done' means. When there are different definitions (i.e., the Blueprint is ready for review, versus the Blueprint has been reviewed and changes captured and incorporated, ready for further use), then this creates problems, particularly with expectations from within other parts of the Programme that are either depending on work coming their way from you (and/or your team).

Although there is often a difference of definitions of '*Done*' between technical people (i.e. developers and testers) and Architects, the concept is the same. When a Developer hands their code over to testing to assess (the point when it is '*Done*'), it is also when that Story is ready for testing to begin. When the Business Architect says '*Done*' to a Story or version of the Story, it means that Story is 'ready to be used both internally and externally on the Programme to further design or implementation work'. 'Done' also means that the Story has been through the governance review and approval process, and can only then be marked or reported as '*Done*'. Having clear and agreed Acceptance Criteria will also help to reinforce the definition of '*Done*' for each Story.



## 8.3 Burn-down Chart

Burn-down Charts is where the fun starts. They show the amount of scope and work that is completed over a given period, but as importantly they play a major role here in reporting and working out 'velocity' - the rate at which work is completed. As with typical Agile Scrum methodology, in **HOBA®** all Stories are assigned points, which are totalled up and '*checked off*' when they're completed. Graphically on a chart this represents the '*run down*' or '*burn down*' rate i.e. the rate that work is completed.

The run-down (or burn-down) rate is a highly understated and underestimated technique that provides a powerful tool to predicting both the rate of work, and whether the current rate is fast enough to complete all the given (and known work) within the time required.

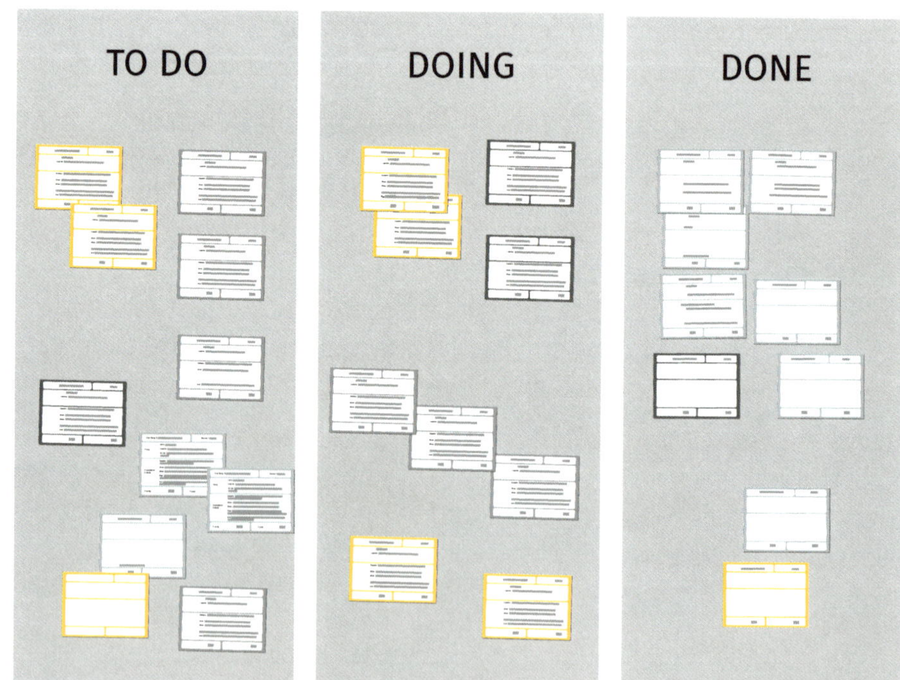


**Figure 6.19** - Example Kanban Storyboard[49]

[49] Ohno, T., (1988) Toyota Production System: Beyond Large-Scale Production

An example of a Business Architecture Burn Down Chart is shown in *Figure 6.20*.

The Business Architecture requirements (i.e. Reference Models, Building Blocks, and Blueprints) are estimated in size at their User Story level. The User Story (*'Story'*) level provides a more accurate (or relatively) realistic estimate of the amount of work required to complete or deliver the requirement in question. More so than trying to estimate larger pieces of work at the Building Block and Reference Model requirements level.

Story points (as I have discussed earlier in this book) are an estimation of the relative size of a piece of work at the User Story level, which when added back up to the higher-level requirements they were decomposed from, help to estimate the size of the work of that Epic, Feature, and also Theme level requirements that they belong too.

The benefit of aggregating up all the Story Points for all the requirements is that they can provide an indication of the total number of points for the whole Programme, and then an early *'guestimate'* of the *'run-rate'* (or 'velocity') required to complete all the work in the time required. This is then used to ask (or question) the team whether they are capable of completing the task in time, given the number of resources available and existing (or other) obligations, or whether additional resources maybe required to assist.

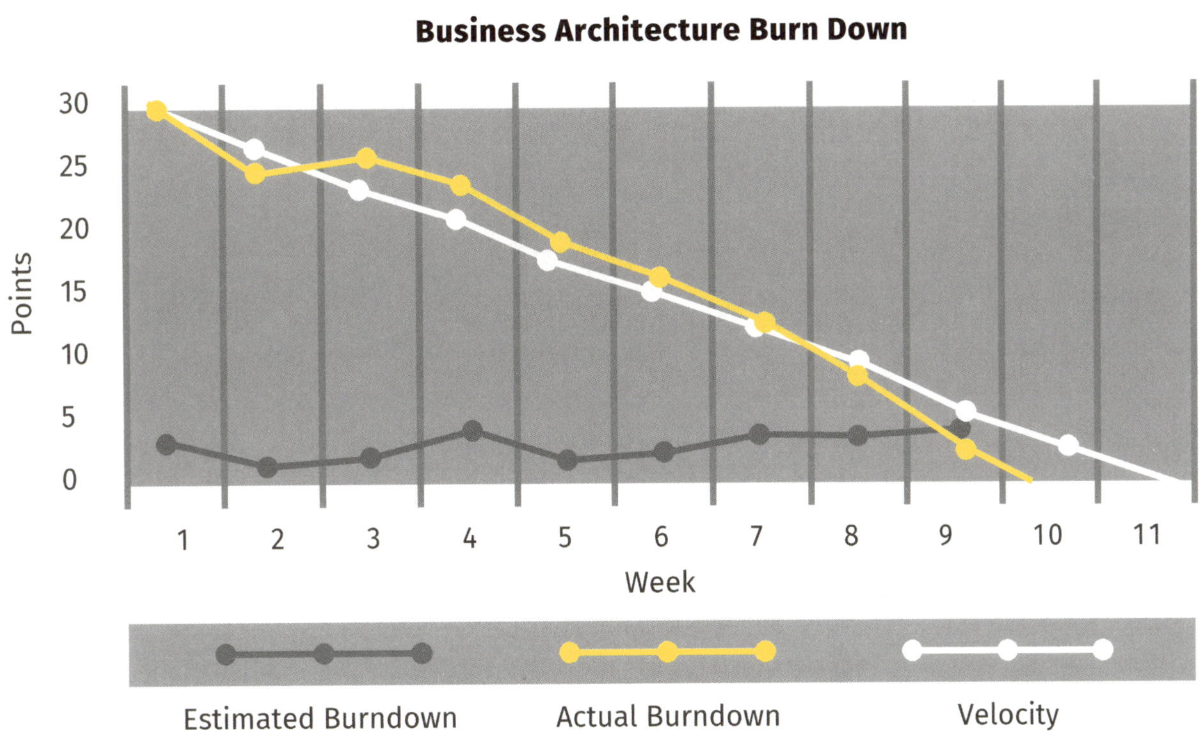


**Figure 6.20** - Example Business Architecture Burn Down Chart

**Inputs**

When it comes to sizing requirements, the approach to how the sizing is to be conducted must be agreed *first*. There are two primary approaches to choose from:

- **High level Requirements** (Theme or Feature), or
- **Low level Requirements** (User Story) [Recommended].

We will discuss these two (2) approaches below.

**High Level Requirement (Theme or Feature) Sizing**

High level requirement (Theme or Feature) sizing is where you provide a rough order of magnitude of size (of the work) required to deliver (or implement) each (Theme or Feature) requirement.

The *advantage* of this approach, is it is a relatively quick way to estimate the amount (i.e. size) of all the work, effort and velocity needed to deliver each high-level requirement, and therefore to finish the Programme within the agreed timeframe.

The *disadvantage* of sizing using Theme or Feature level requirements, is that the sizing is done at a relatively high level without knowledge of the detail of the actual work that is required to complete the Epics and Stories that make up those Features and Themes. This equates into what is essentially a really *'big guess'*.

Depending on the level of knowledge known about the actual work to complete the Epics and Stories, high-level sizing is going to be either – at worse, a *'finger in the air'* guess, or if using similar or past projects of similar size and complexity as the benchmark, a *'well educated'* guess.

**High level size estimates are usually conducted at the start of the Programme, or when the Business Architect is brought onto the Programme, to understand the size and estimated amount of effort needed to complete and deliver the Business Architecture, which are carried out in most cases to assist with resourcing decisions – whether to increase or decrease the number of resources to help deliver the work within the agreed timeframe.**

This margin of error needs to be factored into any decision making, knowing that using lower level requirements (i.e. Epics and User Stories) would provide a more accurate estimate (but would require more time to complete). Sizing using lower level requirement is discussed in the section below.

## Low Level Requirement (User Story) Sizing [Recommended]

User Story level requirements is a more accurate approach to estimating the size of work required, because the estimate is based off the smallest chunk of work expected to be completed in a sprint. The process of sizing the lower requirements is the same as sizing requirements at the higher level, except in this instance the Theme level requirements (i.e. Reference Models) are decomposed into their Feature, Epic and User Story level requirements - the smallest chunk of work that can be delivered in a sprint. It is at this User Story level that the sizing takes place.

Sizing and prioritisation is carried out with the Product Owner and the Scrum Team, sized and prioritised by business value. These scores are then recorded on the User Story Cards and placed on the Kanban board in order of their priority. This approach to estimation is more accurate than the high-level requirement sizing because it is done at the lower level of detail where more is known about the actual size of the expected work. The disadvantage (or issue) with this approach is that all Themes have to be decomposed down to User Story level requirements to get a better or closer estimate of the size, and therefore points to assign to each Story, which takes more time.

The benefit **HOBA®** provides in terms of sizing, is Theme level requirements (i.e. Reference Models) have already been decomposed already into known Features (Building Blocks) and Epics (Blueprints), so there is an existing view of what those User Stories look like (refer to the example of the Business Motivation Reference Model decomposed into its known Building Blocks and Blueprints show in *Figure 6.10*). The only thing to work out the sizing then is to work with the Product Owner and Scrum Team to determine the relative size (i.e. points) and priority against the rest of the work and User Stories that the Scrum Team is tasked with and assign each User Story their respective points.

When prioritising requirements, and negotiating with the Product Owner, you must be aware that the Product Owner (who ultimately, in the project and Programme will approve the priority) may not necessary have an eye on dependencies external to the project or Programme. This is fine as it may not be their role and/or scope to oversee these dependencies. However, *it is your role* as the Business Architect to have sight of this, as both an active member of your Programme's Solution Design Board (being part of the Business Design Authority (BDA)), and also your involvement in external central boards and meetings to bring that awareness to the table (and the Product Owner).

During the sprint, additional sprint activities are carried out (note: these are not *official* Scrum Ceremonies but *Sprints Reviews* or *Retrospectives)* which are a part of the weekly activities within the sprint. These two activities are shown on schedule in Figure 6.18 above for completeness). It is part of the Product Owners role to ensure the User Stories and Product Backlogs are maintained (Maintenance is where the Story details and descriptions may be updated) and the story priority re-evaluated and re-ordered (if required).

The rate the team is completing User Stories – known as *Velocity* (calculated as the 'total number of points *divided* by the total number of weeks', or working days) the team needs to maintain to complete the work, often varies over the duration of the Programme (in most cases due to stories not sized the same). As the team gets better at estimating the size of a story consistency (and completes them at the same rate), the velocity and burn down rates provide early predictions (or warnings) of whether the Stories will be completed within the agreed timeframe. The example in *Figure 6.21* (on the next page) shows the dip in velocity in week 2, causing a chain reaction where the team needed to increase output to increase the burndown rate in order to deliver the Stories within the required timeframe.

As the Business Architect, along with your *'self-organising'* high-performance scrum team (led by the Product Owner), you can use these burn-down charts and velocity (along with the continuous delivery *'plan, do, check, act'* cycle we discussed earlier in the book), in making decisions on the priority and order of the work remaining by quickly determining the increase in velocity required if the amount of work (points) suddenly increased or if there was capacity in the team to accept additional work within the time permitted.

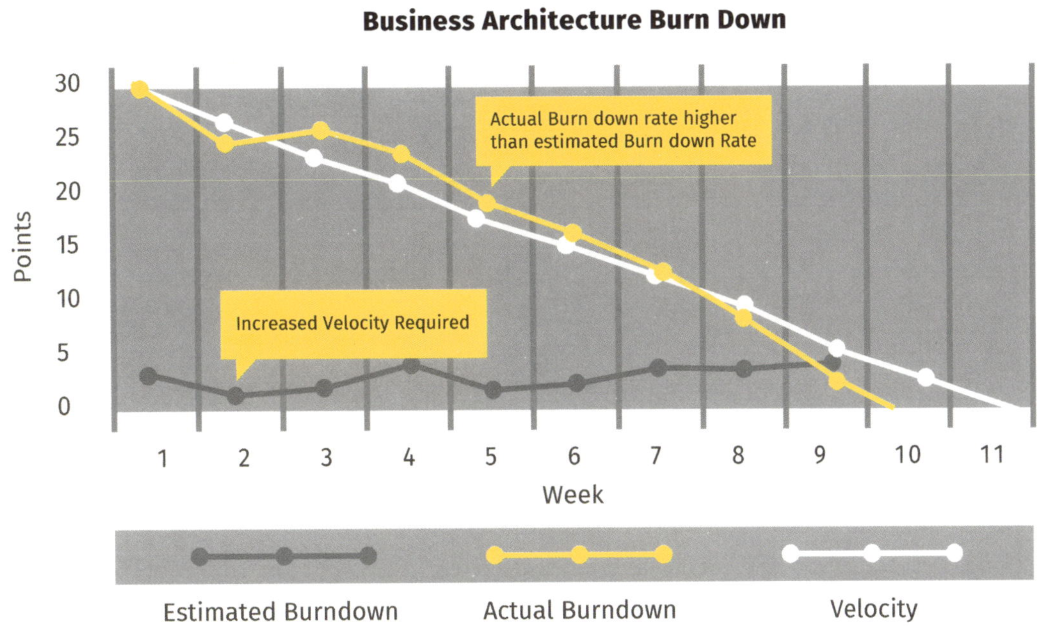


**Figure 6.21 -** Example Business Architecture Burn Down Chart (Marked up)[51]

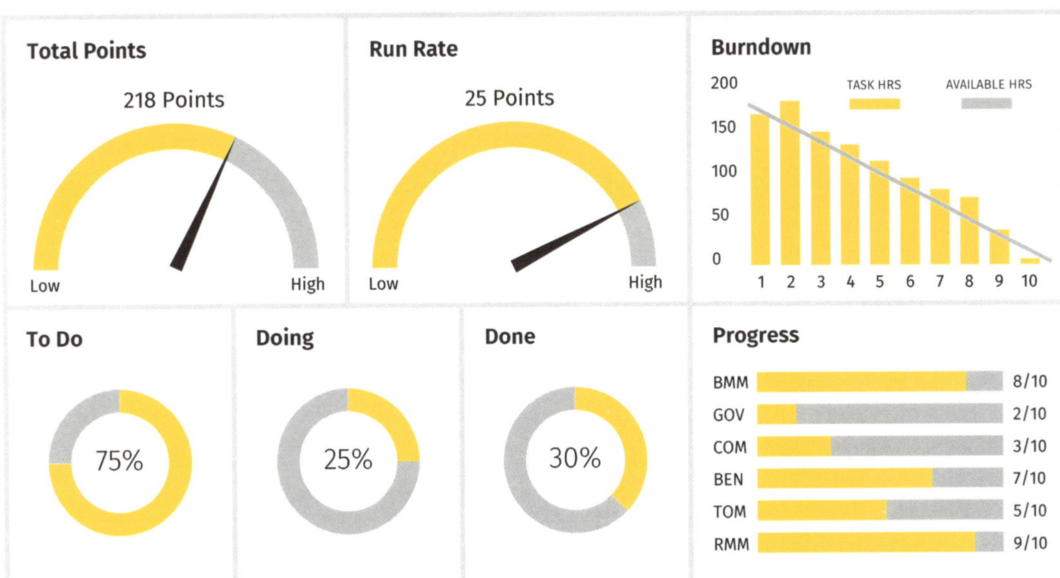


**Figure 6.22-** Sample Business Architecture Dashboard

## 8.4 Dashboard

The last (but not least) method for providing an update of the status and progress of the developing requirements, is in the form of a dashboard. Dashboard's have the advantage of providing a concise view of status and progress, in a single view. You just have to be careful (or conscious) that you are showing the right information that is important to your audience.

An example of a Business Architecture Dash Board is shown in *Figure 6.22* showing both the *progress* through the **Design Process**, and progress through building up the Target State Architecture.

Depending on the type of meeting you are going to (the stakeholder(s), audience, and their specific reporting requirements) you will need to tailor the report type and content to their specific needs.
The following table summarises each type of report we've just discussed as well as its suggested audience, frequency and medium of communication.

Be warned! Don't bombard your stakeholders with too much information, or offer the information too frequently (and at all costs, avoid sending the wrong information!) as this can negatively impact the efforts of you and/or your team.

In order to be successful, you need the Business (and Programme) stakeholders on your side, understanding their reporting requirements and giving them what they want, how they want it, in the format and frequency they want to receive it is going to go a long way in keeping them on side and engaged in the Programme and your work.

[51] Adapted from Evans, J., (2017) Scrum Revealed International Scrum Institute

Report Types for Different Audiences

Table 6.15

| Report Type | Audience | Frequency | Medium |
|---|---|---|---|
| 3-Point (bullet point) | Core Team | Daily | • Face to face<br>• Scrum<br>• Email |
| Kanban | Core Team | Daily | • Face to face<br>• Scrum |
| Summary | • Solution Design<br>• Programme Board | Weekly (end of week) | Email |
| Dashboard | • Solution Design<br>• Programme Board | • Weekly (end of week)<br>• Month end | Email |

## Risks and Mitigations

The risks with developing and agreeing the Governance Framework is the same as with the other Building Blocks and Blueprints – in that is that is set up, but its isn't actually followed. The Governance process can fall down when it gets caught up in the trap of becoming a hollow ritual, i.e. it is talked about, the outcomes are recorded then printed and hung on a wall, but never really followed.

While some of the steps covered in the Governance Framework above appear to be common knowledge (or common sense) to some, and completely foreign to others, the point is, in order to be effective as Business Architects, and Change Agents (as that's what we effectively are), we have to take our Stakeholders on a journey. Both a journey of discovery in (and of) the framework (and process) of how to design and implement the change, as well as a journey of the change itself. There also needs to be adequate controls and measures in place to track and monitor the process (and progress) to allow stakeholders to feel comfortable and confident in the Programme and that is will deliver on its expectations, and deliver value to the Business, and ultimately implement the changes to allow the Business to effectively and efficiently execute its Business Strategy.

## Building Block Wrap-up

In this chapter, we discussed the **Governance Framework** Building Block.

The Governance Framework establishes the framework and processes to manage, track and monitor Business Architecture requirements on the Programme, from discovery to implementation.

The Governance Framework ensures the right stakeholders have the right level of management authority, responsibility and span of control in the Organisation and Programme, and that the Business and Programme (consisting of both Business Architecture, and Technology Architecture) are involved to review and approve the different levels and types of Business Architecture requirements.

The Governance Framework is made up of the **Architecture Governance Framework Blueprint,** and covers the following areas:

- Requirements Management Framework
- Governance Structure
- Governance Authorities
- Review and Approval Process
- Stakeholder (Influence/Impact) Matrix
- Stakeholder Roles and Responsibilities (RACI)
- Meetings and Ceremonies
- Tracking and Reporting

Each one of the above areas is critical to ensuring the Governance Framework is not just established, but *actually* followed routinely. The benefit being, as the team gets better (and/or familiar) at using the framework and process, they will be able to spot issues before they occur, and react quickly to counter them when they do.

## Next Steps

Once you have identified and agreed the Governance framework, the roles and responsibilities and how the Programme is going to run, the next step is to confirm the scope of the Programme, through defining the Design Principles.

# 2.2 Design Principles

## Introduction

Design Principles are the Building Blocks that set the defining principles for the *scope* of the Programme. These principles are the general rules and guidelines used to govern and address the *'What is in (and out of) scope?'* questions asked of the Programme.

Completing this step of the Design Process, and defining the Design Principles Building Block defines the details and conditions under the 'Problem Statement' that the Programme is set up to solve.

The Blueprint that documents the Design Principles is the 'Design Principles Register'. The Design Principles themselves are structured and worded in such a way that there is no ambiguity of what the Programme *thinks* it is going to do, and most importantly, explicitly what it won't be doing.

Design Principles are intentionally structured in such a way that they explain the principle ('statement'), the reason why that principle is in place ('rationale') and the impact to design and scope decisions as a result of the Programme adhering to it ('implications').

An example of a Design Principle 'principle' is shown in Table 6.16.

**When presenting and sharing the Design Principles with (and to) your stakeholders, it's always helpful to provide a summary Table to show the main Stakeholder Concerns addressed and the source of where the Stakeholder Concern has come from, or who provided it. Stakeholder Concerns was discussed in section 1.1 Business Architecture Approach as part of the 1.1.1 Statement of Work (SOW) Blueprint.**

An example of the Design Principles Summary is shown in Table 6.17.

**Example Design Principle**

**Table 6.16**

| Name | Business Process Improvement |
|---|---|
| Statement | We will design to improve or replace all of today's online and paper-based application processes, where it is necessary and cost-effective to do so |
| Rationale | There are a lot of inefficient manual processes that cost the business time and money on wasted effort and resources. Although the primary objective of the Programme is to replace the current legacy system, the Programme will look to take advantage of opportunities to maximize benefits gained from automating work flows and processing where it provides strategic alignment and value for money to do so. |
| Implications | The Programme's primary objective is to replace the legacy Application website, however, where pragmatic we will design to eliminate many current inefficient and manual operational work practices. |

**Example Design Principles Summary**

**Table 6.17**

| # | Design Principle | Concern Addressed | Source |
|---|---|---|---|
| 1 | We will design for the solution to be interoperable and interface with other present, and future systems without undue restriction and with minimal implementation. | Interoperability | Business Case v1.4 Section 1.1 The Vision of the Project |
| 2 | We will design for the solution to be scalable and flexible that our partners can act quickly and at minimal costs to meet current and future data sharing needs. | Scalable / Flexible Solution | Business Case v1.4 Section 1.1 The Vision of the Project |

## Inputs

The inputs used to complete this Building Block are shown in Table 6.18

## Outputs

The Blueprint (output) produced for this Building Block is shown in Table 6.19

## Steps

The steps to complete the Design Principle Blueprint are as follows.

## 2.2.1 Design Principle Register

1. **Record the 'candidate' Design Principle details into the Design Principles Summary table** using the Blueprint Inputs and other documentation from the *Inputs* section above.

An example of the Design Principles table format is shown in Table 6.20 (on the next page)

**Design Principles Building Block Inputs**

**Table 6.18**

| Ref | Blueprint/Documentation | Use |
|---|---|---|
| 1.1.1 | Statement of Work (SOW) | Provides the Problem Statement, description of the Programme and scope, and list of 'Stakeholders Concerns' as potential or candidate 'concerns' (or tensions). |
| N/A | Business Case | Provides potential or candidate 'concerns' (or 'tensions') expressed as or in the form of issues, objectives as well rogramme or project scope, benefits and assumptions. |
| N/A | Project Charter/ Programme Charter | Provides potential or candidate descriptions of design principles (statement, rationale, implication) from list project description, mission, problem statement, goals/ metrics, scope (in/out) and key milestones. |
| N/A | Other existing Programme documentation | Includes any current RAID logs and registers, lessons learned logs and reports, and related Programme documentation that highlights the current issues the business and Programme is attempting and intending to address. |

**Design Principles (Output) Blueprint**

**Table 6.19**

| Ref | Blueprint | Description | Example | |
|---|---|---|---|---|
| 2.2.1 | Design Principles Register | The Design Principles– describe and govern the scope of the Programme and architecture. The Design Principles consists of the 'register' and 'summary' table. | **Name** | **Business Process Improvement** |
| | | | Statement | We will design to improve or replace all of today's online and paper-based application processes, where it is necessary and cost-effective to do so |
| | | | Rationale | There are a lot of inefficient manual processes that cost the business time and money on wasted effort and resources. Although the primary objective of the Programme is to replace the current legacy system, the Programme will look to take advantage of opportunities to maximize benefits gained from automating work flows and processing where it provides strategic alignment and value for money to do so. |
| | | | Implications | The Programme's primary objective is to replace the legacy Application website, however, where pragmatic we will design to eliminate many current inefficient and manual operational work practices. |

Example Design Principles Table Format

Table 6.20

| # | Design Principle | Concern Addressed | Source |
|---|---|---|---|
| 1 | [Design Principle Statement1] | [Concern or Issue addressed1] | [Source document, version and section in document1] |
| 2 | [Design Principle Statement2] | [Concern or Issue addressed2] | [Source document, version and section in document2] |

2. **Elaborate each 'candidate' from Design Principles Summary in Table 6.20 above**, recording the Name, Statement, Rationale and Implications for each Design Principle.

**It is easier and faster to start with the 'Summary Table' first, in a 'top-down' approach, as this takes an externally facing 'macro' level view of the concerns facing the Programme, thereby capturing the 'big ticket concern items'. This is opposed to the 'bottom-up' approach, starting at the 'micro' level, which risks 'missing the trees because of the forest' (i.e. getting stuck in the detail, focusing on one (or two) thing(s), and missing everything else).**

An example of the Design Principles Register format is shown in Table 6.21.

Design Principle Register Format

Table 6.21

| Name | [Name of the Design Principle. Avoid names of technology or ambiguous terms like 'support', or 'good'. You will need to define and explain what they mean later] |
|---|---|
| Statement | [Short and to the point statement to communicate the essence of the principle] |
| Rationale | [The justification for applying this principle] |
| Implications | [The 'now that we have made this principle, how does it affect how the Programme acts and behaves, and decisions it will now take] |

3. **Iteratively socialise, validate and refine the Blueprint** - including any Risks, Assumptions, Issues and Dependencies (RAID) addressed or raised as part of completing this Blueprint), and

4. **Package and publish the Blueprint** – in line with your agreed sprint/release cycle, established back in *Chapter 6 Step 2 – Control*, with the *Governance Model.*

## Risks and Mitigations

There are three (3) main risks (or issues) to be aware of when putting together Design Principles:

- **Not doing enough,**
- **Not doing them at all, and**
- **Not doing them well.**

In terms of **'not doing enough'**– there's no optimum number of Design Principles. The number of Design Principles is going to depend, and be determined by, many things – including the size of the Programme, the number of stakeholders and therefore potential concerns and/or tensions involved.

As a *rule of thumb*, you want to be sure you address the following:

- All stakeholder concerns (and/or tensions) are addressed (if you have 20 concerns for example and they all say similar things, group them under a common theme (e.g. business/process improvement; decision making, Organisation structure etc.).
- Scope items – confirming if something is in or out of scope.
- Implementation options i.e. agile, big bang, use of a pilot of a smaller subset of the end users before rolling out a full implementation; customisation (or no customisation) of off the shelf solutions etc., and
- Any future proof considerations (i.e. will use open source technology and not proprietary software or technology, etc.).

In terms of **'not doing them at all',** the question you should be asking is *'will that cause a problem?'* (BTW, the answer to this is an empathic YES, it *'will'* cause a problem!). Design Principles form part of the *foundation* element of **HOBA®** and the Target State Architecture for a good reason: they are **fundamental** to a strong foundation for a solid architecture.

Despite a strong foundation being favourable, Design Principles are often *'skipped over'*, and not seen or recognised for their importance. I have seen this a lot in Programmes eager to *'crack on'* and get to the *'fun stuff'*, overlooking or missing this step, assuming that these principles are 'well known, agreed and adopted', yet have not actually been verified or validated. A word of advice here, and I cannot emphasis this enough, don't skip this step! Just don't.

In terms of **'not doing them well'**, the following mnemonic (CCC-MUST, explained below) borrowed from our good friends in Business Analysis will help test and clarify your Design Principle statement, rationale and implication descriptions so that they don't raise more questions than they answer.

Once you have drafted your Design Principles Register (or while you are drafting your register), test each design principle against the following CCC-MUST criteria:

- **Complete** – fully defined i.e. enough accurate information to begin planning from.
- **Consistent** – principle should mesh with all other principles on the project or Programme.
- **Correct** – a statement of fact (and not an assumption)
- **Modifiable** – should be able to be updated
- **Unambiguous** – written in such a way that all readers arrive at the same understanding.
- **Stable** – principles should be enduring (i.e. stand the test of time), yet 'modifiable' (above) following a robust review and change process.
- **Testable** – be able to provide evidence testing, examining or demonstrating its existence once in action.

### Building Block Wrap-up

In this section, we discussed the Design Principles Building Block.

This Building Block provides the principles that defines the scope for the Programme and addresses the *'What is in (and out of) scope?'* Question.

This Building Block is made up of the Design Principles Register Blueprint, which is in two (2) parts – the Summary table, and the Design Principles Register:

- The **Summary table** – identifies the Stakeholder Concerns (that were identified back in the Statement of Work (SOW), and the Concern sources;
- The **Design Principles Register** - captures the design principles in such a structured way that there is no ambiguity of what both the Programme thinks is in scope, but also as importantly what is not in scope.

There are a lot of risks with this Building Block. Design Principles are often misunderstood for their importance. They are either *not done enough* (i.e. incomplete), *not done at all* (i.e. overlooked) or *not done well* (i.e. poorly written). This is mostly due to either the misconception or perception that Design Principles are low or no value, or they are already done. If they are already done, then test them against the CCC-MUST criteria (and update where required, or necessary). If not done, the steps above will explain both *Why?* and *How?* to do them. If there is an instance where they aren't yet done, then make sure you do them quickly as a Programme might already be suffering 'scope creep' (with others already be designing off it) based on the perceived scope (which in reality isn't actually in scope at all!).

### Next Steps

Once you have agreed the Design Principles the next step in the Design Process is to validate and manage the Risks, Assumptions, Issues and Dependencies (RAID) affecting the successful design and implementation of the Target Operating Model (TOM).

The RAID Blueprint is discussed in the next section below.

## 2.3 Risks, Assumptions, Issues & Dependencies (RAID)

### Introduction

RAID is the Building Block that is used to both capture the information about the Programmes Risks, Assumptions, Issues and Dependencies (RAID) as well as establish the process to manage them.

The purpose of this Building Block is to clearly identify and manage the risks that can derail the Programme through putting mitigations strategies in place and actioning them, should the need arise.

## Confusion

Before we start, lets clear the air. There are three (3) areas of confusion with RAID. They are to do with:

1. **Definition**
2. **Process**
3. **Timing**

We will discuss each briefly below:

### 1. Definition

The first area of confusion is the name or acronym *"RAID"*. Although there are four (4) elements to RAID, what happens in practise is despite there being 4 elements, *only Risks* are actually tracked and managed, the others being seen either as not important, or are captured but managed elsewhere. The confusion is mostly due to not being clear on definitions.

**So, to be clear, the definition of each RAID element is as follows:**

- **Risk** – the uncertainty of outcome, whether a positive opportunity or negative threat. Project 'risks' are 'issues' that have not occurred, or are waiting to happen.
- **Assumption** – something that is believed as true (but not confirmed) to enable an Organisation to go ahead with a project.
- **Issue** – something that is going wrong now in the project and/or Programme, has occurred, is current and has yet to be properly addressed. An 'issue' is a 'risk' that have eventuated, or come to fruition, which now must be managed.
- **Dependency** – something that must be delivered to enable a project and/or Programme's delivery.

### 2. Process

RAID management is more than just identifying and capturing them on a log or register and ticking a box and saying 'done'. RAID management is about managing the process of managing the risks that can impact the delivery of the Business Architecture. It is about capturing the risks, identifying and agreeing owners, mitigation strategies to address or respond to the risks should they eventuate, as well as managing them through the lifecycle of the Programme and throughout the design and delivery of the Business Architecture.

Managing risks actually follows a circular cycle, as shown in *Figure 6.23.*

So, what the circular process means, is managing risks is not a one-time event, the RAID Log and RAID Registers are just like any other Blueprint – they too need ongoing validating, updating and socializing when new information comes to hand.

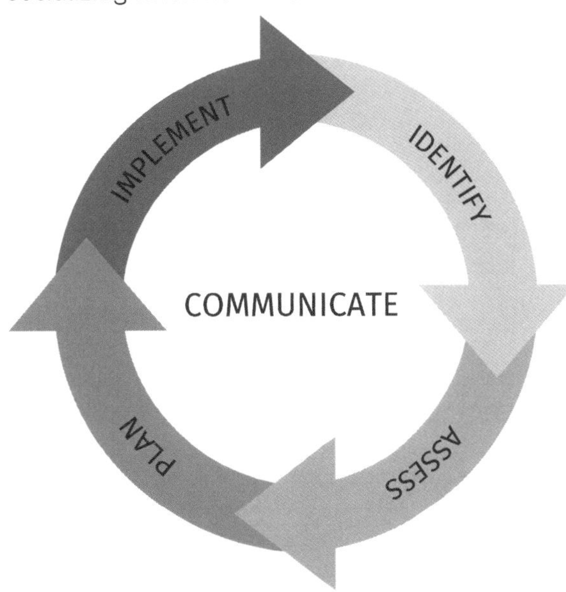


**Figure 6.23-** Risk Management Cycle[52]

[52] Managing Successful Programmes (MSP) (2011), *Cabinet Office*

In terms of that circular process, the first part of the Risk Management Cycle 'Identify' was captured back in the 'Statement of Work (SOW)' Blueprint when the 'initial' Risks, Assumptions, Issues and Dependencies were identified, when the Business Architect was first engaged on the Programme. These 'initial' RAIDs provide the first inputs into the relevant RAID Register discussed later below.

### 3. Timing

Let's be honest, no one likes or wants to go to a separate meeting to discuss Risks. It's not exciting, people would rather 'crack on'. So, what happens is there is one 'Risk' meeting at the start of the Programme. It lasts 1-2 hours, people get annoyed its taking so long as they would rather do more interesting things (like 'crack on'). So they they contribute to the meeting and then hope to never again to be called into another one.

The 'bad taste' of 'losing 2 hours of their life they will never get back' is engrained in everyone's minds so that either two (2) things happen when a new risk arrives:

- **They don't raise it,** and risk having to sit through another 2-hour meeting, or
- **They raise it,** and hope that it's the last they hear about it ('I raised it' is code for "its an entry in the Risk Log, it's in the Risk Log, it's not my problem anymore").

But, what actually happens is the next time they hear about it is when the risk has eventuated and it's too big to brush under the carpet anymore. And guess what? There's a 2-hour meeting to discuss how to deal with it (no surprises there)!

**I'm not sure, but if consultancies changed their business (or revenue) model to be based on 'Programme Outcomes', as opposed to 'Time and Materials', I wonder if Risks would then be properly managed then? It almost seems that some Programmes are set up to fail from the start. Well, it would keep the work flowing in...**

## Solution

To keep RAIDs visible and management of them active, RAIDs are incorporated into the Scrum process as part of the daily routine, as it allows risks to be mitigated before they become issues or unmanageable, which then require the team or team members to take time away from their current tasks to address them. The biggest *faux pas* in Scrum is interrupting the teams flow, who's number one goal is continuous delivery. A big no-no.

RAID's are incorporated into the Scrum, as Scrum provides the short duration, and daily frequency RAID needs for effective visibility and management. Scrum meetings last only 15 minutes – they are intentionally short and occur frequently, which RAIDs need. RAIDs are already discussed in Scrums, being the third (3rd) point in the 3-Point update *"What could prevent you doing your planned work today?"*. How they are managed in the Scrum is as follows:

- **If it is small enough** – it can be dealt with there and then (in the Scrum);
- **If it's small, but can't be addressed in the Scrum** (i.e. would take up the allocated 15mins for the Scrum) – they are taken 'offline' and dealt with there and then (following the Scrum with the Business Architect, Scrum Master and maybe one or two team members); or
- **If they're too big** (to be dealt with between the Business Architect, and Scrum Master) – they are taken to the BDA, TDA, and if needed, the SDA.

I have seen with numerous clients I've assisted, when the need to capture RAIDs arrives, the time it was captured is the only time it was 'actively managed'. The separate RAID meetings didn't happen (although they were in everyone's diaries), and the RAID themselves weren't communicated to the Team, or when it was, it was a link in the bottom of an email to a 'wiki' with the instruction to "go have a look when you have time" (which never happened). As a result, everyone forgot they existed, until of course they developed into something else that needed immediate attention, requiring all hands on deck to fix it.

Ideally Business Architecture RAIDs *should* be registered on the central Programme RAID Log, flagged as 'Business Architecture' and managed centrally. If you have a Project Manager, or better yet – a Project Management Office (PMO) that is tasked to manage the RAID for you, then you are one of the lucky ones. For everyone else, you will maintain your RAIDs in the RAID Log, and/or when necessary (depending on your adopted Programme governance structure and strategy), keep changes updated in the Programmes 'central' RAID Log and manage them yourself.

As a fail-safe, your RAID becomes a standing item at the Solution Design Authority (SDA) Programme wide meeting.

## Inputs

The inputs used to complete this Building Block are shown in Table 6.22 (on the next page).

## Outputs

The Blueprints (outputs) produced for this Building Block are shown in Table 6.23 (on the next page).

## Steps

The steps to complete The RAID Log Blueprint are as follows.

## 2.3.1 RAID Log

The RAID Log Blueprint is made up of the following registers:

1. Risks Register
2. Assumptions Register
3. Issues Register
4. Dependencies Register

We will discuss the above registers in the sections below.

## 1. Risks Register

The Risks Register is where all the information about Risks are captured in a consistent and structured manner. As mentioned earlier in the section above, 'initial' Risks are captured in the 'Statement of Work (SOW)', at the outset of the Business Architects engagement.

An example of a Risk Register (table) is shown in Table 6.24.

Typical impacts include[53] :

- Time
- Cost
- Quality
- Scope
- Benefit
- People
- Resources

Typical mitigation (or responses), and strategies (in parenthesis) include[54] :

- Prevention (terminate the risk)
- Reduction (treat the risk).
- Transference (pass to another or specialist third party, usually by a contract or policy).
- Acceptance (tolerate the risk i.e. do nothing).
- Contingency (planned actions should risk arise).

**RAID Building Block Inputs**

Table 6.22

| Ref | Blueprint/Documentation | Use |
|---|---|---|
| 1.1.1 | Statement of Work (SOW) | Provides the initial list of Risks, Assumptions, Issues and Assumptions (RAID) captured at the outset of the Programme/Business Architects involvement on the Programme. |
| N/A | Business Case | Provides (potential) list of RAIDs from issues, problem statement, and objectives. |
| N/A | Project/ Programme Charter | Provides (potential) list of RAIDs from issues, problem statement, and objectives. |
| N/A | Other existing Business and Programme Documentation | Includes meeting minutes where RAIDs can be raised. |

**RAID (Output) Blueprint**

Table 6.23

| Ref | Blueprint | Description | Example |
|---|---|---|---|
| 2.3.1 | RAID Log | Contains the separate Risk, Assumptions, Issues and Dependencies (RAID) registers. Used to actively manage the RAIDs in and acros the Programme, and Business Architecture | See Table 6.24 below |

Table 6.24

| ID | Risk | Likeli-hood | Severity | Impact | Mitigation | Owner* |
|---|---|---|---|---|---|---|
| R001 | Current Organisation does not have an agreed Organisation level TOM to base final target state Business Architecture off, that the Programme may not be aligned. | High | Medium | · Time (to make changes;<br>· Cost (of making those changes);<br>· Scope (may increase). | Prevention – the Business Architecture will use the To-Be Business Services as a proxy until an agreed TOM is available, and regular share progress of developing Business Architecture, and check for changes. | Business Architect |
| R002 | OAS Project is | High | High | · Time (to make changes;<br>· Cost (of making those changes);<br>· Scope (may increase). | Prevention – Programme is currently defining the Vision while the Business Architecture develops in parallel. Ongoing reconciliations will be made in parallel. | Business Architect |

[53] Managing Successful Projects with PRINCE2 (2005), *Office of Government Commerce (OGC)*
[54] Managing Successful Projects with PRINCE2 (2005), *Office of Government Commerce (OGC)*

Risk Register Table

Table 6.24

| ID | Risk | Likeli-hood | Severity | Impact | Mitigation | Owner* |
|---|---|---|---|---|---|---|
| R001 | Current Organisation does not have an agreed Organisation level TOM to base final target state Business Architecture off, that the Programme may not be aligned. | High | Medium | · Time (to make changes);<br>· Cost (of making those changes);<br>· Scope (may increase). | Prevention – the Business Architecture will use the To-Be Business Services as a proxy until an agreed TOM is available, and regular share progress of developing Business Architecture, and check for changes. | Business Architect |
| R002 | OAS Project is | High | High | · Time (to make changes);<br>· Cost (of making those changes);<br>· Scope (may increase). | Prevention – Programme is currently defining the Vision while the Business Architecture develops in parallel. Ongoing reconciliations will be made in parallel. | Business Architect |

Example Assumptions Register

Table 6.25

| ID | Assumption | Impact | Owner |
|---|---|---|---|
| A001 | Access to the required specialist resources for the duration of the project. | High | Business Architect |
| A002 | Business Architecture artefacts currently exist in and across the Programme for the Vision, Design Principles, Capability and Process definitions, frameworks and models. These will be utilised as a baseline. Where not available, will be assessed whether warranted, and eveloped where needed. | Medium | Business Architect |

Example Assumptions Register

Table 6.26

| ID | Issue | Impact | Owner |
|---|---|---|---|
| I001 | The Organisation Head Office BDA role and involvement in the Programme governance is unclear and so far, un-utilized. | High | Business Architect |
| I002 | The BDA currently does not have proper business representation from all Product Owners on the Programme. There is a potential gap in the design of the final solution does not meet the business' needs. | High | Business Architect |

## 2. Assumptions Register

The Assumptions register is where all the information about Assumptions are captured in a consistent and structured manner. As mentioned above, *'initial'* Assumptions are captured at the outset of the Business Architects engagement in the 'Statement of Work (SOW)'.

An example of an Assumptions Register (table) is shown in Table 6.25.

## 3. Issues Register

The Issues register is where all the information about Issues are captured in a consistent and structured manner. As mentioned above, *'initial'* Issues are captured at the outset of the Business Architects engagement in the 'Statement of Work (SOW)'.

An example of an Issues Register (table) is shown in Table 6.26.

**Note - The Risk Owner should always be a named individual (as opposed to a role or department shown above, and examples below) who is responsible for the management of all aspects of risk assigned to them, including implementing the mitigation actions to address the risk as and when they come to fruition.**

## 4. Dependencies Register

The Dependencies register is where all the information about Dependencies are captured in a consistent and structured manner. As mentioned above, *'initial'* Dependencies are captured at the outset of the Business Architects engagement in the 'Statement of Work (SOW)'.

An example of a Dependencies Register is shown in Table 6.27.

## Risk and Mitigations

Some of the risks with RAIDs are thinking that capturing them is a *one-off* event, not revisiting them again or actively managing them to a successful conclusion. Either the risk (assumption, issue and/or dependency) didn't cause an issue, or the Programme finished successfully without anything being an issue (unlikely).

The problem with this approach or thinking is that this hardly ever happens. Risks become Issues, Assumptions prove to be wrong, Dependencies weren't identified so they weren't managed and they end up escalating into an Issue extremely quickly.

RAID Management is exactly that - *managing* RAID. It actually involves managing each and every RAID effectively and efficiently from the moment they're captured, to the point where they're no longer an issue, and/or the Programme successfully ends and the RAID is handed over to the Business As Usual (BAU) to manage as part of everyday business (with newly assigned RAID Owners and respective RAID mitigation actions).

Risk Register Table

Table 6.27

| ID | Dependency | Owner | Date Required | Impact |
|---|---|---|---|---|
| D001 | The Post Office will continue to fulfil Biometric Enrolments for Visa Applications. | Project Manager | 30 June 2016 | High |
| D002 | New Card Project will deliver the new strategic card fulfilment service. | Project Manager | 30 June 2016 | High |

The best way to manage RAIDs is *'piece-meal',* as described in the sections above – a little bit each day with smaller 'bite-sized' issues addressed locally and bigger issues escalated and taken centrally.

## Building Block Wrap-up

In this section, we discussed the RAID Building Block.

The RAID Building Block provides both the means to capture the RAIDs as well as the process of managing them through the lifecycle of the Programme from discovery to implementation (and beyond, handing over any open RAIDs to the Business to manage, if any residual RAIDs still exist at the end of the Programme).

The Blueprint to capture and manage the RAIDs is the **RAID Log,** which contains separate registers for each Risk, Assumptions, Issues and Dependencies, intentionally structured to ensure there is no ambiguity on who owns them, and what to do when they come to fruition.

Historically RAIDs are not well managed, and seen as a chore (or bore), but when they are included into the day-to-day routine (as part of the daily Scrum), in 'piece-meal' fashion, with small issues handled locally and bigger issues handled centrally, they become manageable.

### Reference Model Recap

Once the RAID Building Block is completed, this completes the Building Blocks (along with the other Design Principles and Architecture Governance Building Blocks), that make up the *'foundation'* of **HOBA®** - the Governance Reference Model.

By completing the Governance Model, this now means you have:

- Put all the controls and processes in place to manage scope, decisions and risks that affect or impact the successful implementation of the Business Architecture, and Target Operating Model (TOM).

For a full recap of **HOBA®** and the Design Process, refer to the *Recap* section in *Chapter 11 Next Steps* below.

### Next Steps

The next step in the Design Process is Step-3, Analyse. This is where you analyse the state of the Current Operating Model (COM) of the Organisation, which will form the baseline to build the Target Operating Model (TOM) from.

# Chapter 7
# Step 3 – Analyse

## Introduction

Step 3 – Analyse, is about analysis. Analysis of the current or 'As-Is' state of the Organisation and Business Architecture, as it is today. Analysis is provided via the Current Operating Model Reference Model.

*Figure 7.1* shows where Step-3 Analyse fits in the overall Design Process:

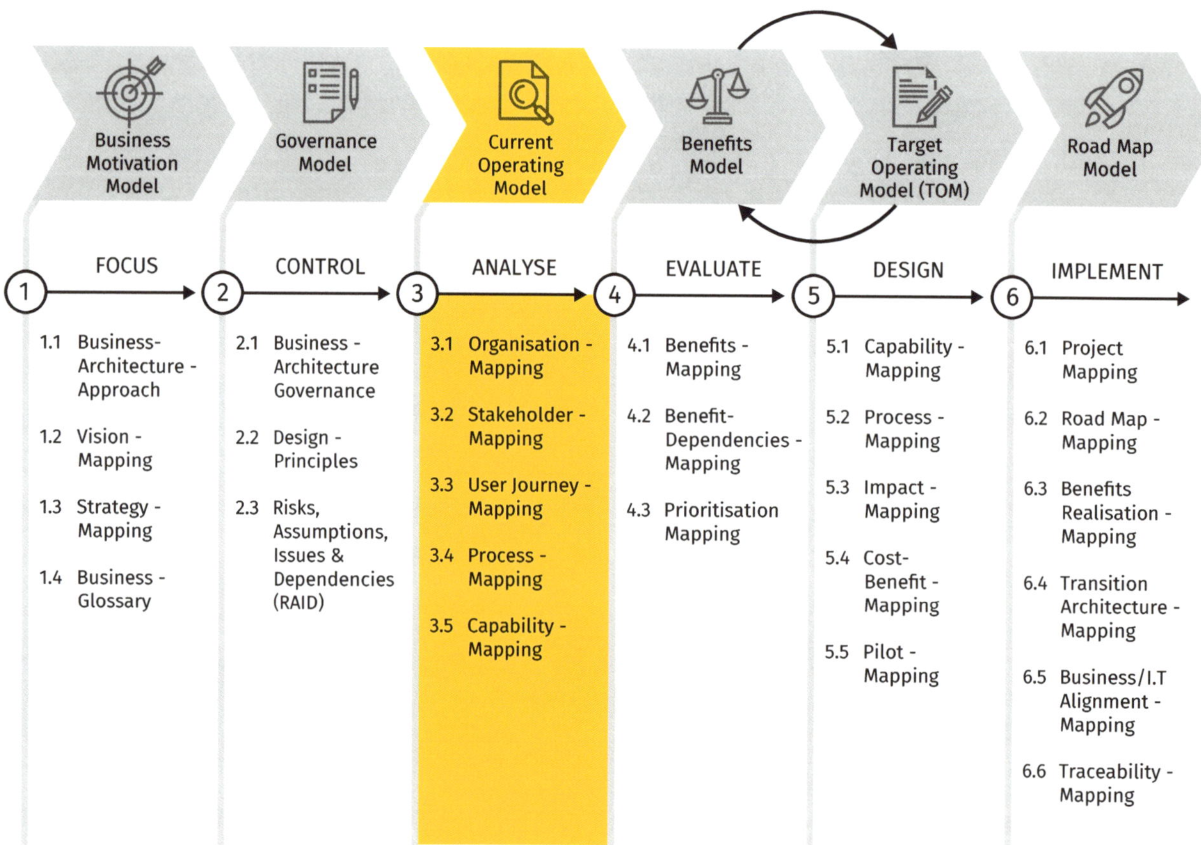


**Figure 7.1** - Design Process – Step 3 Analyse

# Analysis Options

When it comes to defining the Current Operating Model, there are essentially two (2) options or approaches to follow:

1. **Light Touch** (aka the 'fast way')
2. **Full Assessment** (aka the 'thorough, but in most cases, much longer way')

Each option has its own Pros and Cons, which we will briefly discuss below:

### 1. Light Touch

Light touch is where, at the time of conducting the discovery work to build up a draft or initial view of the Current Operating Model, the work that you do, as the Business Architect, is 'high level and only touching the surface'. The Pros and Cons are as follows:

- **Pros** – includes a *'broad-brush'* end-to-end discovery and validation effort of gathering the bare essential information required to understand the concerns and issues (and opportunities) about the Current Operating Model.
- **Cons** - Explicitly excludes doing a *'deep dive'* or analysis in any particular area to understand or assess the performance of it. The problem this creates later is *'you can't improve what you don't measure'.*

### 2. Full Assessment

The Full Assessment is similar to the *'light touch'* in conducting the discovery work to build up the draft or initial view of the Current Operating Model but with a more detailed analysis. The Pros and Cons are as follows:

- **Pros** – The same *'broad-brush'* end-to-end scope as the 'Light Touch' (i.e. same areas of coverage), but deeper analysis of some or all areas to better understand the causes (namely root cause) not just the symptoms, concerns, issues and opportunities that are visible.
- **Cons** – time (and access to the necessary staff and resources needed to complete the Full Assessment).

The reason why this is stated upfront is because this step – whether 'light touch' or 'full assessment' is decided or communicated, what you will find on Programmes is when just the *idea* of assessing the Current Operating Model is raised it is often met with a lot of resistance from the Programme and/or the Business representatives. The reason for the resistance from the Business is generally due to a perceived 'unnecessary need' to complete or define the Current Operating Model to any degree of completeness (or correctness), which is often due to the *perceived* time and (lack of) resource availability and commitment needed to complete and define it. But be warned, this is a trap. I highly recommend you do not skip this step! Irrespective of the source of the 'resistance', I highly recommend you do not skip this step. There is a way to negotiate that *resistance*, which we will discuss below.

In many of the company's I have assisted, the common excuse for not wanting to carry out or establishing a shared understanding of the Current 'As-Is' Operating Model, is often...

> **"We know what the Organisation looks like already, we know what the problem is, we've been living with it for years..."**

And insist on 'cracking on'. What you will find however, after asking ten (10) different individuals about their experiences and views of the issues, concerns and opportunities they face on a day to day basis, is you will receive ten (10) completely different answers (not two being the same).

Defining the Current Operating Model not only provides a baseline to measure progress (which addresses the *'you can't improve what you don't measure'* problem discussed earlier), but importantly also forces those on the Programme to come together and form a consensus and agreement on the state (and nature) of the actual problem(s) they are attempting to solve.

Failing to define the Current Operating Model will make it very hard, if not impossible to get agreement from the stakeholders of what the *'past'* looks like, especially when a Programme has moved 6-months along and they struggle to recall not only what the business looked like, but also how well (or not) it was performing.

In an ideal scenario, when meeting with the key stakeholders and defining and documenting the Current Operating Model, you should also capture the business' performance or success measures, metrics, KPIs, targets and results. This however will (and does) take additional time to capture, record and validate the performance metrics and results with the stakeholders (especially if the Organisation doesn't currently track these types of measures, which is *not* uncommon).

Validating and documenting the business metrics may also cause (or be perceived to cause, even before starting) a *bottleneck* in the process (and progress) of getting the Current Operating Model documented, reviewed and signed off. This is mostly due to key stakeholders not coming to an agreement with your findings, going back-and-forth debating certain performance figures, particularly where incentives and rewards are at stake.

Whether the '*full assessment*' is done upfront, or done later, as the Business Architect, your objective with defining the Current Operating Model is to develop a baseline description of the existing Business Architecture, to the extent necessary to support the Target Operating Model (TOM) design efforts.

If you decide (or are forced) not to do the '*full assessment*' of the Current Operating Model and chose not to capture, record and validate the performance measures and metrics at the time of defining the Current Operating Model, capturing this information should (and must) be done in Step-5 Design, when designing the Target Operating Model (TOM).

## Bottom-Up Analysis Approach

The approach or '*direction*' the analysis takes in defining the Current Operating Model is just as it sounds, 'bottom-up', starting at the foundation of the Organisation – the Organisation structure, and ending up at the centre (or heart) of the Organisation, at the Business Capabilities, as shown in Figure 7.2 below.

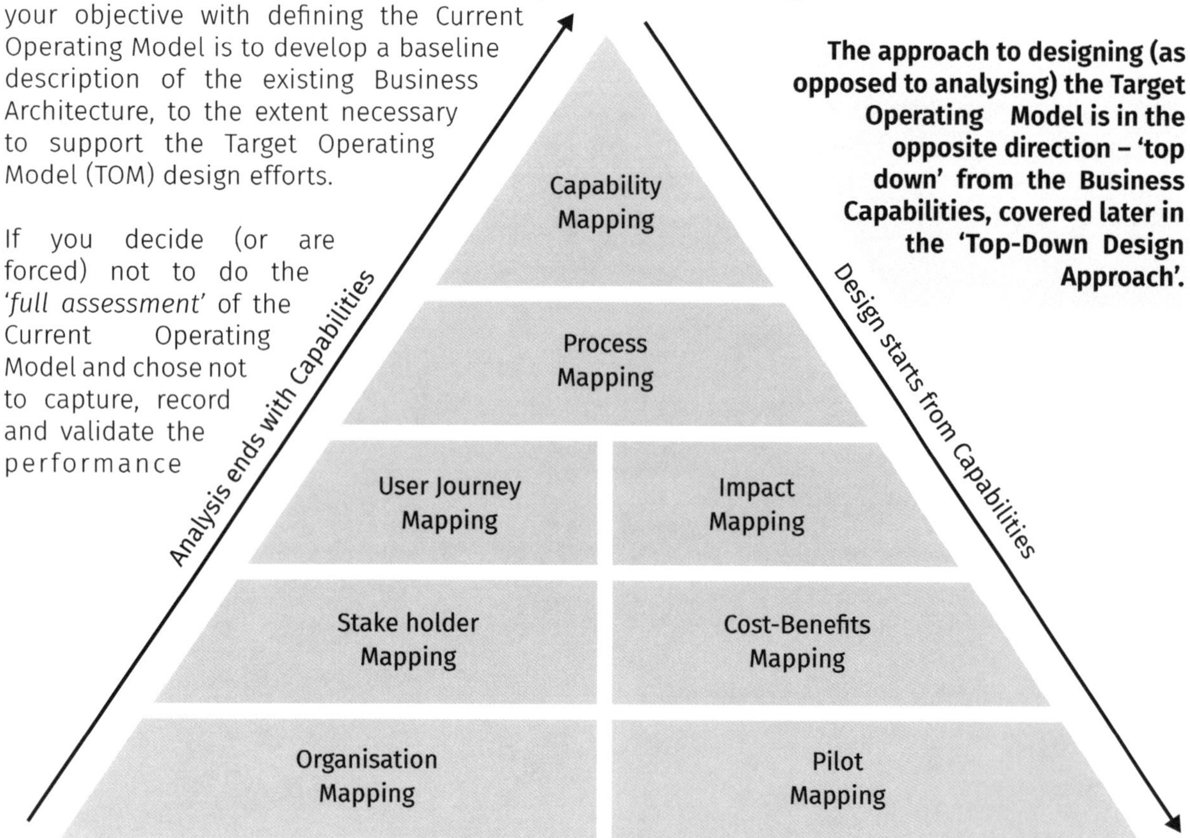


**Figure 7.2 -** HOBA® Analysis/Design Pyramid

## Current Operating Model

Step-3 'Analyse' is about defining the Current Operating Model. The Current Operating Model, also referred to as the 'baseline' or 'as-is' model, provides the 'baseline' to build and design the Target Operating Model (TOM) from.

As mentioned earlier in *Chapter 3 House of Business Architecture®* (**HOBA®**), each **HOBA®** Reference Model addresses a different aspect in the design and implementation of the Target Operating Model (TOM). These different aspects are represented in the following different views:

- Process
- Perspective
- Context, and
- Content

We will briefly discuss each of these views in the section below.

### Process

In terms of process, the Current Operating Model is the third (3rd) step in the Design Process.

Step-3 addresses the areas and activities necessary to defining the Current Operating Model, that establishes the 'baseline' of the Organisation, which the Target Operating Model (TOM) will be built and developed from.

### Perspective

In terms of perspective, the Current Operating Model provides the 'analyse' perspective or 'point of view', where all activities 'analyse' the current state and scope of the Organisation to help establish the baseline of the Organisation and Business Architecture today, from which the Target Operating Model (TOM) will be built and developed from.

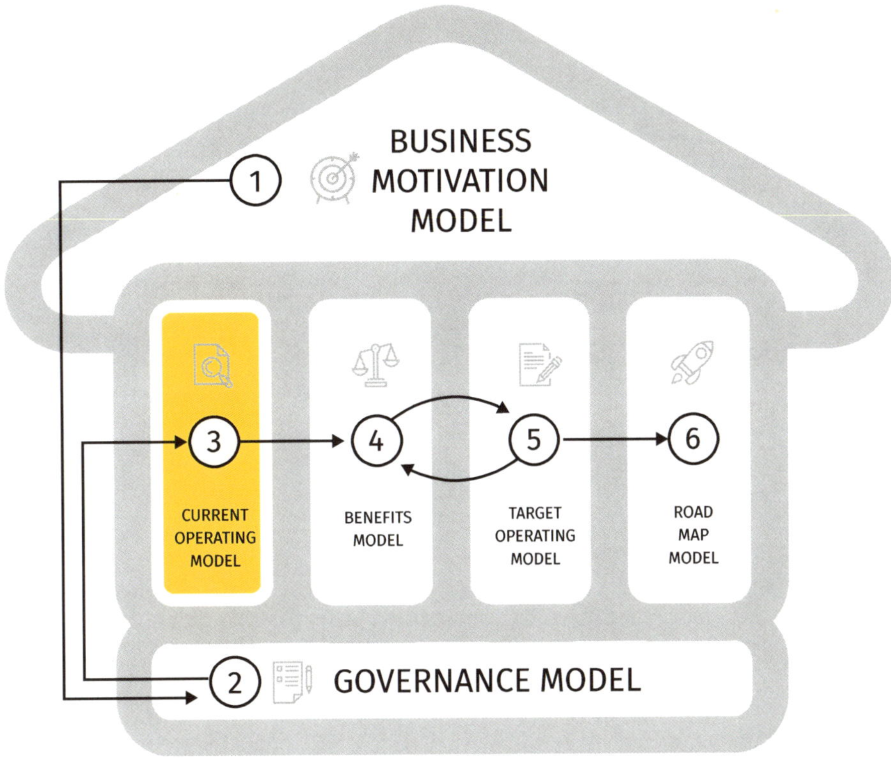


**Figure 7.3** - Current Operating Model - Step 3

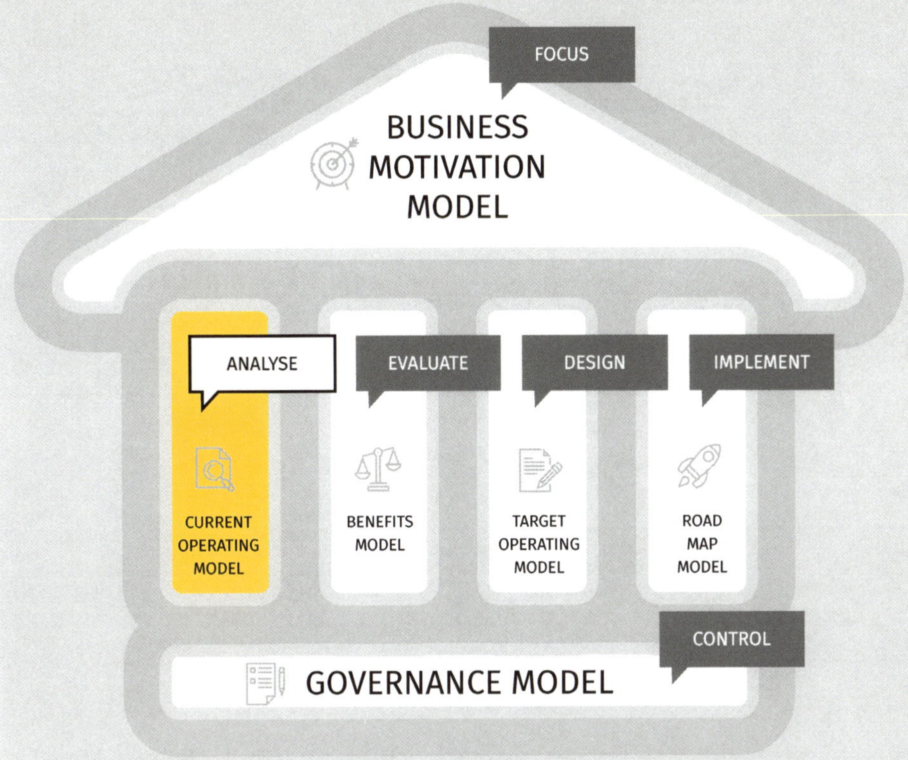


**Figure 7.4** - Current Operating Model – Analyse Perspective

## Context

Business Architecture today, from which the Target Operating Model (TOM) will Context

In terms of context, the Current Operating Model addresses the 'What?' aspect of the *'Why, Who, What, Where, How and When?'* questions asked of both the Business and the Business Architecture:

- What is the current state of the Organisation today?'
- 'What are the baseline measures and metrics of the Business the TOM will be improving from?'
- 'What are the elements (people, process, technology) of the Business that is being touched or changed by the Programme and Business Architecture?'

## Content

In terms of content, the Building Blocks and Blueprints developed here are the Business Architecture content that is necessary to define the current state and baseline measures and metrics of the Organisation which the TOM will be built from.

The list of Building Blocks and respective Blueprints that make up the Current Operating Model are shown in Table 7.1 (on the next page).

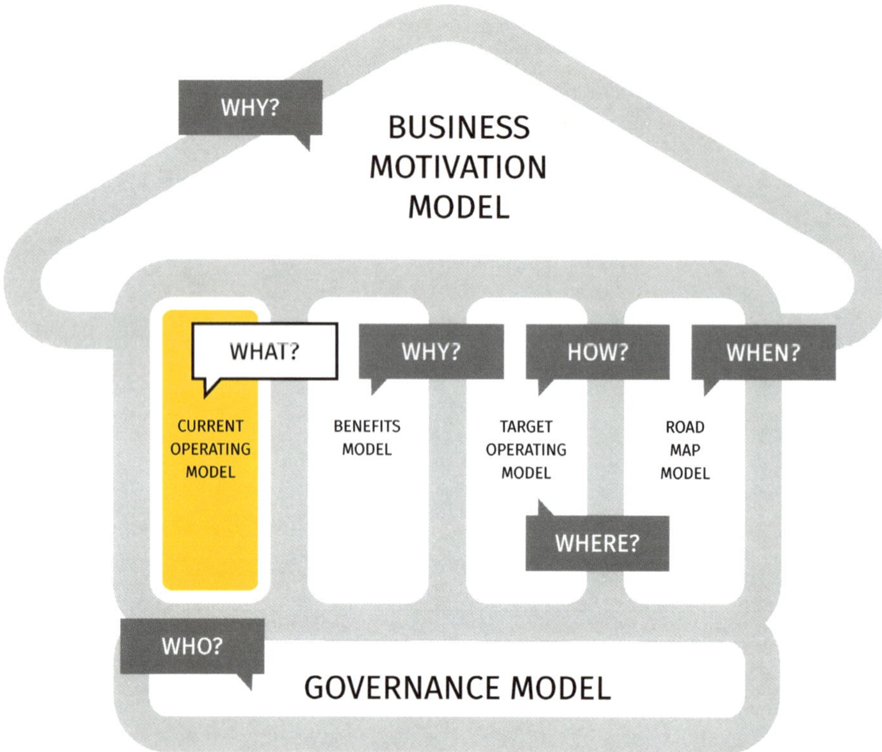


**Figure 7.5 -** Current Operating Model - 'What?'' Context

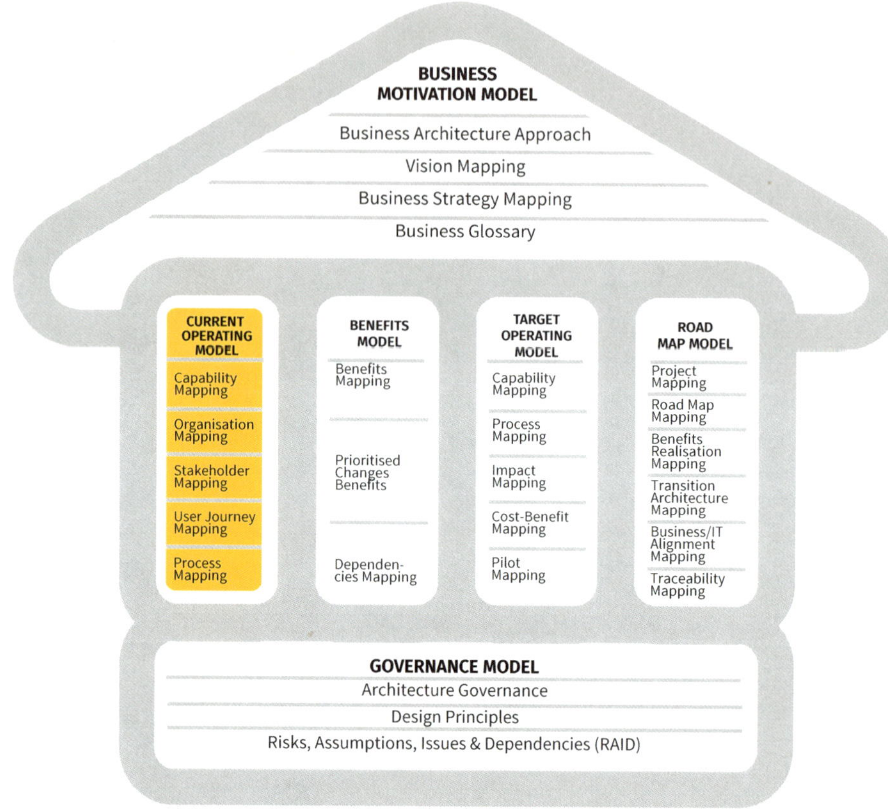


**Figure 7.6 -** Current Operating Model Building Block Content

**Current Operating Model Building Blocks and Blueprints**

**Table 7.1**

| Design Step | Building Block | Purpose | Blueprint |
|---|---|---|---|
| 3.1 | Organisation Mapping | Defines the 'As-Is' state Organisation, and in-scope areas (business units, divisions, functions etc.) that are in-scope for change. | 3.1.1 Organisation Chart |
| 3.2 | Stakeholder Mapping | Defines the 'As-Is' state Stakeholders and roles that are in-scope for change | 3.2.1 Stakeholder Map |
| 3.3 | User Journey Mapping | Defines the 'As-Is' state User Journeys that describes the interaction between a given stakeholder and the Organisation. | 3.3.1 User Journey Maps |
| 3.4 | Capability Mapping | Defines the 'As-Is' state capabilities and capability map(s) that are in-scope for change. | 3.6.1 Capability Maps |
| 3.5 | Process Mapping | Defines the 'As-Is' state processes, and process map(s) that are in-scope for change. | 3.7.1 Process Maps |

# High Level Process (SIPOC)

The Supplier-Input-Process-Output-Customer (SIPOC) process to completing this step – Step-3 Evaluation, and the Current Operating Model are shown in the SIPOC table below.

We will discuss each of the process steps (Building Blocks) within the SIPOC above in the following sections below.

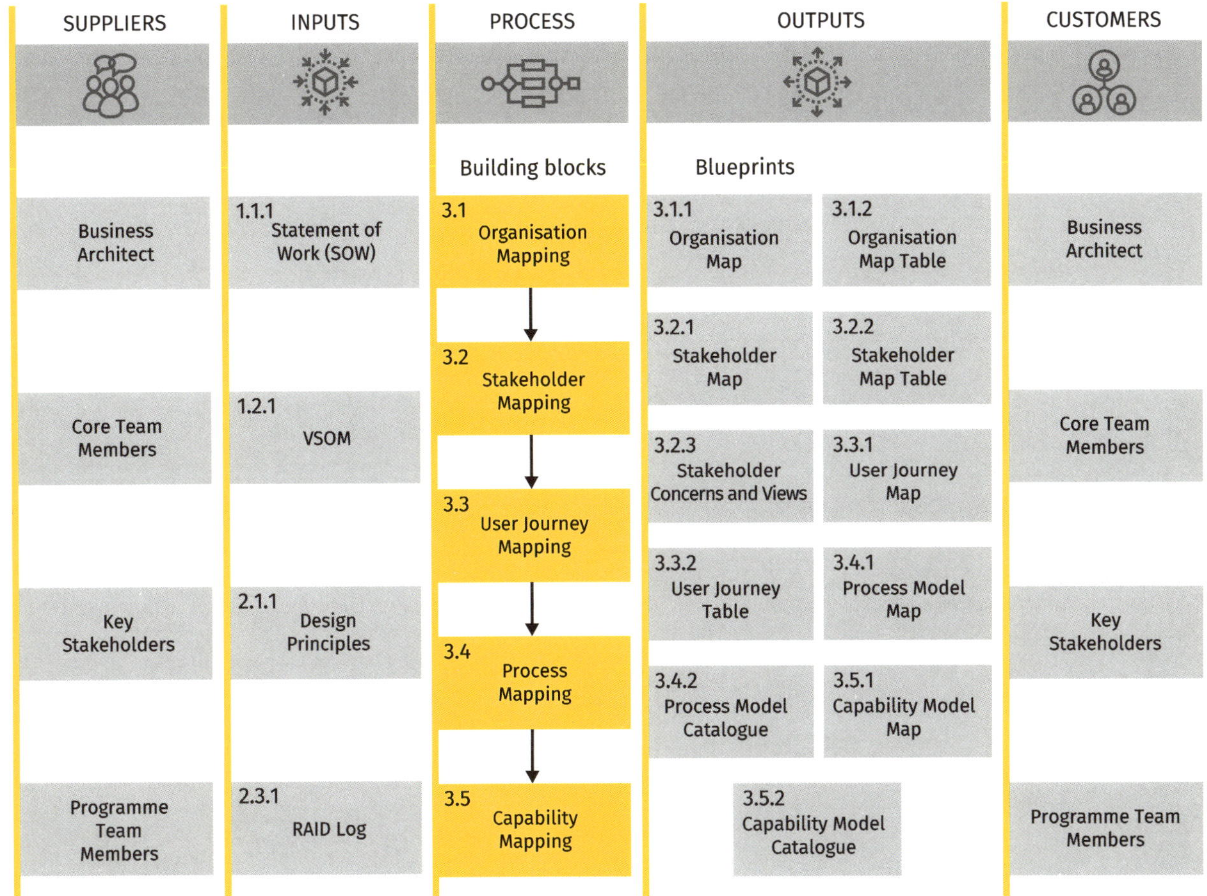


**Figure 7.7** - Current Operating Model SIPOC

# 3.1 Organisation Mapping (As-Is)

## Introduction

Organisation Mapping is a Building Block and first step in building up the Current Operating Model. Organisation Mapping is one part of identifying impacted and affected parts (i.e. business units, divisions, departments etc.) of the Organisation by identifying the changes brought about by the Programme outcomes (the other part is Stakeholder Mapping, the next Building Block in the Current Operating Model).

Organisation Mapping is an externally facing view or perspective from the Programme looking at the Organisation, used to identify which parts are impacted by change, and therefore in scope of the Programme.

Organisation Mapping is not about documenting and agreeing the Programme Organisation Chart or Programme Governance Structure on (or within) the Programme. The mapping of the Programme Organisation Chart, is of course a required activity and should be done, but possibly by the PMO instead of the Business Architect. The Governance Structure for the Programme was discussed earlier in the Design Process, in *Chapter 6 Step 2 – Control* and *the Governance Model.*

## Inputs

The inputs used to complete this Building Block are shown in Table 7.2.

## Outputs

The Blueprints (outputs) produced for this Building Block are shown in Table 7.3.

## Steps

The steps to complete the above Blueprints (Outputs) are as follows.

**Current Operating Model Building Blocks and Blueprints**

Table 7.2

| Ref | Blueprint | Use |
|---|---|---|
| 1.1.1 | Statement of Work (SOW) | Provides the initial Stakeholder list from which Organisation indicating the relevant business units, divisions and/or departments. |
| 2.3.1 | RAID Log | Shown here for completeness. RAID Log is not actually covered until the Governance Model, but should be used as input intothis Blueprint (and all Blueprints) as it contains the register of Risks, Assumptions, Issues and Dependencies that need to be checked against and updated as part of completing this Blueprint |
| N/A | Existing Business/ Programme Documentation | Include existing Organisation documentation, business case, existing project or Programme material that provide background information to the structure of the Organisation |

**Organisation Mapping Building Block (Outputs) Blueprints**

Table 7.3

| Ref | Blueprint | Description | Example |
|---|---|---|---|
| 3.1.1 | Organisation Map | The Organisation Map Blueprint provides the visual representation of the structure of the Organisation showing the relationships of the divisions, business units or departments. | 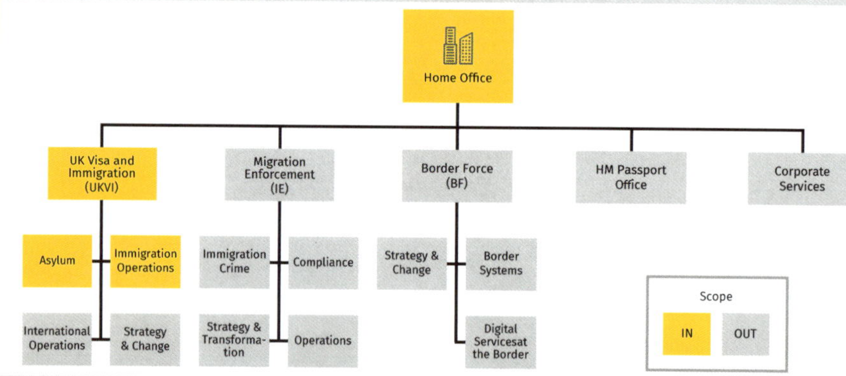 |
| 3.1.2 | Organisation (Map) Table | The Organisation (Map) table provides the Organisation Map details in tabular form for manageability, and later traceability. | |



| Organisation | Business Unit | Division | Location | In Scope |
|---|---|---|---|---|
| Home Office | UK Visa and Immigration (UKVI) | Asylum | Leeds, UK | Yes |
| | | Immigration Operations | London, UK | Yes |
| | | Strategy & Change | Cardiff, UK | No |
| | Immigration Enforcement | Immigration Crime | London, UK | No |
| | | Compliance | London, UK | No |
| | | Operations | London, UK | No |
| | | Strategy & Transformation | London, UK | No |
| | Border Force (BF) | Strategy & Change | London, UK | No |
| | | Border Systems | London, UK | No |
| | | Digital Services at the Border | London, UK | No |
| | HM Passport Office | N/A | N/A | No |
| | Corporate Services | N/A | N/A | No |

## 3.1.1 Organisation Map

### 1. Develop the Organisation Map

Using the Blueprint Inputs and other documentation from the 'Inputs' section above, analyse and identify the totality of the Organisations business units, divisions and/or departments (which every way the Organisation is set up), and plot the business units, departments etc. on the Organisation Map, marking the business areas/unit in/out of scope as appropriate.

An example of an Organisation Map is shown in Figure 7.8.

**Note – the above Organisation Map (Organogram) is not intended to represent an actual Organisation, but shown for illustration purposes only providing a rough approximation of the case study Organisation as stated in the Case Study section.**

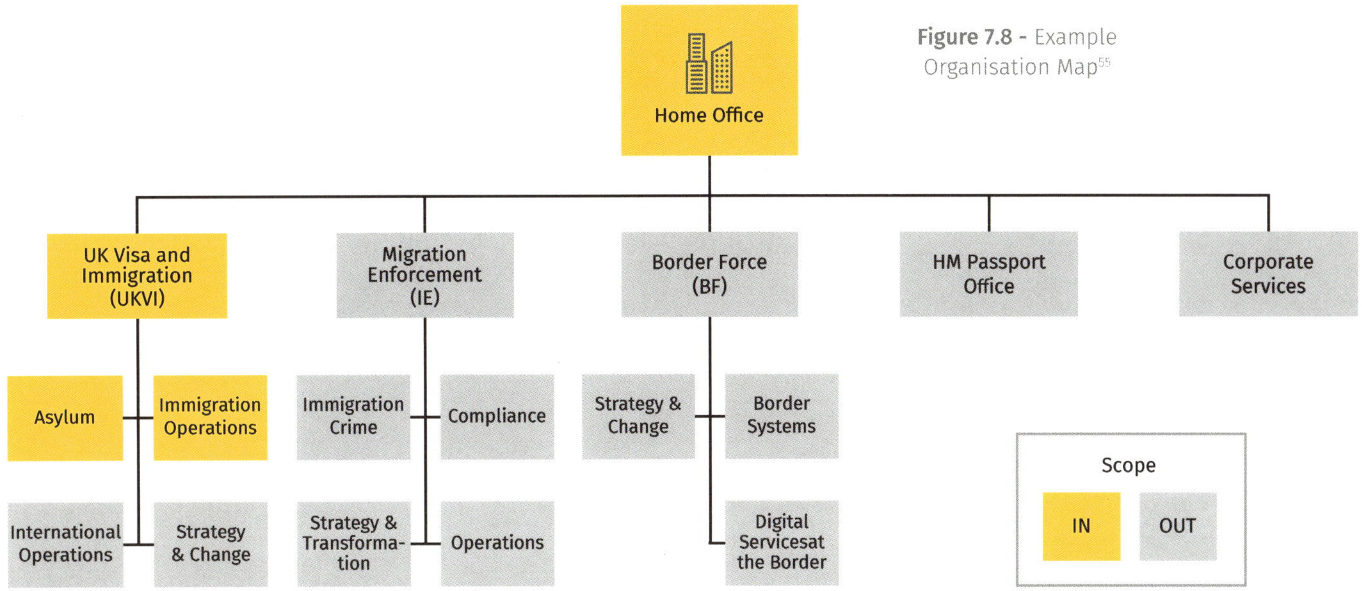


**Figure 7.8** - Example Organisation Map[55]

Example Organisation (Map) Table

**Table 7.4**

| Organisation | Business Unit | Division | Location | In Scope |
|---|---|---|---|---|
| Home Office | UK Visa and Immigration (UKVI) | Asylum | Leeds, UK | Yes |
| | | Immigration Operations | London, UK | Yes |
| | | Strategy & Change | Cardiff, UK | No |
| | Immigration Enforcement | Immigration Crime | London, UK | No |
| | | Compliance | London, UK | No |
| | | Operations | London, UK | No |
| | | Strategy & Transformation | London, UK | No |
| | Border Force (BF) | Strategy & Change | London, UK | No |
| | | Border Systems | London, UK | No |
| | | Digital Services at the Border | London, UK | No |
| | HM Passport Office | N/A | N/A | No |
| | Corporate Services | N/A | N/A | No |

## 3.1.2 Organisation (Map) Table

### 2. Record the Organisation Map Details

Capture the Organisation Map details in the Organisation (Map) Table, as shown in Table 7.4.

[55] Adapted from Data.gov.uk https://data.gov.uk/organogram/home-office (last updated 31 March 2016)

**3. Iteratively socialise, validate and refine the Blueprint(s)** (including any Risk, Assumptions, Issues and Dependencies (RAID) addressed or raised as part of completing these Blueprints), and

**4. Package and publish the map(s)** – in line with the agreed sprint/release cycle, established back in *Chapter 6 Step 2 – Control* and the *Governance Model*.

## Risks & Mitigations

The risk with Organisation Mapping and Org(anisation) Charts, is that they can quickly get complicated, or have the tendency too. Org Charts are rather simple models, intended to show the scope of the Organisation that is *in-scope* – as in, they are 'directly impacted' (or 'changed' by the changes being implemented) by the Programme, and their relationship to each other.

Org Charts tell us explicitly *'who'* (business unit/ department) and *'where'* (location/geography-wise) in the Organisation are within scope of the Programme, and therefore the Business Architecture.

What the Organisation Chart *doesn't* tell us however, is 'who' are those impacted and interested Stakeholders. They are Stakeholders within the Organisation that expect to benefit from the changes brought about by the outcomes implemented by the Programme and Business Architecture, being either:

- **'Primary' Stakeholders** – stakeholders that are directly impacted by the change the Programme delivers, through improved efficiencies the Programme is responsible for delivering (e.g. improved data or information, streamlined business processes etc.), or
- **'Secondary' Stakeholders** – stakeholders who are 'indirectly' impacted by the changes the Programme delivers, as either a 'customer' (A 'buyer' of the Business' products) or a 'consumer' (A 'user' of the Business' products) of the solutions that are delivered by the Programme.

What happens in practice is that the Organisation Map ends up containing everything (i.e. the parts of the Organisation that are affected *and* the Stakeholders involved) including the roles and responsibilities of those Stakeholders.

Building Business Architecture is like building a house. Building a house requires specific plans or Blueprints that show a particular view of the house for that Blueprints intended audience. There is a *plan* for the Plumber, the Electrician, and the Builder (among other 'impacted' primary stakeholders). Each plan provides a view that addresses a specific concern for its intended stakeholder. The Plumber wants to see where to run the pipes; the Electrician - where to run the cables, and the Builder - the floors, walls, and windows. The Plumber is concerned about the pipes being located in the correct place (and not hitting the electricity cables); the Electrician is concerned about running the wires where they need to go (so as not to hit the plumbing), and the Builder is concerned with the structure, so that he puts the floors, walls and windows in the right places so the other two can do their job.

If you have seen (or not seen) a set of house Blueprints, you will know that each stakeholder (i.e. Plumber, Electrician, Builder) has a separate plan or set of plans (and not a single plan, that combines all 3 sets of plans). This is because there would be too much detail, be almost impossible to read and be very confusing! The same applies to Business Architecture Blueprints i.e. the Organisation Chart for business units and locations is on one plan, and the Stakeholder Map for roles and responsibilities (and concerns) exists in another, and for good reason, to avoid causing confusion. So keep them separate (if you don't want to confuse your stakeholders, or overwhelm with too much information).

**The Organisation Chart is a simple and easy to use tool being intuitive and easy to understand. There are many permutations cross-mapping to other Blueprints, which is helpful, but this step is about defining the scope of the Organisation, not what the nature of the relationships between different elements of the Business Architecture are. The mapping to other elements or Blueprints is covered in Step-5 Design, as part of defining the Target Operating Model Reference Model.**

## Building Block Wrap-up

In this chapter, we discussed the Organisation Mapping Building Block.

The Organisation Mapping Building Block is critical to setting and agreeing the Scope for the Business Architecture and Programme, and consists of the following two (2) Blueprints:

- The **Organisation Chart,** which provides the visual (hierarchical view) and scope of the Organisation, highlighting which business units or departments are in and out of scope for the Programme, and
- The **Organisation Chart Table**, which captures and tables the Organisation Chart information.

The Organisation Chart forms the *first* of a two-part view of who are the stakeholders impacted by the changes being implemented by the Programme and Business Architecture. The second part is Stakeholder Mapping, which tells us the business role those stakeholders play in the Organisation and the degree to which their requirements are included (fully or partly) into the design of the Business Architecture.

**Next Steps**

Once the Organisation Mapping is completed and agreed related to the *in* (and *out* of) scope business units, divisions and/or departments, and where they are located (location/geographically).

The next step in the **Design Process** is to identify and validate the role(s) and responsibilities (and concerns) these Stakeholders play in the Organisation, and their role in the design of the Business Architecture.

# 3.2 Stakeholder Mapping (As-Is)

## Introduction

Stakeholder Mapping is the Building Block used to identify and confirm the stakeholders (including systems) that are in-scope for the Programme. It is also about identifying the interested parties that are impacted by the changes brought about by the Programme and assess their level of involvement both in the Programme, and the design of the Business Architecture.

The purpose of this Building Block is to build on the key stakeholders within the business units, departments and/or divisions (identified in the *Statement of Work (SOW)* and *Organisation Chart* Blueprints), and assess their 'role' in the Programme, and in developing the Business Architecture.

This Building Block builds on the initial Core Team (the stakeholders you will be working with on a day to day basis on the Programme) as identified in the *Statement of Work (SOW)*, and validates their role and involvement (which hasn't been done up until now). These stakeholders will become *'key'*, as they are both vital for the success of the Programme, in that they have both significant influence, and/or importance over decisions affecting the success of the Business Architecture and the Programme overall.

The benefit of Stakeholder Mapping – having confirmed all the key stakeholders have been identified and their level of involvement and influence has been determined for the Programme and for developing the Business Architecture, you can be sure:

1. You have the right stakeholders in the room (i.e. the stakeholders mostly impacted by the changes the Programme and Business Architecture is implementing, and the authority to make decisions for those impacted by those changes).
2. You are eliciting the needs and concerns from the right people.
3. You are not eliciting anything (i.e. requirements, needs or concerns) from anyone that isn't related to point (1) and (2) above.

**Remember, the *Statement of Work (SOW)* that was completed at the start of the Business Architects engagement on the Programme is in most cases completed between the Business Architect and the Programme Manager (PM), which is the PMs interpretation of events. Completing the Stakeholder Mapping is the first time the Business Architect will have contact with the Stakeholders directly, or via the Product Owner to validate those Stakeholders themselves and their concerns.**

Stakeholder Mapping also aims to prevent (the wrong) stakeholders *'assuming'* a role on the Programme and therefore the Business Architecture (in terms of either being Responsible, Accountable, Consulted and Informed (RACI)). It serves as a way to highlight if a person is either (1) not suitable for, and/or (2) doesn't concern themselves to the degree they would like (or believe). By getting the Stakeholder Mapping done, and done early

(Stakeholder Mapping is intentionally placed up front early in the Design Process for that reason), you will be able to identify who the right stakeholders are and what their actual stake in the Programme is, to set yourself up early for success.

**What often happens on large Programmes is everyone wants to get involved. Especially individuals impacted from your Programme who also have Programmes (or agendas) of their own which have been approved (are either delayed or are having issues getting funding). In cases such as this, they individuals often see your Programme as an opportunity to conveniently 'slide' their Programmes requirements into yours, for your Programme to deliver, effectively as a 'free ride'. This is a common tactic (or strategy) to get their Programme effectively delivered in whole (or part, in most cases it's the extensive, big cost items) without providing any commitment of additional budget or resources to pay for their requirements and (your) additional scope. This is obviously not only frustrating, spending time on requirements that aren't your own, but also time wasting. When your Stakeholders see this (which they often do), they become disheartened which in turn impacts their involvement and commitment on your Programme as they begin to believe their efforts maybe either side tracked or not return the benefits they are expecting.**

The Blueprint to capture the stakeholders is the Stakeholder Map. This map can take many forms. The objective is to make clear - who is in scope, and why? The Stakeholder 'Onion diagram' (below) provides a powerful and simple visual tool that clearly shows who the stakeholders are on your project or Programme (internal and external) and their role, which also shows by way of omission – who is not there, and any potential gaps (stakeholders or systems) that haven't been currently considered, or who may have even been overlooked.

An example of a Stakeholder Map is shown in the *Figure 7.9.*

## Inputs

The inputs used to complete this Building Block are shown in Table 7.5 (on the next page).

## Outputs

The Blueprints (outputs) produced for this Building Block are shown in Table 7.6 (on the next page).

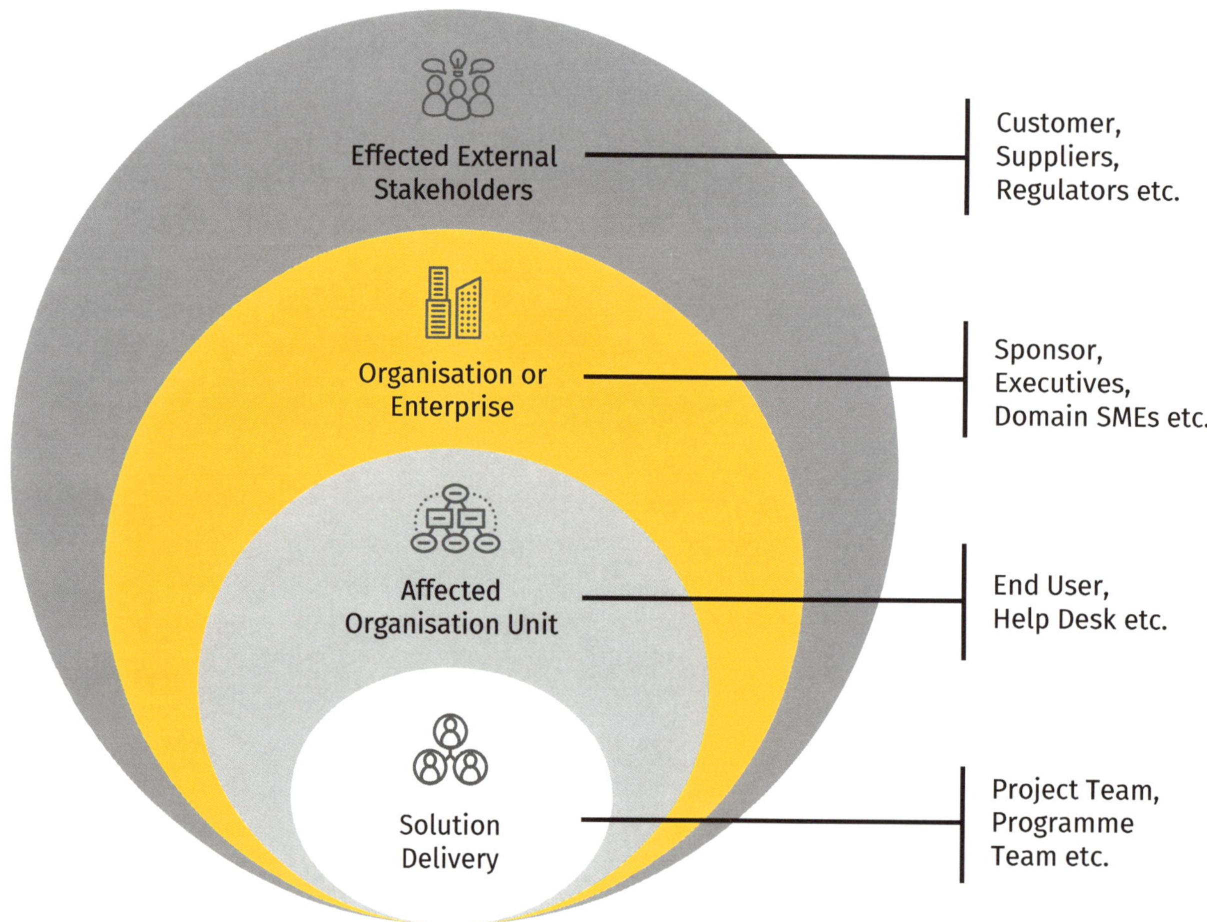


**Figure 7.9 -** Stakeholder Map Layout

## Stakeholder Mapping Building Block Inputs

**Table 7.5**

| Ref | Blueprint | Use |
|---|---|---|
| 1.1.1 | Statement of Work (SOW) | Provides the Problem Statement, end-to-end business process(es) impacted or affected, initial Stakeholder list and list of 'Stakeholders Concerns' as potential or candidate 'concerns' (or tensions). |
| 2.1.1 | Organisation Map | Provides the Divisions, Business Units and Departments to build, elaborate and validate the Stakeholder roles from. |
| N/A | Existing Business Documentation | Includes existing policies and procedures, manual, reference guides and process maps. |

## Stakeholder Mapping (Output) Blueprints

**Table 7.6**

| Ref | Blueprint | Description | Example |
|---|---|---|---|
| 3.1.1 | Stakeholder Map | A visual representation of the structure of the stakeholders affected by changes brought about by the Programme and Business Architecture, showing the relationships of people and systems both within and outside the Organisation. | 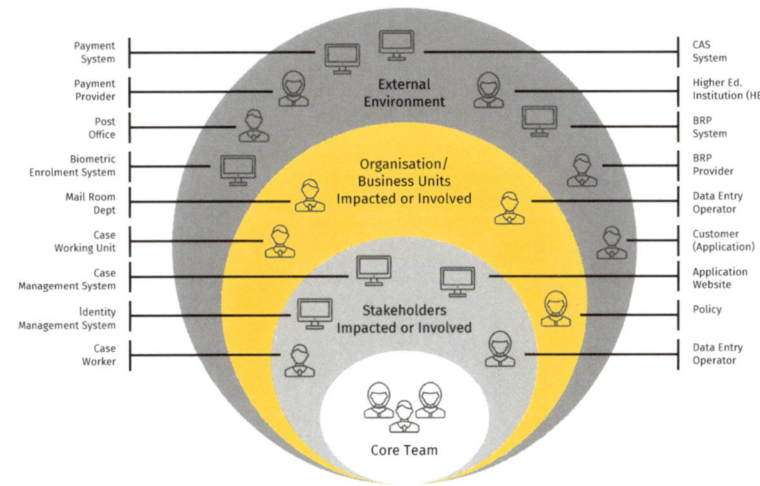 |
| 3.1.2 | Stakeholder (Map) Table | Documents the Stakeholder name/group, Organisation level, roles and date captured. | |



| Organisation Level | Stakeholder Name / Group | Stakeholder Role | Date Identified |
|---|---|---|---|
| Core Team | Product Owner | Represents business on the Programme | May 2016 |
| | Project Manager | Run and deliver the project within agreed time, quality and budget. | |
| | Scrum Master | Facilitate high performing, self-organizing team. | |
| | Business Architect | Design & Delivery of Business Architecture | |
| | Business Analyst | Articulate requirements into User Stories | |
| | Benefits Manager | Benefits identification and management | |
| | Technical Architect | Design & delivery of Technical Architecture | |
| | Test Manager | Systems Testing across the Programme | |
| | Software Development Mgr. | Delivery of successful code and software applications. | |
| Stakeholders Impacted or Involved | Case Worker | Case work & decide on Application | June 2016 |
| | Data Entry Operator | Data entry application details | |
| | Case Mgt. System | Record application & decision details | |
| | Identity Mgt. System | Used to search & update identity records | |
| | Application Website | Stores paper application(s) for download | |
| Organisation Business Unites Impacted or Involved | Case Working Unit | Manages casework for all applications | |
| | Mail Room Dept. | Handles all incoming & outgoing mail (incl. fraud check and payments) | |
| | Data Entry Dept. | Data entry for all paper applications | |
| | Policy Dept. | Ensure policy is implemented & maintained | |
| External Environment | Post Office | Registers Application biometrics (photo & fingerprints) | June 2016 |
| | Payment Provider | Processes Application payments fees | |
| | Higher Ed. Institution | Issue CAS to studies to complete application | |
| | Biometric Enrolment System | Records photo and finger prints | |
| | Payment System | System to process application fees | |
| | Cert. Acceptance Studies (CAS) System | System to manage CAS details | |
| | BRP Provider | Process requests for & send BRP cards | |
| | BRP System | Generate BRP cards | |
| | Customer (Applicant) | Makes and pays for application (student visa) | |

Stakeholder Mapping (Output) Blueprints

**Table 7.6**

<table>
<tr><th>Ref</th><th>Blueprint</th><th>Description</th><th>Example</th></tr>
<tr><td>3.1.3</td><td>Stakeholder Concerns Catalogue</td><td>Documents the Stakeholders Concerns, Needs (CTC), Measures of success (CTQ) and Business Architecture 'View' (Blueprint) concern is addressed in</td><td>
<table>
<tr><th>Stakeholder</th><th>Concern</th><th>CTC (Needs)</th><th>CTQ (Measures)</th><th>In Scope</th></tr>
<tr><td>Applicant (Student)</td><td>Application details are not available online and need to call the contact centre and ask for the progress or status of application and how far until a decision is made or expected.</td><td>Application status and progress information is available online, when requested.</td><td>Can log into an online system at any time (7 days a week, 24 hours a day) and view application status and progress.</td><td>· User Journey Map<br>· Process Model Map</td></tr>
<tr><td>Payment Provider</td><td>Need to ensure connectively throughout transition from Current to Future Process</td><td>Payment interface is available, when requested.</td><td>Applicant is able to processa payment when completing the application during service availability.</td><td>· Process Model Map<br>· Business Architecture Road Map<br>· Transition Architecture Map<br>· Business/IT Alignment Map</td></tr>
</table>
</td></tr>
</table>

## Steps

The Stakeholder Mapping Building Block is made up of the following Blueprints:

- Stakeholder Map
- Stakeholder (Map) Table
- Stakeholder Concerns and Views

We will discuss each of these Blueprints in the steps below.

### 3.1.1 Stakeholder Map

**1. Construct the Stakeholder Map** using the Blueprint *Inputs* and other documentation from the Inputs section above, particularly the end-to-end business process(es), placing each stakeholder/stakeholder group in the appropriate 'ring' location as shown in *Figure 7.10*.

### 3.1.2 Stakeholder (Map) Table

**2. Record the Stakeholder Map information** (Organisation level, name, group and business role they play) in the Stakeholder (Map) Table. An example of a Stakeholder (Map) Table is shown in Table 7.7.

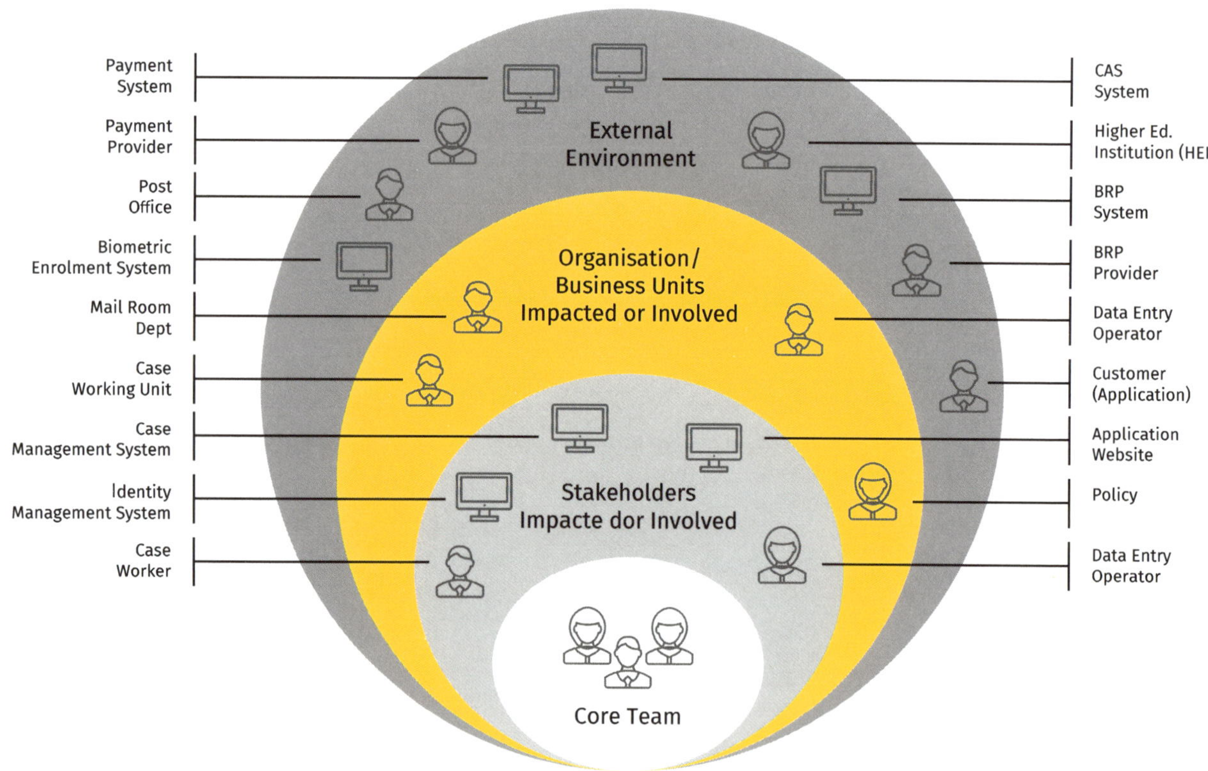


**Figure 7.10-** Example Stakeholder Map

Stakeholder (Map) Table

Table 7.7

| Organisation Level | Stakeholder Name / Group | Stakeholder Role | Date Identified |
|---|---|---|---|
| Core Team | Product Owner | Represents business on the Programme | May 2016 |
| | Project Manager | Run and deliver the project within agreed time, quality and budget. | |
| | Scrum Master | Facilitate high performing, self-organizing team. | |
| | Business Architect | Design & Delivery of Business Architecture | |
| | Business Analyst | Articulate requirements into User Stories | |
| | Benefits Manager | Benefits identification and management | |
| | Technical Architect | Design & delivery of Technical Architecture | |
| | Test Manager | Systems Testing across the Programme | |
| | Software Development Mgr. | Delivery of successful code and software applications. | |
| Stakeholders Impacted or Involved | Case Worker | Case work & decide on Application | June 2016 |
| | Data Entry Operator | Data entry application details | |
| | Case Mgt. System | Record application & decision details | |
| | Identity Mgt. System | Used to search & update identity records | |
| | Application Website | Stores paper application(s) for download | |
| Organisation Business Unites Impacted or Involved | Case Working Unit | Manages casework for all applications | |
| | Mail Room Dept. | Handles all incoming & outgoing mail (incl. fraud check and payments) | |
| | Data Entry Dept. | Data entry for all paper applications | |
| | Policy Dept. | Ensure policy is implemented & maintained | |
| External Environment | Post Office | Registers Application biometrics (photo & fingerprints) | June 2016 |
| | Payment Provider | Processes Application payments fees | |
| | Higher Ed. Institution | Issue CAS to studies to complete application | |
| | Biometric Enrolment System | Records photo and finger prints | |
| | Payment System | System to process application fees | |
| | Cert. Acceptance Studies (CAS) System | System to manage CAS details | |
| | BRP Provider | Process requests for & send BRP cards | |
| | BRP System | Generate BRP cards | |
| | Customer (Applicant) | Makes and pays for application (student visa) | |

Note:
- Stakeholder Name / Group - is the name of the business or functional group within the Organisation the stakeholder belongs to.
- Stakeholder Role – is the role the stakeholder plays in their Organisation level.
- Date Identified – is the date this assessment took place, used to baseline when this activity was carried out.

### 3.1.3 Stakeholder Concerns and Views

**3. Identify (and validate) the stakeholder's explicit needs**, in context of their business role (identified above), using a LEAN/Six Sigma Voice of the Customer (VOC) technique that identifies the following:

- Customer's needs – known as 'Critical to Customer' (or CTCs), and
- Measures of those needs - known as 'Critical to Quality' (or CTQs).

The 'Customer' in this context, includes external (to the Organisation) customers (i.e. Visa Applicant), but also internal (to the Organisation) customers (e.g. Operations Department Users).

Using the initial Stakeholder Concerns from the *Statement of Work (SOW)* taken from the *Inputs* section (above), validate and record their CTCs and CTQs in the Stakeholder Concerns and Views table.

An example of a Stakeholder Concerns and Views Table is shown in Table 7.8 below.

Note:
- Critical to Quality (CTQ) is different to Critical to Customer (CTC):
  - CTC - is about what is important to the customer (i.e. needs),
  - CTQ - provides the quantitative measure of that need.
- A Person or Role can occur more than once in the table, and may have more than one row. Repeat where a Person or Role has more than one issue.

**4. Iteratively socialize, validate and refine each Blueprint** (including any risk, assumptions, issues and dependencies addressed or raised as part of completing this Blueprint), and

**5. Package and publish the Blueprints** – in line with your agreed sprint/release cycle, established back in the Governance Model in *Chapter 6 Step 2 – Control.*

Example Stakeholder Concerns and Views Table

Table 7.8

| Stakeholder | Concern | CTC (Needs) | CTQ (Measures) | View |
|---|---|---|---|---|
| Applicant (Student) | Application details are not available online and need to call the contact centre and ask for the progress or status of application and how far until a decision is made or expected. | Application status and progress information is available online, when requested. | Can log into an online system at any time (7 days a week, 24 hours a day) and view application status and progress. | • User Journey Map<br>• Process Model Map |
| Payment Provider | Need to ensure connectively throughout transition from Current to Future Process | Payment interface is available, when requested. | Applicant is able to processa payment when completing the application during service availability. | • Process Model Map<br>• Business Architecture Road Map<br>• Transition Architecture Map<br>• Business/IT Alignment Map |

## Risks and Mitigations

There are a few risks and issues with Stakeholder Mapping you should be aware of.

There is the risk with **'over doing'** Stakeholder Mapping with the tendency to spend too much time, energy and effort potentially *'trying to make a silk purse out of a pig's ear'.* This is where you spend too much time doing the analysis of where the stakeholders should be placed on the map, and spending too much time deciding on the *'best'* map or model to present the findings in. Simplicity is the key to avoid overdoing things.

There is also the risk that your Stakeholder Map gets *too busy* and is crowded with too many (unnecessary) Stakeholders on it. If you have an extensive stakeholder list and therefore a (potentially) busy Stakeholder Map, your Business Architecture design, development and sign off will face an uphill battle. You will struggle getting not only the right level of management oversight and buy-in, but the velocity of continuously producing regularly updated (and workable) Blueprints out to the Programme is going to be negatively affected. You want the right level and number of stakeholders involved, so you have to manage this. To manage this, assign a *'Must, Should, Could and Won't (MoSCoW)'* rating to each stakeholder concern, and group (or remove) stakeholders where there is a concentration (or lack of concentration) represented in a specific Stakeholder category or area of the business.

There is also the risk of confusing the Stakeholder Mapping and Stakeholder Maps with the *RACI Matrix,* and *RACI Stakeholders.* Although there are similarities, Stakeholder Mapping is not about identifying the stakeholders who are responsible or accountable for sign-off of the Business Architecture Blueprints on and across the Programme (that was completed as part of the Governance Model). In most cases, the Product Owner is representing the Business, and Business Representatives, and acts as the conduit between the Programme and the Business, taking and making most decisions for these Stakeholders, on their behalf.

The relationship between the Stakeholder Map and RACI is shown in *Figure 7.11.*

Most (if not all) of these Stakeholder Map 'business roles' are represented on the Programme and Business Architecture via the Product Owner. The Product Owner is the Voice of the Customer (VoC) for the customer/roles, being the single point of contact. All questions, issues and concerns regarding stakeholder's roles, needs etc. in the first instance should go to, and through the Product Owner first, and then directly to the roles and individuals concerned (if required). This could be done via focus groups – led by the Product Owner, and supported and/or initiated by you (as and when needed).

There is the risk that Stakeholder Mapping is 'not done at all', or 'over looked' as it was incorrectly assumed it has been already completed by another part of the Programme. This happens when it is not clear (or has been mistakenly assumed) that another part of the Programme has already completed this, as this task (Stakeholder Mapping) is often completed by the Project or Programme Management Office (PMO), Business Analysis or Project Manager – and not the Business Architect or Business Architecture. What often happens in practice is it is assumed they are done, but in actual fact stakeholder mapping was started, but never signed off.

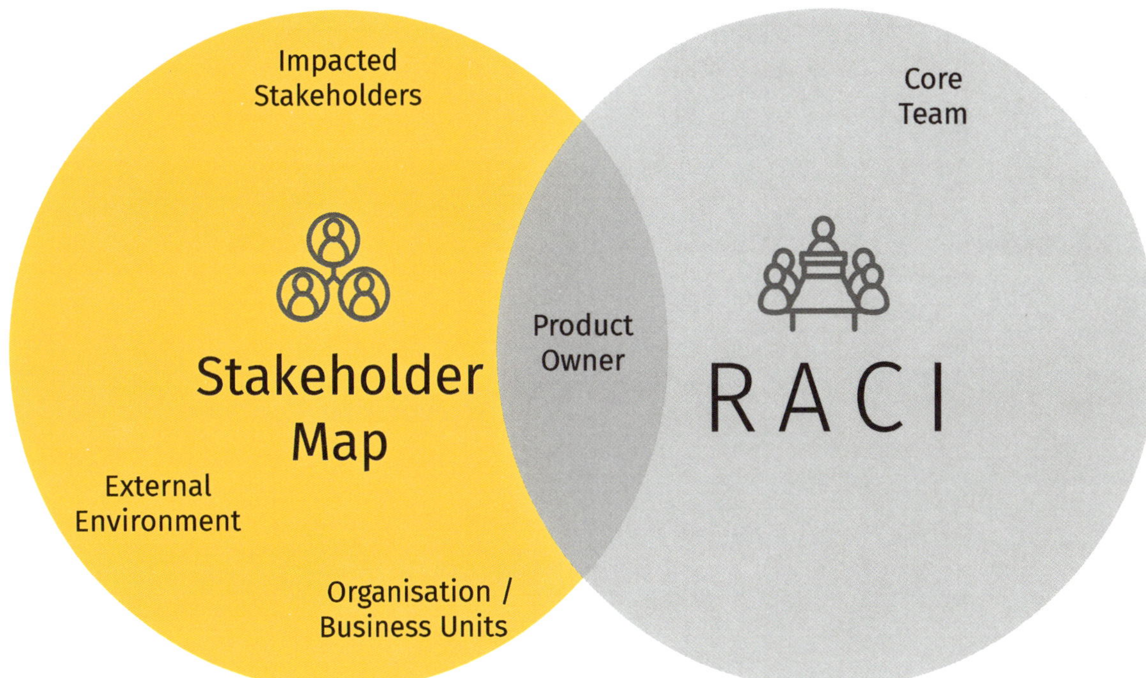


**Figure 7.11 -** Relationship Between Stakeholder Map and RACI

Getting the key stakeholder roles and responsibilities and concerns clearly articulated and agreed, puts the Customer needs first and foremost in the Design Process, and in developing the design of the TOM. It also provides the visibility to the Business, that by articulating their issues and needs upfront and early in the Design Process and Programme lifecycle, that there is no ambiguity of what their needs and concerns are, how to measure success and which Business Architecture view they should expect to see their needs and concerns addressed in.

**Without a clear definition of who the Key Stakeholders are, their individual issues and needs, and how to measure success (i.e. the conditions present confirming their needs have been addressed), the Programme is set to spin around and around as participants debate these facts later in the project and Programme lifecycle. If you are told it has been completed (which is often the case with large Programmes), but no one can find or produce any documented evidence of it, it hasn't been done. These key stakeholders and their needs are (or will become) the centre and subject of all the other Building Blocks and Blueprints, and ultimately the success of the Programme.**

### Building Block Wrap-up

In this chapter, we discussed the Stakeholder Mapping Building Block.

The Stakeholder Mapping Building Block validates and agrees who are the key stakeholders on the Programme, their business role (and responsibilities), as well as their concerns, CTCs (needs) and CTQs (measures).
This Building Block is made of the following three (3) Blueprints:

- Stakeholder (Onion Diagram) Map – provides the visual representation and categorisation of the Stakeholders (people and systems) both within and outside the Organisation affected by the Programme and Business Architecture;
- Stakeholder (Map) Table – documents the Stakeholder name/group and Business role; and
- Stakeholder Concerns and Views – documents the Stakeholders Concerns, Needs (Critical to Customer or 'CTC'), Measures (Critical to Quality or 'CTQ') and Business Architecture Blueprint (View) the Stakeholder concerns are addressed in.

There is a lot of confusion and challenges with Stakeholder Mapping – including its purpose, level of detail, who to include or whether it was actually carried out or not. Several strategies were provided above to address those challenges.

Stakeholder Mapping plays an important role in gaining buy-in and confidence from the Organisation and Key Stakeholders that the Business Architecture correctly identifies and validates the Key Stakeholders, their concerns, CTCs and CTQs, and which Business Architecture Blueprint(s) (view) will address their concerns and needs.

### Next Steps

Once the Stakeholder Mapping Building Block has been agreed, the next step in the **Design Process** is to complete the User Journey Building Block to define the journey and the experience (i.e. good, bad or indifferent) the Customer User has with the Organisation and identify opportunities for improvement.

User Journeys are discussed in the User Journey Mapping Building Block in the section below.

# 3.3 User Journey Mapping (As-Is)

## Introduction

The User Journey Mapping Building Block describes the interactions between the User (in most cases, the external Customer) and the Organisation. User Journeys provide the scope of the Programme and problem statement in context of the Customer and their interaction with the Organisation.

The User Journey (*'User Journeys'*) Map Blueprint is used to show the Customer/Organisation interaction, as the sequence of steps that are undertaken by the Customer in the end-to-end process and interaction with the Organisation.
The purpose of User Journeys is to:

- Help show and understand the key business functions that are involved during the User's interaction with the Organisation in terms of:
  - **Process** - What happens to the Customer during their interaction with the Organisation,
  - **Goals** – What is the Customer intending to gain at each stage of the process,
  - **Experience** - How the customer feels (concerns, issues) about what happens to them during the interaction, and
  - **Improvement Opportunities** – changes to the Organisation that could improve the Customer experience.
- Visualise the interaction (and dependencies) between the User (in their Journey) and the

different Building Blocks and Blueprints of the Business Architecture (e.g. capabilities) to show where and how their concerns and issues are addressed.

The benefits of User Journeys and User Journey Mapping is they:

- Provide a single cross-business view of the customer's interaction and experience with all the Organisations facing and supporting functions;
- Help define key enabling requirements (people, process, technology, etc.), and
- Highlight areas of importance (areas that are critical to the delivery of the User journey, and experience), areas of concern and improvement opportunities to maintain or improve the User's experience.

**User Journeys leverages and builds off Blueprints completed earlier (namely the SOW and the Stakeholder Map), to provide the context of where the User and Key Stakeholders concerns are visible. The idea of User Journeys is to elaborate on the predecessor Blueprints, validate and uncover new or different concerns as well used to help prioritise the order that these concerns will be addressed in.**

The value of User Journeys 'feel' perspective, is they help to understand and put into context both what the customer 'feels' (issues, concerns), as well as 'where' in their interaction with the Organisation they experience it. By knowing 'what' this experience feels like and 'where' in the User's Journey with the Organisation they experience it, the Organisation in turn is able to address their frustrations when developing the TOM, and put the User (and their frustrations) first in the planning and design work to improve their experience and satisfaction by addressing their frustrations directly.

## Inputs

The inputs used to complete this Building Block are shown in Table 7.9..

## Outputs

The Blueprints (outputs) produced for this Building Block are shown in Table 7.10 (on the next page).

## Steps

The steps to complete the above Blueprint (Outputs) are as follows

## 5.3.1 User Journey Map

### 1. Develop the User Journey Map

Using the Blueprint *Inputs* from the Inputs section above, define and list the high-level end to end Business Process for the External User(s). Analyse the External User's Journey and plot each of the User Journey elements for each high-level business process phase:

- **User Goal**
- **Interaction 'touch' points** (between the User and the Organisation)
- **User Experience*** (Concerns, Thoughts & Overall Experience)
- **Improvement Opportunities****

An example of a User Journey Map is shown in Figure 7.12 (on page 169).

**Notes:**

- **(*) 'User Experience' (*Concerns, Thoughts*) captured here should reconcile and validate the Stakeholder *Issues* and *Concerns* already captured previously from the Stakeholder Mapping Blueprint. Use the Stakeholder Mapping 'Issues and Concerns' to both cross-check that all the known concerns are captured (i.e. no gaps) and still valid.**
- **(**) 'Improvement Opportunities' captured here are a first attempt or initial thinking on possible solutions that will directly address the Stakeholders concerns. These will be built on later, and validated in the Benefits Model, and Benefits Dependencies Mapping which defines the 'Enabler' and 'Business Changes' that directly impact and drive the intended Business Benefits the Organisation intends to realise.**

RAID Building Block Inputs

Table 7.9

| Ref | Blueprint/Documentation | Use |
|---|---|---|
| 1.1.1 | Statement of Work (SOW) | Provides the initial Stakeholder List, Concerns and Views. |
| 1.2.1 | Vision (VSOM) | Provides the Vision, and articulated business goals (strategy, objectives and measures) that all requirements including the 'improvement opportunities' should align to and support. |
| 2.2.1 | Design Principles | Provides the scope and boundaries of the Programme, Business Architecture, and improvement opportunities |
| 2.3.1 | RAID Log | Contains register of Risks, Assumptions, Issues and Dependencies that need to be checked against (and updated) as part of completing this Blueprint. |

## Table 7.10

| Ref | Blueprint | Description | Example |
|---|---|---|---|
| 3.3.1 | User Journey Map | A visual representation of the interaction and touch points (physical and online), the User goals, concerns, thoughts), overall rating as well as opportunities for improvements* between the User and Organisation across the User Journey. (*) Note – these will inform 'Enablers' and 'Business Changes' as part of Benefit- Dependencies Map(s). | 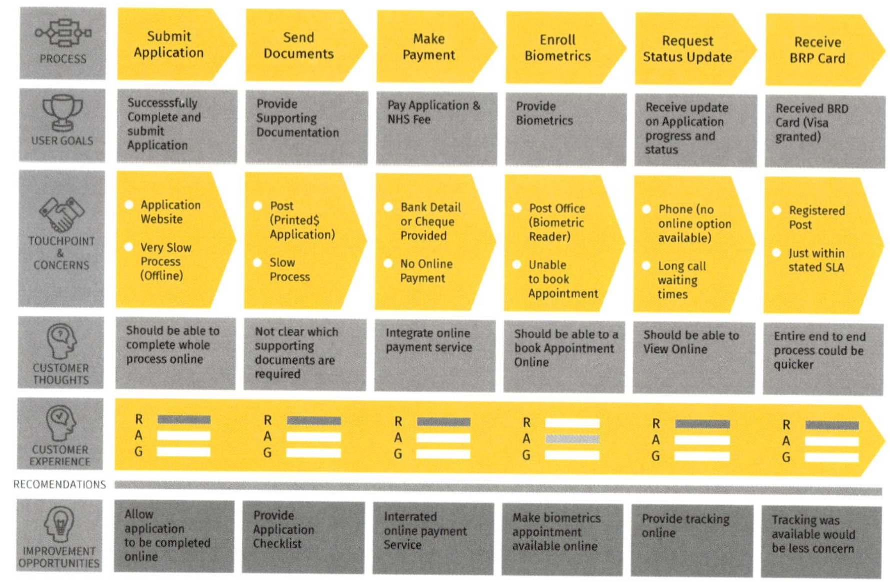 |



| Ref | Blueprint | Description |
|---|---|---|
| 3.3.2 | User Journey (Map) Table | List of all User Journey Maps, including User, Journey, Start and End Points. |

| User Journey | User | Phase No. | Phase Name | Goal | Touch Point | Concern | Exp. | Improve |
|---|---|---|---|---|---|---|---|---|
| Student Visa Appl'n | Student | 1 | Submit Application | Submit Regist'n Online | Appl'n Website | View Slow | RED | Complete Appl'n online |
| | | 2 | Send Documents | Provide Support Doc's | Post | Slow Process | RED | Provide Appl'n checklist |
| | | 3 | Make Payment | Fee Paid | Online (own) Banking | No online payment (within process) | RED | Integrate online payment Service |
| | | 4 | Enrol Biometrics | Provide Biometric | Post Office | Unable to book Ap't | AMBER | Ability to book online |
| | | 5 | Request Status | Update on progress | Call Centre (phone) | Long call wait times | RED | Provide online tracking |
| | | 6 | Receive BRP Card | Card received (Visa granted) | Registered Post | Slow process (just within SLA) | RED | Tracking would elevate stress |
| | Data Entry Op'ator | 1 | Submit Application | Manually input missing data | Case working System | Double entry from App Site to Case System | RED | Remove double entry; User entry populate Case System directly |
| | | 2 | Send Documents | Receive Physical doc's | Mail room | Typos on Users entry | RED | Validation at time of entry (online) |

| PROCESS | Submit Application | Send Documents | Make Payment | Enroll Biometrics | Request Status Update | Receive BRP Card |
|---|---|---|---|---|---|---|
| USER GOALS | Successsfully Complete and submit Application | Provide Supporting Documentation | Pay Application & NHS Fee | Provide Biometrics | Receive update on Application progress and status | Received BRD Card (Visa granted) |
| TOUCHPOINT & CONCERNS | • Application Website<br>• Very Slow Process (Offline) | • Post (Printed$ Application)<br>• Slow Process | • Bank Detail or Cheque Provided<br>• No Online Payment | • Post Office (Biometric Reader)<br>• Unable to book Appointment | • Phone (no online option available)<br>• Long call waiting times | • Registered Post<br>• Just within stated SLA |
| CUSTOMER THOUGHTS | Should be able to complete whole process online | Not clear which supporting documents are required | Integrate online payment service | Should be able to a book Appointment Online | Should be able to View Online | Entire end to end process could be quicker |
| CUSTOMER EXPERIENCE | R A G | R A G | R A G | R A G | R A G | R A G |
| RECOMENDATIONS | | | | | | |
| IMPROVEMENT OPPORTUNITIES | Allow application to be completed online | Provide Application Checklist | Interrated online payment Service | Make biometrics appointment available online | Provide tracking online | Tracking was available would be less concern |

Figure 7.12 - Example User Journey Map

## 5.3.2 User Journey (Map) Table

**2. Develop the User Journey (Map) Table.** For completeness and traceability, record the User Journey Map details in the User Journey (Map) Table, as shown in Table 7.11.

**3. Repeat (for each of the Internal Users)** their User Journey for each phase of the External Users journey (as shown in Table 7.11),

**4. Iteratively socialise, validate and refine the Blueprint(s)** (including any Risks, Assumptions, Issues and Dependencies (RAID) addressed or raised as part of completing these Blueprints), and

**5. Package and publish the Blueprint**s – in line with the agreed sprint/release cycle, established back in *Chapter 6 Step 2 – Control* and the *Governance Model.*

Example User Journey (Map) Table

**Table 7.11**

| User Journey | User | Phase No. | Phase Name | Goal | Touch Point | Concern | Exp. | Improve |
|---|---|---|---|---|---|---|---|---|
| Student Visa Appl'n | Student | 1 | Submit Application | Submit Regist'n Online | Appl'n Website | View Slow | RED | Complete Appl'n online |
| | | 2 | Send Documents | Provide Support Doc's | Post | Slow Process | RED | Provide Appl'n checklist |
| | | 3 | Make Payment | Fee Paid | Online (own) Banking | No online payment (within process) | RED | Integrate online payment Service |
| | | 4 | Enrol Biometrics | Provide Biometric | Post Office | Unable to book Ap't | AMBER | Ability to book online |
| | | 5 | Request Status | Update on progress | Call Centre (phone) | Long call wait times | RED | Provide online tracking |
| | | 6 | Receive BRP Card | Card received (Visa granted) | Registered Post | Slow process (just within SLA) | RED | Tracking would elevate stress |
| | Data Entry Op'ator | 1 | Submit Application | Manually input missing data | Case working System | Double entry from App Site to Case System | RED | Remove double entry; User entry populate Case System directly |
| | | 2 | Send Documents | Receive Physical doc's | Mail room | Typos on Users entry | RED | Validation at time of entry (online) |

## Risks & Mitigations

The risks and mitigations with User Journey Mapping is that User Journeys aren't given the credit or creditability they deserve. This is mainly due to their mistaken identity. User Journeys are often (and wrongly) mistaken for Process Maps, or Value Maps.

User Journeys and User Journey Mapping are different to Process Maps or Value Maps in that User Journeys are designed to describe how the User *'feels'* about their experience with the Organisation, whereas Process Maps and Value Maps are designed to describe *'what happens'* to a User (throughout that journey). Although the process might be efficient, and cost effective for the Organisation, if it's not a rewarding or beneficial experience for the Customer (or worse it becomes a painful experience), it is likely that they will not continue business with the Organisation and any improvements gained in creating a Target Operating Model (TOM) are effectively nullified.

## Building Block Wrap-up

In this section, we discussed the User Journey Building Block.

The User Journey Building Block is critical to visualise a cross Organisation view of the External (and Internal) User experience in their interaction with the Organisation, and consists of the following two (2) Blueprints:

- User Journey Map, which provides the visual representation of the External Users journey, goals, touchpoints, experience (concerns, thoughts, ratings) and improvement opportunities, and
- User Journey (Map) Table, which captures and tables the User Journey Map information details.

User Journeys is a key tool in putting the User (i.e. External and Internal Customers) issues and concerns in the forefront of any planning and development of the TOM, by providing the visual context of the Users experience and interaction with the Organisation, highlighting 'what' the Customer feels (issues, concerns), and 'where' in the interaction with the Organisation this occurs.

By knowing 'what' this experience feels like and 'where' in the Users Journey with the Organisation they experience it, the Organisation is able to directly address their frustrations in the development of the TOM.

## Next Steps

Once the User Journey Mapping is agreed, the next step in the Design Process is to identify and validate the business processes across the Organisation and explicitly which business process are in scope (and not in scope) for changes as a result of the Programme and implementing the TOM.

# 3.4 Process Mapping (As-Is)

## Introduction

Process Mapping is the Building Block that defines the Organisations Process Model, and framework to identify the totality of all processes across the Organisation and specifically the processes the Programme is impacting in developing the Target Operating Model (TOM). It is with this agreed and defined Process Model, that the Business Architect will then work with the Business Analyst and hand over the in-scope high level processes for detailed mapping, discovery and analysis with their expertise detailed mapping and analysis skills.

This approach may fly in the face of what you may have been taught in regards to Process Mapping, and *'Who does what?'*. So, if you're thinking the Business Architect isn't really doing the 'mapping' per se, you are correct. You will recall the differences (and similarities) between Business Architecture/Business Architects and Business Analysis/Business Analysts were discussed earlier in this book, in the Challenge #1: What is Business Architecture? section so we won't go over old ground (but it's worth going over the main points). There are five (5) points of difference between Business Architecture and Business Architects compared with Business Analysis and Business Analysts:

- They have a different focus.
- They operate at a different Organisation level.
- They are engaged at different times (or phase) within the Programme.
- They have similar tools, but use them differently.
- The scale of change is different.

Figure 7.13 (on the next page) shows that Business Architecture is involved earlier in the 'planning' stages in the Organisation and Programme and has a longer-term strategic focus, versus the Business Analyst who is engaged or involved later in the Programme lifecycle, once the problem and requirements for a solution have been identified with their shorter-term 'delivery' focus to translate the business requirements into implementation requirements.

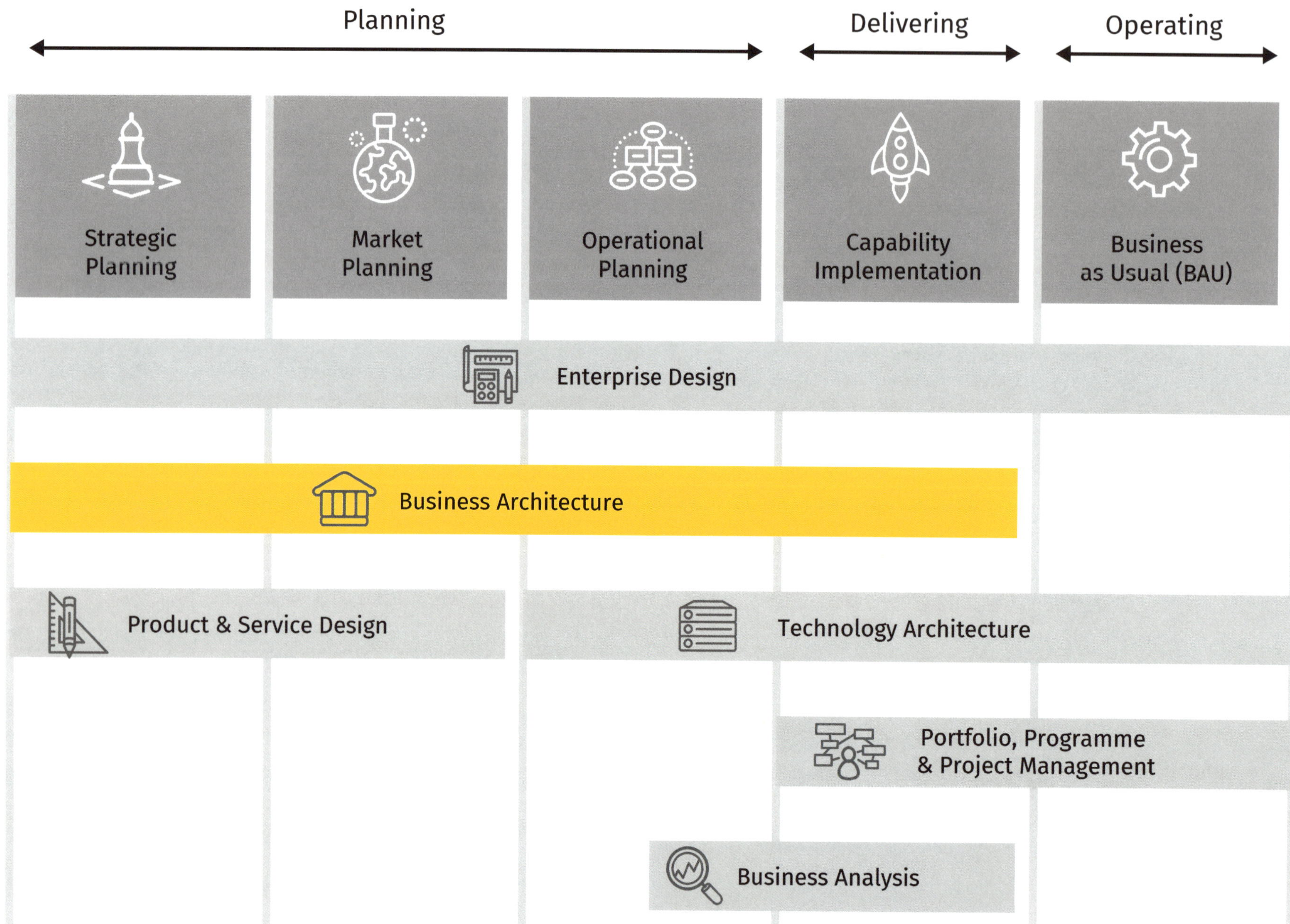


**Figure 7.13** - Example User Journey Map[56]

[56] Martin, C., (2014) 'Driving your BA Career - From Business Analyst to Business Architect'

The Business Architect's objectives with Process Mapping has two (2) parts:

**1. Scope:**

- To identify the totality of the Organisations processes, and ensure (plus assure) that for ALL the Organisation's processes, we have identified not only all of them but (working with the Business Analyst, and the key stakeholders) we have identified and agreed which ones are actually in-scope for the Programme.

**2. Alignment:**

- To ensure (and assure) that (1) only processes that are identified and are in-scope have a direct impact in supporting the strategic objectives of the Organisation, and (2) any changes that are made to these processes do so in such a way that they support or enable the Organisation to deliver its Business Strategy, business (and strategic) objectives and realisation of planned Business Benefits.

However, despite Process Modelling and Process Mapping playing a critical role in the development of the Business Architecture, and indeed the Target Operating Model, Process Mapping is one of the most troubled areas when it comes to defining the Business Architecture. The main reason for this has to do with the time and place when the Business Architect (and the Business Architecture) stops, and the Business Analyst (and Business Analysis) takes over.

As a reminder of the handover between the Business Architect and the Business Analyst, *Figure 7.14* below (from the *Business Architecture is not Business Analysis* section) shows that handover happens between level 3 and level 4 processes.

[57] Adapted from American Productivity & Quality Centre (APQC) (2015), Process Classification Framework (PCF) ver 7.0.2

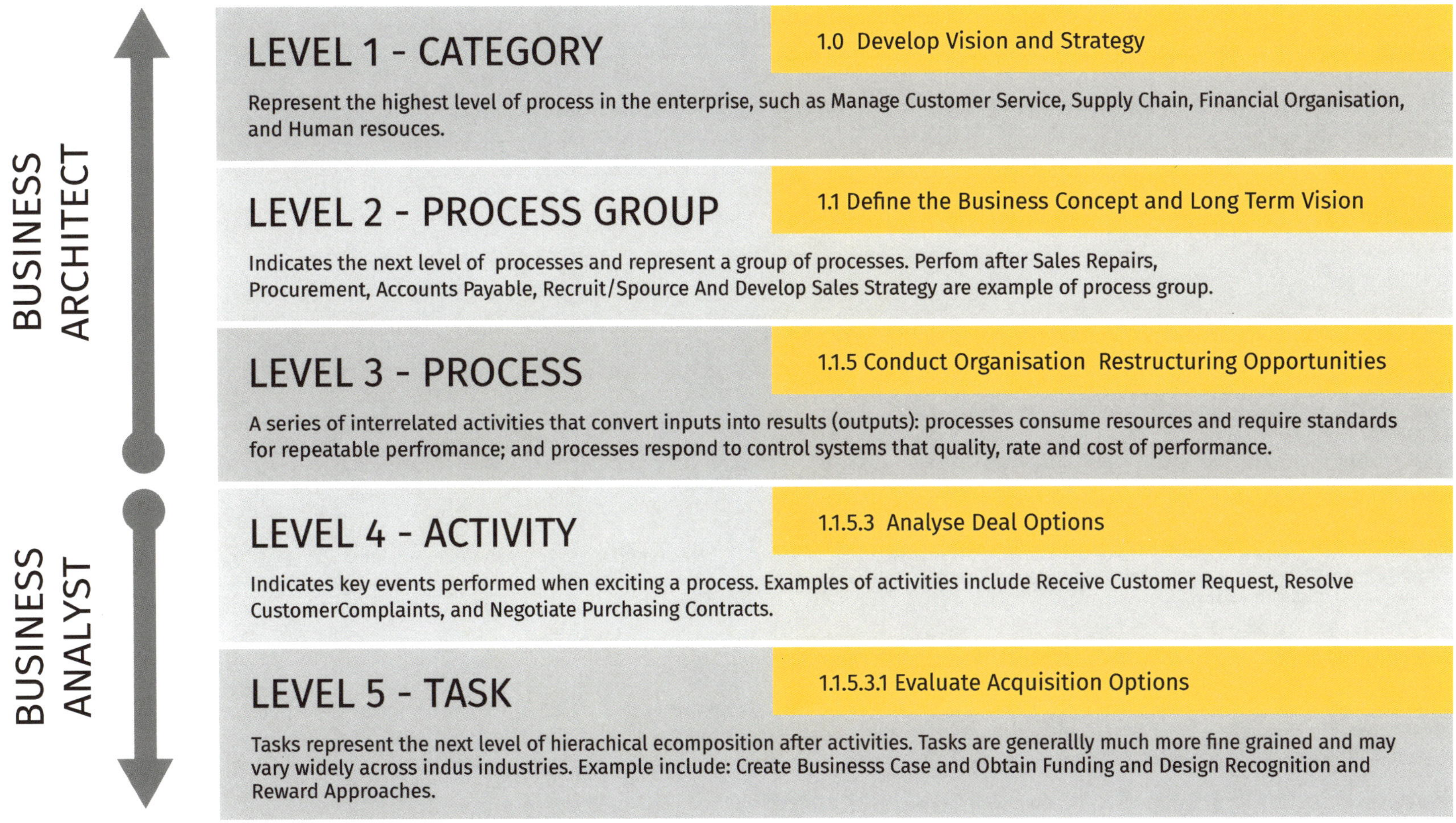


**Figure 7.14** - Business Architect and Business Analyst Process Focus[57]

What this means in terms of the mapping the different levels of an Organisation's processes, is that the Business Architect works at a different level to the Business Analyst. This is a higher level focus (conceptual, abstract and strategic) of the process maps, mapping and developing the Process Model for the Organisation. This *higher-level* focus identifies the totality of processes in the Organisation, and most importantly the in-scope processes for the Programme, before handing over and working with the Business Analyst. Once the Business Analyst has been given the *direction* of what processes are in-scope (and why), the Business Analyst will use those identified processes, to define the detailed (physical, delivery and implementation) level processes and process maps.

In terms of what these different processes visually look like, the following diagram below shows an example of the level of detail for each of the different levels (Level 1, 2, 3, and 4) of the Process Model.

- **Level 1 – Process Landscape.** Is a high level view of the end-to-end business processes and process categories, which usually span the entire organization, and show (the names of the) Level 1 & Level 2 Process maps.
- **Level 2 – Main Processes**. These decompose the level 1 process into their composite (level 2) parts.
- **Level 3 – Processes.** These decompose the Level 2 process into lower level processes (some may contain sub-processes that need to be decomposed still further).
- **Level 4 – Activity.** These decompose Level 3 processes into the lowest level that is 'mapped'.
- **Level 5 – Task:** (not shown in the diagram above). These are not actually process maps per se, but 'tables' of descriptions of the tasks carried out at each step.

## Inputs

The inputs used to complete this Building Block are shown in Table 7.12 (on the next page).

## Outputs

The Blueprints (outputs) produced for this Building Block is shown in Table 7.13 (on the next page).

[58] Adapted from Rosa, M., (2015) IAB203 – Business Process Modelling *Process Architecture Part II Presentation*

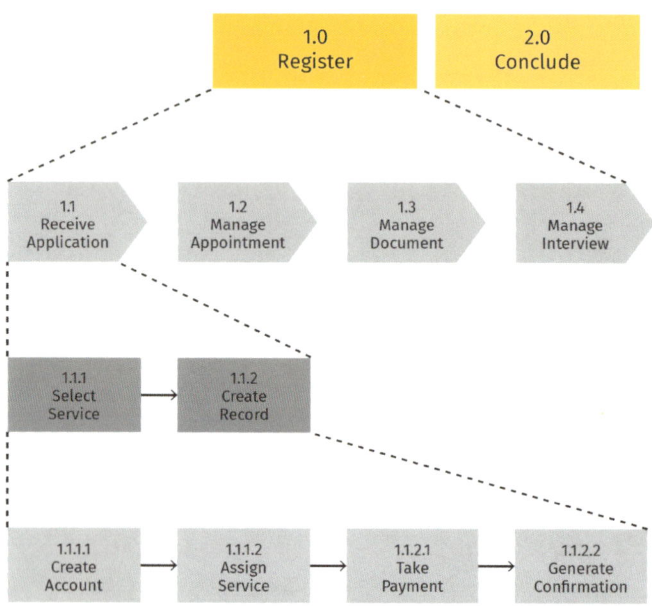


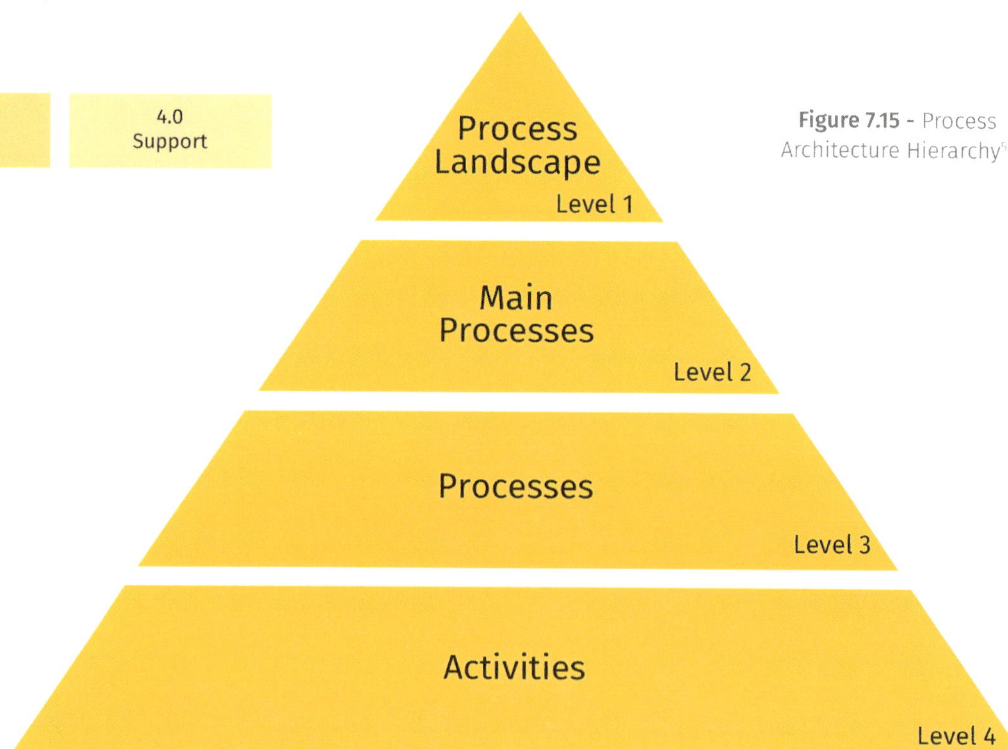


**Figure 7.15** - Process Architecture Hierarchy[58]

## Process Mapping Building Block Inputs

**Table 7.12**

| Ref | Blueprint | Use |
|---|---|---|
| 1.1.1 | Statement of Work (SOW) | Contain the initial set/list of scenarios and issues, that provide candidates for the process maps |
| 2.2.1 | Design Principles Register | Not directly involved here, but you should be mindful, that the Design Principles define the scope of the Programme, Business Architecture and charges, as well as define scope of potential solutions that will solve the problems made visible by these process maps. |
| 2.3.1 | RAID Log | Contains the register of Risks, Assumptions, Issues and Dependencies that need to be checked against and updated as part of completing this Blueprint. |
| 3.2.1 | Stakeholder Maps | Contain the list of Stakeholders that need to be addressed and covered by the process maps. |
| 3.3.1 | User Journey Maps | Provide candidates for the processes to be mapped. |
| N/A | Existing Organisation Documentation | Includes existing process maps, policies and procedures documents and manuals, and existing project or Programme material that provide background information on existing processes. |

## Process Mapping (Output) Blueprints

**Table 7.13**

| Ref | Blueprint | Description | Example |
|---|---|---|---|
| 3.4.1 | Process Model Map | The Process Model Map provides the visual framework for identifying the totality of all processes across the Organisation, which systematically and structurally decomposes the top-level processes (level 1) down to their lowest level (level 5) processes. | |
| 3.4.2 | Process Model Catalogue | Provides the list of all Process Model Map processes from level 1 to level 5, including the level 4 SIPOC. | |

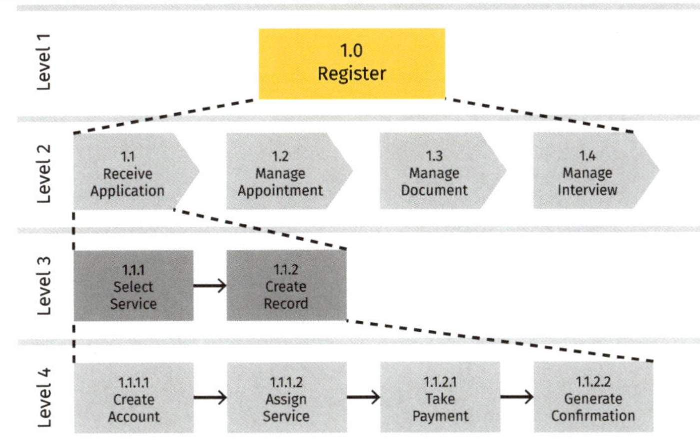


| Ref | Level 1 | Description | Ref | Level 2 | Description | Ref | Level 3 | Description | Ref | Level 4 | Description |
|---|---|---|---|---|---|---|---|---|---|---|---|
| 1.0 | Register | | 1.1 | Receive Application | | 1.1.1 | Select Service | | 1.1.1.1 | Create Account | |
| | | | | | | | | | 1.1.1.2 | Assign Service | |
| | | | | | | 1.1.2 | Create Record | | 1.1.2.1 | Take Payment | |
| | | | | | | | | | 1.1.2.2 | Generate Confirmation | |
| | | | 1.2 | Manage Biometrics | | 1.2.1 | Request Biometrics | | 1.2.1.1 | Receive Bio. Request | |
| | | | | | | | | | 1.2.1.2 | Produce Enrol. Letter | |
| | | | | | | 1.2.2 | Capture Biometrics | | 1.2.2.1 | Confirm Identity | |
| | | | | | | | | | 1.2.2.2 | Record Biometrics | |
| | | | 1.2 | Manage Biometrics | | 1.2.1 | Book Appointment | | 1.2.1.1 | Identify Locations | |
| | | | | | | | | | 1.2.1.2 | Offer Appointment | |
| | | | | | | | | | 1.2.1.3 | Confirm Appointment | |
| | | | | | | | | | 1.2.1.4 | Allocate Sources | |

## Steps

The Process Mapping Building Block is made up of the following Blueprints.

### 3.4.1 Process Model Map

#### 1. Identify the Level 1 Process Categories

Using the Blueprint Inputs and other documentation from Table 7.12, and Establish the Organisation wide level 1 Process Categories. An example of Level 1 Process Categories is shown in *Figure 7.16*.

#### 2. Identify the Level 2 Process Groups

Decompose the level 1 map based on audience, purpose and differentiator (i.e. business object e.g. Application, Appointment etc.), and repeat for each process. The following example decomposes the Level 1 Process Category (1.0 Register) into Level 2 Process Groups.

#### 3. Identify the Level 3 Processes

Decompose the level 2 processes based on the same standards (audience, purpose and differentiator), and repeat for each process. The following example decomposes the Level 2 Process Group (1.1 Receive Application) into Level 3 Process(es).

**The 'arms' shown in the above diagrams from '1.0 Register' are for illustration purposes only (and are not technically 'mapping standards'). These are used purely to show the relationship between the 'parent' and the decomposed 'child(ren)' processes.**

**Figure 7.16** - Process Model Map (Level 1)

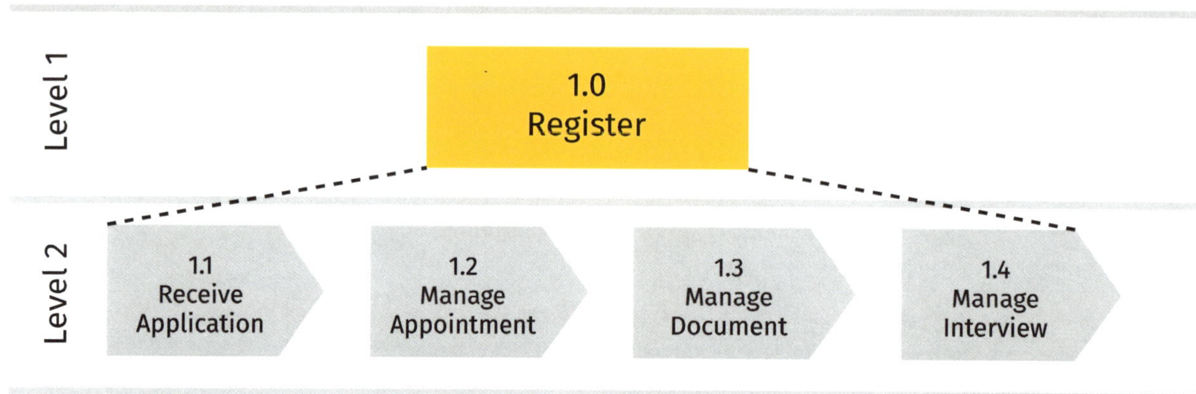


**Figure 7.17** - Process Map Model (Level 1 and 2)

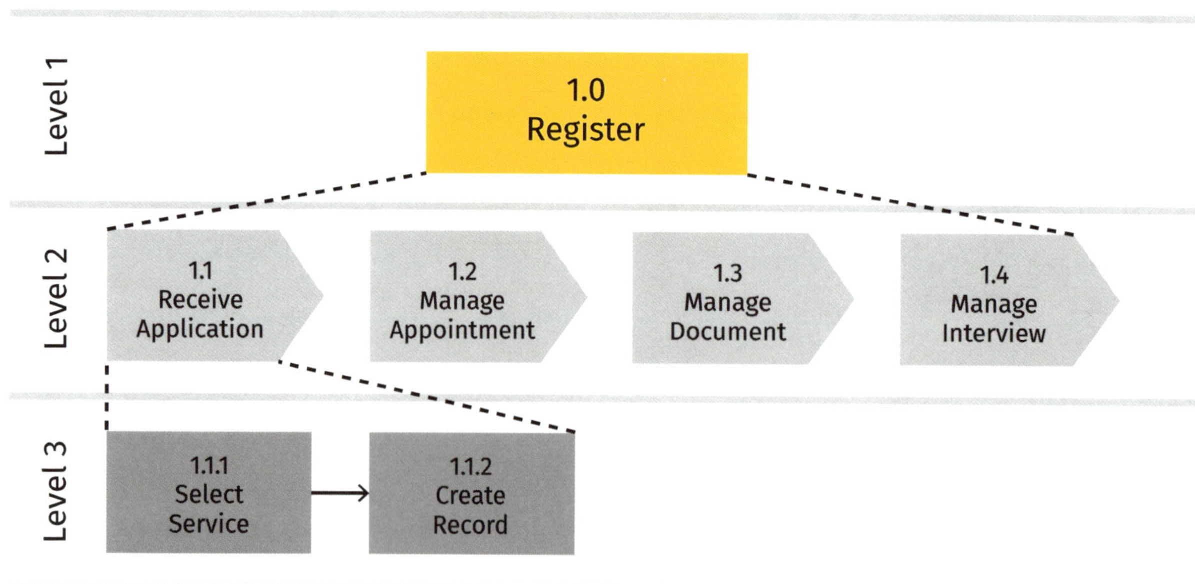


**Figure 7.18** - Process Map Model (Level 1, 2 and 3)

**4. Identify the Level 4 Process Activities**

Decompose each of the level 3 processes based on the same standards (audience, purpose and differentiator), repeat for each level 3 process. Where known, mark the appropriate process which is in/out of scope. In the following example, the level 2 Process (1.1 Receive Application) is decomposed into two (2) Level 3 Process(es) (1.1.1 Select Service, 1.1.2 Create Record), 1.2 Manage Appointment is greyed out (as out of scope), and repeat the decomposition for each level 1, 2, and 3 down to level 4 process(es).

## 3.4.2 Process Model Catalogue

**5. Record the Process Details**

Record the process information is the Process Model Catalogue, including a brief description of the process at each level. An example of the format and structure for the Process Catalogue is shown in Table 7.14 (on the next page).

For completeness, and scope manageability - with each level 4 process, record the Supplier, Input, Process, Output, Customer (SIPOC) details, as shown in the example in Table 7.15 (on page 179).

**6. Iteratively socialize, validate and refine each Blueprint** - including any Risk, Assumptions, Issues and Dependencies (RAID) addressed or raised as part of completing these Blueprints, and

**7. Package and publish the Blueprints** – in line with your agreed sprint/release cycle, established back in the Governance Model in *Chapter 6 Step 2 – Control*.

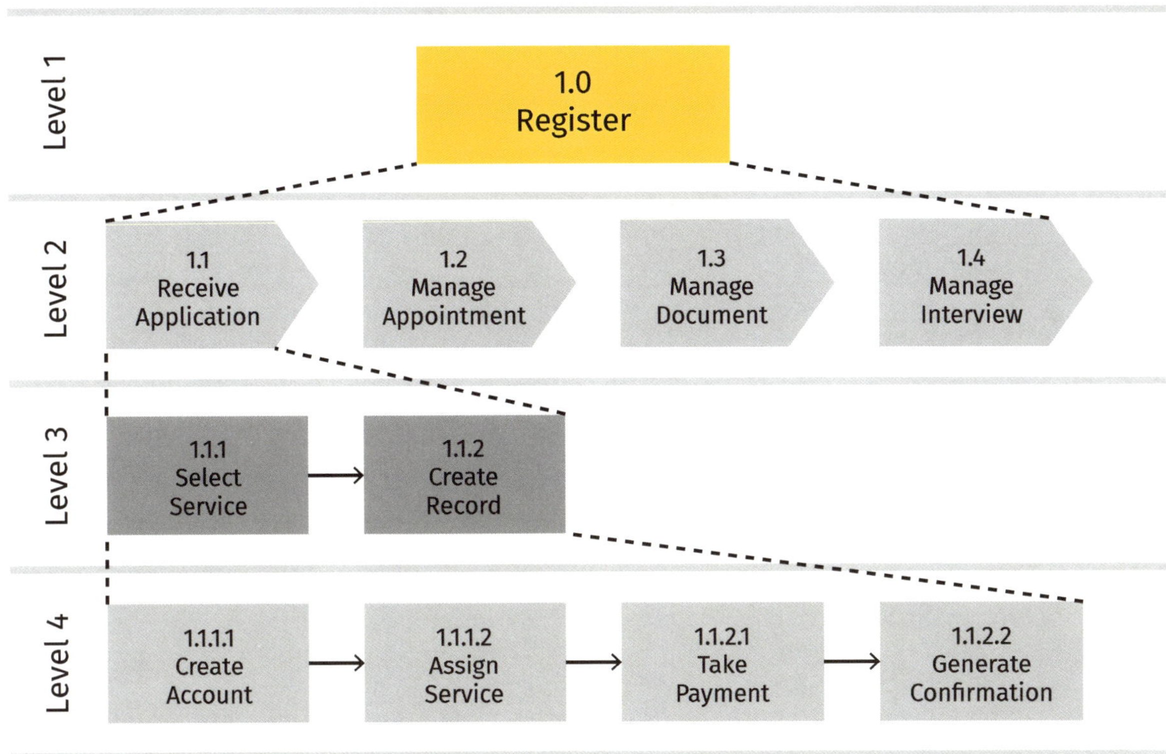


Figure 7.19 – Process Map Model (Level 1, 2, 3 and 4)

**The SIPOC helps define and confirm the scope of each process, to avoid (and identify) process 'scope creep' where separate processes overlap.**

Now, this is where process-mapping gets interesting.

The main objective of putting together the Process Model and Catalogue was to get the single source of truth – the single *'superset'* list of all processes across the Organisation, and therefore the Programme. If you're *lucky*, you were able to identify which processes were in (and out) of scope for your Programme. I wouldn't recommend trying to do those two activities at once, but if you were able to pull that off at the same time, well done! For those that didn't, or didn't get it completed, now is the time to do this activity.

To aid those *'scope'* conversations with your Key Stakeholders, *'mark-up'* or colour code in the Process Model Map the processes that are in scope (and out of scope) for the Programme. The Process Model Map will provide the visuals to help those conversations in providing a single and consistent view of the processes being touched (and changed) by the Programme as well as identify any potential areas of duplication, or gaps where some projects actually *think* certain processes are out of scope for their project, but are actually not (i.e. they're actually in scope).

Table 7.14

Example Process Model Catalogue Structure

| Ref | Level 1 | Description | Ref | Level 2 | Description | Ref | Level 3 | Description | Ref | Level 4 | Description |
|---|---|---|---|---|---|---|---|---|---|---|---|
| 1.0 | Register | | 1.1 | Receive Application | | 1.1.1 | Select Service | | 1.1.1.1 | Create Account | |
| | | | | | | | | | 1.1.1.2 | Assign Service | |
| | | | | | | 1.1.2 | Create Record | | 1.1.2.1 | Take Payment | |
| | | | | | | | | | 1.1.2.2 | Generate Confirmation | |
| | | | 1.2 | Manage Biometrics | | 1.2.1 | Request Biometrics | | 1.2.1.1 | Receive Bio. Request | |
| | | | | | | | | | 1.2.1.2 | Produce Enrol. Letter | |
| | | | | | | 1.2.2 | Capture Biometrics | | 1.2.2.1 | Confirm Identity | |
| | | | | | | | | | 1.2.2.2 | Record Biometrics | |
| | | | 1.3 | Manage Appointment | | 1.3.1 | Book Appointment | | 1.3.1.1 | Identify Locations | |
| | | | | | | | | | 1.3.1.2 | Offer Appointment | |
| | | | | | | | | | 1.3.1.3 | Confirm Appointment | |
| | | | | | | | | | 1.3.1.4 | Allocate Sources | |

Sample Level 4 SIPOC Table

Table 7.15

| Ref | Level 4 | Description | Supplier | Input | Process | Output | Customer |
|---|---|---|---|---|---|---|---|
| 1.1.1.1 | Create Account | | | | | | |
| 1.1.1.2 | Assign Service | | | | | | |
| 1.1.2.1 | Take Payment | | | | | | |
| 1.1.2.2 | Generate Confirmation | | | | | | |
| 1.2.1.1 | Receive Bio. Request | | | | | | |
| 1.2.1.2 | Produce Enrol. Letter | | | | | | |
| 1.2.2.1 | Confirm Identity | | | | | | |
| 1.2.2.2 | Record Biometrics | | | | | | |
| 1.3.1.1 | Identify Locations | | | | | | |
| 1.3.1.2 | Offer Appointment | | | | | | |
| 1.3.1.3 | Confirm Appointment | | | | | | |
| 1.3.1.4 | Allocate Sources | | | | | | |

As an example, with one client I assisted, the Programme already had a 'Process Model' for the Organisation, however the *'framework'* as it was called, did not have consistent levelling or process decomposition, descriptions or rationale to the levels, or indications when a process started and stopped. As there was no consistency in the levelling and decomposition, it was difficult to identify when a process ended, and another one started. This ended up causing two of the three projects under the Programme inadvertently working on changes to the same level 4 process, resulting in one project effectively undoing the work of the other, and one *in-scope* level 4 process *not* being touched at all, which caused a last minute formal change request to the board to include the *'new'* scope. This all could have been prevented had it been brought to their attention earlier and had the Process Model Map been completed using the consistent levelling and decomposition approach above.

With this validated Model and Catalogue (which goes through iterations and releases as gaps and changes are identified), you hand over and work with the Business Analyst to carry out the 'discovery' analysis and detailed process mapping. The Business Analysts role at this point will be to identify *not only* the implementation and system requirements, but production of the Level 4 Activity level process map(s). In doing so also identifies and validates the in-scope stakeholders, dependences, problem areas, measures and metrics, as well as any areas that are delivered by another project or Programme(s), similar to the level 4 process map from the Case Study shown in Figure 7.20 below.

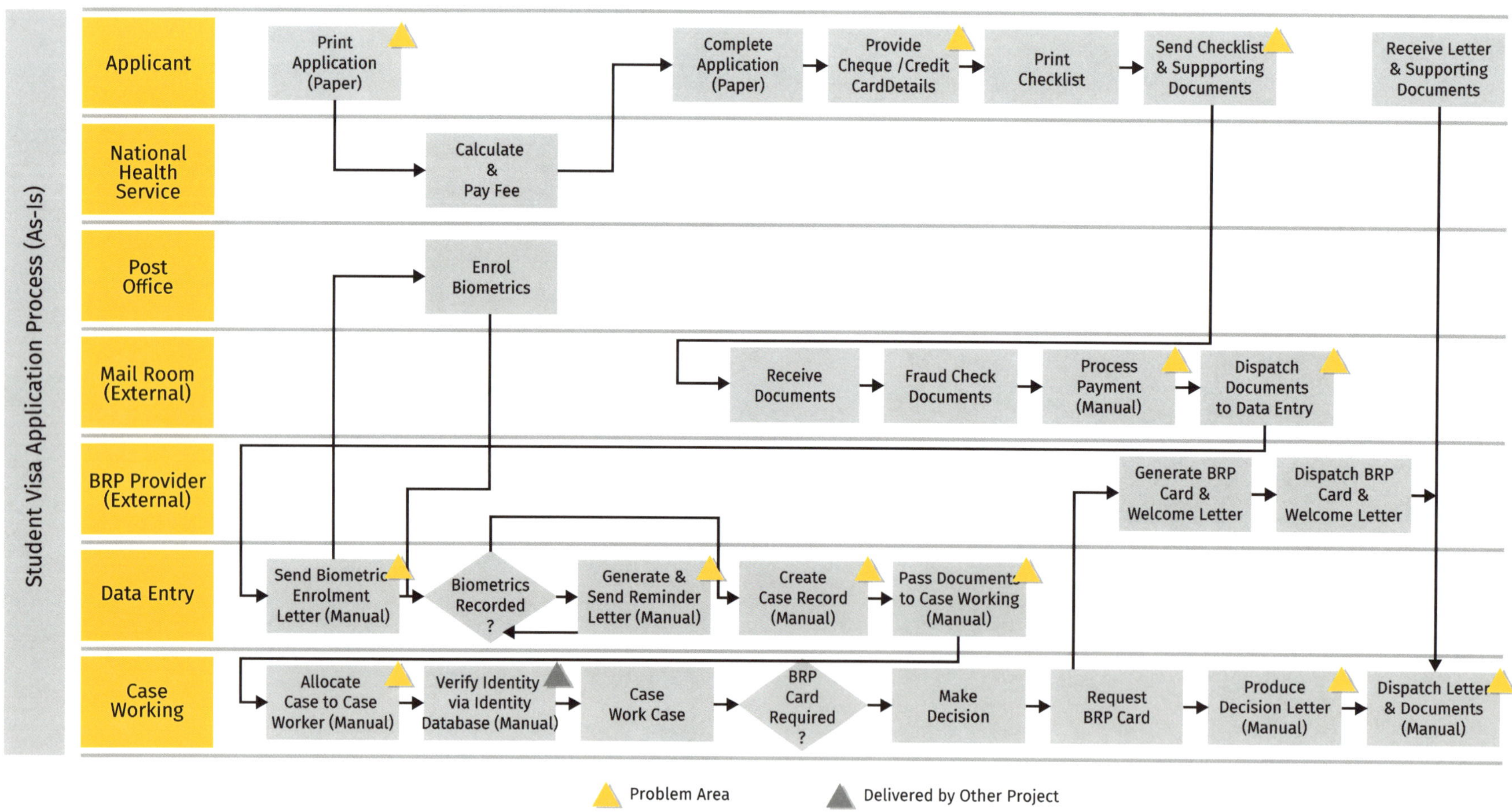


**Figure 7.20 -** Sample Level 4 (Student Visa Application) Process Map

The key to the Business Analysts process mapping activities is the processes that are mapped, or referenced from (and to) the other processes, *are from* the Process Model. There shouldn't be any other processes created or referenced that *are not* in that Process Model, or listed on the Process Catalogue. If there are, it's because there genuinely are new processes, or a gap has now been identified.

**This last step – where the Business Analysis develops the 'actual' level 4 Process Maps is where the Business Analyst gets to flex their process mapping muscles and map out the physical process(es) with all the agreed process mapping notation (e.g. UML, BPMN etc.), symbols, decision and escalation points etc.**

## Risks and Mitigations

The point where the Business Architects hands over to the Business Analyst to carry out the detailed process mapping work, calls for some degree of coordination, and timing.

When it comes time to mapping the Organisation's processes, it is likely either of the following scenarios have occurred:

1. **Process Mapping has already been completed**, and all (at least the 'high level') process maps have been created; or
2. **Process Mapping at any level across the Organisation and within scope for the Programme hasn't yet kicked off.**

Now, if the former (where some form of process mapping has already occurred), then it's just ('just' used very lightly) a reconciliation and mapping exercise to ensure that all of the Organisations processes are mapped, and decomposed to the same and consistent level of detail, while ensuring that no processes or sub-processes have fallen through the gaps.

If the scenario is the latter, and the Organisations processes haven't been mapped, you're in luck, and have the advantage of setting and establishing consistent mapping, decomposition and level standards from the offset. I say *'luck'* because if there are existing maps and mapping that already exist in the Organisation, there has probably been some (or more) effort that has gone into mapping already, and any talk or suggestion of reviewing these could be or might be met with some resistance for any type of interrogation to review them for consistency (i.e. levelling and decomposition), completeness or correctness. As *'uncomfortable'* as it may appear or sound, I highly recommend you persist your interrogations. The benefit of this exercise, to have all the Organisations processes (and therefore in-scope processes for the Programme) not only identified, listed, and decomposed to a consistent structured manner – makes it simpler to identify the Programme and project scope. For instance, where there are gaps and overlaps between different projects within the same Programme inadvertently working on making changes to the same lower level processes, as well as taking on work that is best suited to be delivered by another (or separate) project altogether.

One of the biggest areas mappings can go wrong in, is with decomposing the processes to the same consistency. The easiest way to avoid decomposing and levelling issues is to agree a few basic rules and standards early on. For example, always think of a small process consisting of 2 parts - an input and an output, and for larger (potentially complex) process, consisting of 3 parts – an input, a throughput, and an output. As a *general rule* for decomposition, consider the following:

- A **level 1 'Process Category'** process can always be decomposed into at least 2 or more lower level (level 2) sub-processes;
- A **level 2 'Process Group**' process should be able to be decomposed into at least 2 or more lower level (level 3) sub-processes;
- A **level 3 'Process' process** could be able to be decomposed into at least 2 lower level (level 4) sub-processes,
- A **level 4 'Activity' process** – as this is the lowest level *'mapped'* process it is the exception to the rule and ideally won't be decomposed into lower level processes, and
- A **level 5 process** – is the text/textual version of the Level 4 process above, being simply 'captured'.

To help with the *decomposition* and *levelling*, think of the levels in terms of their audience, purpose and differentiator:

- **Level 1** – external to the Programme, or Organisation. Communicates a process scope, and is easily recognisable to this stakeholder group (e.g. Register, Decide, Conclude, Support). Outputs produce a defined result.
- **Level 2** – external to the Programme. These are the high-level processes that provide context and decomposed from level 1 processes (e.g. Manage Appointment). Outputs produce a defined set of products or services.
- **Level 3** – Programme staff. Provide the list of sub-processes that make up the level 2 process(es) (e.g. Create Appointment, Cancel Appointment etc.). Outputs are used as inputs into other, subsequent process (or as an end product in of itself).
- **Level 4 & 5** – Operational staff. Decompose a process into steps that explain in detail what the implementation process looks like. These levels show the operational roles involved.

For *consistency*, you may want to adopt the following standards:

- Assign each process, at every level a prefix reference number, and assign child (sub) processes sequential prefix reference numbers (i.e. 1.0, 1.1.; 1.1.1 etc.). It will also aid traceability (and is a good mapping practice in general).

- Agree mapping notation (i.e. BPMN, UML etc.) for each process level, namely lower level processes (i.e. Level 4) where the *'real'* mapping takes place.
- Process Steps should be named using active 'verb+noun' present tense formats (e.g. Conduct Interview).
- Processes (at all levels) are mapped from left to right (and top to bottom).
- Use annotations in your maps to assist understanding.

Other standards include (but not restricted to) – limit the number of steps in a process to between 8 to 10 steps (this can help decomposition, if the process has too many steps, it should be broken down. Long winded processes *don't* tend to be very efficient when there is a lot of steps involved); *swim lanes* should bear the name of the stakeholder involved; and you should always use established mapping standards or notation that is in use or agreed in other parts of the Organisation (where necessary and appropriate).

There can also be a tendency to *'over-egg'* process mapping, and create a whole cottage industry on (and for) process maps. While process maps (namely level 4 process maps) are (or at least can be) very pretty and colourful, the key is to develop the process maps in a similar way to how Dell Computers famously created their computers, using the *"Just In Time (JIT)"* method. For Business Architects and Business Architecture, that means – creating the least amount of work (processes, process mapping and process information) possible while still enabling further work to be undertaken (namely discovery) to understand the problem effectively, and then to design and implement a solution or solutions to address the problem(s).

With many of the clients I've assisted, I've seen whole 'war rooms' (aka Design Rooms), with very large colourful power-point presentations full of 'super process maps' that attempt (or intended to) define every single process within the Programme, and indeed the Organisation. While these may seem 'necessary', and (arguably) important, we have to bring everything we do back to first principles and ask the fundamental question – 'WHY?'. 'Why are we doing this?'. Remember, the objective with this Process Model (and Catalogue) Building Block is to identify the totality of processes within (and across) the Organisation, agreeing which are in (and out of) scope for the Programme, and work with (and guide) the Business Analyst towards the lower level processes that need further mapping and analysis. Remember it's not about creating or defining as many process maps as possible, they will only become expensive, colourful shelf ware.

## Building Block Wrap-up

In this section, we discussed the Process Mapping Building Block.

The Process Mapping Building Block provides the visual framework for identifying the totality of all the processes across the Organisation, which systematically and structurally decomposes the top-level processes (level 1) down to their lowest level (level 5) processes, and consists of the following two (2) Blueprints:

- **Process Model Map**, which provides the visual representation of all the processes across the Organisation, used to identify the in (and out of) scope processes for the Programme, and
- **Process Model Catalogue**, which provides the list of all Process Model processes, used as the record of the process information and confirm the scope of each process (as well as identify any gaps, duplication of effort and process scope creep)

Both these Blueprints provide a single source of truth, as the *'superset'* list of all processes across the Organisation, and therefore the Programme. As a visual tool, together they help the *'scope'* conversations in providing a single and consistent view of processes being touched (and changed) by the Programme, as well as identify any potential areas of duplication of effort or gaps where some projects actually *think* certain processes are out of scope for their project (when they should be in scope), or where there is another project (or Programme) that is better suited to delivering changes that the project currently working on them.

## Next Steps

Once the Process Mapping and the in (and out of) scope processes for the Programme have been agreed to (and the Business Analyst has been given the list of processes that require detailed analysis and mapping to identify and validate the in-scope stakeholders, dependencies, problem areas, measures and metrics), the next step in the **Design Process** is to define the Capability Model and the in-scope Business Capabilities that are to be changed because of the Programme.

These concerns are discussed in the Capability Mapping Building Block in the following section.

# 3.5 Capability Mapping (As-Is)

## Introduction

Capability Mapping is the Building Block that defines the business' capabilities that are being enhanced or created by the Programme. Business Capabilities ('Capabilities') are a powerful tool when used to their full potential, however - just as there is confusion and misconception about what is Business Architecture and its value, there is also some confusion and misconception about what Business Capabilities are and their value. So, hopefully, once and for all, I'll clear up the confusion and misconception and get you and the Business (and Programme) talking the same language, to use them correctly.

So, just what are Business Capabilities ('Capabilities')? Well, in short, capabilities are the 'What' the business does. Capabilities define the Organisation's ability to execute its Business Strategy. What is important with Business Capabilities is that they intentionally ignore the 'How' (the Organisation does what it does), and the 'Who' (within the Organisation that does it).

The purpose of modelling capabilities is to model 'What' the business does, based on a 'static' and stable view of the Business. The way (the 'how') a business does what it does can and does change over time, but 'what' it does remains quite stable. For example, an internet provider not so long ago would have a capability of proving an internet service to its customers (the 'what'), but 'how' it did that was back then, via 'dial-up' modems. Today, that business is still in the business of providing an internet service (the 'what') to its customers, but now the 'how' is not by dial-up anymore, but instead by broadband, cable and even wireless.

So why is this stability so important? Well the goal is to model the business on its most stable elements. Over time, and even on a daily basis, the underlying elements making up the capability (i.e. people, process and technology) may change, however the capabilities themselves remain stable, and active. It is through this stability, and business centric view that it makes capabilities ideal to look over the whole Organisation, and identify and focus on the areas of strategic importance.

In terms of where Business Capabilities sit relative to Business Architecture and Technology Architecture, Business Capabilities can be considered as the 'glue' that brings them together. It is the Business Capability 'Technology' element that is the common denominator between the two architectures, as shown in *Figure 7.21* below.

[59] Adapted from Bhatt, A., (2015) Business Capabilities: Challengers and Value Proposition for a Large Enterprise, *Wells Fargo Bank Presentation*

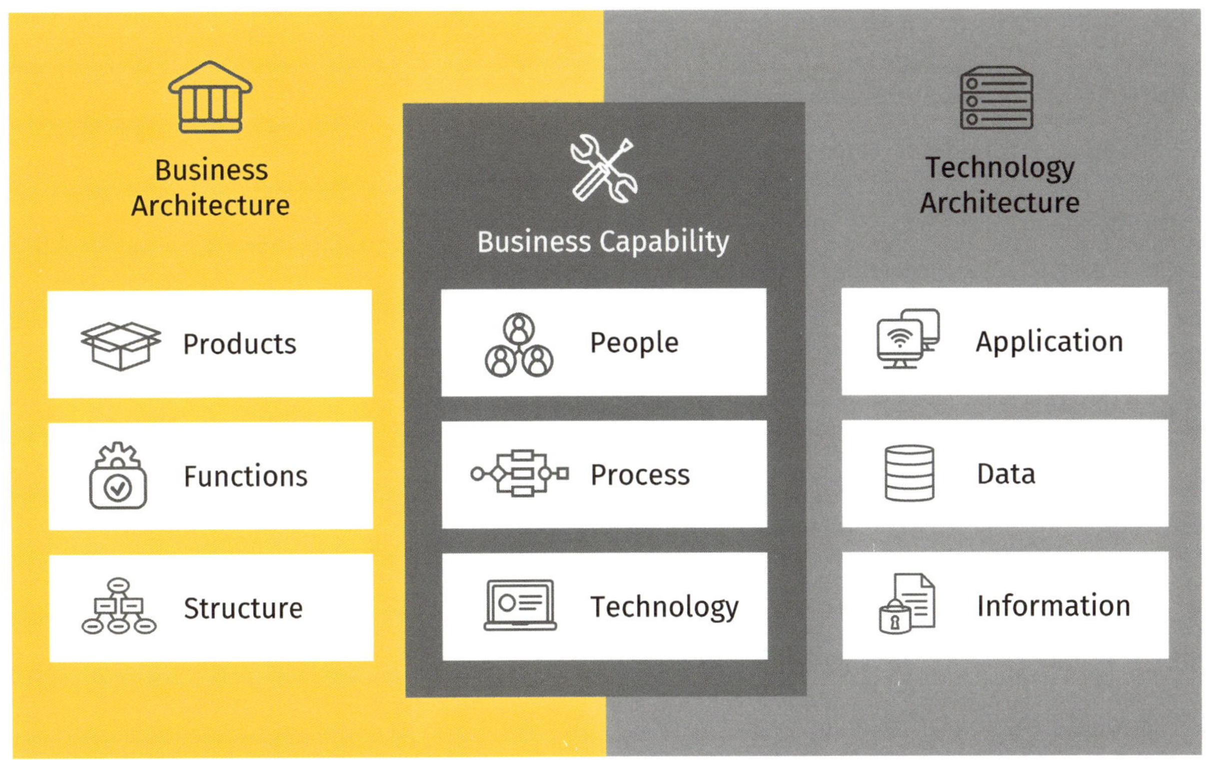


**Figure 7.21** - Business Capability – the link between Business & IT[59]

Capability Mapping is also a useful exercise when the Business doesn't already know what its core or key capabilities are. Capability Mapping will help identify these core or key capabilities and use this information to (re)focus the Organisation on the areas of strategic importance. As Business Architects, our intent and purpose for mapping an Organisations capabilities is to ensure that not only is the current business (as usual) activity and investment aligned to delivering its current Business Strategy, but we as Business Architects design a TOM that aligns to the future Business Strategy, as well as addresses any challenges that the business is currently facing, building on its strengths, and minimising its weaknesses with the current operating model.

In terms of an organisation and its ability to execute its strategy, in a lot of cases (if not all cases), investment spend would (and should) focus on strengthening the Organisations core capabilities. It is those core capabilities, and effective use of those capabilities, that are usually what give the Organisation its competitive advantage. By looking at Business Capabilities, and the Business Capability Model, looking through different perspectives (such as investment spending for example), Business Capability Mapping can show where the Organisation is spending money – on its capabilities where:

- It needs to be **'above market'** average (ideally the core capabilities),
- Where it can be **'at market'** average, and
- Where it is also **'below market'** (but happy to do so, as it is aligned to its Business Strategy and core capabilities).

So now we know what Capabilities are, and what they can be used for. The next questions we have to answer are (1) what are they made of, and (2) how do you model them in practise?

**To an Organisation, it should be of concern if 'cross mapping' capabilities to investment spending showed either spending (or high) costs incurred on capabilities that weren't aligned to the Business Strategy, was all over the shop or worse, not on it's core capabilities at all.**

## What are Capabilities Made of?

Business Capabilities are made up of essentially three (3) elements – *people, process*, and *technology*. Each of these elements can be broken down into the following:

- **People** – these are the people in the Organisation, their roles, responsibilities and skills. This can also include knowledge, behaviours and culture.
- **Process** – including the way a business-Organisation is organised.
- **Technology** – these include tools, systems and data.

## How do you model Capabilities in practise?

Architect we have to decide which capabilities are important? An Organisation for example can have the capability to provide internet service or access, the capability to take payments from the customer, and the capability to make payments to staff or contractors. This leads to the question, so *'which capabilities are important?'*. We are interested in the capabilities that give or support the business to give it a competitive advantage in its markets, the business' *'key capabilities'*.



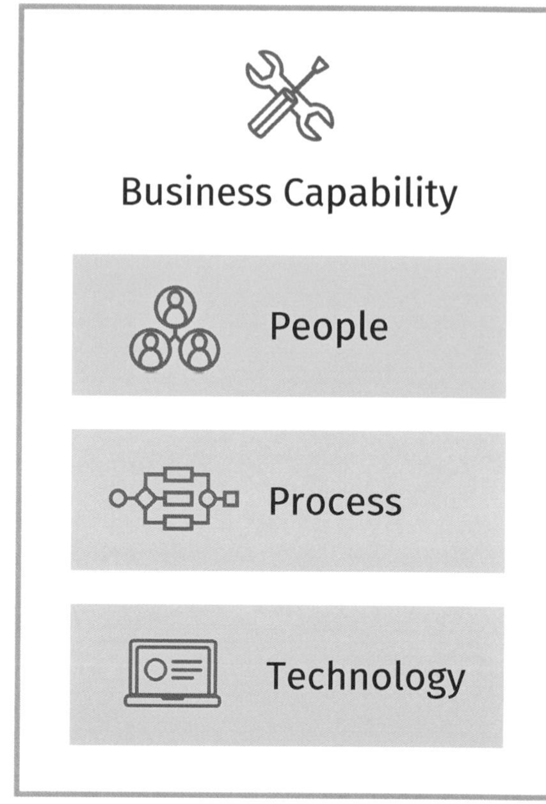


**Figure 7.22 -** Capability Elements

Key capabilities have different perspectives that look at the Organisation through specific views, called *'tiers'*. These tiers are similar to how the APQC Process Classification framework divides processes into 'tiers', depending on their role:

- **Strategic** (or *direction setting* – externally facing to the market),
- **Core** (also called *Operational* or *Customer Facing* – visible to the customer), and
- **Supporting** (behind the scenes, not often seen or visible to the customer).

Within each tier (Strategic, Operational, Supporting), the capability is decomposed into further levels of detail and granularity. At each different and lower level, each successive level shows a lower level of detail, to show a specific view for a specific audience.

The conventional wisdom (and best practice) is three (3) levels is an ideal and optimum number of levels to decompose capabilities down too. These levels are level 1 (top-level), level 2 (mid-level) and level 3 (lower-level), as shown in Figure 7.23 below.

Before you begin developing the Capability Model, it is always preferable to establish some guidelines. These guidelines include the following (depending on the particular issues, goals and even culture of your Organisation):

- **Agree the levels** and naming convention (i.e. Strategic, Operational, Support)
- **Agree the naming convention** for each level. Remember, capabilities describe the business *at rest*. A typical name for the top-level capability would use 'management' in the name (Business Strategy Management) to clearly state and signal that (1) this is something the business does (i.e. 'management'), and (2) this is the business at rest. Naming a capability 'Define Business Strategy' or 'Develop Business Strategy' are descriptions of the business in motion, and not names of capabilities (more suited to business processes, that are probably part of the level 1 'Business Strategy Management' capability).
- **Agree depth and width** you will go to with the modelling. You need to be pragmatic and only do what's necessary, in line with the business priorities and Business Strategy. If the Programme you are working on is focusing on capabilities that are customer facing for example (such as Customer Management), and less on Regulatory Management, then prioritise time and effort on the areas, and levels that are necessary. A level 2 decomposition might be suitable for Regulatory Management, whereas Customer facing is more important right now, so decompose Customer Management et al. to level 3.
- **Use Business Terms**. Business Capabilities speak the business' language. Resist the temptation to impose Programme or technical terms on to the Business. When decomposing capabilities down to lower level capabilities, the language and terms used at the lower levels doesn't change from Business, to technical. If this is the case, you're probably talking about a process (and not a capability).
- **Focus the differentiator on the 'business' or 'information' object** when decomposing capabilities to their respective lower level capabilities, that separates them (i.e. Application, Account, Case etc.)

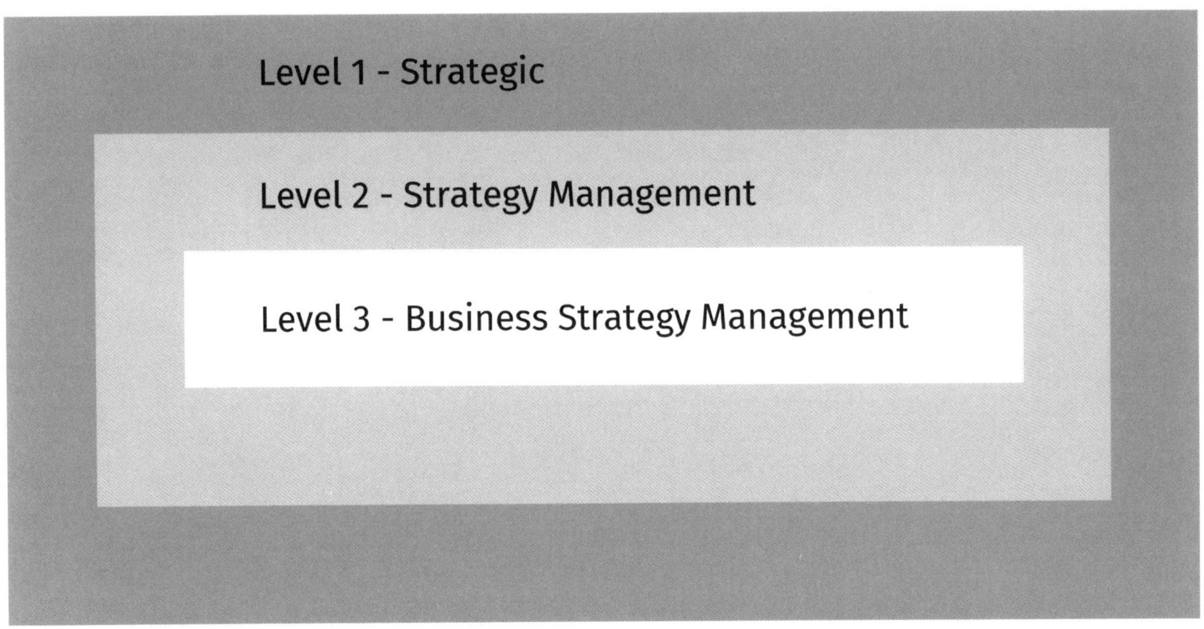


**Figure 7.23** – Business Capability Levelling

## Inputs

The inputs used to complete this Building Block are shown in the table below.

## Outputs

The Blueprints (outputs) produced for this Building Block is shown in the table below.

## Steps

The steps to complete the above Blueprints (Outputs) are as follows.

### Capability Mapping Building Block Inputs

**Table 7.16**

| Ref | Blueprint | Use |
|---|---|---|
| 1.4.1 | Terms & Definitions | Provides the key business or information objects (e.g. application, account, case) that the business needs to manage (Case Management). |
| 3.1.1 | Organisation Map | The different business units or divisions (Insurance Business Unit, Banking Business unit) provide potential candidates for level 1 capabilities – Product Management, Risk Management, Asset Management, Policy Management etc. |
| 3.6.1 | Process Map(s) | Provide context of what business or information object they are handling, and therefore Capability they are supporting (e.g. Process) |
| N/A | Existing Organisation Documentation | Include the existing Organisation, Programme and Business Architecture documentation, that may have provide clues into the type of capabilities or capability maps that already exist. |

### Capability Mapping (Output) Blueprints

**Table 7.17**

| Ref | Blueprint | Description | Example |
|---|---|---|---|
| 3.5.1 | Capability Model Map | Business Capability Model showing all 3 levels of Business Capabilities across the 3 tiers - Strategic, Operational, Supporting. | 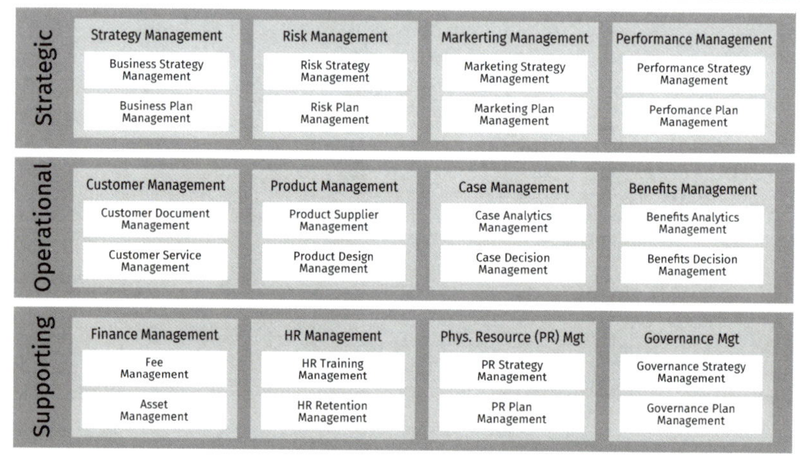 |
| 3.5.2 | Process Model Catalogue | Descriptions behind each Capability of the Business Capability Model. | (see catalogue below) |



| Tier | Level | Capability | Definition |
|---|---|---|---|
| 1 | 2 | Strategy Management | Ability to define, agree and communicate the Organisations strategy. |
| 1 | 3 | Business Strategy Management | Ability to define and communicate the strategies to support the Organisations vision. |
| 1 | 3 | Business Plan Management | Ability to define and agree a plan to achieve one or more business objectives. |
| 1 | 2 | Risk Management | Ability to define and manage the risks facing the Organisation |
| 1 | 3 | Risk Strategy Management | Ability to define and communicate the risk management strategies to manage and mitigate the risks facing the Organisation. |
| 1 | 3 | Risk Plan Management | Ability to articulate a course of action and mitigation actions to reduce the probability and impact of a given risk(s). |
| 1 | 2 | Marketing Management | Ability to define, agree and communicate marketing activities to support the Organisation vision. |
| 1 | 3 | Marketing Strategy Management | Ability to define and communicate marketing strategies to support the Organisations vision. |
| 1 | 3 | Marketing Plan Management | Ability to articulate a course of action to execute a given marketing activity. |

## 3.5.1 Capability Model Map

### 1. Create the first level 1 (or tiers) capabilities

Using the inputs from the *Inputs* section above, working in a *'top-down'* fashion (from level 1 to level 3), develop the first level 1 (tier 1) capabilities, discussed earlier (i.e. Strategic, Operational, Supporting), as shown in *Figure 7.24* below.

Your Organisation might have variations, but essentially there should be – Strategic (forward or external facing), Operational (customer facing or servicing) and support (what holds it altogether).

In one company I assisted, they only had one (1) level – all items (strategic, management, change, compliance, knowledge, and operations) were lumped into one level. This may have been helpful for understanding what the breath of *'what the business does'*, but wasn't helpful in understanding what it was good at (core competencies), or where they should be investing (in strategic capabilities or support capabilities), so agreeing the tiers is important.

**The trick to Capability Mapping is balance. Our objective is to agree 'what' the business does, so that we can identify the capabilities that (1) we are changing, and (2) align any and all changes to these capabilities that the Programme is working on to maximise the impact of any changes by - synchronizing any changes within the Programme, as well as acorss the organsation, and at the same time, reducing any duplication of effort, dependencies and delivery risk.**

**2. Decompose the Level 1 capabilities, to level 2 for each tier,** and plot on the map, as shown in *Figure 7.25 below.*

**Figure 7.24** - Level 1 (3-tier) Capabilities

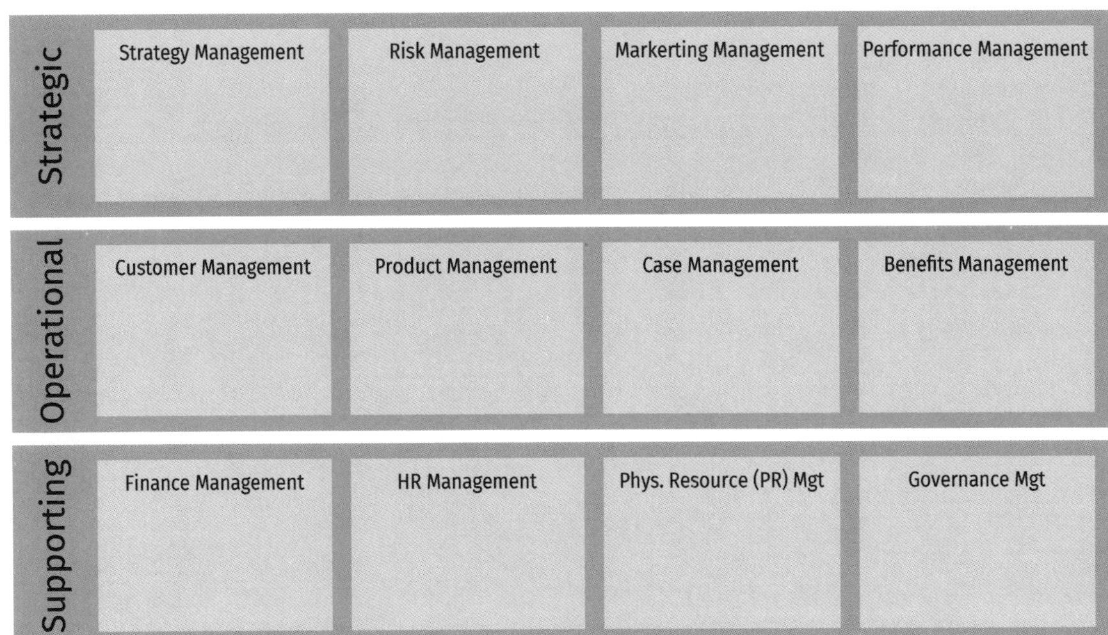


**Figure 7.25** - Example Level 1 Capabilities decomposed to Level 2

Depending on your type of company, examples of level 1 & 2 capabilities *could* include the following:

- **Strategic** - Business Plan Management, Investment Management, Partner & Channel Management, External Stakeholder Management, Marketing Management, etc.
- **Operational** - Policy Management, Financial Solutions Management, Claims & Recoveries Management etc.
- *Supporting* - Legal Management, Training Management, Programme Management, I.T. Management, Event Management etc.

Where your Organisation holds, or places a capability as either Strategic, Operational or Supporting will depend on how the Organisation is currently using it, what industry they are in, or what their current strategy is. For example, an IT Services company might place Product Management as a strategic capability, as their strategy might be to provide market leading, innovative IT solutions and products to its customers, whereas a Financial Services company could have Product Management as an operational capability as they are more reactive, and develop products in response to new customer demands

A note on decomposing level 1 capabilities:

- **Focus on business outcomes to help define and describe a capability**. If there is a definitive business outcome, it's a good candidate for a capability. 'Design Review' would not be a capability because it has not a clearly defined outcome (what is the design of?), however 'Product Design' would be a suitable name as it a defined outcome i.e. a new or modified 'product'.
- **Capabilities are unique, and based on the business or information object they manage and/or use**. An information object is dealt with by one level 1 capability and not shared across two level 1 capabilities. For example, level 2 Case Decision Management would sit under level 1 Case Management, due to the same information object (i.e. case). Case Analytics Management would come under the same level 1 Case Management capability, but not Risk Management as there is no association and usage of the common information object (case).

**3. Decompose the Level 2 capabilities,** to level 3 for each tier, as shown in the table below.

A few rules on decomposing level 2 into level 3 capabilities:

- Lower level capabilities still describe the 'what' the business does. They don't change to 'how' the business does what it does. It just describes the decomposed capability in its wider, full scope. For example, Level 1 Product Management, for the banking business unit (described above), would have a level 2 capability 'Bank Account Management', and possibly 'Bank Account Design Management' – one to manage its existence, another to manager its creation.
- Keep the naming convention of the lower level capabilities aligned to the parent capability, and borrow the noun (information object) element of the name. For example, for the lower level capabilities 'Order Management' (level 1), 'Order Information Management' (level 2), 'Order Execution Management' (level 3). This will also aids in readability (and association) for the reader to easily recognise the association of the capability to the upper and lower level capabilities.

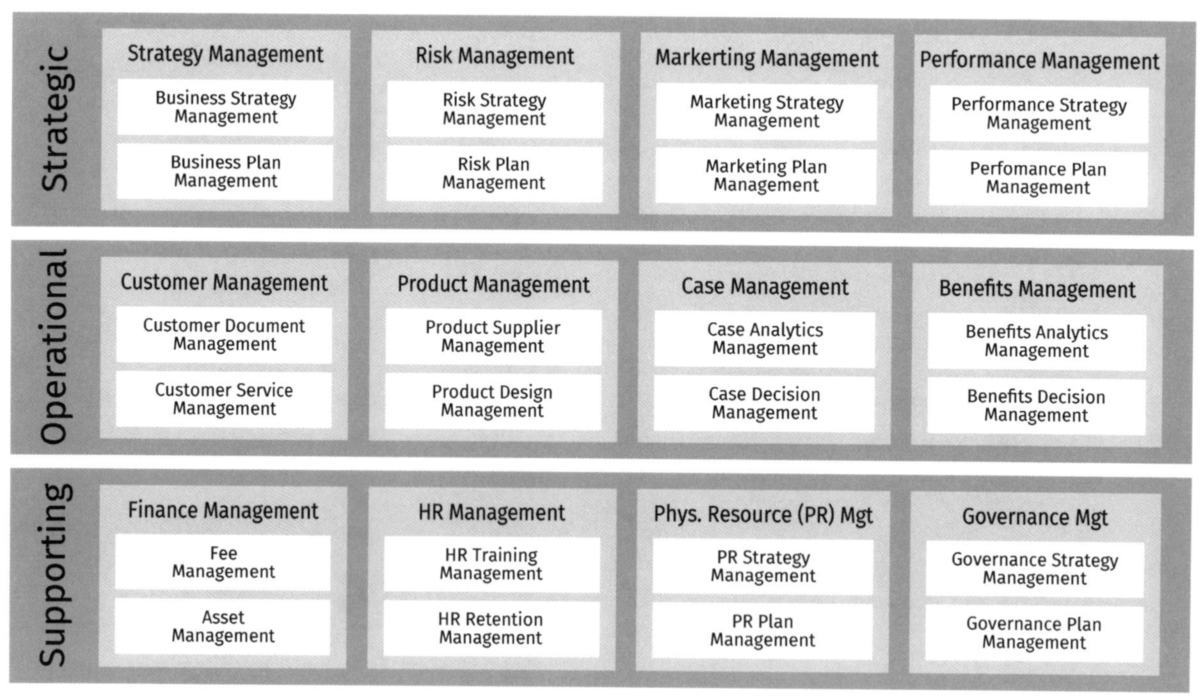


**Figure 7.26 -** Example Level 2 Capabilities decomposed to Level 3

**4. Record the Capability Model information in a Capability Model Catalogue** (table) for record keeping and traceability, now that you have a strawman for discussion and validation with your Product Owner (and/or Key Stakeholders). An example showing Level 1 Strategic capabilities is shown in Table 7.18 below.

**The example in Table 7.18 above shows the definitions for Tier 1 Strategic capabilities, for illustration purposes only. In practice, the Capability Mapping Catalogue should contain all capabilities (including the other Tier 1 Operational and Supporting capabilities not shown above).**

**5. Iteratively socialize, validate and refine each Blueprint** - including any Risk, Assumptions, Issues and Dependencies (RAID) addressed or raised as part of completing these Blueprints, and

**6. Package and publish the Blueprints** – in line with your agreed sprint/release cycle, established back in the Governance Model in *Chapter 6 Step 2 – Control.*

## Risks and Mitigations

The risk with Capability Mapping is getting too excited and trying to map and decompose everything. To avoid these traps, consider the following:

***Levels and decomposing:***

- Don't get in the trap of decomposing capabilities too deep. Decomposing a capability, *'decomposes'* a capability to, yet another (further) capability. In one company I assisted, the Programme decomposed their capabilities to level 4 and 5, and at these levels, the definitions were described as 'steps' and 'activities', which is synonymous with a *process.*

Capability Mapping Catalogue (showing Tier-1) (sample)

Table 7.18

| Tier | Level | Capability | Definition |
|---|---|---|---|
| 1 | 2 | Strategy Management | Ability to define, agree and communicate the Organisations strategy. |
| 1 | 3 | Business Strategy Management | Ability to define and communicate the strategies to support the Organisations vision. |
| 1 | 3 | Business Plan Management | Ability to define and agree a plan to achieve one or more business objectives. |
| 1 | 2 | Risk Management | Ability to define and manage the risks facing the Organisation |
| 1 | 3 | Risk Strategy Management | Ability to define and communicate the risk management strategies to manage and mitigate the risks facing the Organisation. |
| 1 | 3 | Risk Plan Management | Ability to articulate a course of action and mitigation actions to reduce the probability and impact of a given risk(s). |
| 1 | 2 | Marketing Management | Ability to define, agree and communicate marketing activities to support the Organisation vision. |
| 1 | 3 | Marketing Strategy Management | Ability to define and communicate marketing strategies to support the Organisations vision. |
| 1 | 3 | Marketing Plan Management | Ability to articulate a course of action to execute a given marketing activity. |

A capability (if you recall from above) is made up of – People, Process and Technology, but not steps or activities. A 'process' however does have steps and activities. If (or when) you get to a level where you are describing the capability as steps and activities, you have reached the last level of decomposing the capability, and are (most likely) describing a process that supports that capability.

***Scope of the Capability Model:***

- Capabilities for an Organisation, the scope of the Capability Model Map (also called Business Capability Model (BCM)) is the scope of the Organisation. It is *not* the scope of the Programme. One of the common misconceptions with BCMs is that they can be at the project or Programme level. If this happens, what the project or Programme will do is essentially create a BCM of a sub-set of the Organisation's total capabilities, and not a representation (or accurate representation) of the Organisations total capabilities. You want to avoid this.
- When there is more than one Programme underway within the Organisation, and the other (or another) Programme is also developing its own BCM, it will become an issue when it comes to obtaining funding for the Programme (or to pass a phase gate) and justify the spend and investment on a certain capability as there is no clarity on which capability is being touched or enhanced, how it is actually being touched or enhanced and who is doing it.
- When there is more than one BCM for an Organisation (*not* recommended), which in most cases *aren't* identical, it makes it hard (if not near impossible) to trace the strategy down through the BCM to the actual capability where the change, and investment in time, resources and materials are happening. In one company I assisted, they had not two, but *three* capability maps for the one Organisation, each with their different layers, tiers, and decompositions. This made it extremely hard for each individual Programme to explain which business capability they were delivering changes too, as reconciling the capabilities across the 3 Programmes all resulted in 3 different versions of capabilities, with no two capabilities alike. What made it even more difficult was each of the Programmes argued that the BCM was correct and applicable for their Programme. The problem was, it was for the same, single Organisation.
- To prevent you from creating capabilities for *'capabilities-sake'*, only keep those capabilities that have a direct impact to the goals or supporting objective of the Organisation, and include the process (from the Process Model), people and technology that implements the capability, as shown in Table 7.19 below.

Sample Capability Implementation Table

**Table 7.19**

| Customer Management Capabilities | | Implementing Elements | | | Supporting Objective |
|---|---|---|---|---|---|
| **Capability** | **Capability Description** | **Process** | **People** | **Technology** | |
| Customer Document Management | Ability to receive, scan, digitalise, store and retrieve customer documents. | 1.3 Manage Documents | Mailroom Operator (external) | Scanning Solution (external) | • Improved Application Process<br>• Improved Decision Making Process |
| Customer Service Management | Ability to define and manage customer needs and service standards in a consistent and coordinated manner. | 1.1 Manage Registration | Contact Centre Officer | Application Website (legacy) | • Improved Application Process<br>• Decommission legacy case working system & application website |

**In an ideal world, all the capabilities on the Capability Implementation Table should list all the processes that *implement* those capabilities from the Process Model.**

### Building Block Wrap-up

In this section, we discussed the Capability Mapping Building Block.

The Capability Mapping Building Block provides the visual representation of the totality of all Business Capabilities that exist across the Organisation, which systematically and structurally decomposes the top level (tier 1) capabilities to their lowest level (tier 3), and consists of the following two (2) Blueprints:

- Capability Model Map (also called Business Capability Model (BCM)) - provides the visual representation of all the capabilities across the Organisation, used to identify what's in (and out of) scope for the Programme, as well as alignment to the Business Strategy and investment spend (to name a few), and
- Capability Model Catalogue, which provides the list of all Capability Model capabilities, used as the record of the capability information and to confirm the scope of each capability (as well as identify any gaps and duplication of effort and capability scope creep)

Similar to the Process Model and the Process Model Blueprints, the Capability Mapping Blueprints provide the single source of truth, as the *'superset'* list of all capabilities across the Organisation, and the therefore the Programme. As a visual tool, together they help the 'scope' conversations in providing a single and consistent view of capabilities being touched (and changed) by the Programme, as well as identify any potential areas of duplication of effort or gaps where some projects *'think'* (i.e. assumed, and unconfirmed) certain capabilities are out of scope for their project, but they are actually not (they are in scope), or where there is another project (or Programme) that is better suited to delivering changes instead of them.

### Reference Model Recap

Once the Capability Mapping Building Block is completed, this completes the Building Blocks [along with the Organisation Mapping, Stakeholder Mapping, User Journey Mapping and Process Mapping Building Blocks) that make up the Current Operating Model Reference Model.

By completing the Current Operating Model, this now means you have:

- Assessed the state of the Current 'as-is' Operating Model, and have taken a 'bottom-up' analysis approach and identified and agreed the in-scope and impacted business areas and stakeholders (including their roles, concern, needs and measures);
- Identified and documented the User Journeys, which provide the scope of the Programme in context of the Customer and their interaction with the Organisation and identified where in the Customers journey their concerns are visible, and improvement opportunities to address them;
- Identified the processes and capabilities that the Programme is impacting (including defined the only process model and capability model for the Organisation), and
- Agreed the impacted processes and capabilities are in scope for the Programme, and synchronised any changes to the in-scope processes and capabilities both within the Programme, and across the Organisation – agreeing early (i.e. now), who is doing what changes, why and when to reduce any duplication of effort, dependencies and delivery risk from this point on.

For a full recap of **HOBA®** and the **Design Process,** refer to the *Recap* section in *Chapter 11 Next Steps below.*

### Next Steps

The next step in the **Design Process** is to define the Benefits Model, in order to identify, validate and prioritise the Business Benefits the Organisation intends to realise through implementing the Target Operating Model (TOM).

The Benefits Model is discussed in the following chapter.

# Chapter 8

# Step 4 – Evaluate



## Introduction

Step 4 – Evaluate, is about evaluation of both the Business Benefits the Organisation is intending to achieve from its Business Strategy and transformation Programme, as well as evaluation of the Business Capabilities ('Capabilities') that the Organisation is considering investing in, that they are the right capabilities that will lead to the realisation of the Business' intended Business Benefits, in the order and priority the Organisation wants and needs them.

*Figure 8.1* below shows where Step-4 Evaluate fits in the overall Design Process.

Business Benefits and Benefits Realisation Management (BRM) was discussed in the *Alignment with Other Approaches* section, so we won't go over old ground here.

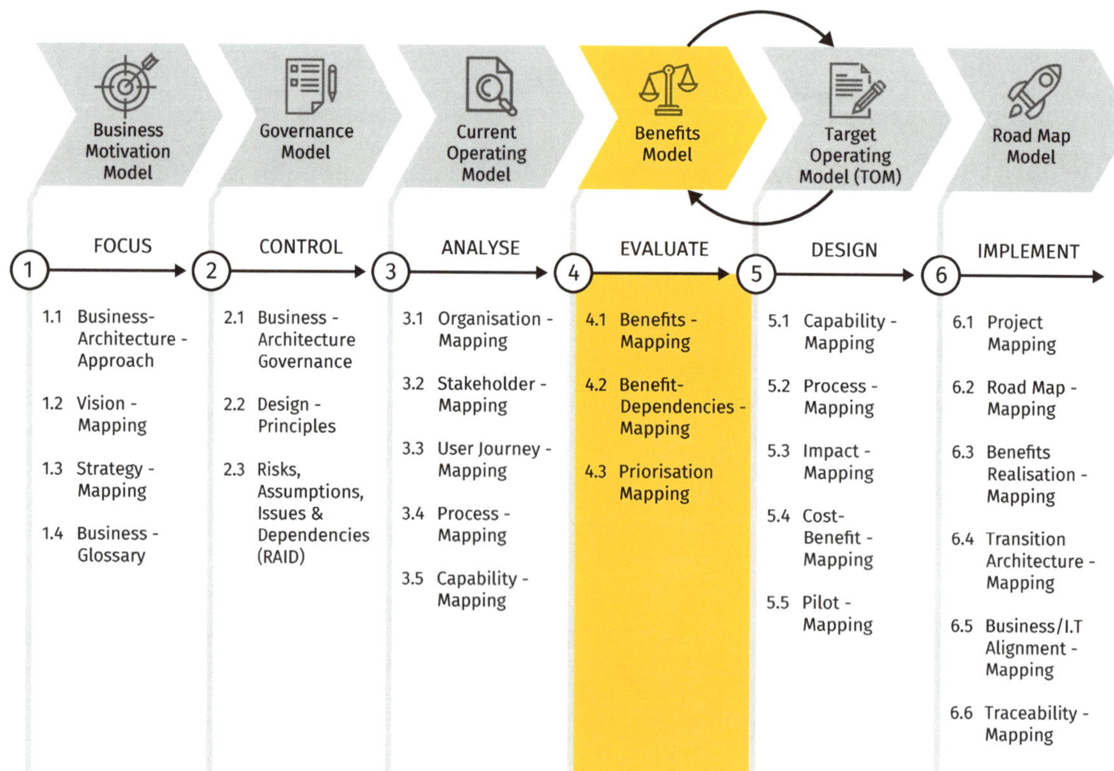


**Figure 8.1** – Design Process – Step 4 Evaluate

Benefits Management is the missing link in Business Architecture today. Benefits are what should be used to drive the selection of Capability investment options. It is in these Capabilities where investments are made, and costs are incurred to either enhance or create new ones. It should also only be when the 'benefits' realised from using those Capabilities outweigh the cost to *enhance or create* new ones, should any decision be made to proceed.

Despite their importance (discussed earlier in the *Benefits Realisation Management* (BRM) section), Benefits has suffered the same *'retrospective'* treatment Business Architecture has faced with its involvement on the Programme – looking back to validate the *'solution decision'*, as opposed to pro-actively to justify any *'solution investment'* in advance. The typical scenario for Benefits, Benefits Identification and Benefits Management is that it is not brought in at Programme inception, but later in the Programme lifecycle, once the Programme is already formed with the clear instruction to:

**"identify the benefits and manage their realisation"**

In order to be successful with our Business Architecture, and our Programmes, we need to make sure the Benefits are realised, and to do that we need to raise Benefits visibility. So, in order to raise Benefits visibility, and show its importance, **HOBA®** was intentionally built *around* the Benefits Model, incorporating it as one of the core pillars, and in the middle of the Target State Architecture **Design Process** ('Design Process'), Step 4 of 6.

# Benefits Model

In Step 4 Evaluate, evaluation is provided through the Benefits Model. The Benefits Model is where you identify, evaluate and prioritise the Business Benefits ('Benefits') the Business is intending to realise from the Capabilities the Programme creates or enhances.

As mentioned earlier in *Chapter 3 House of Business Architecture® (HOBA®)*, each **HOBA®** Reference Model addresses a different aspect in the design and implementation of the Target Operating Model (TOM). These different aspects are represented in the following different views:

- Process
- Perspective
- Context, and
- Content

We will briefly discuss each of these in the section below.

## Process

In terms of process, the Benefits Model is the 4th Step in the Design Process.

Step 4 addresses the areas and activities necessary to define the Benefits Model and prioritise the investment in the Business' Capabilities that directly drive the realisation of the Business' Benefits, in the order and priority the Business wants and needs them.

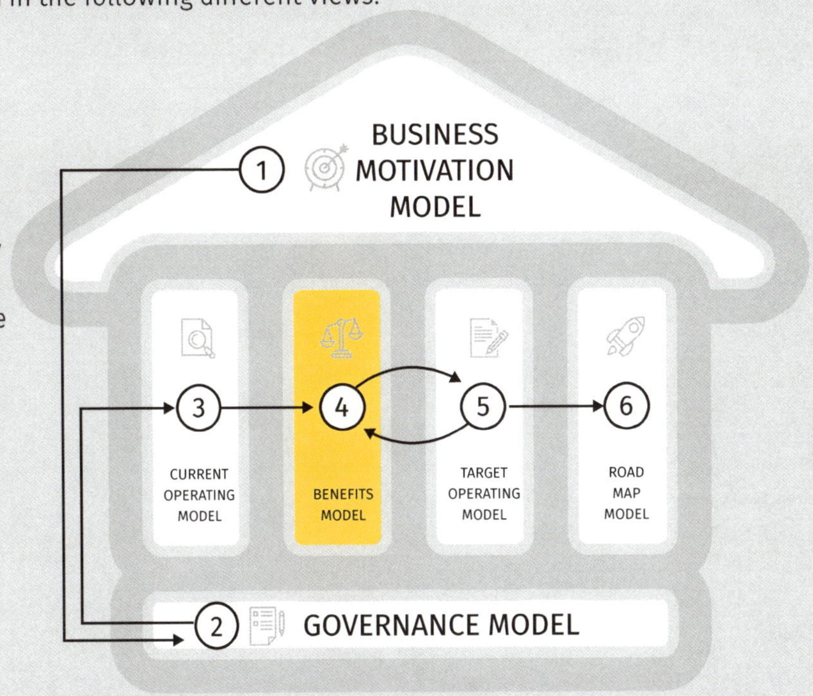


**Figure 8.2** - Benefits Model – Step 4

## Perspective

In terms of perspective, the Benefits Model provides the criteria and method to identify and evaluate the benefits the Business intends to realise, and the Capability solution options available to realise its planned Benefits and Business Strategy.

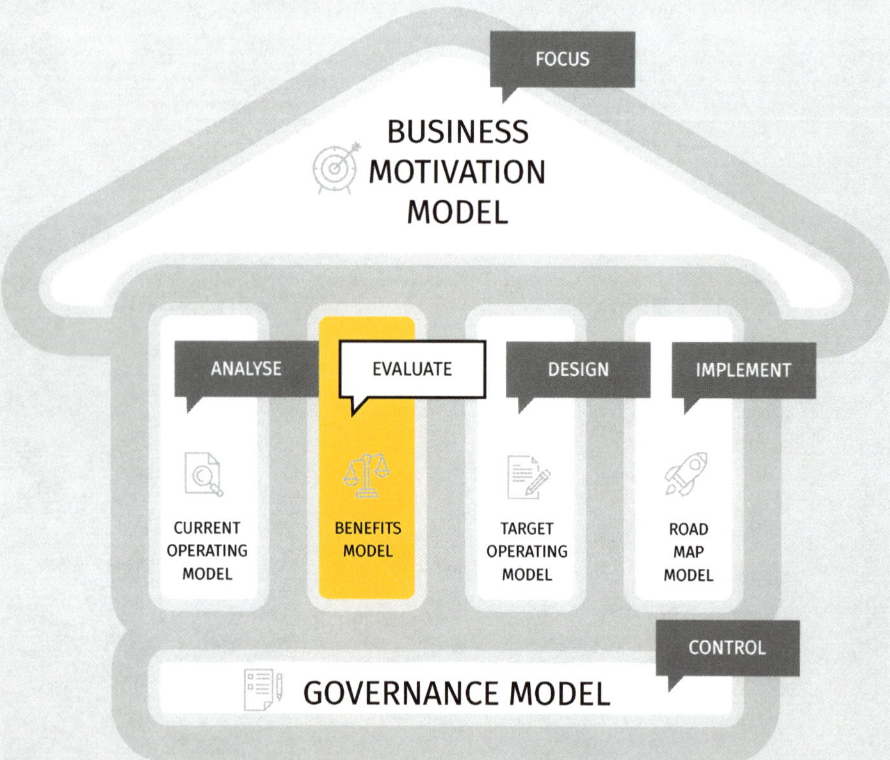


**Figure 8.3 -** Benefits Model – 'Why?' Context

## Context

In terms of context, the Benefits Model addresses the aspect and 'Why?' question asked of the Business, and Business Architecture?

- Why are we doing this? and
- What are the benefits the Organisation intends to realise?

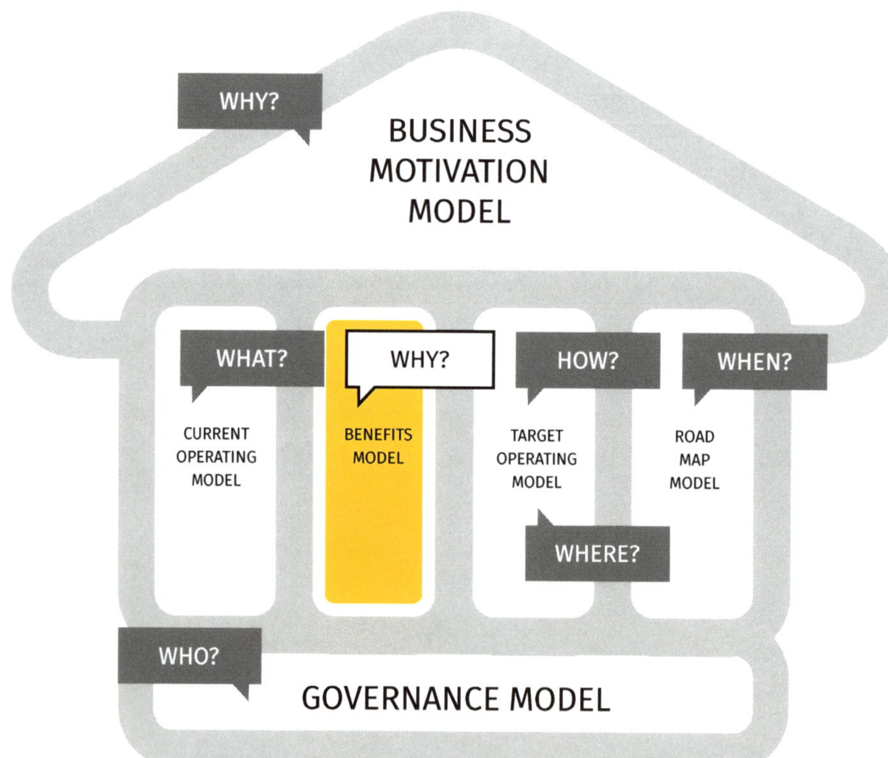


**Figure 8.4-** Current Operating Model - Step 3

## Content

In terms of content, the Building Blocks and Blueprints developed here are the Business Architecture content used to identify and validate the intended Business Benefits that the Business intends to realise, identify and prioritise the capabilities (Business Changes and Enablers) needed to realise those Benefits.

The list of Building Blocks and Blueprints that make up Benefits Model are shown in the table below:

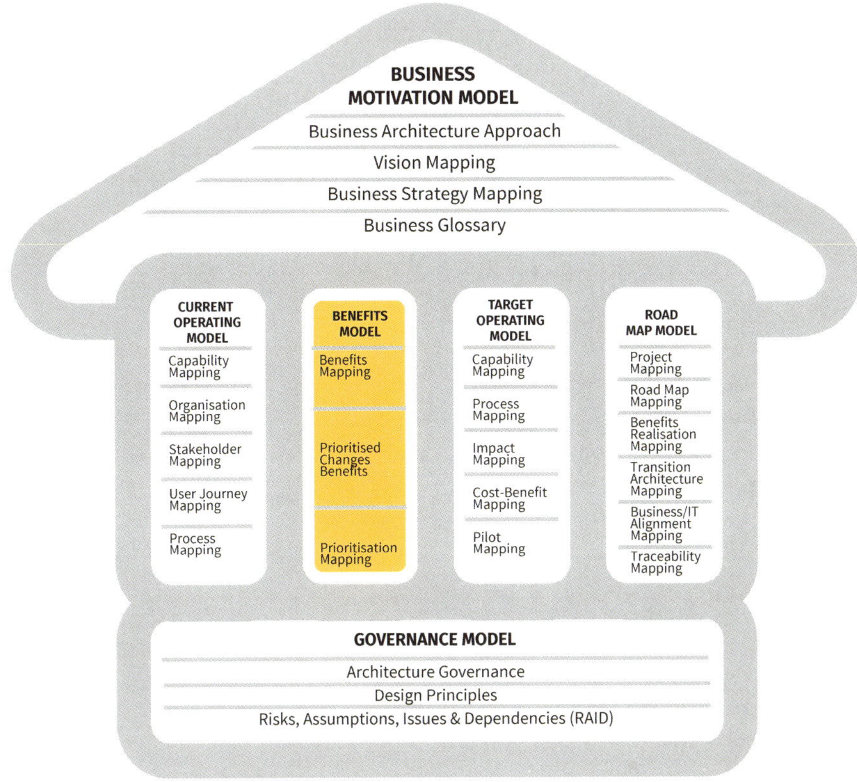


**Figure 8.5** - Current Operating Model - Step 3

**Benefits Model Building Blocks and Blueprints**

**Table 8.1**

| Design Step | Building Block | Purpose | Blueprint |
|---|---|---|---|
| 4.1 | Benefits Mapping | Identify and analyse the all the potential benefits for the key stakeholders | • 4.1.1 Benefits Profile<br>• 4.1.2 Benefits Map |
| 4.2 | Benefit- Dependencies Mapping | Identify and analyse potential solution options to support the benefits | • 4.2.1 Benefits-Dependency Map<br>• 4.2.2 Benefits-Dependency Catalogue |
| 4.3 | Prioritisation Mapping | Evaluate and prioritise the Capabilities the Programme will produce or enhance that directly drive the realisation of the Business' planned Benefits. | • 4.3.1 Prioritised Changes Map<br>• 4.3.2 Prioritised Changes Register |

# High Level Process (SIPOC)

The high level 'Supplier, Input, Process, Output, Customer' (SIPOC) process to complete Step-4 Evaluate, of the Design Process, and the Benefits Model, is shown in the process steps (Building Blocks), and outputs produced (Blueprints) in the SIPOC in *Figure 8.6* below.

We will discuss each of the process steps (Building Blocks) within the SIPOC (above) in the following sections below.

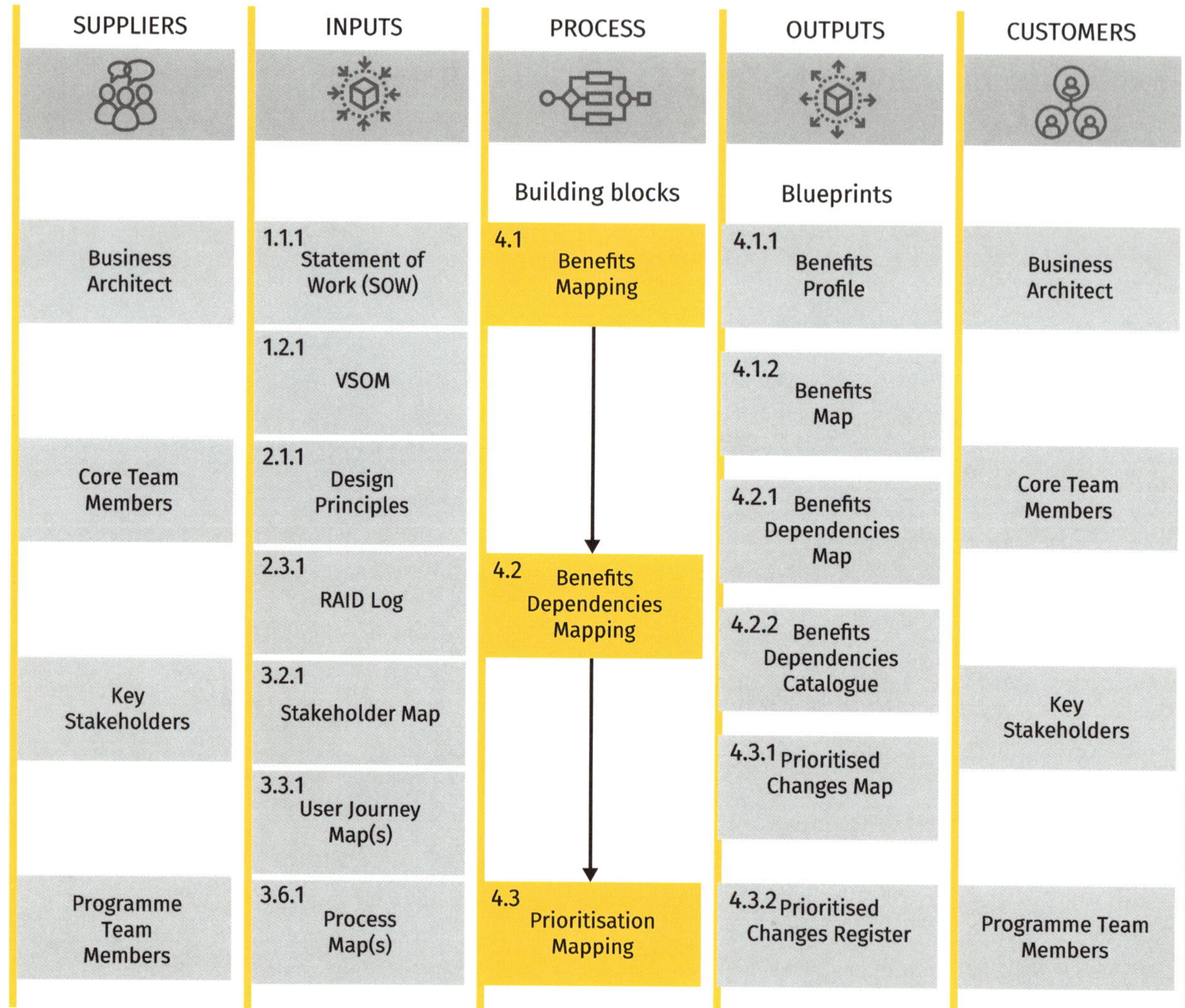


**Figure 8.6** - Benefits Model SIPOC

# 4.1 Benefits Mapping

## Introduction

Benefits Mapping is the Building Block and first step in defining the Benefits Model. This is where the Business Architect works with the Key Stakeholders to identify and assess the Business Benefits ('Benefits') they seek to achieve from the Programme. Remember, it is these benefits that provide the rationale for the Organisation and the Programme to make the investment in creating or enhancing existing Business Capabilities (namely, people, process and technology) that align the Business to the Business Strategy. It is then through the implementation and use of these new (or enhanced) capabilities the business is able to realise the intended benefits. The timing of when the Benefits Model is defined intentionally appears early in the Design Process, before any solution or design is chosen or underway in order to provide the rationale for investment, and not the other way around, to justify the investment, which so often happens in practice. For example, what usually happens in practice is a solution is chosen, or worse – delivered, and the Business Architect is asked to retro-fit and design the Business Architecture around the solution, as opposed to develop a solution to fit the design of the Business Architecture.

You may recall we discussed Benefits Realisation Management (BRM) in the Alignment with Other Approaches section, it was the Programme 'outputs' that, when used by the business, produce 'outcomes', which through their use, the Business is able to realise the intended Benefits, as shown in *Figure 8.7* below

One of the first steps in making sure the likelihood the intended Benefits are going to be realised, is making sure the Organisation and Programme invest in the capabilities that directly impact the realisation of those Benefits. As the Business Architect, our role here in the BRM process is to not only to identify those capabilities but also identify the order and priority the Business wants (and needs) those Benefits realised in.

## Inputs

The inputs used to complete this Building Block are shown in the table below.

## Outputs

The Blueprints (outputs) produced for this Building Block is shown in the table below.

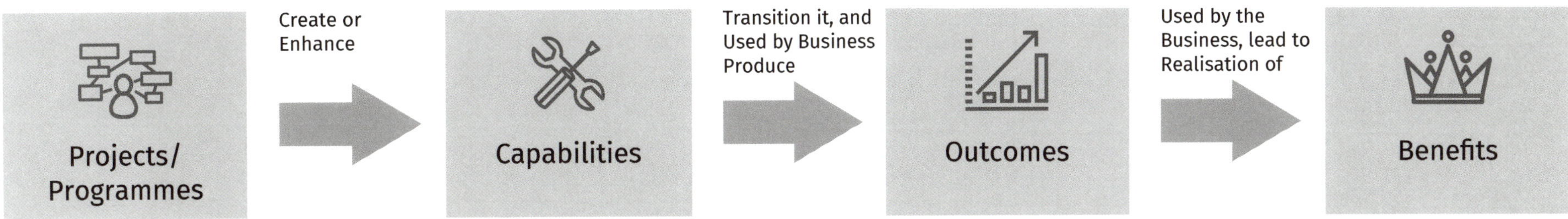


**Figure 8.7 -** Actual Relationship Between Capabilities and Benefits

**Process Mapping Building Block Inputs**

Table 8.2

| Ref | Blueprint | Use |
|---|---|---|
| 1.2.1 | Vision (VSOM) | Provide the Vision and articulated business goals (strategy, objectives and measures), that all requirements including the candidate Business Changes and Enablers must align to and support. |
| 2.2.1 | Design Principles Register | Provide the scope and boundaries of the Programme and Business Architecture, which the Benefits and candidate Business Changes and Enablers must fall within. |
| 2.3.1 | RAID Log | Provide the Risks, Assumptions, Issues and Dependencies that need to be checked against (and updated, where necessary) as part of completing this Blueprint. |
| 3.1.1 | Stakeholder Maps | Provide the list of stakeholders whom benefits will be provided for. |
| 3.1.3 | Stakeholder Concerns and Views | Provide the Voice of the Customer (VOC) – Concerns, Needs (CTC) & Measures (CTQ) that the Business Architecture must address. |
| 3.3.1 | User Journey Map(s) | Provide Improvement Opportunities (as candidate Business Changes and Enablers) to improve User(s) journey and experience. |
| 3.6.1 | Process Maps | Provide context of where and when the benefits are identified. |
| N/A | Existing Programme Documentation | Include the Project Charter, or Project Brief, which may have provided (some) benefits and dis-benefits that have already been identified. |

Table8.3

<table>
<tr><th>Ref</th><th>Blueprint</th><th>Description</th><th>Example</th></tr>
<tr><td>4.1.1</td><td>Benefits Profile</td><td>A detailed description of a benefit, how it is measured and who owns it.</td><td>
<table>
<tr><th>Name</th><th>ID</th><th>Type</th><th>Description</th><th>Measures</th><th>Current Value</th><th>Target Value</th><th>Start Time</th><th>Time</th><th>Value</th><th>Strategic Objective</th><th>Benefits Owner</th></tr>
<tr><td>Increased Volume of Applications Processed</td><td>B001</td><td>Financial (cashable)</td><td>Number of applications that pass 'decision' phase.</td><td>Number of processed applications (start Sept - end Nov)</td><td>20K month</td><td>22K month<br><br>(10% increase)</td><td>00:00:00 1/01/2015</td><td>11:59:59sec 30/12/2015</td><td>£2.4M increase sales per annum</td><td>Improved Application Process</td><td>Product Owner</td></tr>
<tr><td>Less Errors/ Error Handling</td><td>B002</td><td>Financial (cashable)</td><td>Less errors payment processing (less staff costs to process)</td><td>Less manual rocessing of payment errors</td><td>300 errors per month (10 per day)</td><td>60 errors per month (2 per day)<br><br>(80% reduction)</td><td>00:00:00 1/01/2015</td><td>11:59:59sec 30/12/2015</td><td>£50K saving per year<br><br>(2* FTE @ £25K each)</td><td>Improved Application Process</td><td>Product Owner</td></tr>
<tr><td>Reduced Calls to Contact Centre</td><td>B003</td><td>Financial (cashable)</td><td>Applicant can view status online; less calls to Contact Centre</td><td>Reduced application status inquiries to Contact Centre</td><td>840 Calls per month</td><td>168 Calls per month<br><br>(80% reduction)</td><td>00:00:00 1/01/2015</td><td>11:59:59sec 30/12/2015</td><td>£50K saving per year<br><br>(2* FTE @ £25K each)</td><td>Improved Application Process</td><td>Product Owner</td></tr>
</table>
</td></tr>
<tr><td>4.1.2</td><td>Benefits Map</td><td>Visual representation of the relationship between immediate, final benefits and their cause and effect relationship to strategic objectives.</td><td>
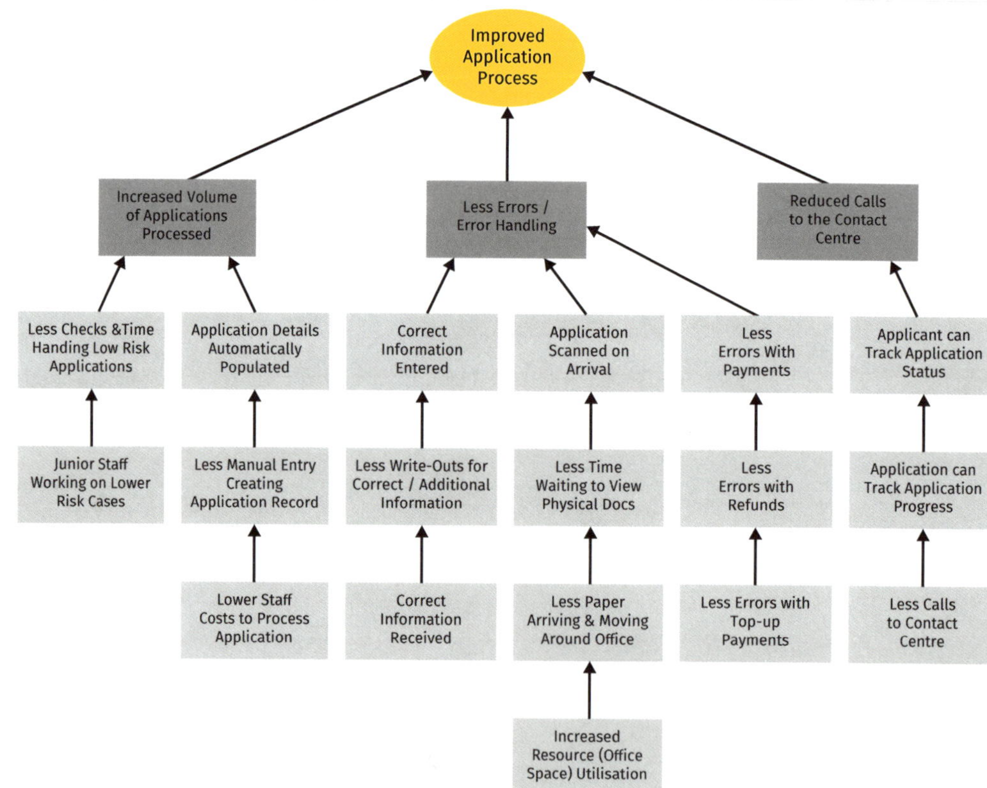

</td></tr>
</table>

## Steps

The steps to complete the above Blueprints (Outputs) are as follows.

### 4.1.1 Benefits Profile

**1. Confirm the Benefits Owners**

This is where you confirm the stakeholders that are accountable for the realisation of the Benefits. Owners aren't necessarily the Beneficiaries, but if they were it would also help as that would provide more incentive to ensure they would be realised.

The SRO is the *ultimate* Benefits Owner, who has the overall accountability that the Programme delivers the identified benefits. The SRO may however delegate the identification, definition and validation of the Benefits to specific roles, Key Stakeholders or directly with the Product Owner.

**2. Develop the Benefits Profile**

The purpose of this step here is to qualify and quantify the details for each benefit, and capture the Benefit details in the Benefit Profile table.

Using the inputs from the *Inputs* section above (particularly Stakeholder Concerns, Needs and Measures, and the User Journey Maps with the Stakeholder Goals and Improvement Opportunities), work with the Product Owner and/or Key Stakeholders as the delegated Benefits Owner, developing the Benefits Profile for each of the Key Stakeholders (or stakeholder group(s)).

An example of a Benefits Profile is shown in Table 8.4 below.

**The Benefit(s) for each of the key stakeholders/stakeholder groups should be represented on the Benefits Map, as one of the final (end) benefits, discussed below.**

The Benefits Profile terms and definitions are shown in the Table 8.5 below.

Sample Benefits Profile Table

Table 8.4

| Name | ID | Type | Description | Measures | Current Value | Target Value | Start Time | Time | Value | Strategic Objective | Benefits Owner |
|---|---|---|---|---|---|---|---|---|---|---|---|
| Increased Volume of Applications Processed | B001 | Financial (cashable) | Number of applications that pass 'decision' phase. | Number of processed applications (start Sept - end Nov) | 20K month | 22K month<br>(10% increase) | 00:00:00 1/01/2015 | 11:59:59sec 30/12/2015 | £2.4M increase sales per annum | Improved Application Process | Product Owner |
| Less Errors/ Error Handling | B002 | Financial (cashable) | Less errors payment processing (less staff costs to process) | Less manual rocessing of payment errors | 300 errors per month (10 per day) | 60 errors per month (2 per day)<br>(80% reduction) | 00:00:00 1/01/2015 | 11:59:59sec 30/12/2015 | £50K saving per year<br>(2* FTE @ £25K each) | Improved Application Process | Product Owner |
| Reduced Calls to Contact Centre | B003 | Financial (cashable) | Applicant can view status online; less calls to Contact Centre | Reduced application status inquiries to Contact Centre | 840 Calls per month | 168 Calls per month<br>(80% reduction) | 00:00:00 1/01/2015 | 11:59:59sec 30/12/2015 | £50K saving per year<br>(2* FTE @ £25K each) | Improved Application Process | Product Owner |

Benefit Profile Descriptions

**Table 8.5**

| Term | Description |
|---|---|
| ID | Unique benefit ID |
| Type | • Financial:<br>- Cashable (give immediate bankable returns);<br>- Non-cashable (e.g. efficiency gains leading to less time to come a required task, but can't be easily converted into a reduction in headcount or costs).<br>• Non-financial:<br>- Measurable (i.e. greater customer satisfaction, measured by a performance rating or survey results);<br>- Non-measurable (i.e. improved culture);<br>• Dis-benefit:<br>- Outcomes that are perceived as having a negative impact of change on performance of the Organisation |
| Benefits Description | What will this benefit (i.e. the outcome) change? What are the impacts of the changes? |
| Measures | How will you know when the benefit is achieved – what measures will you use? Business Architecture customer satisfaction, measured using a performance indicator or survey results. |
| Current Value | Baseline value from which you will measure this benefit |
| Target Value | Future value (KPI), and interim targets until you achieve the final target |
| Start Time | Expected start period measuring to start |
| End Time | Anticipated end period measuring will end |
| Value | Value of the benefit to the Organisation |
| Strategic Objective | The strategic objective the benefit contributes to |
| Benefits Owner | Stakeholder responsible for the definition and realisation of the benefits |

## 4.1.2 Benefits Map

### 3. Develop the Benefits Map

The Benefits Map Blueprint shows the *actual* mapping of the 'Immediate Benefits' that drive the 'final benefits', ultimately driving the Strategy Objective, as shown in *Figure 8.8* below.

**Figure 8.8 -** Sample Benefits Map (showing relative time to benefits realisation)

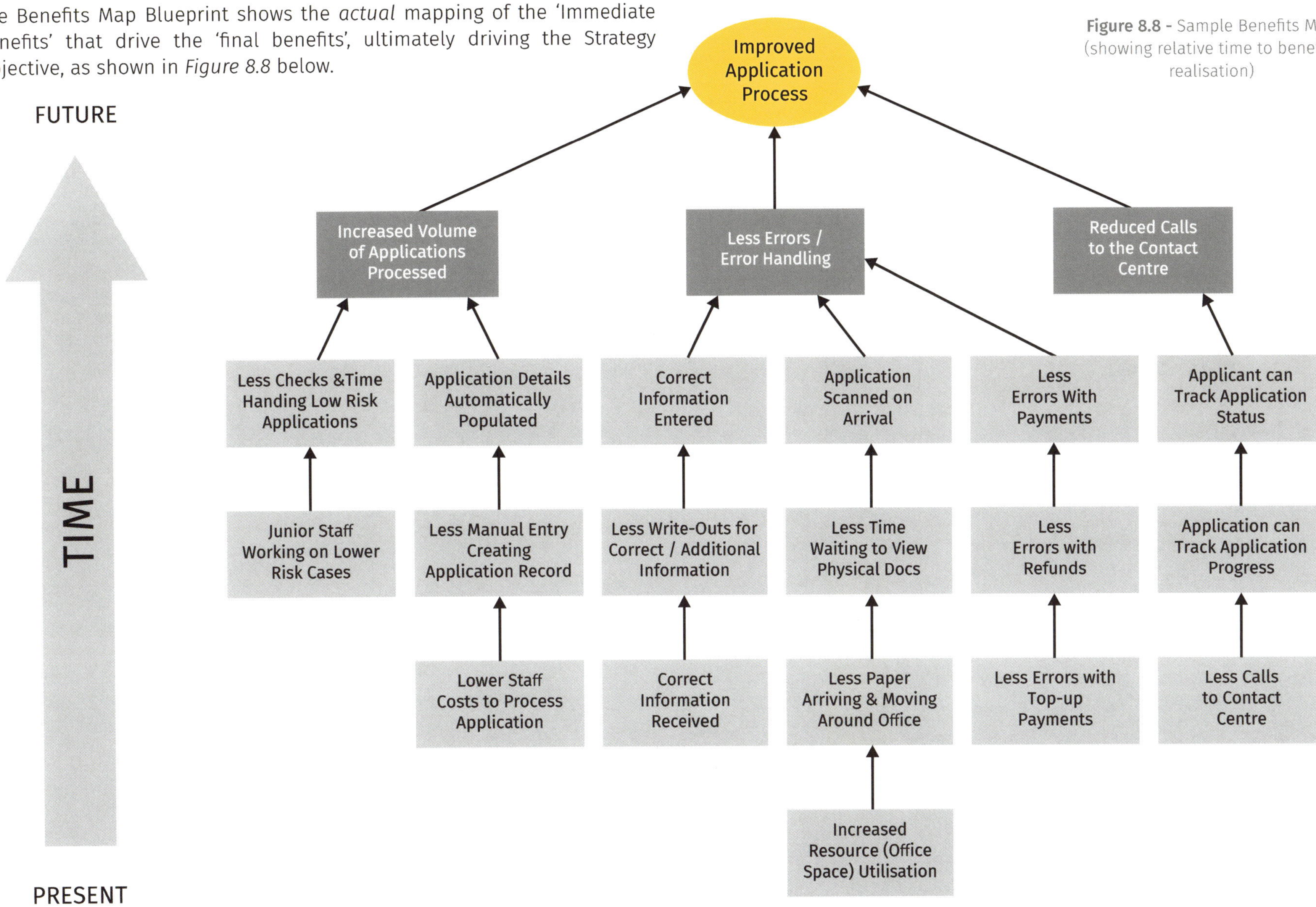

The Benefit Map elements are shown in the table below.

**(*) Note - *Dis-benefits* has been included in the above table for completeness. For simplicity to allow for dis-benefits in Mapping, the value of a corresponding benefit it relates too should be reduced to allow for the dis-benefit negative impact.**

The starting position to begin the mapping is the Strategic Objective, working in the *'top-to-bottom'* fashion, as shown below.

**Figure 8.9 -** Starting point for Benefits Mapping – the Strategic Objective

For every Strategic Objective identified in the Vision (VSOM) Blueprint, that the Programme is responsible for delivering, there *ideally* should be a new Benefits Map created for each Strategic Objective.

**In mapping the Benefits, and producing the Benefit Maps, where the Programme is accountable for implementing the Capabilities to support more than one Strategic Objective, the Programme will have more than one Benefit Map – one for each of the Strategic Objectives.**

**Benefit Map Elements**

**Table 8.6**

| Element | Description | Symbol |
|---|---|---|
| Strategic Objective | The strategic objective, fromthe Vision (Vision, Strategy, Objectives and Measures) Blueprint. | Improved Application Process |
| Final (End) Benefit | An ultimate benefit of a Programme or Project. Achievement of a final benefit is dependent on the achievement of one or more Immediate Benefits. | Final Benefit |
| Immediate Benefit | Benefits which occur between the mplementation of early changes and the realisation of the End Benefits. | Immadiate Benefit |
| Dis-benefit* | An outcome that is seen as negative to a particular stakeholder.<br>Note – a particular outcome maybe a dis-benefit to one stakeholder, but a benefit to another. | Disbenefit |

## 4. Identify the final benefits

With the help from your Product Owner (and/or Key Stakeholders), decompose the Strategic Objective and identify a comprehensive set of realistic Final Benefits, which support the Objective(s) but are also owned by the key stakeholders.

For a single Strategic Objective, the Final Benefits collectively fully represent the Strategic Objective. As a rule of thumb, a Strategic Objective will decompose to a minimum of three (3) Final Benefits, as shown in *Figure 8.10* below.

The test to check that the Final Benefits fully support the Objective be fulfilled is called the 'fulfilment test'. The fulfilment test is done by removing one of the Final Benefits at a time, and asking 'if these remaining benefits were realised, would the objective be fulfilled?':

- **If Yes** – all the Final Benefits have been identified;
- **If No** – then continue looking at other options or areas within the scope of the Business (and Programme), that could address the gap and continue running the 'fulfilment test' until all Final Benefits are identified.

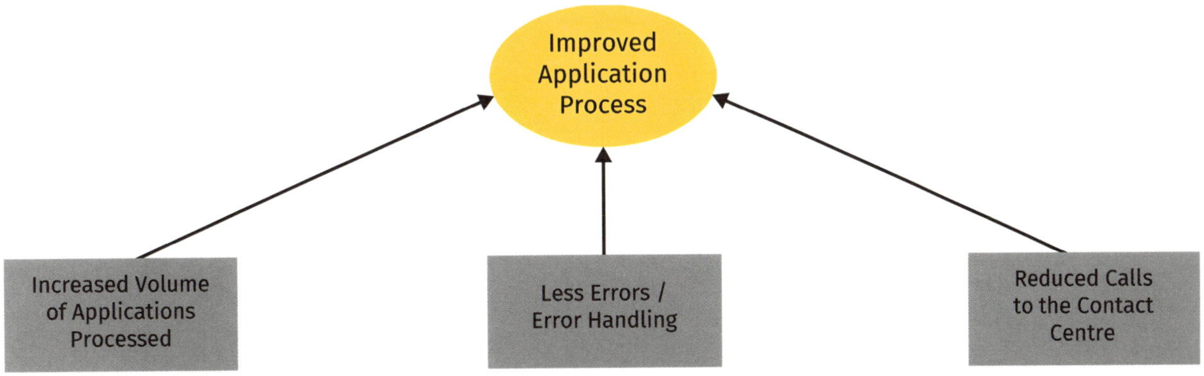


**Figure 8.10 -** Strategic objective decomposed into contributing final benefits

### 5. Identify the Immediate Benefit (that contribute to the final benefits)

The realisation of a Final Benefit is often dependent on the realisation of an earlier Benefit. These earlier benefits are the *'immediate'* Benefits. Identifying the Immediate Benefits is where the Final Benefits are decomposed into contributing ('immediate') Benefits that lend themselves to the realisation of the Final Benefit in a similar 'case-and-effect' relationship that the Final Benefits did with the Strategic Objectives.

An example of the 'cause and effect' relationship between immediate and final benefits is shown in *Figure 8.11* below

Benefits, as shown in *Figure 8.10* below.

The process and test to identify the contributing *'immediate'* benefits to each of the final benefits is the same *'fulfilment test'* as identifying the (final) benefits as discussed above, i.e. decompose the final benefit into its contributing benefits, and run the fulfilment test as mentioned above and systematically remove one Immediate Benefit at a time, and ask 'if these remaining Benefits were realised, would the Objective be fulfilled?':

- **If Yes** – all the Immediate Benefits have been identified;
- **If No** – then continue looking at other options or areas within the scope of the business, and Programme, that could address the gap and continue running the 'fulfilment test' until all Immediate Benefits are identified.

**Immediate Benefits at the bottom of the map represent the quick wins, with the Final Benefits at the top on the Benefits Map, and longer term Benefit(s), hence their relationship to the longer term 'Strategic Objective'. Reading the map from bottom-up, the Immediate Benefits positioned on bottom will be the benefits that are the quickest to realise, and the ones up at the top near the Final Benefit (and Strategic Objective), the furthest in time to realise.**

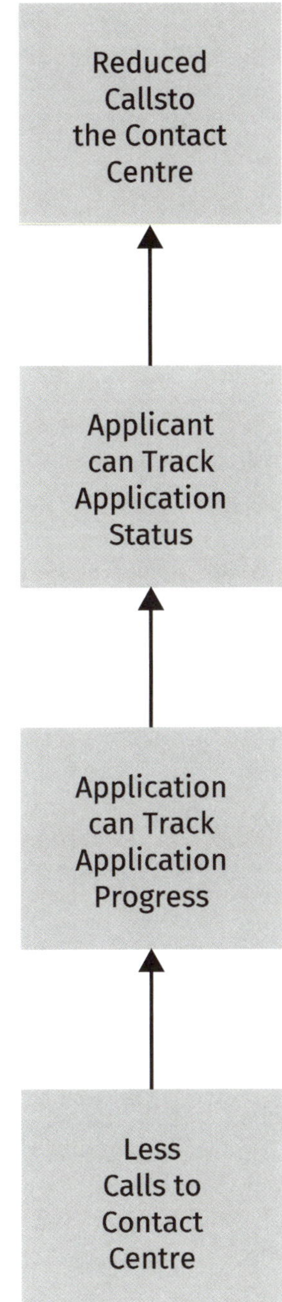


**Figure 8.11 -** Cause and effect relationship between Immediate and final benefits

Repeat decomposing each new/identified Immediate Benefit and running the fulfilment test, until the Immediate Benefits can't be decomposed any more.

As a *general rule*, the relationship between benefits is as follows:

- Each Final Benefit will have 2-3 Immediate Benefits,
- Immediate Benefits may have between 1-3 'earlier' Immediate Benefits.

Once all the decomposing is finalised, the completed Benefits Map should look like Figure 8.12 below.

**When adding the Immediate Benefits to the Benefits Map, the relevant contributing Immediate Benefits in a 'top-to-bottom' reverse chronological order, these should be placed beside other Immediate Benefits that occur or are expected to occur at the same time should sit on the same horizontal level *across* the map. While it's important to show where an Immediate Benefit maps to more than one subsequent Immediate Benefit, what's even more important is to the *'degree'* or *'weight'* that Immediate Benefit contributes to another Immediate Benefit. This weighting is discussed in the prioritisation section below.**

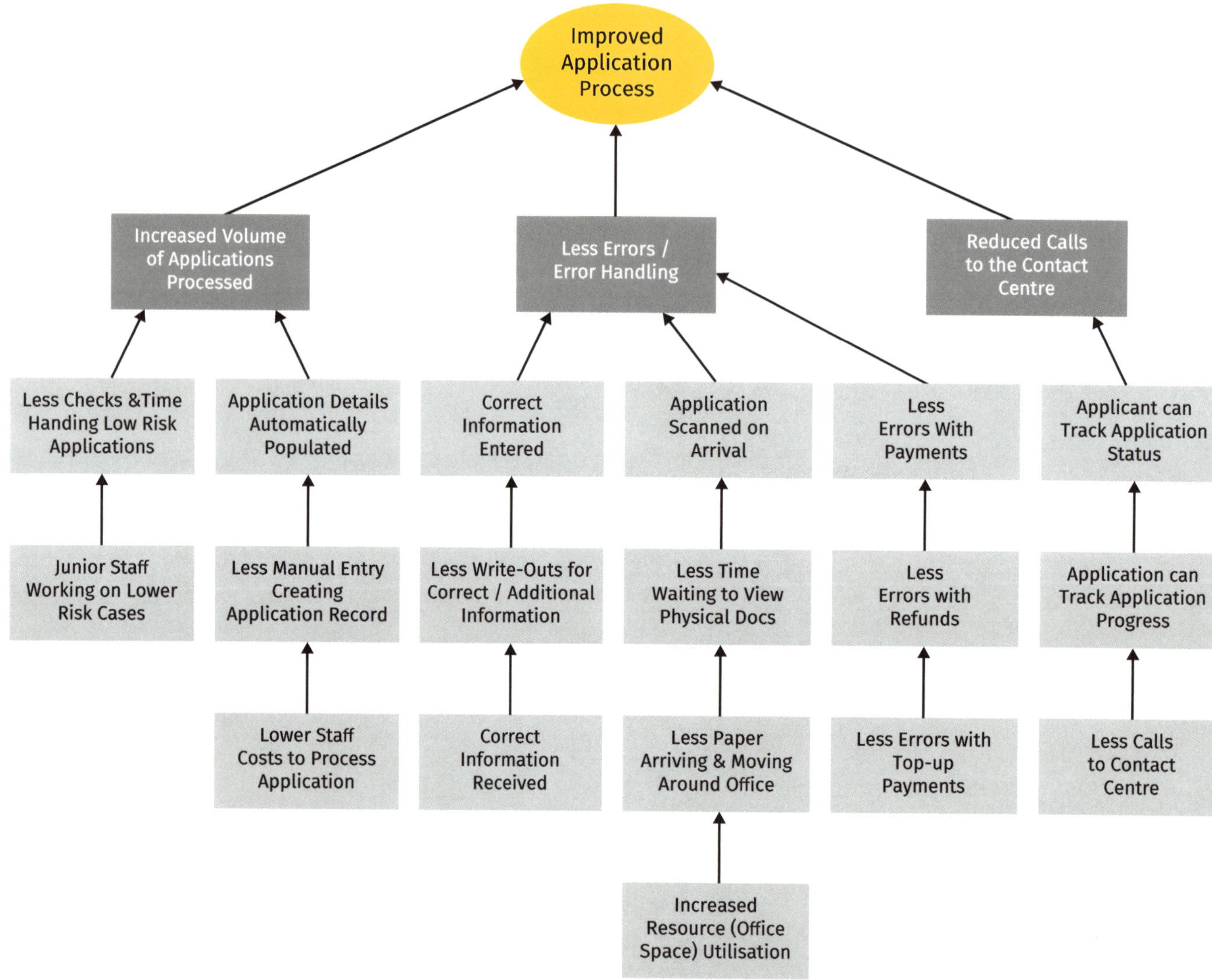


**Figure 8.12** - Benefits Map showing Strategic Objective, Final Benefits and Immediate Benefits

**6. Iteratively socialize, validate and refine each Blueprint** (including any Risk, Assumptions, Issues and Dependencies (RAID) addressed or raised as part of completing these Blueprints), and

**7. Package and publish the Blueprints** – in line with your agreed sprint/release cycle, established back in the Governance Model in *Chapter 6 Step 2 – Control*.

## Risks and Mitigations

Benefit Maps are powerful visual tools to use to get all Key Stakeholders on board with what the Programme and Business

Architecture is to achieve, but there are a few risks to be aware of, as discussed below:

***Valuing Benefits:***

- Valuing Benefits can be tricky, particularly when it comes to quantifying *non-cash* benefits. Wherever possible, always look to quantify and measure a Benefit. Cash or money, is the most obvious (but not the only) measure. Where possible transfer or convert non-cash Benefits *to* cash Benefits.

  By *not* converting non-cash Benefits to cash-equivalent or measurable Benefits, and having some Benefits as cash, and others non-cash, is like comparing apples and oranges. This also applies to *intangible* Benefits (like 'improved brand', or 'improved staff morale'). Wherever possible, you should also always aim to convert intangible Benefits to tangible ones (or something that can be measured). Improved customer service for example can be converted from intangible and measured (by a star rating for example), making it tangible, and measurable. If there is a Benefit that can't be measured, you need to ask if it's a benefit at all? It's worth asking that question because you are going to be expected to show your progress towards delivering the capability that supports that 'benefit'. If you can't measure it, it's going to be very hard (if not near impossible) to show progress towards it.

***Too many immediate Benefits:***

- Having more than 2-3 Immediate Benefits per Final Benefit and/or 1-3 'earlier' Immediate Benefits per Immediate Benefit can create very large (and potentially complicated) maps, which can reduce the effectiveness of these maps as a communication tool to provide the visibility and clarity on how Benefits are related to each other. Try to keep within the 'earlier' Benefits general '1-3 rule'.

***Workshopping Benefit Profile Information:***

- Capturing Benefit Profile information can be done either in a one-on-one situation with the Product Owner or each Key Stakeholder individually, or in a Benefits workshop. Workshops are an efficient forum to encourage collaboration and creative thinking, as well as creating a sense of ownership amongst the stakeholders that they are being involved in the change process. There is a risk however that some members may refrain or withhold their opinion and true thoughts due to the presence of certain other team members. Some 'investigation' beforehand may identify the 'ideal' constructive composition of the workshop participants. Alternatively, run the workshop on a subset of the intended group, or focus group and play back to the broader group to validate your findings.

***Overlapping Benefits:***

- The Vision (VSOM) Blueprint decomposed the Vision into its discrete components i.e. Strategy, Objectives and Measures in a one-to-many (not a many-to-many) relationship which makes them easy to trace and see the relationships between the Vision, and the decomposed parts. Aim to replicate this one-to-many (not a many-to-many) relationship between the Strategic Objective(s) and Final Benefits, and Immediate Benefits and 'earlier' Immediate Benefits. i.e. don't have more than one final benefit mapped to the Strategic Objective. There may be of course situations where Immediate Benefits are shared across 'earlier' Immediate Benefits. If this does occur, you will need to question the rationale for the connection as they are so 'near term' that the strength of the relationship to multiple Final Benefits later in time will become 'diluted' and subjective, it may end up being more of a hindrance than a help when sharing and communicating benefits with your stakeholders.

***Out of Scope Benefits:***

- The idea with benefit maps is to visualize the in-scope items the Programme is responsible for. As part of visualizing the in-scope items for the Programme, there is the possibility you also discover Final or Immediate Benefits that your Programme is not responsible for. When this happens, you effectively have two choices:

  - **Disclose the out-of-scope benefits** (and show them on the map), or
  - **Not show or disclose** those benefits at all.

When it comes to disclosure, you should always be honest and transparent (it's the best policy!). Show these *out of scope* items, immediate or final benefits (and capabilities – discussed in the Prioritisation Mapping Building Block in the next section below) on the map, however make sure to mark them 'out of scope'.

If these out-of-scope items are covered by another project or Programme, reference the Programme that is responsible for their delivery. Referencing other or external parties responsible for pieces of work or benefits you have identified (be they internal of external), and confirming that responsibility with that other project or Programme is not simply good corporate manners and responsibility, but shows that the Business Architecture is *'joined up'* with the other parts of the Organisation, and not working in isolation (known as being in the 'ivory tower', disconnected from the Business and reality, which Business Architecture has historically accused of).

### Building Block Wrap-up

In this section, we discussed the Benefit Mapping Building Block.

This Building Block qualifies, quantifies and maps the Business Benefits the Organisation intends to realise from using the Capabilities (that are directly attributable to the realisation of the planned benefits) that the Programme is responsible for delivering.

This Building Block is made up of the following two (2) Blueprints:

- **Benefits Profile** - a detailed description of a Benefit, how it is measured and who owns it, and
- **Benefits Map** - the visual representation of the relationship between Immediate, Final Benefits and their cause and effect relationship to Strategic Objectives.

Both Blueprints are powerful tools to provide visibility of the Benefits the Programme is responsible for, delivering not only capabilities that support those Benefits, but also putting into context the number, size and dependencies between each benefit, and their cause and effect relationship with the Strategic Objective(s).

### Next Steps

Once the Benefits Mapping has been completed and agreed, the next step in the **Design Process** is to identify the candidate capabilities (i.e. people, process and/or technology changes) as the set of Business Changes and Enablers that the Business is dependent on for the realisation of the planned Benefits.

Benefit 'dependencies' are discussed in the next section.



# 4.2 Benefit Dependencies Mapping

## Introduction

Benefit Dependencies Mapping is the Building Block that identifies the optimum set of capabilities (people, process and technology) which are to become the set of 'Business Changes' and 'Enablers' that the identified Benefits are dependent on for their realisation. These Business Changes and Enablers are also the changes to the Current Operating Model that form the Target Operating Model (TOM) and align the Business to the Business Strategy.

According to Gerald, 'Benefit Realisation Management: A Practical Guide to Achieving Benefits' (2010), Enablers are "technology and information"; while business changes are classified as "people, culture, strategies/policies, processes, practices and procedures", which in Business Architecture translate to technology and 'people and process' elements of Business Capabilities, as shown in Table 8.7 below.

**(*) Note – culture, strategies/policies, practices and procedures are implicitly included as part of 'People and Process' elements of Capabilities, as they are by default required to deliver the 'people' and 'process' changes.**

The Benefit Dependencies Map developed here is shown in Figure 8.13 below (annotated; showing the cause-and-effect relationship from the Business Changes and Enablers 'means', and how they impact the Immediate Benefits 'ways', to bring to affect the final benefits, and ultimate the Strategic Objective 'ends').

Each of the 'cause-and-effect' elements are described in Table 8.8 below.

The objective with Benefits Dependencies mapping is to:

1. **Identify and prioritise the candidate** capabilities that will enable the realisation of the planned benefits, and
2. **Validate early in the process the identified candidate capabilities** are likely *in-scope* and *achievable* within the scope (and budget) of the project or Programme.

Capability Terms Translate into Benefits Model Terms

Table 8.7

| The following Capability terms... | In the Benefits Model, equate to... |
|---|---|
| Technology (non-people, and non-process) element of a business capability | Enablers |
| People and Process element of a business capability | Business Change* |

Figure 8.13 - Benefits Dependencies Map – Cause and Effect elements

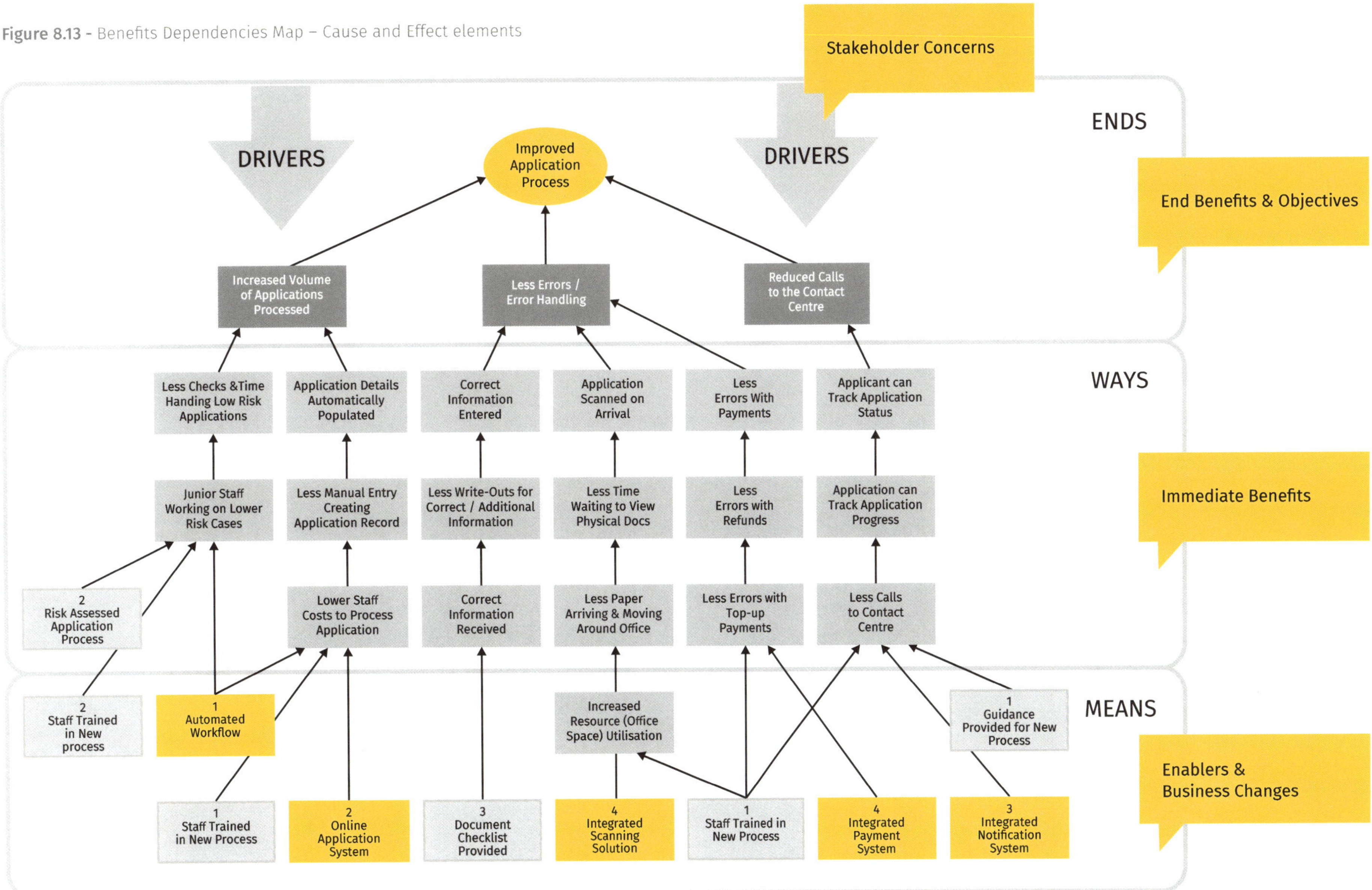

Both of these (identified and in-scope capabilities) need to be confirmed before any detailed design or planning work commences, which is why there is the visible circular feedback loop between the (Step 4) 'Evaluate' and (Step 5) 'Design' in the **Design Process**, as shown in *Figure 8.14* below).

The intentional feedback loop between Step 4 and 5 represents the *iterative* nature of the evaluation/design work, to allow for the identification of the benefits in Step 4, to be costed and validated in Step 5 (Design), until the right cost/benefit combination is found and agreed.

## Inputs

The inputs used to complete this Building Block are shown in the table below.

## Outputs

The Blueprints (outputs) produced for this Building Block is shown in the table below.

## Steps

The steps to complete the above Blueprints (Outputs) are as follows.

## 4.2.1 Benefits-Dependencies Map

### 1. Identify the Business Changes

Using the 'input' from the *Inputs* above, identify the Business Changes (i.e. people and process) that are needed to realise the intended Benefits, starting in reverse order used for identifying Immediate Benefits – *'bottom-to-top'* (as opposed to *'top-to-bottom'*), keeping in mind it is due to

Benefits-Dependencies Map – Cause-and-Effect elements

Table 8.8

| Cause-and-effect element | Description | Example |
|---|---|---|
| Driver | What is creating the need for change | Concern (stakeholder) |
| End | What we want | Strategic Objective<br>End Benefit |
| Ways | What to do | Immediate Benefit<br>Immediate Dis-benefit |
| Means | What you use | Enablers<br>Business Change<br>Project |

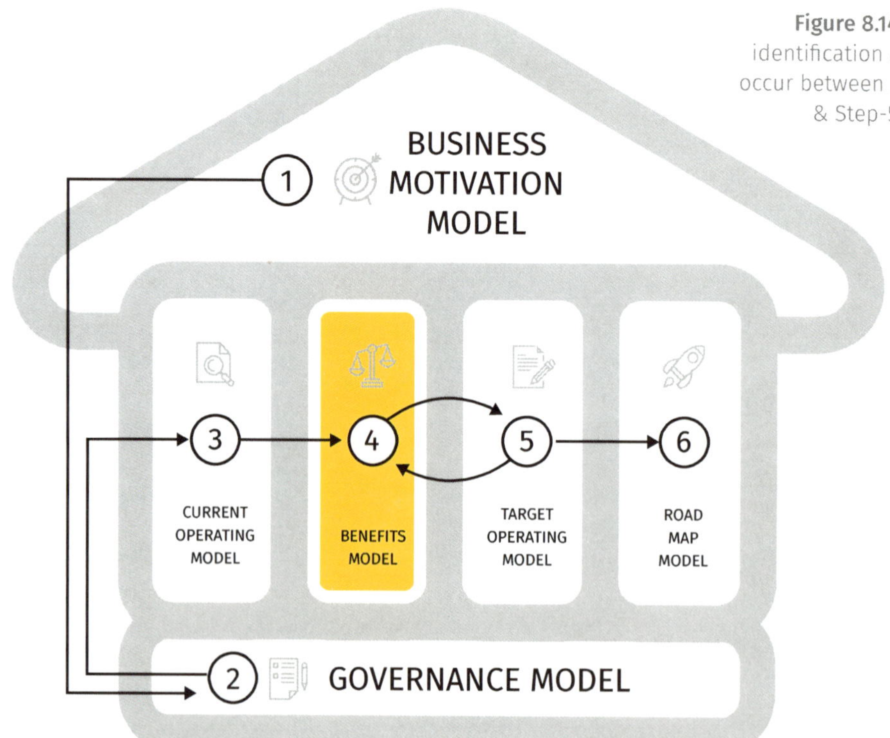


**Figure 8.14** - Benefit identification and validation occur between Step-4 Evaluate & Step-5 Design

## Benefits Mapping Inputs

**Table 8.9**

| Ref | Blueprint | Use |
|---|---|---|
| 4.1.1 | Benefits Profile | Detailed description of a benefit, how it is measured and who owns it. |
| 4.1.2 | Benefits Map | Visual representation of how benefits (immediate and final) relate to each other, and to the strategic and Programme objectives. |

## Process Mapping Building Block Inputs

**Table 8.10**

| Ref | Blueprint | Description | Example |
|---|---|---|---|
| 4.2.1 | Benefits Dependencies Map | A Benefits Map showing the Enablers (technology and information) and Business Changes (people and process elements of capabilities) required to realise the planned benefits. | See diagram below |
| 4.2.2 | Benefits Dependencies Matrix | Matrix of benefits and dependencies (Business Changes and Enablers) showing their relationship to each benefit. | See matrix below |

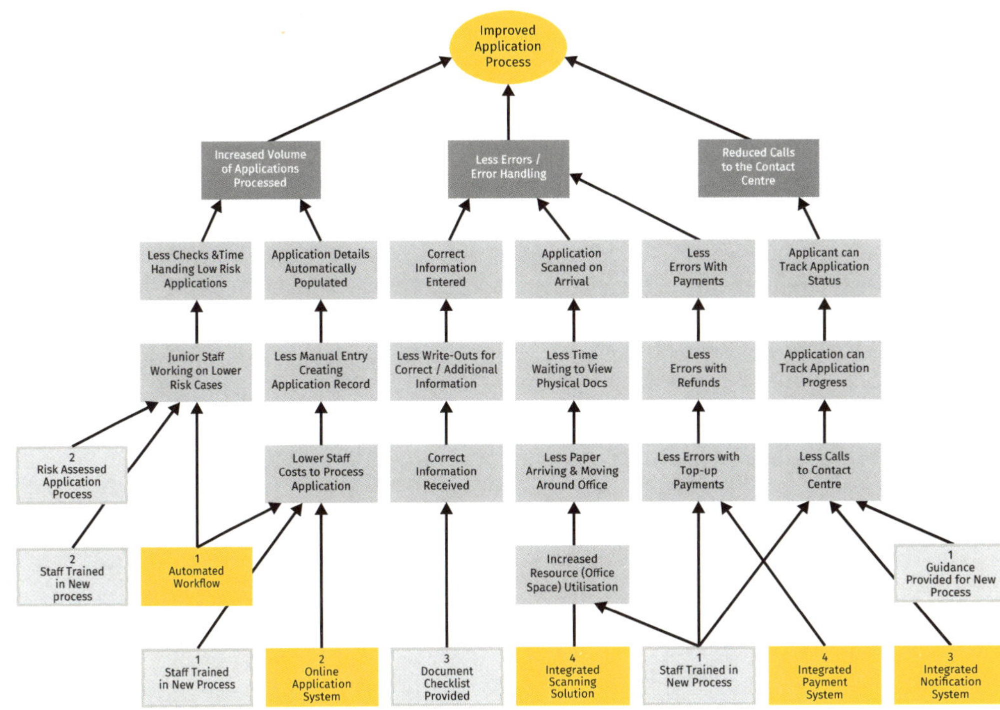


| | Enabler | Business Change | Business Change | Enabler | Business Change | Business Change | Enabler | Business Change | Enabler | Business Change | Enabler | Business Change | Business Change |
|---|---|---|---|---|---|---|---|---|---|---|---|---|---|
| Benefit | Automatic workflow | Risk Assessed Application Process | Staff Trained in New Process | Online Application System | Document Checklist rovided | Staff Trained in New Process | Integrated Scanning Solution | Staff Trained in New Process | Integrated Payment System | Staff Trained in New Process | Integrated Notification System | Staff Trained in New Process | Guidance rovided for New Process |
| Increased Volume of Applications Processed | X | X | X | X | | | | | | | | | |
| Less Errors/ Error handling | | | | X | X | X | X | X | X | | X | X | |
| Reduced Calls to Contact Centre | | | | | | | | | | X | | | |

the 'cause-and-effect' relationship between the 'Business Changes and Enablers' that lead to the Immediate Benefits being realised, then final benefits (then ultimately the Strategic Objectives) being achieved.

Use the *'If-Then'* question and answer in the Table 8.11 below to help identify the 'earliest' Business Change, repeating for all Immediate Benefits.

**Some Immediate Benefits will not have a Business Change (or Enabler) linked to it. Not every Immediate Benefit will. The link to a Business Change or Enabler may be indirectly through another Benefit. Don't create an unnecessary link when there isn't one, that will only make the map look unnecessary complex and complicated.**

### 2. Identify the Enablers

Once Business Changes have been identified, the next step is to identify the Enablers (technology and information) elements that will realise the Benefits.

The process is similar to identifying Enablers, as it was for identifying Business Changes earlier (above), which starts with the *'earliest'* (bottom of map) Immediate Benefit, but also includes the newly identified Business Changes as they too may require Enablers to make them effective.

Use the *'If-Then'* question and answer in the Table 8.12 below to help identify the 'earliest' Enablers, repeating for all Immediate Benefits.

**There may be other means and ways of identifying Business Changes – that may be more creative (such as a brainstorming session or workshops with your key stakeholders), or something more structured, like a structured requirements session. Whichever you chose, ensure the above STAR questions are asked to keep the identified Business Changes and Enablers in the scope of the project or Programme.**

Questions to identify and quantify Business Changes

Table 8.11

| Question | If | Then.. |
|---|---|---|
| Can this Benefit be realised by a Business Change (i.e. more people, better process)? | Yes | This may be a Business Change, but needs to be quantified to confirm whether it is in scope or not, by answering the following STAR goal setting question:<br>• Can you be Specific (i.e. measureable, as opposed to be vague, or non-specific)?<br>• Can you Test it (i.e. can you test whether you can achieve the goal)?<br>• It is Attainable (i.e. is the benefit in scope for the project or Programme)?<br>• Is it Realistic (i.e. does the Programme have the power to influence the benefit)? |
| | No | • There is no Business Change (i.e. people or process) that could improve the realisation of this benefit, and<br>• Skip to the next Immediate Benefit. |

Questions to identify and quantify Business Changes

Table 8.12

| Question | If | Then.. |
|---|---|---|
| Can this Benefit be realised by an Enabler (i.e. better system/ technology, better/ richer/faster data)? | Yes | This may be an Enabler, but needs to be quantified to confirm whether it is in scope or not, by answering the following STAR goal setting question:<br>• Can you be Specific (i.e. measureable, as opposed to be vague, or non-specific)?<br>• Can you Test it (i.e. can you test whether you can achieve the goal)?<br>• It is Attainable (i.e. is the benefit in scope for the project or Programme)?<br>• Is it Realistic (i.e. does the Programme have the power to influence the benefit)? |
| | No | • There is no Enablers (technology or information) that could improve the realisation of this benefit, and<br>• Skip to the next Immediate Benefit. |

### 3. Develop the Benefit Dependencies Map

Using both the newly identified Business Changes, Enablers, and Benefits Map plot the Business Changes and Enablers on the Benefits-Prioritisation Map, as shown from the Case Study in *Figure 8.15* below:

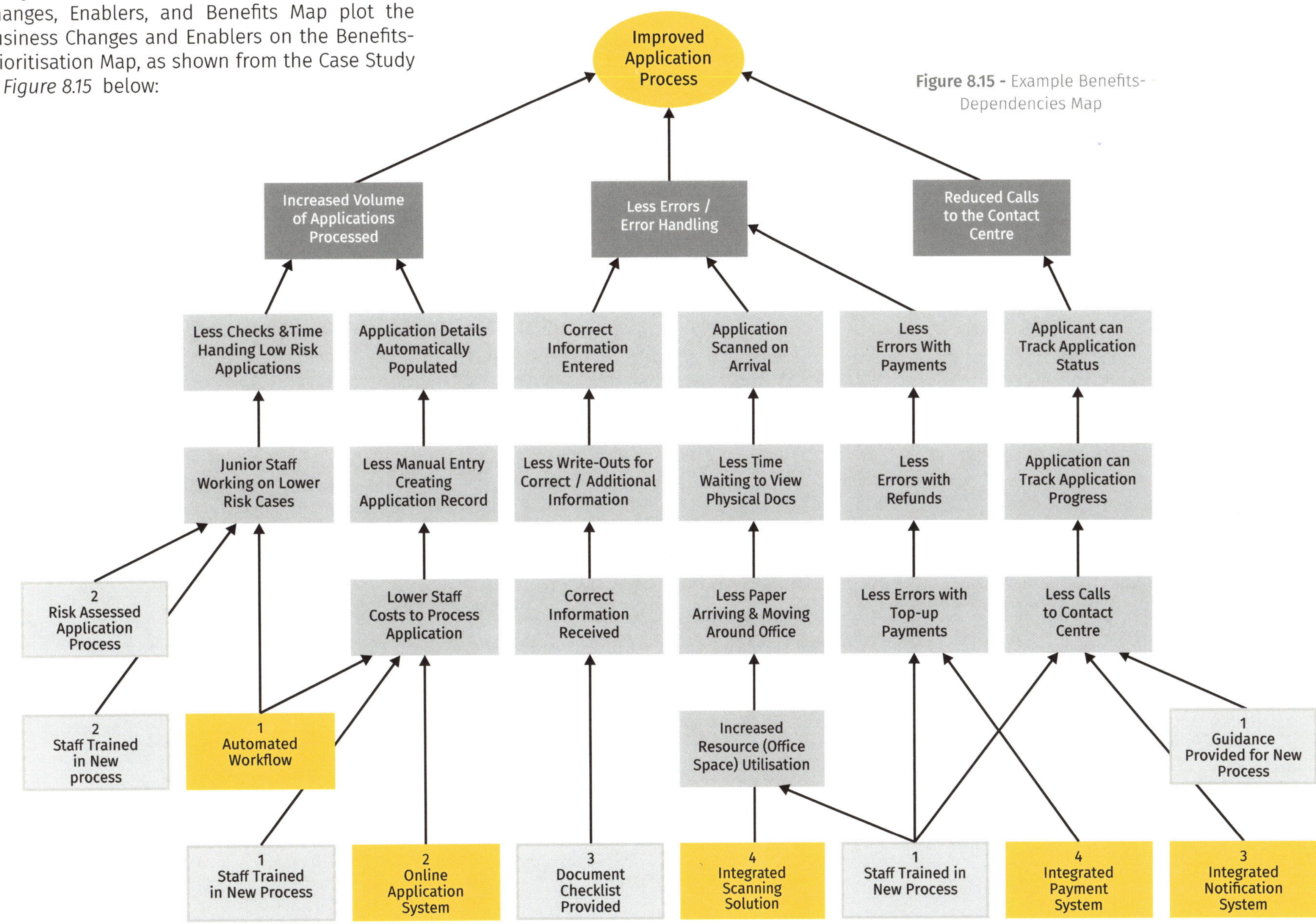


**Figure 8.15 -** Example Benefits-Dependencies Map

The elements making up the Benefits-Dependencies Map are described in the table below.

Questions to identify and quantify Business Changes

Table 8.13

| Element | Description | Symbol |
|---|---|---|
| Enabler | Part of a capability (Technology or Information), that can be developed or purchased to enable the realisation of a/the benefit. | Enabler |
| Business Change | Part of a capability (people and process) that is required to realise a benefit. | Business Change |

## 4.2.2 Benefits-Dependencies Matrix

**4. Develop the Benefit Dependencies Matrix**

Once all Business Changes and Enablers have been identified and plotted on the Benefits-Dependencies Map(s), record the dependencies (i.e. Business Changes and Enablers) on the Benefits-Dependencies Matrix, as shown from the Case Study in Table 8.14 below.

**The Benefit-Dependencies Matrix provides another perspective on Benefits, and the dependencies of achieving each Benefit. The matrix allows you to see which Benefit(s) has a proportionally higher dependency on one or more 'dependent' Business Change(s) and Enabler(s) needed to realise a particular Benefit, to prompt further assessment and/or conversations with your stakeholders to verify (and validate) these findings and assumptions. A Benefit that has a 'full row' of Business Changes and Enablers could mean it is at relatively higher risk of being achieved – and therefore may need to be closely assessed or monitored. It could also mean that you and your stakeholders may need to review the Benefits and their definitions as they might be unattainable with so many dependencies.**

**5. Iteratively socialise, validate and refine the map** (and details – including any Risk, Assumptions, Issues and Dependencies (RAID) addressed or raised as part of completing this step), and

**6. Package and publish the map(s)** – in line with your agreed sprint/release cycle, established back in *Step-2 Control* with the Governance Model.

Example Benefits-Dependencies Matrix

Table 8.14

| | Enabler | Business Change | Business Change | Enabler | Business Change | Business Change | Enabler | Business Change | Enabler | Business Change | Enabler | Business Change | Business Change |
|---|---|---|---|---|---|---|---|---|---|---|---|---|---|
| Benefit | Automatic workflow | Risk Assessed Application Process | Staff Trained in New Process | Online Application System | Document Checklist rovided | Staff Trained in New Process | Integrated Scanning Solution | Staff Trained in New Process | Integrated Payment System | Staff Trained in New Process | Integrated Notification System | Staff Trained in New Process | Guidance rovided for New Process |
| Increased Volume of Applications Processed | X | X | X | X | | | | | | | | | |
| Less Errors/ Error handling | | | | X | X | X | X | X | X | | X | X | |
| Reduced Calls to Contact Centre | | | | | | | | | | X | | | |

#### Risks and Mitigations

The risk with Benefit Dependency Mapping is constructing overtly complex benefit maps, which makes them too complicated and hard to interrupt. This is easily done on large Programmes, or with many Strategic Objectives, as well as shared immediate and/or End Benefits across Programmes.

To help restrict *boiling the ocean* and creating unnecessary Benefits (and therefore a lot of potential Business Changes and Enablers) in the Benefit Dependencies Map, keep the following questions in mind:

- **Does the Benefit strongly align to the Strategic Objective? and**
- **Will the project or Programme deliver changes needed for the Business to realise the proposed Benefit?**

If the relationships between Benefits becomes too complex, consider grouping related Benefits together, and capturing the details in the Benefit Profiles.

If the map is starting to look like a spider's web i.e. there are a lot of links between the different elements on the map, consider removing 'less important' links, keeping in mind the audience of the map, and ensuring their concerns are addressed in the map.

### Building Block Wrap-up

In this section, we discussed the Benefit Dependencies Building Block.

This Building Block identifies the Business Changes and Enablers (the set of Business Architecture / Business Capability 'people and process' and 'technology' changes) that the Business is dependent on for the realisation of the Business' planned Benefits.

The Building Block is made up of the following two (2) Blueprints:

- **Benefits Dependencies Map** – a Benefits Map showing the Enabler and Business Changes required to realise the planned Benefits, and
- **Benefit Dependencies Matrix** – the matrix (table) of dependencies (Business Changes and Enablers) showing the dependencies of achieving each Benefit, as well as highlighting high risk or potentially unachievable Benefits (i.e. benefits that have a relatively high number of dependencies).

Both the Benefit-Dependencies Map and the Benefits-Dependencies Matrix provide valuable tools to visualise and articulate the benefits and dependencies that affect and impact the realisation of the Benefits the Programme and Organisation plans to realise from the new or enhanced capabilities the Programme will be delivering. The timing of carrying out Benefit Dependency Mapping is also important, as it occurs early in the **Design Process,** as an input into design conversations and decisions, before any design decisions have been made.

#### Next Steps

Once Benefit Dependencies Mapping has been completed and agreed, the next step in the **Design Process** is to rank the dependencies in order of business priority.

Dependency prioritisation is discussed in the Prioritisation Mapping Building Block in the next section.

## 4.3 Prioritisation Mapping

### Introduction

Prioritisation Mapping is the Building Block where the Business Changes and Enablers that were identified in the Benefit Dependencies Map are prioritised. It is these Business Changes and Enablers that are used to drive the selection of the capabilities that are enhanced or created, and where the investment(s) are made (in the costs that are incurred in those capabilities). It is also only when the 'benefits' realised from the use of these capabilities outweigh the cost of developing and implementing those changes that the decision be made to proceed.

The purpose of Prioritisation Mapping is to identify (and agree) the order (i.e. priority) of the implementation of the candidate Business Changes and Enablers from the Benefits-Dependencies Map that are needed to realise the Organisations' planned Benefits.

Prioritisation Mapping helps the Programme address the following 'benefit' related questions:

- **'Why' are we doing this?** (i.e. What is the benefit?),
- **'Where' do we see this?** (i.e. what changes are needed to the business?), and
- **'When' should we do this?** (i.e. what is the relative delivery time – near, far, further?)

The objective of Prioritisation Mapping is to help stakeholders understand and appreciate the implementation priority of the candidate capabilities in the order that maximises the business value to the Business. These capabilities are called *'candidate'* until they are confirmed as *'the'* capability the Programme has selected. There are several factors that play on whether a candidate capability becomes the actual, selected capability to be developed or enhanced. These includes such things as cost, benefit, payback period, return on investment and risk.

## Inputs

The inputs used to complete this Building Block are shown in the table below.

## Outputs

The Blueprints (outputs) produced for this Building Block is shown in the table below.

## Steps

The steps to complete the above Blueprints (Outputs) are as follows.

### 4.3.1 Prioritised Changes Map

**1. Assign a nominal value to the Strategic Objective**

Assign a nominal value (e.g. 1000) to the strategic objective. This nominal value is the starting point (and value) that will be disseminated down (and among) the *'earlier'* benefits to the proportion and degree they contribute to the *'later'* benefits.

**Figure 8.16** - Strategic Objective (nominal value = 1,000)

Prioritisation Mapping Building Block Inputs

**Table 8.15**

| Ref | Blueprint | Use |
|---|---|---|
| 1.2.1 | Vision (VSOM) | Contain Vision and articulated business goals (strategy, objectives and measures) that all requirements including prioritised changes must align to and support. |
| 2.2.1 | Design Principles Register | Not directly involved here, but you should be mindful that the Design Principles define the scope of the Programme, Business Architecture as well as the prioritised changes (Business Changes and Enablers). |
| 2.3.1 | RAID | Contains register of Risks, Assumptions, Issues and Dependencies that need to be checked against and updated as part of completing this Blueprint. |
| 4.2.1 | Benefits Dependencies Map | Benefits Map with dependencies (Business Changes and Enablers) that directly influence the intended final benefits and strategic objectives, that are to be prioritised. |

Table 8.16

| Ref | Blueprint | Description | Example |
| --- | --- | --- | --- |
| 4.3.1 | Prioritised Changes Map | Updated Benefits Dependencies Map showing prioritised weighted ranking of all the Enablers and Business Change(s). | |

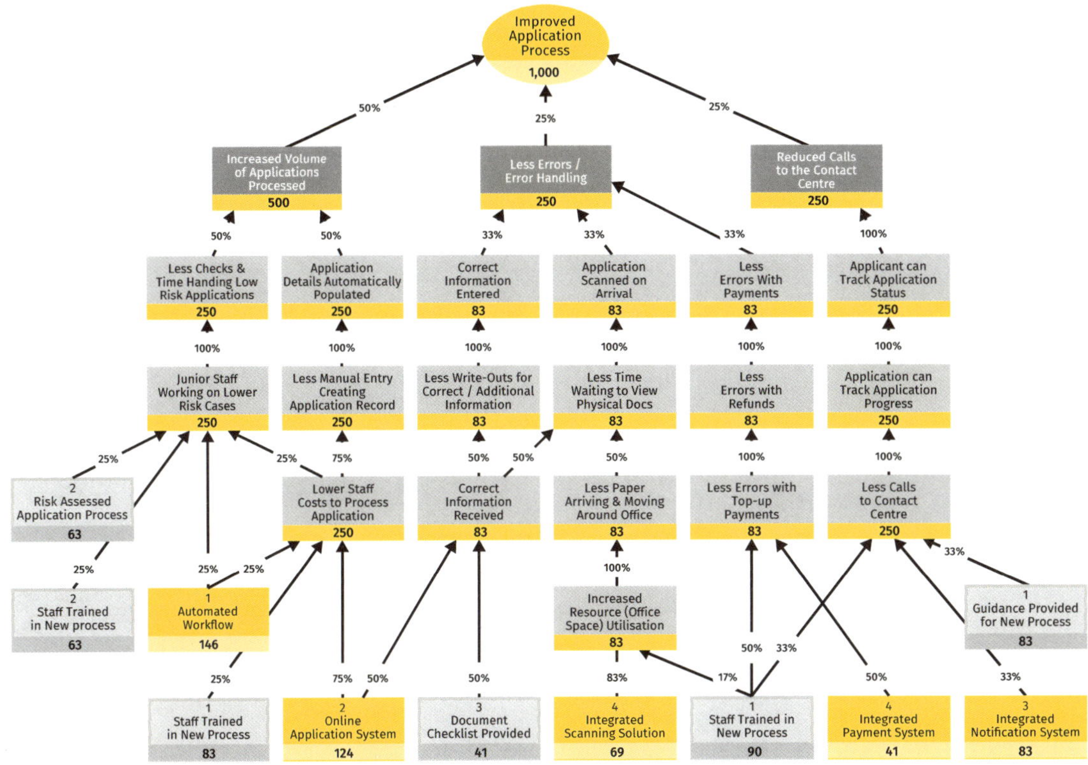


| Ref | Blueprint | Description |
| --- | --- | --- |
| 4.3.2 | Prioritised Changes Catalogue | Register of the Benefit Dependencies Map details, including weighted score, priority (ordered score), owner, start and end date, related final benefits and strategic objective. |

| Enabler/ Business Change | Score | Priority | Owner | Start Date | End Date | Related Final Benefit | Related Strategic Objective |
| --- | --- | --- | --- | --- | --- | --- | --- |
| Automatic workflow | 146 | 1 | Product Owner | Jun-15 | Jul-16 | Increased Volume of Applications Processed | Improved Application Process |
| Risk Assessed Application Process | 63 | 5 | Product Owner | Jun-15 | Jul-16 | Increased Volume of Applications Processed | Improved Application Process |
| Staff Trained in New Process | 63 | 5 | Product Owner | Jun-15 | Jul-16 | Increased Volume of Applications Processed | Improved Application Process |
| Online Application System | 125 | 2 | Product Owner | Jun-15 | Jul-16 | Increased Volume of Applications Processed | Improved Application Process |
| Document Checklist Provided | 41 | 6 | Product Owner | Jun-15 | Jul-16 | Less Errors/ Error handling | Improved Application Process |
| Staff Trained in New Process | 83 | 3 | Product Owner | Jun-15 | Jul-16 | Increased Volume of Applications Processed | Improved Application Process |

**2. Allocate the relative contribution each Final Benefit has to the Strategic Objective.**

**A starting nominal value of '1' could have been used (instead of 1,000) however this will get unnecessarily complicated (and possibly require a scientific calculator, and not the back of a napkin or cigarette packet) to work out the contribution of final and Immediate Benefits to the strategic objective in the next steps, dealing in minute fractions or decimals.**

Calculate the relative contribution each Final Benefit has to the Strategic Objective. This could be done from past experience, previous Programmes or business cases or brainstorm in a workshop. This is not an exact science, and still (slightly) subjective (my preferred method is discussed in the text box below).

**My preferred method for determining the relative contribution of 'earlier' to 'later' benefits is to think in terms of fractions (1/5, ¼, 1/3, ½ etc.) and pick a well known or understood relationship between an End Benefit and strategic objective then use that as the benchmark and reference point, assigning a contribution (i.e. increase in volume of applications processed will be the single biggest contributor to the realisation of the Strategic Objective e.g. 50%).**

Using that first (left hand side) End Benefit as the starting point, assign the remaining contribution to the remaining End Benefits based on their relative contribution. For example, if there are three (3) End Benefits and each is equal, assign a weighting of 33%, or if there are three (3) End Benefits and there is one dominate End Benefit, assign a weighting of 50% and 25% each to the remaining two (2) End Benefits.

Once the weightings are assigned, calculate the score of each of the End Benefits based on their respective contribution to the strategic objective (i.e. weighting x strategic objective score), repeating for each Final Benefit.

### 3. Allocate the relative contribution to each successive benefit

The process to allocate the relative contribution each immediate (and successive) benefit has to the final benefit is much the same as Step 2 (above), i.e. pick an Immediate Benefit that is well known (or better understood) as the starting point and assign its contributing weighting, repeating for the remaining contributing Immediate Benefits.

Calculate the score for each Immediate Benefit based on their respective contribution to the End Benefit (i.e. weighting x final benefit score). Repeat for each contributing Immediate Benefit.

### 4. Calculate the score and ranking of each change

This is where the relative priority of each of the candidate changes becomes visible. Calculate (a simple sum of) the percentage contributions from the 'last' (i.e. earliest) contributing Immediate Benefits. Using the total scores of each of the changes (Business Changes and Enablers), rank them in order of highest (1) to lowest (n).

**A higher score is generally an indication of the relative greater contribution to the immediate and final benefits, and ultimately the strategic objective. A high scoring dependency shouldn't be looked at in isolation of its ranking alone however. Other factors, such as risk should also be considered. To factor in a degree of risk, the percentage weighting of the dependency can be 'scaled down' by a factor of 10%, 20%, or 30% to allow for a low, medium or high risk premium.**

## 4.3.2 Prioritised Changes Catalogue

### 5. Prioritise the Changes

Once you have captured the Business Changes and Enablers in the Benefit-Dependencies Map, record the Enablers and Business Changes centrally in the Benefit-Dependencies Catalogue, as shown from the Case Study example in Table 8.17 below

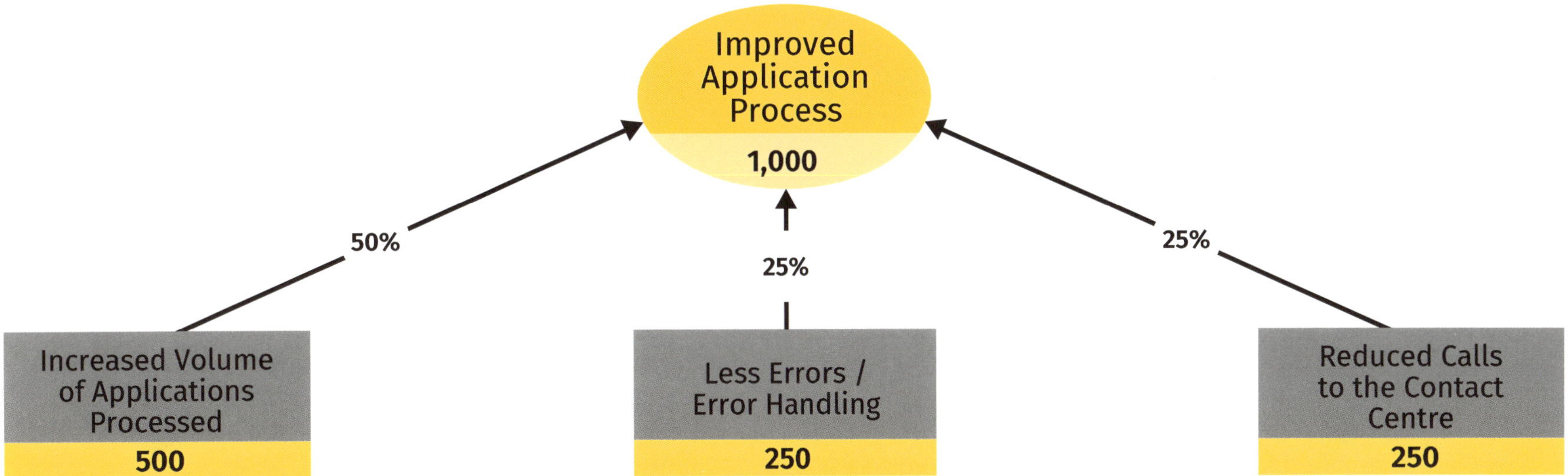


**Figure 8.17** - BDM with scored and weighted paths.

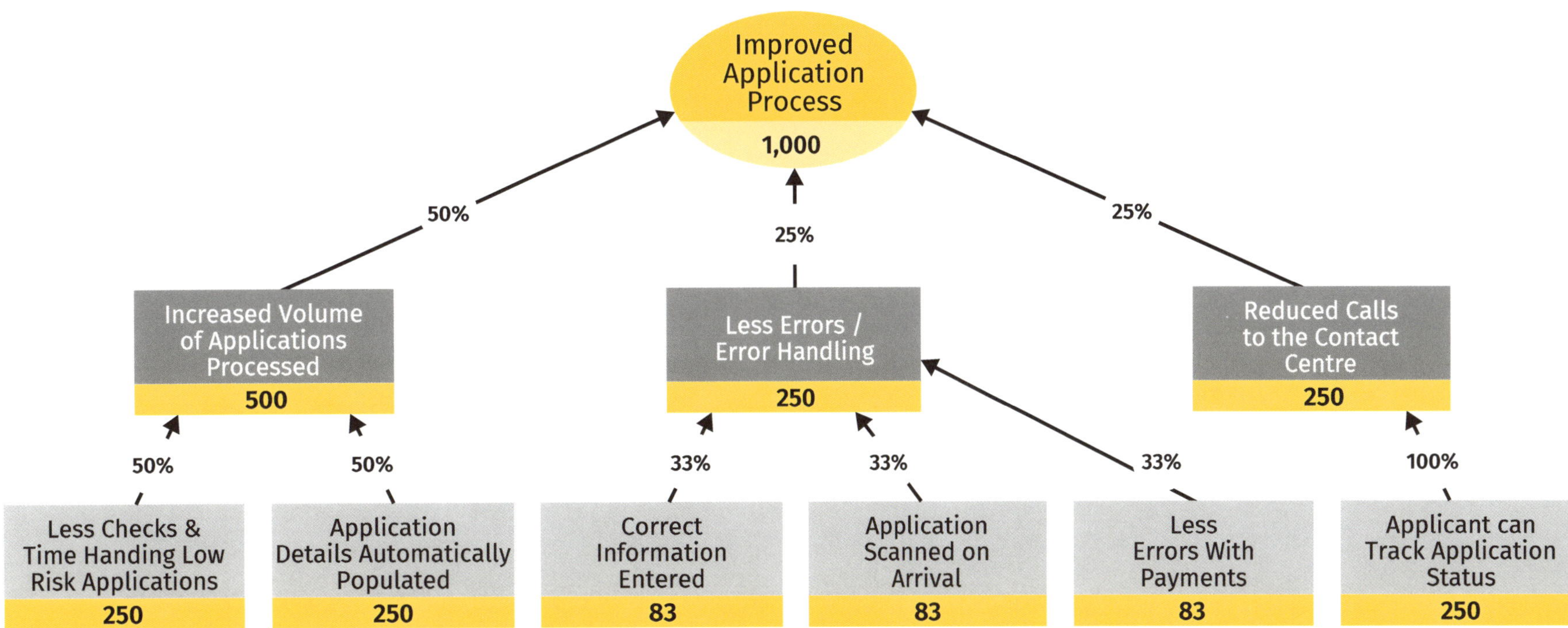


**Figure 8.18** - BDM showing scored and weighted paths from Strategic Objective, Final and Immediate Benefits

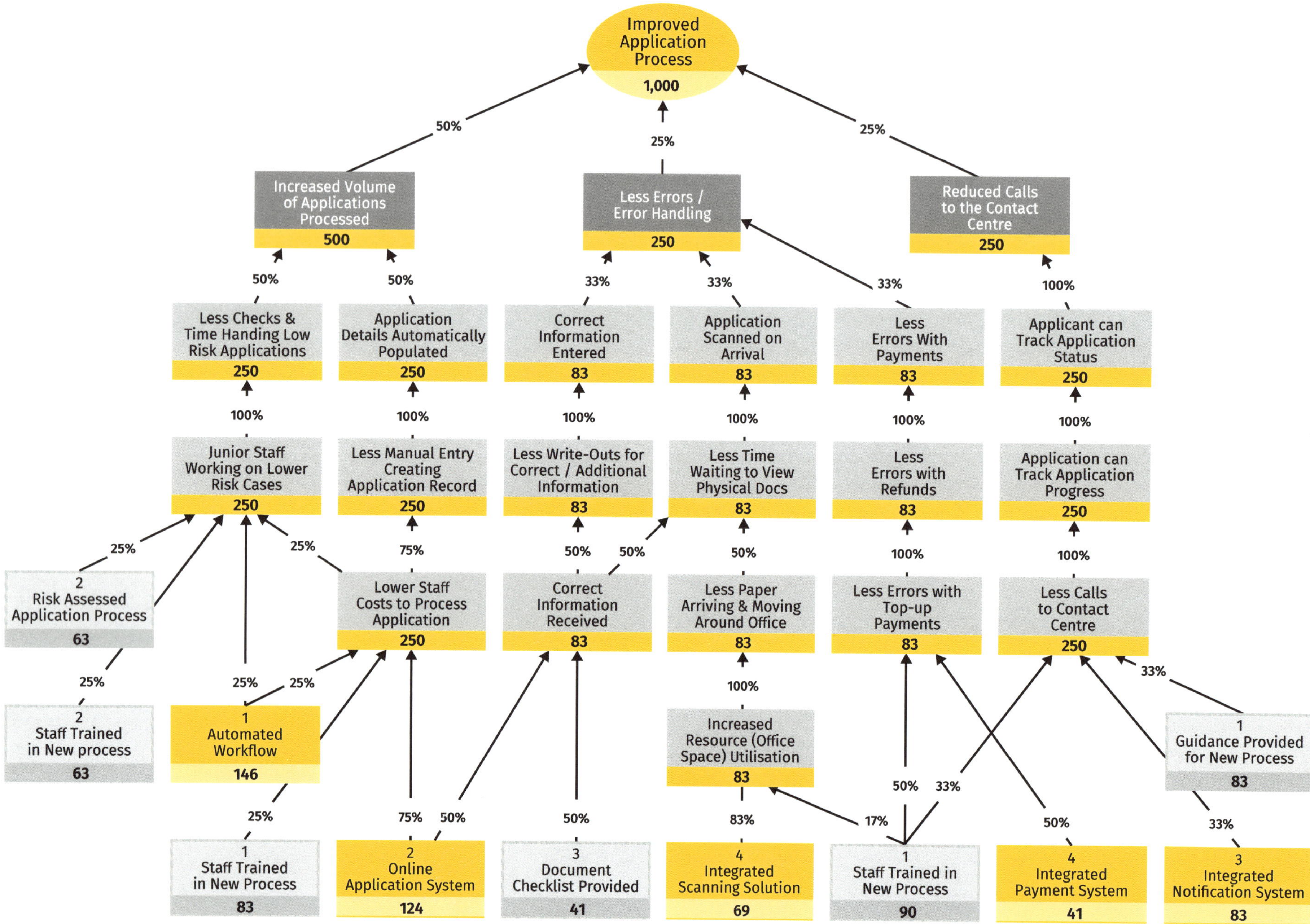


Figure 8.19 - Prioritised Changes Map

Example Prioritised Changes Catalogue

Table 8.17

| Enabler/ Business Change | Score | Priority | Owner | Start Date | End Date | Related Final Benefit | Related Strategic Objective |
|---|---|---|---|---|---|---|---|
| Automatic workflow | 146 | 1 | Product Owner | Jun-15 | Jul-16 | Increased Volume of Applications Processed | Improved Application Process |
| Risk Assessed Application Process | 63 | 5 | Product Owner | Jun-15 | Jul-16 | Increased Volume of Applications Processed | Improved Application Process |
| Staff Trained in New Process | 63 | 5 | Product Owner | Jun-15 | Jul-16 | Increased Volume of Applications Processed | Improved Application Process |
| Online Application System | 125 | 2 | Product Owner | Jun-15 | Jul-16 | Increased Volume of Applications Processed | Improved Application Process |
| Document Checklist Provided | 41 | 6 | Product Owner | Jun-15 | Jul-16 | Less Errors/ Error handling | Improved Application Process |
| Staff Trained in New Process | 83 | 3 | Product Owner | Jun-15 | Jul-16 | Increased Volume of Applications Processed | Improved Application Process |
| Integrated Scanning Solution | 69 | 4 | Product Owner | Jun-15 | Jul-16 | Less Errors/ Error handling | Improved Application Process |
| Staff Trained in New Process | 14 | 7 | Product Owner | Jun-15 | Jul-16 | Less Errors/ Error handling | Improved Application Process |
| Integrated Payment System | 41 | 6 | Product Owner | Jun-15 | Jul-16 | Less Errors/ Error handling | Improved Application Process |
| Staff Trained in New Process | 83 | 3 | Product Owner | Jun-15 | Jul-16 | Reduced Calls to Contact Centre | Improved Application Process |
| Integrated Notification System | 41 | 6 | Product Owner | Jun-15 | Jul-16 | Less Errors/ Error handling | Improved Application Process |
| Staff Trained in New Process | 41 | 6 | Product Owner | Jun-15 | Jul-16 | Less Errors/ Error handling | Improved Application Process |
| Guidance Provided for New Process | 83 | 3 | Product Owner | Jun-15 | Jul-16 | Reduced Calls to Contact Centre | Improved Application Process |

**You may choose to list the Enablers and Business Changes in order of their scoring (highest to lowest), or in the order that they appear on the first, and sequential Benefit-Dependencies Maps. You have the option to filter (or order) the results by priority, or group them around the final benefit they relate to, depending on the area your audience is interested in. Listing and ranking in order of highest to lowest score maybe a sensible approach for stakeholders who are more interested in reading headlines, and will generally focus on the first few lines (normally senior management).**

As per all Blueprints (and Building Blocks), once the above steps are completed:

**6. Iteratively socialise, validate and refine the Blueprints** (and details – including any Risks, Assumptions, Issues and Dependencies (RAID) addressed or raised as part of completing this step), and

**7. Package and publish the Blueprint(s)** – in line with your agreed sprint/release cycle, established back in *Step 2 – Control*, with the *Governance Model.*

### Risks and Mitigations

The risk with Prioritisation Mapping is their potential to become large and complicated, given the scale and size of the Programme. There is however always this risk, with All architectures – Business and Technology, and all Blueprints, which comes back to the skill of the Business Architect, and knowing the audience of the different Blueprints, and being conscious to only showing the detail, or information that is important to that audience that specifically addresses their needs and concerns.

To keep the Prioritisation Mapping Blueprints uncluttered and not busy, it may pay to only map and measure the critical (i.e. 'must' have) changes, and not the 'nice to have' changes. To make sure you only map and measure the critical changes, the first step (having already confirmed the changes are in scope for the Programme) is to identify and agree the 'critical' changes. This could be done, and agreed with the Product Owner.

### Building Block Wrap-up

In this section, we discussed the Prioritisation Mapping Building Block.

This Building Block systematically and structurally identifies the relative order and priority candidate capabilities (i.e. Business Changes and Enablers – People and Process, and Technology elements of business capabilities) need to be implemented in order to maximize the realisation of the planned benefits, that directly contribute to the Strategic Objectives, and therefore the Business Strategy.

The Prioritisation Mapping Building Block is made up of the following Blueprints:

- **Prioritised Changes Map** - an updated Benefits-Dependencies Map, showing the prioritised weighted ranking of all Business Changes, Enablers, immediate and final benefits contributing to achieving the Strategic Objective.
- **Prioritised Changes Register** - captures the details and most importantly the register of the Benefit Dependencies Map, including the weighted score, priority (ordered score), owner, start and end date, related final benefits and strategic objective

Both the Prioritised Changes Map, and Prioritised Changes Register provide powerful tools to allow the Key Stakeholders to visualise and rationalise the order specific Business Changes and Enablers needed to be implemented to bring about the greatest biggest value to the Business.

### Reference Model Recap

Once the Prioritisation Mapping Building Block is complete (along with the other Benefits Mapping and Benefit Dependencies Building Blocks), the Benefits Reference Model is complete.
By completing the Benefits Reference Model, this now means you have:

- Identified and quantified the Business Benefits the Organisation intends to realise from the Programme and identified and prioritised the business capabilities (i.e. Business Changes and Enablers – People and Process, and Technology elements of business capabilities) that when implemented and used by the Business, 'enable' the Business to realise those intended benefits, and
- As part of completing this Reference Model, have produced the Blueprints that visualise and rationalise the business changes and enablers needed that provide the relative order all business changes and enablers within the Programme should be implemented to maximise both the realisation but also the value of the planned Business Benefits. It is also through these specific business changes and enablers, and their specific order of implementation, that when used by the Business, enable the Organisation to achieve its Strategic Objectives, and ultimately execute its Business Strategy.

For a full recap of **HOBA®** and the **Design Process,** refer to the Recap section in *Chapter 11 Next Steps* below.

### Next Steps

The next step in the **Design Process** is Step-5 Design. This is where you use these prioritised changes (i.e. the prioritised Business Changes and Enablers) to design the Target Operating Model (TOM).

The TOM is discussed in the following chapter.

Step 5 – Design

Chapter 9

# Introduction

Step 5 – Design, is about the design of the Target Operating Model (TOM). In a capability-driven design approach, Step-5 'Design' starts with the capabilities (people, process and technology) identified and prioritised from Step-4 'Evaluate', with the Benefits Model. It is these identified and prioritised capabilities, that directly drive the planned Benefits the Business is intending to realise.

*Figure 9.1* below shows where Step-5 Design fits into the overall Design Process.

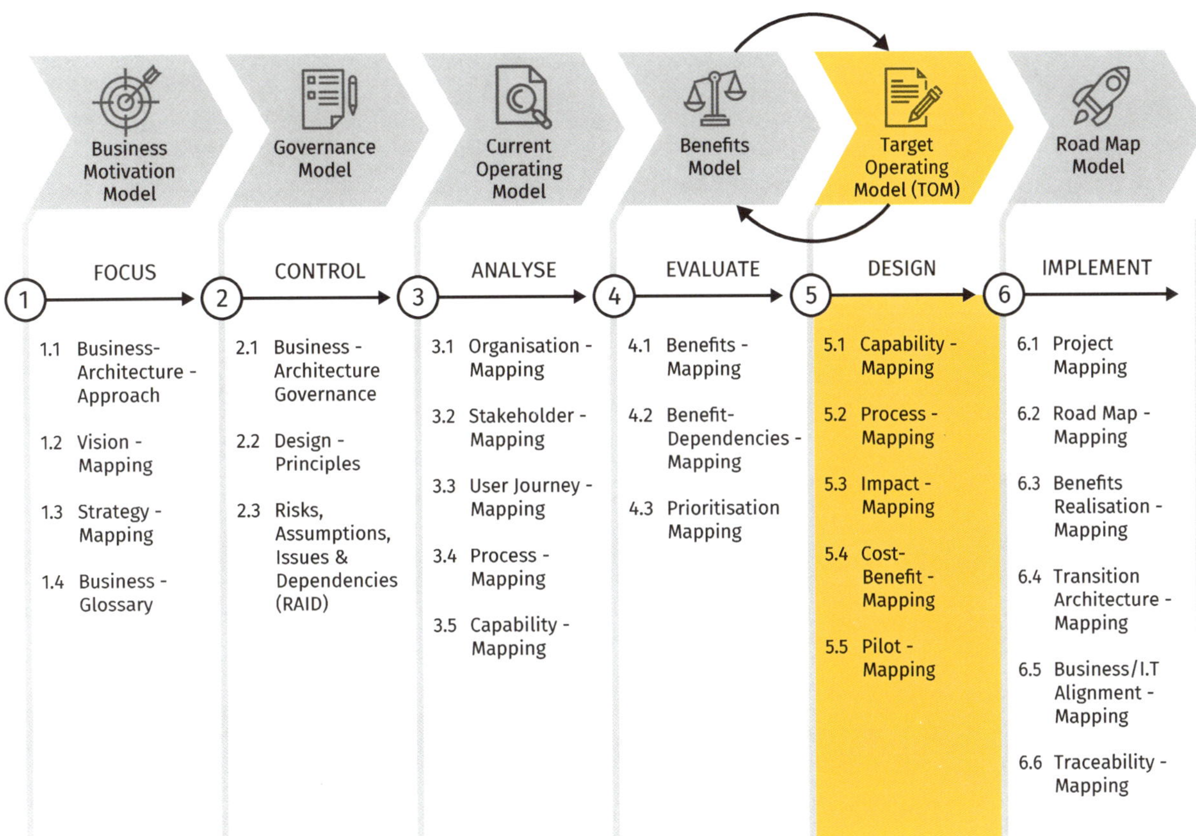


**Figure 9.1** - Design Process – Step 5 Design

# Target Operating Model Implementation Options

In a similar fashion to *defining* the Currently Operating Model there are two (2) options available to *implementing* the Target Operating Model (TOM):

1. **Pilot** (the MVP – Minimum Viable Product), or
2. **Full implementation.**

Each option also has its own Pros and Cons, which need to be considered in *designing* the TOM, as discussed briefly below:

## Pilot

Pilot or 'piloting' means to trial the candidate capabilities (that were identified in the Benefits Model) on a sample population size in the physical Business to test the identified capabilities will actually work *'in practice'* (as opposed to *'on paper')* before making the decision whether to, implement the full solution, tweaking the solution or deciding on another option altogether. The Pros and Cons are as follows:

- **Pros** – the Business gets to validate the candidate capabilities are indeed the right capabilities that will likely achieve the planned Business Benefits (and ultimately the Business Strategy) before the decision (and more costs are incurred and/or committed) for a full implementation.
- **Cons** – perception of additional time and cost necessary to 'test' the solution now, which could have been spent on the 'actual' full Implementation.

## Full Implementation

The full implementation is where the implementation of the physical Business Architecture is implemented in a 'staggered' (or 'phased') approach or the dreaded 'big bang' (aka *'all-or-nothing'*) approach - without (or very limited) testing beforehand. The pros and cons are as follows:

- **Pros** – *'relatively'* quick implementation time (as there is no *'test'* phase), helpful when there is a high degree of confidence or certainty the chosen design and implementation is fit for purpose or there is a time constraint where the solution must be fully implemented quickly.
- **Cons** – the capabilities are not tested in actual operation before full implementation, there is a *'high'* degree of both implementation risk, and operational risk, that the actual full implementation, and the full operation of the implemented capabilities do not go as well as planned, potentially resulting in lost time, money and resources due to unforeseen issues arising from implementing the 'untested' solution.

While both Pilot (MVP) and Full Implementation options each have their pro's and con's, the degree to which either one is seen as an advantage or disadvantage to the Organisation depends on many (and often) competing factors such as the Organisation's (or Programme's) risk appetite, timeline, budget, available resources and experience.

The reason why I am calling this out now – to *'pilot or not to pilot'* is despite the almost clear and obvious benefits of *piloting* (mainly reducing implementation risk that the implementation of the changes to the Business cause minimal disruption and are more likely to achieve the intended benefits), as the Business Architect raising or suggesting the idea of Piloting, you are likely going to face some resistance and/or criticism on this approach – mainly due to lack of knowledge and understanding of what actually is involved in a Pilot and its benefits.

If (or *when*) you face any resistance on the *'pilot'* approach, keep in mind the following:

- The **Business Changes and Enablers** identified in the Benefits Model are untested, which need (and should) be tested. **Pilots allow for the validation of the Enablers, Business Changes and implementation option are *'fit for purpose'*** (and not just *'look good on paper')*.
- **Pilots follow is a lean-start-up technique**, which is based on two (2) principles – *'fail fast'*, and *'Build, Measure, Learn'* as shown in *Figure 9.2* below. That is, build the Minimum Viable Product (MVP), test it on a small-scale implementation to see if you can break it, if it breaks (i.e. doesn't yield expected results), tweak it (or throw it out), if it doesn't break - roll out the full-scale implementation.
- **Pilots (MVPs) allow for better communication and stakeholder engagement.** Through testing the MVP on a small number or scale of stakeholders, the stakeholder communication can be simplified and targeted. By having a smaller number of participants in the pilot allows for a greater level of collaboration between the Programme team and pilot participants. The pilot participants then

become *'champions'* to promote and endorse the changes from their first-hand experience, and because you are dealing with actual representatives from the Business, you (and the Programme) get actual, real User feedback, which can be fed back into the design to make changes to both improve their experience and meet the goals and objectives of the Organisation.

So, to ensure Pilots don't suffer the same fate, forgotten or overlooked (similar to how Benefits, and Benefits Management was previously treated, which is why **HOBA®** put Benefits into its core), Pilots are included in **HOBA®** by default as its own Building Block to ensure it gets the visibility and attention it needs to test the candidate capabilities and implementation options before deciding to 'change, pivot or proceed' with the full implementation.

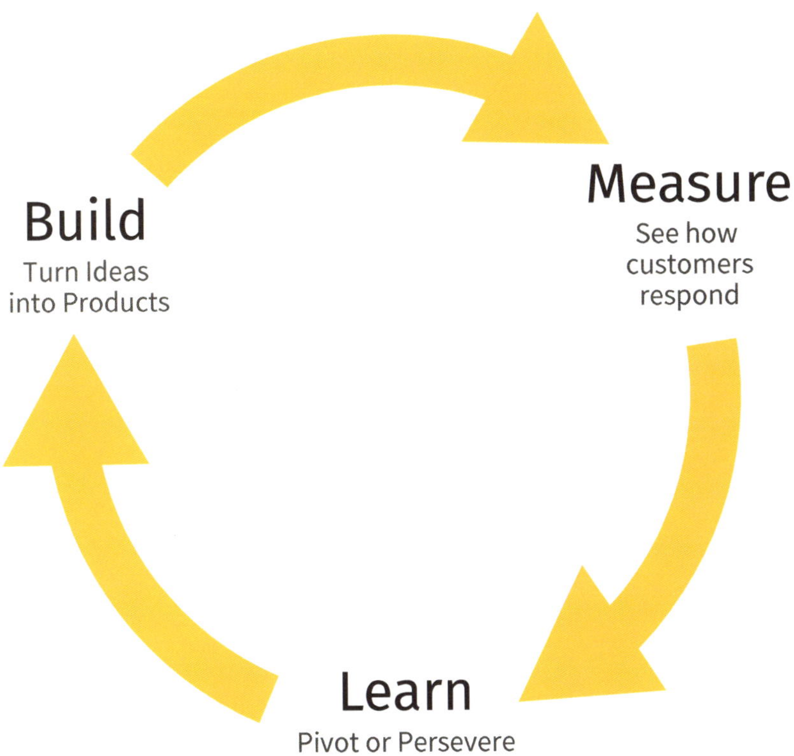


**Figure 9.2 -** The Lean Start Up Continuous Innovation Cycle[60]

[60] Adapted from Ries, E., (2011) The Lean Start-up *How Constant Innovation Creates Radically Successful Businesses*

# Top-Down Design Approach

The approach to design the Target Operating Model (TOM) is a 'top-down' direction, starting at the Business Capabilities ('Capabilities') - in opposite direction to analysing the Current Operating which ended with the Capabilities, as shown in *Figure 9.3* below.

**Remember, the point of HOBA® is to develop the design of the TOM and oversee the implementation of the physical TOM so that it aligns to the design. It is *not* to make Blueprints for Blueprints sake. Only by exception when designing the TOM will it be necessary to create *'To Be'* versions of User Journeys, Stakeholder and Organisation Maps. These exceptions include Merger and/or Acquisition (M&A), formation of a Joint Venture (JV) or divestment, where the structure of the Organisation has fundamentally changed.**

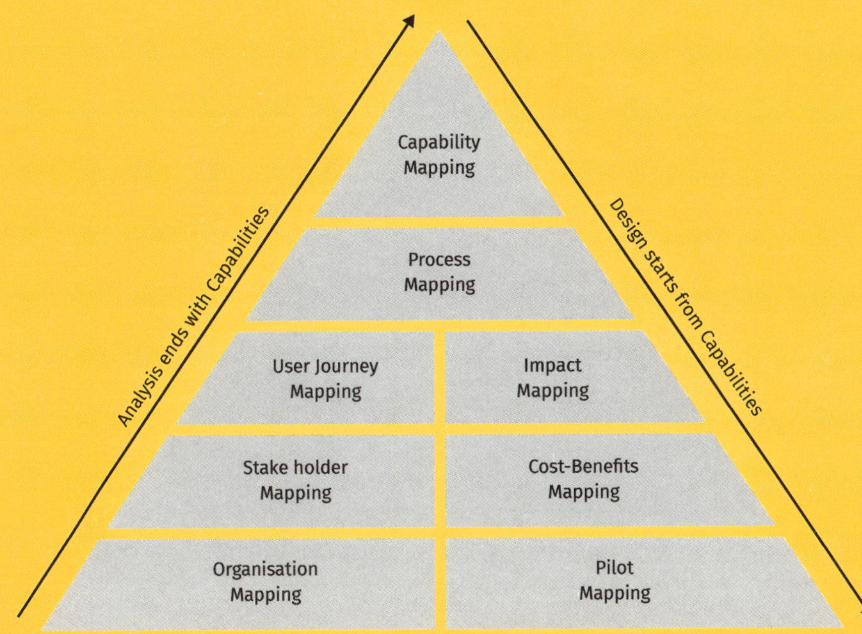


**Figure 9.3 -** HOBA® Analysis/Design Pyramid

This top-down *'capability first'* approach is about achieving the following objectives:

- **Overcome and avoid the 'solution-first' error.** You will recall from the *Benefits Model*, it was with the Benefits Model where the *'solution'* i.e. Business Changes and Enablers (people, process and technology elements of business capabilities) was identified as the changes needed to the Current Operating Model to align the Business to the Business Strategy. The *'solution'* was not in this case created or developed by a product or Vendor to shoe-horn the problem into *fit a predetermined solution*, but correctly, the *solution was identified as the true best fit for the problem* – the Stakeholder concerns and needs, and

- **Encourage the analysis before the design of the TOM** (which includes the analysis and definition of the Current Operating Model) to explicitly include the analysis and definition of the Current Operating Model. As mentioned previously in the *Analysis Options* section, the current misconception in (and of) Business Architecture is to jump (mistakenly) straight into developing the design of the TOM, without regard, or necessary consideration of where the business is today (i.e. defining the Current Operating Model). That isolated (and narrow) view of developing the design of the TOM without looking at the Current Operating Model, would also exclude (mistakenly) identifying the Stakeholder concerns, and needs recorded in the Stakeholder Mapping, or improvement opportunities recognised in the User Journey Mapping, or establishing an agreed view of the Organisations processes and capabilities with the Process and Capability Models, to know which processes and capabilities were being enhanced or created to address the Stakeholder concerns and needs. Everything I've just mentioned is thankfully accounted for in the analysis and definition of the Current Operating Model, which is incorporated into the design of the TOM through the Capabilities, which were identified in the analysis of the Current Operating Model

In many of the companies I've assisted over the years, there have been numerous situations where a solution had already been identified and (worse) sometimes selected, even before the issues, needs and concerns of the Stakeholders and Current Operating Model was well known or defined to effectively determine whether the selected solution was even fit for purpose. In those *'cart-before-the-horse'* situations, the role of the Business (and Business Architecture) was to design a TOM that would effectively attempt to reverse engineer the Business to fit the solution (as opposed to the other and correct way around - the *'horse before the cart'* approach - engineering the solution to fit the business), which often leads to the value of the solution never being fully realised, or the problem the solution was supposed to fix not fully being solved.

The objective with the *'capability-first'* design approach is to overcome and avoid the situation and problems the *'solution-first'* approach causes, by enhancing or creating the right capabilities, in the right order that directly supports the realisation of the intended Business Benefits while and at the same time aligning the Business to the Business Strategy and Vision.

# Target Operating Model (TOM)

As mentioned earlier in *Chapter 3 House of Business Architecture® (HOBA®)*, each HOBA® Reference Model addresses a different aspect in the design and implementation of the Target Operating Model (TOM). These different aspects are represented in the following different views:

- Process
- Perspective
- Context, and
- Content

Each view is discussed in the section below.

## Process

In terms of process, the Target Operating Model Reference Model is the 5th step in the Design Process.

Step-5 takes the identified and prioritised Business Changes and Enablers, from Step-4 Evaluate (Benefits Model), that directly address the Stakeholder concerns and needs that were identified in Step 3-Analyse (Current Operating Model), to develop the design of the Target Operating Model (TOM).

## Perspective

In terms of perspective, the Target Operating Model Reference Model provides the 'design' perspective, to develop and validate the 'design' of the Target Operating Model (TOM).

Figure 9.4 - Target Operating Model - Step 5

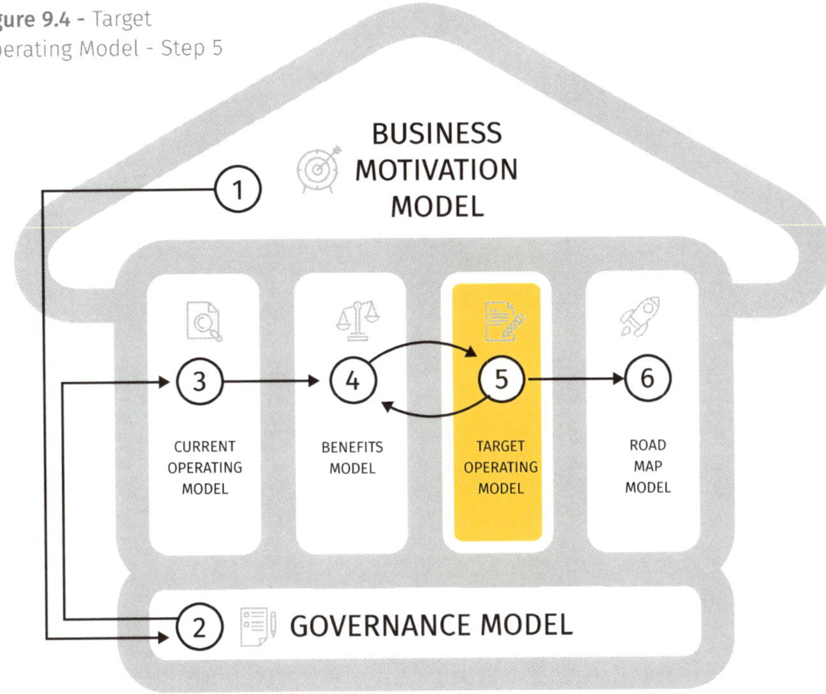


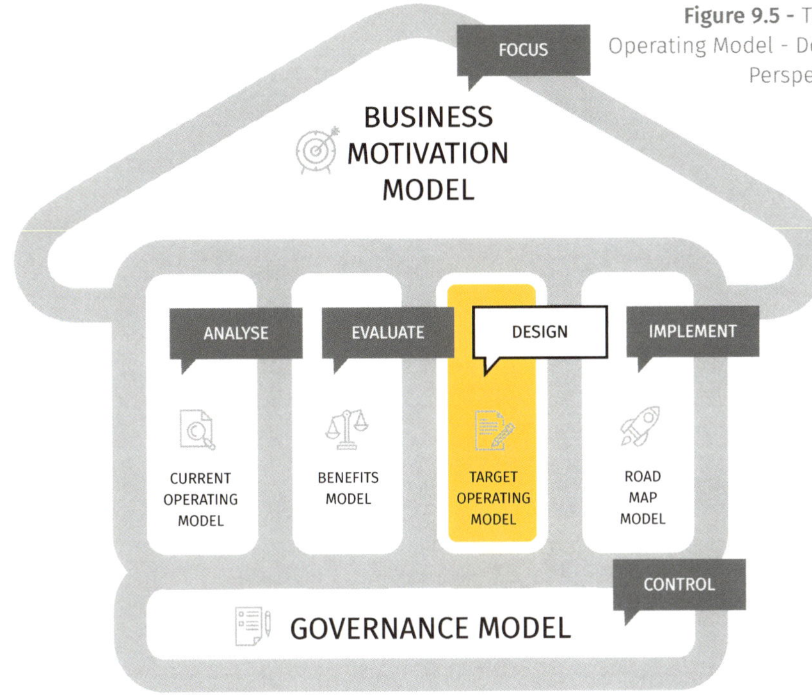


Figure 9.5 - Target Operating Model - Design Perspective

## Context

In terms of Context, the Target Operating Model Reference Model addresses both the aspects and the 'how' and 'where' questions asked of the both the Business and the Business Architecture:

1. How is the Business changed to create the Target Operating Model (TOM) that supports the Business Strategy? and
2. Where are the changes made in the Business to create the TOM?

In this step, the outputs from the Benefits Model – the identified Enablers (technology changes), and Business Changes (people & process changes) are used as inputs into the design of the TOM. It is those inputs that inform the 'where' and 'how' the Current Operating Model needs to change to create the TOM. It is also those changes to the Current Operating Model that create a future 'target' operating model that is designed explicitly and directly to maximize the realisation of planned benefits, return on investment, and ultimately the execution of the Business Strategy.

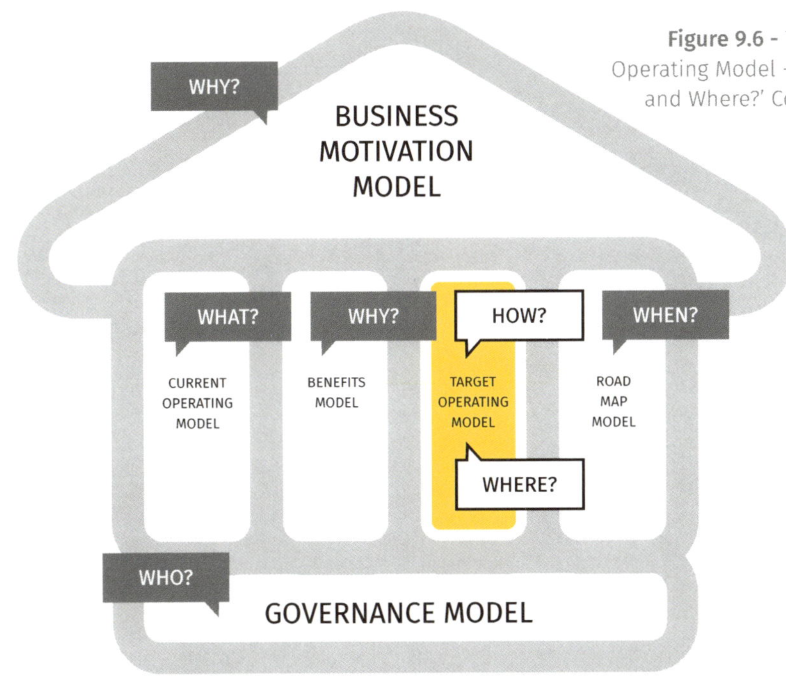


Figure 9.6 - Target Operating Model - 'How and Where?' Context

## Content

In terms of Content, the Building Blocks and Blueprints developed here are the Business Architecture content used to develop and validate the design of the Target Operating Model (TOM) that aligns the Business to the Business Strategy.

The list of Building Blocks and respective Blueprints that make up the Target Operating Model Reference Model, are shown in the table below

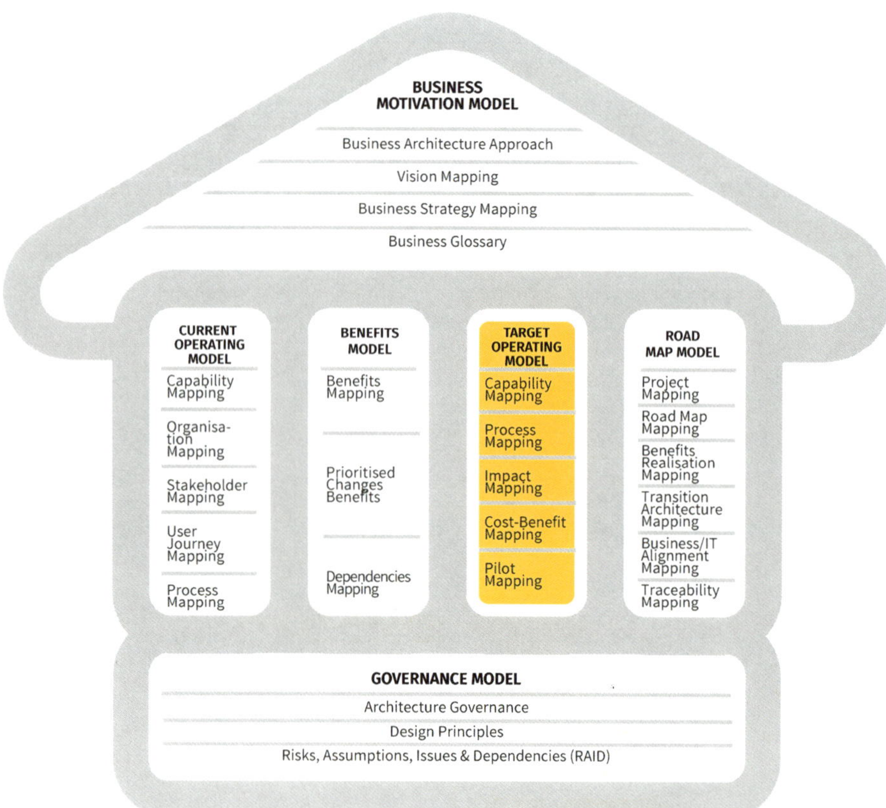


**Figure 9.7 -** Target Operating Model Building Block Content

**Target Operating Model Building Blocks and Blueprints**

**Table 9.1**

| Design Step | Building Block | Purpose | Blueprint |
|---|---|---|---|
| 5.1 | Capability Mapping (To-Be) | Defines the capabilities needed to support the TOM | • 5.1.1 Process Model-Capability Model Map Cross Map<br>• 5.1.2 Capability Model Map (To-Be)<br>• 5.1.3 Process Model-Capability Matrix |
| 5.2 | Process Mapping (To-Be) | Defines the processes needed to support the TOM. | • 5.2.1 Process Map-Process Model Cross Map<br>• 5.2.2 Process Model Map (To-Be)<br>• 5.2.3 Process Map-Process Model Matrix (To-Be) |
| 5.3 | Impact Mapping | Defines the degree of change(s) required to the identified processes, and solution options to support the TOM. | • 5.3.1 Change/ Impact Assessment<br>• 5.3.2 Process Model Heat Map<br>• 5.3.3 Capability Model Heat Map |
| 5.4 | Cost-Benefit Mapping | Provides the cost-benefit evaluation of the costs incurred to realise the intended benefits against the benefits received, including recommendation. | • 5.4.1 Solution Options<br>• 5.4.2 Cost-Benefit Assessment |
| 5.5 | Pilot Mapping | Provides the Pilot/ Min. Viable Product (MVP) of recommended solution - outline, milestones, process maps to validate proposed solution before full i mplementation. | • 5.5.1 Pilot Brief |

# Process (SIPOC)

The high level 'Supplier, Input, Process, Output, Customer' (SIPOC) process to completing this step, Step-5 Design and the Target Operating Model (TOM) are shown in *Figure 9.8* below.

**(*) Note – these Blueprints are shown for completeness here and should be included and considered in the development and sign-off of all subsequent Blueprints as they collectively define the vision, scope and risks that all following work and Blueprints developed and agreed need to consider and align to.**

We will discuss each of the process steps (Building Blocks) in the sections below.

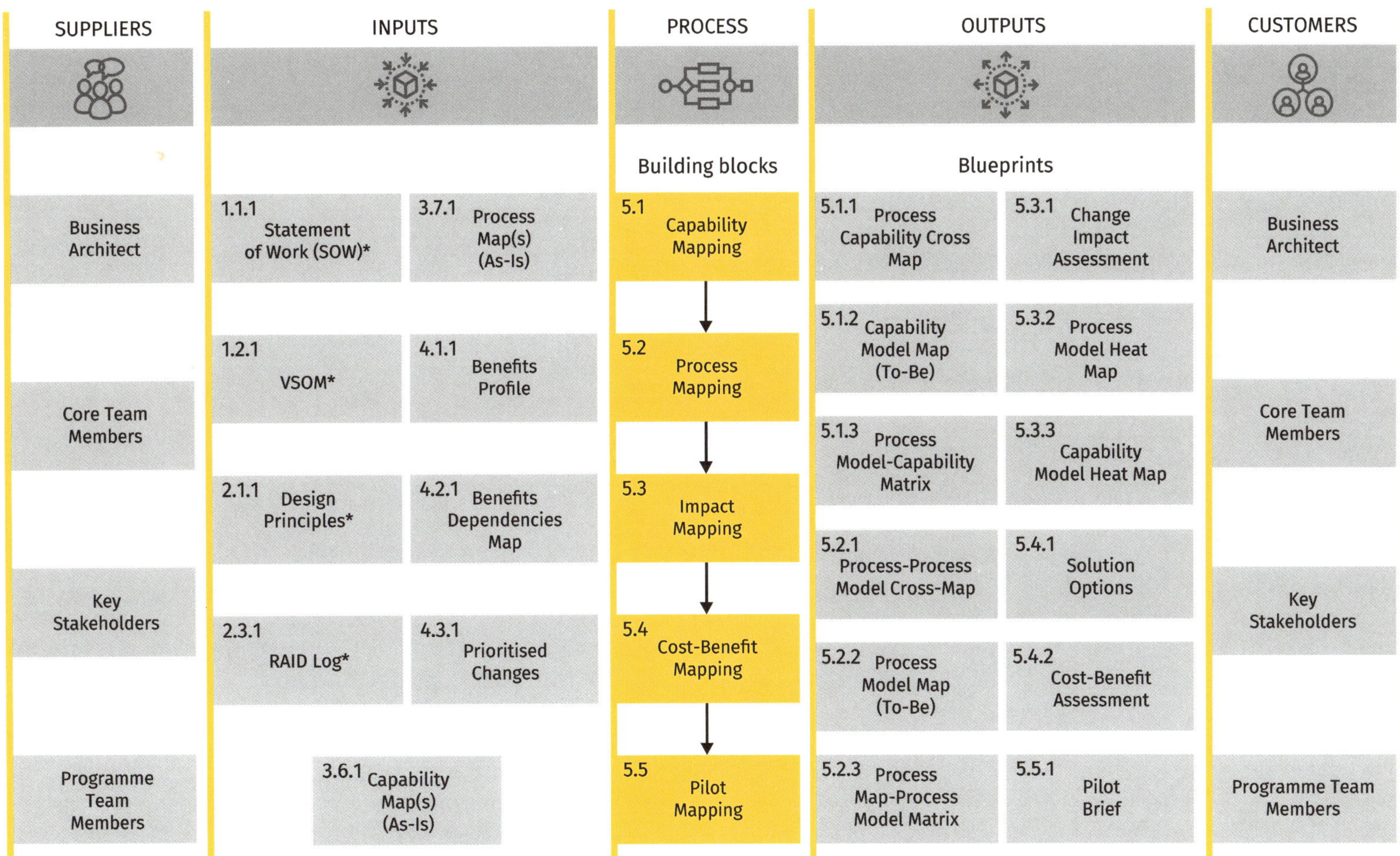


**Figure 9.8**- Target Operating Model SIPOC

# 5.1 Capability Mapping (To-Be)

## Introduction

Capability Mapping (To-Be) is the Building Block that identifies the Business Capabilities ('Capabilities') that need to be created or enhanced in order to align the Business to the Business Strategy.

The objective for Capability Mapping is to identify on the one central single Organisation-wide Capability Model Map (also referred to as Business Capability Model (BCM)) which candidate capabilities are being created or enhanced that specifically address the identified and validated stakeholder's concerns, and directly contribute to the Organisation realising the planned Business Benefits.

The purpose for identifying the candidate capabilities on the central single Organisation-wide Capability Model Map is to produce and use the 'To-Be' Capability Model Map to inform conversations with Key Stakeholders both within (and outside) the Programme to confirm the following:

- **There is no gap, or duplication of work** (i.e. two or more Programmes are not inadvertently working on the same capabilities, or delivering similar functionality, but for different capabilities), and
- **If (or where) there is duplication**, identify any potential dependencies and opportunities to collaborate.

The benefit of using Capability Mapping in this way (identifying dependencies or conflicts with other pieces of work, i.e. other projects and Programmes, or duplicating work), is to have the visibility and therefore conversations (and negotiations) early with other parties across the Organisation *before* any 'change debt' – small or large, technical or non-technical (i.e. design and development of physical architecture) occurs, to reconcile any differences, timings and ultimately align the separate pieces of work.

Figure 9.9 below shows an example of what can happen when the 'left hand' is *not* talking to the 'right hand'. There is either a duplication of effort where two (or more) areas inadvertently work on the same capability, or there is a gap where one or both parties expect a certain capability was out of scope (and therefore no time or budget had been allowed for, i.e. 'Product Supplier Management') but was in fact *in-scope*, which in this actual situation resulted in a last minute scope change (a very costly and frustrating exercise).

The reason why the Capability Model is used to align, and reconcile the differences of changes across the Organisation is because of the strategic perspective the Capability Model view provides:

- **Capability Model** - provides the *strategic level* view across the Organisation, focused at the *planning and design* level, more suitable for Programme/ Design and Architecture team members and Key Stakeholders, who are the decision makers with their Strategic/Executive concerns.
- Conversely, the **Process Model** (discussed and showed later in the Process Mapping (To-Be) Building Block in the next section) - shows a lower, *operational level view* across the Organisation, focused at the delivery/ implementation level, which is suitable for conversations with Project/ Delivery level team members and the Product Owner, who are the decision makers with their Operational/Implementation concerns.

It's important to have these early reconciling and negotiating conversations with other parts of the Programme and Organisation to avoid silos developing. Silos develop not just in Business, but on Programmes with at least two (2) projects under it; more than two (2) Programmes running at the same time and almost definitely where change is happening within (and across) an Organisation that has multiple physical locations in operation.

Silos develop between different projects on the same Programme (and across the Organisation) just as silos occur between the different business units of the Organisation with the people, processes and systems that service their specific markets and customers. While these different business units serve different customers and markets, there is often a great deal of duplication in the capabilities that service and support them.

Customers of phone companies for example are notorious for complaining that they seem to provide the same information over and over to the one- phone company, but still end up receiving multiple communications (Mobile, Landline, Internet etc. including bills) from separate departments

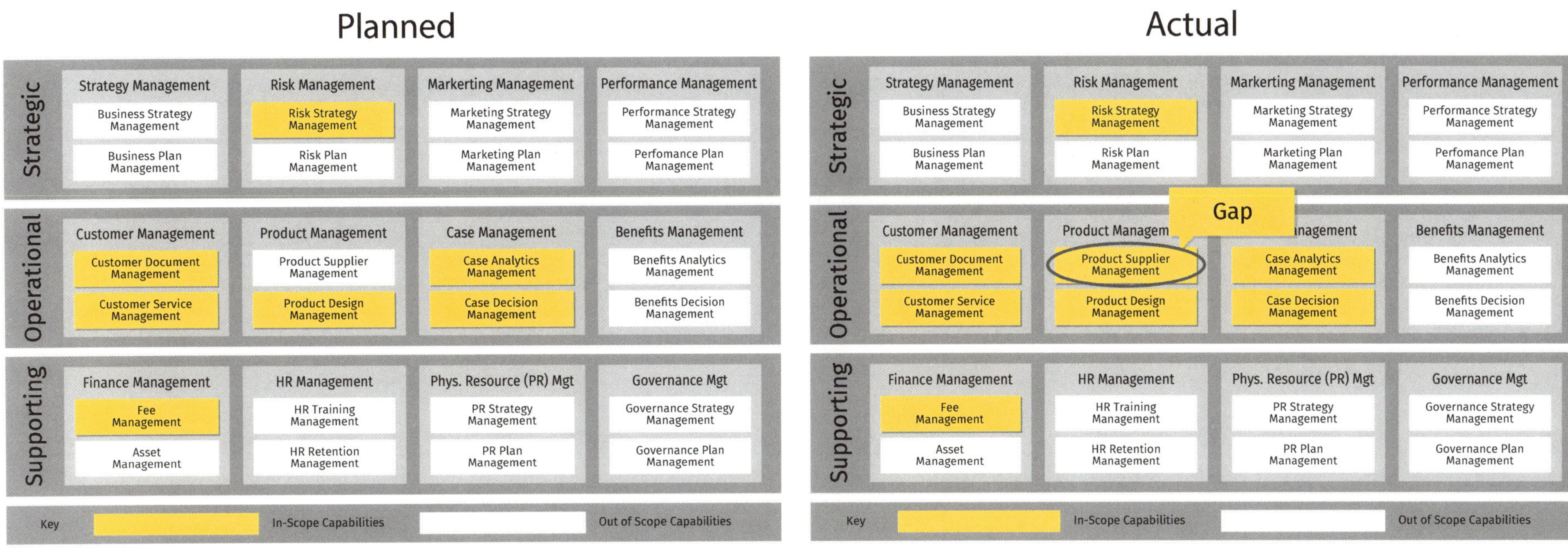


**Figure 9.9 -** 'Planned' vs 'Actual' Capability Model

within that one company (all using the same reporting, billing, mailing and account management capabilities within the same Organisation) - as if they were dealing with three (3) completely different companies, potentially a lot of duplication of time, effort and resources carrying out the same functions.

The Capability Model provides that end-to-end, Organisation wide view of *'what they Organisation does'*, so that silos don't develop and so the 'left hand' is talking to the 'right hand'. As the Business Architect, by knowing what capabilities are being impacted by proposed changes across the *entire* Organisation, you will be able to coordinate and streamline all those changes across the Organisation, minimising disruption to both the Organisation and the Customers and maximise the return on time, and investment in those changes.

## Inputs

The inputs used to complete this Building Block are shown in the table below.

**Capability Mapping (To-Be) Building Block Inputs**

Table 9.2

| Ref | Blueprint | Use |
|---|---|---|
| 3.6.1 | Process Model Map (As-Is) | Provide the baseline process model map, as the agreed starting point to design To-Be processes maps from. |
| 3.7.1 | Capability Model Map (As-Is) | Provide the baseline capability model map, as the agreed starting point to design To-Be capability model map from. |
| 4.2.1 | Benefits Dependencies Map | Provide the Business Changes and Enablers needed to realise the planned benefits. |
| 4.3.1 | Prioritised Changes Map | Provide the prioritised changes - Enablers (technology & data elements of business capabilities), and Business Changes (people and process elements of business capabilities) as candidate changes to business capabilities needed to realise the intended Business Benefits, and support the Business Strategy. |
| N/A | Existing Programme documentation | Includes 'As-Is' Process Maps drawn up with or by the Business Analyst (Business Change or Product Owner) |

## Outputs

The Blueprints (outputs) produced for this Building Block is shown in the table below.

**Capability Mapping (To-Be) (Output) Blueprints**

Table 9.3

<table>
<tr><th>Ref</th><th>Blueprint</th><th>Description</th><th>Example</th></tr>
<tr><td>5.1.1</td><td>Process Model/ Capability Model Cross-Map</td><td>Cross map between the Level 4 Process Map(s), and the 'As-Is' Capability Model Map.</td><td>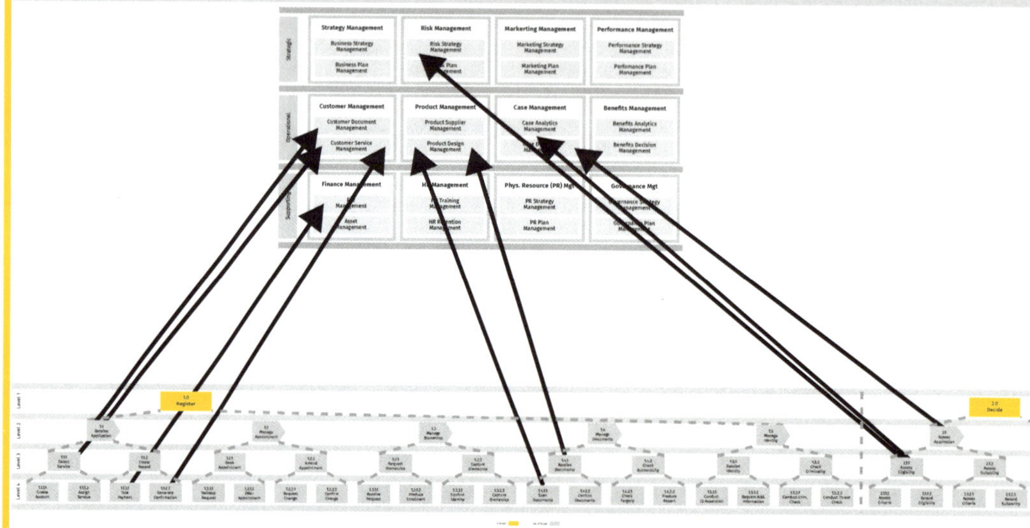</td></tr>
<tr><td>5.1.2</td><td>Capability Model Map (To-Be)</td><td>Updated 'As-Is' Capability Map highlighting in/out of scope capabilities that are impacted by changes to the 'As-Is' Process Model Map.</td><td>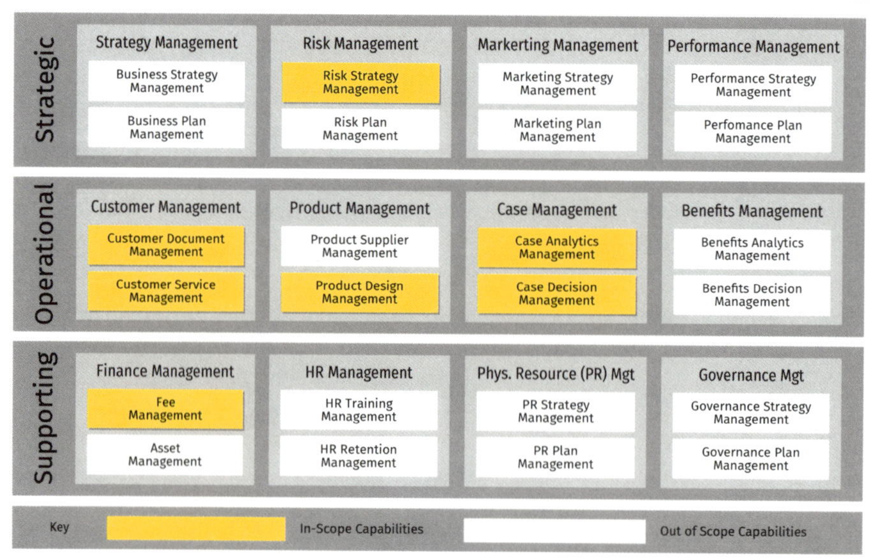
</td></tr>
</table>

Table 9.3

| Ref | Blueprint | Description | Example |
|---|---|---|---|
| 5.1.3 | Process Model/ Capability Model Matrix | Matrix between the Process and Capability Models, showing the relationship and processes that implement that Organisation's Capabilities. | (see matrix below) |

Example

| Ref | Process | Ref / Capability | 1.1 Strategic Management | 1.1.1 Business Strategy Management | 1.1.2 Business Plan Management | 1.2 Risk Management | 1.2.1 Risk Strategy Management | 1.2.2 Risk Plan Management | 1.3 Marketing Management | 1.3.1 Marketing Strategy Management | 1.3.2 Marketing Plan Management | 2.1 Customer Management | 2.1.1 Customer Document Management | 2.1.2 Customer Service Management | 2.2 Product Management | 2.2.1 Product Supplier Management | 2.2.2 Product Design Management | 2.3 Case Management | 2.3.1 Case Analytics Management | 2.3.2 Case Decision Management | 3.1 Finance Management | 3.1.1 Fee Management | 3.1.2 Asset Management | 3.2 HR Management | 3.2.1 HR Training Management | 3.2.2 HR Retention Management | 3.3 Physical Resource Management | 3.3.1 PR Strategy Management | 3.3.2 PR Plan Management |
|---|---|---|---|---|---|---|---|---|---|---|---|---|---|---|---|---|---|---|---|---|---|---|---|---|---|---|---|---|---|
| 1.0 | Register | | | | | | | | | | | | | | | | | | | | | | | | | | | | |
| 1.1 | Receive Application | | | | | | | | | | | | ■ | | | | | | | | | | | | | | | | |
| 1.1.1 | Select Service | | | | | | | | | | | | | ■ | | | | | | | | | | | | | | | |
| 1.1.1.1 | Create Account | | | | | | | | | | | | | ■ | | | | | | | | | | | | | | | |
| 1.1.1.2 | Apply Service | | | | | | | | | | | | | ■ | | | | | | | | | | | | | | | |
| 1.1.2 | Create Record | | | | | | | | | | | | | ■ | | | | | | | | | | | | | | | |
| 1.1.2.1 | Take Payment | | | | | | | | | | | | | | | | | | | | | ■ | | | | | | | |
| 1.1.2.2 | Generate Confirmtn | | | | | | | | | | | | | ■ | | | | | | | | | | | | | | | |
| 1.2 | Manage Appointmt | ■ | ■ | ■ | ■ | ■ | ■ | ■ | ■ | ■ | ■ | ■ | ■ | ■ | ■ | ■ | ■ | ■ | ■ | ■ | ■ | ■ | ■ | ■ | ■ | ■ | ■ | ■ | ■ |
| 1.2.1 | Book Appointment | ■ | ■ | ■ | ■ | ■ | ■ | ■ | ■ | ■ | ■ | ■ | ■ | ■ | ■ | ■ | ■ | ■ | ■ | ■ | ■ | ■ | ■ | ■ | ■ | ■ | ■ | ■ | ■ |
| 1.2.1.1 | Validate Request | ■ | ■ | ■ | ■ | ■ | ■ | ■ | ■ | ■ | ■ | ■ | ■ | ■ | ■ | ■ | ■ | ■ | ■ | ■ | ■ | ■ | ■ | ■ | ■ | ■ | ■ | ■ | ■ |
| 1.2.1.2 | Offer Appointment | ■ | ■ | ■ | ■ | ■ | ■ | ■ | ■ | ■ | ■ | ■ | ■ | ■ | ■ | ■ | ■ | ■ | ■ | ■ | ■ | ■ | ■ | ■ | ■ | ■ | ■ | ■ | ■ |
| 1.2.2 | Amend Appointmt | ■ | ■ | ■ | ■ | ■ | ■ | ■ | ■ | ■ | ■ | ■ | ■ | ■ | ■ | ■ | ■ | ■ | ■ | ■ | ■ | ■ | ■ | ■ | ■ | ■ | ■ | ■ | ■ |

## Steps

The steps to complete the above Blueprints (Outputs) are as follows.

### 5.1.1 Process Model / Capability Model Cross-Map

#### 1. Develop the Process-Capability Model Cross Map

Using the inputs from the Inputs section above, the first step is to identify the 'candidate' capabilities. The term 'candidate' is used as these are 'earmarked' capabilities that haven't actually been validated. They need to be validated (the purpose of this step) so that they are the best set of capabilities addressing the Stakeholder concerns and needs while ensuring no other areas of the Organisation are also looking and considering making changes to them.

The starting point for 'To-Be' Capability Model Map is the 'As-Is' Process Model Map because it contains the last known (and most up to date) list of all the Organisations business processes – the same business processes that implement an Organisations business capabilities.

Using your knowledge of the Business, the Business Representatives (namely the Product Owner, and possibly other Key Stakeholders, if needed), and the Process Model Catalogue Blueprint, identify the candidate Capabilities that implement the specific capabilities on the Capability Model Map, as shown in *Figure 9.10* below.

**The following Process Model and Capability Model Maps are used for illustration purposes only, showing a sample of what the full Process and Capability Models would look like in practice. In reality, both would be expected to be a lot larger, and contain the full spectrum of the Organisation's processes, as well as its capabilities.**

**A more accurate Process-to-Capability mapping could occur using the 'To-Be' Process Model (to be completed in the following Building Block). These activities could be completed in parallel, however, in terms of timing, urgency and decisions made at the planning/design/ strategic level, a priority should be placed on getting the 'To-Be' Capability Model agreed quickly, starting with the latest version of the Process Model, while the development (and reconcile) of the 'To-Be' Process Map happens concurrently in the background.**

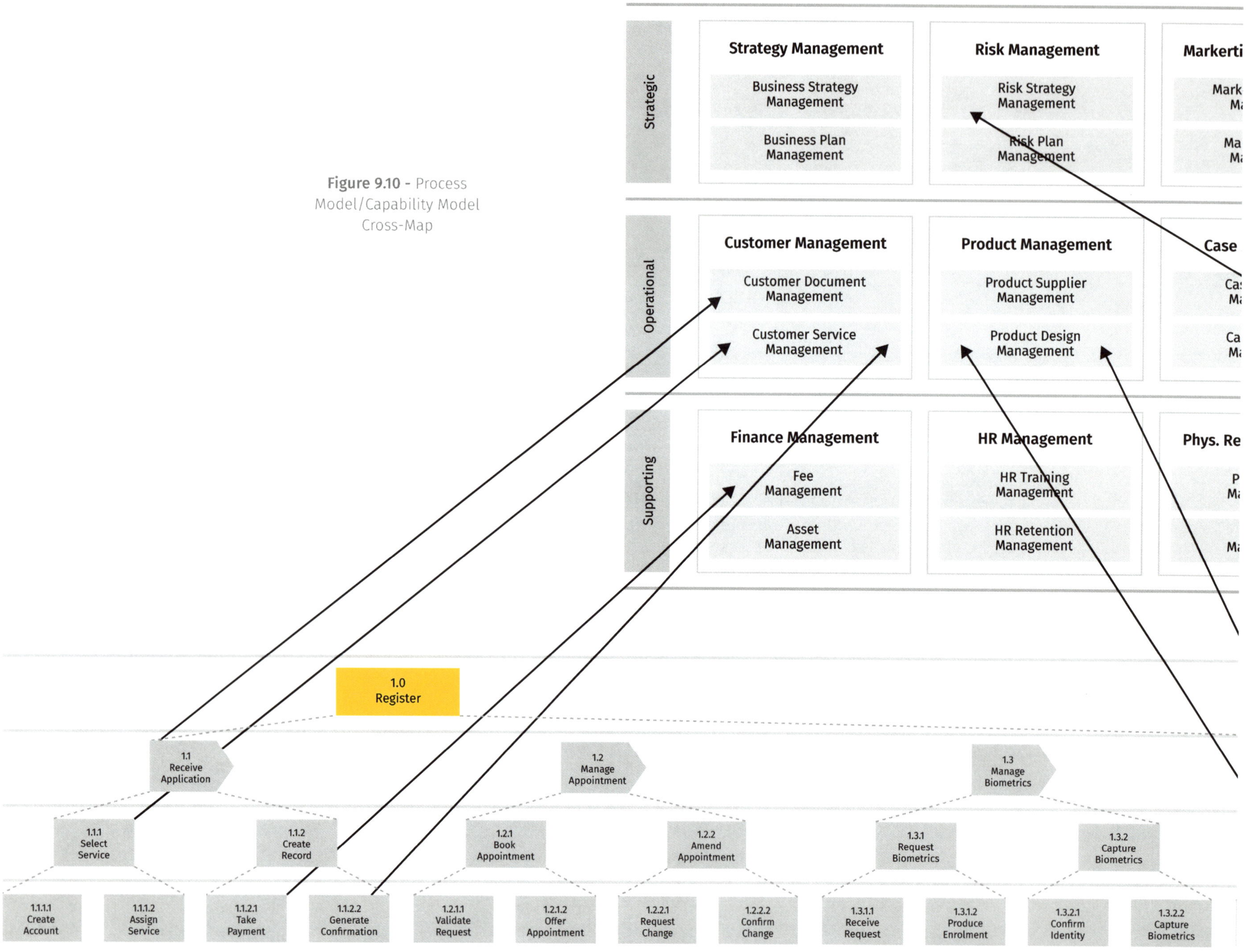


**Figure 9.10 -** Process Model/Capability Model Cross-Map

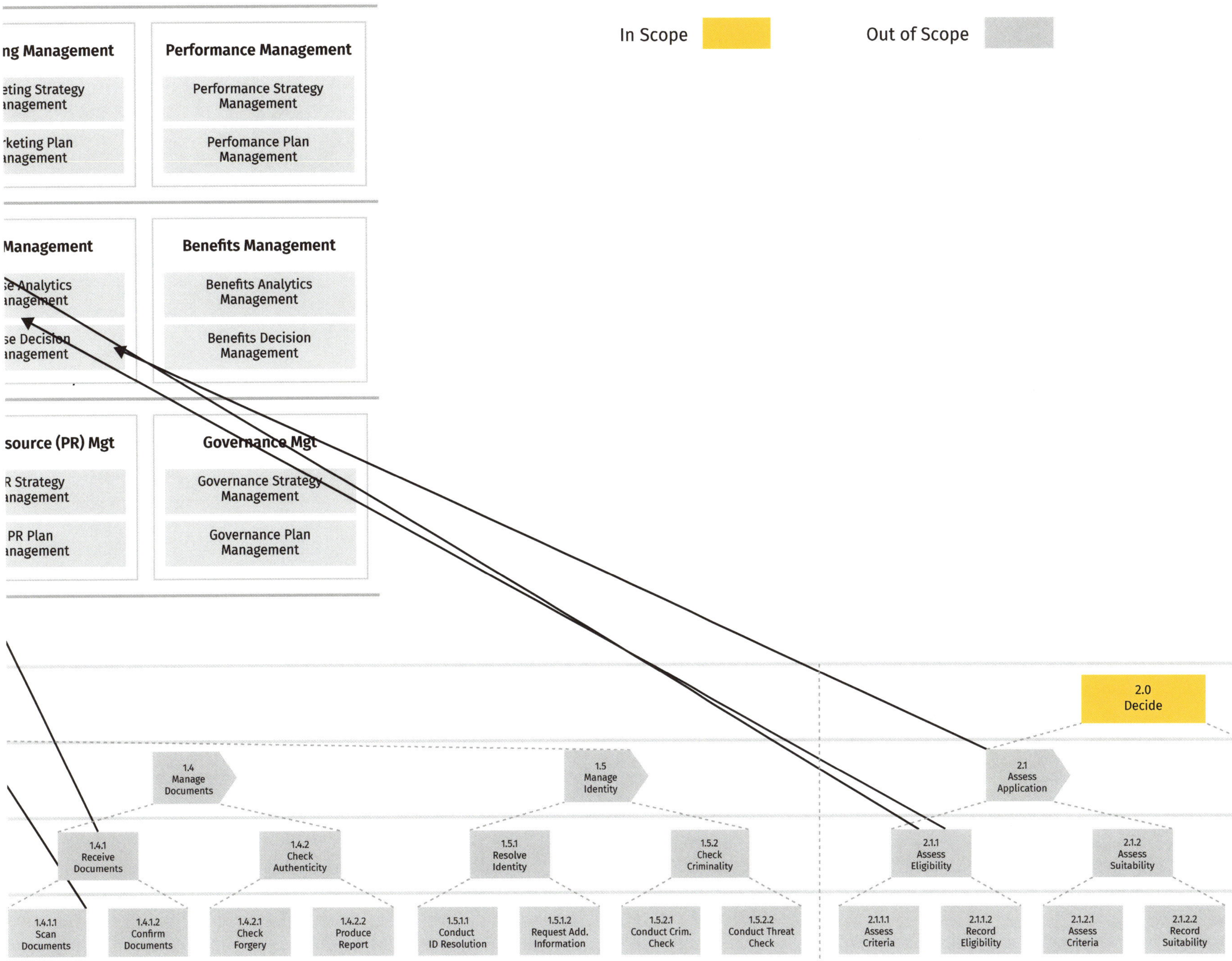
In Scope
Out of Scope
ng Management
eting Strategy
nagement
rketing Plan
nagement
Performance Management
Performance Strategy Management
Perfomance Plan Management
Management
se Analytics
nagement
se Decision
nagement
Benefits Management
Benefits Analytics Management
Benefits Decision Management
source (PR) Mgt
R Strategy
nagement
PR Plan
nagement
Governance Mgt
Governance Strategy Management
Governance Plan Management
2.0 Decide
1.4 Manage Documents
1.5 Manage Identity
2.1 Assess Application
1.4.1 Receive Documents
1.4.2 Check Authenticity
1.5.1 Resolve Identity
1.5.2 Check Criminality
2.1.1 Assess Eligibility
2.1.2 Assess Suitability
1.4.1.1 Scan Documents
1.4.1.2 Confirm Documents
1.4.2.1 Check Forgery
1.4.2.2 Produce Report
1.5.1.1 Conduct ID Resolution
1.5.1.2 Request Add. Information
1.5.2.1 Conduct Crim. Check
1.5.2.2 Conduct Threat Check
2.1.1.1 Assess Criteria
2.1.1.2 Record Eligibility
2.1.2.1 Assess Criteria
2.1.2.2 Record Suitability

## 5.1.2 Capability Model Map (To-Be)

**2. Mark and highlight the in-scope capabilities on the Capability Model Map.**

The 'As-Is' Capability Model Map effectively now becomes the unconfirmed (or draft/yet to be confirmed) 'To-Be' Capability Model Map showing the 'in and out of scope' capabilities.

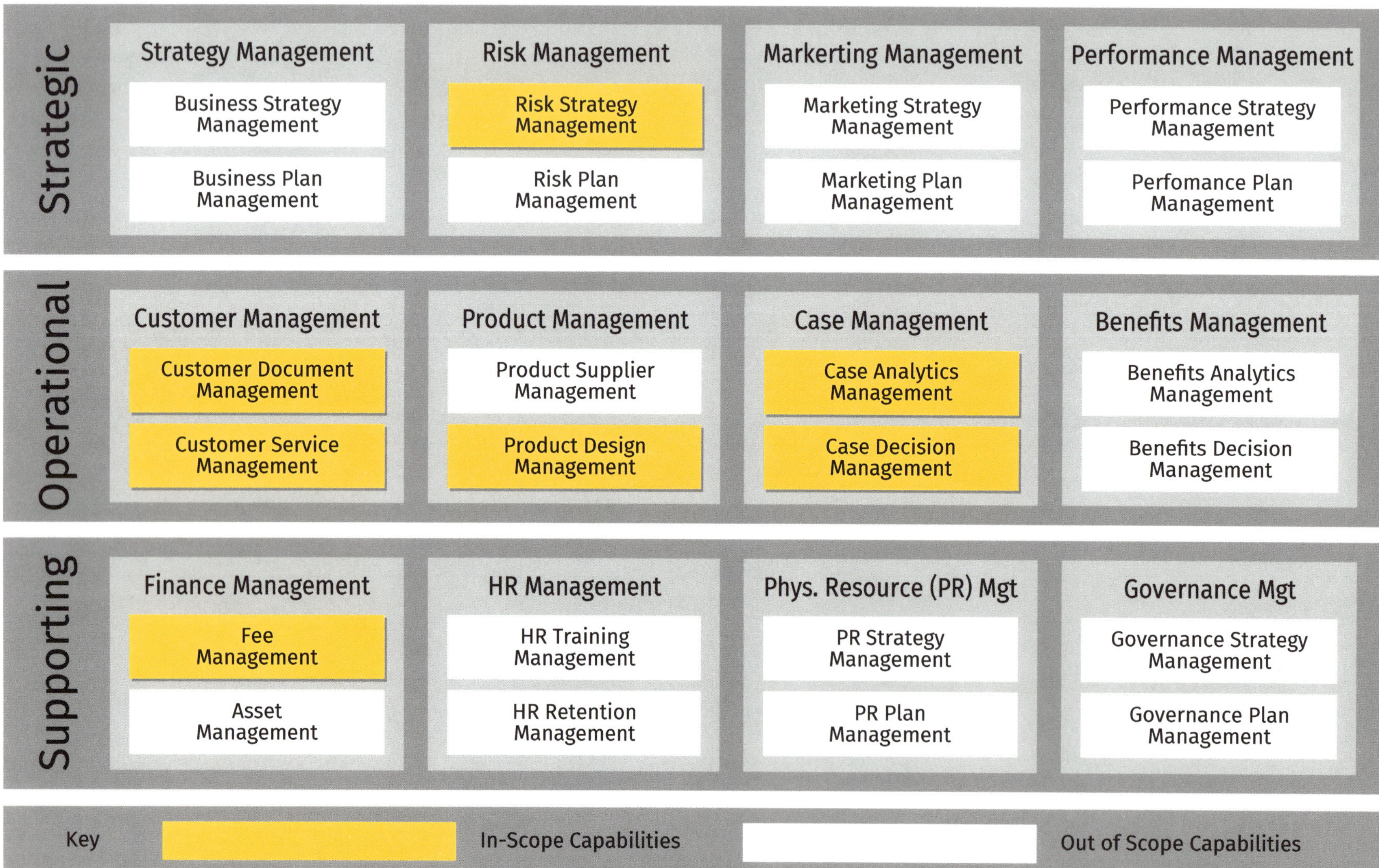


**Figure 9.11 -** Example Capability Model Map (To-Be)

# 5.1.3 Process Model/Capability Model Matrix

**3. Record the Process Model-Capability cross-mapping in the matrix**, indicating the intersection of which process from the Process Model is using the capability from the Capability Model (and for completeness which processes from the Process Model are out of scope), as shown in *Figure 9.12* below.

**Note – in practice, the Process Model/Capability Model Matrix will cover all the processes from the Process Model. The example below shows an extract of the complete Process Model, showing only the subset of all the processes from the Process Model.**

| | | Capability | Strategic Management | Business Strategy Management | Business Plan Management | Risk Management | Risk Strategy Management | Risk Plan Management | Marketing Management | Marketing Strategy Management | Marketing Plan Management | Customer Management | Customer Document Management | Customer Service Management | Product Management | Product Supplier Management | Product Design Management | Case Management | Case Analytics Management | Case Decision Management | Finance Management | Fee Management | Asset Management | HR Management | HR Training Management | HR Retention Management | Physical Resource Management | PR Strategy Management | PR Plan Management |
|---|---|---|---|---|---|---|---|---|---|---|---|---|---|---|---|---|---|---|---|---|---|---|---|---|---|---|---|---|---|
| **Ref** | **Process** | Ref | 1.1 | 1.1.1 | 1.1.2 | 1.2 | 1.2.1 | 1.2.2 | 1.3 | 1.3.1 | 1.3.2 | 2.1 | 2.1.1 | 2.1.2 | 2.2 | 2.2.1 | 2.2.2 | 2.3 | 2.3.1 | 2.3.2 | 3.1 | 3.1.1 | 3.1.2 | 3.2 | 3.2.1 | 3.2.2 | 3.3 | 3.3.1 | 3.3.2 |
| 1.0 | Register | | | | | | | | | | | | | | | | | | | | | | | | | | | | |
| 1.1 | Receive Application | | | | | | | | | | | | ■ | | | | | | | | | | | | | | | | |
| 1.1.1 | Select Service | | | | | | | | | | | | | ■ | | | | | | | | | | | | | | | |
| 1.1.1.1 | Create Account | | | | | | | | | | | | | ■ | | | | | | | | | | | | | | | |
| 1.1.1.2 | Apply Service | | | | | | | | | | | | | ■ | | | | | | | | | | | | | | | |
| 1.1.2 | Create Record | | | | | | | | | | | | | ■ | | | | | | | | | | | | | | | |
| 1.1.2.1 | Take Payment | | | | | | | | | | | | | | | | | | | | | ■ | | | | | | | |
| 1.1.2.2 | Generate Confirmtn | | | | | | | | | | | | | ■ | | | | | | | | | | | | | | | |
| 1.2 | Manage Appointmt | ▨ | ▨ | ▨ | ▨ | ▨ | ▨ | ▨ | ▨ | ▨ | ▨ | ▨ | ▨ | ▨ | ▨ | ▨ | ▨ | ▨ | ▨ | ▨ | ▨ | ▨ | ▨ | ▨ | ▨ | ▨ | ▨ | ▨ | ▨ |
| 1.2.1 | Book Appointment | ▨ | ▨ | ▨ | ▨ | ▨ | ▨ | ▨ | ▨ | ▨ | ▨ | ▨ | ▨ | ▨ | ▨ | ▨ | ▨ | ▨ | ▨ | ▨ | ▨ | ▨ | ▨ | ▨ | ▨ | ▨ | ▨ | ▨ | ▨ |
| 1.2.1.1 | Validate Request | ▨ | ▨ | ▨ | ▨ | ▨ | ▨ | ▨ | ▨ | ▨ | ▨ | ▨ | ▨ | ▨ | ▨ | ▨ | ▨ | ▨ | ▨ | ▨ | ▨ | ▨ | ▨ | ▨ | ▨ | ▨ | ▨ | ▨ | ▨ |
| 1.2.1.2 | Offer Appointment | ▨ | ▨ | ▨ | ▨ | ▨ | ▨ | ▨ | ▨ | ▨ | ▨ | ▨ | ▨ | ▨ | ▨ | ▨ | ▨ | ▨ | ▨ | ▨ | ▨ | ▨ | ▨ | ▨ | ▨ | ▨ | ▨ | ▨ | ▨ |
| 1.2.2 | Amend Appointmt | ▨ | ▨ | ▨ | ▨ | ▨ | ▨ | ▨ | ▨ | ▨ | ▨ | ▨ | ▨ | ▨ | ▨ | ▨ | ▨ | ▨ | ▨ | ▨ | ▨ | ▨ | ▨ | ▨ | ▨ | ▨ | ▨ | ▨ | ▨ |
| 1.2.2.1 | Request Change | ▨ | ▨ | ▨ | ▨ | ▨ | ▨ | ▨ | ▨ | ▨ | ▨ | ▨ | ▨ | ▨ | ▨ | ▨ | ▨ | ▨ | ▨ | ▨ | ▨ | ▨ | ▨ | ▨ | ▨ | ▨ | ▨ | ▨ | ▨ |
| 1.2.2.2 | Confirm Change | ▨ | ▨ | ▨ | ▨ | ▨ | ▨ | ▨ | ▨ | ▨ | ▨ | ▨ | ▨ | ▨ | ▨ | ▨ | ▨ | ▨ | ▨ | ▨ | ▨ | ▨ | ▨ | ▨ | ▨ | ▨ | ▨ | ▨ | ▨ |
| 1.3 | Manage Biometrics | ▨ | ▨ | ▨ | ▨ | ▨ | ▨ | ▨ | ▨ | ▨ | ▨ | ▨ | ▨ | ▨ | ▨ | ▨ | ▨ | ▨ | ▨ | ▨ | ▨ | ▨ | ▨ | ▨ | ▨ | ▨ | ▨ | ▨ | ▨ |
| 1.3.1 | Request Biometrics | ▨ | ▨ | ▨ | ▨ | ▨ | ▨ | ▨ | ▨ | ▨ | ▨ | ▨ | ▨ | ▨ | ▨ | ▨ | ▨ | ▨ | ▨ | ▨ | ▨ | ▨ | ▨ | ▨ | ▨ | ▨ | ▨ | ▨ | ▨ |

| Ref | Process | Capability | Strategic Management | Business Strategy Management | Business Plan Management | Risk Management | Risk Strategy Management | Risk Plan Management | Marketing Management | Marketing Strategy Management | Marketing Plan Management | Customer Management | Customer Document Management | Customer Service Management | Product Management | Product Supplier Management | Product Design Management | Case Management | Case Analytics Management | Case Decision Management | Finance Management | Fee Management | Asset Management | HR Management | HR Training Management | HR Retention Management | Physical Resource Management | PR Strategy Management | PR Plan Management |
|---|---|---|---|---|---|---|---|---|---|---|---|---|---|---|---|---|---|---|---|---|---|---|---|---|---|---|---|---|---|
| | | Ref | 1.1 | 1.1.1 | 1.1.2 | 1.2 | 1.2.1 | 1.2.2 | 1.3 | 1.3.1 | 1.3.2 | 2.1 | 2.1.1 | 2.1.2 | 2.2 | 2.2.1 | 2.2.2 | 2.3 | 2.3.1 | 2.3.2 | 3.1 | 3.1.1 | 3.1.2 | 3.2 | 3.2.1 | 3.2.2 | 3.3 | 3.3.1 | 3.3.2 |
| 1.3.1.1 | Receive Bio Req'st | ▒ | ▒ | ▒ | ▒ | ▒ | ▒ | ▒ | ▒ | ▒ | ▒ | ▒ | ▒ | ▒ | ▒ | ▒ | ▒ | ▒ | ▒ | ▒ | ▒ | ▒ | ▒ | ▒ | ▒ | ▒ | ▒ | ▒ | ▒ |
| 1.3.1.2 | Produce Enrol Let. | ▒ | ▒ | ▒ | ▒ | ▒ | ▒ | ▒ | ▒ | ▒ | ▒ | ▒ | ▒ | ▒ | ▒ | ▒ | ▒ | ▒ | ▒ | ▒ | ▒ | ▒ | ▒ | ▒ | ▒ | ▒ | ▒ | ▒ | ▒ |
| 1.3.2 | Capture Biometrics | ▒ | ▒ | ▒ | ▒ | ▒ | ▒ | ▒ | ▒ | ▒ | ▒ | ▒ | ▒ | ▒ | ▒ | ▒ | ▒ | ▒ | ▒ | ▒ | ▒ | ▒ | ▒ | ▒ | ▒ | ▒ | ▒ | ▒ | ▒ |
| 1.3.2.1 | Confirm Identity | ▒ | ▒ | ▒ | ▒ | ▒ | ▒ | ▒ | ▒ | ▒ | ▒ | ▒ | ▒ | ▒ | ▒ | ▒ | ▒ | ▒ | ▒ | ▒ | ▒ | ▒ | ▒ | ▒ | ▒ | ▒ | ▒ | ▒ | ▒ |
| 1.3.2.2 | Capture Biometrics | ▒ | ▒ | ▒ | ▒ | ▒ | ▒ | ▒ | ▒ | ▒ | ▒ | ▒ | ▒ | ▒ | ▒ | ▒ | ▒ | ▒ | ▒ | ▒ | ▒ | ▒ | ▒ | ▒ | ▒ | ▒ | ▒ | ▒ | ▒ |
| 1.4 | Manage Documents | | | | | | | | | | | | | | | | | | | | | | | | | | | | |
| 1.4.1 | Receive Documents | | | | | | | | | | | | | | | | ■ | | | | | | | | | | | | |
| 1.4.1.1 | Scan Documents | | | | | | | | | | | | | | | | ■ | | | | | | | | | | | | |
| 1.4.1.2 | Confirm Documents | | | | | | | | | | | | | | | | ■ | | | | | | | | | | | | |
| 1.4.2 | Check Authenticity | | | | | | | | | | | | | | | | | | | | | | | | | | | | |
| 1.4.2.1 | Check Forgery | | | | | | | | | | | | | | | | | | | | | | | | | | | | |
| 1.4.2.2 | Produce Report | | | | | | | | | | | | | | | | | | | | | | | | | | | | |
| 1.5 | Manage Identity | ▒ | ▒ | ▒ | ▒ | ▒ | ▒ | ▒ | ▒ | ▒ | ▒ | ▒ | ▒ | ▒ | ▒ | ▒ | ▒ | ▒ | ▒ | ▒ | ▒ | ▒ | ▒ | ▒ | ▒ | ▒ | ▒ | ▒ | ▒ |
| 1.5.1 | Resolve Identity | ▒ | ▒ | ▒ | ▒ | ▒ | ▒ | ▒ | ▒ | ▒ | ▒ | ▒ | ▒ | ▒ | ▒ | ▒ | ▒ | ▒ | ▒ | ▒ | ▒ | ▒ | ▒ | ▒ | ▒ | ▒ | ▒ | ▒ | ▒ |
| 1.5.1.1 | Conduct ID Res. | ▒ | ▒ | ▒ | ▒ | ▒ | ▒ | ▒ | ▒ | ▒ | ▒ | ▒ | ▒ | ▒ | ▒ | ▒ | ▒ | ▒ | ▒ | ▒ | ▒ | ▒ | ▒ | ▒ | ▒ | ▒ | ▒ | ▒ | ▒ |
| 1.5.1.2 | Request Add. Info | ▒ | ▒ | ▒ | ▒ | ▒ | ▒ | ▒ | ▒ | ▒ | ▒ | ▒ | ▒ | ▒ | ▒ | ▒ | ▒ | ▒ | ▒ | ▒ | ▒ | ▒ | ▒ | ▒ | ▒ | ▒ | ▒ | ▒ | ▒ |
| 1.5.2 | Check Criminality | ▒ | ▒ | ▒ | ▒ | ▒ | ▒ | ▒ | ▒ | ▒ | ▒ | ▒ | ▒ | ▒ | ▒ | ▒ | ▒ | ▒ | ▒ | ▒ | ▒ | ▒ | ▒ | ▒ | ▒ | ▒ | ▒ | ▒ | ▒ |
| 1.5.2.1 | Conduct C-Check | ▒ | ▒ | ▒ | ▒ | ▒ | ▒ | ▒ | ▒ | ▒ | ▒ | ▒ | ▒ | ▒ | ▒ | ▒ | ▒ | ▒ | ▒ | ▒ | ▒ | ▒ | ▒ | ▒ | ▒ | ▒ | ▒ | ▒ | ▒ |
| 1.5.2.2 | Conduct T-Check | ▒ | ▒ | ▒ | ▒ | ▒ | ▒ | ▒ | ▒ | ▒ | ▒ | ▒ | ▒ | ▒ | ▒ | ▒ | ▒ | ▒ | ▒ | ▒ | ▒ | ▒ | ▒ | ▒ | ▒ | ▒ | ▒ | ▒ | ▒ |
| 2.0 | Decide | | | | | | | | | | | | | | | | | | | | | | | | | | | | |
| 2.1 | Assess Application | | | | | | | | | | | | | | | | | | | ■ | | | | | | | | | |
| 2.1.1 | Assess Eligibility | | | | | | ■ | | | | | | | | | | | | ■ | | | | | | | | | | |

Figure 9.12 - Process Model/Capability Model Matrix (extract)

■ In Scope ▒ Out of Scope

**4. Iteratively socialise, validate and refine the Blueprint(s)** and matrix – including any Risks, Assumptions, Issues and Dependencies (RAID) addressed or raised as part of completing this step.

With these Blueprints in hand, you can with great confidence engage, and communicate with other projects within your Programme, or other projects in other Programmes (and Programmes themselves), that are also looking at other change initiatives.

In those conversations, if you or other projects (or Programmes) are impacting the same capabilities, then this is where you can now look for opportunities to co-ordinate efforts, or even share work and costs. Where there is similar work going on across the Organisation, at the very least, this exercise should raise questions – *Why?* 'Why is anyone else looking at creating or enhancing these exact capabilities?' followed by 'What Business Benefit(s) do they intend to realise?', and 'What Strategic Objective(s) are they supporting?'

**The other pertinent question to ask at this time 'When?' as in 'When are these proposed changes intended to be implemented?', is discussed in the Road Map Reference Model in *Chapter 10 Step 6 – Implement.***

**5. Package and publish the Blueprint(s)** – in line with your agreed sprint/release cycle, established back in Step-2 Control, with the Governance Model.

## Risks and Mitigations

The main risk with 'To-Be' Capability Mapping is not doing it, not having or delay holding those alignment and reconciliation conversations across the Programmes. Without this enterprise-wide view the 'To-Be' Capability Map provides, you run the risk of making changes in insolation and potentially duplicating effort and/or creating gaps.

When projects and Programmes get into the *'swing of it'*, they have momentum and don't want to stop. These reconciliation and alignment meetings are seen by some as more a hindrance than a help, so you should expect some resistance when requesting this with your counterparts across the Organisation.

For those seasoned professionals amongst us, it is well known that it takes time to *'down tools'*, stop the machine, and align activities. It's also very hard to do, once suppliers have been engaged, and even harder when contracts have been signed and financial incentives (and disincentives) are involved that the technology/technical folk are only too eager to deliver (despite in some cases, there are obvious overlaps and duplication in work and outcomes).

Despite the resistance you will face, the benefits of persisting to complete this activity and Building Block far outweigh the costs. It's also easier and cheaper to identify issues, agree alignment, coordinate changes in scope and/or direction early than finding out half way through implementation that another Programme has been working on the same capability, or alternately, where a dependent capability you expected to be delivered before yours now won't be.

The key to any reconciliation and alignment effort is all parties (or Programmes) are speaking the same language (i.e. same business terms and definitions), ideally talking to the same Capability Model Map. Ideally, there should only be one capability map for the whole Organisation, and if not the case, then this is probably the point to start at.

Just as (or even more) effective in reconciling and alignment with other Programmes, is at the level that physically implements the Organisations capabilities, the process level, using the 'To-Be' Process Model. The 'To-Be' Process Model is developed in the 'To-Be' Process Mapping Building Block in section *5.2 Process Mapping (To-Be)* below

.

## Building Block Wrap-up

In this section, we discussed the Process Mapping (To-Be) Building Block.

This Building Block identifies and highlights the capabilities that are in scope for changes that directly contribute to the realisation of the intended Business Benefits and align the Business to the Business Strategy.

The Building Block is made up of the following three (3) Blueprints:

- **Process/Capability Model Cross-Map** - Cross map between the Level 4 Process Map(s), and the 'As-Is' Capability Model Map;
- **Capability Model Map (To-Be)** - Updated 'As-Is' Capability Map highlighting the in/out of scope capabilities that are impacted by changes to the 'As-Is' Process Model Map, and
- **Process/Capability Model Matrix** - Matrix between the Process and Capability Models

showing the relationship and processes that implement the Organisation's Capabilities.

All Blueprints are used to highlight any interdependencies between the different Programmes across the Organisation, to coordinate and align change activities and avoid duplication and gaps.

The 'To-Be' Capability Model provides the strategic level view across the Organisation, focused at the *planning and design* level, more suitable for Programme/Design and Architecture team members and Key Stakeholders and decision makers at the Strategic/Executive level in both the Programme and Organisation. The 'To-Be' Process Model view on the other hand, discussed in the Process Mapping (To-Be) Building Block in the next section below, shows a lower *operational level* view across the Organisation, focused at the *delivery/implementation* level, which is suitable for conversations with Project/Delivery level team members and Product Owner, as decision makers at the Operational/Implementation level, in both the Programme and Organisation.

### Next Steps

Once the Capability Mapping (To-Be) Building Block has been completed (which includes aligning, reconciliation and coordination of any identified changes as a result of any duplication or gaps), the next step in the Design Process is to reconcile and co-ordinate those changes and differences at the ('As-Is') Process Model level, as part of the ('To-Be') Process Model Mapping Building Block.

The Process Model Mapping (To-Be) Building Block is discussed in the next section.



# 5.2 Process Mapping (To-Be)

## Introduction

Process Mapping (To-Be) Building Block is used to identify the Organisations Business Processes that are the actual processes that are changed (or created) in order to align the Business to the Business Strategy.

The objective for Process Mapping (To-Be) is similar to the objective of the 'To-Be' Capability Mapping – being to identify on the central, single Organisation-wide model (Process Model in this case), the processes that are being created or enhanced in order to align the Business to the Business Strategy.

It is those lower operation level processes, changed by the Business Changes and Enablers (identified back in the Benefits Model as the Benefit-Dependencies) that address both the stakeholders concerns as well as being the actual *Programme outputs* (discussed earlier in Benefits *Realisation Management (BRM)* section) that are delivered and implemented into the business. It is these *Programme outputs* that when used by the Business generate positive Business Outcomes, which ultimately lead to the realisation of the Organisations planned Business Benefits.

The Organisations processes are mapped on to the Process Model, as the Process Model standardises (at a process level) where in the Organisation (i.e. process level) the proposed changes will actually take place - that enable the Business to realise its intended Business Benefits, and align the Business to the Business Strategy.

The purpose for identifying the candidate processes on the central Organisation-wide process model is to produce (and use) the 'To-Be' Process Model Map to inform conversations with Key Stakeholders both within (and outside) the Programme and confirm the following:

- **That no gap, or duplication of work exists** (i.e. two or more Programmes are not inadvertently working on the same processes, or inadvertently delivering similar functionality, but for different processes), and
- **If (or where) there is duplication or overlapping of work,** it identifies any potential dependencies and opportunities to collaborate.

The benefit of using the 'To-Be' Process Mapping in this way of identifying any dependencies or conflicts, is for the same reasons as the 'To-Be' Capability Mapping is for Capability Maps – that is, to have the visibility and therefore conversations early (and negotiations, where necessary) with other parties across the Organisation, before any change debt – small or large, technical or non-technical (i.e. design and development of physical architecture) occurs, to reconcile any differences, timings and ultimately align the separate pieces of work.

Although both the Capability and Process Models provide the single source of truth of what the Organisation does, the Process Model provides the view of the Organisation – of *'how'* the business what it does, however at a more granular level than Capabilities (which describe 'what' the business does). It is at the lower *operational process level* where the actual changes will take place, and is therefore a more accurate picture of *'how the Organisation is changing'* and *'where are actual changes are being made?'*.

As mentioned earlier, the different perspectives of the Process Model and Capability Model make them suitable for conversations with different stakeholders:

- The **'To-Be' Process Model** provides a lower *operational* level view across the Organisation, focused on *delivery and implementation*, suitable for conversations with Project/Delivery level team members and stakeholders, who are the decision makers with operation and implementation concerns; and
- The **'To-Be' Capability Model** provides a higher *strategic* level view across the Organisation, focused on *planning and design*, suitable for conversations with Programme/Design and Architecture team members and stakeholders, who are the decision makers with strategic concerns.

As an example, Figure 9.13 below shows what can happen with Process Mapping when the *'left hand'* is not talking to the *'right hand'*, the potential for duplication in effort or for gaps to materialise where one or both parties expect an area to be out of scope (or in scope). In this example (as actually did happen), the 'Manage Validation' process (and sub-processes) highlighted below, were originally *thought* as out of scope, but after this exercise was performed, the '(To-Be) Process Model' highlighted that there was a gap in one of the processes that was now being 'in-sourced'. The current 'out-sourced' provider didn't just receive and send mail, when they received an Applicant's application and supporting documentation, they carried out an 'initial document forgery check', which was *not* in scope for the 'in-sourced' business unit taking over the process. This caused as a result, a change in scope, and an immediate change request (which no time nor budget had been allowed for).

## Inputs

The inputs used to complete this Building Block are shown in the table below.

Capability Mapping (To-Be) Building Block Inputs

Table 9.4

| Ref | Blueprint | Use |
|---|---|---|
| 3.6.1 | Process Model Map (As-Is) | Provides the baseline process model map, as the agreed starting point to design To-Be processes maps from. |
| 4.3.1 | Prioritised Changes Map | Provides the prioritised changes – Enablers (technology & data elements of business capabilities), and Business Changes (people and process elements of business capabilities) that are the changes that are made to the 'As-Is' Process Maps, which are mapped to the Process Model. |
| N/A | Existing Programme documentation | Includes 'As-Is' Process Maps drawn up with or by the Business Analyst (Business Change or Product Owner) |

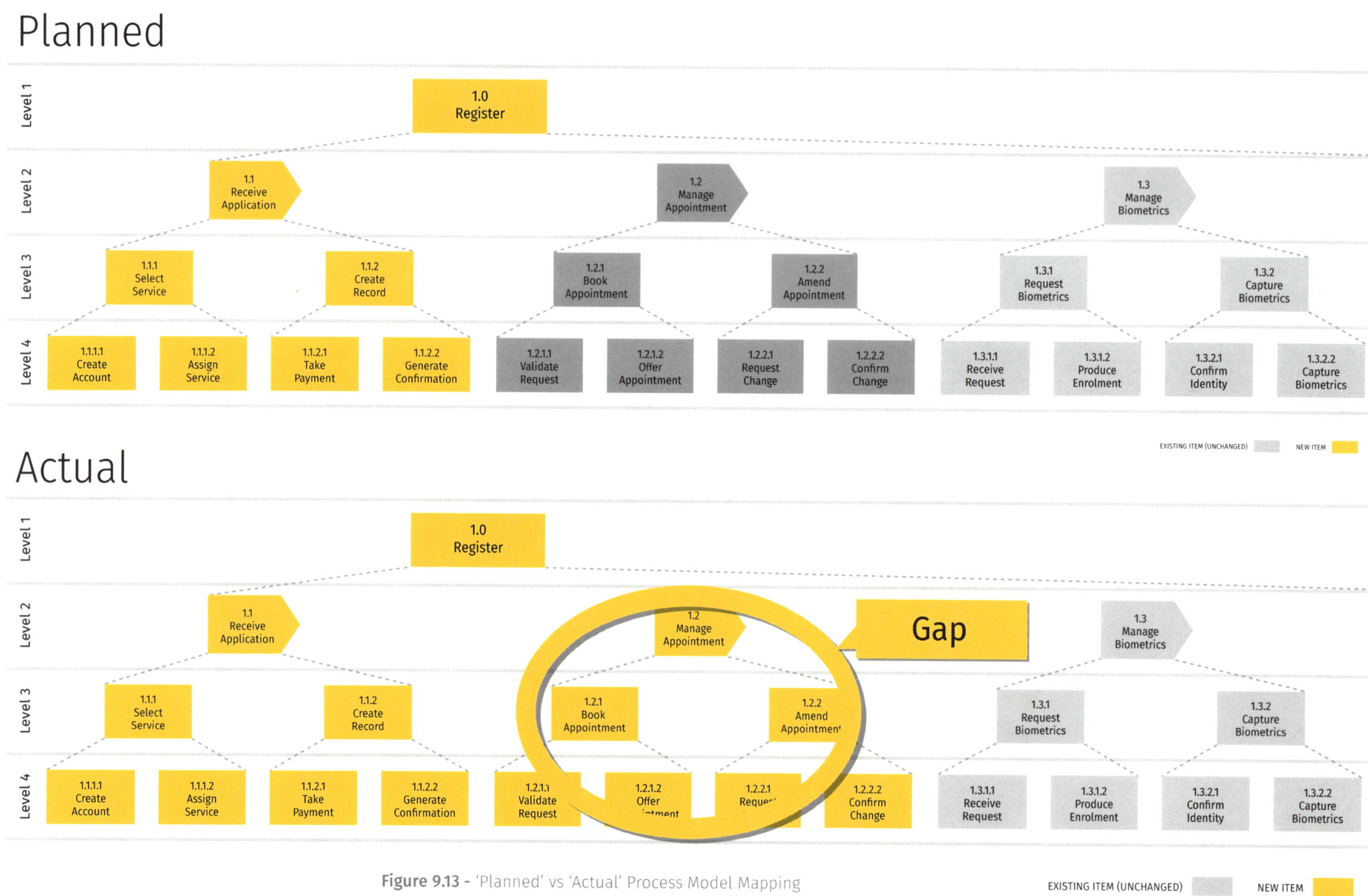


**Figure 9.13** - 'Planned' vs 'Actual' Process Model Mapping

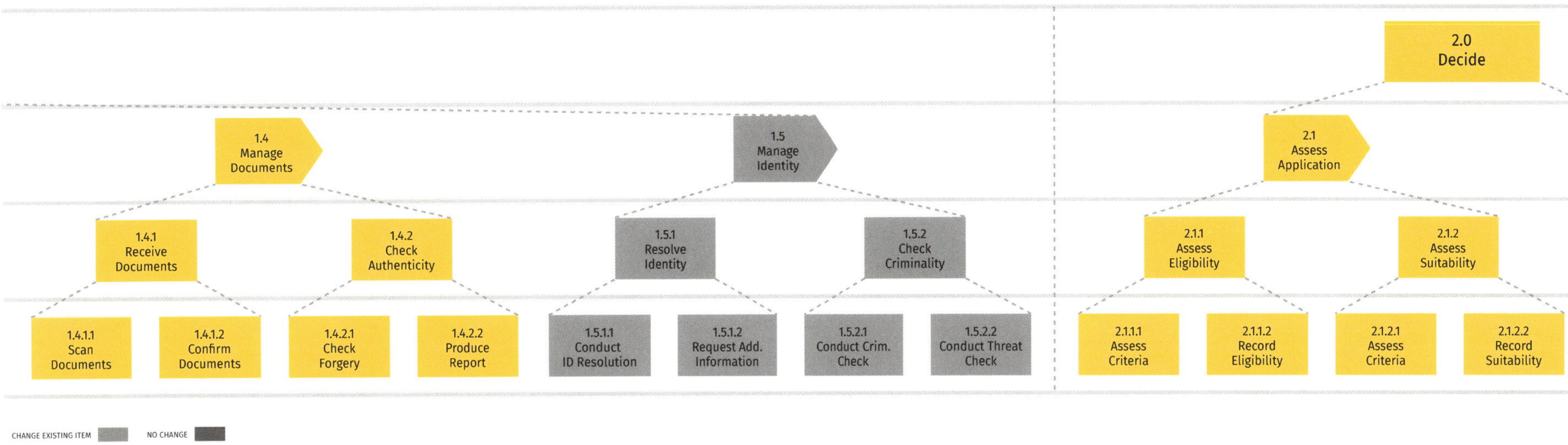
2.0 Decide
1.4 Manage Documents
1.5 Manage Identity
2.1 Assess Application
1.4.1 Receive Documents
1.4.2 Check Authenticity
1.5.1 Resolve Identity
1.5.2 Check Criminality
2.1.1 Assess Eligibility
2.1.2 Assess Suitability
1.4.1.1 Scan Documents
1.4.1.2 Confirm Documents
1.4.2.1 Check Forgery
1.4.2.2 Produce Report
1.5.1.1 Conduct ID Resolution
1.5.1.2 Request Add. Information
1.5.2.1 Conduct Crim. Check
1.5.2.2 Conduct Threat Check
2.1.1.1 Assess Criteria
2.1.1.2 Record Eligibility
2.1.2.1 Assess Criteria
2.1.2.2 Record Suitability
CHANGE EXISTING ITEM
NO CHANGE

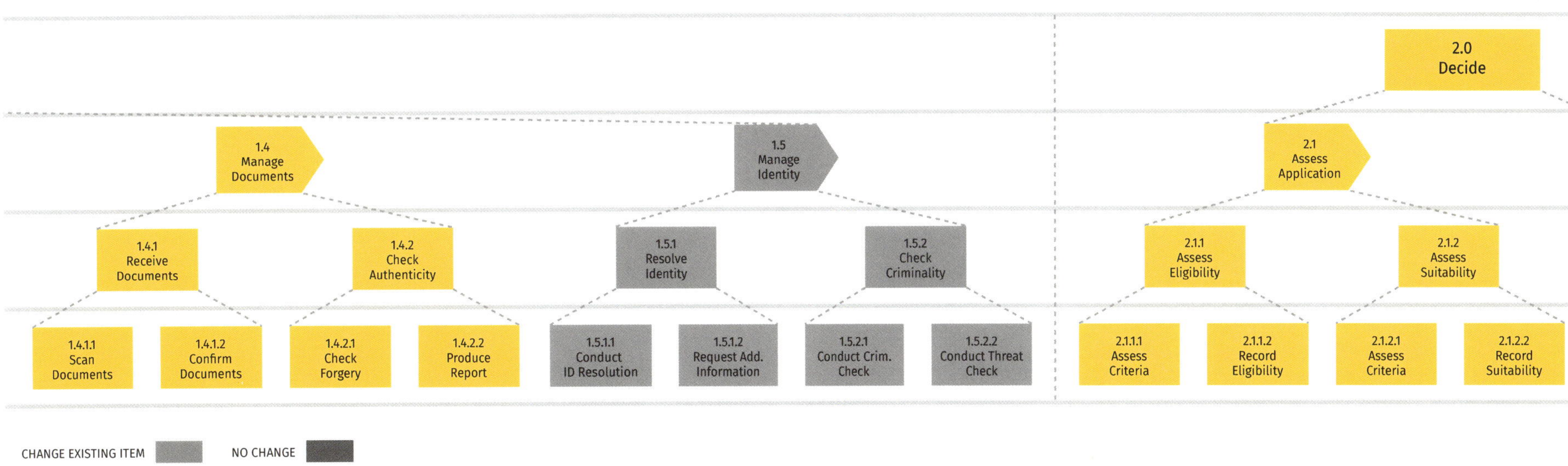
2.0 Decide
1.4 Manage Documents
1.5 Manage Identity
2.1 Assess Application
1.4.1 Receive Documents
1.4.2 Check Authenticity
1.5.1 Resolve Identity
1.5.2 Check Criminality
2.1.1 Assess Eligibility
2.1.2 Assess Suitability
1.4.1.1 Scan Documents
1.4.1.2 Confirm Documents
1.4.2.1 Check Forgery
1.4.2.2 Produce Report
1.5.1.1 Conduct ID Resolution
1.5.1.2 Request Add. Information
1.5.2.1 Conduct Crim. Check
1.5.2.2 Conduct Threat Check
2.1.1.1 Assess Criteria
2.1.1.2 Record Eligibility
2.1.2.1 Assess Criteria
2.1.2.2 Record Suitability
CHANGE EXISTING ITEM
NO CHANGE

# Output(s)

The Blueprints (outputs) produced for this Building Block are shown in the table below:

**Process Mapping (To-Be) (Output) Blueprints**

Table 9.5

| Ref | Blueprint | Description | Example |
|---|---|---|---|
| 5.2.1 | Process Map/ Process Model Cross-Map | Cross map between the low-level process map(s), 'As-Is' Process Model Map, showing which processes are in scope | 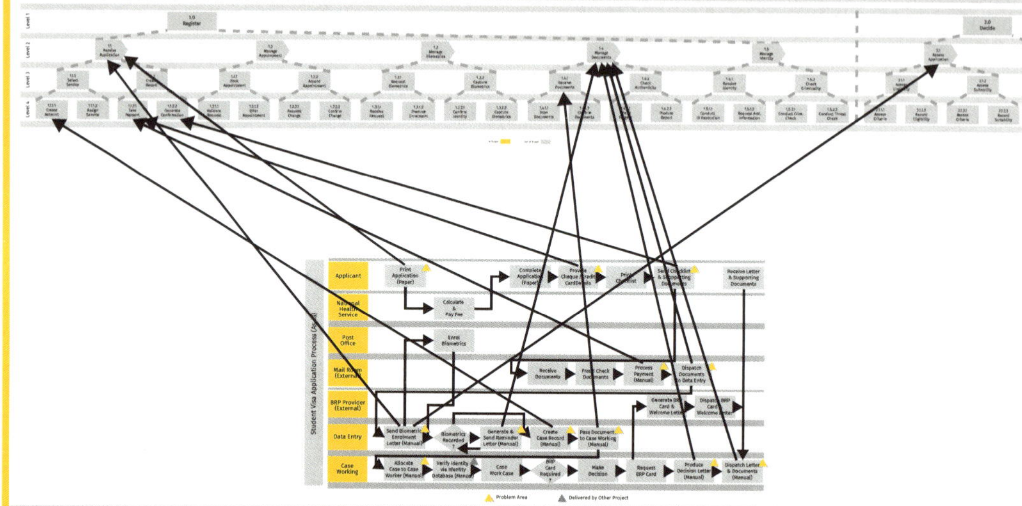 |
| 5.2.2 | Process Model Map (To-Be) | Updated 'As-Is' Process Model Map showing the in-scope processes on the single enterprise wide Process Model Map. | 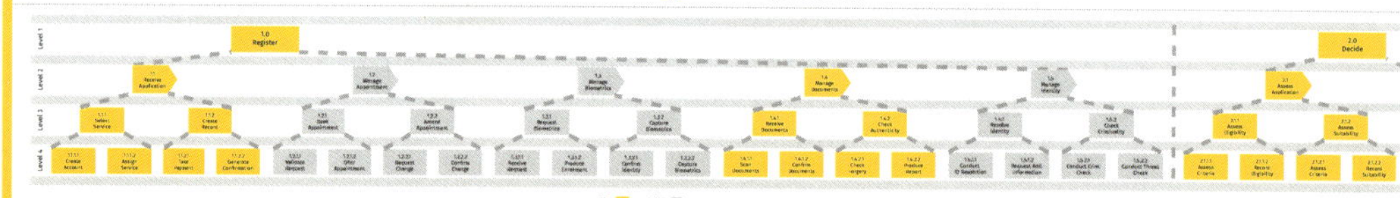 |
| 5.2.3 | Process Map/ Process Model Matrix | Matrix showing the relationship between the lower level process maps, and the process model processes | 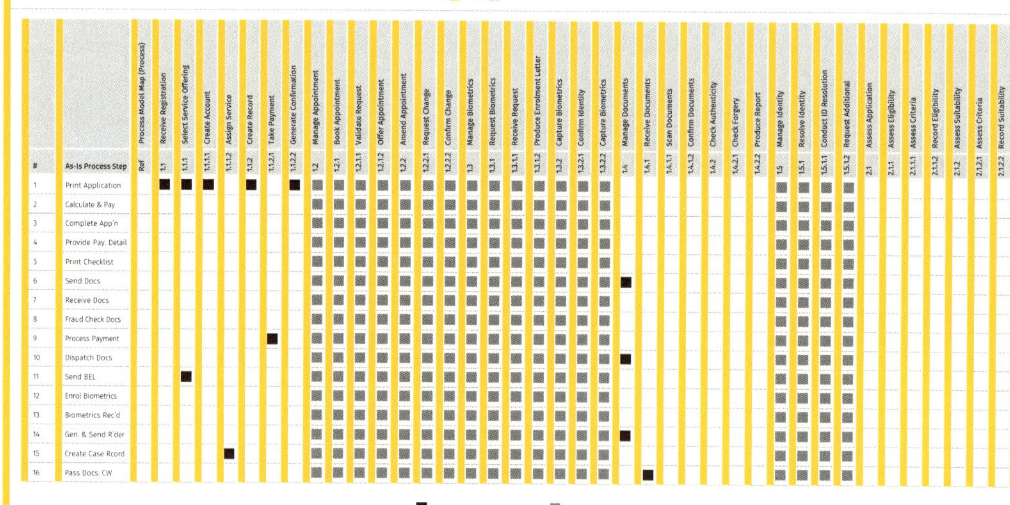 |

## Steps

The steps to complete the above Blueprints (Output) are as follows.

### 5.2.1 Process Map/Process Model Cross Map

**1. Develop the Process Map/Process**

Using the inputs from Table 9.4 above, namely the in-scope 'As-Is' process maps (worked up with or by the Business Analyst), and working with the Business Analyst, and Product Owner, identify and map the in-scope processes on to the Process Model (As-Is), as shown in *Figure 9.14* below.

### 5.2.2 Process Model (To-Be)

**2. Mark and highlight the in (and out of) scope processes** on the Process Model Map, as shown in *Figure 9.15* below.

### 5.2.3 Process Map/Process Model Matrix

**3. Record the Process Map/Process Model cross-mappings** for traceability in the matrix as shown in *Figure 9.16* below

***Figure* 9.15 simply an example of a full Process/Process Model Matrix. In practice, the Blueprint would cover a great deal more including all the lower level processes across the Organisation, and all the processes from the Process Model Map.**

**4. Iteratively socialise, validate and refine the Blueprints** (and matrix - including any Risks, Assumptions, Issues and Dependencies (RAID) addressed or raised as part of completing this step).

As with the Capability Mapping (To-Be) outputs – by (also) using these Blueprints that provide the *'How'* and *'Where'* the Organisation is being changed, you can engage, and communicate with other projects within your Programme or other projects in other Programmes (and Programmes themselves), that are also looking at other change initiatives, and identify which processes are being touched and changed, including where there are overlaps and dependencies, to be clear on scope and expectations.

**The *'When?'* aspect of 'When are these changes intended to be implemented?', are discussed in the Road Map Reference Model in *Chapter 10 Step 6 – Implement.***

**5. Package and publish the Blueprint(s)** – in line with your agreed sprint/release cycle, established back in *Step 2 – Control, with the Governance Model* .

**Risks and Mitigations**

At this point in the Design Process, you have identified the Benefits, Enablers, Business Changes and the Processes (and Capabilities, in the previous Building Block), but not what these actual operational/physical changes *actually* mean to the Organisation, or what is the impact of the proposed changes *will* have on the Business (Impact Mapping is covered in the 5.3 Impact Mapping section below).

This step highlighted the business processes that are responsible for aligning the Business to the Business Strategy, and the realisation of the Business Benefits. The knowledge gained and the Blueprints created in completing this Building Block will allow you to have informed and constructive conversations across the Programme, other Programmes and the Organisation of pending changes, in effort to align all pieces of work. Without this *enterprise-wide* view you run the risk of making changes in insolation and potentially duplicating effort, or creating gaps.

As an example, on one client I have assisted had already into delivery stage when this activity was carried out. The Business Architect discovered and identified that two (2) work streams within the same Programme were inadvertently building on a process ('Conduct [document] Forgery Assessment'), that another work stream was also changing named 'Perform [document] Initial Assessment'. Because this *enterprise-wide* Process Model view was not available at the time these two parallel pieces of work were inadvertently undertaken, it wasn't visible, picked up or called out - despite the various and numerous meetings and conversations between the two (2) work streams about each other's respective work and scope. What this Process Model view also highlighted was a gap in the Process Model that hadn't been addressed – the 'insourcing of the mailroom function that scanned original documents received with the application', which would also print and send the welcome (or reject) letter with the submitted documents back to the Applicant. The generation and maintaining of the decision letter template, as well as the generation of the physical accept/ reject letter and returning with the submitted original documents was not in scope for the new 'in-sourced mail function'. Presenting this 'new'

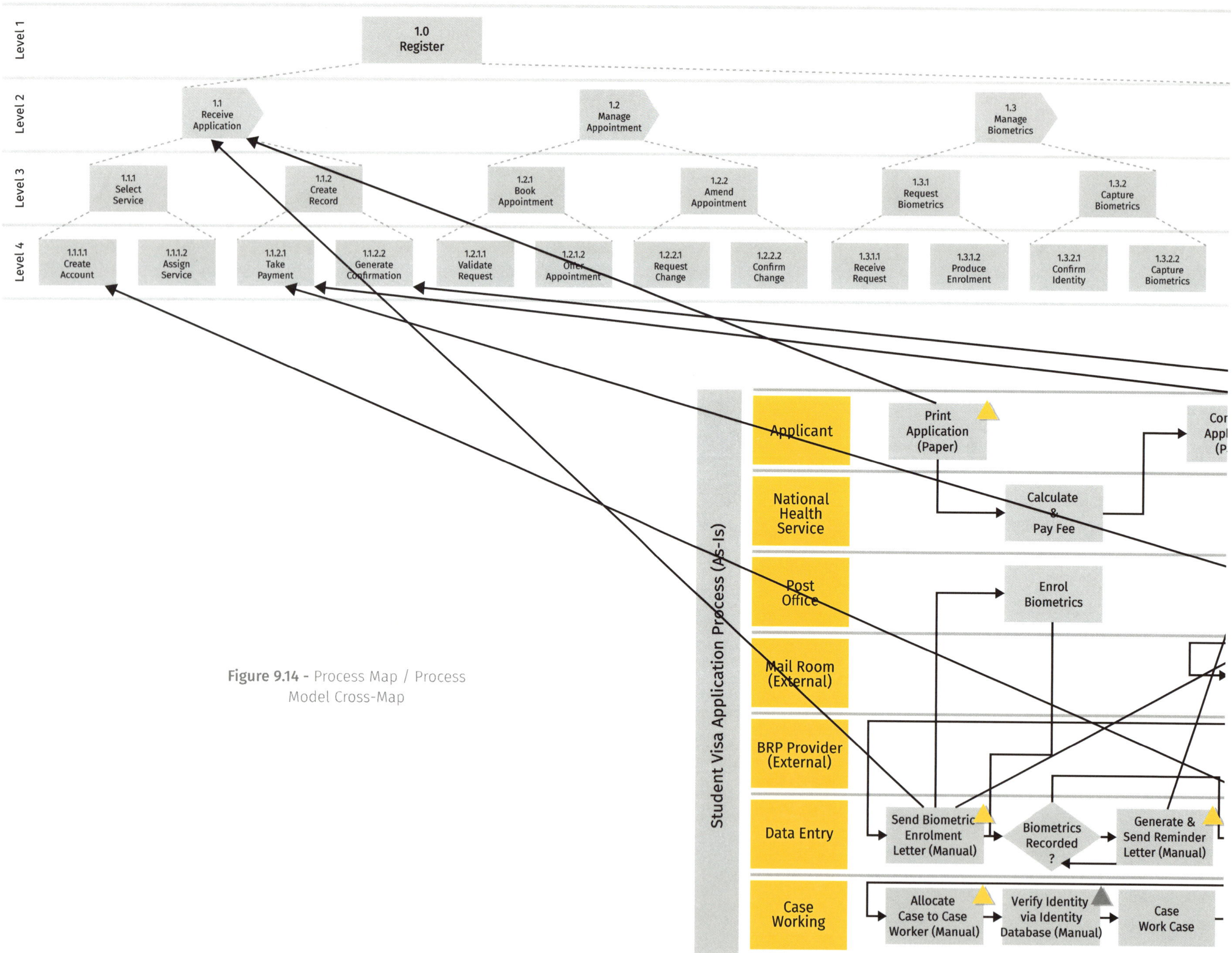


**Figure 9.14 -** Process Map / Process Model Cross-Map

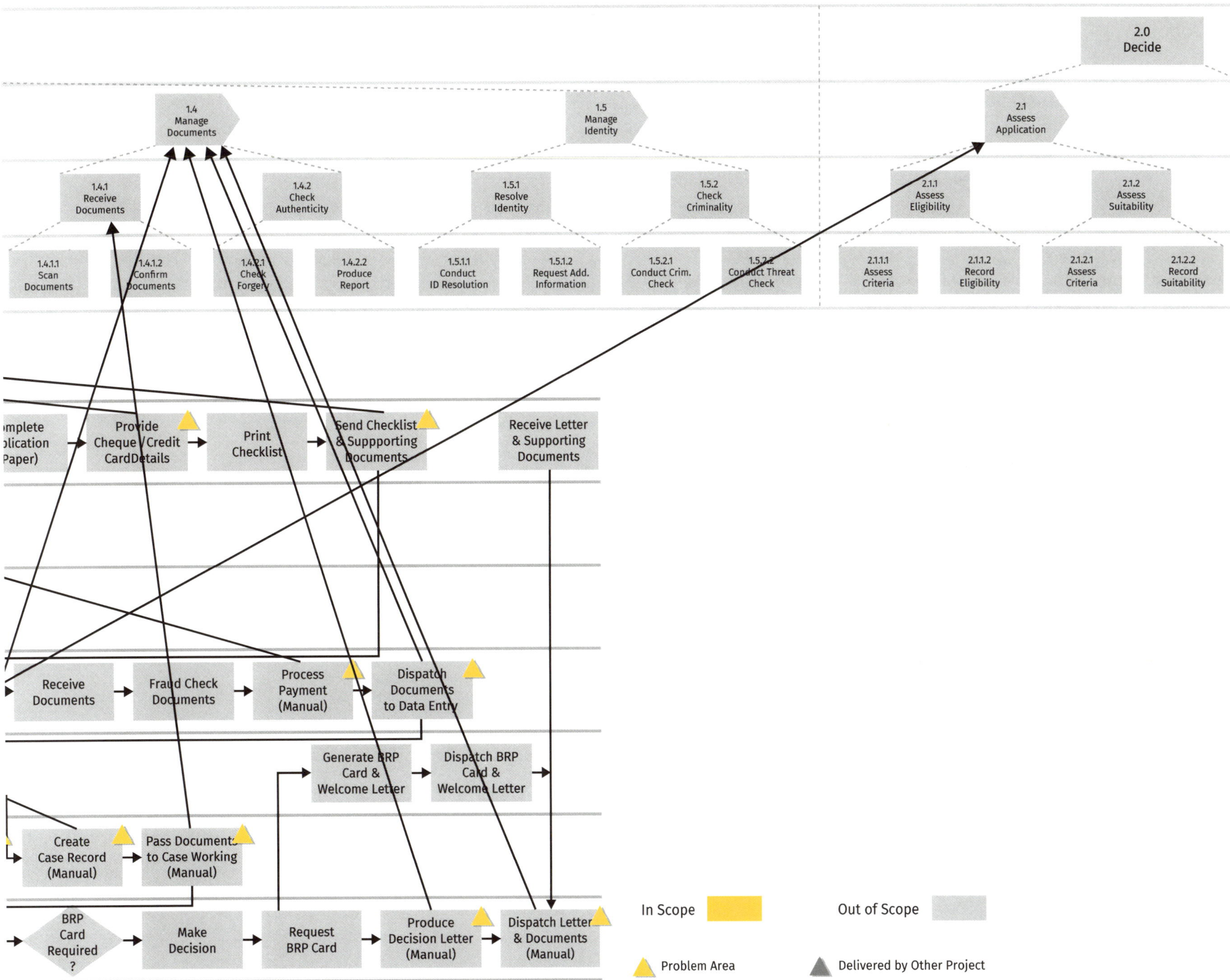
2.0
Decide
1.4
Manage
Documents
1.5
Manage
Identity
2.1
Assess
Application
1.4.1
Receive
Documents
1.4.2
Check
Authenticity
1.5.1
Resolve
Identity
1.5.2
Check
Criminality
2.1.1
Assess
Eligibility
2.1.2
Assess
Suitability
1.4.1.1
Scan
Documents
1.4.1.2
Confirm
Documents
1.4.2.1
Check
Forgery
1.4.2.2
Produce
Report
1.5.1.1
Conduct
ID Resolution
1.5.1.2
Request Add.
Information
1.5.2.1
Conduct Crim.
Check
1.5.2.2
Conduct Threat
Check
2.1.1.1
Assess
Criteria
2.1.1.2
Record
Eligibility
2.1.2.1
Assess
Criteria
2.1.2.2
Record
Suitability
Provide
Cheque/Credit
CardDetails
Print
Checklist
Send Checklist
& Suppporting
Documents
Receive Letter
& Supporting
Documents
Receive
Documents
Fraud Check
Documents
Process
Payment
(Manual)
Dispatch
Documents
to Data Entry
Generate BRP
Card &
Welcome Letter
Dispatch BRP
Card &
Welcome Letter
Create
Case Record
(Manual)
Pass Documents
to Case Working
(Manual)
BRP
Card
Required
?
Make
Decision
Request
BRP Card
Produce
Decision Letter
(Manual)
Dispatch Letter
& Documents
(Manual)
In Scope
Out of Scope
Problem Area
Delivered by Other Project

**Figure 9.15** - Example Process Model Map (To-Be)

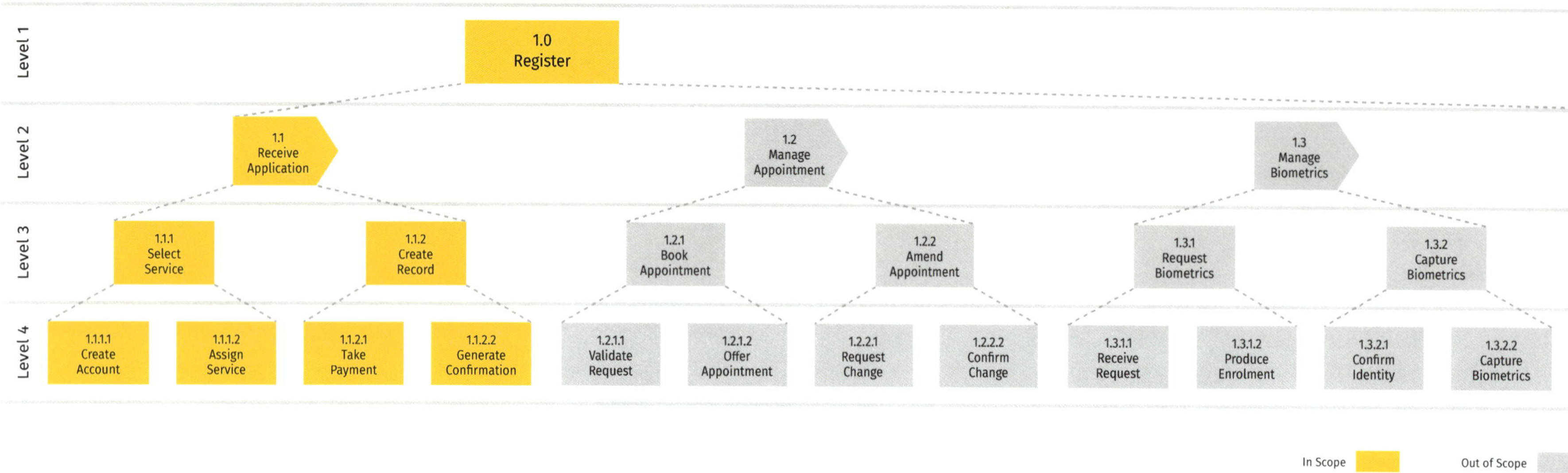


information resulted in a late but necessary change to the scope to the Programme. This then resulted in a formal change (of scope) be taken to the Programme board and agreed.

In terms of changes, this change request impacted the following capability elements:

- **People** – needed to be trained at the internal mailroom to include printing off and picking up the physical accept/reject letter and including that letter when sending the original supporting documentation back to the applicant;
- **Process** – the 'To-Be' business process had to be amended to include the tasks 'generate physical accept/reject letter', and physically 'return Applicant's original supporting documentation' back to the Applicant; and
- **Technology** – the system that was to 'scan the incoming mail' and 'send notifications that the physical supporting documentation had been received by the mailroom', now needed to 'receive accept/reject letter generation requests', including maintenance of the letter template and changes (or a tactical solution quickly be developed and deployed that could handle this, which would be an ever bigger change and impact, requiring the development of a new system!).

This late change request not only required additional time to draft the changes, and understand the impact of the changes, but it took staff away from their existing work, work they had already committed too, in order to help with the change request. This late change, and change itself cost money, and extended the time to delivery, past what was originally planned and budgeted, which all could have been avoided, had there been an enterprise-wide view of all the processes in-scope, validated with all the projects within the Programme highlighting which project is explicitly covering which processes - and not stuck in the detail focused on delivery while missing the big picture.

## Building Block Wrap-up

In this section, we discussed the Process Mapping (To-Be) Building Block. This Building Block identifies and highlights the processes that are in scope the Programme is delivering and implementing changes to, that when used by the Business lead to the realisation of the planned Business Benefits and align the Business to the Business Strategy.

The Building Block is made up of the following three (3) Blueprints:

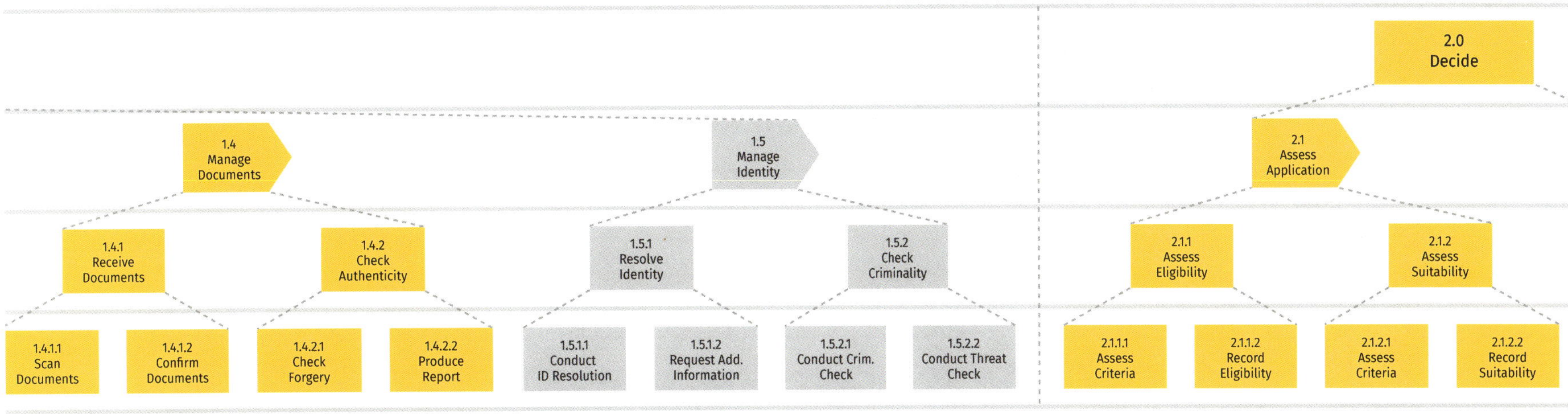


- **Process Map/Process Model Cross-Map** - Cross map between the low-level process map(s) and 'As-Is' Process Model Map, showing which processes are the in-scope processes.

- **Process Model Map (To-Be)** – Updated 'As-Is' Process Model Map showing the in-scope processes on the single enterprise-wide Process Model Map.

- **Process Map/Process Model Matrix** - Matrix showing the relationship between the lower level process maps, and the process model processes.

These Process Mapping Blueprints (like the Capability Mapping Blueprints) help inform and guide conversations across the Programme and Organisation, of 'what processes are earmarked for changes' in an effort to identity any duplications or gaps, and to co-ordinate with other projects and Programmes where necessary (or where it makes sense to do so).

Both the 'To-Be' Process Model Map, and 'To-Be' Capability Map Blueprints have different purposes, and different audiences:

- **Process Model Maps** are more suitable for delivery/implementation focused stakeholders (i.e. Product Owners, Project team members) with their operation/implementation concerns, whereas

- **Capability Maps** are more suited for strategic/planning & design focused stakeholders (i.e. Programme Managers, Senior Executives, Architects) with their strategic concerns.

## Next Steps

Once the Process Mapping (To-Be) Building Block has been completed (which includes aligning, reconciliation and coordinating any changes as a result of any duplication or gaps identified here), the next step in the **Design Process** is to identify what the actual operational/physical changes mean to the Organisation and to understand the impact to the Business and then determine the best set of *solution and implementation options* needed to achieve the intended outcomes, while minimising the impact to the Business.

These concerns are discussed in the Impact Mapping Building Block in the following section.

| | | Process Model Map (Process) | Receive Registration | Select Service Offering | Create Account | Assign Service | Create Record | Take Payment | Generate Confirmation | Manage Appointment | Book Appointment | Validate Request | Offer Appointment | Amend Appointment | Request Change | Confirm Change | Manage Biometrics | Request Biometrics | Receive Request | Produce Enrolment Letter | Capture Biometrics | Confirm Identity |
|---|---|---|---|---|---|---|---|---|---|---|---|---|---|---|---|---|---|---|---|---|---|---|
| # | As-Is Process Step | Ref | 1.1 | 1.1.1 | 1.1.1.1 | 1.1.1.2 | 1.1.2 | 1.1.2.1 | 1.1.2.2 | 1.2 | 1.2.1 | 1.2.1.1 | 1.2.1.2 | 1.2.2 | 1.2.2.1 | 1.2.2.2 | 1.3 | 1.3.1 | 1.3.1.1 | 1.3.1.2 | 1.3.2 | 1.3.2.1 |
| 1 | Print Application | | ■ | ■ | ■ | | ■ | | ■ | ▩ | ▩ | ▩ | ▩ | ▩ | ▩ | ▩ | ▩ | ▩ | ▩ | ▩ | ▩ | ▩ |
| 2 | Calculate & Pay | | | | | | | | | ▩ | ▩ | ▩ | ▩ | ▩ | ▩ | ▩ | ▩ | ▩ | ▩ | ▩ | ▩ | ▩ |
| 3 | Complete App'n | | | | | | | | | ▩ | ▩ | ▩ | ▩ | ▩ | ▩ | ▩ | ▩ | ▩ | ▩ | ▩ | ▩ | ▩ |
| 4 | Provide Pay. Detail | | | | | | | | | ▩ | ▩ | ▩ | ▩ | ▩ | ▩ | ▩ | ▩ | ▩ | ▩ | ▩ | ▩ | ▩ |
| 5 | Print Checklist | | | | | | | | | ▩ | ▩ | ▩ | ▩ | ▩ | ▩ | ▩ | ▩ | ▩ | ▩ | ▩ | ▩ | ▩ |
| 6 | Send Docs | | | | | | | | | ▩ | ▩ | ▩ | ▩ | ▩ | ▩ | ▩ | ▩ | ▩ | ▩ | ▩ | ▩ | ▩ |
| 7 | Receive Docs | | | | | | | | | ▩ | ▩ | ▩ | ▩ | ▩ | ▩ | ▩ | ▩ | ▩ | ▩ | ▩ | ▩ | ▩ |
| 8 | Fraud Check Docs | | | | | | | | | ▩ | ▩ | ▩ | ▩ | ▩ | ▩ | ▩ | ▩ | ▩ | ▩ | ▩ | ▩ | ▩ |
| 9 | Process Payment | | | | | | | ■ | | ▩ | ▩ | ▩ | ▩ | ▩ | ▩ | ▩ | ▩ | ▩ | ▩ | ▩ | ▩ | ▩ |
| 10 | Dispatch Docs | | | | | | | | | ▩ | ▩ | ▩ | ▩ | ▩ | ▩ | ▩ | ▩ | ▩ | ▩ | ▩ | ▩ | ▩ |
| 11 | Send BEL | | | ■ | | | | | | ▩ | ▩ | ▩ | ▩ | ▩ | ▩ | ▩ | ▩ | ▩ | ▩ | ▩ | ▩ | ▩ |
| 12 | Enrol Biometrics | | | | | | | | | ▩ | ▩ | ▩ | ▩ | ▩ | ▩ | ▩ | ▩ | ▩ | ▩ | ▩ | ▩ | ▩ |
| 13 | Biometrics Rec'd | | | | | | | | | ▩ | ▩ | ▩ | ▩ | ▩ | ▩ | ▩ | ▩ | ▩ | ▩ | ▩ | ▩ | ▩ |
| 14 | Gen. & Send R'der | | | | | | | | | ▩ | ▩ | ▩ | ▩ | ▩ | ▩ | ▩ | ▩ | ▩ | ▩ | ▩ | ▩ | ▩ |
| 15 | Create Case Rcord | | | | | ■ | | | | ▩ | ▩ | ▩ | ▩ | ▩ | ▩ | ▩ | ▩ | ▩ | ▩ | ▩ | ▩ | ▩ |
| 16 | Pass Docs: CW | | | | | | | | | ▩ | ▩ | ▩ | ▩ | ▩ | ▩ | ▩ | ▩ | ▩ | ▩ | ▩ | ▩ | ▩ |

Figure 9.16 - Example Process Map/Process Model Matrix

| 1.3.2.2 Capture Biometrics | 1.4 Manage Documents | 1.4.1 Receive Documents | 1.4.1.1 Scan Documents | 1.4.1.2 Confirm Documents | 1.4.2 Check Authenticity | 1.4.2.1 Check Forgery | 1.4.2.2 Produce Report | 1.5 Manage Identity | 1.5.1 Resolve Identity | 1.5.1.1 Conduct ID Resolution | 1.5.1.2 Request Additional | 2.1 Assess Application | 2.1.1 Assess Eligibility | 2.1.1.1 Assess Criteria | 2.1.1.2 Record Eligibility | 2.1.2 Assess Suitability | 2.1.2.1 Assess Criteria | 2.1.2.2 Record Suitability |
|---|---|---|---|---|---|---|---|---|---|---|---|---|---|---|---|---|---|---|
| Out | | | | | | | | Out | Out | Out | Out | | | | | | | |
| Out | | | | | | | | Out | Out | Out | Out | | | | | | | |
| Out | | | | | | | | Out | Out | Out | Out | | | | | | | |
| Out | | | | | | | | Out | Out | Out | Out | | | | | | | |
| Out | | | | | | | | Out | Out | Out | Out | | | | | | | |
| Out | In | | | | | | | Out | Out | Out | Out | | | | | | | |
| Out | | | | | | | | Out | Out | Out | Out | | | | | | | |
| Out | | | | | | | | Out | Out | Out | Out | | | | | | | |
| Out | | | | | | | | Out | Out | Out | Out | | | | | | | |
| Out | In | | | | | | | Out | Out | Out | Out | | | | | | | |
| Out | | | | | | | | Out | Out | Out | Out | | | | | | | |
| Out | | | | | | | | Out | Out | Out | Out | | | | | | | |
| Out | | | | | | | | Out | Out | Out | Out | | | | | | | |
| Out | In | | | | | | | Out | Out | Out | Out | | | | | | | |
| Out | | | | | | | | Out | Out | Out | Out | | | | | | | |
| Out | | In | | | | | | Out | Out | Out | Out | | | | | | | |

In Scope

Out of Scope

# 5.3 Impact Mapping

## Introduction

Impact Mapping is the Building Block that assesses the impact of change associated with delivering the Business Changes and Enablers that directly support the realisation of the Business' planned Benefits, and align the Business to the Business Strategy.

The purpose of this Building Block is to:

- **Establish a common understanding of the impact of change on the Current Operating Model**, in terms of its capabilities (people, process and technology); and
- **Use these insights to help align and coordinate change activities within the Programme, and across the Organisation** to make better design and implementation decisions.

Impact Mapping is primarily a **risk managemen**t and **prioritisation technique,** as it is used to:

- **Visualise the degree of change** across the Organisation and remove any assumptions or ambiguity which areas are subject to the highest degree of change, and
- **Help prioritise the order (and areas) where change should happen**, in order of strategic importance.

By visualising the scale and scope of change, Impact Mapping aims to address two (2) Change Management concerns:

1. **People are intrinsically adverse to change**, so to increase the chances of success, do only one major change at a time (i.e. don't impose change everywhere, all at once), and
2. **People suffer 'change fatigue'** (caused by too much change without prioritisation), use these insights to prioritise the areas of change that can handle it, that offer the best return on investment and time, so that those affected by the change will feel as though it was worth it.

The Impact Mapping Building Block produces two main outcomes, or perspectives – the *Capability Impact Model* (Capability Model Heat Map), and the *Process Impact Model* (Process Model Heat Map), both suitable for conversations with different stakeholder groups:

- **Capability Model Heat Map (and matrix)** – this shows the impact of changes on the enterprise-wide Capability Model, as a *'big picture'* view of change across the Organisation - suitable for Programme/Executive level Stakeholders at the strategic level to show the scale of change and alignment with the strategy, and
- **Process Model Heat Map (and matrix)** – shows the impact of these changes on the enterprise-wide Process Model, which also shows a *'big picture'* view of change across the Organisation, but at the process level – suitable for Project/Operations level Stakeholders who will be implementing the changes, used to show the degree of change and to ask the question – '*can we actually do it* (i.e. handle that much change)?'

The benefit of Impact Mapping is by knowing where the biggest area of change is, across the whole enterprise, considering all the pieces of work that are going on in (and across) the Organisation, is the ability to use that knowledge to prioritise the next steps and future work, in the most *risk effective way.*

As an example, Figure 9.17 (below) shows Impact Mapping (at the process level) when the 'left hand' was not talking to the 'right hand', or where assumptions were not confirmed.

The previous example in Figure 9.14 with 'To-Be' Process Mapping highlighting the 'in scope' processes on the enterprise-wise Process Model, showed the area in question was previously *thought* as 'out of scope' was in fact actually 'in scope'. Now, on closer inspection looking at the diagram below, the Process Model Heat Map has highlighted the scale of change was actually bigger than originally thought i.e. it was a 'New Item' change, and not a 'Change to an Existing Item', which not only brings in a whole lot of new considerations (i.e. timing of turning off redundant systems and processes / turning on new systems and processes, training, handover etc.), but shows the cumulative effect now of all that change on specific (and adjacent) areas which now needs to be taken into account, and asked the question – *'what is possible?'*.

## Inputs

The inputs used to complete this Building Block are shown in the table below.

## Output(s)

The following table provides the Blueprints (outputs) produced in completing this step

**Impact Mapping Building Block Inputs**

**Table 9.6**

| Ref | Blueprint | Use |
|---|---|---|
| 5.1.2 | Capability Maps (To-Be) | Provides enterprise-wide view of the Organisation's capabilities, highlighting the capabilities are in-scope for changes. |
| 5.2.2 | Process Model Map (To-Be) | Provides the enterprise-wide view of which processes are impacted by the Enablers and Business Changes from the benefits-dependencies map, aligned with changes within and across the Programme (and other Programmes). |
| N/A | Existing Process Maps | Includes 'As-Is' (and updated 'To-Be') Process Map drawn up with or by the Business Analyst. |

**Impact Mapping (Output) Blueprints**

**Table 9.7**

| Ref | Blueprint | Description | Example |
|---|---|---|---|
| 5.3.1 | Process Model Heat Map | 'To-Be' Process Model Map, highlighting the degree of change(s). | See below |
| 5.3.2 | Process Model Heat Map Table | Tabular format of results of Process Model Heat Map. | See below |

Example:

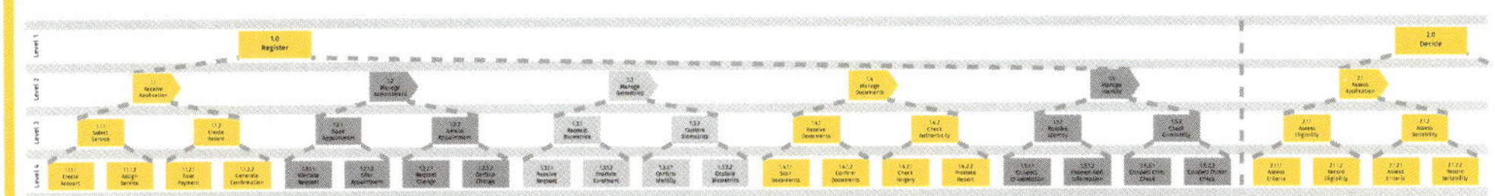

| Level 1 | Level 2 | Level 3 | | Level 4 | | | | Before | After | Impact | Rating |
|---|---|---|---|---|---|---|---|---|---|---|---|
| Register | Manage Registration | Select Service | Create Record | Create Account | Assign Service | Take Payment | Generate Confirm. | Manage customer registration for product or service (via paper application & manual payment by Staff) | Apply online for Visa product or service. | • People: staff to be training in new process; • Process: new (registration, payment, scanning), and • Technology: new (application, payment, scanning) to be implemented | |
| | Manage Appointment | Book Appointment | Amend Appointment | Validate Request | Offer Appointment | Request Change | Confirm Change | Receive and allocate booking requests from Customer | Receive and allocate booking requests from Customer (using replacement system). | • People: internal staff to be trained in new system; • Process: no change (system change only, no impact to process), and • Technology: new booking system to be implemented. | |
| | Manage Biometrics | Request Biometrics | Capture Biometrics | Receive Biometrics Request | Produce Enrolment Letter | Capture Biometrics | Confirm Identity | Request and capture biometric details for the customer. | Request and capture biometric details for the customers (using existing people, process & systems) but integrated into new registration process & case working system. | People: no change (system change only, no impact to customer); • Process: no change (system change only, no impact to process), and • Technology: existing biometric system to be integrated into new online application system & case working system. | |
| | Manage Documents | Receive Documents | Scan Documents | Confirm Documents | Check Authenticity | Check Forgery | Produce Report | Receive, confirm, scan, store and retrieve documents from Customer (by external staff). | Receive, confirm, scan, store and retrieve documents from Customer (from internal staff). | • People: Internal staff to be trained; • Process: new end to end scanning process (including forgery check), and • Technology: new scanning system to be implemented. | |
| | Manage Identity | Resolve Identity | Conduct ID Res. | Request Add. Info | Check Criminality | Conduct Crim. Check | Conduct Threat Check | Verify Customer identity (using legacy systems). | Verify Customer identity (using legacy replacement identity system). | • People: Internal staff to be trained on new system; • Process: no change (system change only, no impact to process), and • Technology: new identity system to be implemented. | |
| Decide | Assess Application | Assess Eligibility | Assess Suitability | Assess Criteria | Record Eligibility | Assess Criteria | Record Suitability | Allocate work (manually) to appropriately trained staff to assess application for suitability and eligibility. | Allocate work (automatically) to appropriately trained staff to assess suitability and eligibility (using legacy replacement system). | • People: internal staff to be trained in new process & system; • Process: new process to allocate applications (cases) to appropriately trained staff, and • Technology: new case working system to be implemented. | |

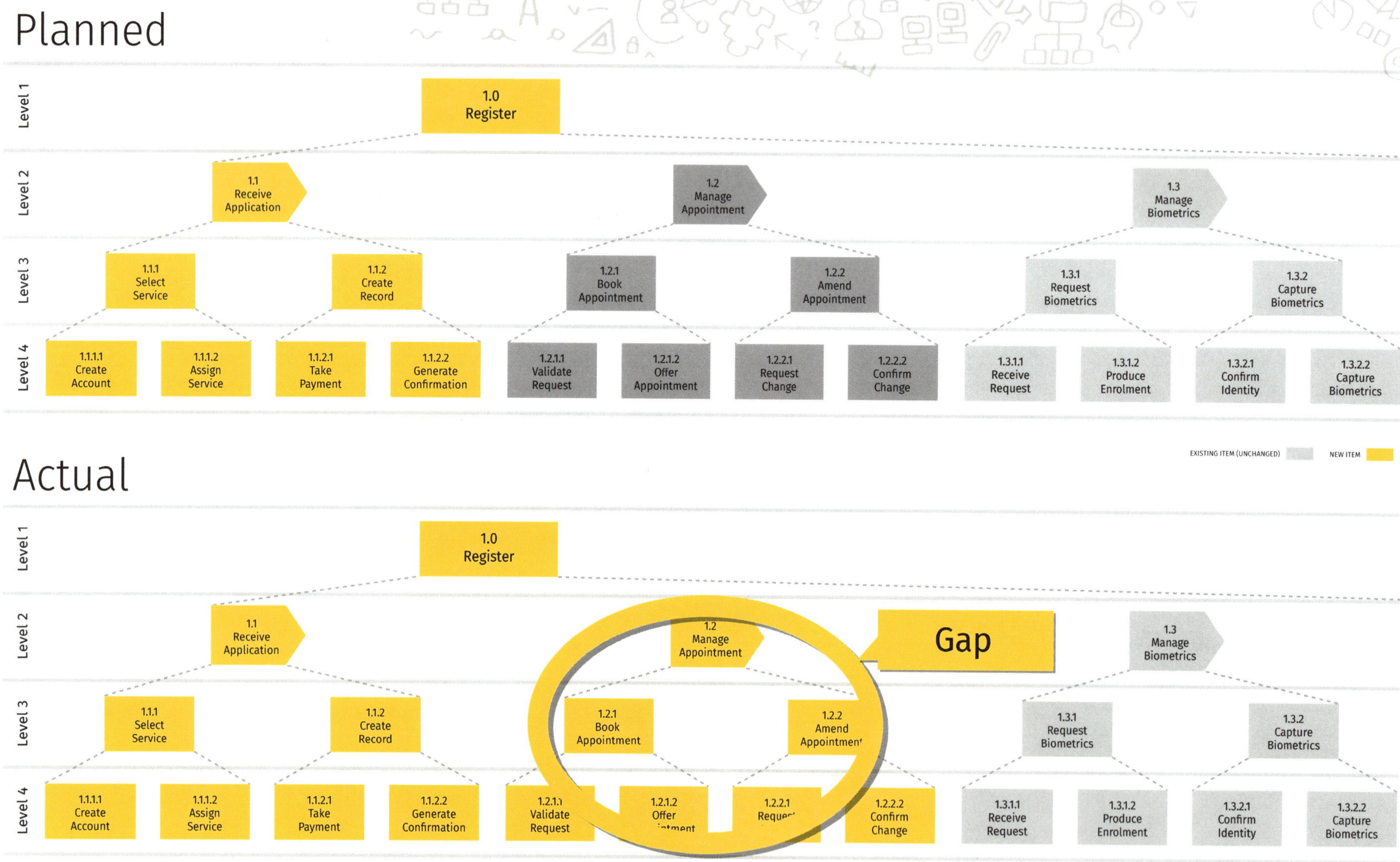


**Figure 9.17** - 'Planned' vs 'Actual' Process Model Heat Map

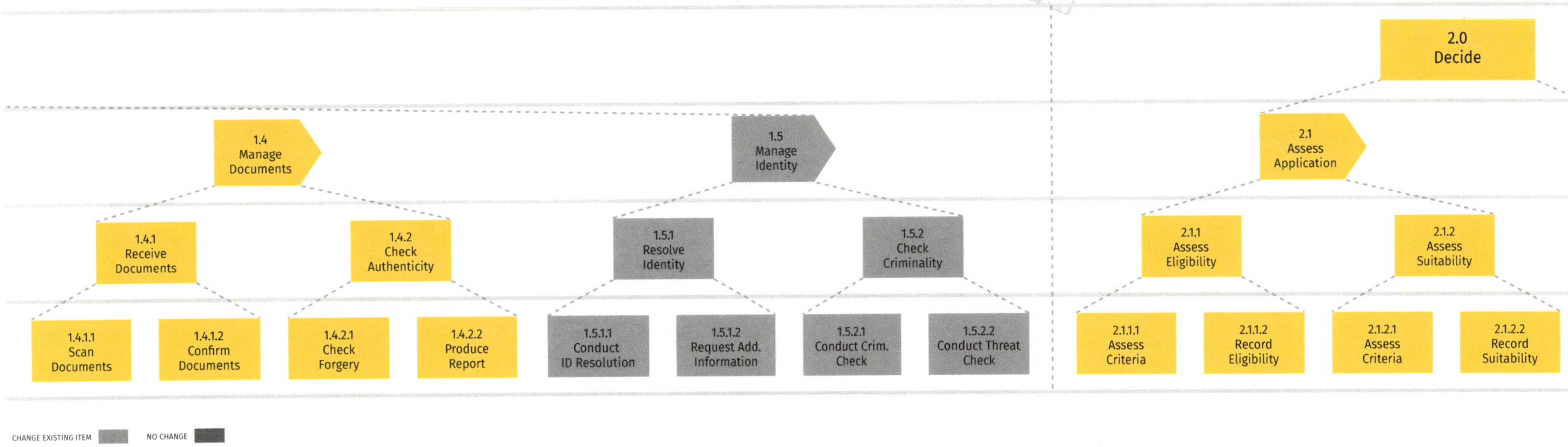
2.0 Decide
1.4 Manage Documents
1.5 Manage Identity
2.1 Assess Application
1.4.1 Receive Documents
1.4.2 Check Authenticity
1.5.1 Resolve Identity
1.5.2 Check Criminality
2.1.1 Assess Eligibility
2.1.2 Assess Suitability
1.4.1.1 Scan Documents
1.4.1.2 Confirm Documents
1.4.2.1 Check Forgery
1.4.2.2 Produce Report
1.5.1.1 Conduct ID Resolution
1.5.1.2 Request Add. Information
1.5.2.1 Conduct Crim. Check
1.5.2.2 Conduct Threat Check
2.1.1.1 Assess Criteria
2.1.1.2 Record Eligibility
2.1.2.1 Assess Criteria
2.1.2.2 Record Suitability
CHANGE EXISTING ITEM
NO CHANGE

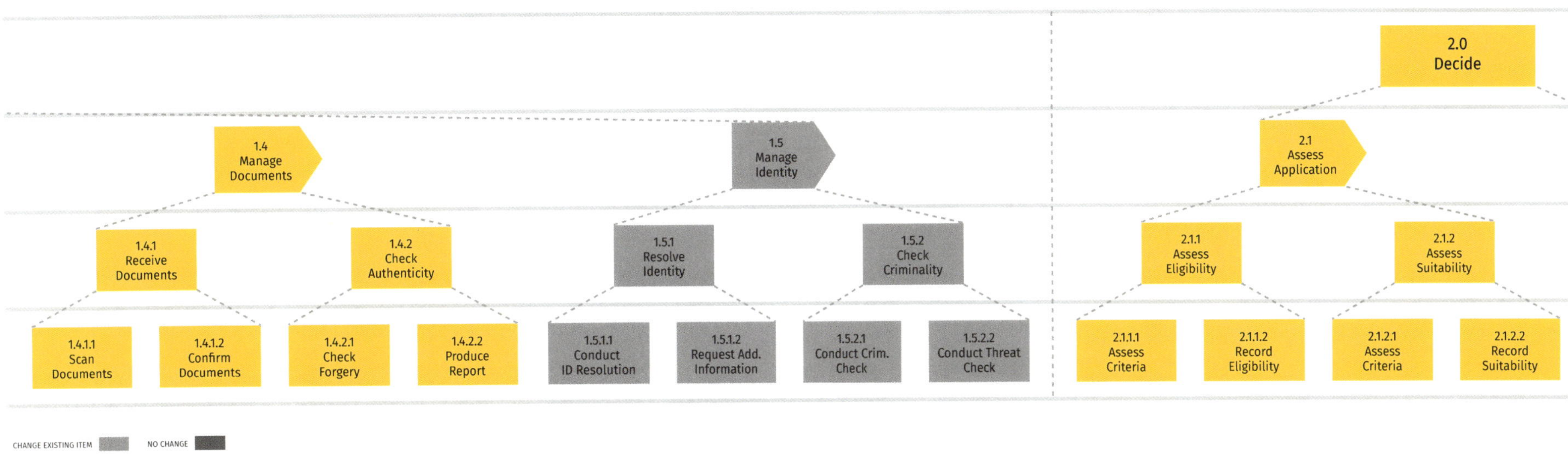
2.0 Decide
1.4 Manage Documents
1.5 Manage Identity
2.1 Assess Application
1.4.1 Receive Documents
1.4.2 Check Authenticity
1.5.1 Resolve Identity
1.5.2 Check Criminality
2.1.1 Assess Eligibility
2.1.2 Assess Suitability
1.4.1.1 Scan Documents
1.4.1.2 Confirm Documents
1.4.2.1 Check Forgery
1.4.2.2 Produce Report
1.5.1.1 Conduct ID Resolution
1.5.1.2 Request Add. Information
1.5.2.1 Conduct Crim. Check
1.5.2.2 Conduct Threat Check
2.1.1.1 Assess Criteria
2.1.1.2 Record Eligibility
2.1.2.1 Assess Criteria
2.1.2.2 Record Suitability
CHANGE EXISTING ITEM
NO CHANGE

Table 9.7

| Ref | Blueprint | Description | Example |
|---|---|---|---|
| 5.3.3 | Capability Model Heat Map | 'To-Be' Capability Model Map, highlighting the degree of change(s). | |

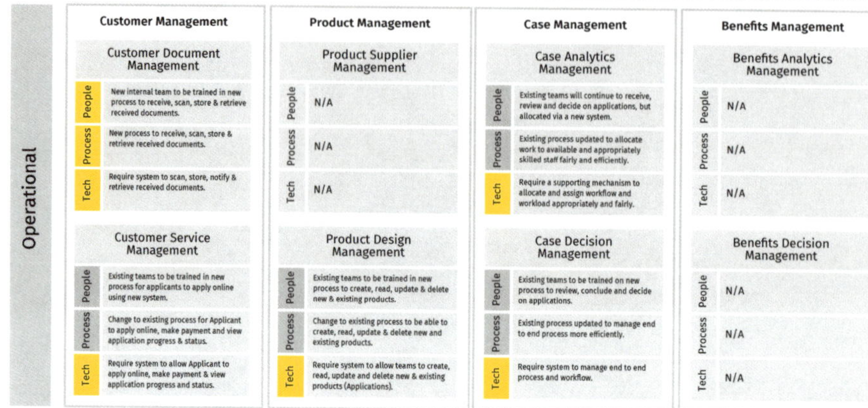


| Ref | Blueprint | Description | Example |
|---|---|---|---|
| 5.3.4 | Capability Model Heat Map Table | Tabular format of results of Capability Model Heat Map | |

| Level 1 | Level 2 | Level 3 | Before | After | Impact | Rating |
|---|---|---|---|---|---|---|
| Strategic | Strategic Management | Business Strategy Management | No Change | No Change | N/A | |
| | | Business Plan Management | No Change | No Change | N/A | |
| | Risk Management | Risk Management Strategy | Ability to define a the risk managem manage and mitigate the risks facing the Organisation. | Communicate Operational risks to Programme and business so that applications are assessed, prioritised and processed based on risk. | • People: existing teams to develop and communicate risk strategy to operational staff to implement; • Process: no change to existing process, and • Tech: no change to existing system. | |
| | | Risk Plan Management | No Change | No Change | N/A | |
| | Marketing Management | Marketing Strategy Management | No Change | No Change | N/A | |
| | | Marketing Plan Management | No Change | No Change | N/A | |
| Operational | Customer Management | Customer Document Management | Ability to receive, store & retrieve c documents (by external supplier). | Ability to receive, scan, digitalise, store & retrieve customer documents (by internal department). | • People: internal (mailroom) staff to be trained in new process; • Process: new (scanning) process to be implemented, and • Tech: new (scanning) system to be implemented to support capability. | |
| | | Customer Service Management | Ability to define and manage customer needs and service standards in a consistent and coordinated manner. | Ability to define and manage customer needs and service standards in a consistent, coordinated manner with minimum human or manual intervention. | • People: Internal (Case Worker) staff to be trained on new registration process; • Process: new registration process to be implemented, and • Tech: new website to allow Applicant to complete and pay for application online. | |
| | Product Management | Product Supplier Management | No Change | No Change | N/A | |
| | | Product Design Management | Ability to create, update, distribute and delete (where necessary) new & existing products & services. | Ability to create, update, distribute and delete (where necessary) new & existing products & services with minimum human or manual intervention. | • People: existing teams to be trained in new process; • Process: existing process to be updated to allocate work to available and appropriately skilled staff fairly, efficiently and electronically, and • Tech: new mechanism to allocate and assign workflow and workload appropriately and fairly. | |
| | Case Management | Case Analytics Management | Ability to assess risk and workload of team and allocate work (applications for processing) to team members. | Ability to assess risk and workload of team and allocate work (applications for processing) using a risk-based approach. | • People: existing teams to be trained in new process; • Process: existing process to be updated to allocate work to available and appropriately skilled staff fairly and efficiently, and • Tech: new system to manage end to end process and workflow. | |
| | | Case Decision Management | Ability to manage the end to end process of assessing & deciding on an application for a product or service. | Ability to manage the end to end process of assessing & deciding on an application for a product or service using risk based approach. | • People: existing teams to be trained in new process to review, conclude and decide on applications; • Process: existing process to be updated to allocate & manage end to end process more efficiently, and • Tech: new system to manage end to end risk based process and workflow. | |
| Supporting | Finance Management | Fee Management | Ability to take fee payment for products and services from Customers and allocate to appropriate debit/credit accounts. | Ability to take fee payments for products and services from Customer (online) and allocate to appropriate debit/credit accounts. | • People: existing teams to be trained in new process for Customers to pay online; • Process: existing process to be updated for Customer to pay online, and • Tech: new payment mechanism to capture and process Customer payment at the time of submitting the application online. | |
| | | Asset Management | No Change | No Change | N/A | |

## Steps

The steps to complete the above Blueprints (Outputs) are discussed in the section below:

### 5.2.1 Process Map Heat Map

**1. Develop the Process Map Heat Map**

Using the inputs from Table 9.6 above, namely the Process Model (To-Be) Map, and working with the Business Analyst, Business Change and Product Owner, map the impact rating showing the degree of change for the in-scope processes, as shown in *Figure 9.18* below.

**The degree/impact of change is based on the following scale:**

- **White – Use an existing unchanged item (i.e. use in the future, as it is today).**
- **Grey – Change an existing item (i.e. this is an existing item, but is changed, enhanced or substituted for an alternative performing the same role).**
- **Yellow – New item required (i.e. this item doesn't currently exist within the Organisation today and needs to be created).**
- **Black – No changes (i.e. not involved in the process today and is out of scope for change).**

### 5.3.2 Process Map Heat Map Table

**2. Record the Process Map Heat Map** details for traceability in the Process Model Heat Map Table, as shown in *Figure 9.19* below.

***Figure 9.18*** **and** ***Figure 9.19*** **above are only a sample of a full Process Model Heat Map and Table. In practice, these Blueprints would be expected to cover *all* the processes from the Process Model Map, even if marked *out of scope.***

### 5.3.3 Capability Model Heat Map

**3. Develop the Capability Model Heat Map**

With the completed Process Model Heat Map, and the 'To-Be' Capability Model Map, map the impact rating onto the Capability Model Heat Map, highlighting the rating and impact summary into each of the people, process and technology elements of the impacted capabilities, as shown in the example in *Figure 9.20* below.

Figure 9.18 - Process Model Heat Map

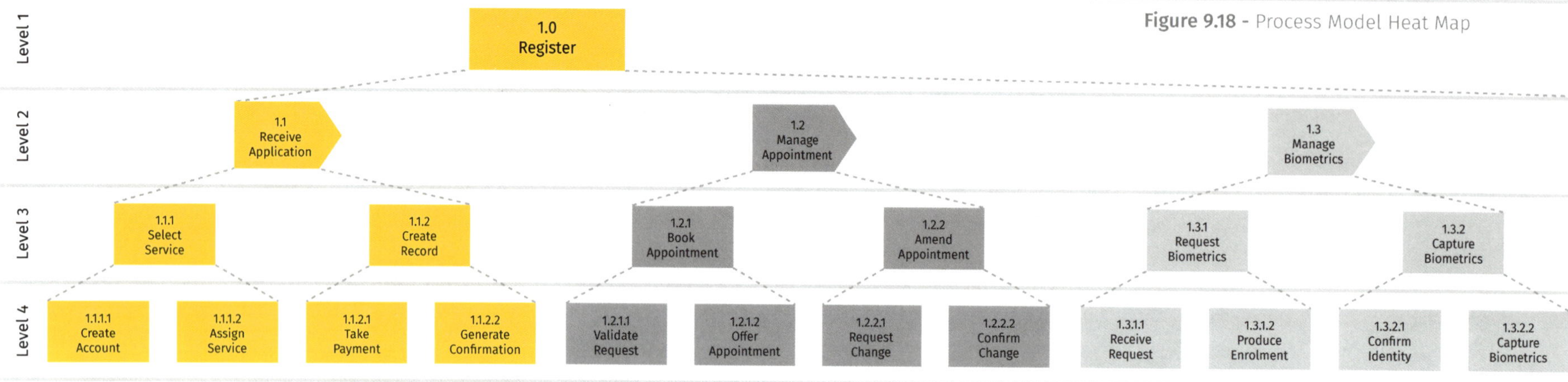


| Level 1 | Level 2 | Level 3 | | Level 4 | | | | Before | After | Impact | Rating |
|---|---|---|---|---|---|---|---|---|---|---|---|
| Register | Manage Registration | Select Service | Create Record | Create Account | Assign Service | Take Payment | Generate Confirm. | Manage customer registration for product or service (via paper application & manual payment by Staff) | Apply online for Visa product or service. | • People: staff to be training in new process;<br>• Process: new (registration, payment, scanning), and<br>• Technology: new (application, payment, scanning) to be implemented | |
| | Manage Appointment | Book Appointment | Amend Appointment | Validate Request | Offer Appointment | Request Change | Confirm Change | Receive and allocate booking requests from Customer | Receive and allocate booking requests from Customer (using replacement system). | • People: internal staff to be trained in new system;<br>• Process: no change (system change only, no impact to process), and<br>• Technology: new booking system to be implemented. | |
| | Manage Biometrics | Request Biometrics | Capture Biometrics | Receive Biometrics Request | Produce Enrolment Letter | Capture Biometrics | Confirm Identity | Request and capture biometric details for the customer. | Request and capture biometric details for the customers (using existing people, process & systems) but integrated into new registration process & case working system. | People: no change (system change only, no impact to customer);<br>• Process: no change (system change only, no impact to process), and<br>• Technology: existing biometric system to be integrated into new online application system & case working system. | |

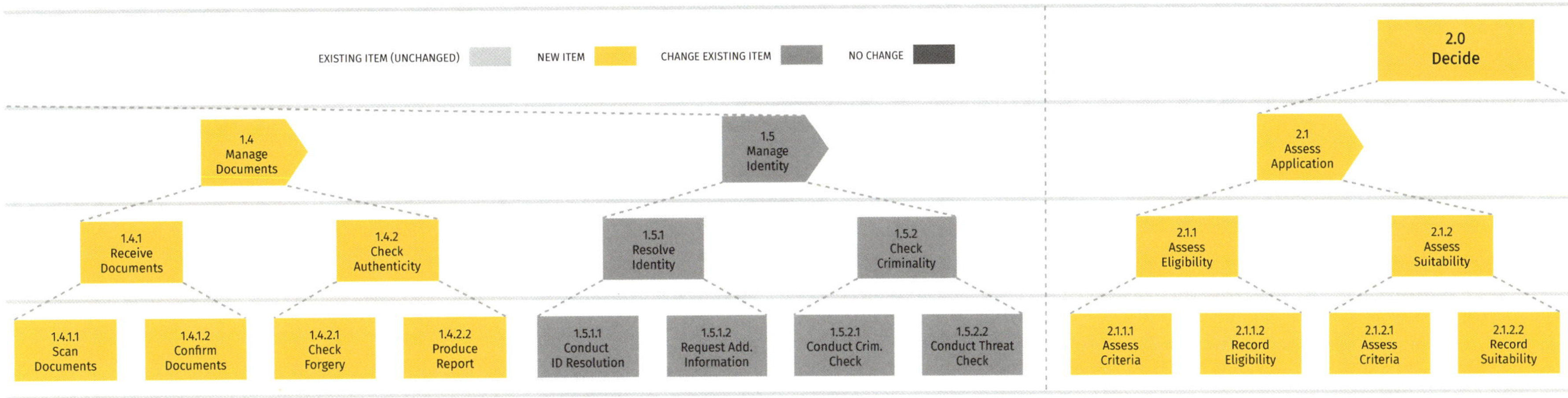


| Level 1 | Level 2 | Level 3 | | Level 4 | | | | Before | After | Impact | Rating |
|---|---|---|---|---|---|---|---|---|---|---|---|
| | Manage Documents | Receive Documents | Scan Documents | Confirm Documents | Check Authenticity | Check Forgery | Produce Report | Receive, confirm, scan, store and retrieve documents from Customer (by external staff). | Receive, confirm, scan, store and retrieve documents from Customer (from internal staff). | • People: Internal staff to be trained; • Process: new end to end scanning process (including forgery check), and • Technology: new scanning system to be implemented. | |
| | Manage Identity | Resolve Identity | Conduct ID Res. | Request Add. Info | Check Criminality | Conduct Crim. Check | Conduct Threat Check | Verify Customer identity (using legacy systems). | Verify Customer identity (using legacy replacement identity system). | • People: Internal staff to be trained on new system; • Process: no change (system change only, no impact to process), and • Technology: new identity system to be implemented. | |
| Decide | Assess Application | Assess Eligibility | Assess Suitability | Assess Criteria | Record Eligibility | Assess Criteria | Record Suitability | Allocate work (manually) to appropriately trained staff to assess application for suitability and eligibility. | Allocate work (automatically) to appropriately trained staff to assess suitability and eligibility (using legacy replacement system). | • People: internal staff to be trained in new process & system; • Process: new process to allocate applications (cases) to appropriately trained staff, and • Technology: new case working system to be implemented. | |

Existing Item    Change Existing    New Item    No Change

**Figure 9.19 -** Process Model Heat Map Table (extract)

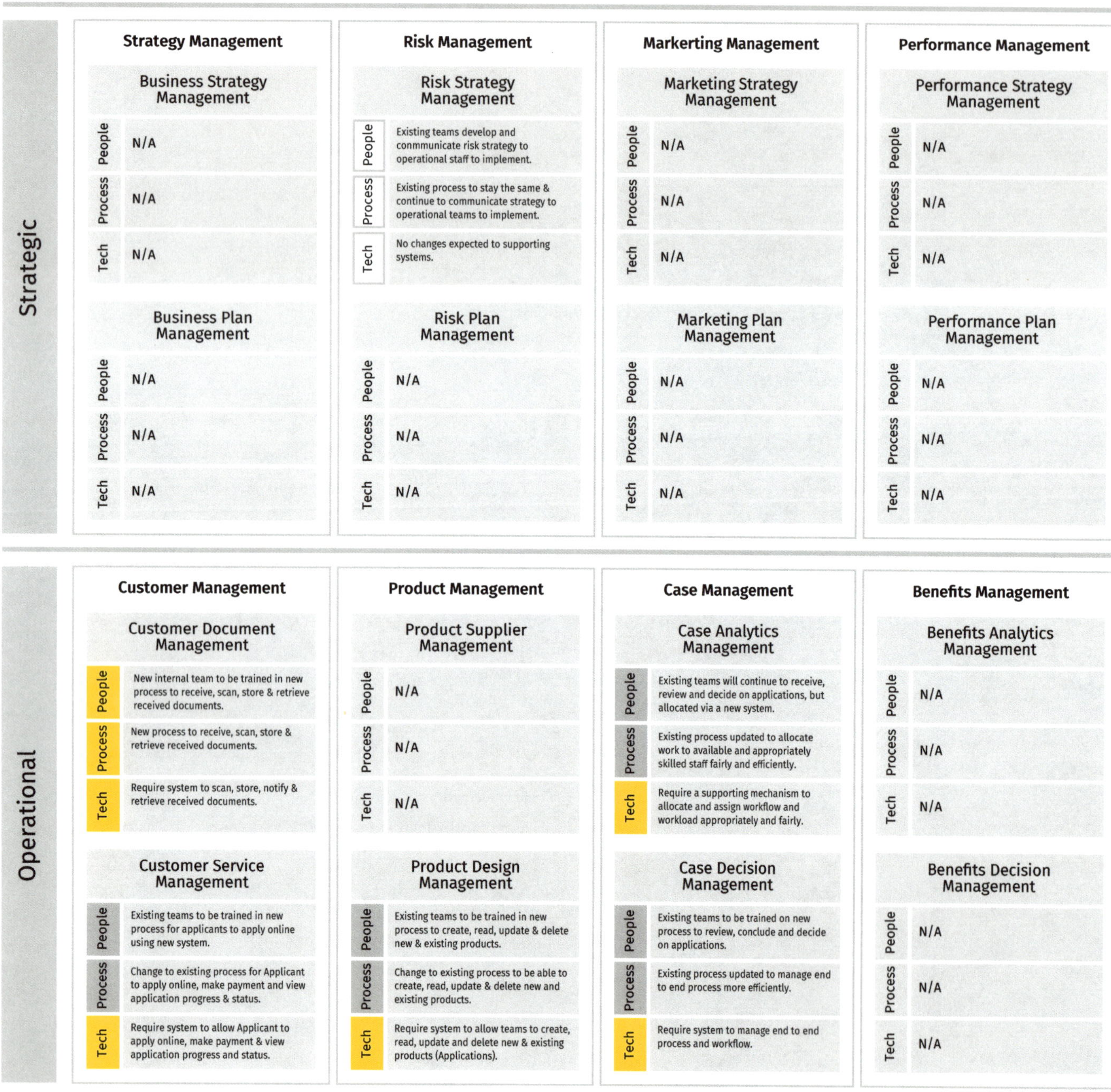


### 5.3.4 Capability Model Heat Map Table

**4. Record the Capability Model Heat Map details** for traceability in the Capability Model Heat Map Table, as shown in *Figure 9.21* below.

**5. Iteratively socialise, validate and refine the Blueprint(s)** - including any Risks, Assumptions, Issues and Dependencies (RAID) addressed or raised as part of completing this step.

**6. Package and publish the Blueprint(s)** – in line with your agreed sprint/release cycle, established back in *Step 2 – Control*, with the *Governance Model*.

**As part of the socialising, validating and refining activities, where these Blueprints raise or highlight duplication, dependencies and/ or gaps, this is the time and place to reconcile and align any differences and update the related and impacted**

**Blueprints to reflect the new alignment, which may also be Blueprints that aren't a part of this Building Block. However, getting the Blueprints agreed and published in line with the Programme (and project) sprint and release cycle is *not* the goal of this exercise, getting the Blueprints agreed and published – reflecting the agreed alignment with the rest of the Programme (and Organisation) is.**

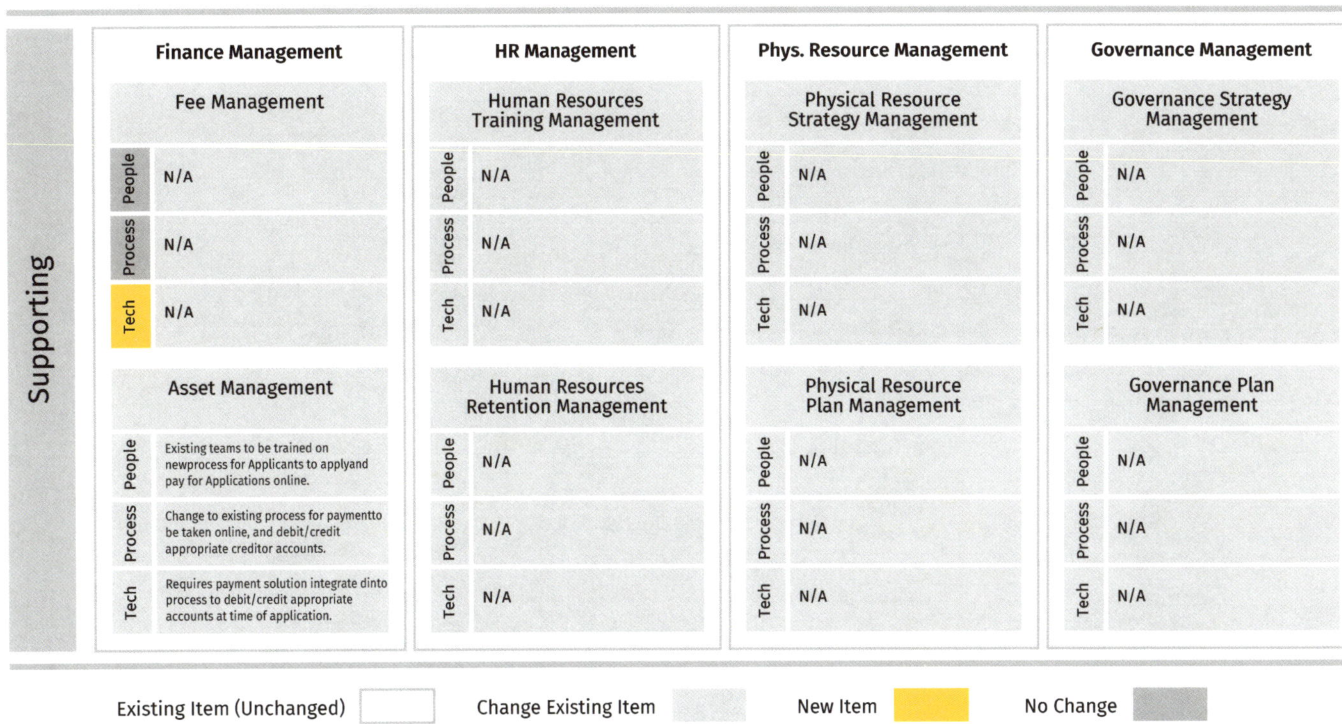


**Figure 9.20 -** Capability Model Heat Map

## Risks and Mitigations

The risks associated with Impact Mapping are the confusion with the value they bring, and comparison with a similar impact assessment – the *'Change Impact Assessment* (CIA)' that is usually (if you are lucky) lead by the Business Change Manager, that results in Impact Mapping not *actually* being done, or there is resistance is supporting it being done.

The CIA and Impact Mapping are *similar* in that they provide a view of the 'scale of change' across the Organisation. Where they *differ* is in the 'level of perspective' they look at, and the 'audience' they appeal too.

Impact Mapping provides the *big-picture* of the impact of change across the Organisation. These views (and Blueprints) are of interest to the Executive level (C-suite), Programme Sponsor(s) and Architects.
Impact Mapping for this group of stakeholders provides (and highlights) how well the Organisation is aligned with its overall strategy and where it is investing its money:

- Into capabilities (and processes) that are strategically aligned, or
- Into capabilities (and processes) that *are* not strategically aligned (i.e. don't support the Organisations vision of the future, and Business Strategy).

| Level 1 | Level 2 | Level 3 | Before | After | Impact | Rating |
|---|---|---|---|---|---|---|
| Strategic | Strategic Management | Business Strategy Management | No Change | No Change | N/A | |
| | | Business Plan Management | No Change | No Change | N/A | |
| | Risk Management | Risk Management Strategy | Ability to define a the risk managem manage and mitigate the risks facing the Organisation. | Communicate Operational risks to Programme and business so that applications are assessed, prioritised and processed based on risk. | • People: existing teams to develop and communicate risk strategy to operational staff to implement;<br>• Process: no change to existing process, and<br>• Tech: no change to existing system. | |
| | | Risk Plan Management | No Change | No Change | N/A | |
| | Marketing Management | Marketing Strategy Management | No Change | No Change | N/A | |
| | | Marketing Plan Management | No Change | No Change | N/A | |
| Operational | Customer Management | Customer Document Management | Ability to receive, store & retrieve cı documents (by external supplier). | Ability to receive, scan, digitalise, store & retrieve customer documents (by internal department). | • People: internal (mailroom) staff to be trained in new process;<br>• Process: new (scanning) process to be implemented, and<br>• Tech: new (scanning) system to be implemented to support capability. | |
| | | Customer Service Management | Ability to define and manage customer needs and service standards in a consistent and coordinated manner. | Ability to define and manage customer needs and service standards in a consistent, coordinated manner with minimum human or manual intervention. | • People: Internal (Case Worker) staff to be trained on new registration process;<br>• Process: new registration process to be implemented, and<br>• Tech: new website to allow Applicant to complete and pay for application online. | |
| | Product Management | Product Supplier Management | No Change | No Change | N/A | |
| | | Product Design Management | Ability to create, update, distribute and delete (where necessary) new & existing products & services. | Ability to create, update, distribute and delete (where necessary) new & existing products & services with minimum human or manual intervention. | • People: existing teams to be trained in new process;<br>• Process: existing process to be updated to allocate work to available and appropriately skilled staff fairly, efficiently and electronically, and<br>• Tech: new mechanism to allocate and assign workflow and workload appropriately and fairly. | |
| | Case Management | Case Analytics Management | Ability to assess risk and workload of team and allocate work (applications for processing) to team members. | Ability to assess risk and workload of team and allocate work (applications for processing) using a risk-based approach. | • People: existing teams to be trained in new process;<br>• Process: existing process to be updated to allocate work to available and appropriately skilled staff fairly and efficiently, and<br>• Tech: new system to manage end to end process and workflow. | |
| | | Case Decision Management | Ability to manage the end to end process of assessing & deciding on an application for a product or service. | Ability to manage the end to end process of assessing & deciding on an application for a product or service using risk based approach. | • People: existing teams to be trained in new process to review, conclude and decide on applications;<br>• Process: existing process to be updated to allocate & manage end to end process more efficiently, and<br>• Tech: new system to manage end to end risk based process and workflow. | |

| Level 1 | Level 2 | Level 3 | Before | After | Impact | Rating |
|---|---|---|---|---|---|---|
| Supporting | Finance Management | Fee Management | Ability to take fee payment for products and services from Customers and allocate to appropriate debit/credit accounts. | Ability to take fee payments for products and services from Customer (online) and allocate to appropriate debit/credit accounts. | • People: existing teams to be trained in new process for Customers to pay online;<br>• Process: existing process to be updated for Customer to pay online, and<br>• Tech: new payment mechanism to capture and process Customer payment at the time of submitting the application online. | |
| | | Asset Management | No Change | No Change | N/A | |
| | HR Management | HR Training Management | No Change | No Change | N/A | |
| | | HR Retention Management | No Change | No Change | N/A | |
| | Physical Resource Management | PR Strategy Management | No Change | No Change | N/A | |
| | | PR Plan Management | No Change | No Change | N/A | |

Existing Item    Change Existing    New Item    No Change

**Figure 9.21-** Capability Model Heat Map Table (extract)

If the strategy was to improve customer experience and satisfaction, and the greatest amount of change (and therefore investment) is taking place or planned to take place within Supporting capabilities (as opposed to Core or Customer facing capabilities), then this would be a cause for concern, which should raise a red flag that the 'actual' implementation of the strategy, is not *aligned* to the 'design' of the strategy, and the changes, timing, and join up across the Programme need to come together (quickly) to address and close the gap between them.

The CIA on the other hand is focused at the *implementation* level where the change is actually felt and carried out to gauge the degree of change, questioning whether the Business is *'change ready'*. Based on the assessment of the Organisations *'change readiness'*, the necessary tools, training and communication needs are then developed and implemented to help the Business through their *'change journey'*.

These outputs of the CIA – the overall assessment, the status of readiness, training, communications etc. are suitable for a different set of stakeholders at the Operational and implementation level, where the change *actually* takes place.

## Building Block Wrap-up

In this section, we discussed the Impact Mapping Building Block.

This Building Block provides the big picture view of where across the Organisation changes occur (i.e. which capabilities, and processes) and the degree of impact of that change, in implementing the Business Changes and Enabler(s) that directly support the realisation of the Business' planned Benefits, thereby aligning the Business to the Business Strategy.

This Building Block is made up of the following four (4) Blueprints:

- **Capability Model Heat Map (and Table)** – showing where across the Organisation changes are expected, and the *degree of change* at the Capability level, used to show Programme/Executive level Stakeholders the *scale of change* at the strategic level, and
- **Process Model Heat Map (and Table)** - showing where across the Organisation changes are expected, and the degree of the change, but at the process level, used to show Project/Operations level Stakeholders who will be implementing the changes, to show the *degree of change* and to ask the question – *can we actually do it (i.e. handle that much change)?*

All the Impact Mapping Blueprints are used to hold and inform conversations within (and across) the Programme and Organisation to align all change activities across the Programme. These alignment conversations are aimed at ensuring (and assuring) that not only are all changes across the Organisation focusing on the right activities, and outcomes (Business Benefits and strategic objectives), but the *'actual'* implementation of the Business Strategy is aligned to the *'design'* of the Business Strategy.

Without these enterprise-wide process and capability views – where the actual changes to the business and Business Architecture take place, there isn't the opportunity or view to ensure that all the *'actual'* change activities across the Programme are delivering to the *'design'* and that there isn't any duplication of effort or unnecessary change debt (business or technical) being inadvertently created.

**Next Steps**

Once Impact Mapping and the degree of change has been agreed (including agreement for any alignment/realignment which needs to happen because of it), the next step in the **Design Process** is to develop a set of solution (and implementation) options to achieve the intended Business Benefits while minimising the disruption the Business.

These concerns are discussed in the Cost-Benefit Mapping Building Block in the following section.

# 5.4 Cost-Benefit Mapping

## Introduction

Cost-Benefit Mapping is the Building Block that proposes a set of solution (and implementation) options for the prioritised Business Changes and Enablers, and cost/benefit analyses providing an assessment of the advantages and disadvantages for each option for the Business to consider.

The objective with this Building Block is to identify and present to the Business the options available (and the costs associated) to implement each option.

The purpose of this Building Block is to give the Business enough information to make a decision about the solution and implementation options available, in order to allow further work to proceed, namely the development and implementation of the physical architecture of the selected option.

Cost-Benefit Mapping and analysis is crucial in supporting the Programme's progression, as well as the 'Go-No-Go' decision – whether its viable to proceed (given the choices available), or not to proceed at all. The decision (and costings) also provides feed back into the Business Case to validate the expected cost/benefit ratio is still within the planned Programme budget and expectations. This feedback loop is shown on the Design Process with the visible feedback loop between 'Step-4 Evaluate and Step-5 Design'.

Based on the outcome of this assessment (and feedback from the Business, namely the Product Owner, key stakeholders and related boards), should the cost/benefits result (determined here as part of this Building Block) not meet expectations, the Benefits can be reviewed again to re-prioritise the Business Changes and Enablers. These can then be fed back through (re-running the Cost-benefit analysis) to generate a different set of options.

The approach to completing this Building Block is to develop a set of implementation options, including the costs and benefits associated with them, and present them to the Business for decision.

In terms of developing the implementation options themselves, which includes the timing, milestones and sequence of events, these options can be developed in a structured interview or via brainstorming and discovery sessions with the Product Owner and other key stakeholders. In these discovery sessions, it is always important to not only focus on the common visible issues and concerns (the symptoms) but also be mindful of the underlying problems and root causes the design should also be trying to address.

Having the Benefits, Business Changes and Enablers defined is one thing, sequencing the implementation of these changes into the Business is another. It involves taking into account factors such as the current business environment including existing contracts with suppliers that are currently in place or outsourced functions that are currently in operation, penalties or incentives to start or break a contract; the current amount of change the business area is currently under and even the current real estate capacity to handle an increase in staff and storage, just to name a few. All these issues (and many more) need to be considered.

To provide you with some context as to why you need to know the current Business environment, let me provide you with an example from another client I assisted. This particular client was also involved in a similar digitalising (Application) Programme to the case study version I have been using within this book. Their Business' objective was to process more applications by removing manual (i.e. human) intervention. The Programme agreed to speed up the process by electronically 'scoring' the application based on pre-defined criteria, to get the Application to the Case Worker as quickly as possible to make a decision (i.e. approve or reject). Although the Case Worker was empowered to 'make the decision', in almost all of the cases (i.e. 99%), the Case Worker would escalate the actual decision to the Supervisor for 'manual override', effectively nullifying the benefits gained from implementing the changes, all because it was later learned - the Case Worker didn't feel their decision would be supported by Management. Had a representative from the Case Team (not just the Case Workers Supervisor) been consulted for input (in a non-threatening manner and environment), this issue could have been identified and addressed well before any design and implementation had taken place.

In terms of costs, they are based on two areas – Capital (i.e. Implementation) costs, and Operational (i.e. running costs). Capital costs are primarily the apportioned project costs, attributable to the costs of implementing the selected Business Change(s) and Enabler(s), while the Operational costs (for our purposes) are based on Full Time Equivalent (FTE) costing. In terms of speed, FTE Costing is a relatively fast measure to calculate, compared with another type of costing known as Activity Based Costing. While the latter can be more accurate (for example looking at costs incurred based on the different activities and tasks that are necessary in completing a process), Activity Based Costing also takes more time to calculate and complete. Even though it's a more thorough alternative, it still has elements of error and assumptions attached to it. Considering this and the fact that both methods have (about) the same amount of estimation to them, I recommend FTE costing for speed, simplicity and getting the assessment and Blueprints in front of the Business sooner to make a decision (as opposed to spending vast amounts of time calculating and attributing costs using Activity Based Costing).

The intention with the Cost/Benefit Assessment is to get an order of magnitude for each option, and make a comparison between the different solution options, but based on the same variables. The assumption (for the illustration, and Case Study examples) is that no new building or real estate, machinery or equipment was purchased or leased as part of any option. If there was such a situation, in practise the share of the capital costs would then also need to be accounted for and included in the costings. However, in the example that follows (again, used for illustration purposes only) any share of capital costs has been intentionally excluded from the assessment.

In terms of Benefits, benefits were already identified (and quantified) as part of the Benefits Model completed earlier. The tricky part with Benefits is when the Benefit Type was non-financial, the cost/benefit assessment becomes subjective (due to the non-financial benefits being extremely difficult to quantify).

## Inputs

The inputs used to complete this Building Block are shown in the table below.

**Capability Mapping (To-Be) Building Block Inputs**

Table 9.8

| Ref | Blueprint | Use |
|---|---|---|
| 4.1.1 | Benefits Profile | Provides the list and description (and valuation) of the Benefits the Solution Options are delivering changes to the Business, that through their use will realise the intended Benefits. |
| 4.3.1 | Prioritised Changes Map | Provides the Benefits Dependencies Map showing prioritised weighted ranking of all the Enablers and Business Change(s). |
| 4.3.2 | Prioritised Changes Register | Register of the Benefit Dependencies Map details, including weighted score, priority (ordered score), owner, start and end date, related final benefits and strategic objective. |
| 5.3.2 | Process Model Heat Map Table | Provides the enterprise wide and level view of the scope and scale of change for processes across the Organisation. |
| 5.3.4 | Capability Model Heat Map Table | Provides the enterprise wide and level view of the scope and scale of change for capabilities across the Organisation |
| N/A | Existing Programme Documentation | Namely Business Case, Project and Programme Brief. |

## Output(s)

The following table provides the Blueprints (outputs) produced in completing this step

## Steps

The steps to complete the above Blueprints (Outputs) are as follows

## Cost-Benefit Mapping (Output) Blueprints

**Table 9.9**

| Ref | Blueprint | Description | Example |
|---|---|---|---|
| 5.4.1 | Solution Options | The solution and implementation options (Summary), and high level timeline (High Level Timeline) of transition from Current Operating Model to the Target Operating Model. | |

| | Do Nothing | Out Source | In Source |
|---|---|---|---|
| Option | Maintain existing decommission plans | Accelerate decommission plans & tactical solution | Accelerate decommission plans & manual process |
| Summary | · Online applications via existing system<br>· Outsourcer remains in place to receive and dispatch docs<br>· Use existing legacy system until new Application system available | · Online applications submitted via existing system<br>· Outsourcer remains in place to receive, scan and dispatch documents<br>· All applications case worked on legacy system until new Application system available | · Online applications submitted via existing system<br>· Outsource contract ended<br>· Manual scanning and dispatch in-house<br>· All Applications case worked in legacy system until new Application system available |
| Pros | · Maintains existing plans (lower risk)<br>· No additional staff training<br>· No tactical solution required | Recruitment of new staff not required | Uses existing process (lower implementation risk) |
| Cons | Changes made to legacy system will create technical debt as eventually decommissioned | · Retains current high staff level<br>· Tactical solution will not replace full Out Source current role | · Need to recruit new staff<br>· Short lead time for training before peak season<br>· Reintroduce paper back into the process |

Example Solution Option Summary

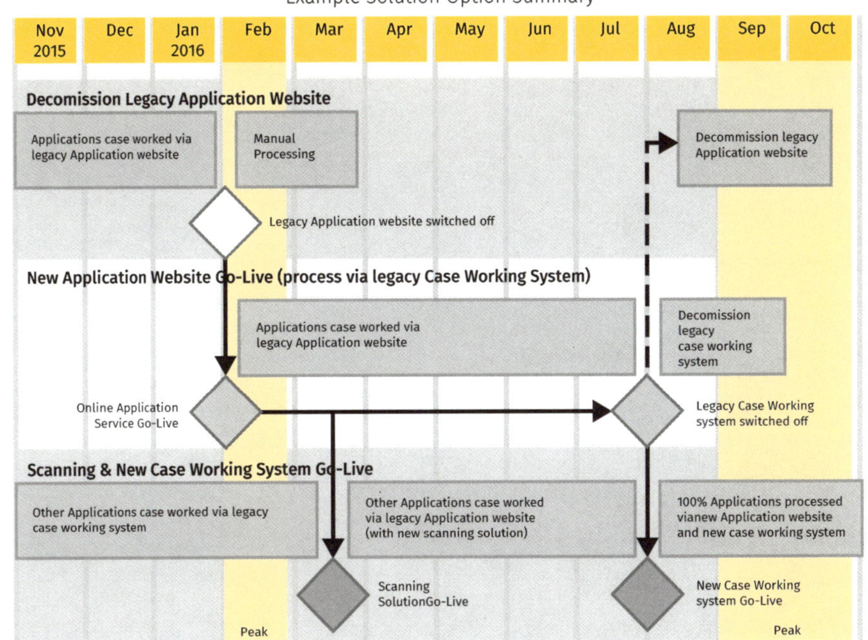


Example Solution Option Summary

Cost-Benefit Mapping (Output) Blueprints

Table 9.9

| Ref | Blueprint | Description | Example |
|---|---|---|---|
| 5.4.2 | Cost-Benefit Assessment | Assessment between the monetary and non-monetary costs and benefits in implementing each Solution Option. | |

| | Option 1 | Option 2 | Option 3 |
|---|---|---|---|
| Capital Costs | £1.5M Project Cost | £0.8M Project Cost | £0.5 Project Cost |
| Operating Costs | £0.0M Staff Costs<br>£1.3M Mail Room<br>£1.2M Outsource Fee | £0.2M Staff Costs<br>£1.3M Mail Room<br>£1.2M Outsource Fee | £1.0M Staff Costs<br>£0.0M Mail Room<br>£1.2M Outsource Fee |
| PV of Costs (Total) | £4.0M | £3.5M | £2.7M |
| **Cost-Benefit Analysis of Monetary Cost and Benefits:** | | | |
| PV of Monetary Benefits | £2.4M Increase sales<br>£0.1M Staff savings | £2.4M Increase sales<br>£0.1M Staff savings | £0.0M Increase sales<br>£0.0M Staff savings |
| PV of Benefits (Total) | £2.5M | £2.5M | £0.0M |
| Net PV | (£1.6M) | (£1.0M) | (£2.7M) |
| **Analysis of Non-Monetary Benefits:** | | | |
| Benefit 1 | Improved Application process (faster, less errors) | Improved Application process (faster, less errors) | |
| Benefit 2 | Less manual entry | Less manual entry | |
| Benefit 3 | Less time spent on low risk cases | | |
| Preferred Option | Best for customer, but higher cost/risk | Tactical solution creates technical debt | Least favourable, introduces paper back into the process |

## 5.4.1 Solution Options

The Solutions Options is made up of the following two (2) areas:

1. **Solution Options Summary**
2. **Solution Options High Level Timeline**

Each of the above areas are discussed in the section below.

### 1. Solution Options Summary

The first area in developing the Solution Options is to provide a summary for each of the options. As a *general rule*, in presenting your options to the Business, there should be at least three (3) options (sometimes 4):

- **Do nothing,**
- **Do as little as possible,**
- **Do what you need to, and**
- **Do more than you need too** (assuming time and money is not a problem)

These choices are otherwise known as *'nothing', 'minimum', 'intermediate',* and *'aspirational'.* For practicality (and sanity) however, I would recommend sticking to the first three.

Using the *inputs* from the Inputs section above, and working with the necessary key stakeholders as mentioned earlier, develop a set of solution options, summarising the Business Change, Enablers and Benefits targeted for each option, and record in the Solution Option Summary, as shown in the example in *Figure 9.22* below.

When looking at these Solution Options, they should have the appropriate mix of the following to be effective:

- A good balance of *'quick, medium and long-term'* wins. Quick wins are those small projects or initiatives that require a small investment, and can be implemented quickly and signal and communicate progress to the rest of the Organisation. Signalling of progress also builds motivation and incentivises the wider Programme and the business because progress is seen to be getting made, while providing leverage to elicit support and resources for the longer-term more resource intensive initiatives, and
- A balance of internal/external and functional/political perspectives and considerations (i.e. satisfy the needs of Stakeholders as identified in the Impact/Influence Map who have the influence to derail the Programme).

| Do Nothing | | Out Source | In Source |
|---|---|---|---|
| Option | Maintain existing decommission plans | Accelerate decommission plans & tactical solution | Accelerate decommission plans & manual process |
| Summary | • Online applications via existing system<br>• Outsourcer remains in place to receive and dispatch docs<br>• Use existing legacy system until new Application system available | • Online applications submitted via existing system<br>• Outsourcer remains in place to receive, scan and dispatch documents<br>• All applications case worked on legacy system until new Application system available | • Online applications submitted via existing system<br>• Outsource contract ended<br>• Manual scanning and dispatch in-house<br>• All Applications case worked in legacy system until new Application system available |
| Pros | • Maintains existing plans (lower risk)<br>• No additional staff training<br>• No tactical solution required | Recruitment of new staff not required | Uses existing process (lower implementation risk) |
| Cons | Changes made to legacy system will create technical debt as eventually decommissioned | • Retains current high staff level<br>• Tactical solution will not replace full Out Source current role | • Need to recruit new staff<br>• Short lead time for training before peak season<br>• Reintroduce paper back into the process |

**Figure 9.22** - Solution Option Summary

### 2. Solution Options High Level Timeline

Using the *inputs* from the Inputs section above, and working with the necessary key stakeholders as mentioned earlier, develop the high-level timeline covering the key processes, milestones and dependences, as shown in the example in Figure 9.23 (below).

**The examples in *Figure 9.22* and *Figure 9.23* show the Summary and High Level Timeline for one single project under the Programme only (from the case study) responsible for delivering the Online Application System, and not the workflow, notifications and payments systems (Enablers) that were also identified in the Benefits Model and Benefits Dependencies Map. The Solutions Options for the whole Programme would include all these (i.e. each individual project solution option).**

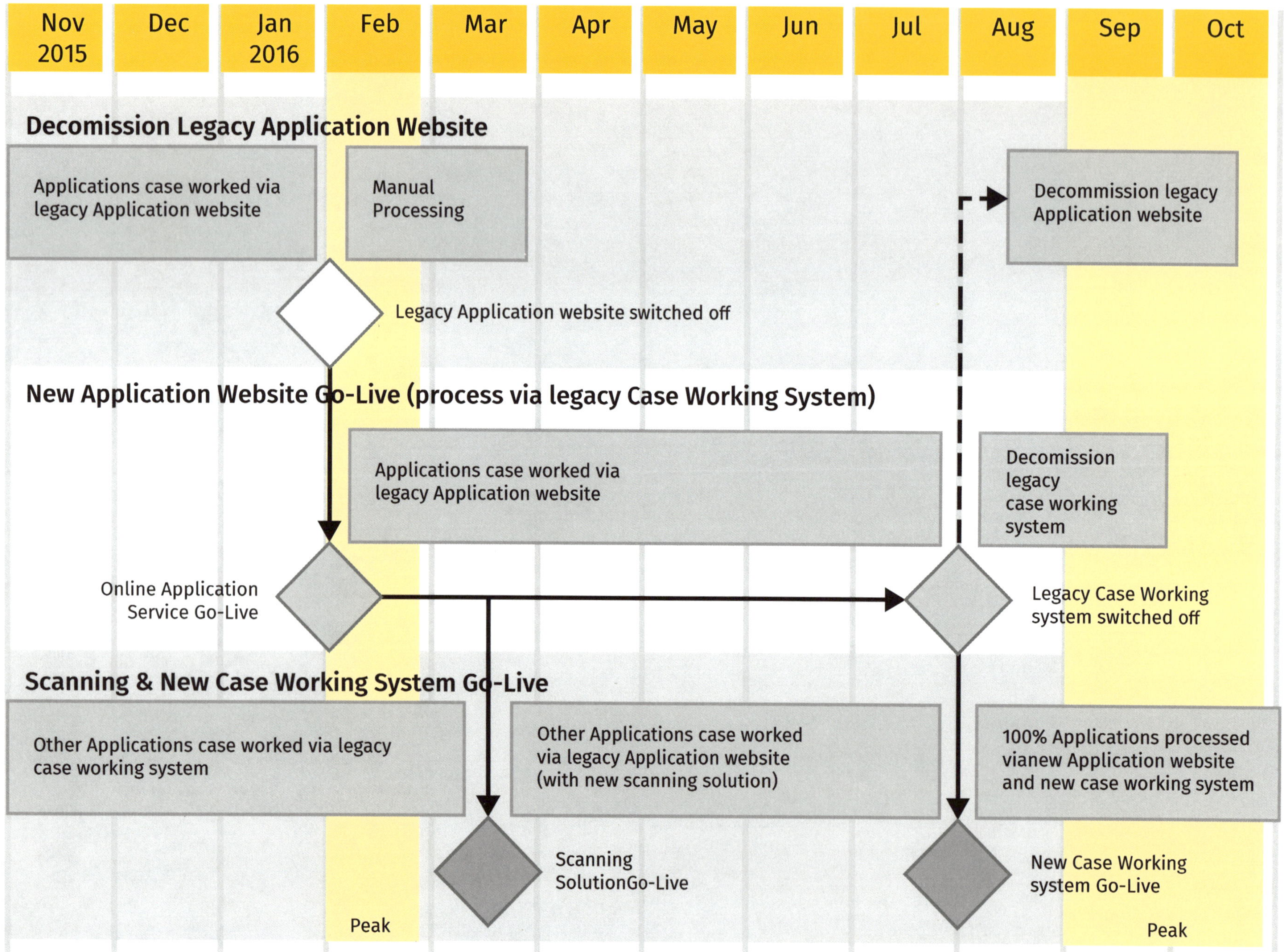


**Figure 9.23** - Solution Option High Level Timeline

## 5.4.2 Cost-Benefit Assessment

### 3 Develop the Cost-Benefit Assessment

Again, using the *inputs* from the Inputs section above, and working with the necessary key stakeholders as mentioned earlier, develop the Cost-Benefit Assessment – accounting for both the monetary (including capital and operating costs) and non-monetary costs and benefits expected from delivering the changes stated in the Summary, as shown in the example in *Figure 9.24* (below):

Based on comment and feedback from key stakeholders, you should re-run any changes to the prioritised capabilities through the Benefits Model, and re-evaluate your cost-benefit analysis here to ensure the selected option meets the desired benefit requirements.

**4. Iteratively socialise, validate and refine the Blueprint(s)** - including any Risks, Assumptions, Issues and Dependencies (RAID) addressed or raised as part of completing this step, and

**5. Package and publish the Blueprint(s)** – in line with your agreed sprint/release cycle, established back in *Step 2 – Control, with the Governance Model.*

| | Option 1 | Option 2 | Option 3 |
|---|---|---|---|
| Capital Costs | £1.5M Project Cost | £0.8M Project Cost | £0.5 Project Cost |
| Operating Costs | £0.0M Staff Costs<br>£1.3M Mail Room<br><br>£1.2M Outsource Fee | £0.2M Staff Costs<br>£1.3M Mail Room<br><br>£1.2M Outsource Fee | £1.0M Staff Costs<br>£0.0M Mail Room<br><br>£1.2M Outsource Fee |
| PV of Costs (Total) | £4.0M | £3.5M | £2.7M |
| **Cost-Benefit Analysis of Monetary Cost and Benefits:** | | | |
| PV of Monetary Benefits | £2.4M Increase sales<br><br>£0.1M Staff savings | £2.4M Increase sales<br><br>£0.1M Staff savings | £0.0M Increase sales<br><br>£0.0M Staff savings |
| PV of Benefits (Total) | £2.5M | £2.5M | £0.0M |
| Net PV | (£1.6M) | (£1.0M) | (£2.7M) |
| **Analysis of Non-Monetary Benefits:** | | | |
| Benefit 1 | Improved Application process (faster, less errors) | Improved Application process (faster, less errors) | |
| Benefit 2 | Less manual entry | Less manual entry | |
| Benefit 3 | Less time spent on low risk cases | | |
| Preferred Option | Best for customer, but higher cost/risk | Tactical solution creates technical debt | Least favourable, introduces paper back into the process |

**Figure 9.24** - Cost-Benefit Assessment

### Risks and Mitigation

There are a couple of issues (or misconceptions) to be aware of with cost-benefit mapping:

1. **A more comprehensive assessment maybe required**
2. **Cost-Benefit Mapping is a *'nice-to-have'***

We will discuss each of these issues below.

**1. A more comprehensive assessment maybe required**

The examples provided in the section above were fairly straight forward and didn't account for Return on Investment (ROI), Payback Period (PB) or Net Present Value (NPV). While these type of financial analysis (as opposed to *cost-benefit* analysis) is valid and important, the objective with Cost-Benefit Mapping here is providing an assessment of the *net-cost* based on the 'changes made in creating the Target Operating Model (TOM) *against* the Benefits gained from delivering those changes'.

The Business Case (whether managed by the Programme Management Office (PMO), the Programme Director, or Business Case Officer) may need those (ROI, PB etc.) numbers, but to be able to calculate those, they will first need to know 'what are the changes being made?', and the 'what are the costs (and benefits) to implement those changes?', which is where the solution options, and cost-benefit analysis comes in – identifying those options, and obtaining and providing the costs and benefits figures of implementing those options.

### 2. Cost-Benefit Mapping is a *'nice-to-have'*

Although the case for conducting the cost-benefit analysis is strong (and a key role in validating not only the direction of the Programme, but also that the actual changes to be implemented are the strongest candidates to realise the planned benefits) – the Cost-benefit analysis itself is still an element in the process of developing the Target Operating Model that is *often overlooked, intentionally missed* or *not done to a great level of detail to do it justice*. In cases where it is done, and the results are not 'favourable' (i.e. don't meet the cost/benefit threshold), the opportunity or feedback loop is not available (or built into) the design process to make changes or trade-offs for and with a different set or combination of capabilities.

In many company's I have assisted, doing the cost-benefit analysis was unfortunately treated as a *'nice to have'* and in most cases not carried out, or when it was, it was carried out too late, because by the time it was requested, a solution (and in most cases it was a supplier provided solution) was already *'pre-selected'* – even before properly validating the solution was *fit for purpose* or indeed the right one in the first place.

By incorporating both the Cost-Benefit Mapping Building Block and assessment Blueprint into the **Design Process** (so it isn't overlooked), and intentionally placing the feedback loop into the Benefits Model, so solution options and benefits can be re-evaluated if the cost-benefit does not meet the intended returns and planned costs, you can get the design and costings to the point quickly where a decision (including the *'go-no-go'* decision) can be made, to provide approval to either proceed; not proceed or alternatively revisit the benefits once more and develop a new set of options for consideration.

## Building Block Wrap-up

In this section, we discussed the Cost-Benefit Mapping Building Block.

This Building Block provides the solution options – as the set of solution, and implementation options to implement the changes (i.e. Programme outputs) that, when used by the Business, realise the planned benefits and align the Business to the Business Strategy; and the cost-benefit assessment of the net cost (of implementing those changes) and creating the Target Operating Model (TOM), against the Benefits gained from delivering those changes.
This Building Block is made up of the following two (2) Blueprints:

- **Solution Options** – provides the solution and implementation options (Summary), and high level timeline (High Level Timeline) of the transition from Current Operating Model to the Target Operating Model (TOM), and
- **Cost-Benefit Assessment** - Assessment between the monetary and non-monetary costs and benefits in implementing each Solution Option.

The cost-benefit assessment provides an assessment of the cost versus the benefits gained from implementing the suggested changes. The cost-benefit assessment is not the financial analysis, but would feed into the financial analysis (using figures out of the cost benefit assessment table similar to the example table provide above). Should this cost-benefits (or financial analysis) assessment not meet the 'anticipated or expected' returns, before any further design or development is authorised, the benefits and Business Changes that directly contribute to the realisation of those planned benefits should be re-evaluated as part of the Benefits Model, and feed through to the Target Operating Model Reference Model (TOM) in order to develop a new set of options for (re) consideration.

## Next Steps

Once the Cost-Benefit Mapping is completed and a (solution) option has been agreed, the next step in the **Design Process** is to agree on a pilot to test that the solution option is both actually feasible and achievable (or make the changes if necessary) before full solution.

The Pilot is discussed in the Pilot Mapping Building Block in the following section.

# 5.5 Pilot Mapping

## Introduction

Pilot Mapping is the Building Block where you validate the candidate Enablers and Business Changes via a 'pilot' – the Minimal Viable Product (MVP).

The objective is to test the selected solution option from the previous Building Block (Cost-Benefit Mapping), and evaluate both the solution, and the implementation of the solution, on a small scale (limited in scope, budget and/or time), before a full-scale implementation.

The purpose of the Pilot is primarily to make full-scale implementation more effective, by gathering data about the results, and identifying any issues so they can be addressed before a full-scale implementation.

Typically, the pilot is run and coordinated by the Business Change Manager, with the support of the Business Analyst (and technical team – developers, testers, test managers etc.). Your role as Business Architect is to assure (and ensure) the Enablers and Business Changes that were identified and validated as part of the Benefits Model produce the expected results in order to move onto full scale implementation. Where the outcome of the pilot (and therefore the Business Changes and Enablers that are being tested) don't meet the expected results, then this would (and should) trigger a review and possibly reprioritisation of the selected Business Changes and Enablers, and then following this, another re-run of the Cost-Benefit Mapping analysis.

Provided the results of the pilot (i.e. the tested Enablers and Business Changes) meet the expected results, these then form part of the project brief(s), roadmap and benefits realisation plan (and related Blueprints) as part of (and in preparation of) full scale implementation. These Blueprints are both addressed and completed as part of the next step in the Design Process, with the Road Map Model, covered in Step 6 – Implement, in the following section.

## Inputs

The inputs used to complete this Building Block are shown in the table below.

## Output(s)

The following table provides the Blueprints (outputs) produced in completing this step

**Pilot Mapping Building Block Input**

**Table 9.10**

| Ref | Blueprint | Use |
|---|---|---|
| 5.4.1 | Solution Options | Provides the overview and timeline of the solution and implementation option of the candidate capabilities (and Enablers and Business Changes) needed to realise the Organisation' planned Business Benefits, and align the Business to the Business Strategy. |

Pilot Mapping (Output) Blueprint

Table 9.11

| Ref | Blueprint | Description | Example |
|---|---|---|---|
| 5.5.1 | Pilot Brief | Outline of the pilot, the capabilities (people, process and technology) to be tested on a small scale, to evaluate both the solution and implementation options before full scale implementation. | See example below |

| | Description |
|---|---|
| Scope | The part of the business that is in scope to be tested. |
| Objective | The Business Changes and Enablers that are to be tested. |
| Outcome | The benefit(s)to be gained from the successful completion of the pilot |
| Final Benefit | Related Final Benefit |
| Strategy Objective | Related Strategy Objective |
| Enablers | Related Enabler(s) |
| Business Changes | Related Business Changes |
| Business Capability | Related Business Capability |
| Business Process | Related Business Process |
| Success Criteria | Measure of success pilot will be measured by |
| Start Date | Date pilot expected to start |
| End Date | Date pilot expected to end |
| Current | Baseline measure for set period |
| Expected | Target measure (for agreed period) |
| Result | Pass/Fail |

## Steps

The steps to complete the above Blueprint (Output) are discussed in the section below:

## 5.5.1 Pilot Brief

### 1. Develop the Pilot Brief

Using the inputs from the Inputs section above, working with the Product Owner (and other necessary key stakeholders) develop the Pilot details (i.e. scope, objectives, outcomes etc.), and record them on a Pilot Brief template, as shown in the example below.

An example of the Pilot Brief for the Online Application Project is shown in *Figure 9.26* below.Using the inputs from the Inputs section above, working with the Product Owner (and other necessary key stakeholders) develop the Pilot details (i.e. scope, objectives, outcomes etc.), and record them on a Pilot Brief template, as shown in the example below.

An example of the Pilot Brief for the Online Application Project is shown in *Figure 9.26* below.

**2. Iteratively socialise, validate and refine the Blueprint** - including any Risks, Assumptions, Issues and Dependencies (RAID) addressed or raised as part of completing this Blueprint, and

**3. Package and publish the Blueprint** – in line with your agreed sprint/release cycle, established back in *Step 2 – Control*, with the *Governance Model.*

| | Description |
|---|---|
| Scope | The part of the business that is in scope to be tested. |
| Objective | The Business Changes and Enablers that are to be tested. |
| Outcome | The benefit(s)to be gained from the successful completion of the pilot |
| Final Benefit | Related Final Benefit |
| Strategy Objective | Related Strategy Objective |
| Enablers | Related Enabler(s) |
| Business Changes | Related Business Changes |
| Business Capability | Related Business Capability |
| Business Process | Related Business Process |
| Success Criteria | Measure of success pilot will be measured by |
| Start Date | Date pilot expected to start |
| End Date | Date pilot expected to end |
| Current | Baseline measure for set period |
| Expected | Target measure (for agreed period) |
| Result | Pass/Fail |

**Figure 9.25** - Pilot Brief Template

| | Case Study Example |
|---|---|
| Scope | Online Application Process for Student Visa Application (Registration only). |
| Objective | • Enabler – Online Application System (and integration with existing case working system).<br>• Business changes – Staff training |
| Outcome | • Customers are able to submit their application online<br>• Remove manual data entry by Data Entry Officer<br>• Customer Record created automatically |
| Final Benefit | Increase volume of applications processed |
| Strategy Objective | Improved Application Process |
| Enablers | Online Application System (new) |
| Business Changes | Staff Training (on updated online application process) |
| Business Capability | Customer Service Management |
| Business Process | Manage Registration |
| Success Criteria | Number of applications processed (received and records created) through the Online Application System |
| Start Date | May 01 2016 |
| End Date | May 31 2016 |
| Current | 10,000 Applications (for month of May) |
| Expected | 12,500 Application (for month of May) |
| Result | Pass |

**Figure 9.26** - Pilot Brief Case Study Example

## Risks and Mitigations

There is a whole science and process for running effective pilots, which includes identifying and training appropriate team members, understanding and executing clear communications, identifying possible failure points and mitigation actions, as well as data collection, and monitoring and evaluation of results.

While this is all important and necessary, your role as the Business Architect is to ensure (and assure - from the Business Architecture perspective) that the capabilities (Enablers and Business Changes) that have been selected, prioritised and modelled as the solution option(s) will produce the intended results.

This will involve close cooperation and a working relationship with the Business Change Manager to feed in requirements and expectations, as well as monitoring of progress and results.

Any deviation from the expected results would form *lessons learned* and would need to be communicated to your key stakeholders to solicit feedback and potential re-evaluation of all the Enablers and Business Changes in scope, and for the full-scale implementation.

This re-evaluation may involve revisiting (and potentially reordering) the priority of the already agreed candidate Enablers and Business Changes. The resulting design (and any updates) from the pilot will form part of the *final design* for the full large scale rollout and implementation.

## Building Block Wrap-up

In this section, we discussed the Pilot Brief Building Block.

The Pilot Brief provides the outline of the pilot, that lists the capabilities (Enablers and Business Changes) to be tested in a 'pilot' before full scale implementation.

The objective of the pilot is to evaluate both the solution (i.e. the candidate Business Changes and Enablers) and implementation options, to ensure they produce the expected results on a small scale before embarking on a full-scale implementation. Any changes or lessons learned from the pilot are then fed back to the Business and Programme (as per the review and approval process), before being incorporated into the final Target Operating Model (TOM) design.

## Reference Model Recap

Once the pilot has run successfully (or lessons learned fed back into the design from an unsuccessful pilot, and depending on the degree of success/failure, re-run again), and all other TOM Reference Model Building Blocks (i.e. Capability Mapping, Process Mapping, Impact Mapping and Cost-Benefit Mapping) are complete, the TOM Reference Model is complete.

By completing the TOM Reference Model, this now means you have:

- Defined the capabilities and processes needed to support the TOM (including agreed, aligned and reconciled change activities across the Programme and organisation at the strategic/strategy level with the capability model, and at the operational/implementation level with the process model that there is no gaps or duplication of effort);
- Agreed the actual impact to the Organisation and taken a risk-management approach to determine the best set of solution and implementation options to achieve the Organisations intended outcomes (business strategy and strategic objectives), while minimising the impact to the Business;
- Conducted the cost-benefit analysis and presented the results and indicative high level (implementation) timeline to the Business for approval;
- Used the preferred solution and implementation options and developed and ran the pilot to test the chosen business changes and enablers on a small scale before a full-scale implementation;
- Taken a capability-driven approach, and used the identified and prioritised business capabilities (people, process and technology) from the Benefits Reference Model to design the TOM, and
- Finally (but by no means, least) avoided the 'solution-first' error (i.e. attempting to design the business to fit a pre-determined or pre-selected solution as opposed to develop a solution fit for the business) and avoided 'solution-mode' (jumping straight into design of the TOM without regard or necessary consideration of where the business is today), which is the cause of lot of failed transformation Programmes today.

For a full recap of **HOBA®** and the **Design Process,** refer to the Recap section in *Chapter 11 Next Steps* below.

## Next Steps

The next step in the **Design Process** is to define the Road Map Reference Model. This is where you use the prioritised (and tested business capabilities and implementation option, provided you ran the pilot), and develop the plans to implement the business capabilities. It is also where you setup the process to manage, track and report on benefits realisation, develop the transition architecture plan, insure the alignment between the Business with the Technology and Data Architectures, and provide the traceability that all stakeholder concerns are covered and addressed.

The Road Map Reference Model is also where you develop the plans to deliver the design of the TOM, which makes this part of **Design Process** (Step-6) developing the plans to deliver the design of the TOM, one of the exceptions in that, although Step-6 of the Design Process is the last step in the process, it doesn't mean developing the plans to deliver the design can't be started earlier. This is discussed further in *6.1 Project Mapping*, and *6.2 Road Map Mapping* as part of the Road Map Reference Model in the following chapter.

# Chapter 10
# Step 6 – Implement

## Introduction

Step 6 – Implement, is about the implementation* of the both the 'design' of the Target Operating Model (TOM), as well as the 'physical' Business Architecture that the TOM describes. In terms of HOBA®, implementation is provided via the Road Map Model Reference Model.

*Figure 10.1* below shows where Step-6 Implement fits in the overall Design Process:

**(*) Note – As discussed in the Challenge #5: What is the role of the Business Architect (and when do we engage them)? section, the Business Architects role is two parts – developing and delivering the design of the Business Architecture (namely the Target Operating Model (TOM)) to the Business, as well as assuring (and ensuring) the implementation of the physical TOM is aligned to the design. This Step-6 Implement, covers both the delivering the design to the Business, and the overseeing the implementation of the physical architecture that the design describes.**

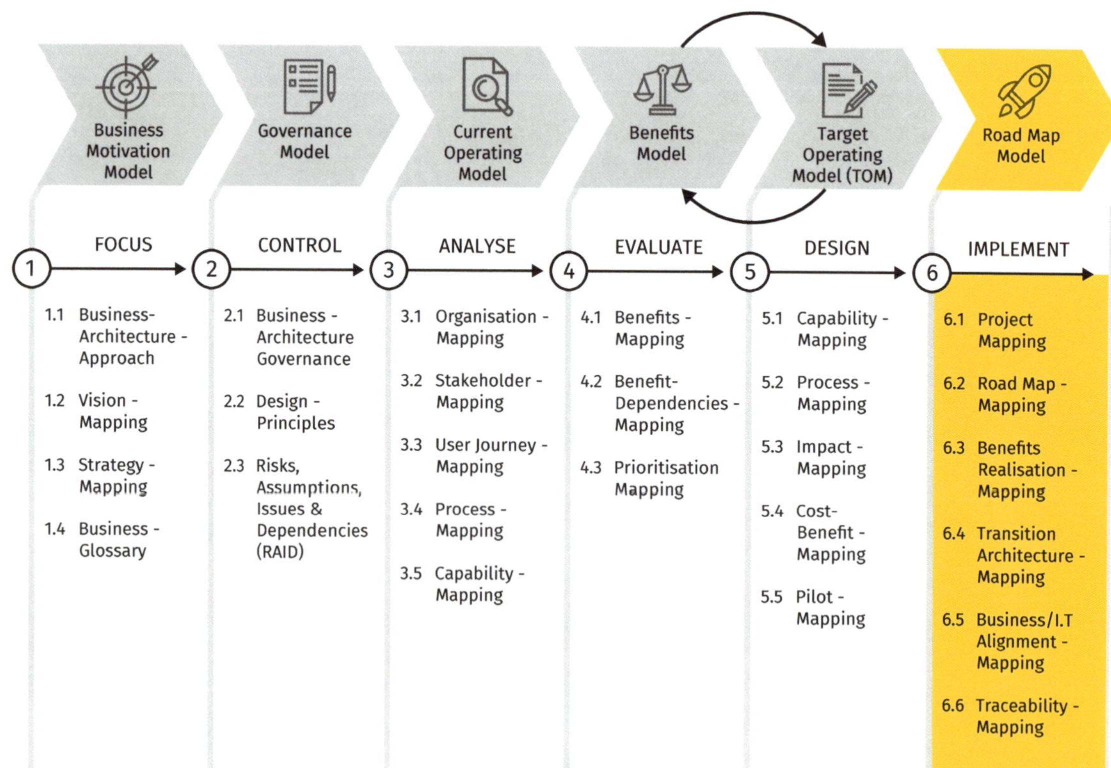


**Figure 10.1** - Design Process - Step 6

# Road Map Model

As mentioned earlier in Chapter 3 House of Business Architecture® (HOBA®), each HOBA® Reference Model addresses a different aspect in the design and implementation of the Target Operating Model (TOM). These different aspects are represented in the following different views:

- Process
- Perspective
- Context, and
- Content

We will briefly discuss each of these in the section below.

## Process

In terms of process, the Road Map Model is the 6th (and last) step of the Design Process, as shown in *Figure 10.2* below.

Step-6 brings it all together, all the work done in the previous steps comes together here, in developing the design, of the TOM, and implementing the physical Business Architecture that the aligns to the design.

## Perspective

In terms of 'perspective', the Road Map Model provides the 'implement' perspective of developing and implementing the TOM, that is all the activities needed to develop the design and oversee the implementation of the physical Business Architecture that it is aligned to the design of the TOM.

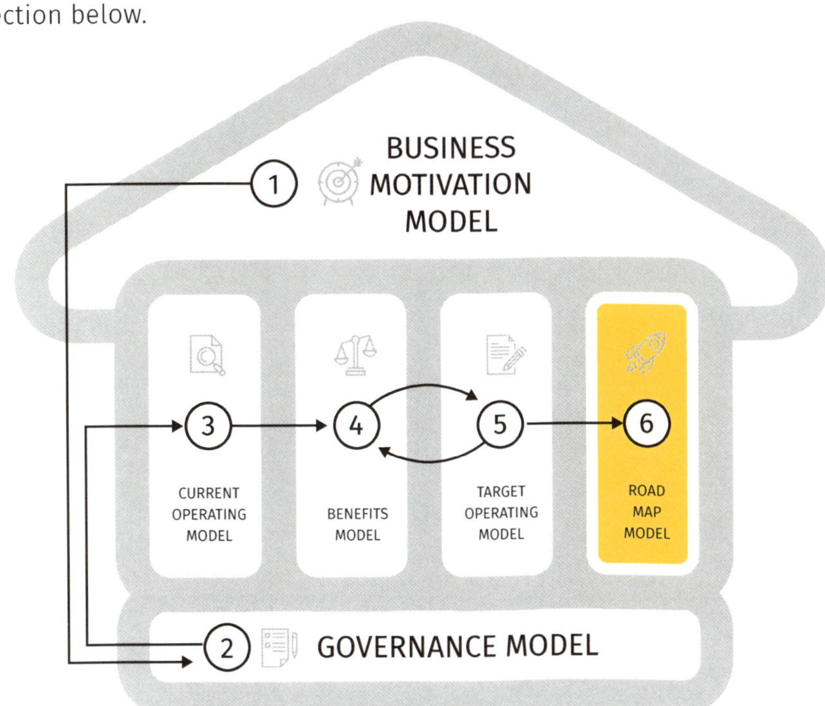


**Figure 10.2 -** Road Map Model – Step 6

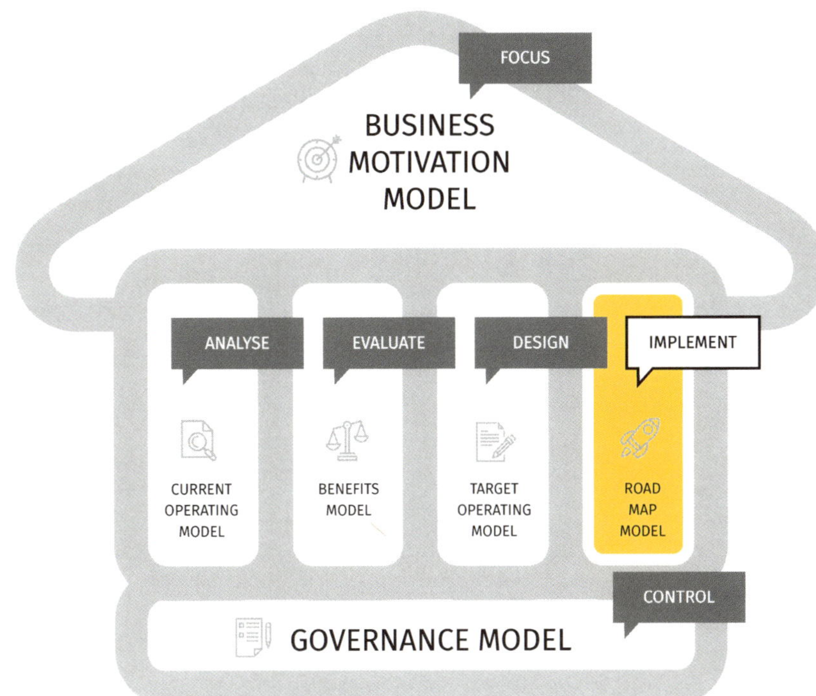


**Figure 10.3 -** Road Map Model – Implement Perspective

## Context

In terms of context, the Road Map Model addresses the aspect and 'When?' question asked of the both the Business and the Business Architecture:

- When will the design of the Target Operating Model be developed, and delivered? and
- When will the physical Business Architecture be implemented?

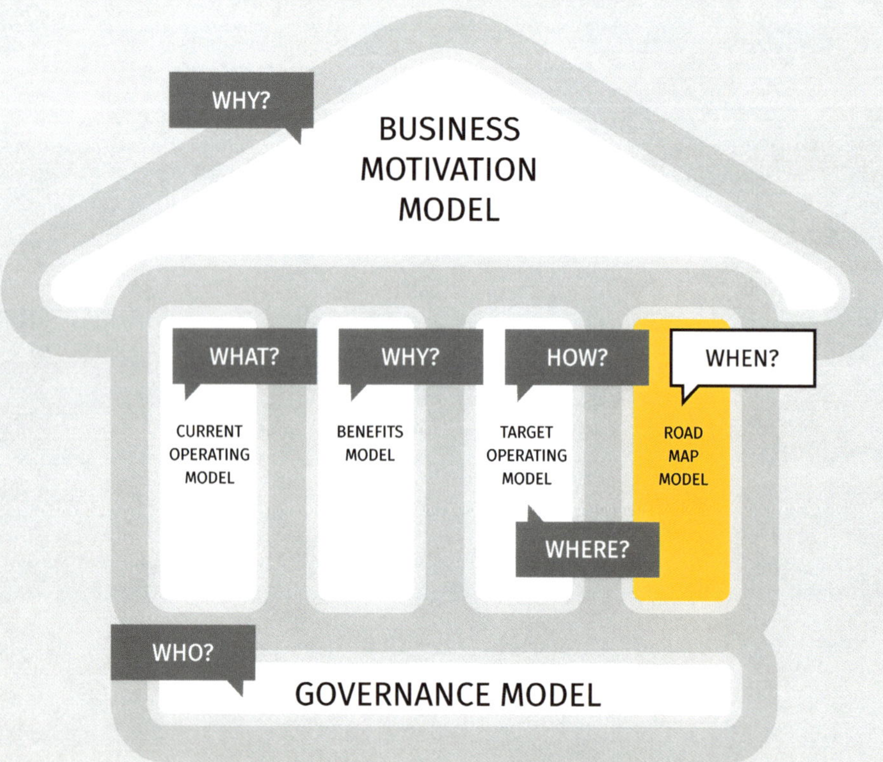


**Figure 10.4 -** Road Map Model – 'When?' Aspect



## Content

In terms of content, the Building Blocks and Blueprints developed here are the Business Architecture content used to deliver the design of the TOM, and manage the alignment of the implementation of the physical TOM with the design.

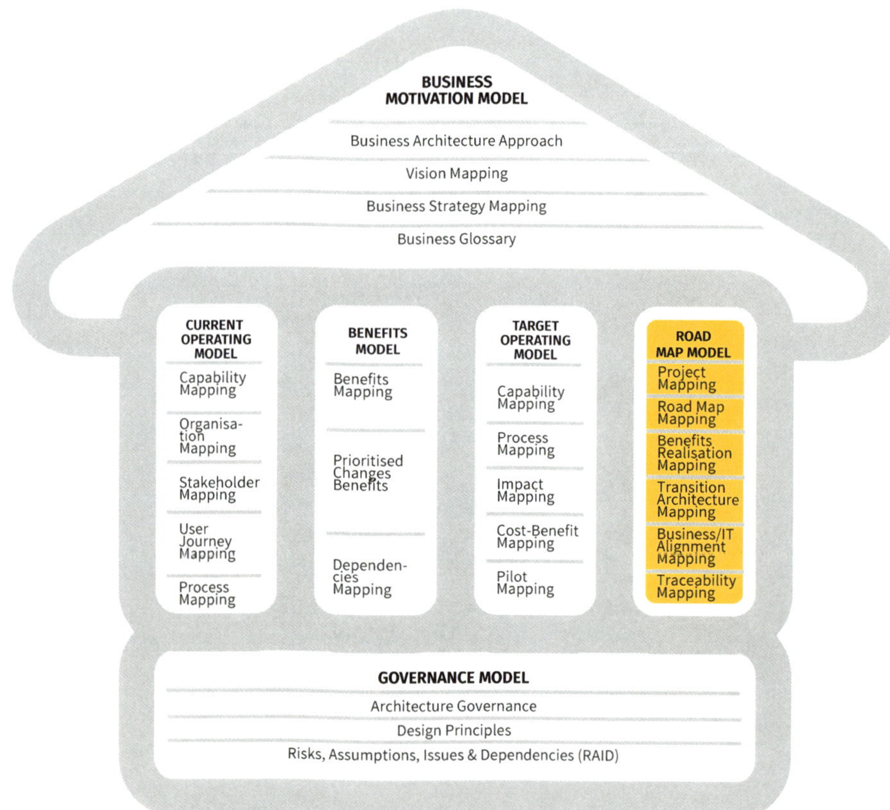


**Figure 10.5 -** Road Map Model Building Block Content

The Building Blocks and their respective Blueprints that make up the Road Map Model are shown in the table below:

**Road Map Model Building Blocks and Blueprints**

**Table 10.1**

| Design Step | Building Block | Purpose | Blueprint |
|---|---|---|---|
| 6.1 | Project Mapping | Provides the outline of the projects (including in/out of scope changes, objectives, benefits, approach etc.) needed to implement the physical TOM. | • 6.1.1 Project Brief<br>• 6.1.2 Project-Benefits Map |
| 6.2 | Road Map Mapping | Defines the outline implementation roadmap of the activities needed to develop and deliver the TOM design, and the activities to develop and implement the changes and implement the physical TOM. | • 6.2.1 Business Architecture Road Map<br>• 6.2.2 Programme Road Map |
| 6.3 | Benefits Realisation Mapping | Defines the activities and Blueprints to capture, track and report on benefits realisation progress and status. | • 6.3.1 Benefits Realisation Register<br>• 6.3.2 Benefits Realisation Map |
| 6.4 | Transition Architecture Mapping | Defines the activities and Blueprints to show the views (Transition Architecture Strategy and Transition Architecture Plan, and Maps) of the architectural significant states between the 'baseline' Current Operating Model and the 'future' Target Operating Model (TOM). | • 6.4.1 Transition Architecture Strategy Map<br>• 6.4.2 Transition Architecture Phase Map |
| 6.5 | Business/IT Alignment Mapping | Defines the Technology (and Data) Architecture that is needed to support and align with the Business Architecture, and Target Operating Model (TOM). | • 6.5.1 Business/IT Alignment Map<br>• 6.5.2 Business/IT Alignment Table |
| 6.6 | Traceability Mapping | Defines the activities and Blueprints to manage the traceability between Stakeholders concerns and HOBA® Blueprints. | • 6.6.1 Stakeholder Concerns Traceability Matrix<br>• 6.6.2 Blueprint Traceability Matrix |

# High Level Process (SIPOC)

The high level 'Supplier, Input, Process, Output, Customer' (SIPOC) process to completing this step - Step-6 Implement, and the Road Map Model is shown in *Figure 10.6* below:

| SUPPLIERS | INPUTS | | PROCESS | OUTPUTS | | CUSTOMERS |
|---|---|---|---|---|---|---|
| | | | Building blocks | Blueprints | | |
| Business Architect | 1.1.1 Statement of Work (SOW)* | 4.2.1 Benefits Dependencies Map | 6.1 Project Mapping | 6.1.1 Project Brief | 6.4.1 Transition Architecture Strategy Map | Business Architect |
| | 1.2.1 VSOM* | 4.3.1 Prioritised Changes | ↓ 6.2 Road Map Mapping | 6.1.2 Project-Benefits Map | 6.4.2 Transition Architecture Phase Map(s) | |
| Core Team Members | 2.1.1 Architecture Governance Framework* | 5.1.2 Process Model Map (To-Be) | ↓ 6.3 Benefits Realisation Mapping | 6.2.1 Business Architecture Road Map | 6.5.1 Business/IT Alignment Map | Core Team Members |
| Key Stakeholders | 2.2.1 Design Principles* | 5.4.1 Solution Options | ↓ 6.4 Transition Architecture Mapping | 6.2.2 Programme Road Map | 6.5.2 Business/IT Alignment Table | Key Stakeholders |
| | 2.3.1 RAID Log* | 5.4.2 Cost-Benefit Assessment | ↓ 6.5 Business/IT Alignment Mapping | 6.3.1 Benefits Realisation Register | 6.6.1 Stakeholder Concerns Traceability Matrix | |
| Programme Team Members | 4.1.1 Benefits Profile | 5.5.1 Pilot Brief | ↓ 6.6 Traceability Mapping | 6.3.2 Benefits Realisation Map | 6.6.2 Blueprint Traceability Matrix | Programme Team Members |

**Figure 10.6** - Road Map Model SIPOC

**(*) Note – these Blueprints are shown for completeness here and should be included and considered in the development and sign-off of all subsequent Blueprints, as they collectively define the vision, scope and risks that all following work and Blueprints developed and agreed will need to consider and align to.**

We will discuss each of the process steps (Building Blocks) in the sections below.

# 6.1 Project Mapping

## Introduction

Project Mapping is the Building Block that identifies and allocates the prioritised Enablers and Business Changes needed to develop the Target Operating Model (TOM) to the discrete projects that will develop and implement those aspects of the physical Business Architecture.

The purpose of Project Mapping is to provide a clear view of the responsibly of which projects are delivering the specific Business Changes and Enablers that directly support the planned benefits and the relative timeline these will be delivered, and benefits realised, relative to the other (or all) projects within the Programme.

The objective of Project Mapping is to provide clear lines of responsibility of which projects are delivering what changes, and to provide input into determining the prioritisation and relative delivery timeline of these changes. The benefit of Project Mapping is it helps facilitate *benefits traceability, prioritisation* and *reporting* of issues that you, as the Business Architect are responsible for. Project Mapping does that by providing the visualisation of which Projects within the Programme that are delivering the different Business Changes and Enablers relative to each other; their individual contribution to (immediate and final) benefits, as well as the Project's relative contribution to the overall Strategic Objective(s).

Project Mapping provides that visualisation of which projects are delivering the Business Changes and Enablers that, when used by the Business, realise the intended Business Benefits. This visual view provides the *benefits traceability* via the Project-Benefits Map, which shows the relative contribution each project has to the overall strategy objective. As the Business Architect, knowing the relative contribution each project has to the overall strategic objective, you are able to provide the Organisation with a guide to the prioritisation of the order of the different projects (and therefore Business Changes and Enablers) needed to be implemented for the Business to realise the planned benefits (in the order that it requires them in).

As an example, it was not clear to the Portfolio, Programme or Benefits Team for one client I assisted whether a single Programme was responsible to delivering changes against which benefit or collectively as a 'group'? This was despite the Portfolio itself having its own Benefits Map, and each Programme having its own Programme Charter (listing the benefits which each Programme was impacting by the Business Changes and Enablers it was responsible for implementing). It also didn't help that the Benefits Map looked like a spider's web, with almost every Programme contributing to the realisation of almost every benefit on the map, making it visually unrecognisable which particular Programme or project was contributing to which benefit.

This is often the case when Benefits, and Benefits Mapping, are done retrospectively (as discussed previously in *Step 4 – Evaluate* as part of defining the *Benefits Model*) used to 'validate' the chosen Business Changes and Enablers, as opposed to defining benefits *proactively* to 'justify' the investment in the Business Changes and Enablers.

Doing Project Mapping here and now, before any development or build takes place ensures not only that the Objectives of each project (and Programme) are aligned, but that there are clear dividing lines between projects (and Programmes) that are impacting and contributing to specific benefits. This allows the projects to coordinate and prioritise the order the Business Changes and Enablers are implemented, to allow the Business to realise the Benefits from using the implemented Business Changes and Enablers, in the order and priority the Benefits are needed in.

## Inputs

The inputs used to complete this Building Block are shown in the table below:

**Project Mapping Building Block Inputs**

**Table 10.2**

| Ref | Blueprint | Use |
|---|---|---|
| 4.1.1 | Benefits Profile | Provides the detailed description of a benefit, how it is measured, related strategic objective and who owns it. |
| 4.2.1 | Benefit-Dependencies Map | Provides the Business Changes and Enablers that directly influence the intended (immediate and) final benefits and strategic objectives. |
| 4.2.2 | Benefits-Dependencies Matrix | Shows the relationship between the dependencies (Business Changes and Enablers) and each benefit. |
| 5.4.1 | Pilot Brief | Provides the outline of the pilot, the capabilities (people, process and technology) to be tested on a small scale, to evaluate both the solution and implementation options before full scale implementation. |

## Output(s)

The Blueprints (outputs) produced for this Building Block are shown in the table below:

Table 10.3

| Ref | Blueprint | Description | Example |
|---|---|---|---|
| 6.1.1 | Project Brief | Provides the project outline (i.e. scope, outcomes, approach etc.) that is responsible for delivering the Business Changes and Enablers for each project under the Programme. | See below |

**Project Online Application Project Brief**

**Project Description**

New Online Application Service (OAS) to replace existing Online Application website, allowing Users (Visa Applicants) to complete the Application online and pay for a Visa Application. The new OAS will integrate with existing Workflow/Case working system (or replacement) and payment service.

| Project Sponsor | Project Manager or Involved Parties | Key Stakeholders |
|---|---|---|
| Programme Sponsor | Project Manager | · Product Owner (Visa Application Centre (VAC) Manager)<br>· Operations (VAC) Worker<br>· Policy Officer |

| In Scope | Out of Scope |
|---|---|
| · Enabler(s) - Online Application Service (OAS) (including integration with existing Workflow / Case working service and Payment services)<br>· Business Change(s) – Staff trained in updated process; document checklist provided<br>· Business Capability – Customer Management (Customer Document Management, Customer Service Management)<br>· Business Process(es) – 1.1 Receive Application, 1.1.1 Select Service, 1.1.1.1 Create Account, 1.1.1.2 Apply Service, 1.1.2 Create Record, 1.1.2.2 Generate | · Enablers - Workflow/Case working Service (changes to); Online Booking service (integration or changes to)<br>· Business Change(s) – Staff trained in updated process; (new) risk assessment application process<br>· Business Capability – Product Design Management<br>· Business Process(es) – 1.4 Manage Documents, 1.4.1 Receive Documents, 1.4.1.1 Scan Documents. |
| **Projected Outcomes/Objectives** | **Expected Benefits** |
| · Customer application data integrated into Workflow/Case Working system<br>· Improved data quality<br>· Payments taken online | · Reduced rework<br>· Reduced work returning invalid applications<br>· Reduced work for data entry teams<br>· Increase volume Applications processed |
| **Project Assumptions** | **Business Assumptions** |
| Pilot will be run (start and end) during off-peak period and will cost postal route only when volumes are both low and staff number are available to support running of the pilot. | Off peak period occurs 2nd week of January for a period of 10-weeks, when volumes are low, suitable for running pilot and testing new process and systems. |

**Key Dependencies on Other Projects**

Document scanning and digital storage will go live and be available prior to the start of the Pilot.

| Indicative Timeframe/milestones | Risks |
|---|---|
| · OAS ready and tested (Jan 10)<br>· Applicants apply via OAS (from Jan 15)<br>· Applications processed via OAS for 8 weeks (till Mar 15) | · Document Scanning not available<br>· Digital Storage not available<br>· OAS not available |
| **Recommended Approach** | **Current Actions/Next Steps** |
| Staff training to be carried out, system integration to be completed, manual backup | Confirm Digital Scanning and Digital Storage available and proceed according to plan. |

**Project Online Application Project Brief**

| | |
|---|---|
| process ready (if needed) | |

Project Mapping (Output) Blueprints

Table 10.3

| Ref | Blueprint | Description | Example |
| --- | --- | --- | --- |
| 6.1.2 | Project-Benefits Map | The graphical view of the combined Project Briefs for all the projects under the Programme, showing the relative timeline of delivery of Enablers and Business Changes that support the realisation of the (immediate and final) benefits leading to the realisation of the Strategy Objective(s) and ultimately the Organisation Vision. | 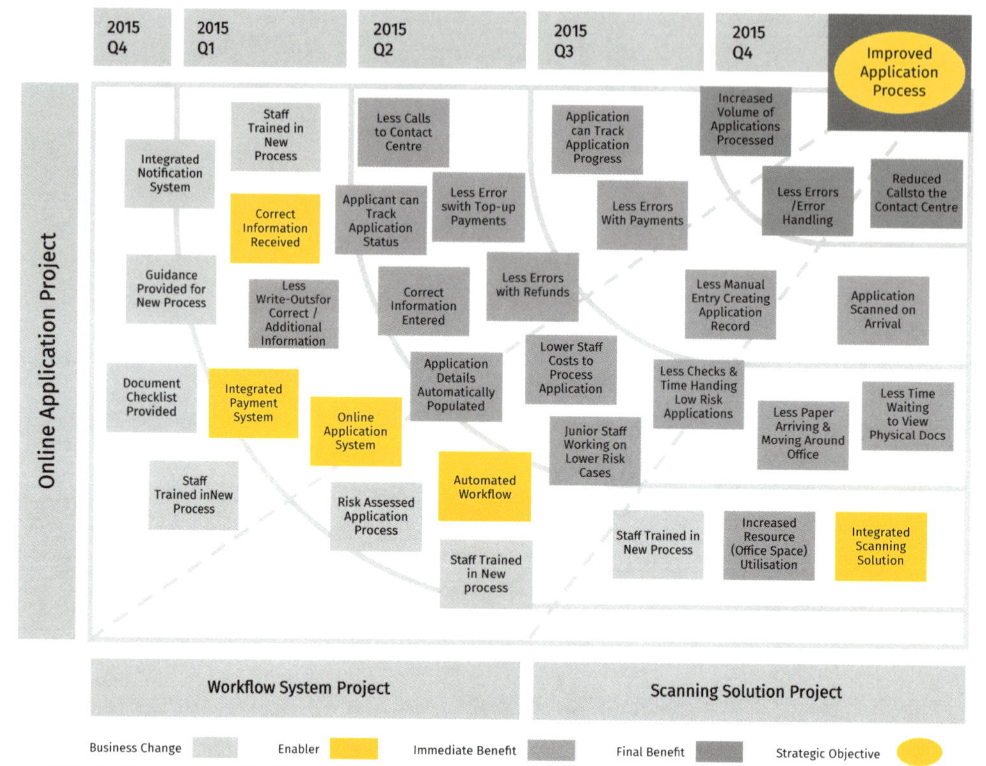 |



## Steps

The steps to complete the above Blueprints (outputs) are as follows.

## 6.1.1 Project Brief

### 1. Develop the Project Brief(s)

Using the input from the *Inputs* section above, and working with the Product Owner and/or other Key Stakeholders, develop the Project Brief for each project under the Programme. An example Project Brief is shown in *Figure 10.7* below:

| Project Online Application Project Brief |
|---|
| **Project Description** |
| New Online Application Service (OAS) to replace existing Online Application website, allowing Users (Visa Applicants) to complete the Application online and pay for a Visa Application. The new OAS will integrate with existing Workflow/Case working system (or replacement) and payment service. |

| Project Sponsor | Project Manager or Involved Parties | Key Stakeholders |
|---|---|---|
| Programme Sponsor | Project Manager | • Product Owner (Visa Application Centre (VAC) Manager)<br>• Operations (VAC) Worker<br>• Policy Officer |

| In Scope | Out of Scope |
|---|---|
| • Enabler(s) - Online Application Service (OAS) (including integration with existing Workflow / Case working service and Payment services)<br>• Business Change(s) – Staff trained in updated process; document checklist provided<br>• Business Capability – Customer Management (Customer Document Management, Customer Service Management)<br>• Business Process(es) – 1.1 Receive Application, 1.1.1 Select Service, 1.1.1.1 Create Account, 1.1.1.2 Apply Service, 1.1.2 Create Record, 1.1.2.2 Generate Confirmation. | • Enablers - Workflow/Case working Service (changes to); Online Booking service (integration or changes to)<br>• Business Change(s) – Staff trained in updated process; (new) risk assessment application process<br>• Business Capability – Product Design Management<br>• Business Process(es) – 1.4 Manage Documents, 1.4.1 Receive Documents, 1.4.1.1 Scan Documents. |

**Figure 10.7-** Project Brief Example

| Projected Outcomes/Objectives | Expected Benefits |
|---|---|
| • Customer application data integrated into Workflow/Case Working system<br>• Improved data quality<br>• Payments taken online | • Reduced rework<br>• Reduced work returning invalid applications<br>• Reduced work for data entry teams<br>• Increase volume Applications processed |
| **Project Assumptions** | **Business Assumptions** |
| Pilot will be run (start and end) during off-peak period and will cost postal route only when volumes are both low and staff number are available to support running of the pilot. | Off peak period occurs 2nd week of January for a period of 10-weeks, when volumes are low, suitable for running pilot and testing new process and systems. |
| **Key Dependencies on Other Projects** | |
| Document scanning and digital storage will go live and be available prior to the start of the Pilot. | |
| **Indicative Timeframe/milestones** | **Risks** |
| • OAS ready and tested (Jan 10)<br>• Applicants apply via OAS (from Jan 15)<br>• Applications processed via OAS for 8 weeks (till Mar 15) | • Document Scanning not available<br>• Digital Storage not available<br>• OAS not available |
| **Recommended Approach** | **Current Actions/Next Steps** |
| Staff training to be carried out, system integration to be completed, manual backup | Confirm Digital Scanning and Digital Storage available and proceed according to plan. |
| **Project Online Application Project Brief** | |
| process ready (if needed) | |

Figure 10.7- Project Brief Example

## 2. Develop the Project-Benefits Map

Using the input from the Inputs section above including the Project Brief Blueprint(s), plot the respective Enablers and Business Changes for each project under the Programme on the Project-Benefits Map, in chronological order within the respective project.

An example of a Project-Benefits Map is shown in *Figure 10.8* below:

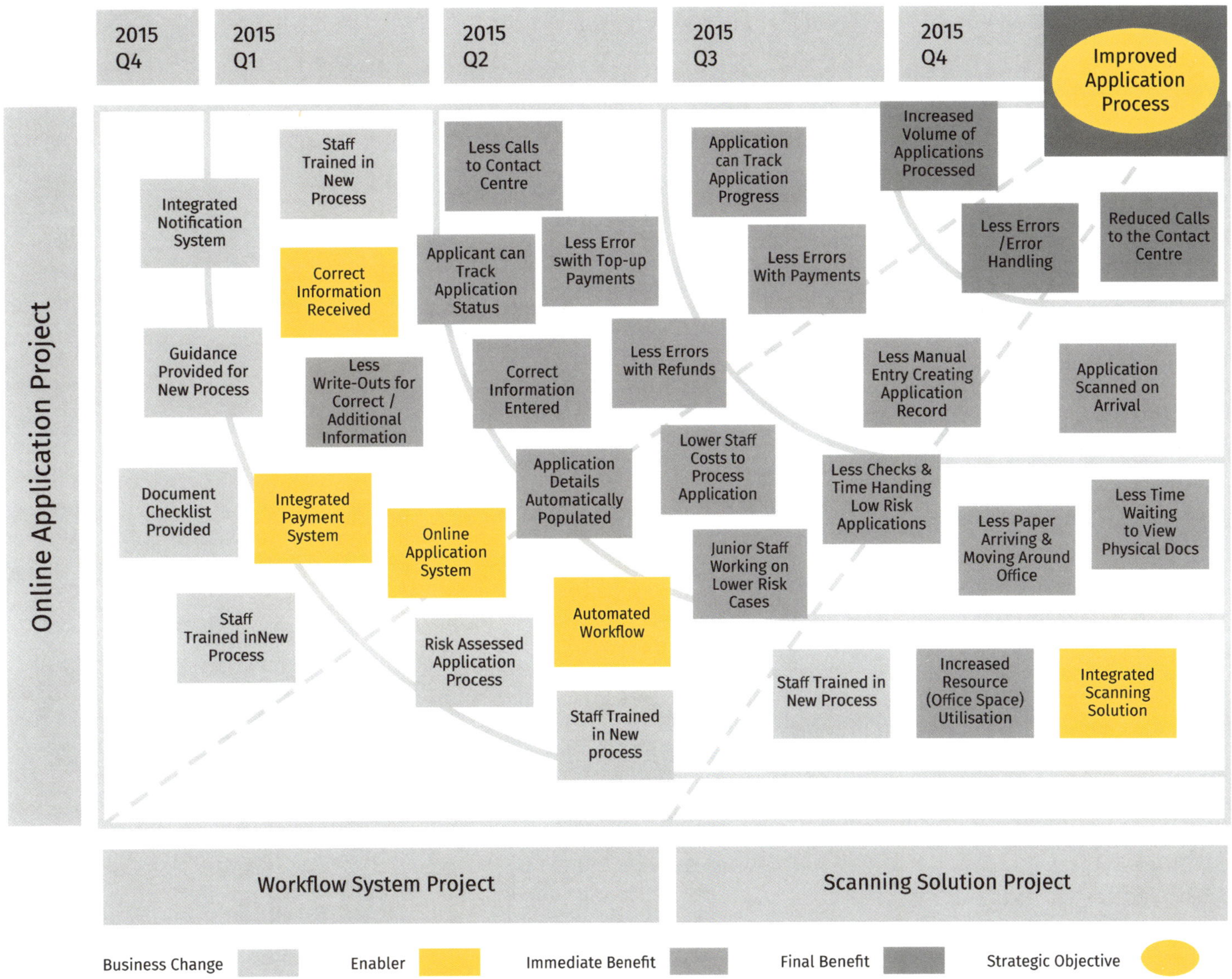


**Figure 10.8** - Sample Project-Benefits Map

**3 Repeat steps 1 and 2 (above) for each Project under the Programme,**

**4. Iteratively socialise, validate and refine the Blueprint(s)** - including any Risks, Assumptions, Issues and Dependencies (RAID) addressed or raised as part of completing this step, and

**5. Package and publish the Blueprint(s)** – in line with your agreed sprint/release cycle, established back in *Step 2 – Control*, with the *Governance Model.*

## Risks & Mitigations

In terms of risks and mitigations, the thing to be aware of here is the timing and when the Project Mapping can be carried out.

Project Mapping is one of the exceptions in that, although Step 6 of the **Design Process** is the last step in the process, it doesn't mean Project Mapping can't be started earlier. This Building Block can be done *in parallel* with other Building Blocks. In fact, it should actually be done at the beginning of the Programme (or close to the beginning as possible).

In an ideal world, in a well planned (and executed) Programme, when the Programme is conceived, the Projects within the Programme are also conceived and defined at the same time. This makes it relatively easy to identify and assign the different Benefits, Enablers and Business Changes that each project is responsible for delivering as the Benefits, Business Changes and Enablers are identified at the time of Programme conception.

However, in practice what tends to happen (more times than not) is new projects are created midway through the Programme lifecycle – either conceived halfway through as a result of newly discovered scope (scope deemed too big to include under a project within the Programme), an 'orphan' project or a project (inherited from another Programme) is added to an existing Programme. This creates alignment, coordination and timing issues around which particular project is solely (or jointly) delivering capabilities that support the realisation of specific benefits as the lines of responsibility become blurred, and projects complete for shared resources, for what they are told are for '*shared benefits*'.

As an example, one client I assisted was implementing an Identify and Access Management (IAM) system with a Programme which only had one testing environment to 'test' in. This test environment was booked up solid, however when a new project joined the Programme mid-stream, they needed immediate access to *go-live* with some new functionality. The project that was booked in next was on the critical path but wasn't ready to get into the test environment earlier (and definitely couldn't start later), so the project currently in the test environment had to cut their testing short and were instead forced to make a decision of either releasing less functionality to the business as originally promised, or release promised changes to the business but with untested (and potentially error prone) functionality. All apparently 'acceptable' allowances, as it was described as "it is for the greater good (i.e. benefit) of the Programme". Clearly this line of thought benefited for some within the Organisation, but to the detriment of the others. Had a clear view of what benefit(s) were being delivered by each project, and by how much each project was *actually* contributing to those benefits been available, it would have proved very helpful to aid prioritising which project stayed in the test environment, and which has to wait.

So, if you find yourself in the position of getting a new project joining midway through the Programme, before jumping straight in and adding it into the Project-Benefits Map, start at the Benefits Model and re-run the Benefits Dependences, and the Prioritized Changes Blueprints with the new project included. This will give each (new and existing) project in the Programme fair and equal representation of their contribution to the relevant Benefits. This can then be used to then determine any (re) prioritisation of which project should and need to get priority treatment due to the 'earlier' benefits they are impacting. Once completed, you can then use this Project Mapping (and the Project-Benefits Map) to provide a clear view of the responsibility of each project to the overall Programme (and business) objectives to help the alignment, coordination and timing. Doing so also avoids any rushed or rash decisions that could have a negative impact on the Programme, and the Business as a whole.

## Building Block Wrap-up

In this section, we discussed the Project Mapping Building Block, which identifies and allocates the prioritised Business Changes and Enablers needed to develop the Target Operating Model (TOM), into discrete projects that will develop and implement the physical Business Architecture.

This Building Block is made up of the following two (2) Blueprints:

- **Project Brief** - provides the high-level project outline (i.e. scope, outcomes, approach) that are responsible for delivering the Business Changes and Enablers for each Project under the Programme, and

- **Project-Benefits Map** – which provides the graphical view of the combined Project Briefs for all the projects under the Programme, showing the relative timeline of delivery of Enablers and Business Changes that support the realisation of the (immediate and final) Benefits.

The objective of Project Mapping is to provide clear lines of responsibility of which projects are delivering what Business Changes and Enablers, and impacting which (immediate and final) benefits. This is also done to provide input into determining the prioritisation and relative delivery timeline of those changes, so the changes they are delivering will be implemented in the timeframe when the Business Benefits they contribute to are expected (and needed) to be realised.

### Next Steps

Once the Project Mapping Building Block is complete, the next step in the **Design Process** is to define the Project and Programme Roadmaps – for both the development and delivery of the *'design'* of the TOM, but also the development and implementation of the *'physical'* Business Architecture, as part of the Road Map Mapping Building Block.

These concerns are discussed in the Roadmap Mapping Building Block in the following section.

# 6.2 Road Map Mapping

## Introduction

Road Map Mapping is the Building Block which provides the high level timeline of the chunks of work to develop and deliver both the *'design'* of Target Operating Model (TOM), as well as develop and implement the *'physical'* Business Architecture as part of Target Operating Model (TOM).

The Road Map Mapping Building Block effectively provides two (2) road maps:

1. **The 'design' road map** - for developing and delivering the *design* of the Target Operating Model (TOM), and
2. **The 'physical' road map** - for the development and implementation of the *physical* Business Architecture that is aligned to the design of the Target Operating Model (TOM).

The purpose of this Building Block is to visualise and communicate the activities needed to develop the *design* of the TOM, and to develop and implement the *physical* Business Architecture.

The objective of both road maps is to provide not only the view of what activities are needed to develop and deliver the *design* and *physical* Business Architecture, but to also build confidence from the Programme stakeholders that there is a solid and realistic plan to achieve the Programmes outcomes and the Programme being able to deliver its intended changes so the Business can realise its intended Benefits, resulting in the Organisation having a higher degree of confidence in it achieving its strategic objectives.

Now, because there are two road maps (with one feeding the other), there is an (ideal) order and sequence to developing each road map (i.e. the *'design'* road map should clearly lead and inform the *'physical'* road map). The added benefit of HOBA® having already defined all the work, and deliverables (i.e. Reference Models, Building Blocks and Blueprints) is the list of the potential work and deliverables is already known, and this list is actually already agreed in the Statement of Work (SOW) at the outset of the Business Architecture/Business Architect engagement, which you, the Business Architect would have already agreed with the Programme. This includes the Reference Models that are in scope, and therefore the activities needed to complete the respective Building Blocks and Blueprints. At the very least, at the time the SOW was signed off, you already had the inputs into developing the outline strawman of the *'design'* road map as the deliverables and activities were already known.

So, although Road Map Mapping appears at the end of the Design Process (Step 6), it doesn't mean that you can't or couldn't start this step earlier, especially if you have eager or restless stakeholders that want to get a sense of the scale and scope of work required to develop the design of the Target Operating Model (TOM), and complete the Programme. **HOBA®** Reference Models, Building Blocks, and Blueprints allows you to draft a strawman relatively quickly and get it out to the Programme and Business for comment. It is also an effective stakeholder management strategy to involve your stakeholders early, get them involved and on board with the change journey so they feel part of the change, as opposed to having changed forced upon them (which never really works or inspires lasting change).

In terms of developing the '*physical*' road map, this step could not have been started any earlier (i.e. at the same time as the '*design*' road map), or not at least until the Enablers and Business Changes were identified and prioritised to know the changes and the order (and project for that matter), with the latter having only been completed in the Project Mapping Building Block as outlined in the previous step. It is important to point out here however that some of the '*physical*' road map foundations have already been partially developed (in true 'Building Block' fashion, building off previous Building Blocks), through the development of the 'input' Building Blocks and Blueprints already completed earlier.

In terms of approaches to completing each road map, there are two (2) planning approach options[61]:

1. **Start from Present Day** - and plan out from today the activities and necessary time needed to deliver the design and implement the physical changes, or
2. **Start at a Future Date** - (i.e. expected delivery date) and work backwards to present day.

Each option clearly has its own pros and cons that need to be considered before deciding which option is best to choose, as shown in the table below:

[61] Managing Successful Projects with PRINCE2 (2005), Office of Government Commerce (OGC)

Road Map Mapping Planning Approach Options

**Table 10.4**

| # | Planning Approach Option | Pros | Cons |
|---|---|---|---|
| 6.1 | Start from Present Date (and 'plan out') | Useful when the start date is fixed (and the finish date is rough or fluid). | The actual Project finish date is not fixed (i.e. ends when the last activity ends, which may not be when the 'expected' finish date). |
| 6.2 | Start from Project finish date (and 'plan backwards') | Useful when there is a known fixed finish date. | Some (or all) tasks will be compressed to fit within the fixed finish date and the start date. |

**For illustration purposes – Option 1 (above) will be used in the following example (i.e. Steps section) discussed below to show the activities necessary to deliver both the *design* of the TOM, and to implement the *physical* Business Architecture. In practice, the duration of each activity might not be so uniform.**

## Inputs

The inputs used to complete this Building Block are shown in the below:

Road Map Mapping Building Block Inputs

**Table 10.5**

| Ref | Blueprint | Use |
|---|---|---|
| 1.1.1 | Statement of Work (signed) | Provides the list of in scope Business Architecture deliverables (i.e. Reference Model, Building Blocks etc.) that were agreed at the outset of the Business Architecture/Business Architect engagement, that form part of the 'design' Road Map. |
| 2.1.1 | Requirement Management Framework | Provides the Architecture Requirement Hierarchy and relationship between HOBA® elements (Reference Model, Building Blocks and Blueprints) and Architecture Requirements (theme, feature, epics and stories). |
| 6.1.1 | Project Brief | Provides the scope, approach, timeline, Business Changes and Enablers that are to be delivered, and mapped onto the Road Map. |
| 6.1.2 | Project-Benefits Map | Provides indicative timeline for the delivery of the in-scope Business Changes and Enablers to be delivered by the project(s). |

# Output(s)

The Blueprints (outputs) produced for this Building Block are shown in the table below:

**Project Mapping (Output) Blueprints**

**Table 10.6**

| Ref | Blueprint | Description | Example |
|---|---|---|---|
| 6.2.1 | Business Architecture ('design') Road Map | Business Architecture Road Map setting out the Business Architecture deliverables required to develop and deliver the design of the Target Operating Model (TOM). | 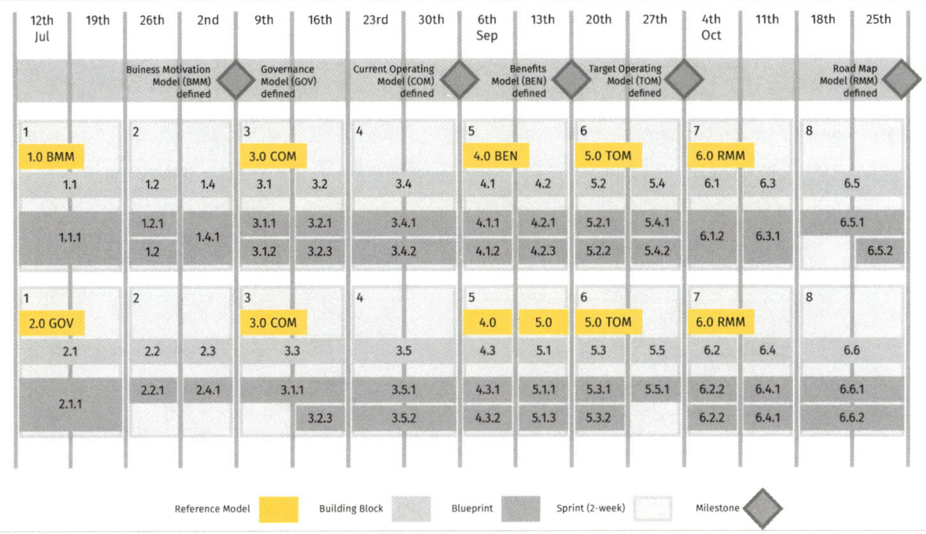 |
| 6.2.2 | Business Architecture ('physical') Road Map | Programme Road Map setting out the activities for each project within the Programme required to develop and implement the Business Changes and Enablers to create the physical Target Operating Model (TOM). | 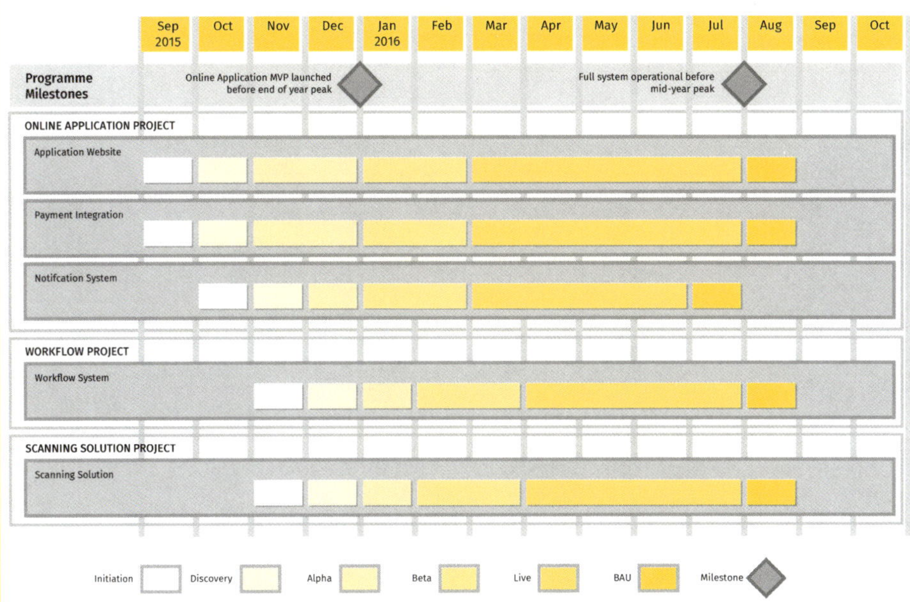 |

## Steps

The Road Map Mapping Building Block is made up of the following Blueprints:

- **Business Architecture Road Map,** and
- **Programme Road Map**

We will discuss each of these Blueprints in the steps below:

### 6.2.1 Business Architecture Road Map

**1. Develop the Business Architecture 'design' Road Map**

Using the inputs from the *Inputs* section above, and working with the Product Owner (and other necessary Key Stakeholders), map the agreed in-scope Reference Models, Building Blocks and Blueprints on to the Road Map, starting from the Programme start date.

An example Business Architecture Road Map is shown in *Figure 10.9* below.

**The above example shows successive Building Blocks and Blueprints starting when the predecessor Building Block and/or Blueprint begins. As in most cases, the predecessor Blueprints are inputs into the subsequent Blueprint. In practice however, there may be some overlap and several activities may run in parallel at the same time, particularly where the Organisation and Programme has been through this process before, there will be re-usable Building Blocks and Blueprints to re-employ as templates, and with the experience gained this process (and activity) will get progressively quicker and better.**

### 6.2.2 Programme Road Map

**2. Develop the Programme 'physical' Road Map**

Once the Business Architecture *'design'* Road Map is drafted and activities and dates are laid out, these should provide an indicative starting point (or start date) for the activities or phases of activities for the discovery, design, build and implementation of the changes to the physical Organisation to begin.

Using the Project Brief Map (with the prioritised changes – Business Changes and Enablers), map the phases of activities from the starting point or date dictated from the Business Architecture *'design'* Road Map.

An example Business Architecture Road Map is shown in *Figure 10.10* below.

**You will recall from the *Challenge #1: What is Business Architecture?* section, that Business Architecture is involved mostly in the Planning stages in Organisation design, which in most cases is before the Programme is born, which means the Business Architecture activities and *design* roadmap should start well *before* the activities and dates in the *physical* (Programme) road map, which uses the *design* road map to guide the implementation of the *physical* road map.**

**3. Iteratively socialise, validate and refine both maps** - including any Risks, Assumptions, Issues and Dependencies (RAID) addressed or raised as part of completing this step, and

**4. Package and publish the map(s)** – in line with your agreed sprint/release cycle, established back in *Step 2 – Control* with the *Governance Model.*

**Risks and Mitigation**

Both the Business Architecture and the Programme Road Maps have been intentionally kept both relatively high level. Both road maps also intentionally ignored *'effort'* (in favour of *'duration'*) needed to complete the tasks and activities that make up the Road Map here.

Duration is a better measure to use (in my opinion and experience) as it focuses the tasks to identify

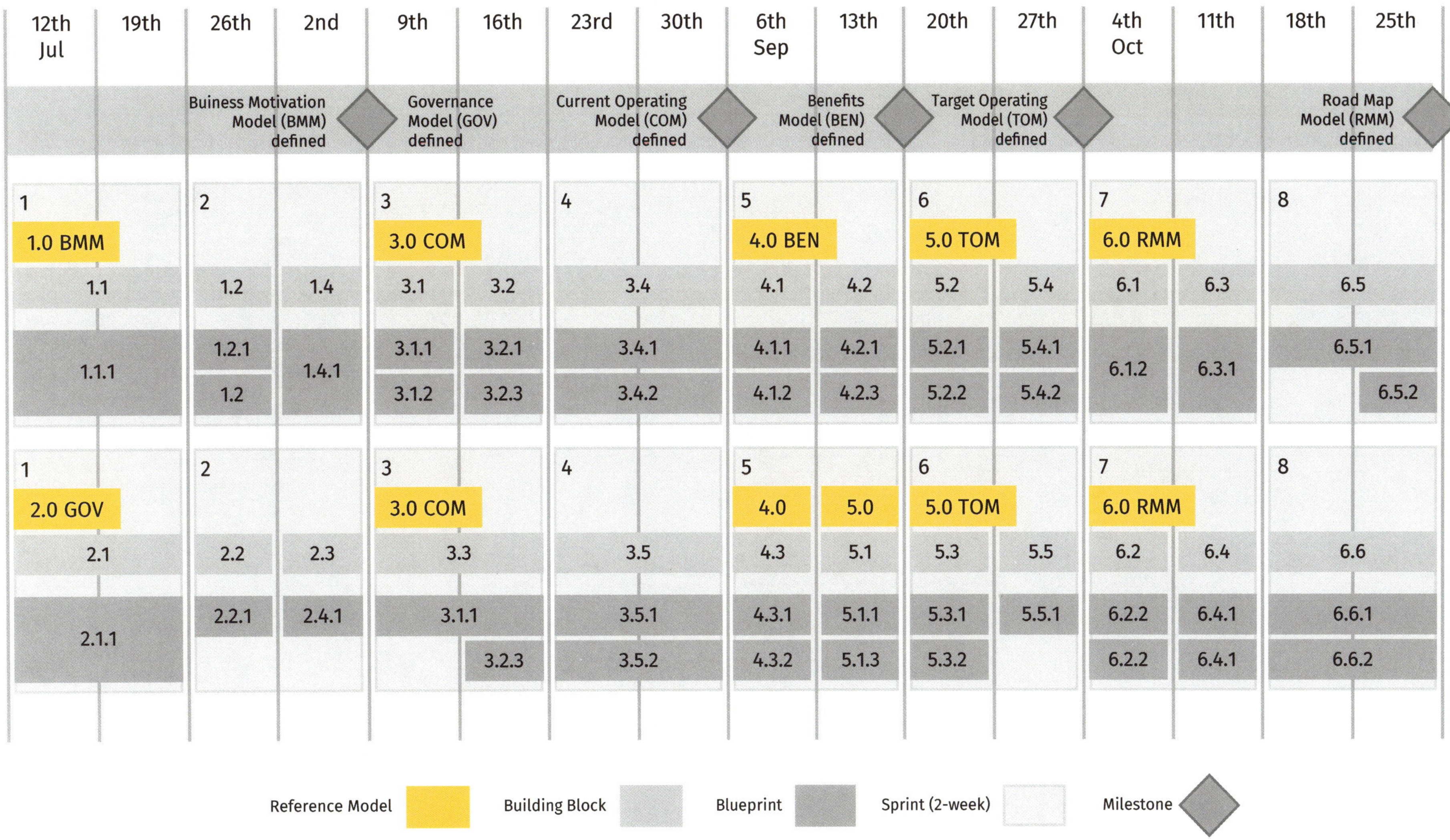


**Figure 10.9 -** Sample Business Architecture Road Map

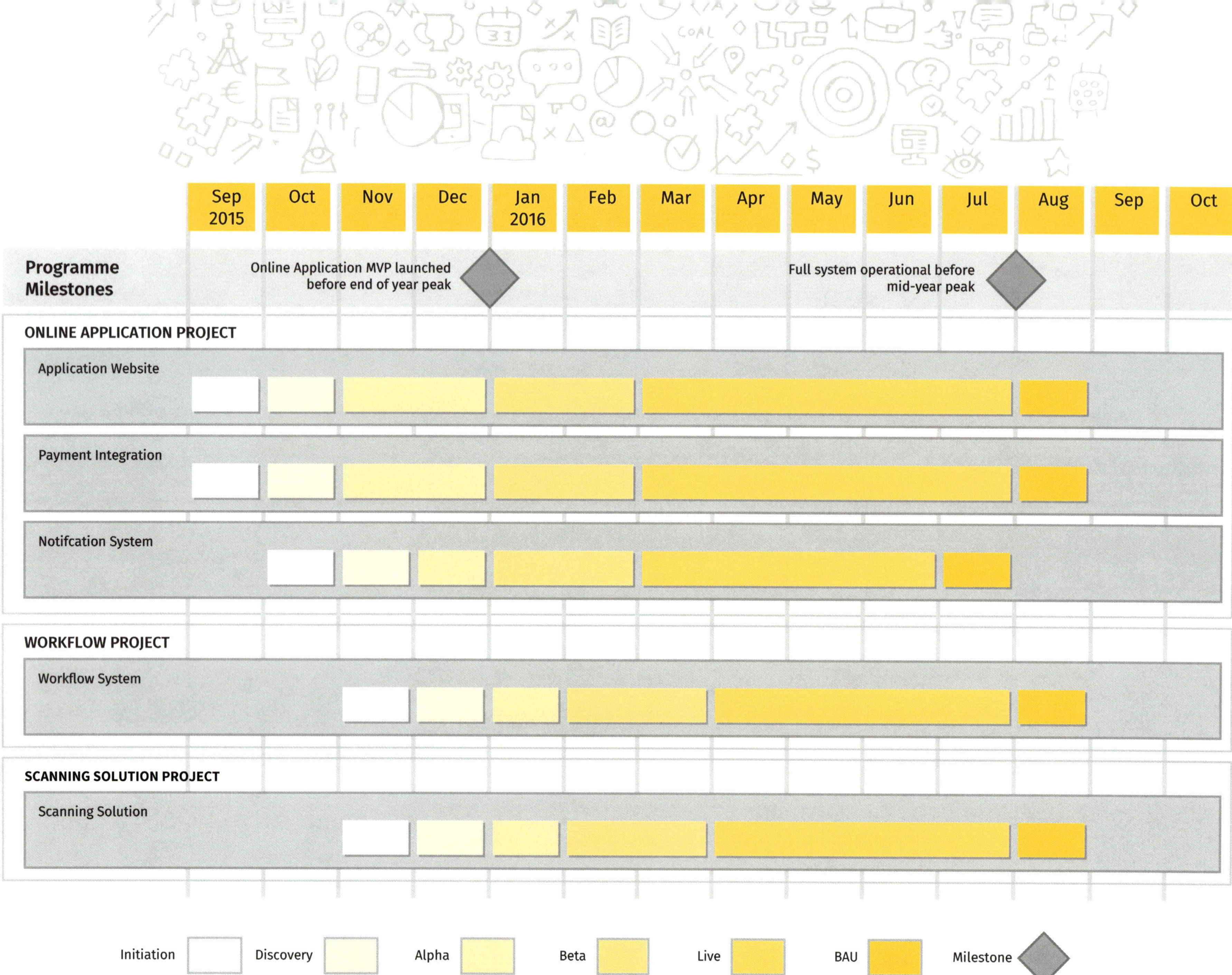


**Figure 10.10 -** Sample Programme Road Map

and anticipate the time required and (most importantly) the dependencies between the different tasks to complete each deliverable. These tasks include all the required drafting, viewing, updating and sign off activities that are required to call a deliverable '*done*', which is the Business Architects main concern – cadence, getting the updated latest versions of the deliverables, agreed and issued at regular intervals. All those '*behind the scenes*' tasks are all factored into '*duration*'. Effort on the other hand, is a little trickier, as it depends on many things, including resource availability, working hours, experience, skill and a host of other considerations. Effort is also a measure that is often more appealing to the financial interests of the Programme (because time is usually charged against the 'number of work units' e.g. hours, to complete a task), however this is outside the scope for our purposes (i.e. getting the road maps drafted and agreed).

In terms of getting a feel of the '*size*' (and therefore 'duration') of each architecture requirement, sizing is a relative measure to all other requirements (not just architecture requirements, but technical and business requirements as well), which is a team activity, and is carried out with other members of the Scrum Team. For simplicity however, and to mock up the strawman of the Road Map and get it out to the Programme (and Business) for discussion, the easiest and quickest method is to assign an arbitrary length of time (e.g. 1-week) to each Blueprint, to get the discussions going. This of course in practice might not be the case (or even possible), as some will take less than a week, like the Statement of Work – if you are lucky, or over a week like the Vision, Strategy, Objectives and Measures (VSOM) Blueprint, as shown in *Figure 10.9 – Sample Business Architecture Road Map* above. If you are extremely unlucky it may take even longer, as was the case with one client I assisted where it took no less than *2-months* to get the Vision statement agreed (not including setting the measures that success of the Programme would be measured by!).

## Building Block Wrap-up

In this section, we discussed Road Map Mapping, which is about developing the two (2) road map Blueprints – the Business Architecture, and the Programme Road Maps:

- **The Business Architecture Road Map** – which provides the view of the timeline and plan to design and deliver the '*design*' of the Business Architecture, being the Business Architecture requirements and deliverables making up the design of the Target Operating Model (TOM), and

- **Programme Road Map** – which provides the view of the timeline and plan to implement the '*physical*' Business Architecture, creating the physical TOM.

The Road Maps build on the in-scope Business Architecture requirements (i.e. Reference Models, Building Blocks and Blueprints) that was agreed in the Statement of Work (SOW), the prioritised Enablers and Business Changes, and indicative timeline of delivering the physical changes into the Organisation from the Project Brief, and Project-Benefits Map Blueprints.

Because the SOW contains the agreed in scope deliverables (i.e. Reference Models, Building Blocks and Blueprints), the Business Architecture Road Map can at least be drafted earlier in the **Design Process** (and not wait to till Step 6) to give the Programme and key stakeholders a sense of the size, scale and the amount of work (and deliverables) required to deliver the changes and close the Programme. The only caveat is the duration taken to actually complete each deliverable is not known, however having this (even without knowing exact timing) still help's the stakeholders prepare for the amount of work, and changes coming.

## Next Steps

Once the Business Architecture and Programme Road Maps have been agreed, the next step in the **Design Process** is to agree the Benefits Realisation Plan, in order to manage and track the realisation of the planned Business Benefits that the Business Changes and Enablers are supporting, as part of the Benefits Realisation Mapping Building Block.

These concerns are discussed in the Benefits Realisation Mapping Building Block in the following section.

.

# 6.3 Benefits Realisation Mapping

## Introduction

Benefits Realisation Mapping is the building block that is used to manage and track the delivery and realisation of the Business Benefits. Benefits Realisation Mapping is included in **HOBA®** for the same reason the Benefits Model is included in **HOBA®** - to overcome the Benefits current lack of visibility and management and to ensure Benefits are *proactively* included in the development and implementation of the TOM.

The purpose of Benefits Realisation Mapping is to establish and agree the framework to record, monitor and report on Benefits progress and realisation.

The advantage of Benefits Realisation Mapping is by having a framework to monitor and report on Benefits progress, Stakeholders have the visibility to see and assess the overall health of the Programme, enabling them to proactively plan (and take actions if required) as (and when) required to ensure successful Benefits delivery, which is according to Bradley (2010):

**"the purpose of any change should always be the realisation of benefits"**

As discussed earlier in the *Alignment with Other Approaches* section with PMIs Benefits Realisation Management (BRM) process, the (full) realisation of Benefits doesn't actually occur in *'pre-capability delivery'* - equivalent to PMI's Phase-3 'Benefits Delivery' shown in the *Figure 10.11* below. The realisation of Benefits occurs after the capabilities are delivered, when the Business actually gets using them to be able to then start realising the planned Benefits. This Benefits realisation is *'post-capability delivery'*, which in most cases is after the Programme has closed and everything has been handed over to the Business to run 'Business As Usual (BAU)'.

The issue with PMI having the delivery of 'Benefits Delivery' in the wrong place (it is actually *'delivery of capabilities'* in the PMI model), is that the tracking of Benefits realisation is often not monitored until the Final (End) Benefits come to realisation, which includes ignoring any monitoring of any Immediate Benefits that contributed to the realisation of the Final

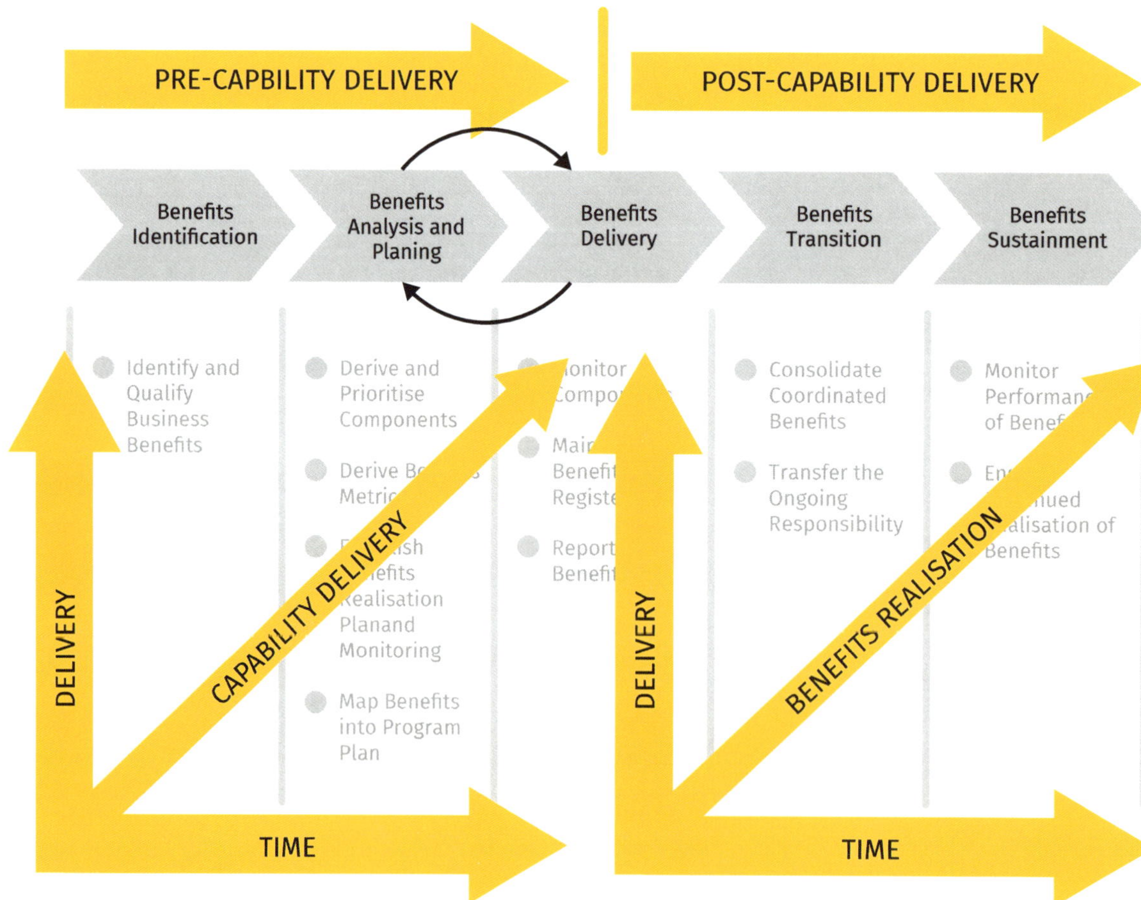


**Figure 10.11** - PMI Benefits Management – Capability Delivery

(End) Benefit themselves. We now know, from completing the Benefits Model, that the Final (End) Benefits are only able to come to realisation *after* the cumulative (compounding) effect of the contributing *'earlier'* Immediate Benefits have been realised (before the respective Final End Benefits themselves).

This Building Block aims to address this short-coming and track the realisation of *all* Benefits the Programme is responsible for impacting, and not just the Final Benefits – to give a full and accurate picture of how the Benefits realisation is tracking and to determine if (and when) mitigation actions need to be taken to correct any slippage in time or realisation, in order to maximize the full value of the Benefits.

The Business Realisation Mapping Blueprints used to track and monitor Benefits realisation are:

- **Benefits Realisation Register**, and
- **Benefits Realisation Map.**

The Benefits Realisation Register is effectively the *'Benefits Realisation Plan'*. It captures how the Benefits are measured, their current and future value, and progress over agreed monitoring periods, providing the *'register'* where benefits will be captured and reported.

The Benefits Realisation Map is the graphical representation of the *Benefits Realisation Register*. It is a snap shot of the Benefits realisation at each of the agreed benefits realisation 'periods' (*phases* of transition), used to provide a visualisation of the state and status of the benefits at specific points in time.

*Figure 10.12* (below) shows an example of a series of Benefit Realisation Maps, as they would appear and change over 4 phases of transition from *phase 0* (current state) to *phase 3* (future state):

**As you can see, the Benefits Realisation Maps mimic the look and feel of the Benefits Maps, and for good reason (for familiarity). Stakeholders reading these find them instantly familiar and recognise the subject matter (i.e. Benefits) and most importantly - the relative position and location of each element and *'cause and effect'* relationship to each other, just like the Benefits Model itself.**

**Where the Benefit Realisation Maps differ from the Benefit Model Maps is the traffic light colour coding to indicate the progress – on track, 25% within target, 25% outside of target, providing an easily recognisable Benefits Realisation *'dashboard'*.**

## Inputs

The inputs used to complete this Building Block are shown in the below:

## Output(s)

The Blueprints (outputs) produced for this Building Block are shown in the table below:

**Benefits Realisation Building Block Inputs**

**Table 10.7**

| Ref | Blueprint | Use |
|---|---|---|
| 4.1.1 | Benefits Profile | Provides the detailed description of a benefit, how it is measured, related strategic objective and who owns it. |
| 4.3.1 | Prioritised Changes Map | Provides the prioritised changes - Enablers (technology & data elements of business capabilities), and Business Changes (people and process elements of business capabilities) that are needed to realise the intended (immediate and final) Business Benefits. |
| 6.1.1. | Project Brief | Provide the outline of the project scope, approach, timeline, project processes, Business Changes and Enablers, benefits, strategic objectives and roles and responsibilities of stakeholders involved in the project. |
| 6.1.2 | Project-Benefits Map | Provides the indicative timeline of the immediate and final benefits. |

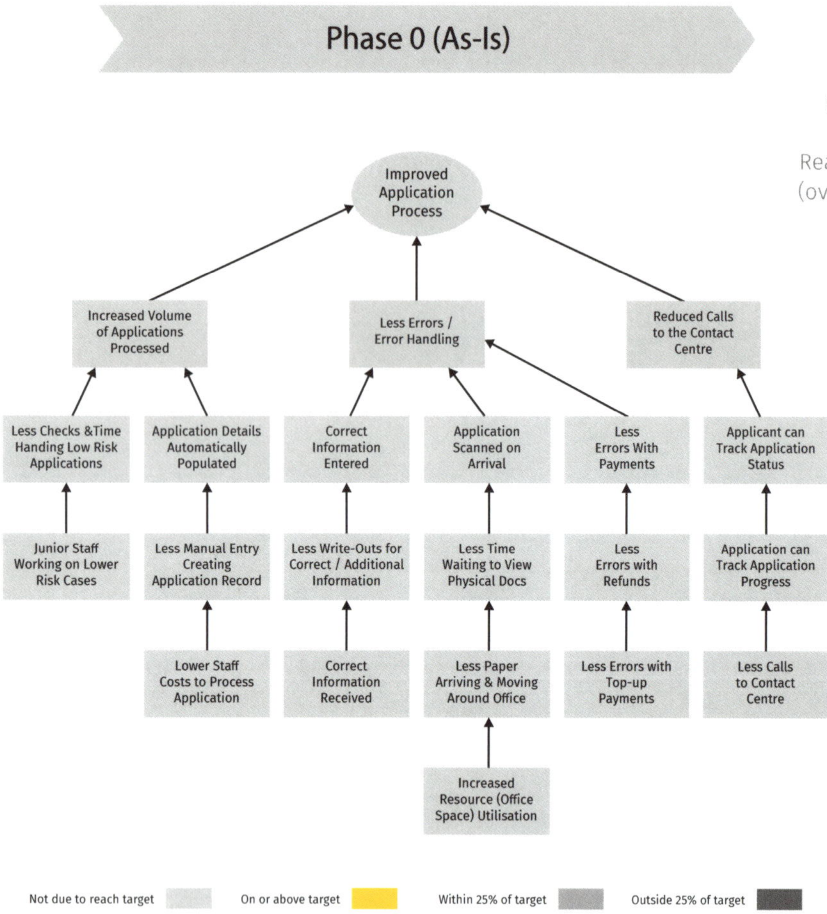


**Figure 10.12** - Benefit Realisation Maps (over 4 phases of transition)

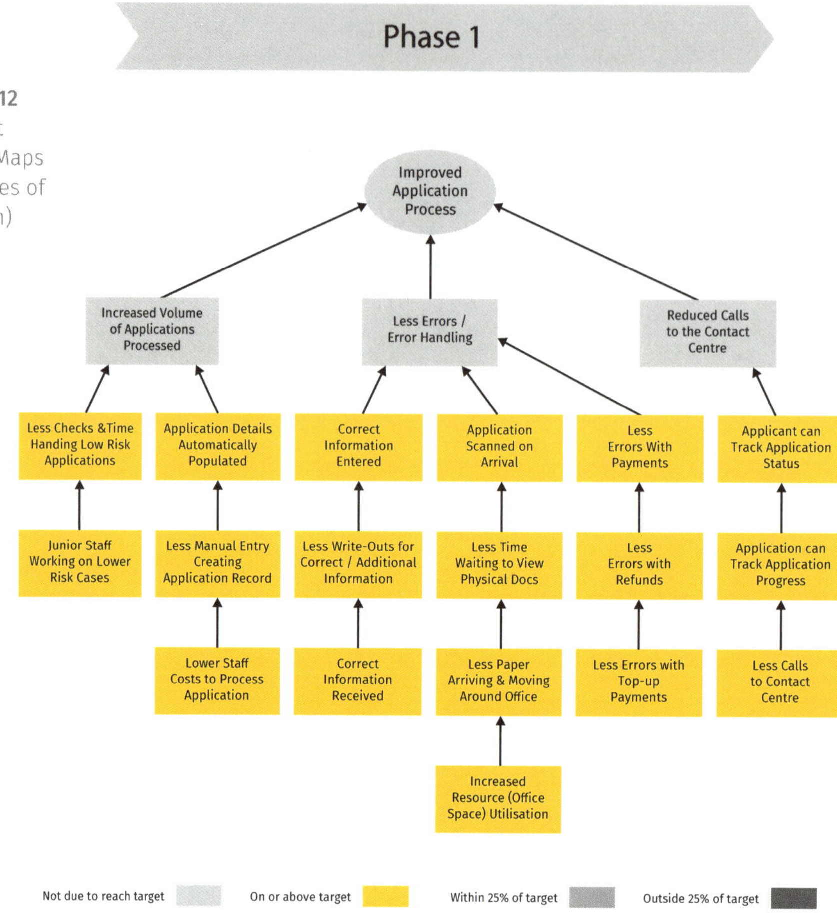


### Benefits Realisation (Output) Blueprints

**Table 10.8**

| Ref | Blueprint | Description | Example |
|---|---|---|---|
| 6.3.1 | Benefits Realisation Register | Register to manage and track the delivery and realisation of Benefits. | (see below) |

| ID | Name | Measure | Baseline Value | Target Value | Period 1 | Period 2 | Period 3 | Period 4 | Benefit Target |
|---|---|---|---|---|---|---|---|---|---|
| B1.0 | Increased Volume of Applications Processed | No. of Applications processed (per period) | 20,000 | 25,000 | 21,000 | 25,500 | 24,000 | 25,500 | |
| B1.1 | Less Checks /Time Handling | Time taken to complete Application (minutes) | 45 | 30 | 45 | 40 | 42 | 37 | |
| B1.2 | Junior Staff-Low Risk Cases | No. of Senior Staff (FTE) involved | 10 | 5 | 10 | 8 | 7 | 6 | |
| B1.3 | Auto Populate Application | No. of errors per 100 Applications | 25 | 10 | 30 | 25 | 20 | 11 | |
| B1.4 | Less Manual Entry | No. of applications needing manual changes (per 100) | 15 | 10 | 15 | 12 | 11 | 10 | |

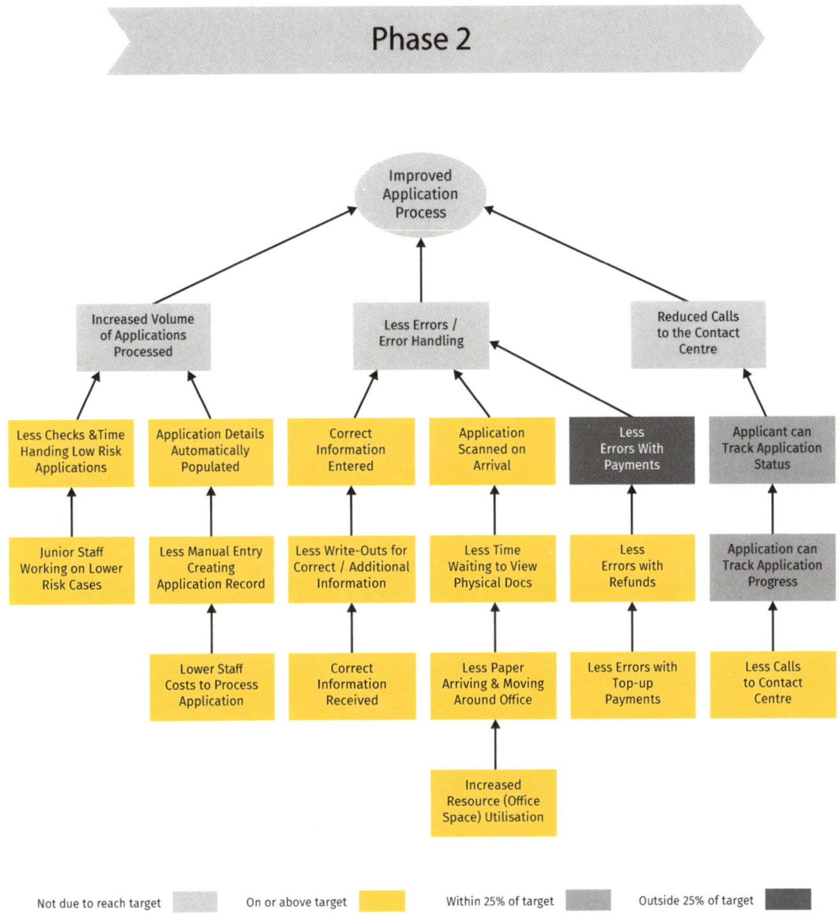


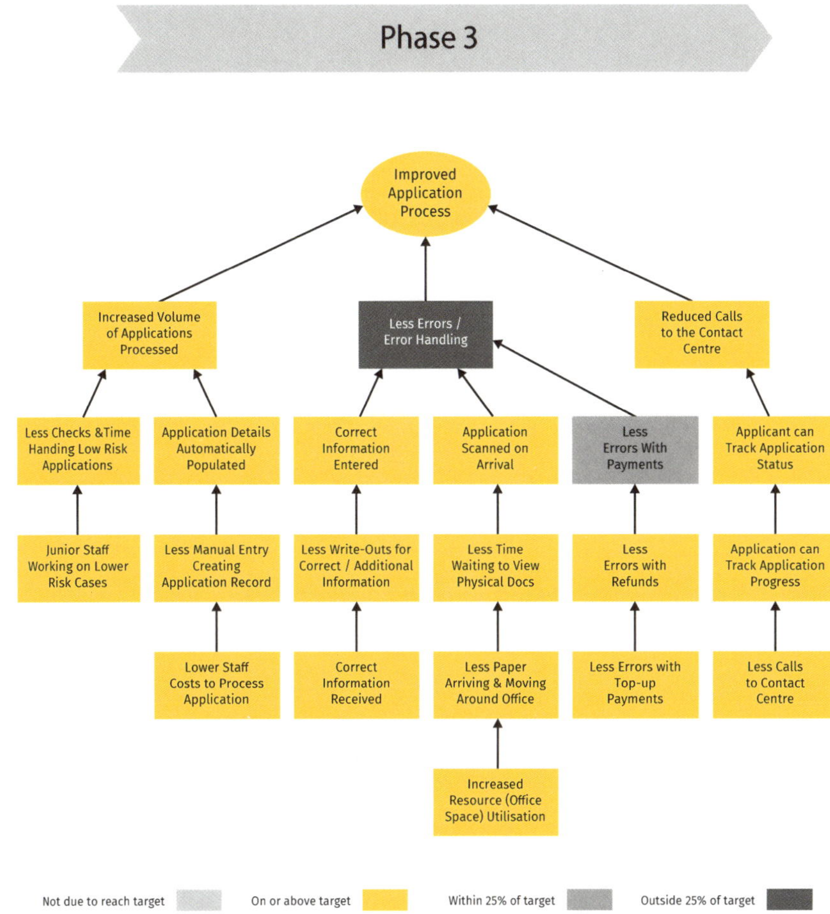


## Benefits Realisation (Output) Blueprints

**Table 10.8**

| Ref | Blueprint | Description | Example |
|---|---|---|---|
| 6.3.2 | Benefits Realisation Map | The graphical representation of the Benefits Realisation Register providing a Benefit Realisation 'dashboard' showing the progress towards Benefits Realisation as percentage (%) realised for each Benefit Realisation period. | 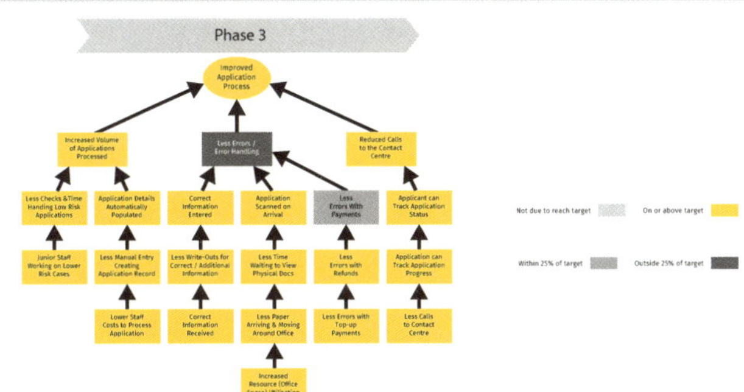  |

## Steps

The steps to complete the above Blueprints (Outputs) are as follows:

### 6.3.1 Benefits Realisation Register

**1. Develop the Benefits Realisation Register**

Using the input for the Inputs section above, and working with the Product Owner and/or other Key Stakeholders, develop the Benefits Realisations Register for each Project under the Programme, by doing the following:

- **Identify the Benefits** (see Benefits Profile),
- **Reconfirm baseline and target measures** (as these might have changed since originally captured),
- **Agree the milestone and key dates** (or periods e.g. 1 period = 3 months) the benefits delivery are to be captured, record and assessed, and
- **Record the details on the Benefits Realisation Register.**

An example Benefits Realisation Register is shown in *Figure 10.13* (below):

| ID | Name | Measure | Baseline Value | Target Value | Period 1 | Period 2 | Period 3 | Period 4 | Benefit Target |
|---|---|---|---|---|---|---|---|---|---|
| B1.0 | Increased Volume of Applications Processed | No. of Applications processed (per period) | 20,000 | 25,000 | 21,000 | 25,500 | 24,000 | 25,500 | |
| B1.1 | Less Checks /Time Handling | Time taken to complete Application (minutes) | 45 | 30 | 45 | 40 | 42 | 37 | |
| B1.2 | Junior Staff-Low Risk Cases | No. of Senior Staff (FTE) involved | 10 | 5 | 10 | 8 | 7 | 6 | |
| B1.3 | Auto Populate Application | No. of errors per 100 Applications | 25 | 10 | 30 | 25 | 20 | 11 | |
| B1.4 | Less Manual Entry | No. of applications needing manual changes (per 100) | 15 | 10 | 15 | 12 | 11 | 10 | |
| B1.5 | Lower Staff Costs to Process Applications | Cost per day (Senior FTE cost per day @ £100 pp) | £1,000 | £500 | £1,000 | £800 | £700 | £750 | |
| B2.0 | Less Errors/Error Handling | No. of applications needing missing information added (per 100 applications) | 10% | 5% | 10% | 10% | 10% | 10% | |
| B2.1 | Correct Information Entered | No. of Applications with user errors (per 100) | 25 | 5 | 25 | 15 | 10 | 20 | |

Within 25% of Target — On or Above Target — Outside 25% of Target

**Figure 10.13** - Example Benefits Realisation Register

**The Benefits Realisation Register *reporting* period duration should be aligned to the Programme critical dates i.e. Programme / Portfolio reporting periods, quarterly or monthly reporting, to ensure Benefits Realisation is tracked and reported on the same time schedule and same critical dates.**

## 6.3.2. Benefits Realisation Map

### 2. Develop the Benefits Realisation Map

The benefits realisation map is a snap shot of Benefits realisation at a given time – from the current state (Period 0) to the future state (Period N), as per the periods provided in the Benefits Realisation Register. At each new period, create a new version of the Benefits Realisation Map, to reflect the benefit measures recorded on the Benefits Realisation Register at each period.

As time passes, at each period, the status and Benefits 'value' within that period is recorded on the Benefits Realisation Map.

An example of the Benefits Realisation Map at Period 3 is shown in *Figure 10.14* below:

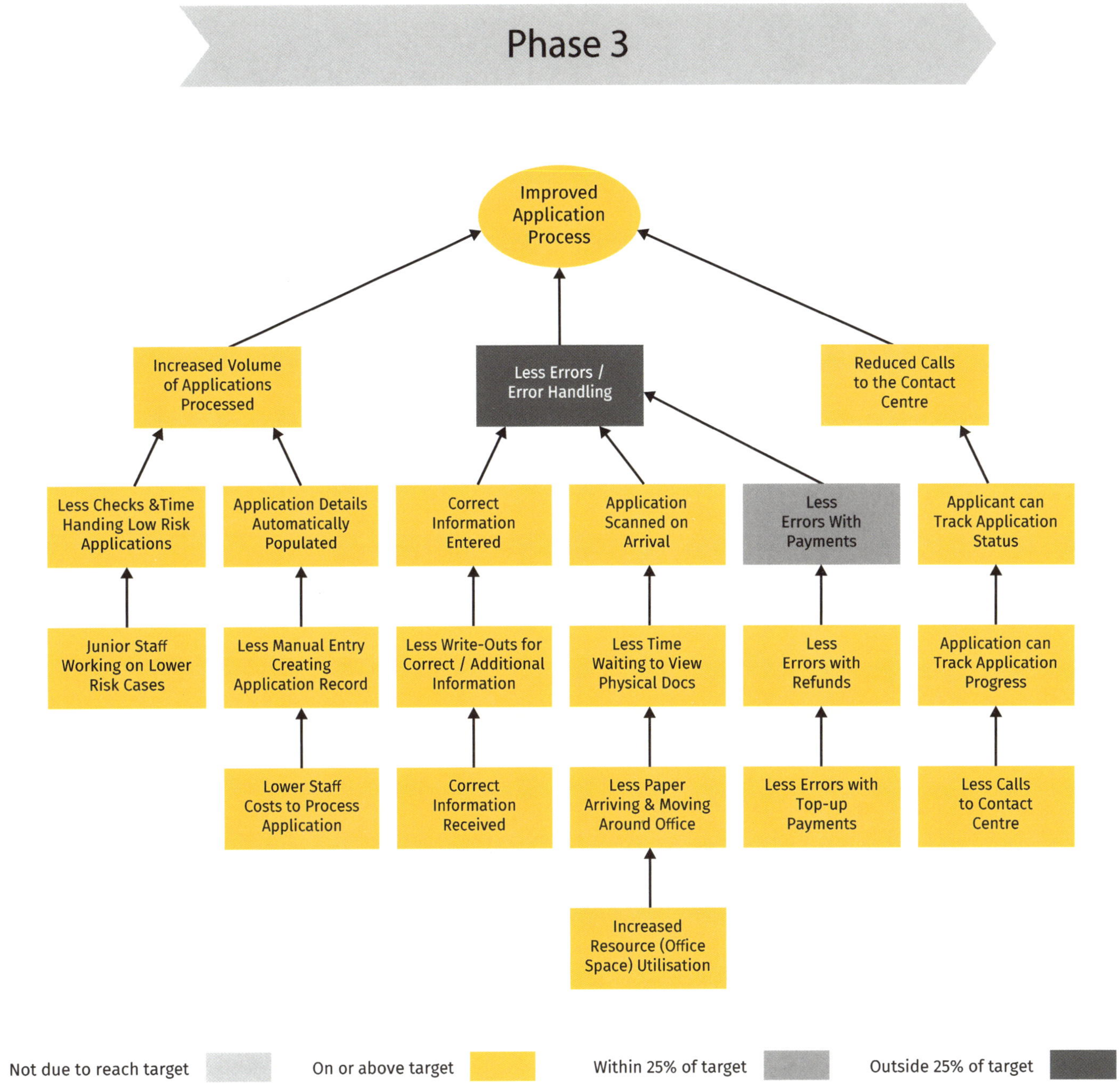


**Figure 10.14 -** Benefits Realisation Map (Phase 3)

### 3. Record any risks if expected Benefits are not likely to be realised at each reporting Period

As you track the Benefits realisation, any risks of the Benefits not being achieved should be added to the Risks Register in the RAID log, to monitor and manage centrally from the one location and repository.

An example of a RAID entry for the Benefit realisation risk, is shown in *Table 10.9* (below):

1. **Iteratively socialise, validate and refine the Blueprint(s)** - including any Risks, Assumptions, Issues and Dependencies (RAID) addressed or raised as part of completing this step, and
2. **Package and publish the Blueprint(s)** – in line with your agreed sprint/release cycle, established back in *Step 2 – Control* with the *Governance Model*.

## Risks and Mitigations

There are two (2) main issues to be aware of with benefits realisation:

1. **No Benefits/Change Manager**
2. **Handover to BAU (Business As Usual)**

We will discuss each of these issues below.

### 1. No Benefits/Change Manager.

Benefit Realisation Management (BRM) (identification, validation, tracking, realisation) is usually a role filled by the Benefits Manager* (if not the Change Manager if you are lucky enough to have one). However, should neither be available, as the Business Architect it then becomes your responsibility, because you are responsible for the identification of Business Changes and Enablers that drive those Benefits.

**(*) Note - 'Benefits Manager' is not the same as 'Benefits Owner'. Benefits Ownership remains unchanged.**

### 2. Handover to BAU (Business As Usual).

The major difference with delivering this Building Block and Blueprints compared to all the others, is that the Customer for these Blueprints here is the actual Business (external to the Programme), and these Blueprints are enduring, intended to live past when the Programme has closed, to manage the Benefits realisation, as part of BAU. As a result, there needs to be a process to handover the responsibility for monitoring the Benefits realisation once the Programme is closed.

As the Product Owner is (in most cases) the Benefits Owner (being the representative of the Business or delegated owner on behalf of the Business stakeholders), he/she would have been actively involved in developing these Blueprints (i.e. they know what this looks like, what it means and how to manage it) so there shouldn't be any surprises.

At the end of the Programme (at Programme close and/or Capability delivery), the Product Owner should simply take full ownership of both the Benefits Realisation Register, and Benefits Realisation Map (along with the RAID – or mitigation actions within the RAID) and manage the Benefits Realisation Management process from that point on, as part of Business As Usual (BAU).

## Building Block Wrap-up

In this section, we discussed the Benefits Realisation Mapping Building Block, which effectively defines the Business Realisation Plan, captured in the Benefits Realisation Register, and visuals represented in the Benefits Realisation Map.

Business Realisation Mapping is made up of two (2) Blueprints – the Business Realisation Register, and Business Realisation Map:

- The Business Realisation Register – effectively provides the Benefits Realisation Plan –

Table 10.9 Example RAID Entry for a Benefits Realisation Mitigation Action

| Risk ID | Risk Description | Likelihood | Impact | Severity | Mitigation Plan | Owner | Status | Date Closed |
|---|---|---|---|---|---|---|---|---|
| R0.2 | Benefit B1.0 Increased Volume of Applications Processed not processing expected number of applications | L | M | M | Check application process, Identify and resolve bottlenecks, Review (and update training, manuals, policies) | Product Owner | Open | |

what the benefits look like, how they are measured, current value, future value, and the period(s) the benefits will be recorded in to check they are being realised as planned (or when to implement the mitigation actions in the instances where they are not coming to realisation), and

- The Benefits Realisation Map – which provides the visual representation of the Benefits Realisation Register, as snap shots at a point in time (the agreed periods), used to provide the visual representation of the state and status of the Benefits as they are realised over time.

Any mitigation actions to address any variations to the expected Benefits Realisation progress are recorded and managed centrally through the RAID Log.

Benefits Realisation Mapping is the only (one off) Building Block and Blueprints that will endure past the Programme close, to be handed over to the Business to manage and track the Benefit realisation as part of BAU.

### Next Steps

Once the Benefits Realisation Mapping has been agreed, the next step in the Design Process is the Transition Architecture Mapping Building Block, which provides the views of the developing Business Architecture as it develops at architecturally significant periods from the Current Operating Model, to the Target Operating Model (TOM).

The Transition Architecture Mapping Building Block is discussed in the following section.

## 6.4 Transition Architecture Mapping

### Introduction

Transition Architecture Mapping is the building block that provides the views of the Target Operating Model (TOM), at specific phases of the physical Business Architecture implementation.

The objective with this Building Block is to show and describe, at architecturally significant points in time, the progression from the '*baseline*' Current Operating Model to the '*future*' Target Operating Model (TOM).

The purpose of Transition Architectures is to provide clear targets along the Business Architecture transition from '*baseline*' state to '*target*' state, by providing an early view of what the TOM will look like at different points in time.

The benefit of the Transition Architecture views (along with showing what each phase of development looks like), is they are an effective stakeholder and risk management tool, by helping stakeholders:

- **Gain confidence the design** will deliver the expected changes and benefits (as well as when they can expect to see the views of what the future Business Architecture looks like, as it develops incrementally over time),
- **Ask questions and challenge the design and implementation decisions** and assumptions before actual implementation (in light of seeing all the changes together in scope for the Programme), and
- **Identify and agree mitigation actions to address any risks** that may prevent the transition states being achieved.

This Building Block is made up of the following Blueprints:

1. **Transition Architecture Strategy Map, and**
2. **Transition Architecture *Phase* Maps**

We will discuss each of these Blueprints below.

#### 1. Transition Architecture Strategy Map

The Transition Architecture Strategy Map provides a template and outline of how the Organisation intends to transition from the 'baseline' Current Operating Model, to the 'future' Target Operating Model, providing a high-level schedule, as shown in the example in *Figure 10.15* (below).

The Transition Architecture Strategy Map provides a view of the people, process and technology changes in a phased approach to implementing these changes to create the physical Target Operating Model (TOM). It is effectively describing the 'best steps' to take to implement the Target Operating Model (TOM), to align the Business to the Business Strategy and support the Organisation to realise the planned Business Benefits and Strategic Objectives.

The steps to put together the Transition Architecture Strategy Map is a 2-Step approach - Business Benefits, and then Risk Management:

| Jan 2017 – Mar | Apr – Jun | Jul – Sep | Oct – Dec |
|---|---|---|---|
| **AS IS**<br>Current State | **PHASE 1**<br>Deliver Workflow & Online Application Systems | **PHASE 2**<br>Deliver Notification & Scanning Solutions | **PHASE 3**<br>Deliver Intergrated Payment Solution |
| **People** | | | |
| • Lots of calls to Contact Centre<br>• Manual entry payments<br>• Sending of physical documents | • Document Checklist provided to Applicant online | • Guidance on notifications provided to applicant | • Risk assessment process integrated into |
| **Process** | | | |
| • Manual process<br>• Manual data entry<br>• Manual payments<br>• Manual sending docs/Letters | • Staff trained in new online application process<br>• Staff trained in new automated workflow system | • Staff trained in new scanning system & process<br>• Staff trained in integrated notification system | • Staff trained on new risk assessment process |
| **Technology** | | | |
| • Applications are printed off website (sent manually for manual keying)<br>• No payment facility (via 3rdParty) | • Automatic workflow system live<br>• Online application system Live | • Integrated notification system<br>• liveIntegrated scanning system llve | • Integrated payment system live |

**Figure 10.15** - Sample Transition Architecture Strategy Map

1. **Business Benefits Approach** – the first step is to use the Prioritised Changes from the Benefits Model as a starting point to guide the order of implementation. This is so the planned Benefits that those Prioritised Changes directly support are implemented in that order (and priority) the Benefits are intended to be realised in. You will recall from the Benefits Model, it was the '*priority*' score from the Prioritised Changes Register that showed the degree of contribution and therefore the priority the respective Business Changes and Enablers have on the Final Benefits.
2. **Risk Management Approach** – the second step is using the '*draft*' map developed from (1) above, and use that view to show all the changes and timing(s) across the Organisation to identify opportunities to reduce the number of changes happening on the Business at any one time or phase. This approach aims to address and reduce the risk of implementation failure. When looking vertically down the map, if there is more than one '*big*' change (e.g. implementing a new system) at the same time, this should raise questions, such as:

- **Is it sensible to proceed with (these) two (or more) big changes at the same time?**
- **Does the Business have capacity to handle that amount of change all at once?**
- **Is it possible to stagger their release or extend the delivery dates** of any one (which might mean pushing out the project milestones or due dates, but maybe at an acceptable trade-off of lowering delivery risk)? or
- **Can we proceed with caution, plan and be ready with other mitigation actions** (or fall back options) should the implementation not go according to plan?

Other factors may also come into play that effect scheduling and potentially changing implementation timelines, such like - IT change freezes, peak business periods, holiday periods etc. These 'blocked out' periods will mean further adjustments to the timing and sequence of certain Business Changes and Enablers can be and/or should be implemented.

## 2. Transition Architecture Phase Map

The Transition Architecture Phase Map Blueprint is the next level of decomposition down from the *Transition Architecture Strategy Map*, which provides a view of the *actual* phases to implement the Transition Architecture Strategy Map. The Transition Architecture Phase Maps are a snap shot in time of the Organisation at each 'transition phase', and puts each phase in context of the Business processes they are impacting.

An example of a Transaction Architecture Phase Map is shown in the *Figure 10.16* below:

The Transition Architecture Phase Maps show all architectural changes on the single view for that phase, over the transition period of implementation (until fully implemented), starting from the current day *(Phase 0)*, to full implementation *(Phase N)*.

Transition Architecture Map Phase 0 (current 'As-Is' state) (*Figure 10.16* below) shows all the changes in their different phases in one view (from Phase 0 to Phase N) as the 'baseline' map, to show the full picture or '*end to end*' view of all architectural changes, while each subsequent phase map following, will show only the changes that occur in that phase.

As an example, (*Figure 10.17* ) below shows each of the different Transaction Architecture Phase Maps for each of the transition phases, from Phase 0 (current state) up to Phase 3 (in this example, the future state).

You will notice how Phase 0 provides the full view of all changes, and each subsequent map highlights the areas that are 'affected, not affected, or not in scope' for that phase.

The benefit of these combined views is that it helps to set stakeholder expectations of what (and where) the changes are, and in what order these changes will be carried out and implemented.

The Transition Architecture Phase Map Blueprint also allows *both* the Business and Technology Stakeholders to have a joined up, clear view and understanding of the actual changes that are planned to happen in a business context as well as where they will happen (i.e. the named Business Processes stated in the Transition Strategy Map, which the Technology needs to support).

## End to End Student Visa Application Process - Phase 0 (As-Is)

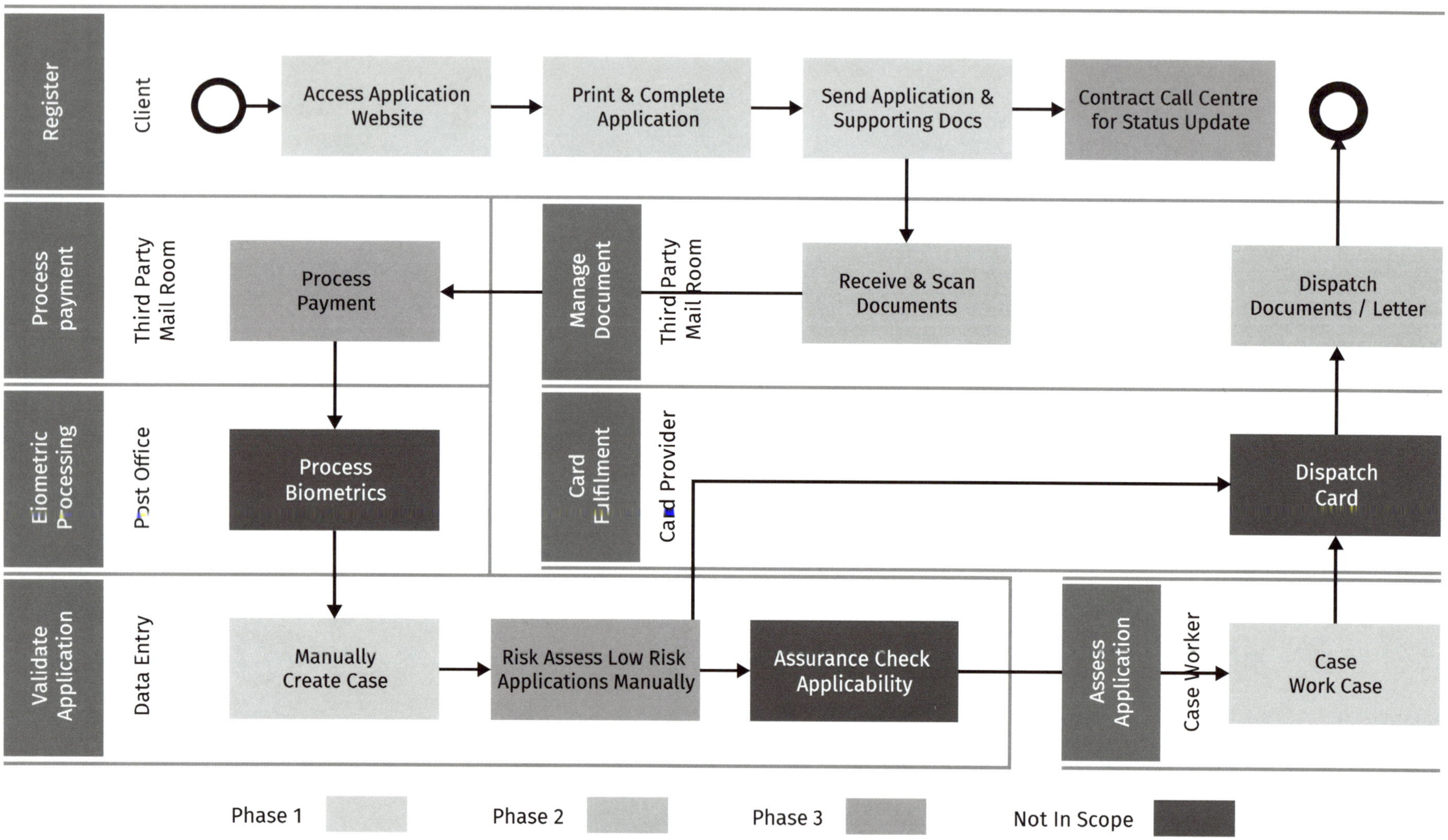


Figure 10.16 - Sample Transition Architecture Phase Map (Phase 0)

You will recall we discussed at the start of this book in the *Current Situation* section, that *'lack of User Input, incomplete requirements and changing requirements'* are the top three (3) reasons why projects fail. The Transition Architecture Strategy (and Phase) Maps addresses these factors by showing these two (2) groups of Stakeholders (i.e. the Business, and Technology stakeholders) the following:

- **Where and when the expected significant architectural changes occur** to the Business, that the *technical/technology* stakeholders are aware of it and can support it, thereby having a common (shared) view of what these changes mean for themselves, and each other, so both parties are ready (and comfortable) with the changes and dependencies, and most importantly –
- **They are able to plan now for any mitigation actions should the implementation of these changes not go as planned** or show to not yield the expected results.

The **Transition Architecture Phase Map Blueprint** itself is made up of the following three (3) areas:

- **Transition Summary** – provides a summary of the architectural phases, changes and milestones at each phase;
- **Transition Phase Map** – provides the visual view of the in-scope, end-to-end, high level business processes impacted by the changes the Programme and TOM bring about, highlighting the architectural significant changes, at each phase of implementation, and
- **Transition Impact Assessment** – provides a summary of the *before* and *after* states, changes and impact of those changes at each architectural phase at the Business Capability level (i.e. people, process, and technology) across the impacted end-to-end business process.

We will discuss the steps to develop and deliver each of these Blueprints in the Steps section below.

**Transition Architecture Building Block Inputs**

Table 10.10

| Ref | Blueprint | Use |
|---|---|---|
| 5.1.2 | Process Model Map (To-Be) | Provides the in-scope / To-Be business processes the Transition Phase Maps are based on |
| 4.3.1 | Prioritised Changes Map | Provides the prioritised list of Business Changes and Enablers, prioritised in order of implementation, which the Transition Architecture Strategy, Transition Architecture Plan, and Transition Architecture Maps are based on. |
| 4.3.2 | Prioritised Changes Register | Provides the details behind the Prioritised Changes Map(s). |

## Inputs

The inputs used to complete this Building Block are shown in the above:

## Output(s)

The Blueprints (outputs) produced for this Building Block are shown in the table below:

## Steps

The steps to complete the above Blueprints (Outputs) are as follows:

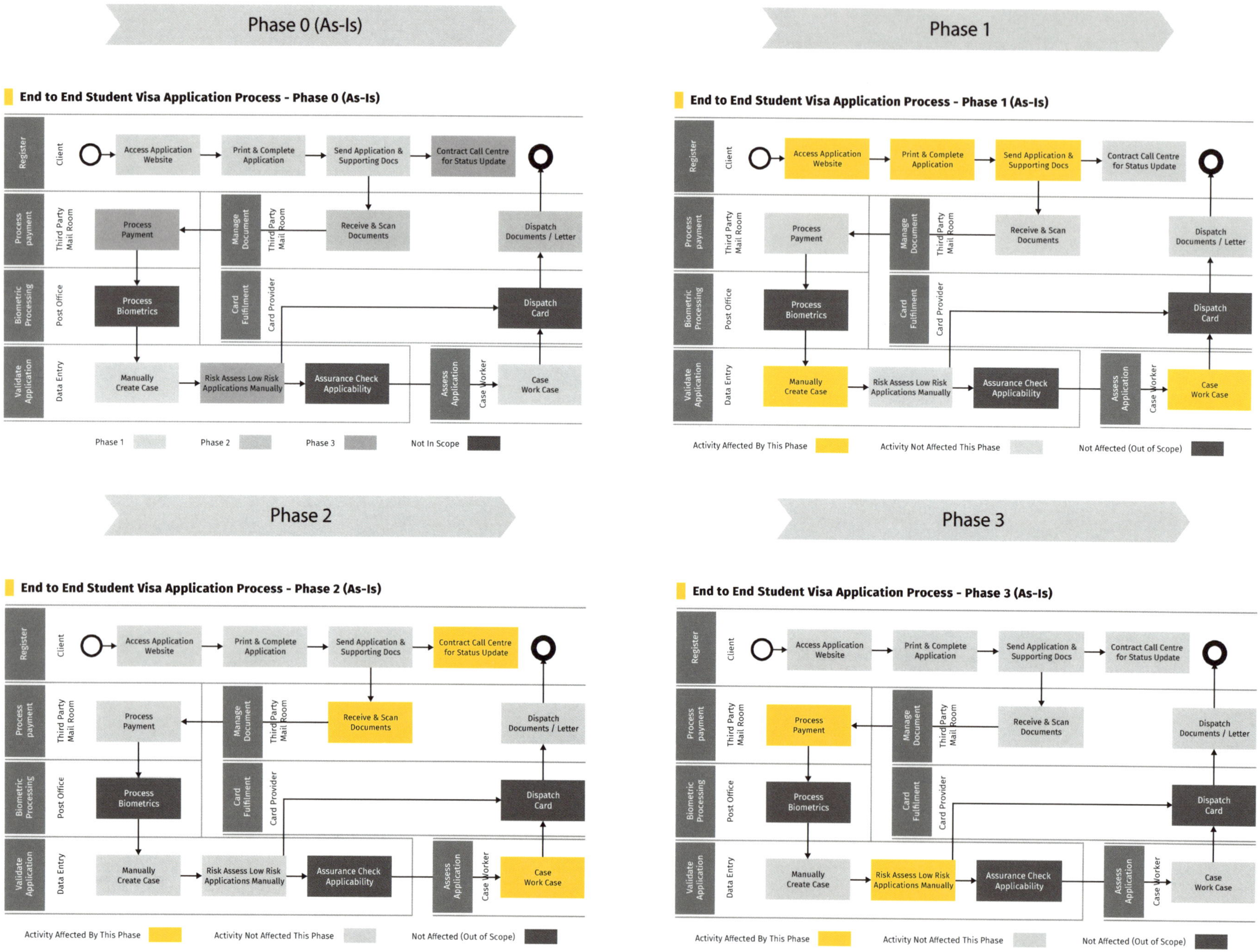


**Figure 10.17 -** Transition Architecture Phase Maps over 4-phases of transition

**Table 10.11**

| Ref | Blueprint | Description | Example |
|---|---|---|---|
| 6.4.1 | Transition Architecture Strategy Map | Provides the outline of order the Business Changes and Enablers (i.e. People, Process and Technology changes) will be implemented to maximize the realisation and timing of the Business Benefits and minimise delivery risk | 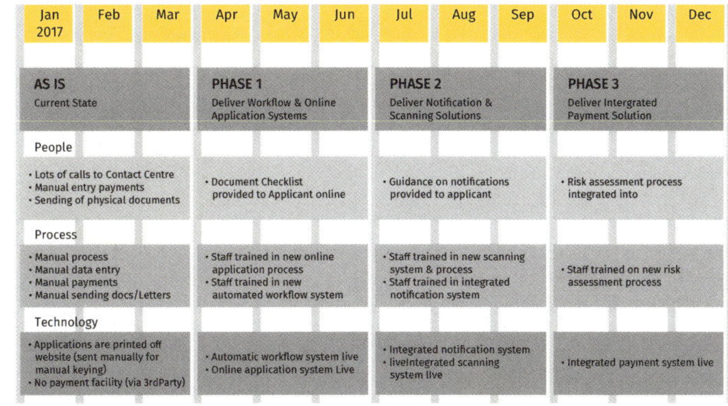 |
| 6.4.2 | Transition Architecture Phase Map | Provides the planned (and implemented) architectural changes at each transition phase.<br>This Blueprint is made up of the three (3) parts:<br><br>• Transition Summary<br>• Transition Phase Map(s)<br>• Transition Impact Assessment | Table 10.12 (below); 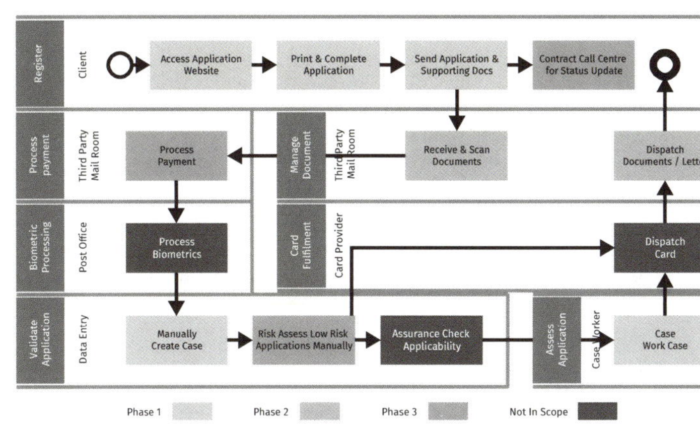 |



**Table 10.12**

| Phase | Name | Period | Business Changes and Enablers Delivered | Current Situation/ Summary of Changes |
|---|---|---|---|---|
| 0 | As-Is | Today | Nil | · Legacy website used to locate & print application<br>· Third party receives postal Applications<br>· Third party scans into legacy workflow<br>· Third party manual makes payments<br>· Third party sends reminder/decision letters<br>· Third party returns supporting docs |
| 1 | Workflow & Online Application | Apr-Jun | · Automated Workflow Ser. (AWS)<br>· Online Application Service (OAS)<br>· Document Checklist<br>· Staff training (OAS& AWS) | · Legacy application website decommissioned<br>· OAS handle all applications<br>· Legacy workflow decommissioned<br>· AWS in place |
| 2 | Notification & Scanning | Jul-Sep | · Integrated Notification Sys. (INS)<br>· Integrated Scanning Service(ISS)<br>· Notification Guidance<br>· Staff Training (INS & ISS) | · Notifications and updates available online<br>· Third party scanning no longer involved<br>· Internal mailroom scanning in place |
| 3 | Integrated Payment | Oct-Dec | · Integrated Risk Assessment Service (IRS)<br>· Integrated Payment System (IPS)<br>· Staff Training (IRS& IPS) | · Low risk applications routed for faster processing<br>· IPS in place |

Example Transition Summary



Example Transition Phase Map

Table 10.11

| Ref | Blueprint | Description | Example |
|---|---|---|---|
| 6.4.2 | Transition Architecture Phase Map | Provides the planned (and implemented) architectural changes at each transition phase.<br>This Blueprint is made up of the three (3) parts:<br>• Transition Summary<br>• Transition Phase Map(s)<br>• Transition Impact Assessment | See Table 10.13 below (Example Transition Impact Assessment) |

Table 10.13

| Area | Before | After | Impact |
|---|---|---|---|
| Client | Downloads application as PDF, prints, completes and returns via post with supporting docs to external mail house | Completes & submits application form online, prints checklist and returns via post to external mail house | • Legacy application website decommissioned<br>• Online Application Service (OAS) handle all applications<br>• Automated Workflow Service (AWS) in place<br>• Legacy workflow decommissioned |
| External Mail House | Receives large volume of mail (application forms and supporting docs), scans and sends physical docs to Case Working | Receives less volume (checklist and supporting docs only), scans and sends physical docs to Case Working | Less volume, less scanning, less physical documents in storage and circulation (faster processing) |
| Data Entry | Receives all applications for manual entry into legacy workflow system | • Receives checklist and supporting docs only<br>• Client record automatically created in legacy workflow system replacement<br>• Correct values record against docs received | • Legacy workflow system decommissioned<br>• AWS record automatically created<br>• Less workload for data entry (faster processing) |
| Post Office | Capture biometrics (when requested and required) via existing biometrics system | No change felt by business | AWS interface into existing biometrics system (Technical change only) |
| Card Provider | Receive card requests in existing card system via legacy workflow system | Receive card request in existing card system via AWS | AWS interface into existing card system (Technical change only) |
| Case Working | Works case in legacy case working system | Works case in legacy replacement (AWS) | Uses AWS to work case (faster processing) |

Example Transition Impact Assessment

## 6.4.1 Transaction Architecture Strategy Map

### 1. Develop the Transition Architecture Strategy Map

Using the inputs from the Inputs section above, and working with the Product Owner (and other Key Stakeholders where necessary), agree the duration of the Phase periods (e.g. 3 months), and plot the prioritised changes on the Transition Architecture Strategy Map in their corresponding 'priority' for each of the Business Changes and Enablers changes under their respective People, Process and Technology sections, as shown in the previously example in *Figure 10.15* – Sample Transition Architecture Strategy Map above.

**The Business Changes (People and Process) and Enablers (Technology) should closely mimic the Prioritised Changes Map and Prioritised Changes Register in terms of the order they are implemented. The only time this will change should be when a priority is amended due to any risk management reprioritization strategy or activity (i.e. technical dependencies or clashes with other parts of the Programme or Organization).**

## 6.4.2 Transaction Architecture Map

### 2. Develop the Transition Summary

Using the *Transition Architecture Strategy Map*, break down the map and capture the following information:

- Phase Number
- Phase Name
- Phase (i.e. date range)
- Business Changes and Enablers Delivered
- Summary of Changes

An example of a Transition Summary is shown in *Table 10.12* below:

Sample Transition Summary

Table 10.12

| Phase | Name | Period | Business Changes and Enablers Delivered | Current Situation/ Summary of Changes |
|---|---|---|---|---|
| 0 | As-Is | Today | Nil | • Legacy website used to locate & print application<br>• Third party receives postal Applications<br>• Third party scans into legacy workflow<br>• Third party manual makes payments<br>• Third party sends reminder/decision letters<br>• Third party returns supporting docs |
| 1 | Workflow & Online Application | Apr-Jun | • Automated Workflow Ser. (AWS)<br>• Online Application Service (OAS)<br>• Document Checklist<br>• Staff training (OAS& AWS) | • Legacy application website decommissioned<br>• OAS handle all applications<br>• Legacy workflow decommissioned<br>• AWS in place |
| 2 | Notification & Scanning | Jul-Sep | • Integrated Notification Sys. (INS)<br>• Integrated Scanning Service(ISS)<br>• Notification Guidance<br>• Staff Training (INS & ISS) | • Notifications and updates available online<br>• Third party scanning no longer involved<br>• Internal mailroom scanning in place |
| 3 | Integrated Payment | Oct-Dec | • Integrated Risk Assessment Service (IRS)<br>• Integrated Payment System (IPS)<br>• Staff Training (IRS& IPS) | • Low risk applications routed for faster processing<br>• IPS in place |

### 3. Develop the Transition Architecture Phase Map (for each phase)

Using the Transition Strategy Map and Transition Summary, plot the changes on the first (Phase 0) Transition Architecture Phase, which shows all phases (0, 1, 2, 3,...N) on a single map. This first Transition Phase Map (Phase 0) shows the changes to be delivered at each phase, shown by the key.

An example of a Transition Phase Map (*Phase 0*) was shown in *Figure 10.16* above. For completeness and reference, this is again shown in Figure 10.18 (below).

Repeat the *Transition Phase Map* for each phase and highlight the relevant changes that are in scope to be changed in that phase.

An example of a Transition Phase Map (*Phase 1*), is shown in *Figure 10.19* below.

An example of a Transition Phase Map (*Phase 2*), is shown in *Figure 10.20* below.

For completeness, an example of the *Transition Phase Map* (Phase 3, the last and final phase), is shown in *Figure 10.21* below.

**Each individual phase maps is intended to highlight only the changes that occur in that specific phase in order to compare each maps differences and changes through the transition from Current State to Future State (i.e. Target Operating Model) highlighting how different parts of the Organisation are changed at different times.**

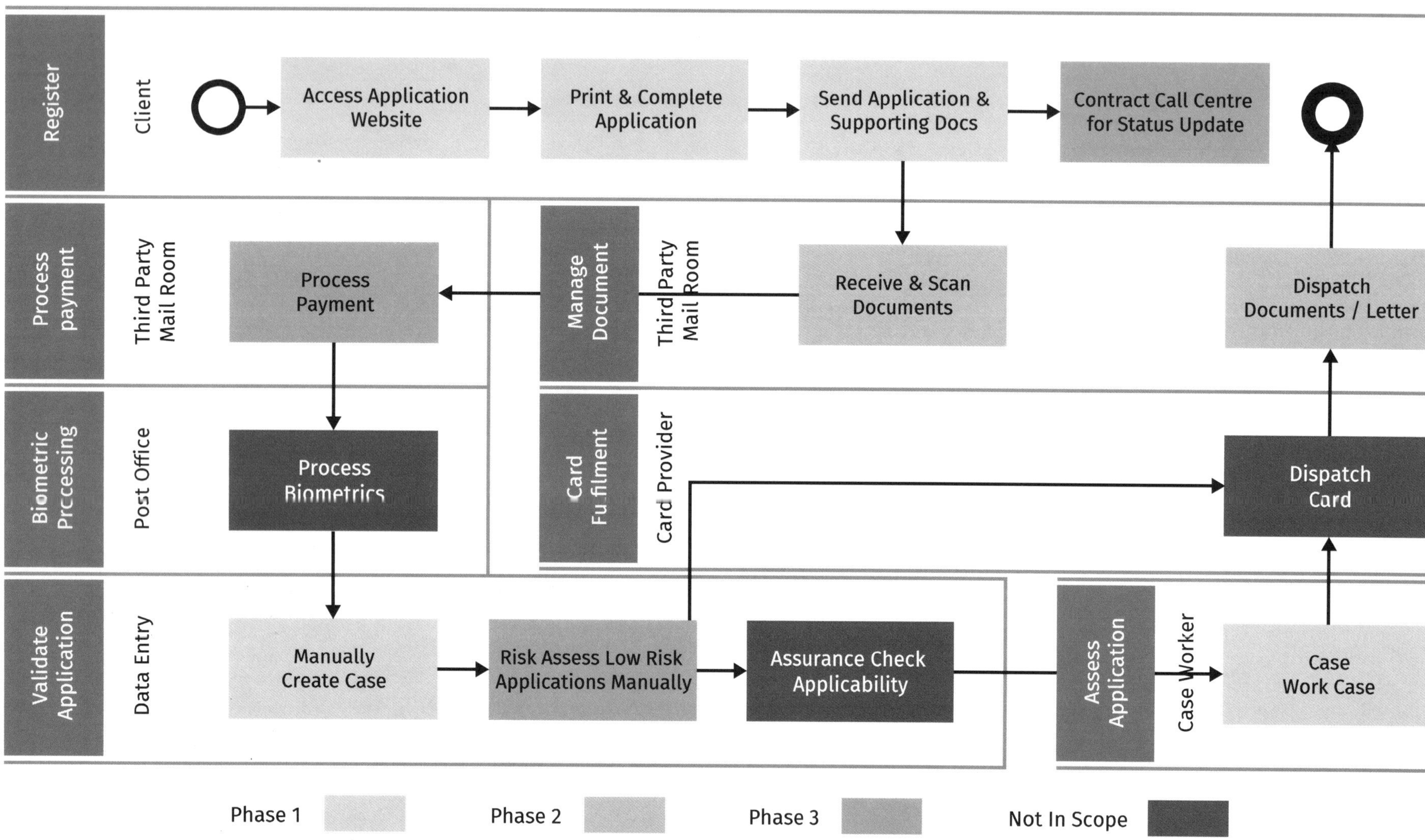


**Figure 10.18** - Sample Transition Phase Map (Phase 0)

## End to End Student Visa Application Process - Phsse 1 (As-Is)

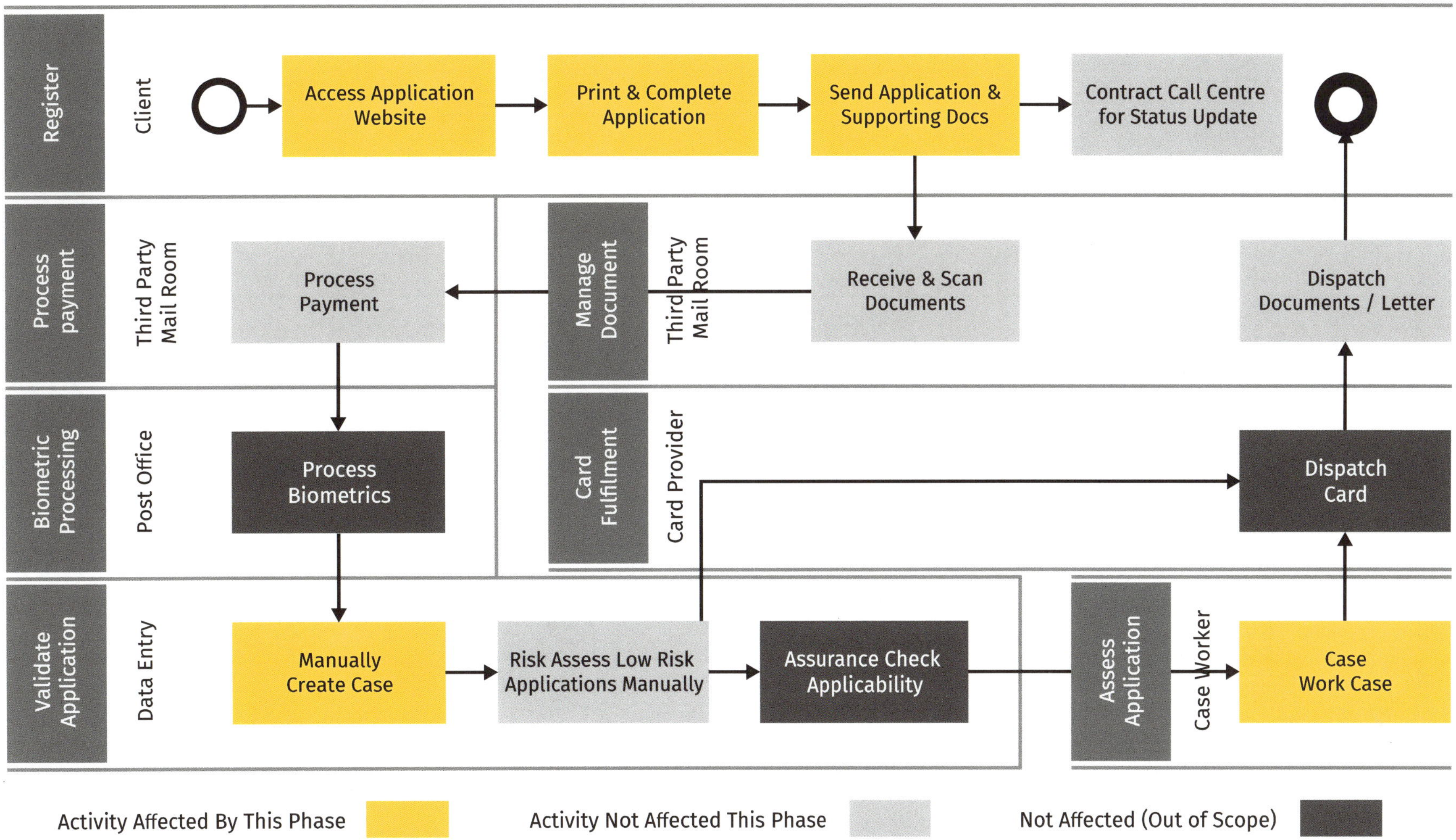


**Figure 10.19 -** Example Transition Map (Phase 1)

## End to End Student Visa Application Process - Phase 2 (As-Is)

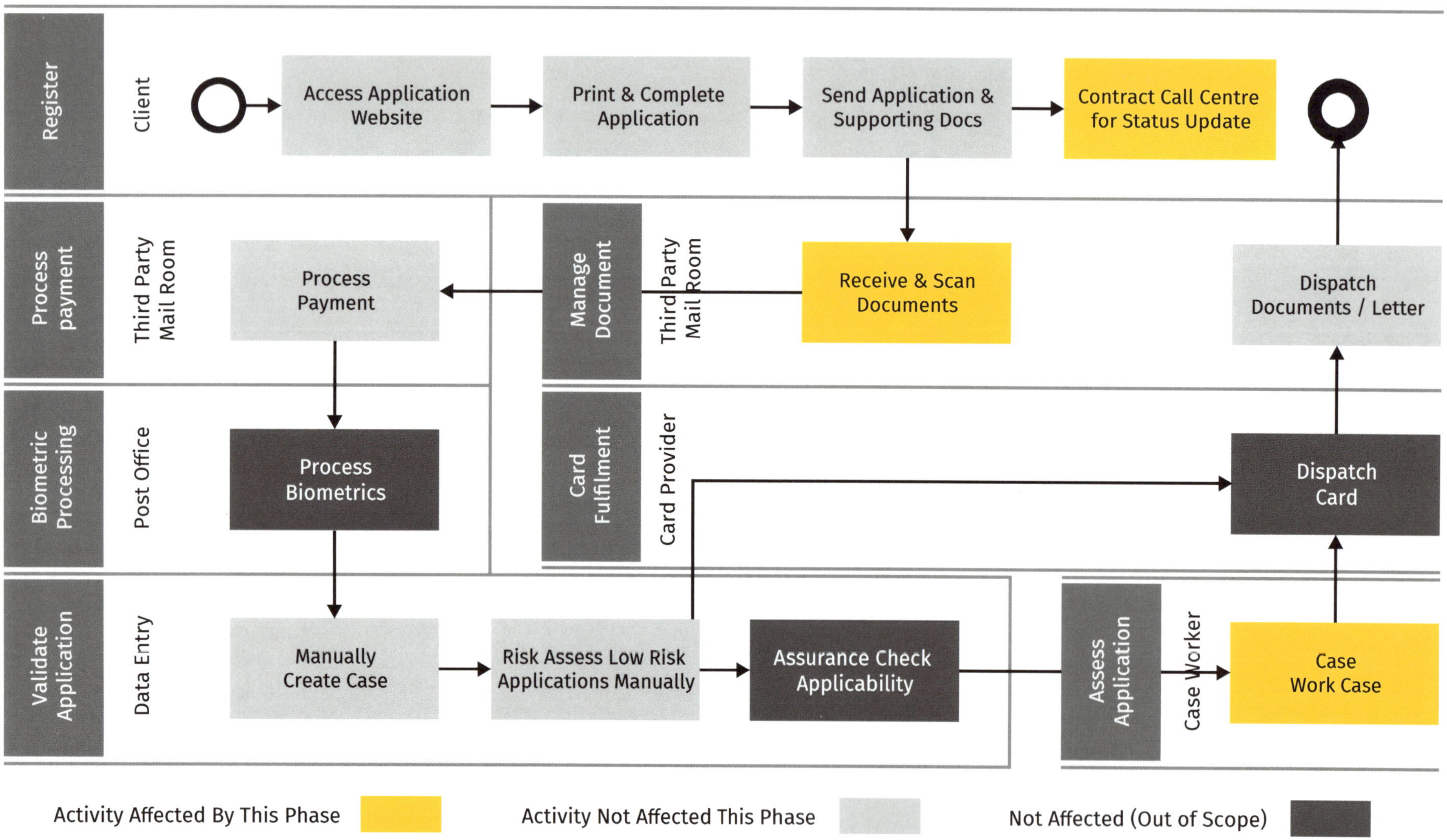


**Figure 10.20 -** Example Transition Map (Phase 2)

## End to End Student Visa Application Process - Phase 3 (As-Is)

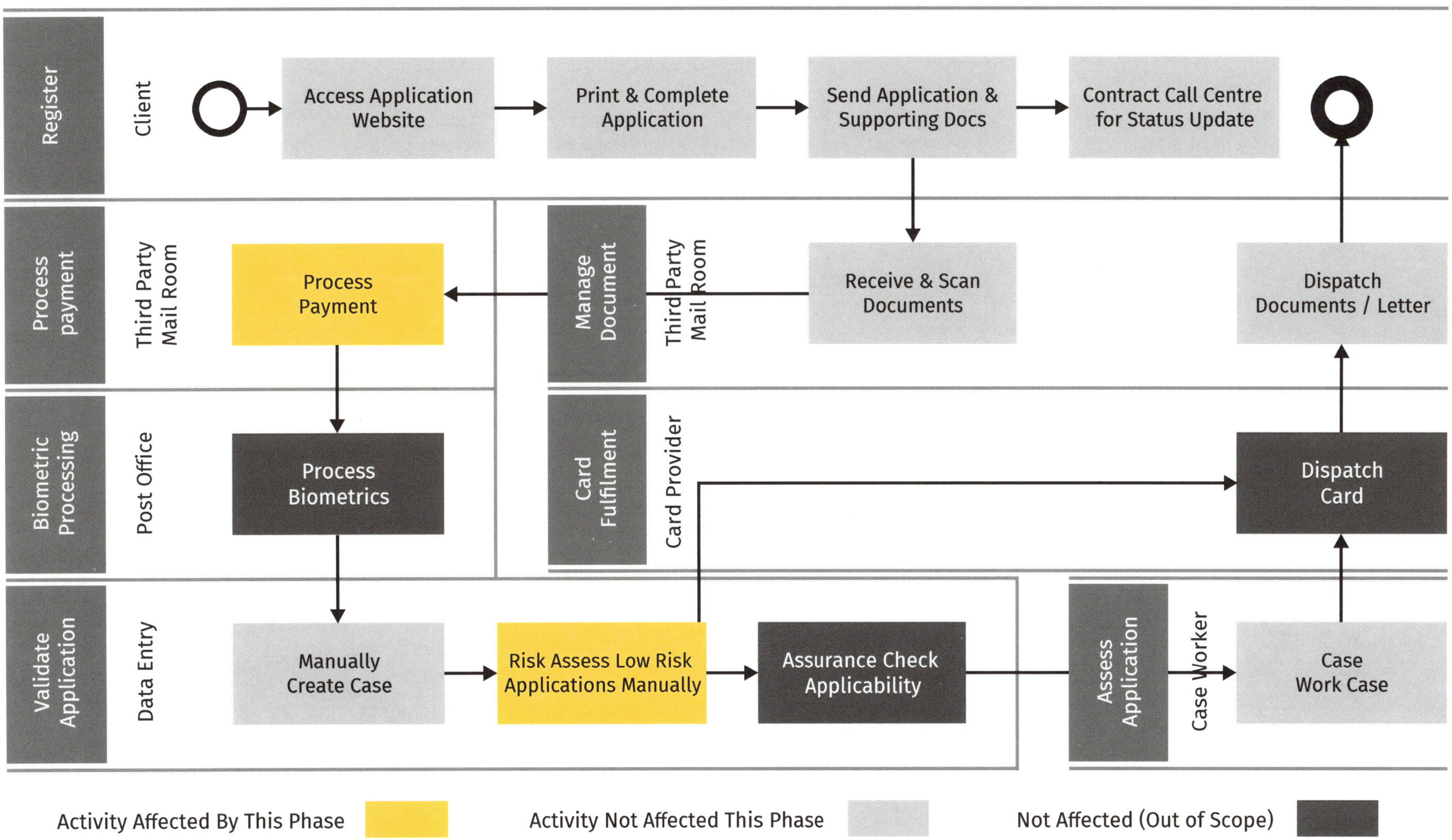


**Figure 10.21** - Example Transition Map (Phase 3)

**4. Develop the Transition Impact Assessment (for each phase)**

For each Transition Phase, carry out the Transition Impact Assessment for each of the Transition Phases, and capture and record the following transition details:

- **Area** (of change)
- **Before** (current phase)
- **After** (at the end of this phase, or result of this phase)
- **Changes/Impact** (as a result of changes taking place at this state)

An example of a Transition Impact Assessment (*Phase 1*), is shown in *Table 10.13* below.

Repeat the *Transition Impact Assessment* for each subsequent phases - highlighting the relevant changes that occur in each phase (including where there a *no changes*). These assessments provide the description and transparency of the changes shown on the *Transition Phase Maps.*

An example of Transition Impact Assessment (*Phase 2)* is shown in *Table 10.14* below:

For completeness, the Transition Impact Assessment (*Phase 3*), is also shown in Table 10.15 (below):

**5. Iteratively socialise, validate and refine each Blueprint** - including any Risks, Assumptions, Issues and Dependencies (RAID) addressed or raised as part of completing this step, and

**6. Package and publish the Blueprints** – in line with your agreed sprint/release cycle, established back in the Governance Model in Chapter 6 Step 2 – Control.



## Risks and Mitigations

The risks associated with putting together the Transition Architectures is not getting the level of decomposition right. That is, not decomposing the changes to the Organisation so they are meaningful to the intended audience – the Business. Where implementation almost always falls apart is at the operational level, which is why there is intentionally a lot of focus on the transition architecture maps (i.e. at the operational and process level).

The Transition Architectures Blueprints intentionally show and describe the changes to the Organisation at the operational and process level. That is to reduce any ambiguity in the Stakeholders minds, so they are clear:

- When significant architectural changes happen (e.g. phase 1, 2 etc.)?
- Where these changes occur (i.e. business unit, business process etc.)?
- What is the state (and status) of the Business was before and after the changes occur?
- What are those changes (e.g. decommission of a legacy system)? and
- What are the impacts of those changes? (e.g. staff training required on new process and systems)

By using the process level, the Business can prepare both physically, mentally (and even emotionally) and ask themselves:

- Am I/we ready for this change?
- Can we handle that change or amount of change?', and
- Do we need to be develop some mitigation actions if it doesn't go according to plan?'

There are other levels, which other approaches tend to focus on, which are mainly conceptual and/or contextual (i.e. very high level) models and views.

Example Transition Impact Assessment (Phase 1)

Table 10.13

| Area | Before | After | Impact |
|---|---|---|---|
| Client | Downloads application as PDF, prints, completes and returns via post with supporting docs to external mail house | Completes & submits application form online, prints checklist and returns via post to external mail house | • Legacy application website decommissioned<br>• Online Application Service (OAS) handle all applications<br>• Automated Workflow Service (AWS) in place<br>• Legacy workflow decommissioned |
| External Mail House | Receives large volume of mail (application forms and supporting docs), scans and sends physical docs to Case Working | Receives less volume (checklist and supporting docs only), scans and sends physical docs to Case Working | Less volume, less scanning, less physical documents in storage and circulation (faster processing) |
| Data Entry | Receives all applications for manual entry into legacy workflow system | • Receives checklist and supporting docs only<br>• Client record automatically created in legacy workflow system replacement<br>• Correct values record against docs received | • Legacy workflow system decommissioned<br>• AWS record automatically created<br>• Less workload for data entry (faster processing) |
| Post Office | Capture biometrics (when requested and required) via existing biometrics system | No change felt by business | AWS interface into existing biometrics system (Technical change only) |
| Card Provider | Receive card requests in existing card system via legacy workflow system | Receive card request in existing card system via AWS | AWS interface into existing card system (Technical change only) |
| Case Working | Works case in legacy case working system | Works case in legacy replacement (AWS) | Uses AWS to work case (faster processing) |

Sample Tranistion Impact Assessment (Phase 2)

Table 10.14

| Area | Before | After | Impact |
|---|---|---|---|
| Client | Call Contact Centre for application progress and updates | Views guidance and status update online | • Less calls to Contact Centre<br>• Faster processing case working staff not interrupted for queries |
| External Mail House | Receives large volume of mail (application forms and supporting docs), scans and sends physical docs to Case Working | Receives less volume (checklist and supporting docs only), scans and sends physical docs to Case Working | • New scanning solution delivered<br>• New process (scanning & payment) for existing internal business unit (Internal Mail House)<br>• External Mail House no longer involved<br>• Legacy files/electronic & physical transferred to internal business unit (Internal Mail House) |
| Data Entry | No Changes | No Changes | No Changes |
| Case Working | Works case in legacy replacement (AWS) | Works case in AWS with integrated scanning (no physical docs) | • All documents scanned into workflow<br>• Paperless process<br>• Faster processing / better office utilization |

While those levels of abstraction are helpful in *painting the broader picture* of what architectural changes are expected, they don't go down far enough into the detail of what it actually means operationally, which still leaves the Business asking the above questions because the level of abstraction wasn't deep or meaningful enough.

There *are* risks with doing a more detailed assessment and mapping than provided above however. These include the possibility that you become stuck in the detail and spend a lot of (unnecessary) time and energy creating, reviewing, agreeing and iteratively updating Blueprints with your stakeholders, when the point could have been made in less time, with less effort.

One of the ways to address this '*need*' while still avoiding becoming stuck in the detail is to leverage the predecessor Blueprints that were used as *inputs* to creating these Blueprints, reminding Stakeholders of previous decisions, and that the ongoing work builds off previously developed and agreed Blueprints (like the rest of **HOBA®** Blueprints). So, unless there has been some fundamental changes or decisions made since the input Blueprint(s) were agreed, then you have a relatively stable baseline to start from, and putting together this Building Block and Blueprints should be a relatively '*quick*' exercise.

## Building Block Wrap-up

In this section, we discussed the Transition Architecture Mapping Building Block, that provides the views of the Target Operating Model (TOM), at specific phases of the physical Business Architecture implementation.

The Transition Architecture Mapping Building Block is made up of the following (2) Blueprints:

- **Transition Architecture Strategy Map** - provides the outline of order the Business Changes and Enablers (i.e. People, Process and Technology changes) will be implemented in to maximize the realisation and timing of the Business Benefits and minimise delivery risk, and

- **Transition Architecture Phase Maps** - Provides the planned (and implemented) architectural changes at each transition phase, and consist of three (3) parts:

Example Transition Impact Assessment (Phase 1)

Table 10.15

| Area | Before | After | Impact |
|---|---|---|---|
| Client | No changes | No changes | |
| Online Application Service (OAS) | No payment through OAS | Client makes payment at time of completing application | • Integrated Payment Service (IPS) delivered<br>• Internal Mail House no longer handles manual payments |
| Internal Mail House | Internal Mail House receives checklist and supporting docs Makes manual payment | High risk applications routed for case working | • IPS delivered<br>• No longer handles manual payments |
| Data Entry | Manually review all applications for processing (and detailed case working) | No change felt by business | • Integrated Risk Assessment Service (IRS) delivered<br>• Low risk applications routed to decision stage |
| Case Working | Works ALL (low and high risk applications) cases in AWS with integrated scanning. | Case work high risk applications in ASW | • Process high risk applications only (low risk applications routed to decision stage)<br>• Faster application processing throughput |

- **Transition Summary** - provides a summary of the architectural phases, changes and milestones at each phase;
- **Transition Phase Map(s)** - provides the visual view of the in-scope, end-to-end, high level business process impacted by the changes the Programme and TOM bring about, highlighting the architectural significant changes, at each phase of implementation, and
- **Transition Impact Assessment** - provides a summary of the before and after states, changes and impacts of those changes at each architectural phase at the capability level (i.e. people, process, and technology) across the impacted end-to-end business process.

Transition Architectures are used to provide the view of the people, process and technology changes in a phased approach in implementing these changes to create the *physical* Target Operating Model (TOM). They effectively describe the 'best steps' to implement the *physical* TOM, to align the Business to the Business Strategy and support the Organisation to realise the planned Business Benefits and Strategic Objectives.

Transition Architectures also make transparent the amount of change happening across the Organisation for the Programme, and at any one time, to highlight any dependencies and raise questions whether the Business *is ready for change*, can handle the change, and where they can't, then plan accordingly.

### Next Steps

Once the Transition Architecture Mapping is agreed, the next step in the **Design Process** is to agree Business and IT (Technology) Architecture alignment.

Business and IT (Technology) Architecture alignment is discussed in the Business/IT Alignment Mapping Building Block in the following section.

# 6.5 Business/IT Alignment Mapping

## Introduction

Business /IT Alignment Mapping is the Building Block that provides the visibility and assurance that the Business Architecture of the Target Operating Model (TOM) are aligned to the Technical Architecture.

The purpose of this Building Block is to show the dependent Technical (and Data) Architecture that is needed to support the aspects of the Business Architecture across the full end-to-end business process of the Target Operating Model (TOM).

The **benefit of the Business/IT Alignment Building Block** is to show from a business perspective:

- **A common (and shared) view of the dependencies** on the target Technical Architecture needed to support the end-to-end Business Architecture in implementing the Target Operating Model (TOM);
- **Provide the transparency** (discussed earlier in the *Challenge #3: What does this value look like?* section), by providing a cross-functional view of the Organisation, informing 'join up' conversations between stakeholders across-Programme and Organisation to identify, agree and synchronise the timing of the delivery of dependent architectures; and
- **Provide a means to enable transparent and ongoing communication and dialogu**e with other parts of the Programme and Organisation to ensure the development and delivery of dependent architectures remain in sync.

You will recall the **role of the Business Architect** is divided into two (2) parts:

Part 1. **Align the Business to the Business Strategy** (which included alignment to other architectures); and to

Part 2. **Ensure the implementation of the *physical* Business Architecture is aligned with the *design*** (by default, this also means it aligns to Technical Architecture as well).

In terms of the Design Process, Part 1 (above - alignment to the Business Strategy) – is completed as part of Steps 4 and 5 within the Benefits Model and Target Operating Model. Part 2 (alignment to the physical Business Architecture, and Technical Architecture), is accounted for via this step (Step 6 – Road Map Model) and this Building Block, specifically in relation to the Business/IT Alignment Map Blueprint.

The **Business/IT Alignment Map Blueprint shows** the following:

- **End-to-end Business process** (from the *6.4 Transition Architecture Mapping*);
- **User Interface** (i.e. the physical and online touchpoints between the User or Customer with the Organisation, from *3.3 User Journey Mapping (As-Is)*);
- **Technical Architecture** (the Technical or Digital Services from the Technical Architecture, provided by the Technical Architect), and
- **Data Architecture** (the Data Clusters and Data Objects from the Data Architecture or Data Objects Model, provided by the Data Architect).

Like all Building Blocks and Blueprints, the *Business/IT Alignment Map* requires input from other Programme Members. In this case, the *Business/IT Alignment Map* requires both the Technical Architect and the Data Architect to provide input from their respective technical perspectives and architectures. It's also important to note here that the Business Analyst must also validate the features and functions the technical services (and data) provides actually meets the Business's business and implementation requirements.

## Inputs

The inputs used to complete this Building Block are shown in the below.

## Output(s)

The Blueprints (outputs) produced for this Building Block are shown in the table below.

### Business/IT Alignment Building Block Inputs

**Table 10.16**

| Ref | Blueprint | Use |
|---|---|---|
| 3.3.1 | User Journey Map | Provides the interaction and touch points (physical and online) between the User and the Organisation, across the User Journey. |
| 6.4.1 | Transition Architecture Strategy Map | Provides the outline of how the Organisation will implement the Business Changes and Enablers (People, Process and Technology changes) in prioritised order to maximize the realisation and timing of the planned Business Benefits and minimize delivery risk. |
| 6.4.2 | Transition Architecture Phase Map(s) | Provides the planned (and implemented) architectural changes at each transition phase, and candidate for the high-level end-to-end business process, made up of the three (3) parts:<br>• Transition Summary<br>• Transition Phase Map(s)<br>• Transition Impact Assessment |
| N/A | Technical Architecture / Services Catalogue | Description (and delivery timing) of the Technical (or Digital) Services that form part of the Technical Architecture (owned by Technical Architecture). |
| N/A | Data Architecture / Data Model | Description (and delivery timing) of the Data Clusters and Data Objects that form part of the Data Architecture (owned by Data Architecture). |

### Transition Architecture Mapping (Output) Blueprints

**Table 10.17**

| Ref | Blueprint | Description | Example |
|---|---|---|---|
| 6.5.1 | Business/ IT Alignment Map | Provides the high-level view of the dependent Technical and Data Architecture that is needed to support the Business Architecture across the Organisation end-to-end business process of the Target Operating Model (TOM). | 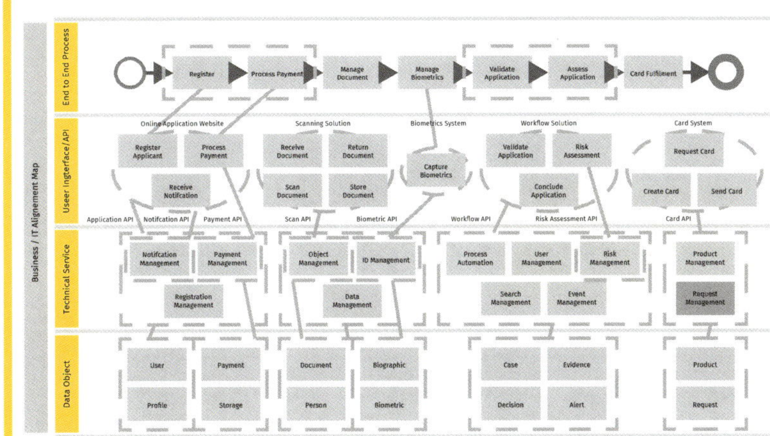 |

Table 10.17

| Ref | Blueprint | Description | Example |
|---|---|---|---|
| 6.5.1 | Business/ IT Alignment Map | Provides the high-level view of the dependent Technical and Data Architecture that is needed to support the Business Architecture across the Organisation end-to-end business process of the Target Operating Model (TOM). | (see below) |

| Business Architecture | | Technical Architecture | | | | Data Architecture | Delivery | | |
|---|---|---|---|---|---|---|---|---|---|
| Process | Description | User Interface | API | Technical Service | Description | Data Cluster | Phase | Date | Who |
| Register | Applicant registers for (visa) product | Online Application Website | Application API | Registration Management | Handles the CRUD of a User registration | User | TBC | | |
| | | | Notification API | Notification Management | Handles the CRUD of a notification when event or application status triggered | Profile | TBC | | |
| Process Payment | Applicant makes payment | Online Application Website | Payment API | Payment Management | Handles the processing of payments | Payment | TBC | | |
| Manage Document | Receiving, scanning, storing checklist & documents | Scanning Solution | Scanning API | Data Management | Handles data storage and retrieval | Storage | TBC | | |
| Manage Biometrics | Request, capture and storage of biometrics | Biometrics System | Biometrics API | ID Management | Handles the checking and matching of biometric and biographic data | Biographic | TBC | | |
| | | | | | | Biometric | TBC | | |
| Validate Application | Check applicability & eligibility | Workflow System | Workflow API | Process Automation | Handles the automated management of cases based on process status | Case | TBC | | |
| Assess Application | Evaluate and decide on application | Workflow System | Workflow API | Risk Management | Handles the automated management of allocating cases based on risk parameters | Decision | TBC | | |
| | | | | User Management | Handles CRUD of Users | Evidence | TBC | | |
| | | | | Search Management | Handles the ability to search for a User or specific events | Alert | TBC | | |
| | | | | Events Management | Handles the CRUD of an event and associate it to another User, Object or Document | Event | TBC | | |
| Card Fulfilment | Management of physical card request | Card System | Card API | Product Management | Handles the CRUD of a product | Product | TBC | | |
| | | | | Request Management | Handles the CRUD request for a product or service | Request | TBC | | |

## Steps

The steps to complete the above Blueprints (Outputs) are as follows:

### 6.5.1 Business/IT Alignment Map

#### 1. Develop the Business/IT Alignment Map

Using the inputs from the *Inputs* section above, and working with the Business representatives, Technical and Data Architects and Business Analyst(s), identify and plot the following respective business, technical and data architecture elements on to the Business/IT Alignment Map, highlighting (where known) the following:

- **In Scope** (elements in-scope for delivery within, and from, the Programme), and
- **Out of scope** (i.e. elements not in scope for the Programme to deliver):

An example the Business/IT Alignment Map is shown in *Figure 10.22* below.

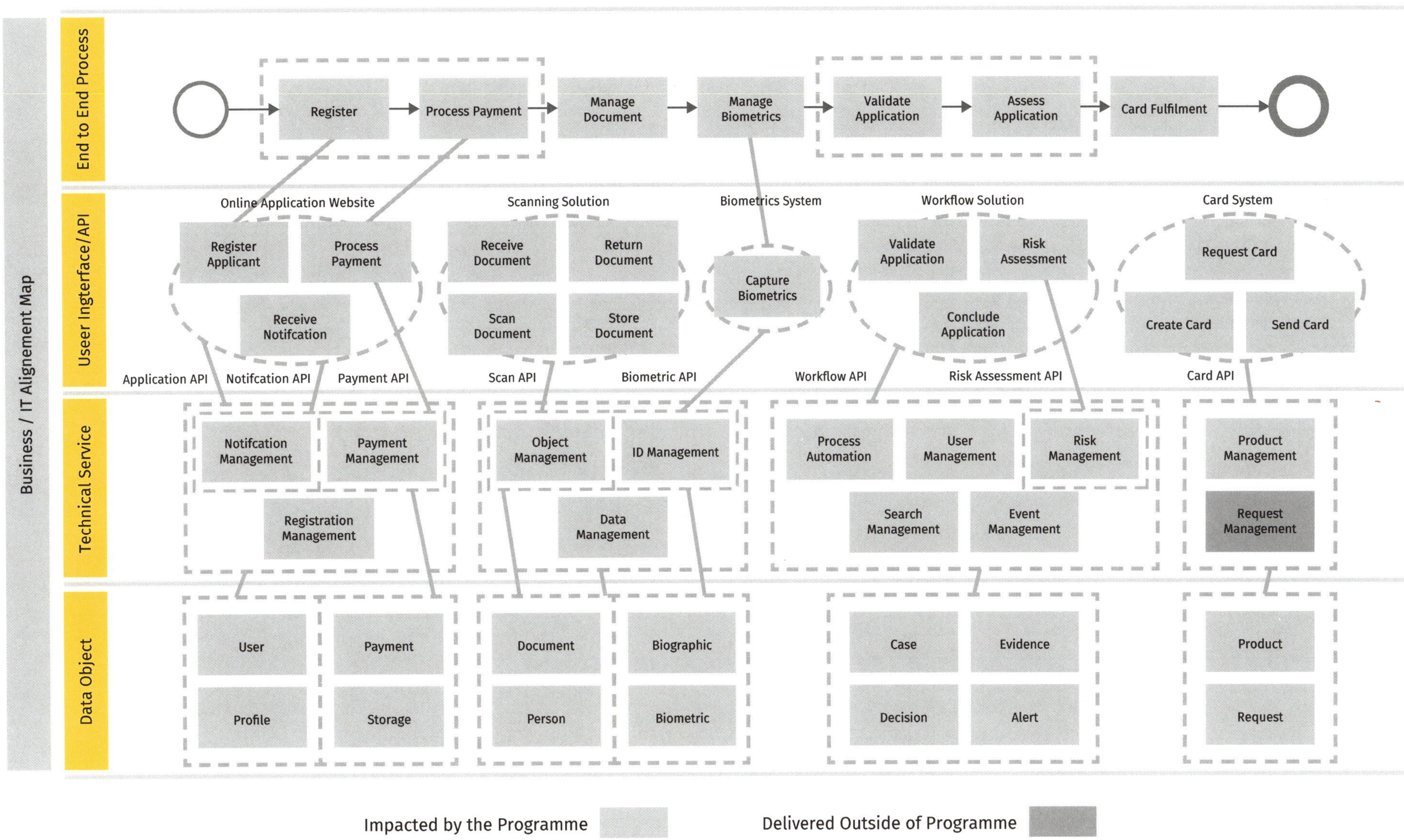


**Figure 10.22 -** Example Business/IT Alignment Map

**2. Develop the Business/IT Alignment (Map) Table**

Document of the Business/IT Alignment Map elements for completeness, traceability and management in the Business/IT Alignment Table.

An example Business/IT Alignment (Map) Table is shown in *Table 10.18* below.

**Use both the Business/IT Alignment Map and Table views to initiate and continue ongoing communication (and negotiation) and gain agreement on the scope, alignment and delivery (phase, date and who) of the dependent technical and data architecture elements.**

**4. Iteratively socialise, validate and refine the Blueprint(s)** - including any Risks, Assumptions, Issues and Dependencies (RAID) addressed or raised as part of completing this step, and

**5. Package and publish the Blueprint(s)** – in line with your agreed sprint/release cycle, established back in *Chapter 6 Step 2 – Control* with the Governance Model.

### Risks and Mitigations

The risk with completing this Building Block relates to the *'version of the truth'* (of the dependent Technical and Data Architecture Model and Catalogues) you are referencing.

Just as you, the Business Architect will be developing your view of the TOM (through developing and publishing different versions of the different Blueprints to develop the full TOM), so too will the Technical and Data Architects be developing their respective architectures!

What this means is you need to keep on top of the different versions of the Technical and Data Architecture Models that you are reflecting and referencing in your model (i.e. the TOM) and respective Blueprints.

The benefit of **HOBA®** and the Governance Reference Model brings is that you would have already agreed on (as part of Step-2 Control - the Governance Reference Model) the Programme sprint/release cycle and the duration and frequency when the up to date versions of Blueprints are released at regular cadence. So, you therefore know that prior to a release (i.e. a first, or updated version of any Blueprint being published), any Stakeholder marked as 'C' (Consulted) on the RACI for the respective document or Blueprint will be Consulted for input before being issued. This means as the Business Architect, you should be consulted for input into both Technical and Data Architectures, and the Technical and Data Architects should be marked 'C' and consulted for input in the relevant Business Architecture Blueprint(s). By marking other Architects as "Consulted" in the relevant Blueprints, ensures that the other Architects are kept aware of the Blueprint (and changes) and are able to contribute and provide input, and importantly, follow what was agreed so that all parties should then update their own Blueprints, thereby keeping everyone in sync.

This Building Block at the very least highlights the need for both the Business and Technical (and Data) Architectures to initiate, and continue ongoing communication and dialogue to ensure all are aligned, particularly as they will (and do) develop at different rates over the course of the Programme.

### Building Block Wrap-up

In this section, we discussed the Business/IT Alignment Building Block.

This Building Block provides the visibility and assurance that the technical and data architecture that is needed to support the Business Architecture as part of the physical Target Operating Model (TOM) is in place, and will be delivered on time.
This Building Block leverages off the phased delivery approach discussed and established in the predecessor Transition Architecture Mapping Building Block, which defined the order and priority of the implementation of the Business Changes and Enablers that lead to the creation of the physical Target Operating Model (TOM).

The Business/IT Alignment Mapping Building Block is made up of the following two (2) Blueprints:

- **Business/IT Alignment Map** - showing the dependent elements of technical and data architecture that is needed to support the Business Architecture across the end to end business process of the TOM, and
- **Business/IT Alignment (Map) Table** – providing the descriptions of those dependent Technical

Table 10.18

| Business Architecture | | Technical Architecture | | | | Data Architecture | Delivery | | |
|---|---|---|---|---|---|---|---|---|---|
| **Process** | **Description** | **User Interface** | **API** | **Technical Service** | **Description** | **Data Cluster** | **Phase** | **Date** | **Who** |
| Register | Applicant registers for (visa) product | Online Application Website | Application API | Registration Management | Handles the CRUD of a User registration | User | TBC | | |
| | | | Notification API | Notification Management | Handles the CRUD of a notification when event or application status triggered | Profile | TBC | | |
| Process Payment | Applicant makes payment | Online Application Website | Payment API | Payment Management | Handles the processing of payments | Payment | TBC | | |
| Manage Document | Receiving, scanning, storing checklist & documents | Scanning Solution | Scanning API | Data Management | Handles data storage and retrieval | Storage | TBC | | |
| Manage Biometrics | Request, capture and storage of biometrics | Biometrics System | Biometrics API | ID Management | Handles the checking and matching of biometric and biographic data | Biographic | TBC | | |
| | | | | | | Biometric | TBC | | |
| Validate Application | Check applicability & eligibility | Workflow System | Workflow API | Process Automation | Handles the automated management of cases based on process status | Case | TBC | | |
| Assess Application | Evaluate and decide on application | Workflow System | Workflow API | Risk Management | Handles the automated management of allocating cases based on risk parameters | Decision | TBC | | |
| | | | | User Management | Handles CRUD of Users | Evidence | TBC | | |
| | | | | Search Management | Handles the ability to search for a User or specific events | Alert | TBC | | |
| | | | | Events Management | Handles the CRUD of an event and associate it to another User, Object or Document | Event | TBC | | |
| Card Fulfilment | Management of physical card request | Card System | Card API | Product Management | Handles the CRUD of a product | Product | TBC | | |
| | | | | Request Management | Handles the CRUD request for a product or service | Request | TBC | | |

(and Data) Architecture elements (from the Business/IT Alignment Map), including the delivery (phase, date, and who).

Both Blueprints are drawn up and agreed with the input from the Business and the Technical Stakeholders, both from within the Programme and also across the Organisation with the Technical Architect providing the descriptions and delivery details of the Technical (or digital) Architecture, and the Data Architect providing the Data Clusters (or objects) as part of the respective Technical and Data Architecture Models.

Both these Blueprints highlight the interdependencies between the Business Architecture and Technical (and Data) Architecture, to initiate and continue ongoing communication and alignment of the architectures, as they develop – ideally with Business Architecture leading, or in parallel, keeping them all in alignment.

**Next Steps**

Once the Business/IT Alignment Mapping is agreed, the next and final step in the **Design Process** is to complete the Traceability Mapping Building Block to ensure the design of the TOM addresses all the Stakeholder Concerns and from an *impact analysis* perspective, provide the means to quickly identify when there is a change to one particular Blueprint, that it is easy to identify the impact of the change and which impacted Blueprints need to be checked (and updated) due to that change.

Traceability Mapping Building Block is discussed in the following section.



# 6.6 Traceability Mapping

## Introduction

Traceability mapping is the Building Block that provides the visibility and assurance that all the Stakeholders Concerns that were raised have been both covered and addressed.

The purpose of Traceability Mapping is to not only identify which Blueprint(s) are said to address the stated Stakeholder Concerns, but also to cross check (i.e. verify and validate) that the Blueprint(s) actually do address the stated concerns.

The objective and benefit of Traceability Mapping is to use the *'traceability'* to carry out the following:

1. **Impact Analysis** – when a Stakeholder Concern or issue (or opportunity) is changed, using the Traceability matrices below, you will as the Business Architect be able to quickly identify the Blueprints impacted by the change, to quickly gauge the size and *'impact'* of the change, and therefore the amount of work needed to review and update the impacted Blueprints (which includes any follow-up work needed because of that change), and
2. **Concerns Coverage** – when Stakeholder Concerns (and/or issues and opportunities) are traced to Blueprints (where they are addressed), Traceability Mapping provides *'some'* assurance that the concerns are actually being addressed (as they need to be physically (or virtually) checked to confirm this is the case. If a concern or issue is not *'traced'* to a Blueprint, this becomes a red flag that the concern has likely not been assessed and therefore excluded in the design of the TOM, which would need to be rectified ASAP.

The approach to carrying out 'traceability' is 'Bi-directional'. This is where you, as the Business Architect, use the (Stakeholder) Traceability Matrix to check that there is a Blueprint(s) against every Stakeholder Concern in a *'forward'* direction (i.e. 'forward traceability'), and then in the *'reverse'* direction (i.e. 'reverse traceability'). This is done by you inspecting the 'traced' Blueprint to confirm the Blueprint actually does address the stated Stakeholder Concern(s).

As a best practice, the Bi-directional approach works best when you have the *Stakeholder Concerns Traceability Matrix* on hand each time a Blueprint is being developed or updated. At the creation of a Blueprint, the matrix can be referred too to check which concern(s) the Blueprint should be addressing, and then when updating that Blueprint, ensuring that the concern(s) is actually addressed. This recommended approach (almost always) avoids having a separate meeting for traceability as it is done each time a Blueprint is created or changed.

## Inputs

The inputs used to complete this Building Block are shown in the below.

**Traceability Mapping Building Block Inputs**

**Table 10.19**

| Ref | Blueprint | Use |
|---|---|---|
| 1.1.1 | Statement of Work (SOW) | Provides initial Stakeholder Concerns list and the agreed Reference Models, Building Blocks (and Blueprints) that are in scope. |
| All | All **HOBA®** Blueprints | All traced Blueprints need to be checked they actually address the stated Stakeholder Concern(s), as well as every HOBA® Blueprint is included in the Blueprint Traceability Matrix. |

## Output(s)

The Blueprints (outputs) produced for this Building Block are shown in the table below.

**Transition Architecture Mapping (Output) Blueprints**

**Table 10.20**

| Ref | Blueprint | Description | Example |
|---|---|---|---|
| 6.6.1 | Stakeholder Concerns Traceability Matrix | The traceability matrix that shows the Blueprints that address the stated Stakeholder Concern(s). | 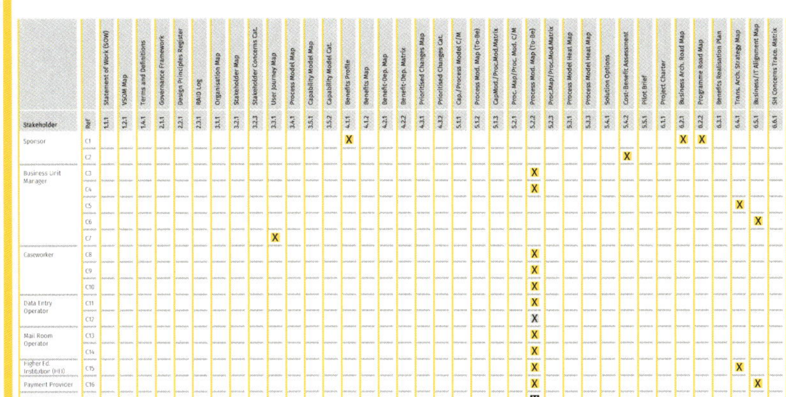 |

Table 10.20

| Ref | Blueprint | Description | Example |
|---|---|---|---|
| 6.6.2 | Blueprint Traceability Matrix | A traceability matrix, showing all the Blueprints that are used as inputs into other Blueprints. | 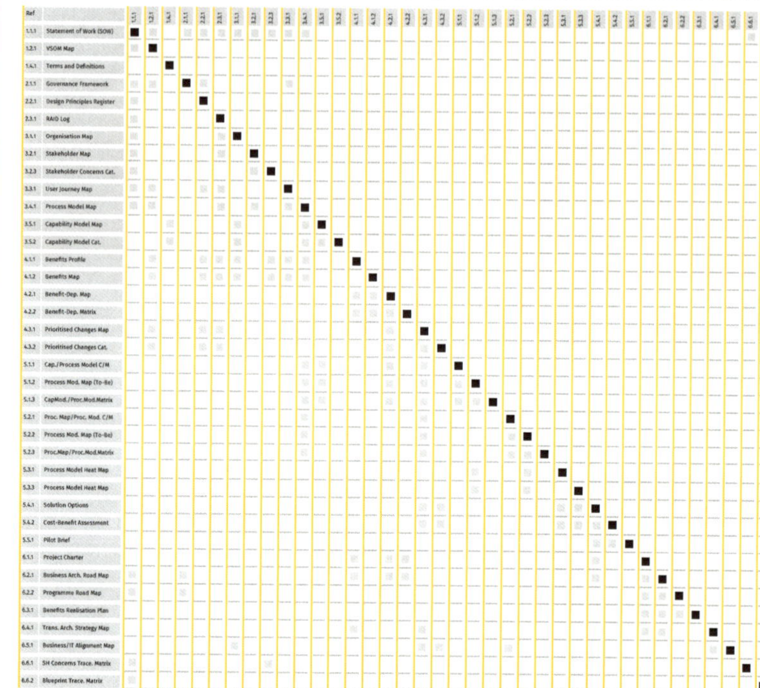 |

## Steps

The steps to complete the above Blueprints (Outputs) are as follows:

## 6.6.1 Stakeholder Concerns Traceability Matrix

### 1. Develop the Stakeholder Concerns Traceability Matrix

Using the inputs from the *Inputs* section above:

- **In a 'forward traceability' approach** - list the Stakeholder and their concerns on the matrix, and then find their corresponding Blueprint and mark with an 'X' where they intersect, and then
- **In a 'reverse traceability' approach** - for each 'X', locate the latest version of that Blueprint, and physically (or virtually) inspect and verify the Blueprint actually addresses the stated concern:
  - For every Blueprint that addresses the mapped concern, record the version number of that Blueprint (e.g. v1.2) in the matrix, and
  - For every Blueprint that is marked 'X' to address a mapped concern, but on inspection of the Blueprint doesn't address the stated concern, leave unchanged. This is a red flag that the Blueprint needs to be reviewed with the Product Owner (and/or named Stakeholder(s)) to understand the changes that are needed to the Blueprint, which you can either arrange a meeting with the Product Owner immediately or address in the following morning daily *scrum*.

An example Stakeholder Concerns Traceability Matrix is shown in *Table 10.21* below:

For the list of Stakeholder Concerns, refer to *Table 5.7 – Example Stakeholder, Concerns and Views Table.*

**As an additional measure to show the 'level' of coverage that a Blueprint actually addresses a stated Stakeholder Concern, you may want to use the following 'traffic light' colour coding system:**

- **Black – Stakeholder Concern (Not Addressed)**
- **Grey – Stakeholder Concern (Partially Addressed)**
- **Yellow - Stakeholder Concern (Fully Addressed)**

## 6.6.2 Blueprint Traceability Matrix

### 2. Develop the Blueprint Traceability Matrix

The benefit of **HOBA®** is as a framework, all the inputs for each Blueprint are already defined. However, as a framework, you have the liberty to adopt the framework to suit your Programme and Organisation, which may mean the recommended Inputs will change.

An example (of a section of the full) Blueprint Traceability Matrix is shown *Table 10.22* below:

**The above Blueprint Traceability Matrix is shown for illustration and example purposes only and shows only a simple subset (the first several Blueprints for each Reference Model) of what would be the full Blueprint Traceability Matrix. In practice, this matrix would contain the complete list of Blueprints, including the 'cross-mapping'.**

**3. Iteratively socialise, validate and refine each Matrix** (as and when needed), ensuring the Stakeholder Concern(s) are addressed – including any Risks, Assumptions, Issues and Dependencies (RAID) addressed or raised as part of completing this step, and

**4. Package and publish the matrix** – in line with your agreed sprint/release cycle, established back in the *Step 2 – Control* with the Governance Model.

**The Blueprint Traceability Matrix can be seen or perceived as more an internal *Business Architecture team/department* facing deliverable than an internal *Programme deliverable*, and is more suited as an internal reference document (or register) that is referred too to carry out an internal impact assessment. If this is the case, make this available to your Key Stakeholders on a 'need to know' or 'inquiry' basis only and exclude from the regular Business Architecture updates, publications and releases. Programme Stakeholders may be interested in it, in cases of an impact assessment, but they maybe be more concerned that the Business Architecture and the Technical Architectures are aligned, or that the Stakeholder Concern(s) are addressed.**

### Risks and Mitigations

The risk with Traceability Mapping (and/or matrices) is that they aren't given the visibility, importance or priority they deserve, and are often not being used the way they should.

Despite their importance (i.e. ensuring all Stakeholder Concerns are addressed, and a quick impact assessment can be carried out when needed), Traceability Mapping (and matrices) are unfortunately seen as a *'nice to have'*, *'let's do it if we have time'*, or worse *'we'll do it if we have too'*. In the rare instances when it's done – it's often done incorrectly as a *'box ticking'* exercise, which is literally cross-checking a concern, or requirement against the Blueprint that 'others' said the Building Block addressed, without actually physically checking. This is not how you do traceability mapping or matrices.

To do traceability 'correctly', you need to *physically* (or virtually) go to that Blueprint, and review it, and ask *'Does this Blueprint address this Stakeholder Concern?'*:

- **If Yes** – record the applicable version in the matrix 'addressed' (and mark 'YELLOW' for 'addressed');

- **If No** – colour code the intersection/cell BLACK (for 'not addressed'), continue checking the whole matrix as a first pass, and then again one by one to inspect each.

**The strategy behind marking the cell BLACK on the 'first pass', is because no one likes to see BLACK or 'not addressed' on the matrix. This as a result actively encourages people (including Key Stakeholders) to take action to rectify it.**

Blueprint to verify and validate the concern(s) are actually addressed/not addressed, and update accordingly.

Sample Stakeholder Concerns Traceability Matrix

**Table 10.21**

| Stakeholder | Ref | Statement of Work (SOW) 1.1.1 | VSOM Map 1.2.1 | Terms and Definitions 1.4.1 | Governance Framework 2.1.1 | Design Principles Register 2.2.1 | RAID Log 2.3.1 | Organisation Map 3.1.1 | Stakeholder Map 3.2.1 | Stakeholder Concerns Cat. 3.2.3 | User Journey Map 3.3.1 | Process Model Map 3.4.1 | Capability Model Map 3.5.1 | Capability Model Cat. 3.5.2 | Benefits Profile 4.1.1 | Benefits Map 4.1.2 | Benefit-Dep. Map 4.2.1 | Benefit-Dep. Matrix 4.2.2 | Prioritised Changes Map 4.3.1 | Prioritised Changes Cat. 4.3.2 | Cap./Process Model C/M 5.1.1 | Process Mod. Map (To-Be) 5.1.2 | CapMod./Proc.Mod.Matrix 5.1.3 | Proc. Map/Proc. Mod. C/M 5.2.1 |
|---|---|---|---|---|---|---|---|---|---|---|---|---|---|---|---|---|---|---|---|---|---|---|---|---|
| Sponsor | C1 | | | | | | | | | | | | | | X | | | | | | | | | |
| | C2 | | | | | | | | | | | | | | | | | | | | | | | |
| Business Unit Manager | C3 | | | | | | | | | | | | | | | | | | | | | | | |
| | C4 | | | | | | | | | | | | | | | | | | | | | | | |
| | C5 | | | | | | | | | | | | | | | | | | | | | | | |
| | C6 | | | | | | | | | | | | | | | | | | | | | | | |
| | C7 | | | | | | | | | | X | | | | | | | | | | | | | |
| Caseworker | C8 | | | | | | | | | | | | | | | | | | | | | | | |
| | C9 | | | | | | | | | | | | | | | | | | | | | | | |
| | C10 | | | | | | | | | | | | | | | | | | | | | | | |
| Data Entry Operator | C11 | | | | | | | | | | | | | | | | | | | | | | | |
| | C12 | | | | | | | | | | | | | | | | | | | | | | | |
| Mail Room Operator | C13 | | | | | | | | | | | | | | | | | | | | | | | |
| | C14 | | | | | | | | | | | | | | | | | | | | | | | |
| Higher Ed. Institution (HEI) | C15 | | | | | | | | | | | | | | | | | | | | | | | |
| Payment Provider | C16 | | | | | | | | | | | | | | | | | | | | | | | |
| Post Office | C17 | | | | | | | | | | | | | | | | | | | | | | | |

| 5.2.2 Process Mod. Map (To-Be) | 5.2.3 Proc.Map/Proc.Mod.Matrix | 5.3.1 Process Model Heat Map | 5.3.3 Process Model Heat Map | 5.4.1 Solution Options | 5.4.2 Cost-Benefit Assessment | 5.5.1 Pilot Brief | 6.1.1 Project Charter | 6.2.1 Business Arch. Road Map | 6.2.2 Programme Road Map | 6.3.1 Benefits Realisation Plan | 6.4.1 Trans. Arch. Strategy Map | 6.5.1 Business/IT Alignment Map | 6.6.1 SH Concerns Trace. Matrix | 6.6.2 Blueprint Trace. Matrix |
|---|---|---|---|---|---|---|---|---|---|---|---|---|---|---|
| | | | | | | | | X | X | | | | | |
| | | | | | X | | | | | | | | | |
| X | | | | | | | | | | | | | | |
| X | | | | | | | | | | | | | | |
| | | | | | | | | | | | X | | | |
| | | | | | | | | | | | | X | | |
| | | | | | | | | | | | | | | |
| X | | | | | | | | | | | | | | |
| X | | | | | | | | | | | | | | |
| X | | | | | | | | | | | | | | |
| X | | | | | | | | | | | | | | |
| X | | | | | | | | | | | | | | |
| X | | | | | | | | | | | | | | |
| X | | | | | | | | | | | | | | |
| X | | | | | | | | | | | X | | | |
| X | | | | | | | | | | | | X | | |
| X | | | | | | | | | | | | | | |

## Building Block Wrap-up

In this section, we discussed Traceability Mapping Building Block.

This Building Block provides the visibility and assurance that all the Stakeholders Concerns that were raised have been covered and addressed, and consist of the following two (2) Blueprints:

- **Stakeholder Concerns Traceability Matrix** – which shows which Blueprints address the stated Stakeholder Concern(s), and
- **Blueprint Traceability Matrix** – which shows all the Blueprints that are used as *inputs* into other Blueprints.

The objective and benefit of Traceability Mapping is to use the 'traceability' to carry out the following:

1. **Impact Analysis** – to quickly gauge the 'size' and 'impact' of the changes to one Blueprint, across other 'impacted' Blueprints, and therefore anticipate the amount of work now required to review and update the impacted Blueprints, and
2. **Concerns Coverage** – to provide assurances that all Stakeholders Concerns are addressed by the stated Blueprints, and therefore the design of the Target Operating Model (TOM).

Once the Traceability Mapping is agreed, you have completed the Road Map Reference Model, and also reached the end of the **Design Process**. However, this is not the end for the Business Architect, the Business Architecture's role or work per se, as discussed in the *Reference Model Recap* and *Next Steps* sections below.

## Reference Model Recap

Once the traceability mapping Building Block is complete (along with the other Project Mapping, Road Map Mapping, Benefits-Realisation Mapping, and Business/I.T Alignment Mapping), the Road Map Reference Model is complete.

Sample Blueprint Traceability Matrix

Table 10.22

| Ref | | 1.1.1 | 1.2.1 | 1.4.1 | 2.1.1 | 2.2.1 | 2.3.1 | 3.1.1 | 3.2.1 | 3.2.3 | 3.3.1 | 3.4.1 | 3.5.1 | 3.5.2 | 4.1.1 | 4.1.2 | 4.2.1 | 4.2.2 | 4.3.1 | 4.3.2 | 5.1.1 | 5.1.2 | 5.1.3 | 5.2.1 |
|---|---|---|---|---|---|---|---|---|---|---|---|---|---|---|---|---|---|---|---|---|---|---|---|---|
| 1.1.1 | Statement of Work (SOW) | ■ | □ | | □ | □ | □ | □ | □ | □ | □ | □ | | | | | | | | | | | | |
| 1.2.1 | VSOM Map | □ | ■ | | | | | | | | | | | | | | | | | | | | | |
| 1.4.1 | Terms and Definitions | | | ■ | | | | | | | | | | | | | | | | | | | | |
| 2.1.1 | Governance Framework | □ | □ | | ■ | □ | | | | | □ | | | | | | | | | | | | | |
| 2.2.1 | Design Principles Register | □ | | | | ■ | | | | | | | | | | | | | | | | | | |
| 2.3.1 | RAID Log | □ | | | | | ■ | | | | | | | | | | | | | | | | | |
| 3.1.1 | Organisation Map | □ | | | | | □ | ■ | | | | | | | | | | | | | | | | |
| 3.2.1 | Stakeholder Map | □ | | | | | □ | | ■ | | | | | | | | | | | | | | | |
| 3.2.3 | Stakeholder Concerns Cat. | □ | | | | | | | □ | ■ | | | | | | | | | | | | | | |
| 3.3.1 | User Journey Map | □ | □ | | | □ | □ | | | | ■ | | | | | | | | | | | | | |
| 3.4.1 | Process Model Map | □ | □ | | | | □ | | □ | | □ | ■ | | | | | | | | | | | | |
| 3.5.1 | Capability Model Map | | | □ | | | | □ | | | | □ | ■ | | | | | | | | | | | |
| 3.5.2 | Capability Model Cat. | | | □ | | | | □ | | | | □ | □ | ■ | | | | | | | | | | |
| 4.1.1 | Benefits Profile | | □ | | | □ | □ | □ | | □ | □ | □ | | | ■ | | | | | | | | | |
| 4.1.2 | Benefits Map | | □ | | | □ | □ | □ | | □ | □ | □ | | | | ■ | | | | | | | | |
| 4.2.1 | Benefit-Dep. Map | | | | | | | | | | | | | | □ | □ | ■ | | | | | | | |
| 4.2.2 | Benefit-Dep. Matrix | | | | | | | | | | | | | | □ | □ | □ | ■ | | | | | | |
| 4.3.1 | Prioritised Changes Map | | □ | | | □ | □ | | | | | | | | | | □ | | ■ | | | | | |
| 4.3.2 | Prioritised Changes Cat. | | □ | | | □ | □ | | | | | | | | | | □ | | □ | ■ | | | | |
| 5.1.1 | Cap./Process Model C/M | | | | | | | | | | | □ | □ | | | | □ | | □ | | ■ | | | |

| 5.2.2 | 5.2.3 | 5.3.1 | 5.3.3 | 5.4.1 | 5.4.2 | 5.5.1 | 6.1.1 | 6.2.1 | 6.2.2 | 6.3.1 | 6.4.1 | 6.5.1 | 6.6.1 | 6.6.2 |
|---|---|---|---|---|---|---|---|---|---|---|---|---|---|---|

By completing the Road Map Reference Model, this means you have:

- Identified and agreed the projects that are delivering the identified and prioritised business changes and enablers that directly support the planned benefits and relative timeline these changes will be implemented and benefits realised;

- Developed and agreed the 'design' road map to deliver the Business Architecture work (i.e. Reference Models, Building Blocks and Blueprints) – providing visibility of the work to come, what to expect and when, and the 'physical' roadmap to develop and deliver the physical Business Architecture, which both help show and build confidence from the Programme stakeholders that there are realistic plans to deliver the intended changes into the Business, and the Business being able to realise the Business Benefits as planned;

- Agreed the process and Blueprints to capture, track and report on benefit realisation progress and status; agreed the specific transition phases of the physical Business Architecture implementation from the Current Operating Model (COM) to the Target Operating Model (TOM), as a stakeholder and risk management tool, helping stakeholders gain confidence in the design that it will deliver the expected changes and benefits, question and challenge any design and implementation decisions, and identify and agree mitigation actions to address any risks that prevent the transition states being achieved;

- Defined and agreed the Technology and Data Architecture with the respective Architects and architecture owners that is needed to support (enable) and align with the Business Architecture and TOM, and

- Finally, you have traced the key stakeholder concerns right the way through the Design, through the specific Blueprints that address their concerns, and provided the Blueprint Traceability Matrix necessary to carry out impact analysis and concerns coverage, to quickly gauge the size and impact of any potential change/change request (which often happens on large Programmes), and give the Programme assurance that all stakeholder concerns are addressed (and which Blueprint provides this).

Sample Blueprint Traceability Matrix

Table 10.22

| Ref | | 1.1.1 | 1.2.1 | 1.4.1 | 2.1.1 | 2.2.1 | 2.3.1 | 3.1.1 | 3.2.1 | 3.2.3 | 3.3.1 | 3.4.1 | 3.5.1 | 3.5.2 | 4.1.1 | 4.1.2 | 4.2.1 | 4.2.2 | 4.3.1 | 4.3.2 | 5.1.1 | 5.1.2 | 5.1.3 | 5.2.1 |
|---|---|---|---|---|---|---|---|---|---|---|---|---|---|---|---|---|---|---|---|---|---|---|---|---|
| 5.1.2 | Process Mod. Map (To-Be) | | | | | | | | | | | □ | □ | | | | □ | | □ | | □ | ■ | | |
| 5.1.3 | CapMod./Proc.Mod.Matrix | | | | | | | | | | | □ | □ | | | | □ | | □ | | □ | □ | ■ | |
| 5.2.1 | Proc. Map/Proc. Mod. C/M | | | | | | | | | | | □ | | | | | | | □ | | | | | ■ |
| 5.2.2 | Process Mod. Map (To-Be) | | | | | | | | | | | □ | | | | | | | □ | | | | | □ |
| 5.2.3 | Proc.Map/Proc.Mod.Matrix | | | | | | | | | | | □ | | | | | | | □ | | | | | □ |
| 5.3.1 | Process Model Heat Map | | | | | | | | | | | | | | | | | | | | | □ | | |
| 5.3.3 | Process Model Heat Map | | | | | | | | | | | | | | | | | | | | | □ | | |
| 5.4.1 | Solution Options | | | | | | | | | | | | | | | | | | □ | □ | | | | |
| 5.4.2 | Cost-Benefit Assessment | | | | | | | | | | | | | | | | | | □ | □ | | | | |
| 5.5.1 | Pilot Brief | | | | | | | | | | | | | | | | | | | | | | | |
| 6.1.1 | Project Charter | | | | | | | | | | | | | | □ | | □ | □ | | | | | | |
| 6.2.1 | Business Arch. Road Map | □ | | | □ | | | | | | | | | | □ | | □ | □ | | | | | | |
| 6.2.2 | Programme Road Map | □ | | | □ | | | | | | | | | | | | | | | | | | | |
| 6.3.1 | Benefits Realisation Plan | | | | | | | | | | | | | | | | | | | | | | | |
| 6.4.1 | Trans. Arch. Strategy Map | | | | | | | | | | | | | | □ | | | | □ | | | | | |
| 6.5.1 | Business/IT Alignment Map | | | | | | | □ | | | | | | | | | | | □ | □ | | | | □ |
| 6.6.1 | SH Concerns Trace. Matrix | □ | | | | | | | | □ | | | | | | | | | | | | | | |
| 6.6.2 | Blueprint Trace. Matrix | □ | | | | | | | | | | | | | | | | | | | | | | |

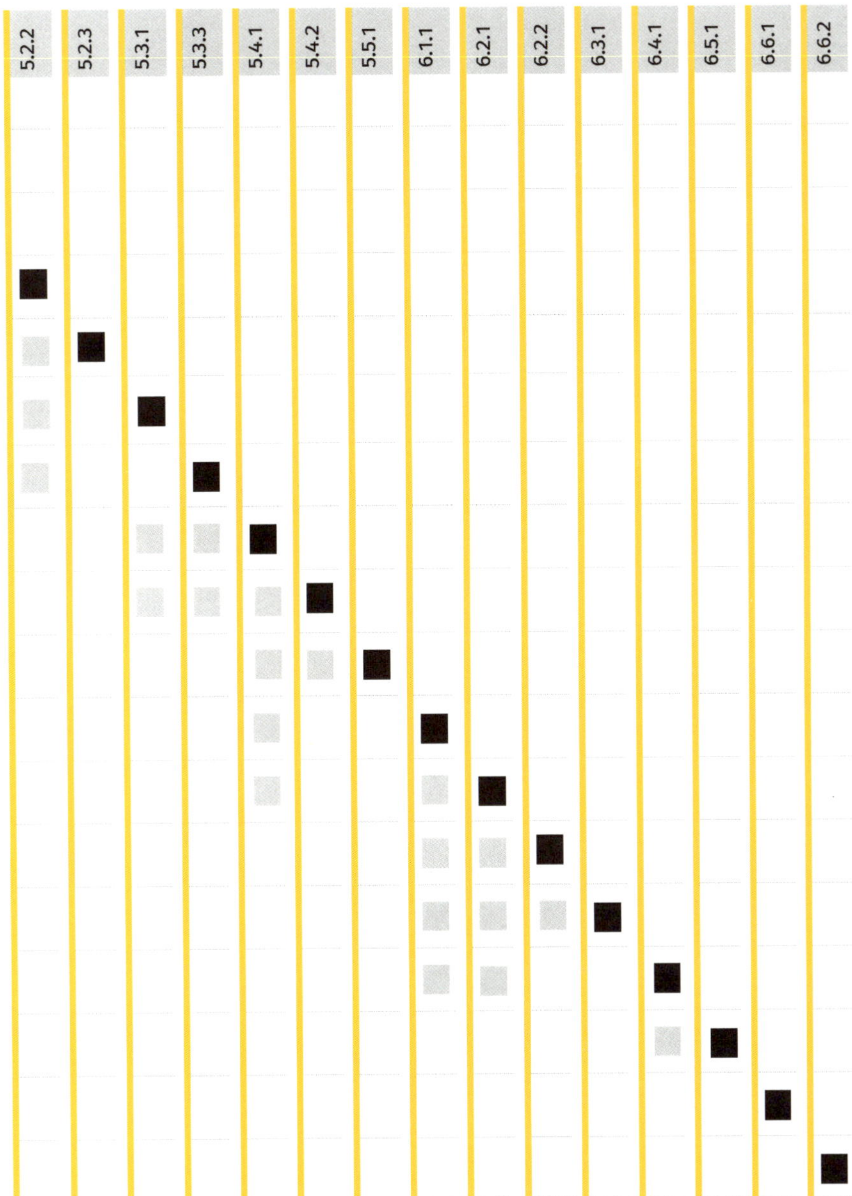


For a full recap of **HOBA®** and the **Design Process**, refer to the Recap section in *Chapter 11 Next Steps* on following page.

## Next Steps

Although you have reached the end of the Road Map Reference Model, as well as the last step (and activity) of the **Design Process**, this is not the end of your work, as the Business Architect, and custodian of the Business Architecture. Your continued role is to ensure and assure the alignment of the Business Architecture from design to implementation, with the other Architectures (Technology and Data). This means that the next steps are to ensure the ongoing updates to any and all Blueprints are released on a regular cadence, in line with the Programme sprint/release cycle, that all Stakeholders Concerns remain addressed, and as importantly – that the Technical and Data Architectures support and align to the Business Architecture.

# PART 3

# DO

Part 3 describes the practical approaches to getting started and using HOBA® in your project, Programme or work place immediately (i.e. today), starting with a Recap of the key points of HOBA® framework and the Design Process, Implementing HOBA®, Free Online Resources, Get In Touch (with the Author, me!), and Appendices.

- **Chapter 11 – Next Steps**, recaps the key points of **HOBA®** and the **Design Process**, Next Steps options (where and how to start using **HOBA®** now), Next book and **HOBA®** Cheat (reference) Sheet of the different elements of **HOBA®**, and the aspect (Why, Who, What, Where, How, and When) they address to help you get off to a flying start!
- **Chapter 12 – Free Online Resources**, take the free online Transformation Test and get your Transformation Scorecard®, assess your strengths and weaknesses to successfully implement your Organisations Target Operating Model (TOM) as part of the business transformation and get your personalised report and tips to improve your score, and visit www.hoba.tech and download the latest free resources – templates, checklists, toolkits and case studies.
- **Chapter 13 – Get In Touch**, comments, credits, training, consulting and talk details, and contact details to connect with the Author (me)!
- **Chapter 14 – Appendix** – contains the important facts that you may want to look up now (as you read), and/or refer to later. Includes the Glossary, Tables list, Figures list, Reference Models, Building Blocks and Blueprints, Additional Reading List and Index.

# Recap

So, if you made it this far, you are ready to set about implementing your Organisations Business Strategy and Target Operating Model (TOM) to transform the Business, congratulations! To (re) set the scene, lets remind ourselves where you are now on your transformation journey. You recall in *Chapter 1 Introduction* (and hopefully throughout the rest of this book) the overriding assumption in terms of starting positions on your Programme and transformation journey is, that you are at the beginning.

In terms of the **HOBA®** and the **Design Process** that 'beginning' means that you are about to, or are going through Step-1 Focus of the **Design Process**, and are working on completing the Business Motivation (Reference) Model, ideally to get the Statement of Work (SOW) Blueprint agreed (at least), which means you know '*who's who in the zoo*' i.e. all the Key Stakeholders, their concerns, the Vision (most importantly) and (as importantly) all in (and out of) scope work you need to deliver.

If that situation (or scenario) is the case, then great, we're on the same page! But what that also means, is there are situations and scenarios that weren't covered (and for good reason). A lack of time and space being one of them, but also the need to '*focus*' on one thing at a time, addressing the biggest problems I saw (and see) every day with business transformation projects and Programmes (which is why I'm asked to come in), is frustrated Business Stakeholders and Product Owners (and even Programme Directors) that are stuck in the middle of their transformation project or Programme and can't make heads or tails of what is going on, questioning whether to pull the pin and start again, or can the whole idea altogether because the transformation journey is so painful!

My intention with this book, and **HOBA®** (and the **Design Process** for that matter) is to share with you the framework and core information in a palatable and digestible format, so that you (and your Key Stakeholders, namely the Business, and Business Stakeholders) would understand it, use it and own it. All the way from the beginning of your Programme and transformation journey (i.e. from design) through to implementation. And the way you do that is in bite size chunks – hence the emphasis on the *Agile* iterative continuous delivery approach and releasing updated views and perspectives of the Business Architecture out to the Business and Programme at a regular cadence, being highly visible and transparent in relation to the process you are following and the progress you are making. All the while remembering to keep your Key Stakeholders not only engaged, but the ones actually driving the design from the start of the Programme to Programme close, and hopefully (if all goes to plan), you would have also addressed each and every one of those Business Architecture Challenges we discussed all the way back in *Chapter 2 The Business Architecture Challenge*!

So, let's recap on what we have covered:

- **HOBA® is the complete and comprehensive framework** for both developing both the *design* of the Target Operating Model (TOM) – including managing the alignment with other architectures, as well as managing the alignment of the implementation of the *physical* Business Architecture with the *design*;

- **HOBA® consists of four (4) complementary frameworks** that look at, and address, the different aspects and *'Why, Who, What, Where, How and When?'* questions asked of the Business and Business Architecture, thereby providing complete picture of what the Business does and wants to do strategically, as well as where, how and when it needs to change operationally to get to its destination (the TOM);
- **HOBA® is made up of three (3) core elements – Reference Models, Building Blocks and Blueprints:**

  1. **Reference Models** - address the *strategic* aspects and *'Why, Who, When, Where, Why and How?'* questions asked of the Business and Business Architecture, and are broken down into Building Blocks;
  2. **Building Blocks** – break down and address a specific aspect of the Reference Model they belong too, and are a collection of Blueprints that drill down and describe a specific perspective of that *'Why, Who, When, Where, Why and How?'* aspect; and
  3. **Blueprints** - provide an increasing focused and detailed view of the Building Block they belong to, capturing and documenting the *operational* aspects of the Business and Business Architecture.

- **HOBA® Reference Models neatly address the different aspects of the Organisation and Business Architecture, a**nd intentionally align to specific steps of **the Design Process:**
  - **Business Motivation Model** – is **Step - 1 'Focus'**, which sets the direction of the Business and Business Architecture, and addresses the **'Why?'** aspect asked of the Business and Business Architecture, establishing the expectations of the Business Architect, the work plan and expected deliverables;
  - **Governance Model** – is **Step - 2 'Control'**, which sets the *control* governance framework, and addresses the **'Who?'** aspect asked of the Business and Business Architecture, establishing the process and roles for making decisions on the Programme and managing changes (a very important model as it sets a solid foundation to build the TOM from, which is also why it is a primary 'foundation' of **HOBA®**);
  - **Current Operating Model** – is **Step-3 'Analyse'**, which is the *'analysis'* step that sets the baseline of the Current Operating Model, from which the Target Operating Model will be designed and built and addressed the '**What?**' aspect asked of the Business and Business Architecture. This is often an over looked step – with Programmes and Businesses often only focusing on *'delivering'*, without a full understanding of the *'current state'* (or at least having a common agreement across the Business and Programme of the current state, which in the end doesn't end well when there is multiple versions of the truth);
  - **Benefits Model** – is **Step-4 'Evaluate'**, which addresses the '**Why?**' aspect of the Business and Business Architecture – Why do this? (i.e. what Business Benefits does the Business intended to realise?), and uses those Benefits to drive the investment and solution options (the Business Changes and Enablers), which are the changes to the business, that align the Business to the Business Strategy. This step is the missing step in Business Architecture today! Benefits are often seen as an afterthought, and only done at the end (or near to the end) of the Programme in a *retrospective* fashion to *validate* investment in certain Business Capabilities and/or solution(s), instead of being used *proactively* (as in should be used) in the **Design Process** to drive and *justify* investment certain Business Capabilities and/or solution(s);
  - **Target Operating Model** – is **Step-5 'Design'**, and addresses the '**How?**' aspect of the Business and Business Architecture i.e. 'How is the Business to be changed? and 'Where are these changes?';
  - **Road Map Model** – is **Step-6 'Implement'**, which addresses the '**When?**' aspect of Business and Business Architecture. That is 'when' will the *design* of the TOM be delivered, and 'when' will the *physical* Business Architecture be implemented? Implementation is also arguably the second most overlooked step in Business Architecture today, leaving the Business and Programme stakeholder scratching their heads asking, 'so now you have come up with the *design* of the Target Operating Model (TOM) - now what?'. Step-6 covers the process, steps and deliverables to manage that delivery of the *design* of the TOM, which includes aligning the Business Architecture with the Technical Architectures, and then by necessity, manage the alignment of the implementation of the *physical* TOM, with the *design*.

- **HOBA® Building Blocks and Blueprints – are the Business Architecture content pieces (the deliverables)** that are produced by the Business Architect that make up the respective Reference Models and specific view of the Business and Business Architecture.
- **Design Process** – the **6 - step** 'design process' process (focus, control, analyse, evaluate, design and implement) **which addresses each of the 'Why, Who, What, Where, How and When' question asked of the Business and Business Architecture.** These are the actual steps offered in a structured order to develop the complete view of the Business and Business Architecture incrementally in an *agile* fashion. They also oversee the implementation of the *physical* Business Architecture to ensure (and assure) it is aligned to the *design*.

So that's what we've covered in a nutshell, based on the position, and assumptions I made in the *Assumptions* section. Which then leaves the question – well, what didn't we cover?

Well, quite a lot actually! But there just wasn't enough time and space within these pages to cover it all here...which brings me conveniently to discuss my...

# Next Book

What wasn't covered within these pages will be the subject of my next book...covering the '*before there was a Programme*' scenario. That is, when a Business wants to (or knows it needs to) come up with a new Business Strategy itself, but needs additional help to work out its new Vision, Strategy, Objectives or Measures. Alternatively, a Business may need to audit its Business Capabilities and see how aligned it is to its current Business Strategy and whether its investing in the right capabilities for where it needs to be. For a Business, this would be either '*above market*' average (ideally speaking about a Businesses core capabilities), '*at market*', or '*below market*' average (where a Business is happy to be if it's intentionally aligned to its Business Strategy).

And these scenarios exist, because that's how the Programme that you have been (currently are, or are about to be) on most likely came about in the first place – the Business needed a new TOM developed and implemented to align to its new Business Strategy.

You may recall from the *Current Situation* section that there's a problem with transformation Programmes right now, where '70% of all Programmes in existing and established businesses are failing to deliver on their [new (or changed)] Business Strategy[62].

This should be a wakeup call that something's not working.

And with '3 out of 4 crowd funding projects also failing'[63], it's probably also safe to say the problem of going from Strategic Planning to Strategy Implementation is just as (if not more) difficult for Business Start-ups. Which is the reason for my next book:

**"HOBA® - The Art of the Possible - Six Strategic Models for Business Architects"**

It's kind of like Star Wars and the trilogy series, part 3 came out first, then the next was the prequel. There was a method in that madness, and that method is the 80/20 rule.

In this book – '**The Business Transformation Playbook – *How to Implement Your Organisation's Target Operating Model (TOM) and Achieve a Zero Percent Fail Rate Using the 6-Step Agile Framework***', I've addressed the question 'how do you do Business Architecture?' in an existing Programme, within an existing Business.

It came about because I wanted to address the pain points which I, my colleagues, fellow Business Architects and other architecture colleagues (Technology, Data etc., all of whom I've either worked with, alongside, spoken to,

---

[62] The Standish Group (2014), Chaos Report
[63] Anglia Ruskin University: Why 3 out of 4 crowdfunding projects fail (Sep 2016) http://www.anglia.ac.uk/news/why-3-out-of-4-crowdfunding-projects-fail

met, heard from and/or surveyed at conferences and quarterly meetings) had often collectively seen and experienced.

Having answered these questions within this book, the next step (and book) was always going to be about the situations '*before there was a Programme*', and '*before there was a Business*'.

Therefore, in my next book I will discuss (and provide solutions for) scenario's where no Programme exists and an Organisation; has either been given a bunch of money (or needs to raise it), has a high level aspirational Vision, and needs to look both within and outside the Organisation to seek out improvement opportunities where it can build on its strengths and reduce its weaknesses while looking to see where it can compete. These scenarios (and others) will be covered in my next book.

In terms of **HOBA®**, that still means using **HOBA®** (the Reference Models, Building Blocks and Blueprints), but from a different perspective with more emphasis on some areas and elements, and less on others.

For example, it will mean a deeper dive into the *Business Strategy Mapping Building Block* which was intentionally glossed over in this book because of the assumption that 'the Organisations Vision and Strategy was already defined', and so the Organisation didn't need help working out what it was, or how it could or wanted to compete in the market because that work was already done.

In my next book, there will be a greater emphasis (and different assessments) of the Organisations Business Capabilities, Process Model, and Cost-Benefit Mapping to get a clear view of how aligned the Organisation is against its current, and even future strategy. We will look at the solution options available to the Business, and the transition roadmap for the Business to make an informed decision about which option(s), or timing of different options are best, given the number of competing variations including where and how the Organisation wants to compete. From these options the Business can then say, '*You know what, given the options available, the Vision, Strategies (developed through the Business Strategy Mapping Building Block(s) that will be covered in the next book), and what we know about our external market (i.e. competitors, strengths, weaknesses, opportunities, threats), let's go with Option 2!*'.

But that's all I will say for now. If you want to know more on this subject then you'll need to keep an eye out for my next book! (If you can wait?)

But enough on that now and let's come back to this book.

So, given where you are, considering what you've now read, consumed and (*hopefully*) learned, the question now is...what's next? well, let's discuss this now in the Getting Started section (below).

# Getting Started

So, you've just read everything, you're at the end of the book, congratulations (and thank you)! If you've read from the beginning, you have walked through the Case Study from start to finish as well so hopefully you have gained some additional insights and learnt how others have used **HOBA®** along the way, so the only logical next step from here is... Action!

Action, in terms of **HOBA®** and the **Design Process**, depends on where your Programme is (i.e. about to start, just started or part way through), what level of certainty or confidence the Programme has on a solid agreed 'true north' and, everyone on the Programme (and across the Organisation if you are a Start-up) are pulling in the same direction. Taking this into consideration there are only two (2) next logical Action Step possibilities:

1. **Start at Step 1** – Focus (with the Business Motivation Model) [Recommended], or

2. **Start at Step 5** – Design (with the Target Operating Model).

We will briefly discuss each of these options below.

## 1. Start at Step 1 – Focus [Recommended]

Starting at Step 1 – Focus (i.e. defining the Business Motivation Model Reference Model, Building Blocks and Blueprints) is the recommended starting position regardless of where the Programme may be in terms of starting (i.e. about to start, just started or part way though)

Step 1 – Focus is the recommended starting position, irrespective of which stage of the Programme the Organisation is in. How you will temper the speed and level of detail you complete in Step 1 is based on you i.e. if your Programme (or Organisation) has no or little appetite for it (for reasons discussed earlier), do it *fast* and do it *light* but make sure you at least have a draft (if not signed off) version of the Statement of Work (SOW) Blueprint drafted and out for review (or at best, you have it signed off). This at least means you agreed the high-level scope, objectives, and measures that both you and the Business Architecture will be assessed against.

As previously mentioned earlier in this book, there is the possibility, regardless of which step you've chosen to start with, that you may face some push back, resistance and pressure from the Programme that the priority is *'delivery'* (not discovery). Most of the time this resistance comes from *'fear of the unknown'* – where they don't know what the process is for developing and delivering the Business Architecture or what it looks like and what's involved.

This can be resolved by employing an education process using **HOBA®** and the **Design Process.** You now have a framework, and process, so make sure you introduce them to **HOBA®** and the **Design Process**, its purpose and benefits, what it looks like and what they can expect to help placate their fears and get yourself off to a great start!

### 2. Start at Step 5 - Design

The assumption here is that you are working on an existing Programme where there will be at least a Programme Charter or Business Case (if not approved, at least drafted). There should also be some Benefits listed (ideally defined as per the Benefits Profile), and you have been given the instruction to design and deliver the Business Architecture that aligns the Business to the Business Strategy. You would also have an agreed definition of the Vision, Current Operating Model and Benefits the Organisation plans to achieve. If this is the case, then Step 5 – Design, is the most sensible place to start. That's because it's where you can still define the Target Operating Model (TOM) based off the definition of the Current Operating Model, and the Benefits the Organisation plans to achieve (You probably haven't been given the instruction to ensure, and assure, the implementation of the physical Business Architecture aligns to the *design*, because they *'don't know what they don't know'*, but that's your added-value!).

Be warned however, starting at Step-5 is the riskiest of the two options, and is not recommended. Starting here is the reason for most problems on Programmes right now – everyone (namely Senior Execs) who are driven by the *'voices in their ear'* - mainly from our *'technical'* friends, have been running around screaming (sometimes literally) the Programme needs a *'hurry along'*, *'need to start delivering'*. But have some patience.

The best response to all that 'noise' is to question *'Deliver what, and for what benefit?'*. If no one can quantify this or what is the relationship between that benefit and the changes being made is (and can they be seen)? then this is a good place to start – understanding those areas first and not focusing on simply the delivery.

If you get push back, again it's because they don't have (or can't see) another tangible option, all they can see is someone (you) putting up a roadblock, saying to them "No, stop, wait!". This is the time to take them on the Business Architecture journey, show them you have a framework (i.e. *HOBA®*), and a process (i.e. **Design Process**), and walk them through it, showing them the purpose, benefits, what it looks like and what to expect.

If you are forced to go down this route (starting at Step 5), then (as suggested in *Chapter 7 Step 3 – Analyse*), do a *'light touch'* of the Current Operating Model while you work on Step 5 simultaneously, and confirm *'on the run'* (so to speak) the baseline and assumptions that are being made with the design. This approach does require you having two different hats on, or rather, looking in two different directions – Backwards to where you (or rather the Business) is coming from, and forwards - in the direction the Business is going to – aware of both situations as opposed to *'blindly'* focused on *'delivering'*, without first knowing or acknowledging what the existing concerns, weaknesses and opportunities the design is intending to address.

Whichever option you chose (or are 'encouraged' to follow), as a matter of best practise, it is always a good idea (whether you started at Step 1 or Step 5), is to get the Statement of Work (SOW) agreed so there is at the very least a documented contract between yourself, the Programme and the Organisation. Once you've got the SOW agreed, continue from your chosen Step.

## HOBA® Cheat Sheet

To help you remember where everything is, the following cheat sheet will provide a quick reference guide of HOBA® and the different elements, aspects and roles:

| Aspect | WHY? | WHO? | WHAT? | WHY? | WHERE? | WHEN? | Requirement |
|---|---|---|---|---|---|---|---|
| Design Step | 1<br>Focus | 2<br>Control | 3<br>Analyse | 4<br>Evaluate | 5<br>Design | 6<br>Implement | |
| Reference Model | Business Motivation Model (BMM) | Governance Model (GOV) | Current Operating Model (COM) | Benefits Model (BEN) | Target Operating Model (TOM) | Road Map Model (RMM) | Theme |
| Building Blocks | • Business Architecture Approach<br>• Vision Mapping<br>• Business Strategy Mapping<br>• Business Glossary | • Governance Framework<br>• Design Principles<br>• Risks, Assumptions, Issues & Dependencies (RAID) | • Organisation Mapping<br>• Stakeholder Mapping<br>• User Journey Mapping<br>• Process Mapping<br>• Capability Mapping | • Benefits Mapping<br>• Benefits-Dependencies Mapping<br>• Prioritisation Mapping | • Capability Mapping<br>• Impact Mapping<br>• Cost-Benefit Mapping<br>• Pilot Mapping | • Project Mapping<br>• Road Map Mapping<br>• Benefits Realisation Mapping<br>• Transition Architecture Mapping<br>• Business/IT Alignment Mapping<br>• Traceability Mapping | Feature |

**Figure 11.1** - HOBA® Cheat Sheet

| Blueprints | | | | | | | Epics & User Stories |
|---|---|---|---|---|---|---|---|
| | • Statement of Work (SOW)<br>• Vison, Strategy, Objectives & Measures (VSOM) Map<br>• Strategy Maps(s)<br>• Terms & Definitions | • Architecture Governance Framework<br>• Design Principles Register<br>• RAIDs Log | • Organisation Map<br>• Organisation (Map) Table<br>• Stakeholder Map<br>• Stakeholder (Map) Table<br>• Stakeholder Concerns and Views<br>• User Journey Map<br>• User Journey (Map) Table<br>• Process Model Map<br>• Process Model Catalogue<br>• Capability Model Map<br>• Capability Model Catalogue | • Benefits Profile<br>• Benefits Map<br>• Benefits Dependencies Map<br>• Prioritised Changes Map<br>• Prioritised Changes Catalogue | • Capability / Process Model Cross-Map<br>• Capability Model Map<br>• Capability / Process Model Matrix<br>• Process Model-Cap Cross-Map<br>• Process Model Map<br>• Process Model Matrix<br>• Process Model Heat Map<br>• Prowess Model Heat (Map) Table<br>• Capability Model Heat Map<br>• Capability Model Heat (Map) Table<br>• Solution Options<br>• Cost-Benefit Assessment<br>• Pilot Brief | • Project Brief<br>• Project Benefits Map<br>• Business Architecture Road Map<br>• Programme Road Map<br>• Benefits Realisation Register<br>• Benefits Realisation Map<br>• Transition Architecture Strategy Map<br>• Transition Architecture Phase Map(s)<br>• Business/IT Alignment Map<br>• Stakeholder Concerns Traceability Matrix<br>• Blueprint Traceability Matrix | |

Figure 11.1 - HOBA® Cheat Sheet

Chapter 12
Free Online Resources

# Get Your Free Transformation Scorecard®

Are you ready to implement your Organisations Target Operating Model (TOM) and transform the business as part of the Organisations business transformation? Take the Transformation Test and get your Transformation Scorecard® and learn your ability to transform your Business using **HOBA®.**

The **Transformation Scorecard®** is a **free online assessment to assess your ability to transform the business** against the different elements of **HOBA®**.

The Transformation Scorecard® is based on the same premises for designing (and implementing) the Target Operating Model (TOM):

- **Starting from an agreed baseline.** For Business Architecture, the starting point is the Current Operating Model. For you, and your ability to implement the TOM and transform the Business as part of its Business transformation is via the Transformation Test, and
- **You can only improve what you measure.**

The **Transformation Scorecard Test** will test your ability to design and implement your Organisations TOM against the different aspects of **HOBA®** and the **Design Process**.

The **Transformation Test** is based on the critical aspects and the *'Why, Who, What, Where, How and When?'* questions asked for each **HOBA®** Reference Model, and most importantly, asks the critical questions at each stage of developing and implementing the Organisations business transformation.

You will test and gauge your ability to help your Organisation achieve its intended outcomes and planned Business Benefits from its business transformation.

The **Transformation Test will ask you questions not covered and addressed (but often alluded to) in this book.** Effective design and implementation of the Organisations Business Architecture and business transformation requires a combination of technical and soft skills:

- **Technical skills** - of knowing and understanding how and when to use the different aspects of HOBA® and the Design Process when designing and implementing the Business Strategy and Business Architecture, and
- **Soft skills** – namely the necessary stakeholder and change management skills so not only are the key stakeholders identified, involved and informed, but also where required, their agreement is obtained for all strategic design and operational implementation decisions.

# Free Online Resources

The **Transformation Scorecard®** will help you

- Get insights into how ready you are to implement your Organisations Target Operating Model (TOM) and increase the level of success you will achieve,
- Discover your *Transformation* Score and increase your ability to transform your Organisation, align the business to the Business Strategy, and implement its Target Operating Model (TOM)
- Identify your personal areas of strength and weakness and improvement opportunities, and
- Provide you with tips of how to improve your score and rating (and ultimately, your level of success in implementing your Organisations transformation).

The Transformation Test is made up of the following:

- **Unique Yes/No questions format across each aspect of the HOBA® framework**
- **60 questions**
- **10 mins (max, no strings attached)**

By completing the Transformation Test you will get the following:

- Your **individual score against each aspect of the HOBA® framework,**
- **Your overall score and rating**
- **Individual 20+ page Transformation Scorecard® Report,** and
- **Tips on how to improve your score**

**To get your free Transformation Scorecard®, go to www.hoba.tech**

For the full list of online resources to help you, go to www.hoba.tech and download the following latest free resources:

- **Transformation Scorecard®** – take the transformation test and get your score and custom Transformation Scorecard® report on your ability to successfully implement your Organisations Business Architecture and business transformation,
- **Templates** – the Building Blocks and Blueprints you need to get you started quickly (or back on track quickly, depending where you are on your Programme and/or business transformation),
- **Checklists** – to help ensure there is no gaps and you are doing the right things (and only the right things, and in the right order),
- **Toolkits** – the set of tools you need as a Business Architect to develop the Business Architecture and transform the business, and
- **Case Studies** – learn how other companies and Organisations are and have used HOBA® to implement their Target Operating Model (TOM) as part of their business and digital transformation.

# Chapter 13 Get In Touch

## Comments

I appreciate you taking the time to read this book, and would appreciate hearing from you! Whether you enjoyed it, have suggestions on ways to improve it or simply want to know more, please feel free to get in touch and send me an email via the contact details below. I look forward to hearing from you!

## Credits

I made strenuous efforts to credit the sources, models, and ideas citied in this book. Having said this I realise there is always the rare chance that I may have unintentionally missed or neglected to mention some people. If you are aware of any piece of work contained here that is not properly credited, please feel free to let me know so that I can make amendments in future editions.

## Workshops, Training, Consultancy and Talks

This book, HOBA® and the Design Process (and everything contained within it), is only the tip of the iceberg in terms of expanding your skills and abilities in this unique industry.

To support what you have read here we also offer support in the form of workshops, training and consultancy services on using HOBA® to design and implement business strategies and Target Operating Models (TOM) as part of Organisations business transformation and digital transformations.

Finally, as the ultimate way to get further insights in what I've covered here, I am also available to speak at your next business conference and training event.

# Get in touch

You can get in touch via the website or contact details below:

**Email:** heath@hoba.tech

**Website (book):** www.businesstransformationplaybook.com

**Website (main):** www.hoba.tech

# Connect

If you would like to connect with me, you can do so here:

**Twitter:**

- @hobatech
- @heath_gascoigne

**Facebook:**

- @HobaTechLtd
- www.facebook.com/HobaTechLtd
- www.facebook.com/heathgascoigne/

**LinkedIn:**

- https://www.linkedin.com/company/hobatech/
- https://uk.linkedin.com/in/heathgascoigne

**Instagram:**

- https://www.instagram.com/hoba.tech
- https://www.instagram.com/heath.gascoigne/

# Join the Community

If you would like to join the community of like-minded Business Transformators®, stay up to date with the latest updates, changes and trends in the industry, receive exclusive content, invites to special events and offers, receive free tips and tricks as well as learn how others are successfully using HOBA® to transform their and/or their clients businesses, you can join our closed Facebook group here:

- www.businesstransformators.com

Thanks for reading '**The Business Transformation Playbook® – *How to Implement Your Organisation's Target Operating Model (TOM) and Achieve a Zero Percent Fail Rate Using the 6-Step Agile Framework***', and I wish you every success!

# Chapter 14 Appendices

This section contains the following appendices:

- Appendix A – Glossary
- Appendix B – Tables List
- Appendix C – Figures List
- Appendix D – Reference Models, Building Blocks and Blueprints
- Appendix E – Additional Reading
- Appendix F - Index

## Appendix A – Glossary

Please note: some of these terms have multiple meanings and uses. This glossary gives definitions only as they're used in this book.

**Activity** - Indicates key events performed when executing a process[64] .

**Agile** - The philosophy designed to deliver the user requirements in a way that allows for flexibility, through incremental iterations to enable more testing and feedback opportunities.

**Agile Manifesto** - The Agile Manifesto, is in effect a contract between the delivery team and the Stakeholder. All work streams, facilitated by the Scrum Master, endeavour to deliver to ensure sprints are guided by the Agile Manifesto.

**Agile Scrum** - An interactive and incremented Agile software development framework for managing software projects and products or application development.

**Application Lifecycle Management (ALM)** – represents the costs (and activities) involved to support an application post implementation, includes maintenance, training and support.

**Artefact** - An architectural work product that describes an aspect of the architecture, generally classified as catalogues (lists), matrices (showing relationships between things) and diagrams (pictures of things)[65] .

**Backlog** - List of requirements (i.e. User Stories, themes, epics), usually prioritised by business value. A Programme can have one or more backlogs. Business Architecture Programme, Work Stream, Spring, Test backlog with each subsequent backlog a subset of other Backlog i.e. Work stream backlog is a subset of the Programme backlog; Sprint backlog is a subset of the works tram backlog; Test Backlog is a subset of the Spring Backlog etc.

---

[64] APQC Process Classification Framework_Ver_6 1_1

[65] The Open Group Architecture Framework (TOGAF®) v9.1, *The Open Group*

**Benefits (Business)** - An outcome of an action or decision that contributes towards meeting one or more business (strategic) objectives. Benefits are the result of capabilities delivered and transitioned into and used by the Business Organisation, that produce positive outcomes for the business, that through their ongoing use, lead to the realisation of benefits.

**Benefit Type** - Intermediate: a benefit that occurs early, that contributes to an End Benefit; End: achievement of a final benefit, that is dependent on the achievement of one or more Immediate Benefits.

**Benefits Map** - A network of benefits, usually linked to one or more primary investment objectives[66] .

**Benefits Owner** - A person responsible for the realisation benefits. Can be an individual or group of stakeholders. According to the Managing Successful Programmes (MSP), this responsibility usually lies with the Senior Responsible Officer (SRO).

**Benefits Profile** - A comprehensive description of a single benefit, including all its attributes and dependencies.

**Benefits Realisation Management (BRM)** - The framework and process of Organisation and managing Benefits, so that planned benefits, arising from investment in change, are actually achieved[67].

**Benefits Realisation Plan (BRP)** - The artefact which shows how and when all benefits, for a particular change initiatives, are expected to be realised.

**Beta** - A phase of a project where the solution is in use and in the process of being improved, through testing within the Programme or in the public domain[68]
Also refers to the *status* of a Business Architecture Blueprint or artefact.

**Blueprint** - A Blueprint is a User Story level Business Architecture requirement and deliverable that describe a specific view or perspective of the Organisation. Blueprints make up HOBA® Business Architecture Building Blocks.

**Building Blocks** - Building Blocks are Epic level Business Architecture Requirements and deliverables. They are made up of Blueprints, that collectively describe a specific view or perspective of the Organisation. Building Blocks make up HOBA® Business Architecture Reference Models.

**Business Architecture** - A description of the structure and interactions between the Business Strategy, organization, functions, business processes, and information needs[69] .

**Business Architecture Approach ('Approach')** - The high-level plan of the series of steps that are both required and followed in a specific and logical order to build up the Business Architecture.

**Business Change/Business Changes** - *Changes* that are needed or made to the business environment (people, skills, processes), to support the realisation of benefits (but excludes technology).

Note – *business change* implicitly includes culture, strategies/policies, practices, procedure as they are necessary to deliver the above mentioned 'people' and 'process'.

**Business Capability** - In Business/Business Architecture context – a business capability is 'what a business does', made up of (essentially) people, process and technology. Each of these can be broken down further into people skills, culture, process steps, action, hardware, software, data etc.
Also see *Capability*

**Business Service** - A concept or abstraction of a business system, where the actual 'Business System' is not known or known about the physical landscape.
Also see *Service*

**Business System** - Something that physically exists i.e. Application software or Technical System.

**Cadence** - A regular rhythm of working.

---

[66] Bradley, G., (2010) Benefit Realisation Management: A Practical Guide to Achieving Benefits
[67] Bradley, G., (2010) Benefit Realisation Management: A Practical Guide to Achieving Benefits
[68] Adapted from GOV.UK How the beta phase works
https://www.gov.uk/service-manual/agile-delivery/how-the-beta-phase-works (last updated Aug 2016, last viewed Aug 2017)
[69] The Open Group Architecture Framework (TOGAF®) v9.1, The Open Group

**Capability** - In Benefits Realisation Management (BRM) context – a capability is 'the set of outputs required to create an outcome'.
Also see *Business Capability*

**CRUD** - Acronym for Create, Read, Update and Delete. Used to describe (shorthand) the basic function or User requirements.

**Change Debt** - Situation where quick and dirty design choice is made to meet a deadline or milestone, which end up costing unnecessary time and effort to undo or correct when time and/or money comes available. Can be both technical (systems and information) or non-technical (people and process) .
Criticality - In terms of assumptions – an indicator of the level of how disruptive the change will be to the Programme.[70]

**Critical to Customer (CTC)** - A Customers needs (or requirement) expected from a given product or service that addresses their stated (or unstated) concern(s).

**Critical to Quality (CTQ)** - The quantitative measure of a Customer (internal or external) need. See *Critical to Customer (CTC)* above.

**Data Cluster** - Logical grouping and representation of a common data store.

**Design Process** - The 6-step process using HOBA® to develop the design of the Target Operating Model (TOM) and manage the alignment of the implementation of the physical TOM with the design.

**Dis-benefit** - An outcome perceived as negative by one or more stakeholders .

Discovery - Phase of the project where the user needs are researched and identified[71].

**Discovery, Alpha, Beta, Live** - Phases of software development (or phases of project management). Also, referred to as Discovery, Design, Build, Deliver.

**Domain** - An enterprise architectural domain, or architectural subsets of an overall enterprise architecture[72] .

**Duration** - Total time to complete the activities based on resources available, and does not include holidays or non-working days, often referred to as work days or weeks.

**Effort** - The number of work units to complete the activity, often referred to as man hours, days or weeks.

**Elapsed Time** - The total calendar time needed to complete the activities, which can include weekends and public holidays.

**Epic** - A Product Backlog Item (PBI) which is not sufficiently defined. These are large story(s) that need to be broken down into User Stories.

**Enabler** - Something that can be developed or purchased to enable the realisation of a/the benefit. Business Architecture capability classifications include – technology and information.

**End Benefit -** An ultimate benefit of a Programme or project. Achievement of a final benefit is dependent on the achievement of one or more Immediate Benefits.

**Enterprise Architecture** - the description of how the Business Organisation is setup and structured in order to deliver on its Business Strategy. Consists of both Business Architecture, and Technology Architecture.
Also see *Business Architecture*, and *Technology Architecture*.

**Feature** - High-level abstractions of User Stories and can include Non-Functional Requirements (NFRs) of discrete '*business visible*' functionality that deliver Business Benefits.

**Full Time Equivalent (FTE)** – an indicator of the cost to the Programme of a full-time worker (on an annual basis).

**Goal** - Final outcome the business or Organisation sets to achieve.
Immediate Benefits - Benefits which occur between the implementation of early changes and the realisation of the End Benefits.

---

[70] Flower, M., (2003) Technical Debit https://martinfowler.com/bliki/TechnicalDebt.html (last viewed Aug 2017)
[71] Letavec, C., (2014) An Introduction to Benefits Realization Management [sic]
[72] The Open Group Architecture Framework (TOGAF®) v9.1, *The Open Group*
[73] Ohno, T., (1988) Toyota Production System: Beyond Large-Scale Production

**Kanban** - Technique for managing a software development process in a highly efficient way. Kanban underpins Toyota's "just-in-time" (JIT) production system.
The technique relies on work being 'pulled' through the system from the downstream process, when the upstream process has capacity to process it. The technique aims to reduce work-in-progress at each step of the process, prevent overproduction and remove bottlenecks[73] .

**Key Performance Indicator (KPI)** - A measure, usually tracked at a corporate level, to monitor overall performance.

**LEAN Process** - An approach designed to increase efficiency, reduce waste and focus on what is important (i.e. maximising the value to the customer).

**Live** - A phase of a project where the service is public and works well, and continually improved to meet user needs.
Also refers to the status of the Business Architecture Blueprint, final and *in-use* yet subject to change based on review and feedback, usually formal change control.

**Measure** - Strategy and objective outcome indicators, used to measure success or progress towards a goal (or Vision).

**Metric** - The Quantifiable level of an indicator that the Organization uses to measure progress.

**Mission** - The purpose for which the Organisation exists.

**MoSCoW** - Method of prioritising requirements – **M**ust have (i.e. critical), **S**hould have (i.e. important but not critical), **C**ould have (i.e. desirable, but not necessary) and **W**ont have (i.e. least critical, lowest payback items or not appropriate at this time).

**Objective** - An answer to the important 'WHY?' question which defined purpose, aim and direction.
Also, referred to as '*Strategic Objective*' – which are the drivers for investment.

**Outcome** - The result of change, or the result of transition that embeds a capability in the business Organisation.

**Output** - The deliverable created by a project (or Programme).

**Phase** - One of the subdivisions of the process (Project Management process, BRM process).

**Primary Objective** - An end objective for a change initiative which helps bound it scope.

**Product Backlog Item (PBI)** - Also referred to as 'Backlog item' or Product Backlog Item. An 'item' representing all the work a team needs to complete, includes requirements and tasks needed to complete to deliver requirement(s).

**Portfolio Management Office (PMO)** - The office responsible for supporting the Portfolio Board in the managing of the whole change Portfolio.

**Programme** - A mechanism for managing projects.

**Programme Board** - A group of senior stakeholders, responsible for providing leadership and direction for the Programme.

**Reference Model** - Describe a specific conceptual view or aspect of the Organisation and Business Architecture. A Reference Model is made up of Building Blocks and Blueprints, which provide increasingly focused detailed level view of that aspect.

**Service** - A logical representation of a repeatable business activity that has a specific outcome. A service is self-contained, maybe composed of other services, and is a "black box" [74] .

**Scrum** - Scrum is an iterative and incremental agile software development methodology for managing product development[75] . Also see *Agile*

**Senior Responsible Officer (SRO)** - Senior Executive or Sponsor for a project or Programme. Ultimately responsible for the realisation of benefits. In BRM, ultimately accountable for benefit realisation.

**Scenarios** - High level business process(es).

---

[74] The Open Group Architecture Framework (TOGAF®) v9.1, The Open Group
[75] Scrum Alliance 'Why Scrum' https://www.scrumalliance.org/why-scrum (last viewed Aug 2017)

**Sprint** - A sprint (or iteration) is the basic unit of development in Scrum. The sprint is a "time boxed" effort; that is, it is restricted to a specific duration. The duration is fixed in advance for each sprint and is normally between one week and one month.

**Sprint Planning** - A core team exercise to estimate the amount of development and testing effort required to deliver a completed a backlog item.

**Sprint Review** - The Sprint Team present work that was completed and not completed during the Sprint.

**Sprint Retrospective** - Core team members discuss the past Sprint to identify areas for possible process improvements.

**Stand-up (daily Scrum Meeting)** - A daily 15 minute '*standing up*' meeting by the core project members to present an update on progress and or impediments which require resolution.

**Story / User Story** -A user story is a very high-level definition of a requirement, containing just enough information so that the developers can produce a reasonable estimate of the effort to implement it.

Typically, a sentence or two that describes who uses the story, the goal they are trying to accomplish, and any additional information that may be critical to understanding the scope of the story, including acceptance criteria. May also include NFRs[76] .

**Storyboard** - A visual depiction of backlog cards organised by their current status, showing a left to right progression through the team's process, that is either '*not started*', '*in progress*' and '*done*'. Also see *Kanban.*

**Strategy** - The 'HOW' is the business going to achieve its Vision question. The plan of action or management mechanism needed to achieve an objective or vision.

**Straw man** - A stage or status of a brainstormed draft outline or proposal intended to generate discussion and generation of new and better proposals. Later stage refined and improved proposals are subsequently named Wooden man, Tinman and Ironman. Originated from Ada Programming language[77] .

**Tactic** - Actions taken to support the Business Strategy.

**Target State Architecture Design Process ('Design Process')** - See '*Design Process*' above.

**Task** - Tasks represent the next level of hierarchical decomposition after Activities[78] .

**Technology Architecture** - the description of how the Technology aspects of the Organisation is structured to support the Business Architecture in delivering on the Business Strategy, and consists of other architectures such as data, application etc.

**Theme** - Strategic investment opportunities. Themes connect the *Vision* to the *Business Strategy*, and provide:

- the context for decision-making at the Portfolio/investment level, and
- the going-forward differentiators from the current state to the future state.

**T-shirt size** - A relatively quick *Agile* estimating technique (compared to 'absolute' estimation) to estimate the 'relative' size (Small, Medium, Large etc.) of a story or piece of work by comparing stories against each other.

**User Story Card (or Story Card)** - User Stories are usually written on index cards, usually referred to as 'cards' and form part of the backlog and are displayed on the Story/Kanban board.

**Vision, Vision Statement** - The 'WHY' is the business doing this? Question. Also, a high-level statement that describes the future state from a business perspective.

**Voice of the Customer (VOC)** - A technique used to qualify and quantify a customer (internal or external to the Organisation) requirements from the customer. Often expressed in CTCs (Critical to Customer) and CTQs (Critical to Quality).

**Work Breakdown Structure (WBS)** - A technique used to define the scope of work and developing estimates of the work. WBS decomposes the project scope into smaller and smaller pieces, creating a hierarchy of work.

---

[76] Agile Modelling 'User Stories: An Agile Introduction http://www.agilemodeling.com/artifacts/userStory.htm (last viewed Aug 2017)
[77] Ada Programming Language, *Project Milestones (archives)* http://archive.adaic.com/pol-hist/history/holwg-93/8.htm#milestones (last viewed Aug 2017)
[78] APQC Process Classification Framework_Ver_6 1_1

# Appendix B – Figures List

# Appendix C – Tables List

# Appendix D – Reference Models, Building Blocks and Blueprints

### 1.0 Business Motivation Model

| Ref | Building Block | Ref | Blueprint | Page (Link) |
|---|---|---|---|---|
| 1.1 | Business Architecture Approach ('Approach') | 1.1.1 | Statement of Work (SOW) | 82 |
| 1.2 | Vision Mapping | 1.2.1 | Vision, Strategy, Objectives and Measures (VSOM) Map | 101 |
| | | 1.2.2 | VSOM Table | 101 |
| 1.3 | Business Strategy Mapping | 1.3.1 | Business Strategy Map | 103 |
| | | 1.3.2 | Balanced Score Card | 104 |
| | | 1.3.3 | Business Model Canvas | 104 |
| | | 1.3.4 | Porters 5-Forces | 104 |
| | | 1.3.5 | SWOT Analysis | 105 |
| | | 1.3.6 | PESTLE Analysis | 105 |
| 1.4 | Business Glossary | 1.4.1 | Terms and Definitions | 107 |

## 2.0 Governance Model

| Ref | Building Block | Ref | Blueprint | Page (Link) |
|---|---|---|---|---|
| 2.1 | Business Architecture Governance | 2.1.1 | Architecture Governance Framework | 115 |
| 2.2 | Design Principles | 2.2.1 | Design Principles Register | 142 |
| 2.3 | Risks, Assumptions, Issues and Dependencies (RAID) | 2.3.1 | RAID Log | 146 |

## 3.0 Current Operating Model

| Ref | Building Block | Ref | Blueprint | Page (Link) |
|---|---|---|---|---|
| 3.1 | Organisation Mapping | 3.1.1 | Organisation Map | 152 |
| | | 3.1.2 | Organisation (Map) Table | 152 |
| 3.2 | Stakeholder Mapping | 3.2.1 | Stakeholder Map | 162 |
| | | 3.2.2 | Stakeholder (Map) Table | 162 |
| | | 3.2.3 | Stakeholder Concerns and Views | 164 |
| 3.3 | User Journey Mapping | 3.3.1 | User Journey Map | 167 |
| | | 3.3.2 | User Journey Table | 170 |
| 3.4 | Process Mapping | 3.4.1 | Process Model Map | 176 |
| | | 3.4.2 | Process Model Catalogue | 177 |
| 3.5 | Capability Mapping | 3.5.1 | Capability Model Map | 187 |
| | | 3.5.2 | Capability Model Catalogue | 189 |

## 4.0 Benefits Model

| Ref | Building Block | Ref | Blueprint | Page (Link) |
|---|---|---|---|---|
| 4.1 | Benefits Mapping | 4.1.1 | Benefits Profile | 199 |
| | | 4.1.2 | Benefits Map | 201 |
| 4.2 | Benefits Dependencies Mapping | 4.2.1 | Benefit-Dependencies Map | 208 |
| | | 4.2.2 | Benefit-Dependencies Matrix | 212 |
| 4.3 | Prioritisation Mapping | 4.3.1 | Prioritised Changes Map | 214 |
| | | 4.3.2 | Prioritised Changes Catalogue | 216 |

## 5.0 Target Operating Model

| Ref | Building Block | Ref | Blueprint | Page (Link) |
|---|---|---|---|---|
| 5.1 | Capability Mapping (To-Be) | 5.1.1 | Capability/Process Model Cross-Map | 229 |
| | | 5.1.2 | Capability Model Map (To-Be) | 232 |
| | | 5.1.3 | Capability/Process Model Matrix | 233 |
| 5.2 | Process Mapping (To-Be) | 5.2.1 | Process Model-Capability Cross Map | 240 |
| | | 5.2.2 | Process Model Map (To-Be) | 240 |
| | | 5.2.3 | Process-Process Model Matrix | 240 |
| 5.3 | Impact Mapping | 5.3.1 | Process Model Heat Map | 253 |
| | | 5.3.2 | Process Model Heat Map Table | 253 |
| | | 5.3.3 | Capability Model Heat Map | 253 |
| | | 5.3.4 | Capability Model Heat Map Table | 256 |
| 5.4 | Cost-Benefit Mapping | 5.4.1 | Solution Options | 264 |
| | | 5.4.2 | Cost-Benefit Assessment | 267 |
| 5.5 | Pilot Mapping | 5.5.1 | Pilot Brief | 270 |

## 6.0 Road Map Model

# Appendix E - Additional Reading

The list of additional reading and material referenced and cited in this book is as follows.


- **The Open Group Architecture Framework (TOGAF®)** - The Open Group (2013)
- **Agile Software Requirements: Lean Requirements Practises for Teams, Programs, and the Enterprise** - Cockburn and Highsmith (2010).
- **The Minto Pyramid Principle: Logical in Writing, Thinking & Problem Solving** - Barbara Minto (2008).
- **Strategy Maps: Converting Intangible Assets into Tangible Outcomes** - R Kaplan, D Norton (2004).
- **Benefits Realisation Management: A Practical Guide to Achieving Benefits Through Change** – Bradley, G (2010).
- **Business Model Generation** – Osterwalder, A. & Pigneur, Y. (2010).
- **The Lean Start-up: How Constant Innovation Creates Radically Successful Businesses** – Ries, E. (2011)
- **Managing Successful Programmes (MSP)** – Crown (The Cabinet Office) (2011).
- **Making Sense of Change Management: A Complete Guide to the Models, Tools and Techniques of Organizational Change** - Cameron, E. & Green, M. (2012).


# Appendix F – Index

**O**



**P**



**R**

CPSIA information can be obtained at www.ICGtesting.com
Printed in the USA
BVIW121612170719
553466BV00036B/55

* 9 7 8 0 9 9 5 7 7 7 9 3 4 *